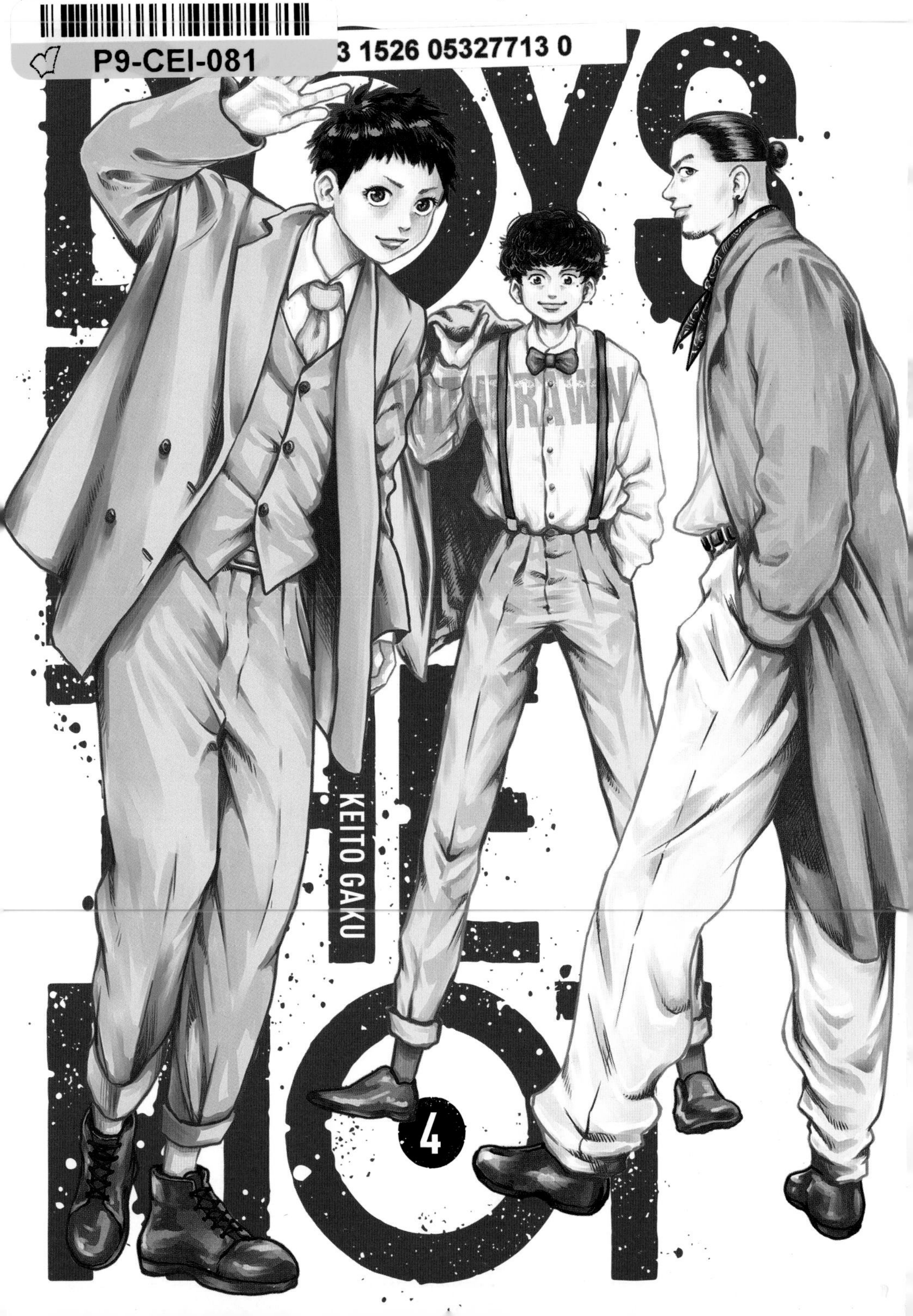
KEITO GAKU
4

CONTENTS

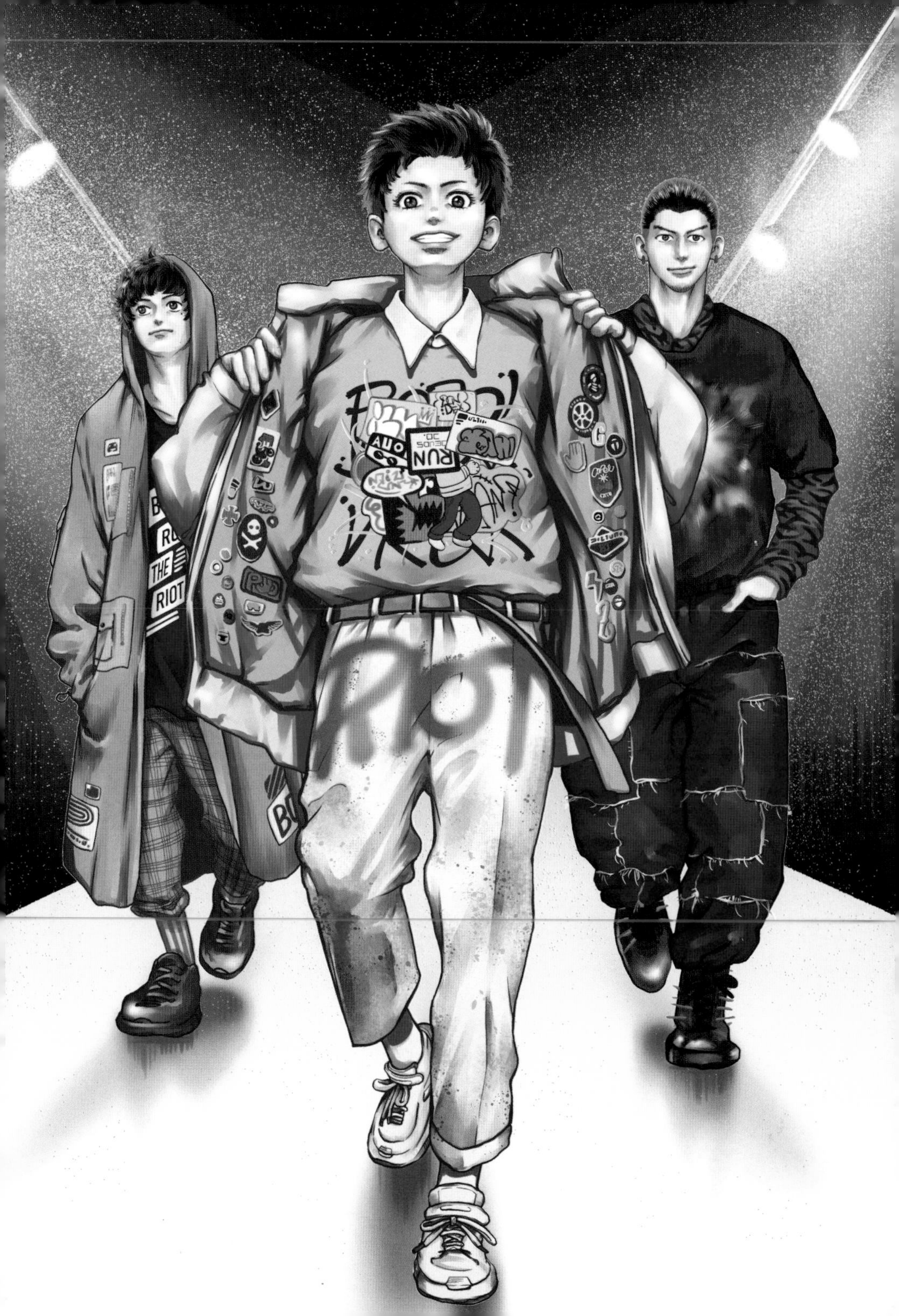
THE
RIOT
RUN
RIOT

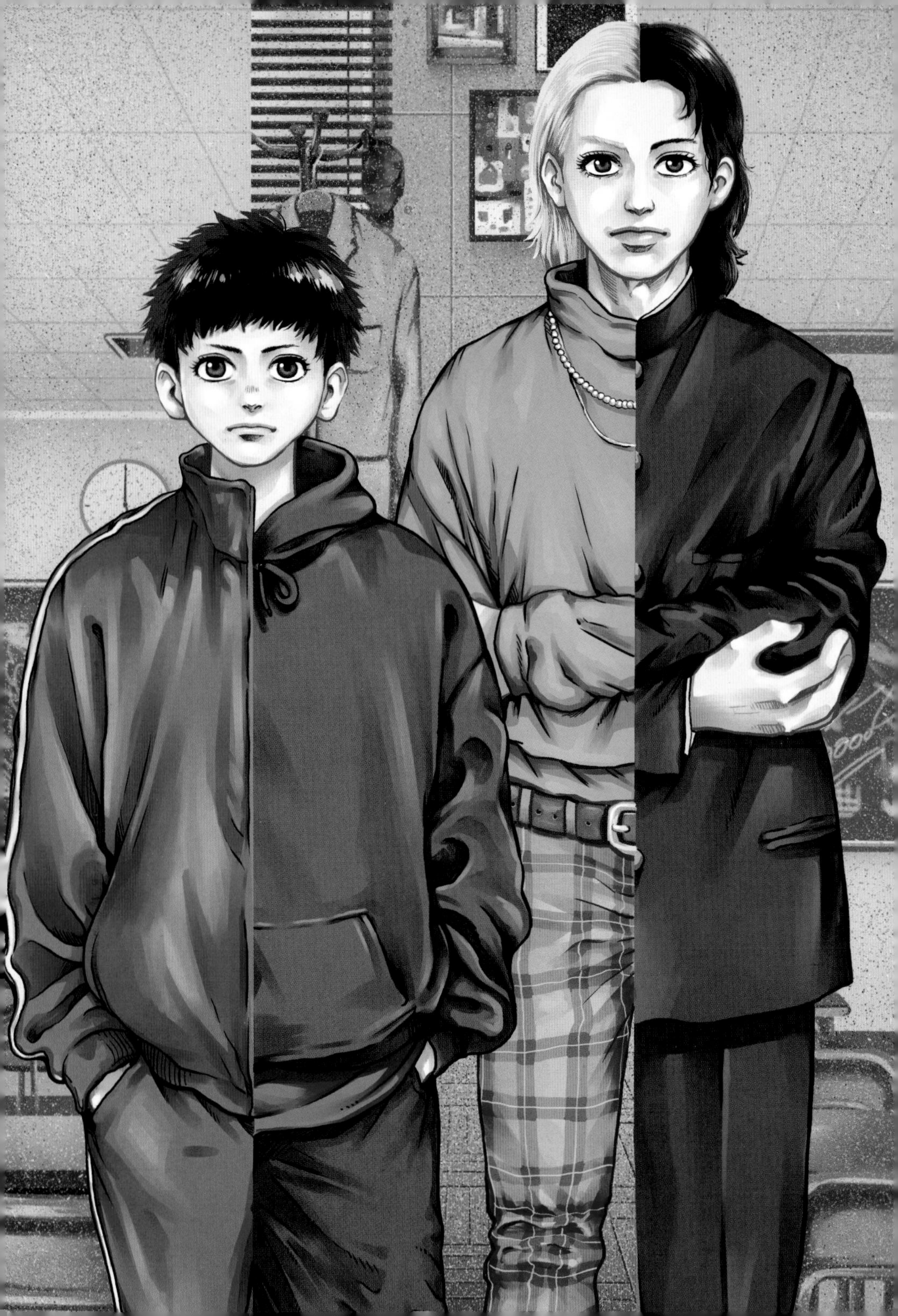

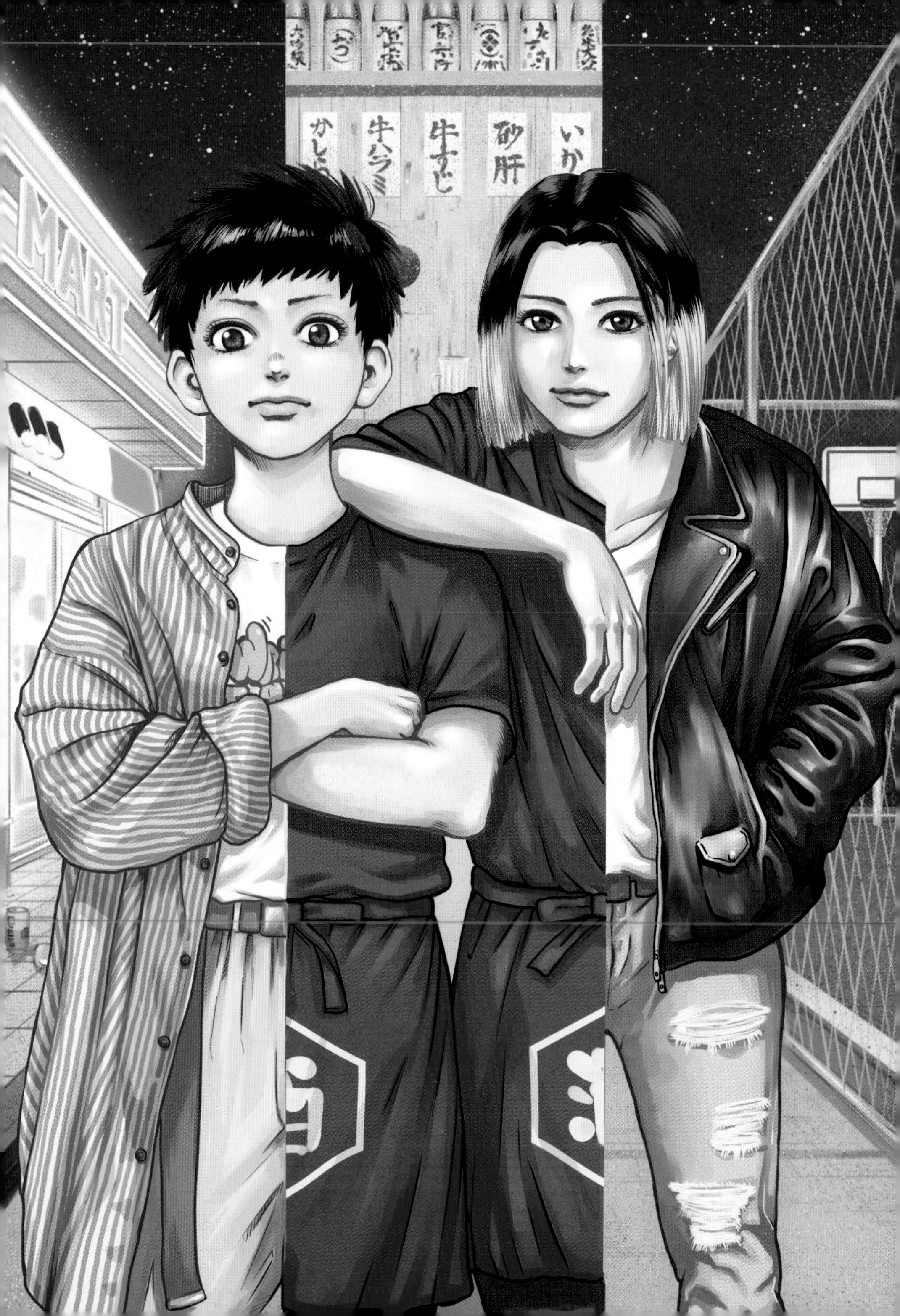

いか
砂肝
牛すじ
牛ハラミ
MART

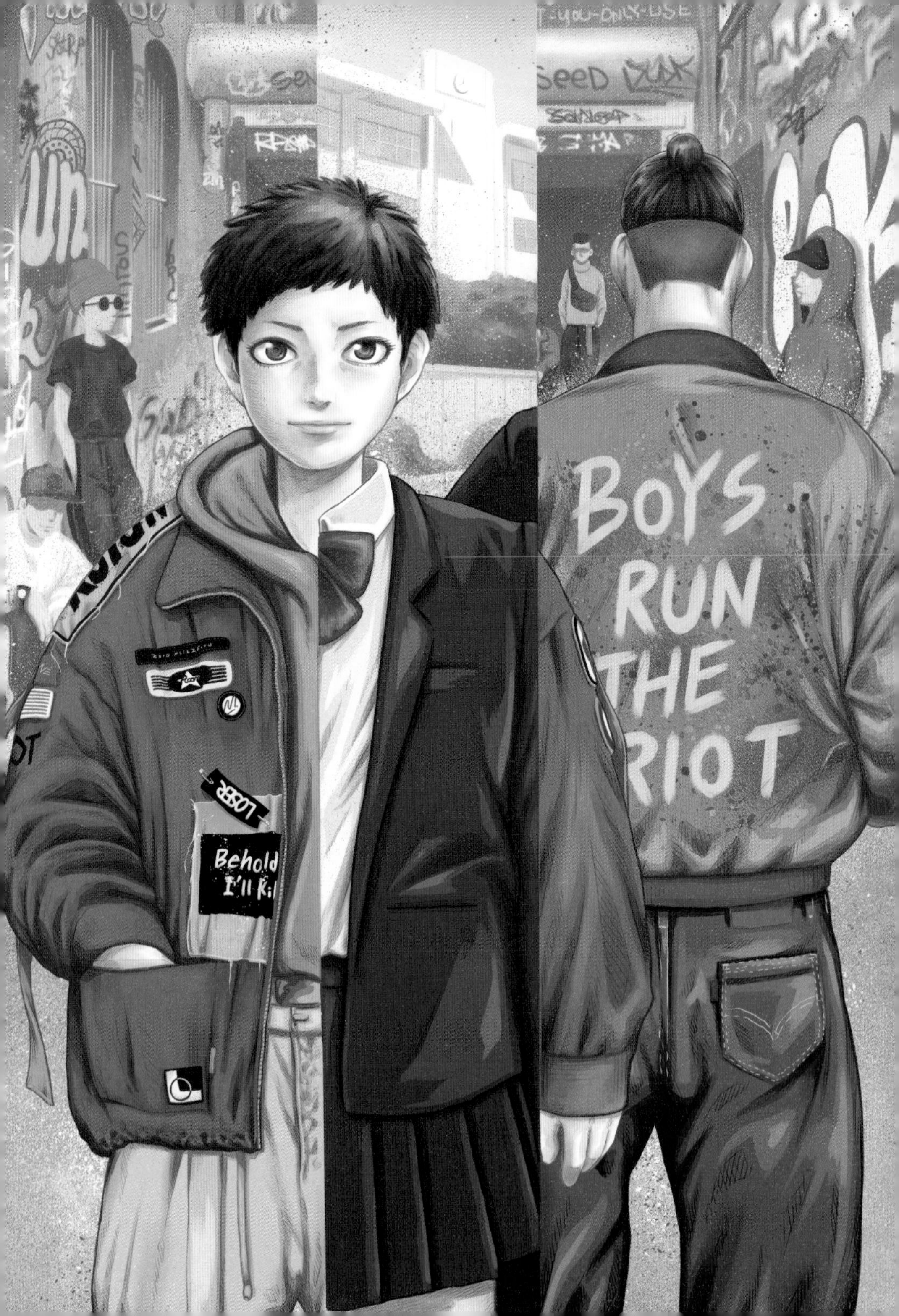
BOYS
RUN
THE
RIOT
LOSER
Behold
I'll Ki

A Kodansha Comics Trade Paperback Original
Boys Run the Riot 4 copyright © 2021 Keito Gaku
English translation copyright © 2021 Keito Gaku

All rights reserved.

Published in the United States by Kodansha Comics, an imprint of Kodansha USA Publishing, LLC, New York.

Publication rights for this English edition arranged through Kodansha Ltd., Tokyo.

First published in Japan in 2021 by Kodansha Ltd., Tokyo as *Boys Run the Riot*, volume 4.

ISBN 978-1-64651-121-1

Printed in the United States of America.

www.kodansha.us

9 8 7 6 5 4 3 2 1
Translation: Leo McDonagh, Rose Padgett
Lettering: Ashley Caswell
Editing: Tiff Joshua TJ Ferentini
Kodansha Comics edition cover design by Phil Balsman

Publisher: Kiichiro Sugawara

Director of publishing services: Ben Applegate
Associate director of operations: Stephen Pakula
Publishing services managing editors: Alanna Ruse, Madison Salters
Assistant production managers: Emi Lotto, Angela Zurlo
Logo and character art ©Kodansha USA Publishing, LLC

MAGIC ● KNIGHT RAYEARTH
25TH ANNIVERSARY EDITION
CLAMP

A BELOVED CLASSIC MAKES ITS STUNNING RETURN IN THIS GORGEOUS, LIMITED EDITION BOX SET!

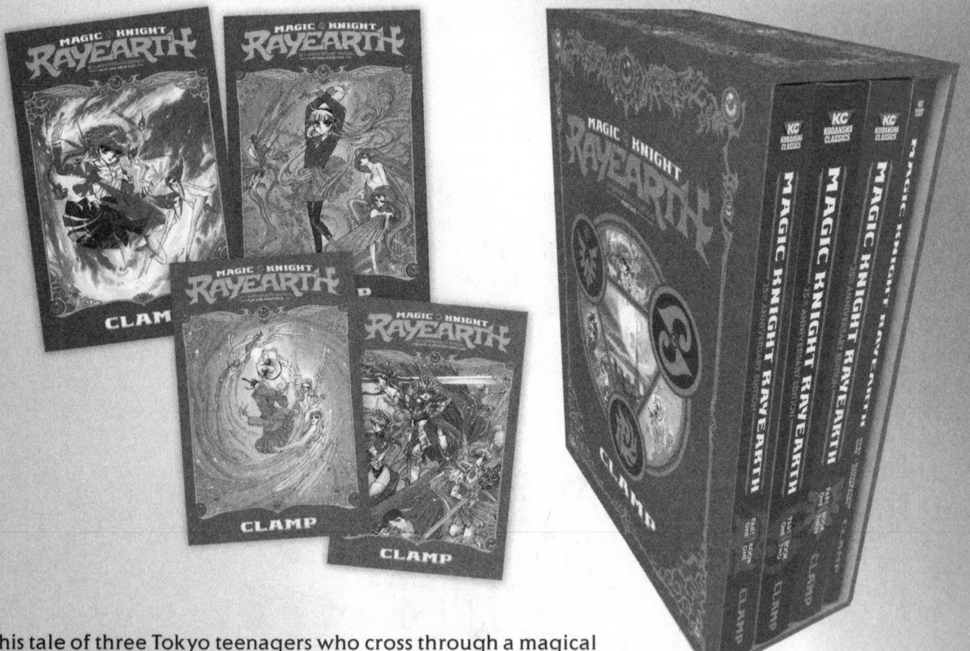

This tale of three Tokyo teenagers who cross through a magical portal and become the champions of another world is a modern manga classic. The box set includes three volumes of manga covering the entire first series of *Magic Knight Rayearth*, plus the series's super-rare full-color art book companion, all printed at a larger size than ever before on premium paper, featuring a newly-revised translation and lettering, and exquisite foil-stamped covers.

A strictly limited edition, this will be gone in a flash!

The beloved characters from *Cardcaptor Sakura* return in a brand new, reimagined fantasy adventure!

"[*Tsubasa*] takes readers on a fantastic ride that only gets more exhilarating with each successive chapter." —Anime News Network

In the Kingdom of Clow, an archaeological dig unleashes an incredible power, causing Princess Sakura to lose her memories. To save her, her childhood friend Syaoran must follow the orders of the Dimension Witch and travel alongside Kurogane, an unrivaled warrior; Fai, a powerful magician; and Mokona, a curiously strange creature, to retrieve Sakura's dispersed memories!

THE WORLD OF CLAMP!

Cardcaptor Sakura Collector's Edition

Cardcaptor Sakura: Clear Card

Magic Knight Rayearth 25th Anniversary Box Set

Chobits

TSUBASA Omnibus

TSUBASA WoRLD CHRoNiCLE

xxxHOLiC Omnibus

xxxHOLiC Rei

CLOVER Collector's Edition

Young characters and steampunk setting, like *Howl's Moving Castle* and *Battle Angel Alita*

Beyond the Clouds © 2018 Nicke / Ki-oon

A boy with a talent for machines and a mysterious girl whose wings he's fixed will take you beyond the clouds! In the tradition of the high-flying, resonant adventure stories of Studio Ghibli comes a gorgeous tale about the longing of young hearts for adventure and friendship!

The adorable new odd-couple cat comedy manga from the creator of the beloved *Chi's Sweet Home*, in full color!

Praise for Chi's Sweet Home

"Nearly impossible to turn away... a true all-ages title that anyone, young or old, cat lover or not, will enjoy. The stories will bring a smile to your face and warm your heart."

—*School Library Journal*

Sue & Tai-chan

Konami Kanata

Sue is an aging housecat who's looking forward to living out her life in peace... but her plans change when the mischievous black tomcat Tai-chan enters the picture! Hey! Sue never signed up to be a catsitter! *Sue & Tai-chan* is the latest from the reigning meow-narch of cute kitty comics, Konami Kanata.

KC
KODANSHA
COMICS

CUTE ANIMALS AND LIFE LESSONS, PERFECT FOR ASPIRING PET VETS OF ALL AGES!

YUZU
THE
PET
VET

1

BY
MINGO ITO

In collaboration with
NIPPON COLUMBIA CO., LTD.

Yuzu the Pet Vet © Mingo Ito / NIPPON COLUMBIA CO.,LTD. / Kodansha Ltd.

For an 11-year-old, Yuzu has a lot on her plate. When her mom gets sick and has to be hospitalized, Yuzu goes to live with her uncle who runs the local veterinary clinic. Yuzu's always been scared of animals, but she tries to help out. Through all the tough moments in her life, Yuzu realizes that she can help make things all right with a little help from her animal pals, peers, and kind grown-ups.

Every new patient is a furry friend in the making!

Knight of the ICE

Yayoi Ogawa

Knight of the Ice ©Yayoi Ogawa/Kodansha Ltd.

SKATING THRILLS AND ICY CHILLS WITH THIS NEW TINGLY ROMANCE SERIES!

A rom-com on ice, perfect for fans of *Princess Jellyfish* and *Wotakoi*. Kokoro is the talk of the figure-skating world, winning trophies and hearts. But little do they know... he's actually a huge nerd! From the beloved creator of *You're My Pet* (*Tramps Like Us*).

Chitose is a serious young woman, working for the health magazine *SASSO*. Or at least, she would be, if she wasn't constantly getting distracted by her childhood friend, international figure skating star Kokoro Kijinami! In the public eye and on the ice, Kokoro is a gallant, flawless knight, but behind his glittery costumes and breathtaking spins lies a secret: He's actually a hopelessly romantic otaku, who can only land his quad jumps when Chitose is on hand to recite a spell from his favorite magical girl anime!

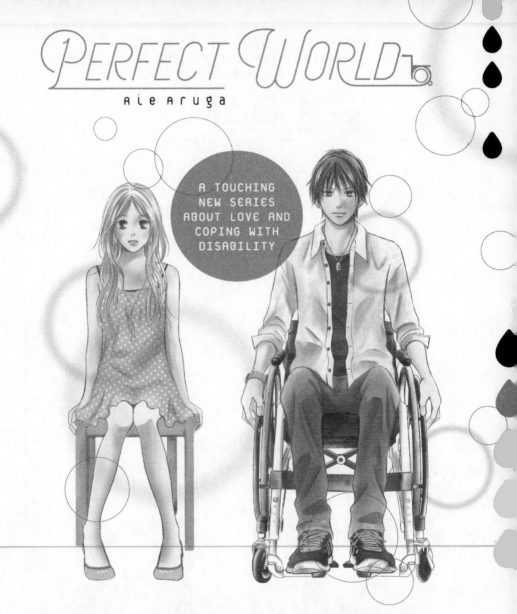

① PERFECT WORLD
Rie Aruga

A TOUCHING NEW SERIES ABOUT LOVE AND COPING WITH DISABILITY

An office party reunites Tsugumi with her high school crush Itsuki. He's realized his dream of becoming an architect, but along the way, he experienced a spinal injury that put him in a wheelchair. Now Tsugumi's rekindled feelings will butt up against prejudices she never considered — and Itsuki will have to decide if he's ready to let someone into his heart...

"Depicts with great delicacy and courage the difficulties some with disabilities experience getting involved in romantic relationships... Rie Aruga refuses to romanticize, pushing her heroine to face the reality of disability. She invites her readers to the same tasks of empathy, knowledge and recognition."
—Slate.fr

"An important entry [in manga romance]... The emotional core of both plot and characters indicates thoughtfulness... [Aruga's] research is readily apparent in the text and artwork, making this feel like a real story."
—Anime News Network

KC KODANSHA COMICS

BOYS RUN THE RIOT VOLUME 4
ORIGINAL U.S. COVER SKETCH
BY AUTHOR KEITO GAKU

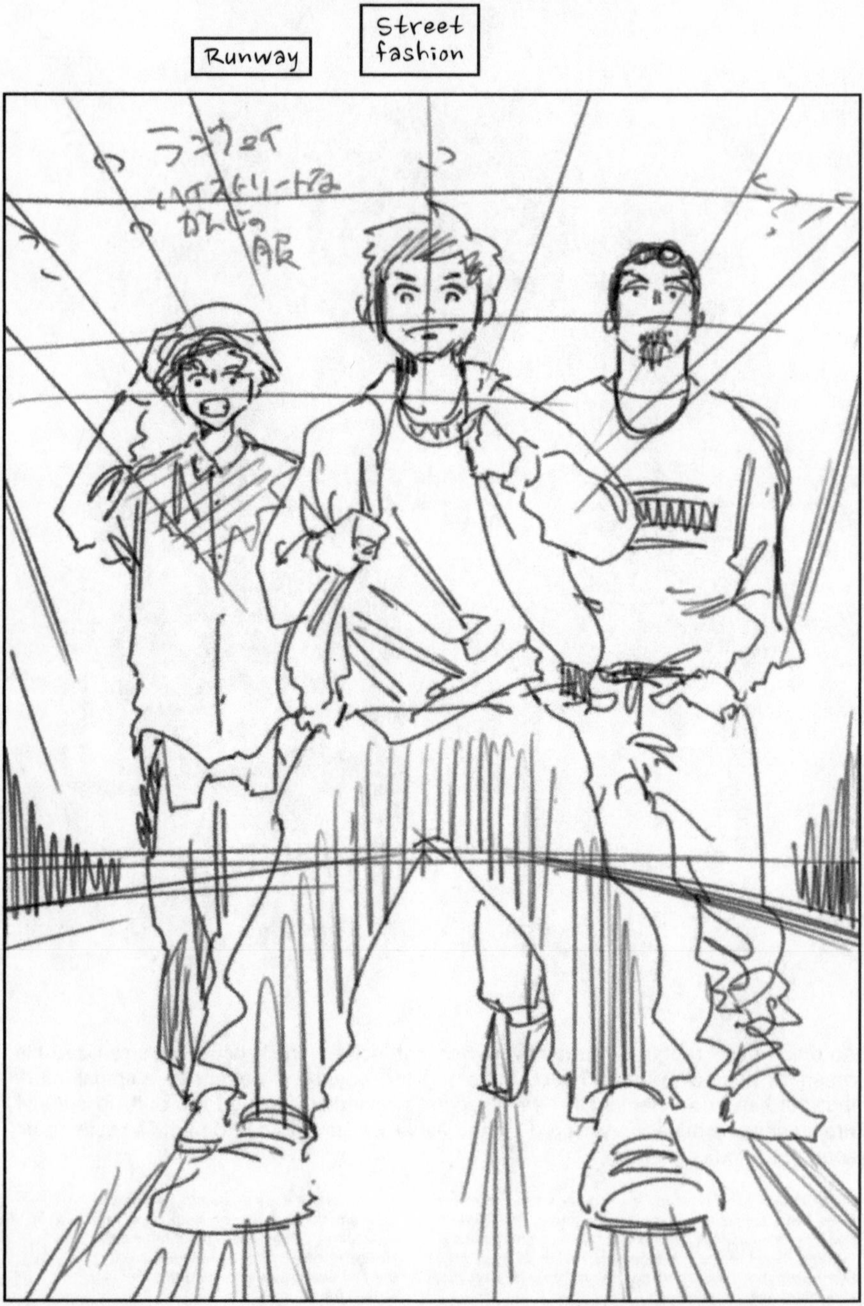
Runway
Street fashion
ランウェイ
ハイストリートなかんじの服

TRANSLATION NOTES

TATSUYA, page 47
The fictional video rental store Ryo visits in this scene is a reference to Tsutaya, a real-life bookstore and video rental chain in Japan.

"WE'RE IN A BAR...", page 111
The type of bar Ryo, Joe, and company are at is an izakaya, an informal Japanese bar that serves alcoholic drinks and snacks.

"ISN'T THAT... NAO'S UNIFORM...?" "...*YES*.", page 132
Throughout the series in the original Japanese, Ryo uses the masculine personal pronoun *ore* to refer to himself in front of people who know he is a boy. In this scene, on page 132, Ryo uses the pronoun *ore* for himself in front of his family for the first time ever as he is coming out to them as a boy.

"...OR SHOULD I SAY, MAKI-*KUN*.", page 209
Here, Kimura switches from addressing Maki as Maki-*san*, a gender neutral honorific used to address someone as Mr./Ms./Mx., to Maki-*kun*. an honorific often attached to the names of boys or younger men.

"I'M SORRY, MR. KIMURA.", page 217
In the original Japanese, Maki is addressing Kimura as Kimura-*tenchou*, or manager.

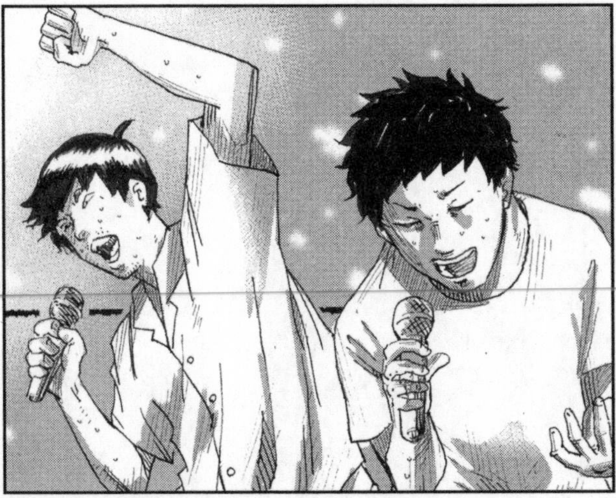

"CHOO CHOO TRAIN" BY EXILE, page 236
The song Kimura is singing on this page is "Choo Choo Train," a 2003 single by the Japanese boy band Exile.

"MOONLIGHT, SUNLIGHT" BY THE HIGH-LOWS, page 240
Here, the boys are singing "Moonlight, Sunlight," (*Gekkou, Youkou*) a 1997 single by the Japanese rock band The High-Lows.

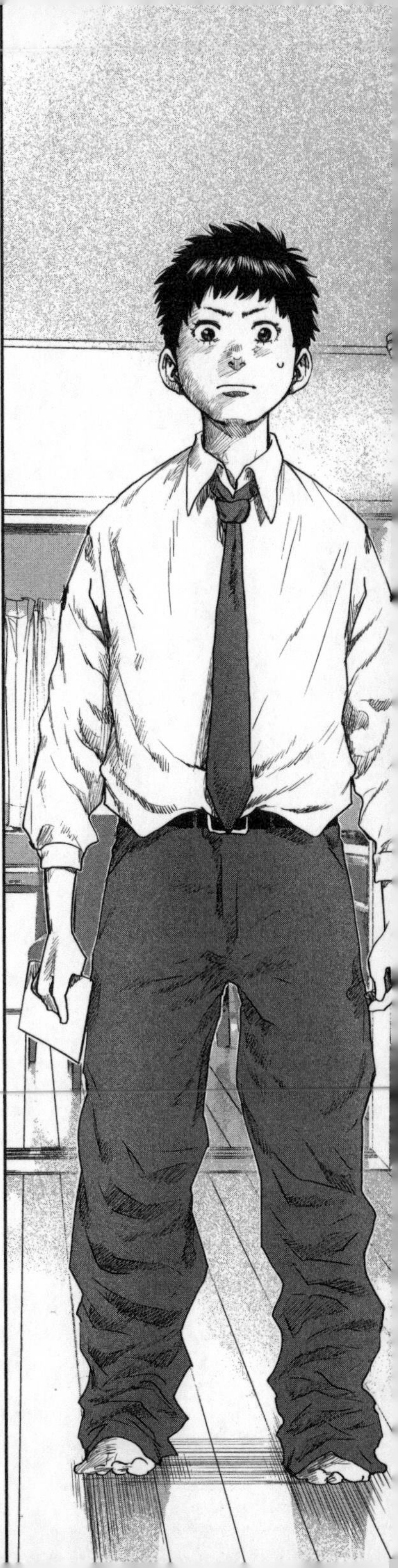

BOYS RUN
ボーイズ・ラン・ザ・ライオット
THE RIOT

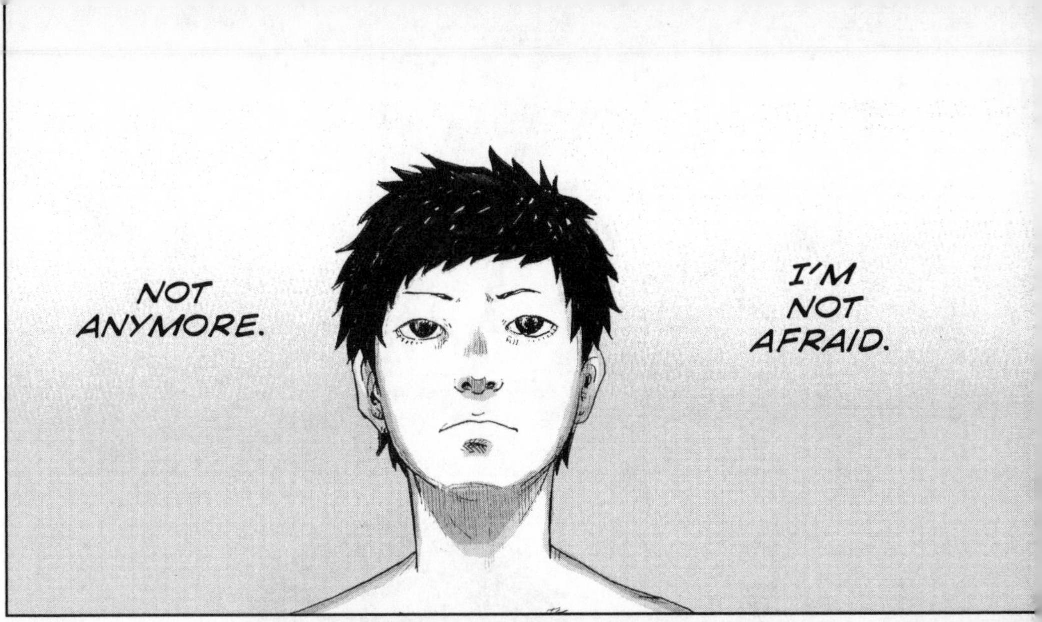
I'M NOT AFRAID.
NOT ANYMORE.
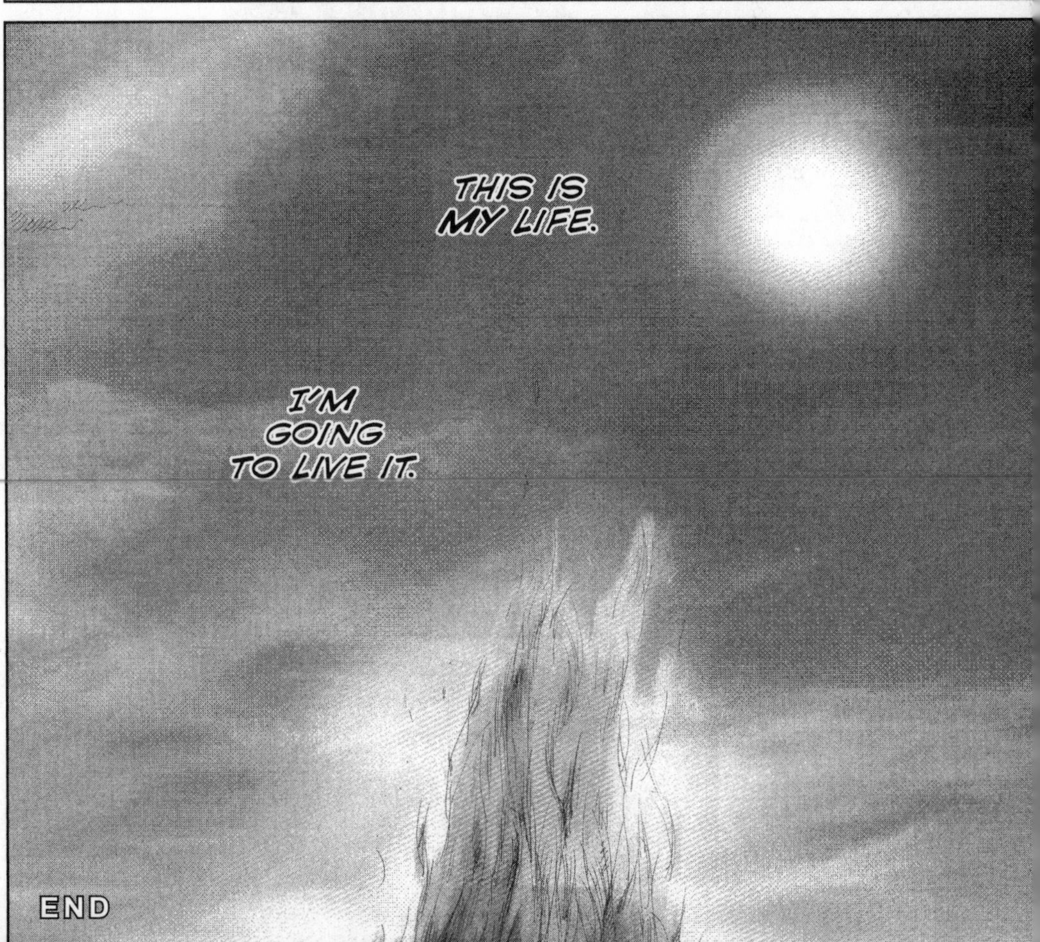
THIS IS MY LIFE.
I'M GOING TO LIVE IT.
END

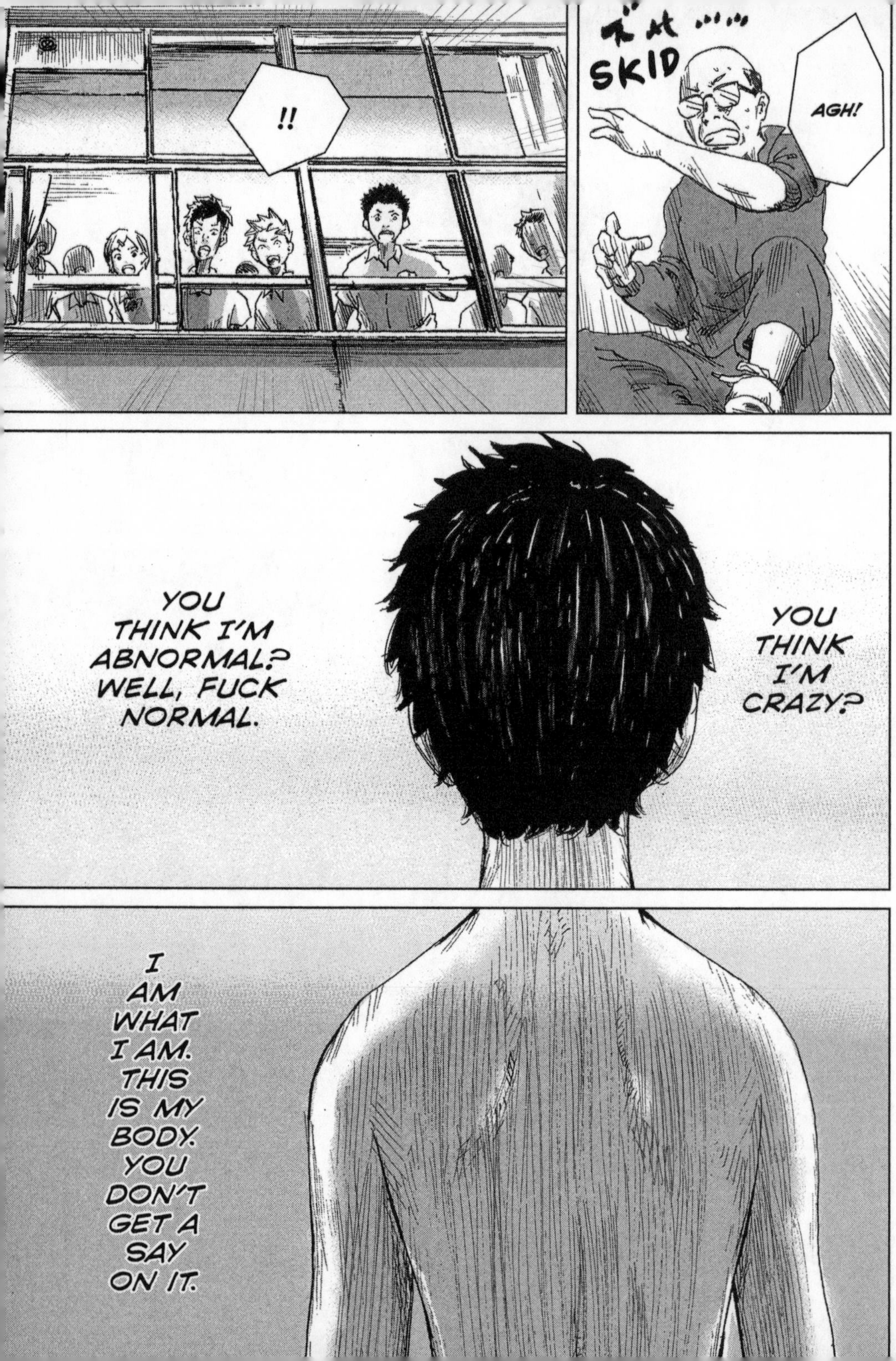
SKID
AGH!
!!
YOU THINK I'M CRAZY?
YOU THINK I'M ABNORMAL? WELL, FUCK NORMAL.
I AM WHAT I AM. THIS IS MY BODY. YOU DON'T GET A SAY ON IT.

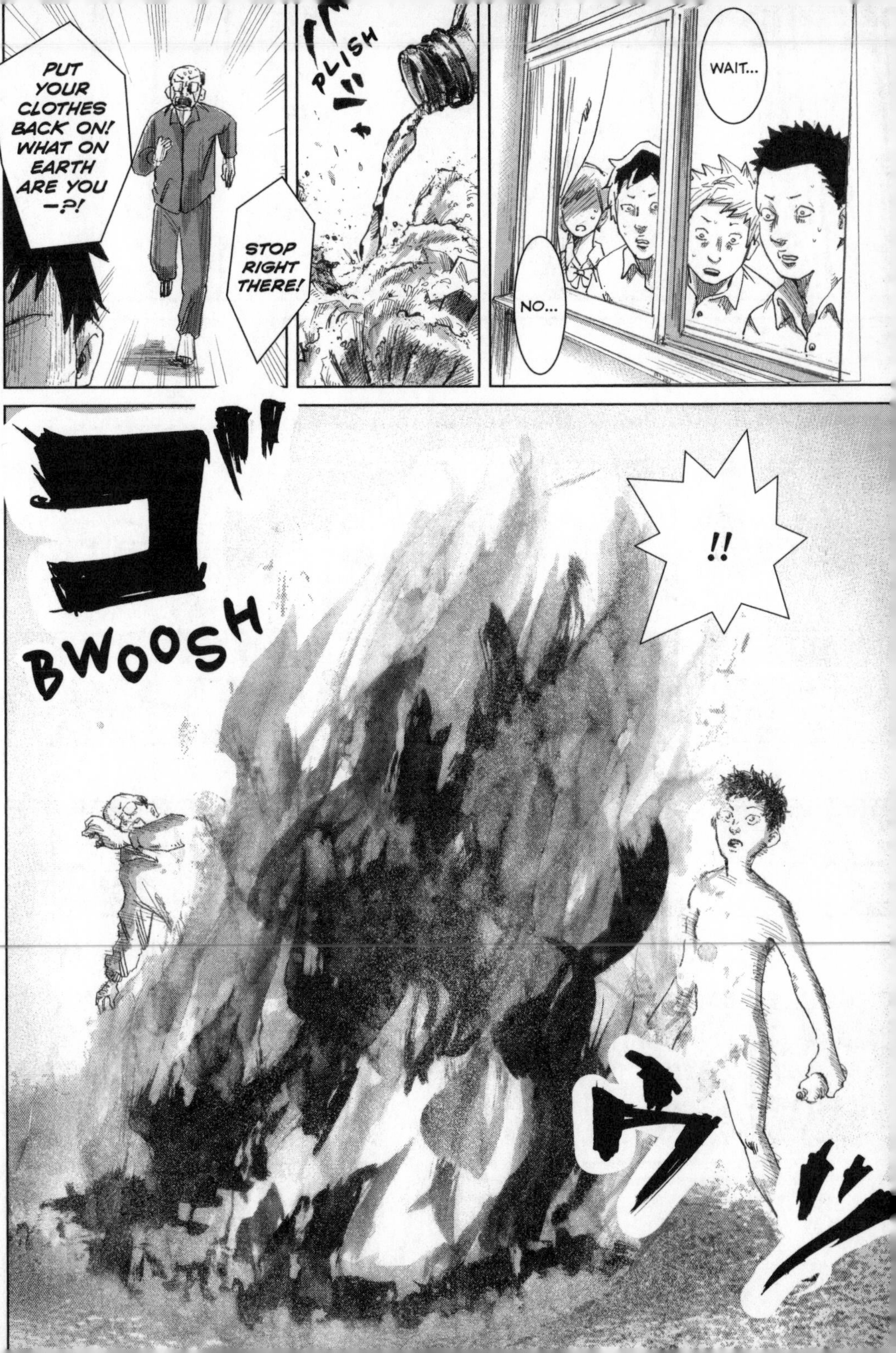
WAIT...
NO...
PLISH
STOP RIGHT THERE!
PUT YOUR CLOTHES BACK ON! WHAT ON EARTH ARE YOU—?!
!!
BWOOSH

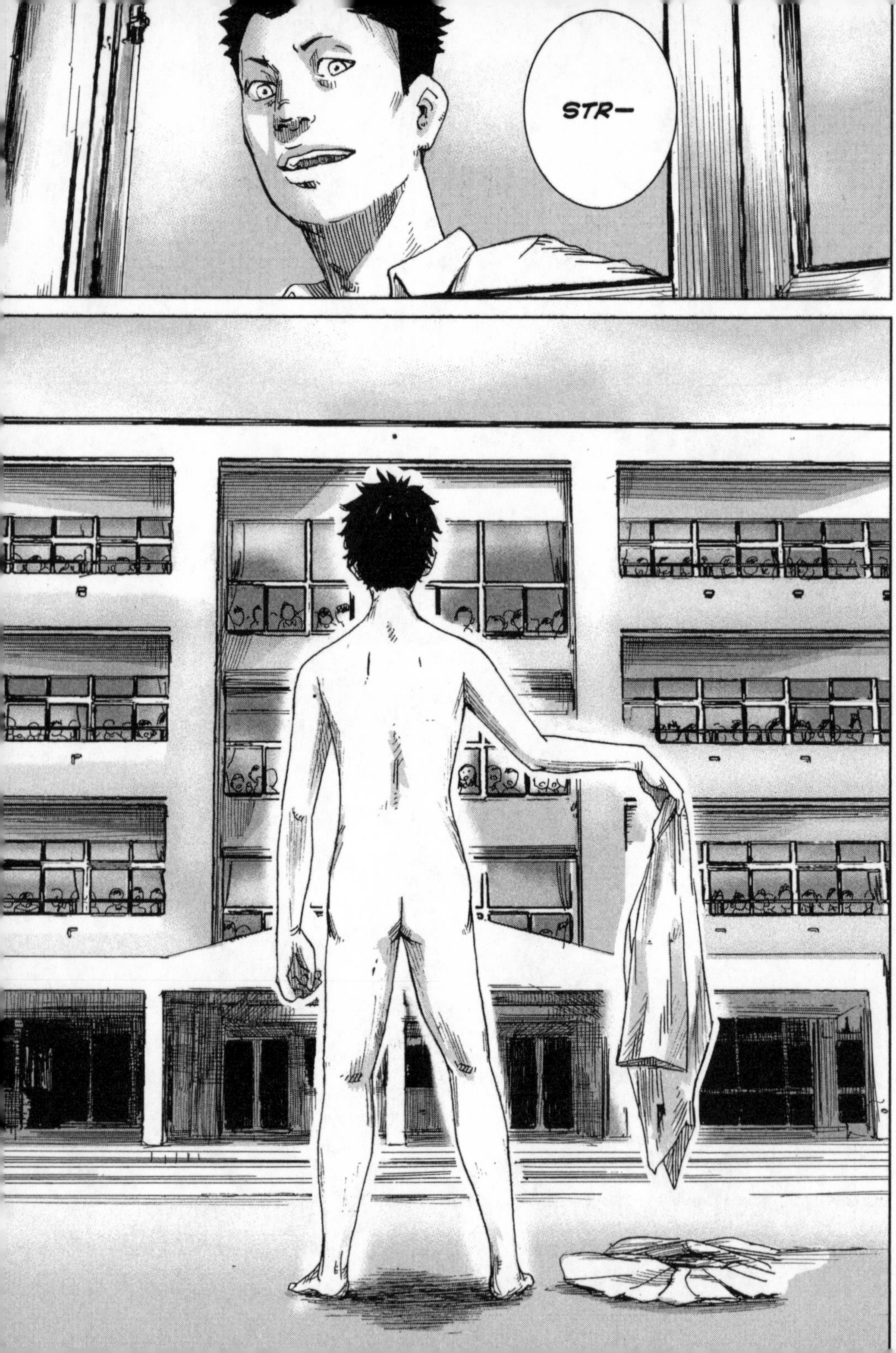
STR—

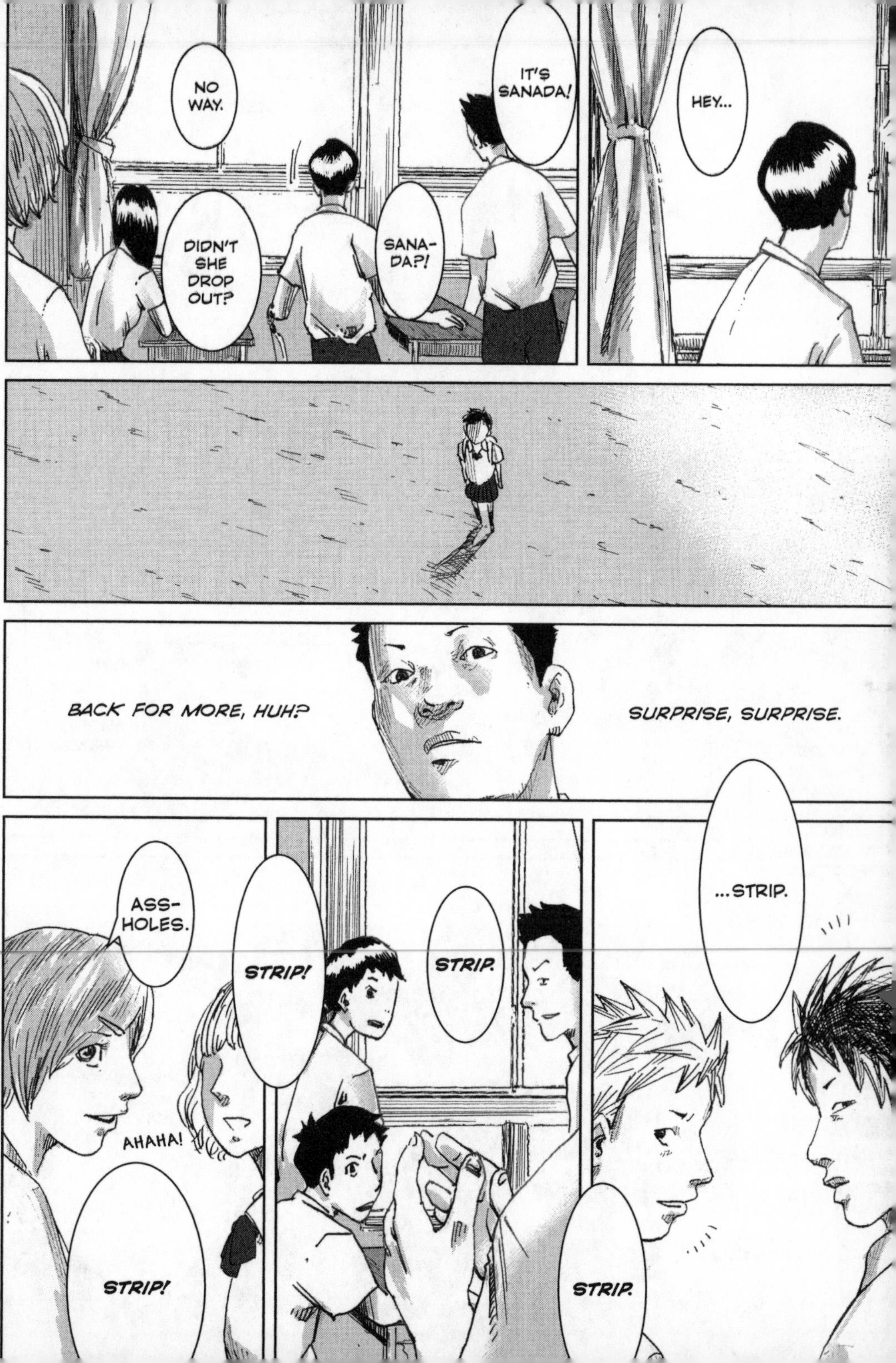
HEY...
IT'S SANADA!
NO WAY.
SANA-DA?!
DIDN'T SHE DROP OUT?
SURPRISE, SURPRISE.
BACK FOR MORE, HUH?
...STRIP.
STRIP.
STRIP.
STRIP!
ASS-HOLES.
AHAHA!
STRIP!

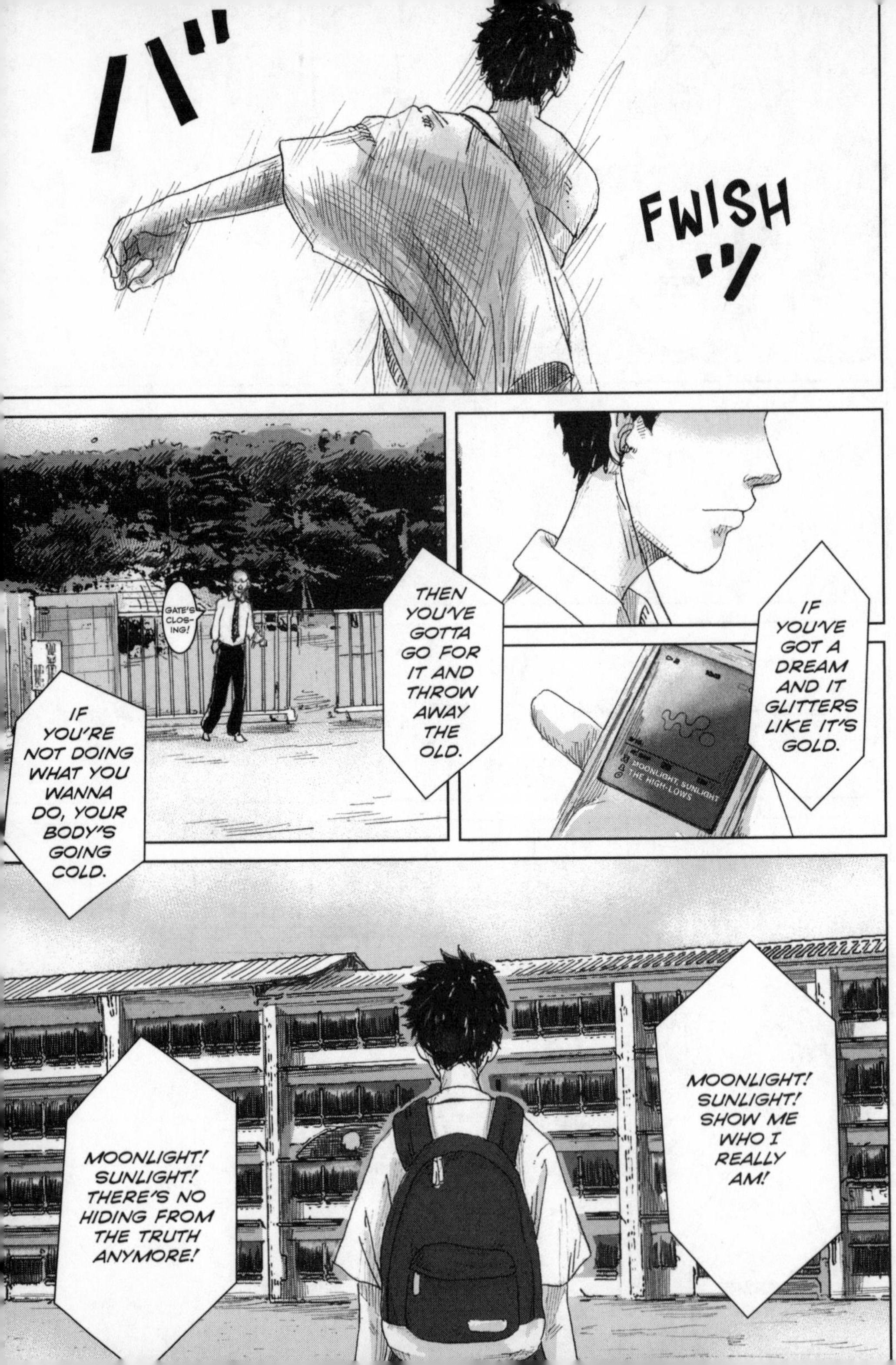
バ
FWISH
ッ
IF YOU'VE GOT A DREAM AND IT GLITTERS LIKE IT'S GOLD.
MOONLIGHT, SUNLIGHT
THE HIGH-LOWS
THEN YOU'VE GOTTA GO FOR IT AND THROW AWAY THE OLD.
GATE'S CLOS-ING!
IF YOU'RE NOT DOING WHAT YOU WANNA DO, YOUR BODY'S GOING COLD.
MOONLIGHT! SUNLIGHT! SHOW ME WHO I REALLY AM!
MOONLIGHT! SUNLIGHT! THERE'S NO HIDING FROM THE TRUTH ANYMORE!

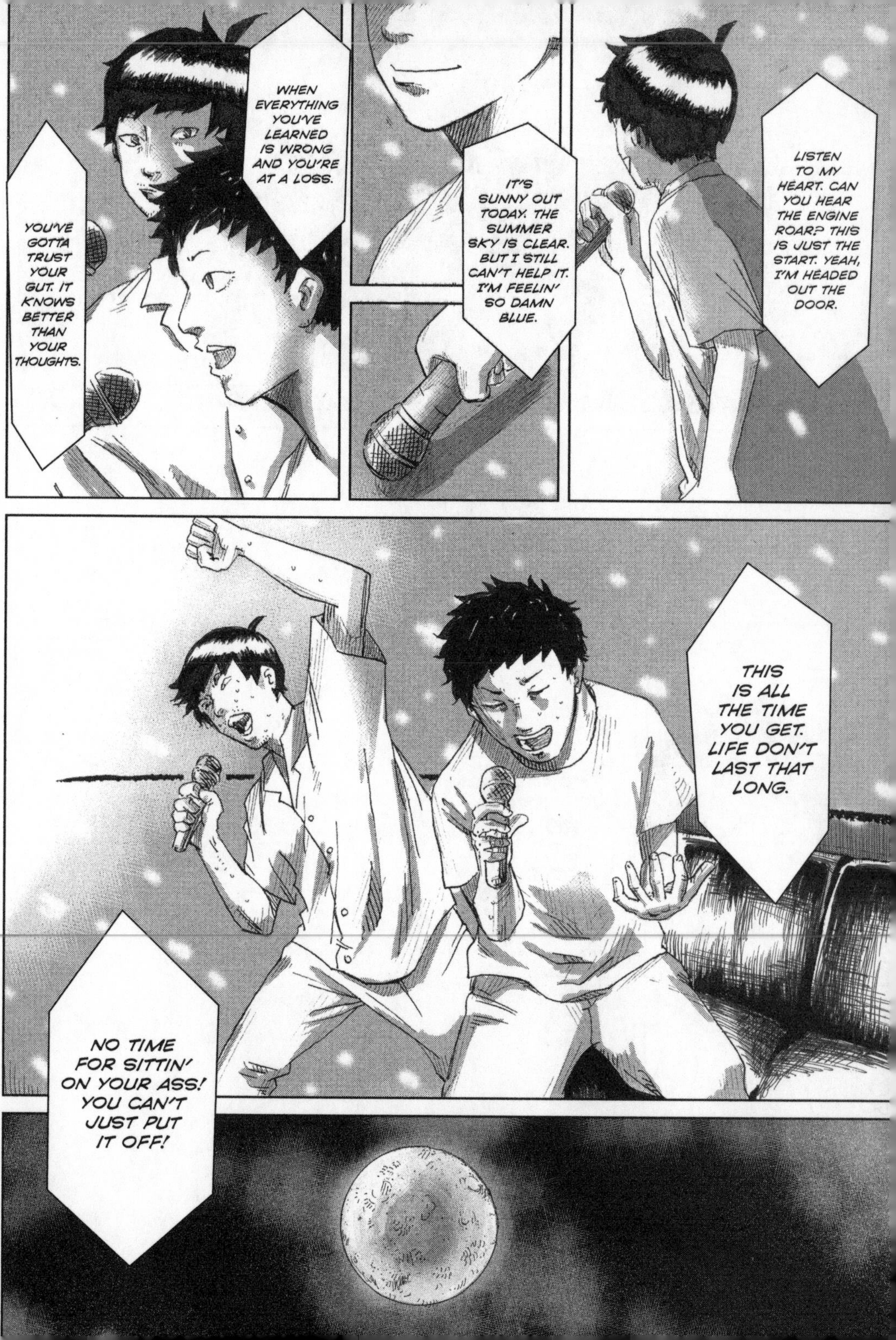
LISTEN TO MY HEART. CAN YOU HEAR THE ENGINE ROAR? THIS IS JUST THE START. YEAH, I'M HEADED OUT THE DOOR.
IT'S SUNNY OUT TODAY. THE SUMMER SKY IS CLEAR. BUT I STILL CAN'T HELP IT. I'M FEELIN' SO DAMN BLUE.
WHEN EVERYTHING YOU'VE LEARNED IS WRONG AND YOU'RE AT A LOSS.
YOU'VE GOTTA TRUST YOUR GUT. IT KNOWS BETTER THAN YOUR THOUGHTS.
THIS IS ALL THE TIME YOU GET. LIFE DON'T LAST THAT LONG.
NO TIME FOR SITTIN' ON YOUR ASS! YOU CAN'T JUST PUT IT OFF!

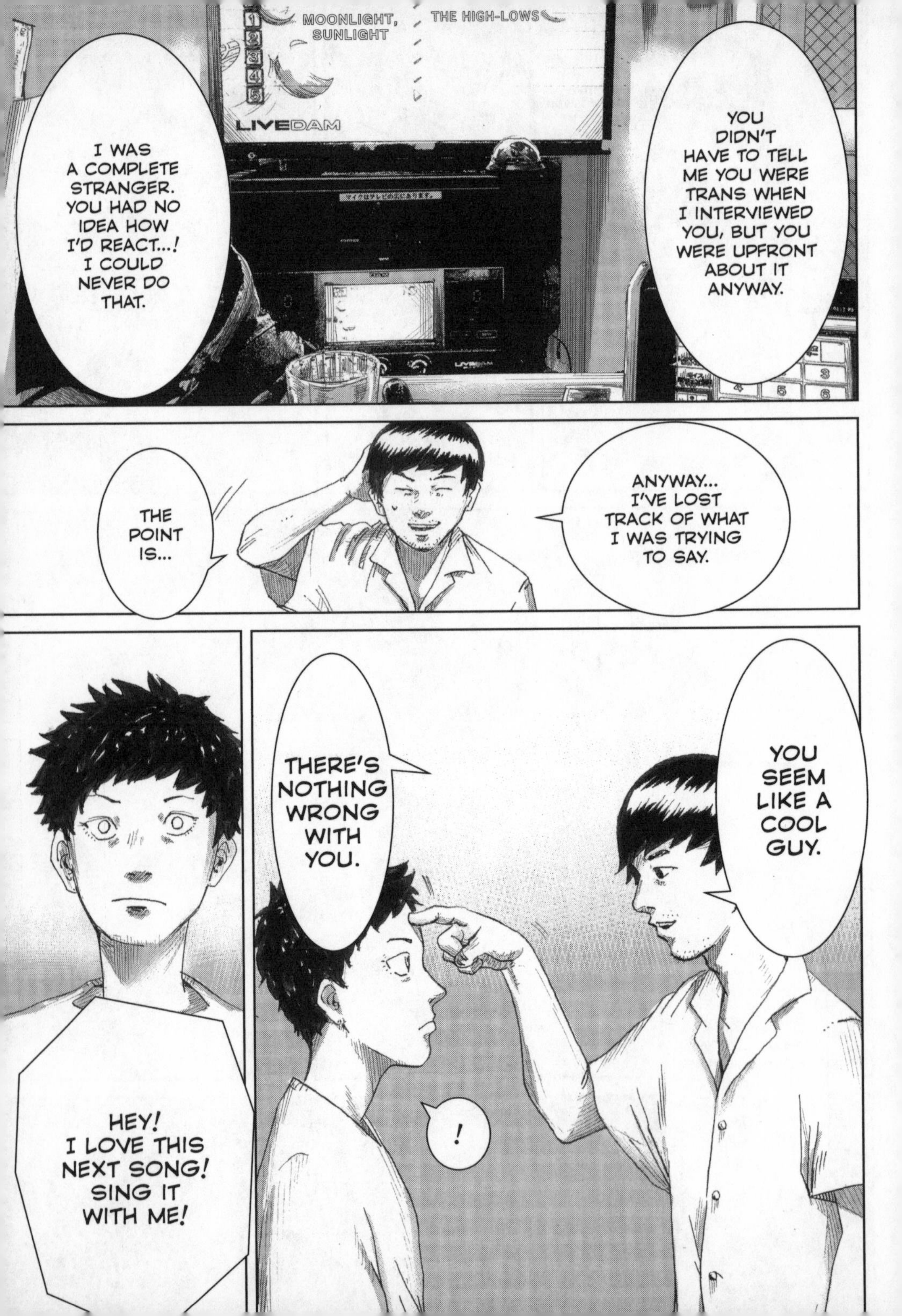
MOONLIGHT, SUNLIGHT
THE HIGH-LOWS
LIVEDAM
YOU DIDN'T HAVE TO TELL ME YOU WERE TRANS WHEN I INTERVIEWED YOU, BUT YOU WERE UPFRONT ABOUT IT ANYWAY.
I WAS A COMPLETE STRANGER. YOU HAD NO IDEA HOW I'D REACT...! I COULD NEVER DO THAT.
ANYWAY... I'VE LOST TRACK OF WHAT I WAS TRYING TO SAY.
...
THE POINT IS...
YOU SEEM LIKE A COOL GUY.
THERE'S NOTHING WRONG WITH YOU.
!
HEY! I LOVE THIS NEXT SONG! SING IT WITH ME!

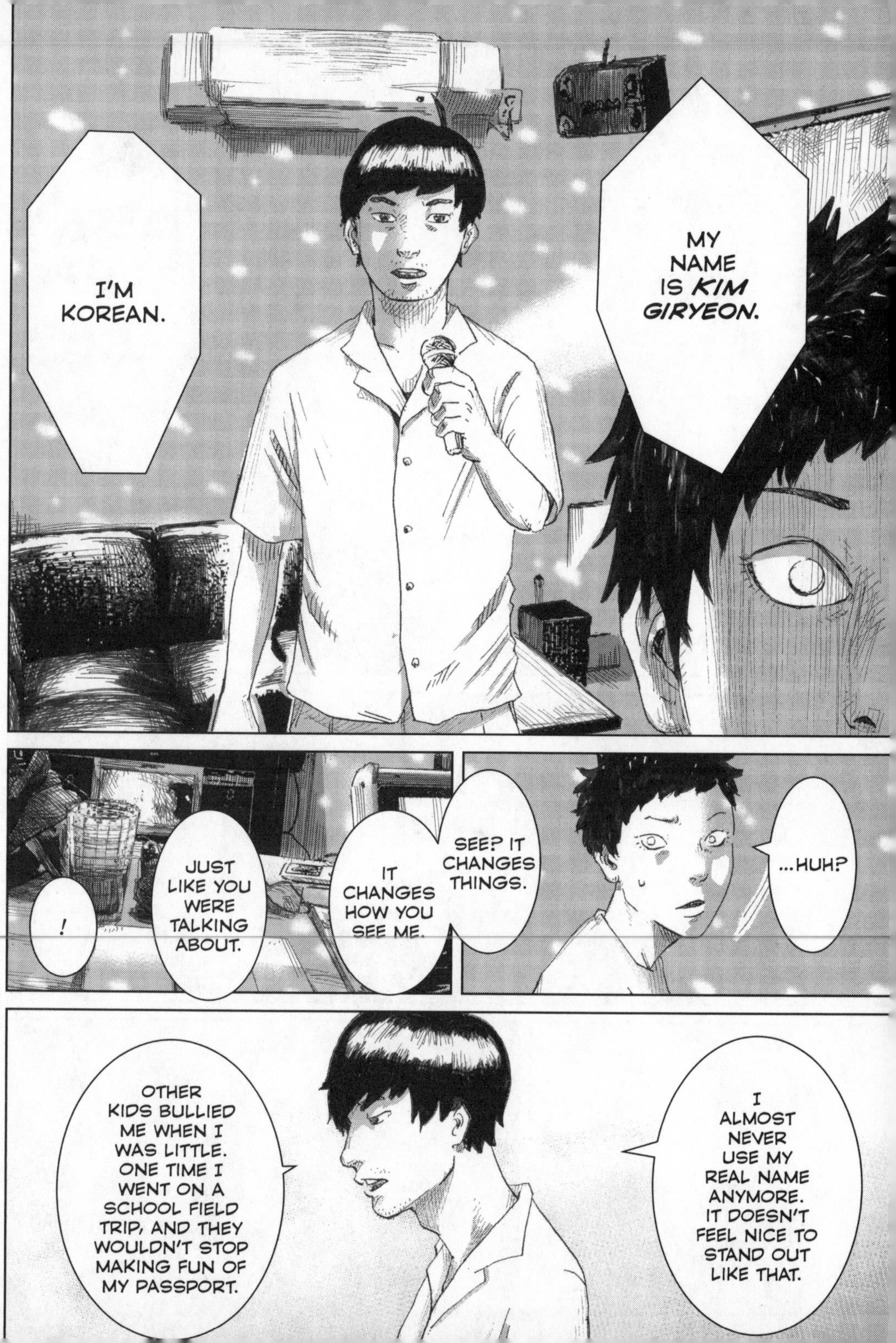
MY NAME IS *KIM GIRYEON*.
I'M KOREAN.
...HUH?
SEE? IT CHANGES THINGS.
IT CHANGES HOW YOU SEE ME.
JUST LIKE YOU WERE TALKING ABOUT.
!
I ALMOST NEVER USE MY REAL NAME ANYMORE. IT DOESN'T FEEL NICE TO STAND OUT LIKE THAT.
OTHER KIDS BULLIED ME WHEN I WAS LITTLE. ONE TIME I WENT ON A SCHOOL FIELD TRIP, AND THEY WOULDN'T STOP MAKING FUN OF MY PASSPORT.

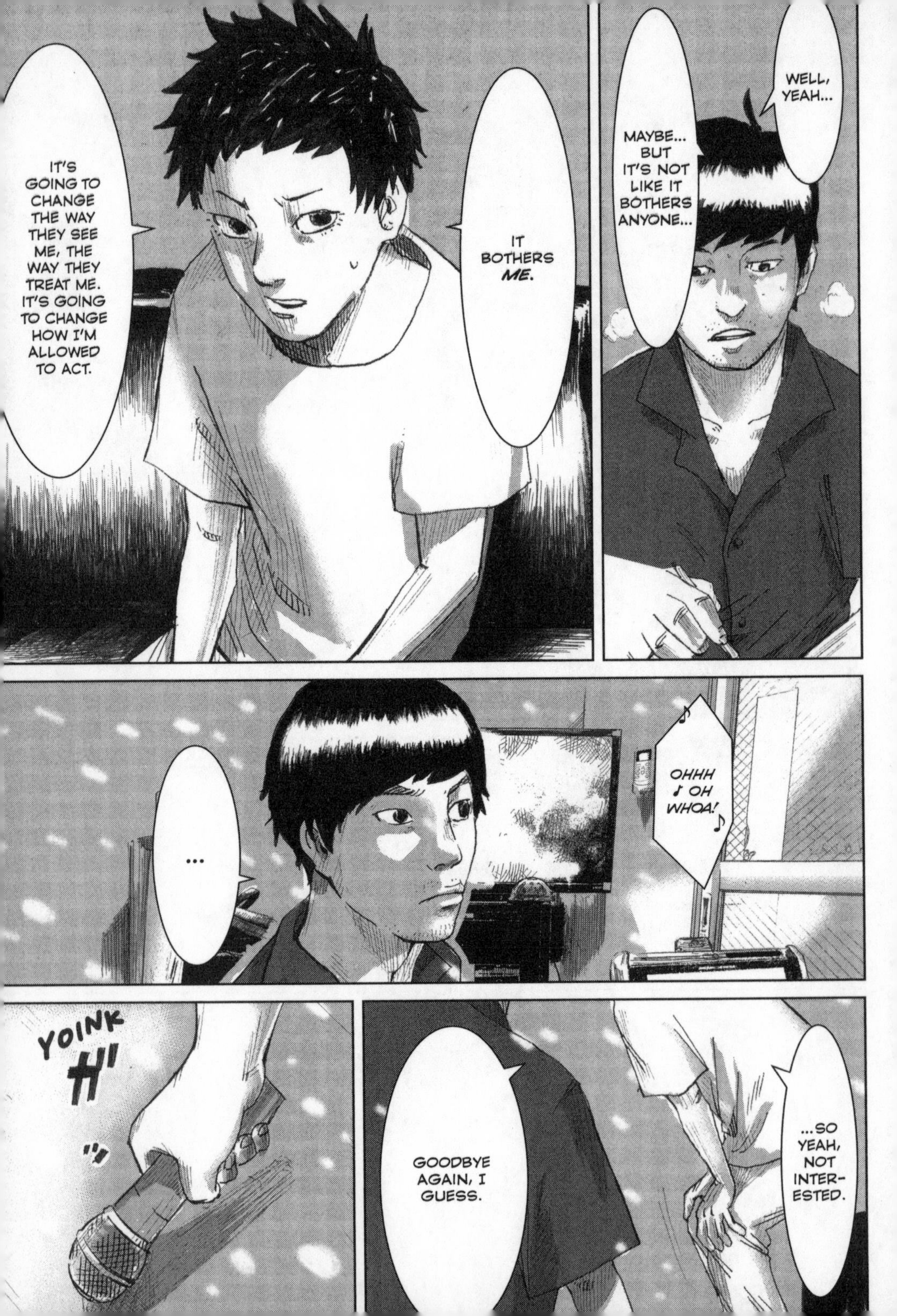
WELL, YEAH...
MAYBE... BUT IT'S NOT LIKE IT BOTHERS ANYONE...
IT BOTHERS *ME.*
IT'S GOING TO CHANGE THE WAY THEY SEE ME, THE WAY THEY TREAT ME. IT'S GOING TO CHANGE HOW I'M ALLOWED TO ACT.
OHHH ♪ OH WHOA! ♪
...
...SO YEAH, NOT INTER-ESTED.
GOODBYE AGAIN, I GUESS.
YOINK

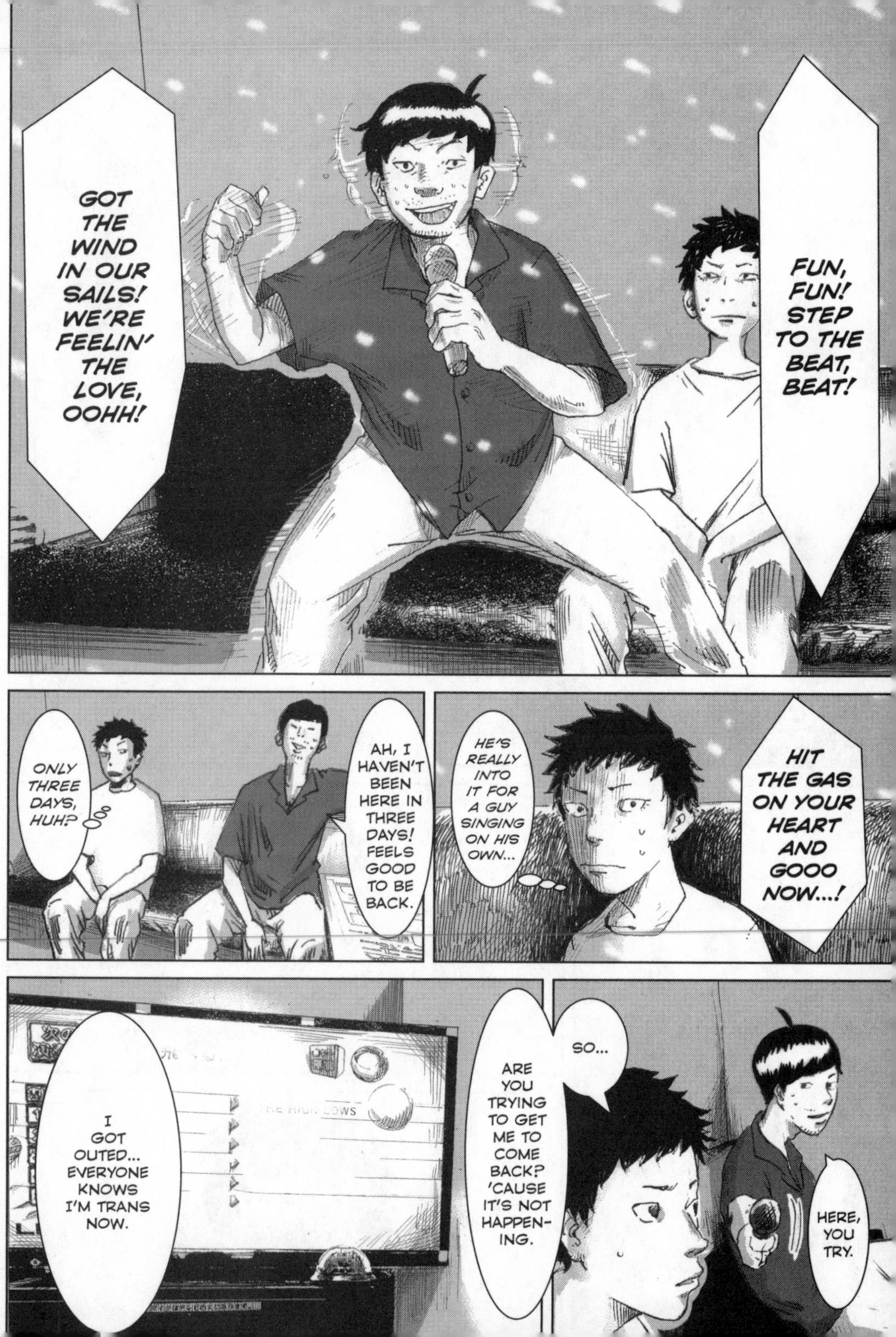
FUN, FUN! STEP TO THE BEAT, BEAT!
GOT THE WIND IN OUR SAILS! WE'RE FEELIN' THE LOVE, OOHH!
HIT THE GAS ON YOUR HEART AND GOOO NOW...!
HE'S REALLY INTO IT FOR A GUY SINGING ON HIS OWN...
AH, I HAVEN'T BEEN HERE IN THREE DAYS! FEELS GOOD TO BE BACK.
ONLY THREE DAYS, HUH?
HERE, YOU TRY.
SO...
ARE YOU TRYING TO GET ME TO COME BACK? 'CAUSE IT'S NOT HAPPEN-ING.
I GOT OUTED... EVERYONE KNOWS I'M TRANS NOW.

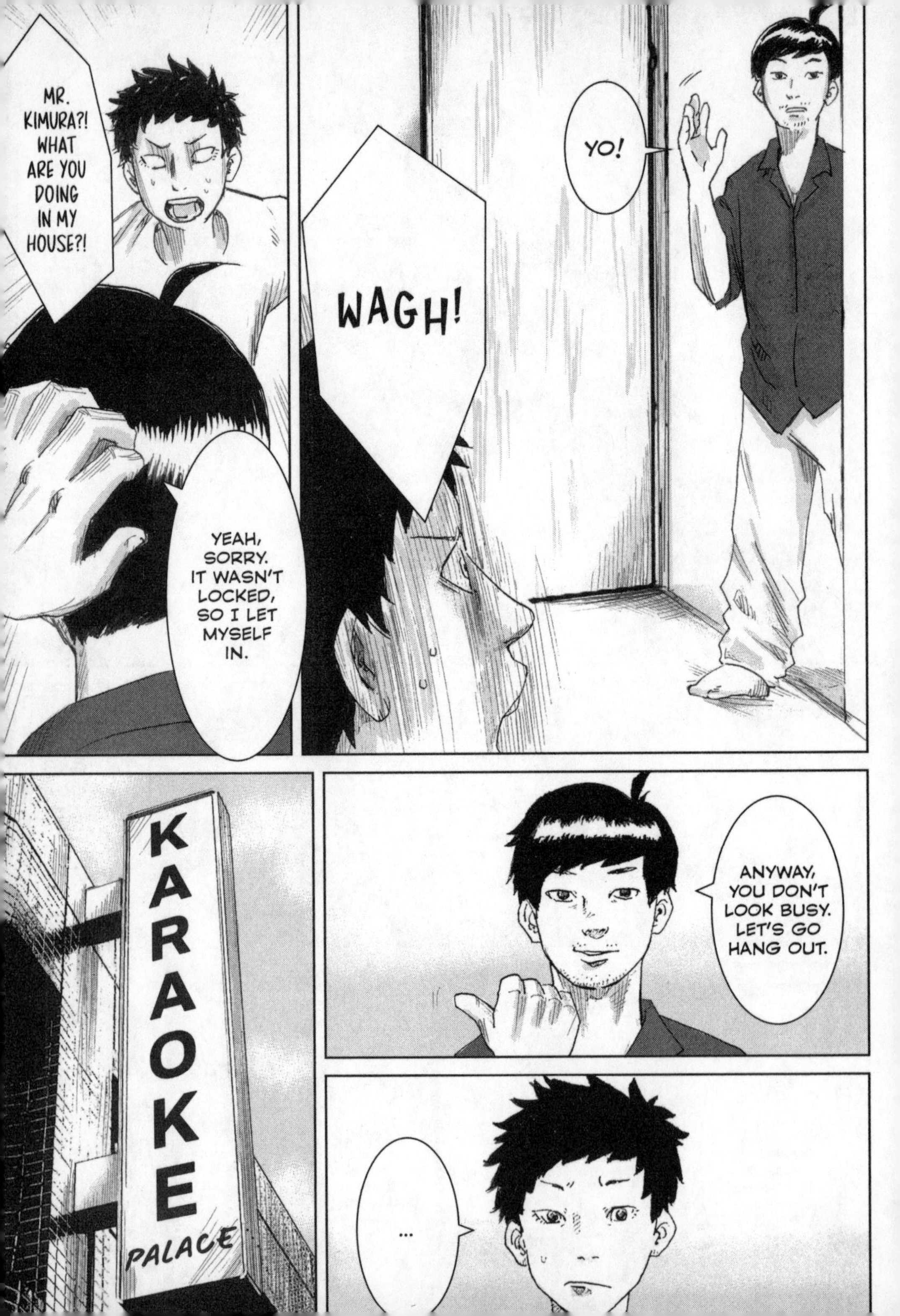
YO!
WAGH!
MR. KIMURA?! WHAT ARE YOU DOING IN MY HOUSE?!
YEAH, SORRY. IT WASN'T LOCKED, SO I LET MYSELF IN.
ANYWAY, YOU DON'T LOOK BUSY. LET'S GO HANG OUT.
...
KARAOKE
PALACE

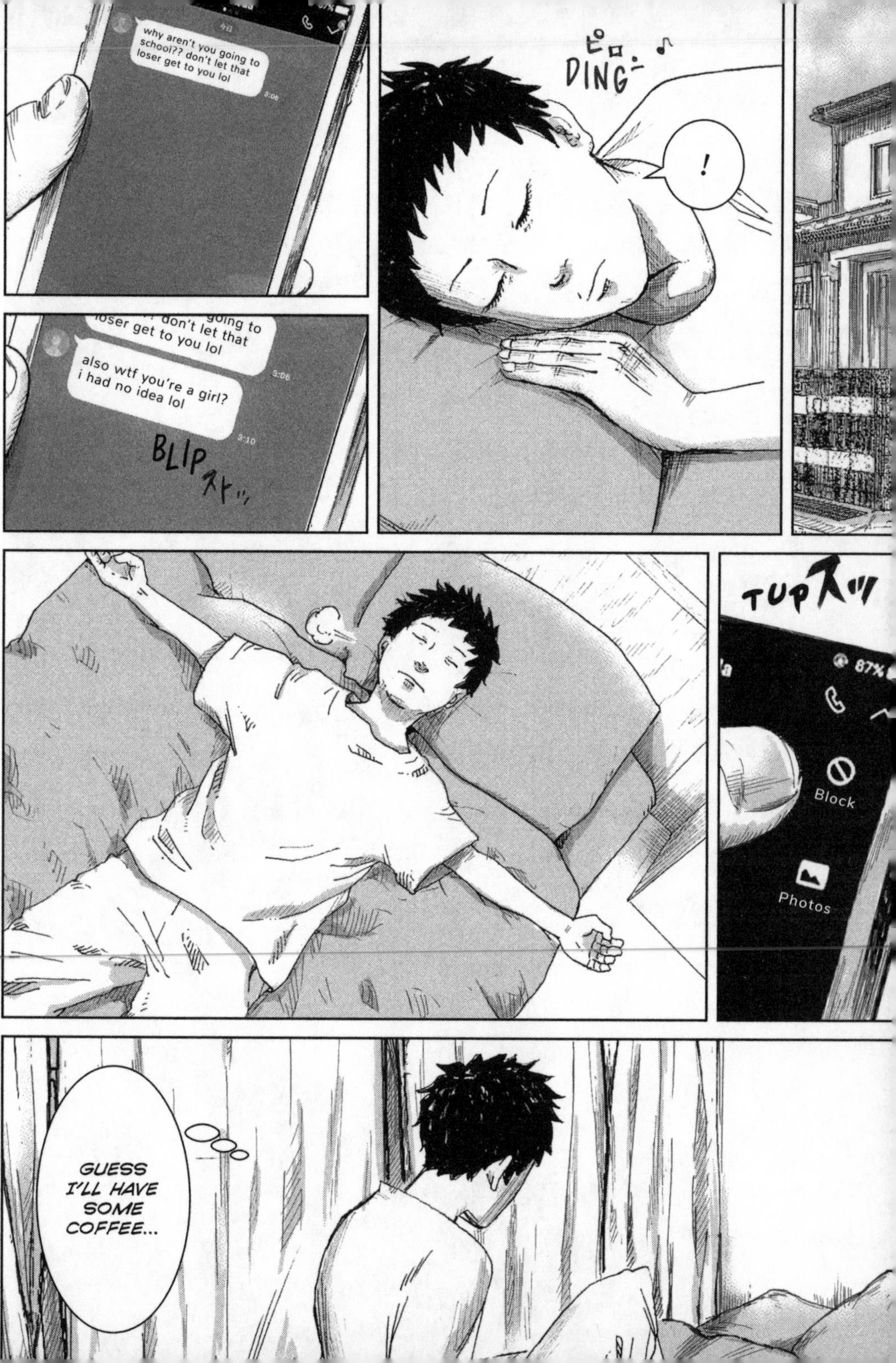

ピロ♪
DING
!
why aren't you going to school?? don't let that loser get to you lol
3:06
loser get to you lol
3:06
also wtf you're a girl? i had no idea lol
3:10
BLIP スッ
TUP スッ
87%
Block
Photos
GUESS I'LL HAVE SOME COFFEE...

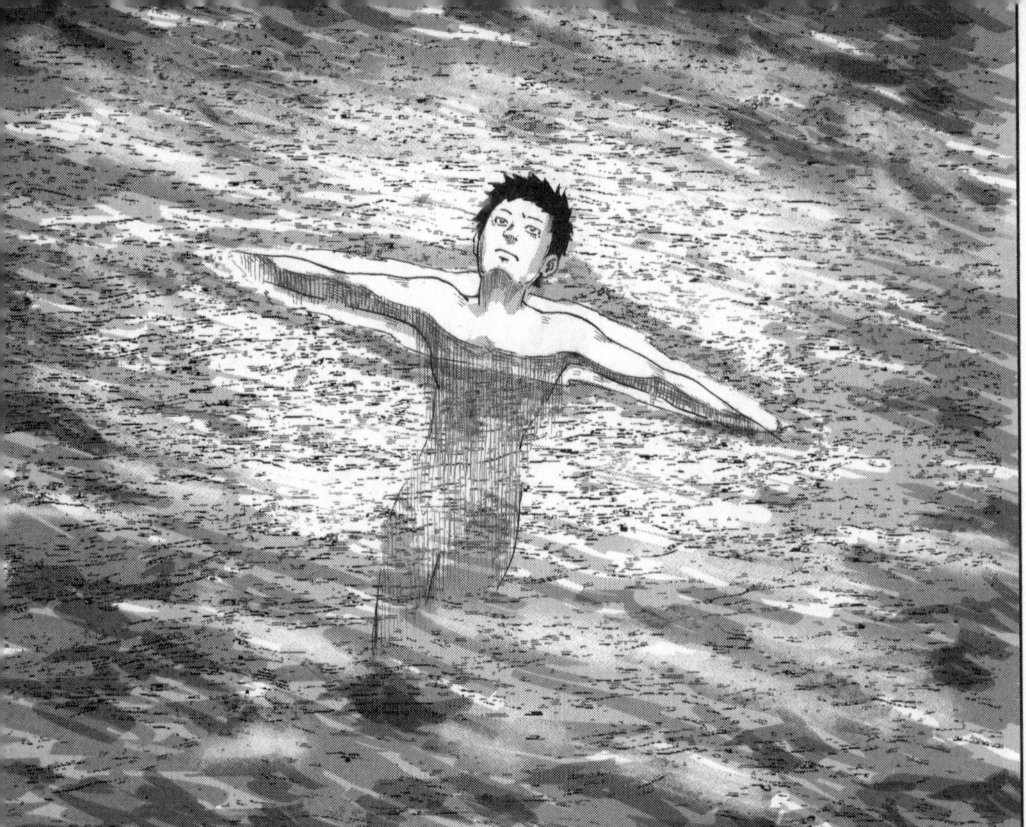
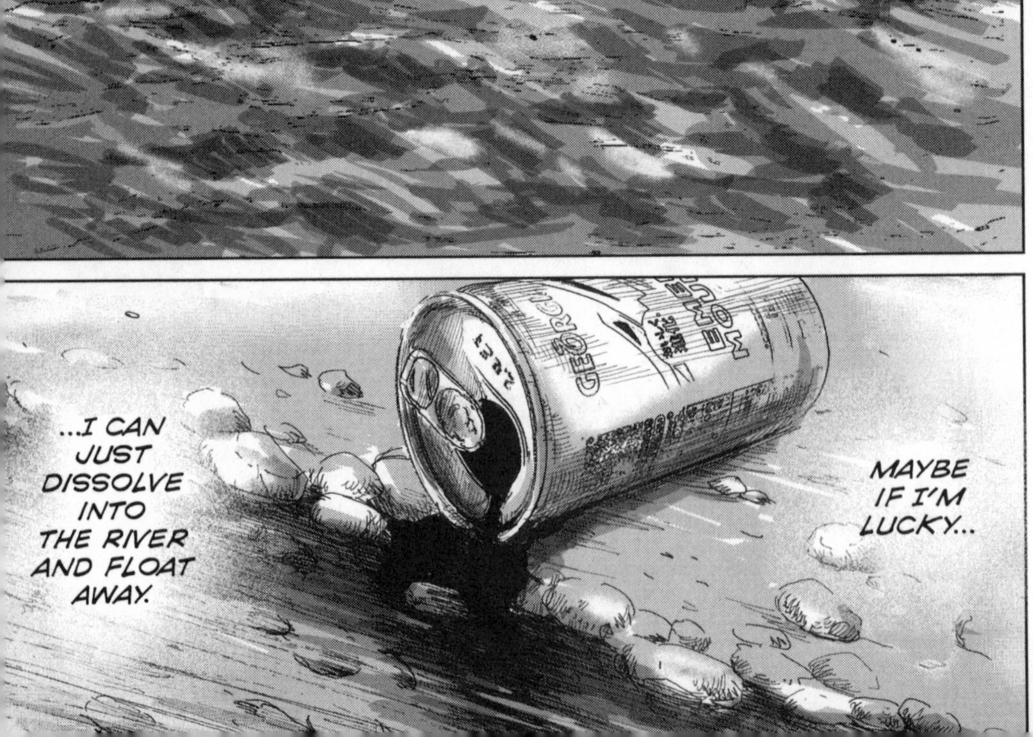
MAYBE IF I'M LUCKY...
...I CAN JUST DISSOLVE INTO THE RIVER AND FLOAT AWAY.

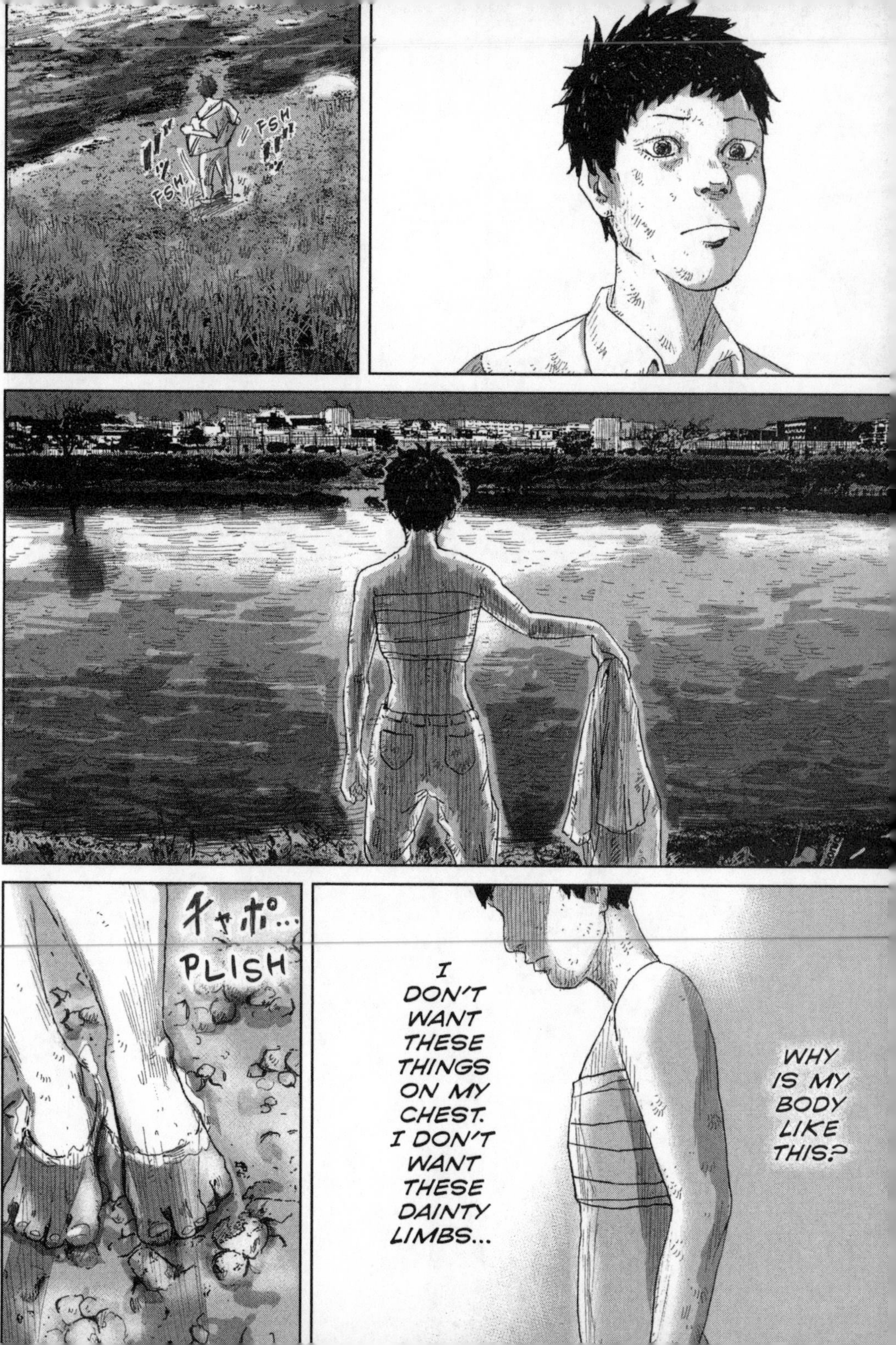
FSH
FSH
WHY IS MY BODY LIKE THIS?
I DON'T WANT THESE THINGS ON MY CHEST. I DON'T WANT THESE DAINTY LIMBS...
チャポ…
PLISH

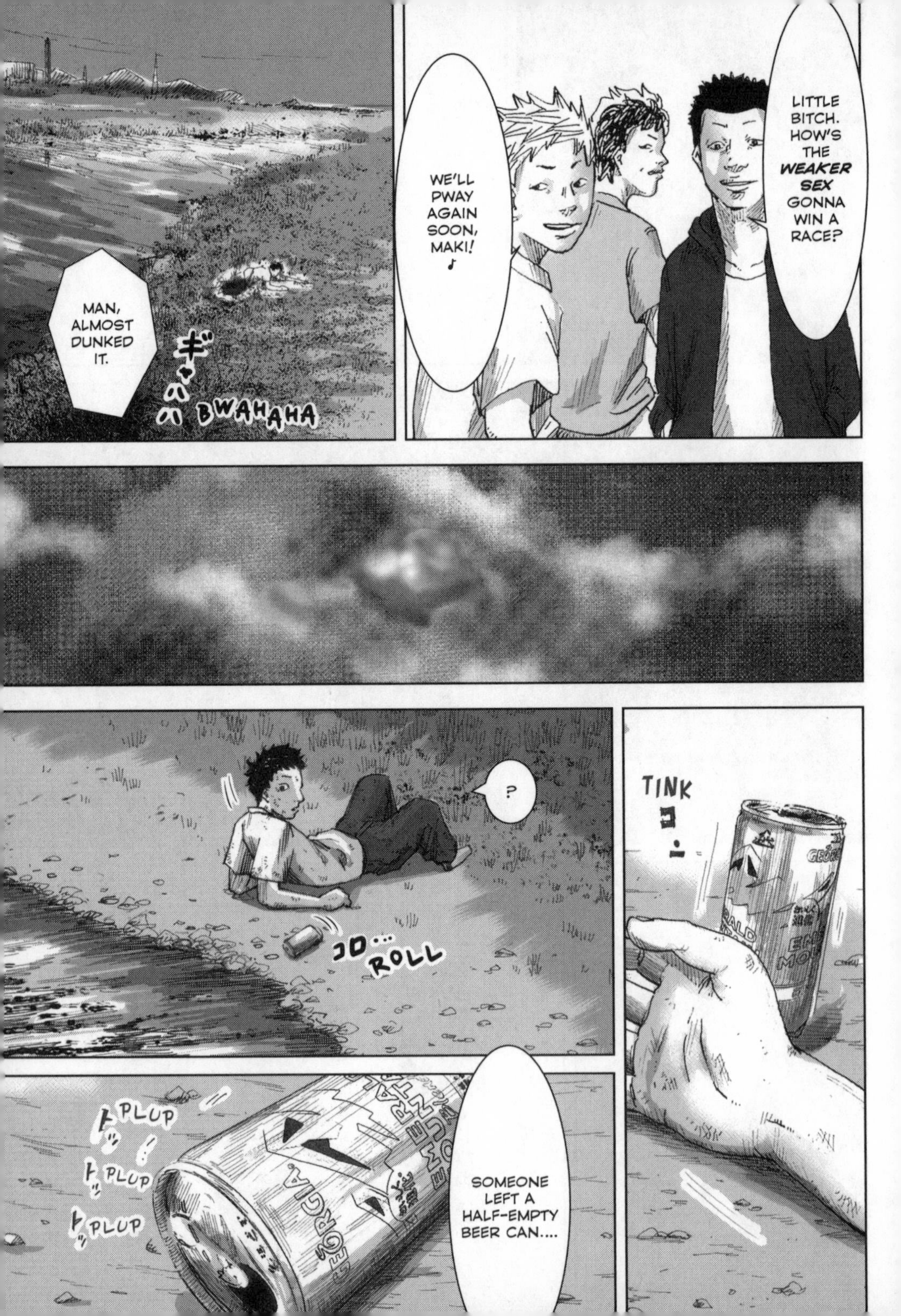
LITTLE BITCH. HOW'S THE **WEAKER SEX** GONNA WIN A RACE?
WE'LL PWAY AGAIN SOON, MAKI! ♪
MAN, ALMOST DUNKED IT.
BWAHAHA
TINK
?
ROLL
PLUP
PLUP
PLUP
SOMEONE LEFT A HALF-EMPTY BEER CAN....

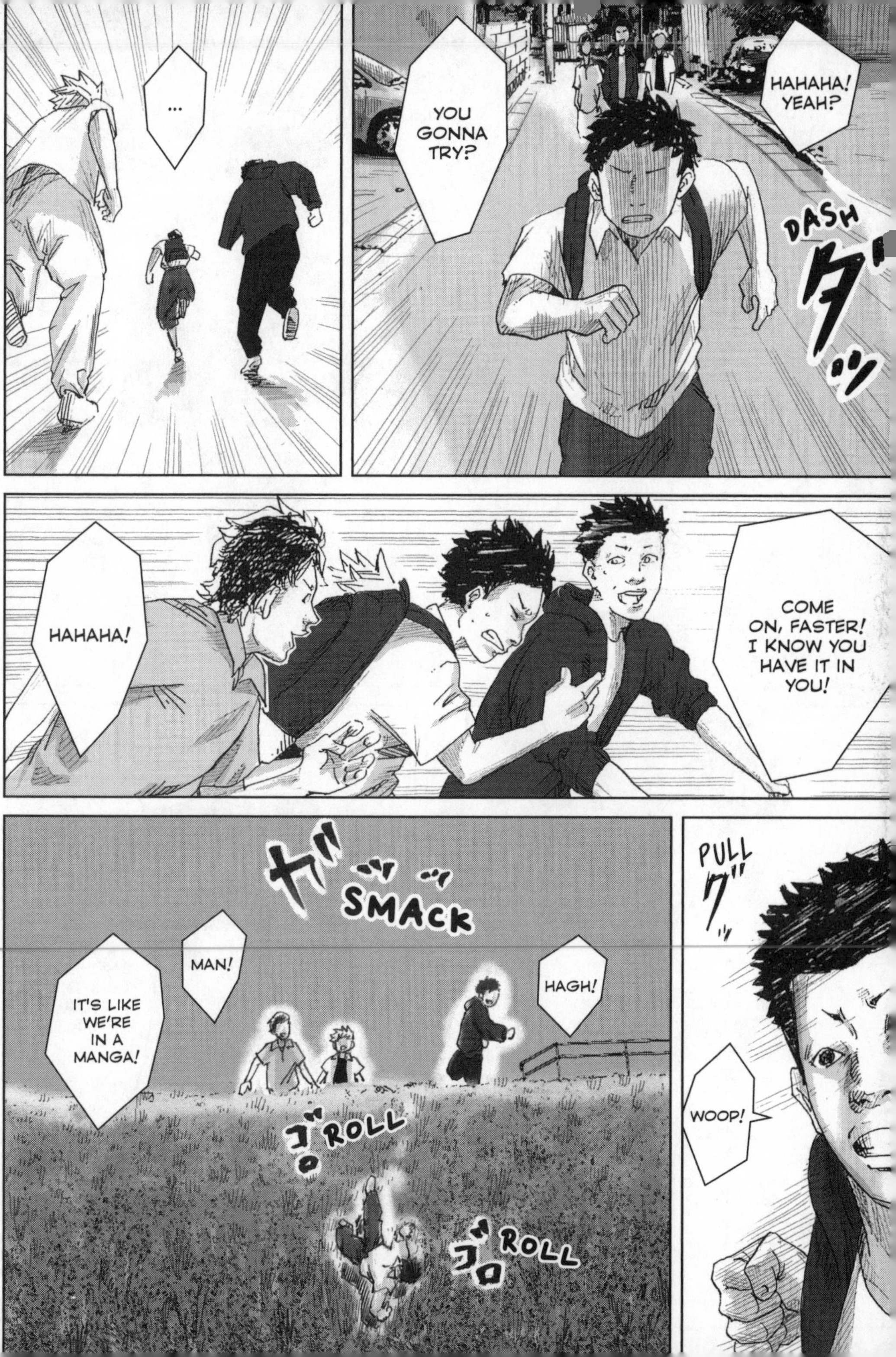
HAHAHA! YEAH?
YOU GONNA TRY?
DASH
...
COME ON, FASTER! I KNOW YOU HAVE IT IN YOU!
HAHAHA!
PULL
WOOP!
SMACK
HAGH!
MAN!
IT'S LIKE WE'RE IN A MANGA!
ROLL
ROLL

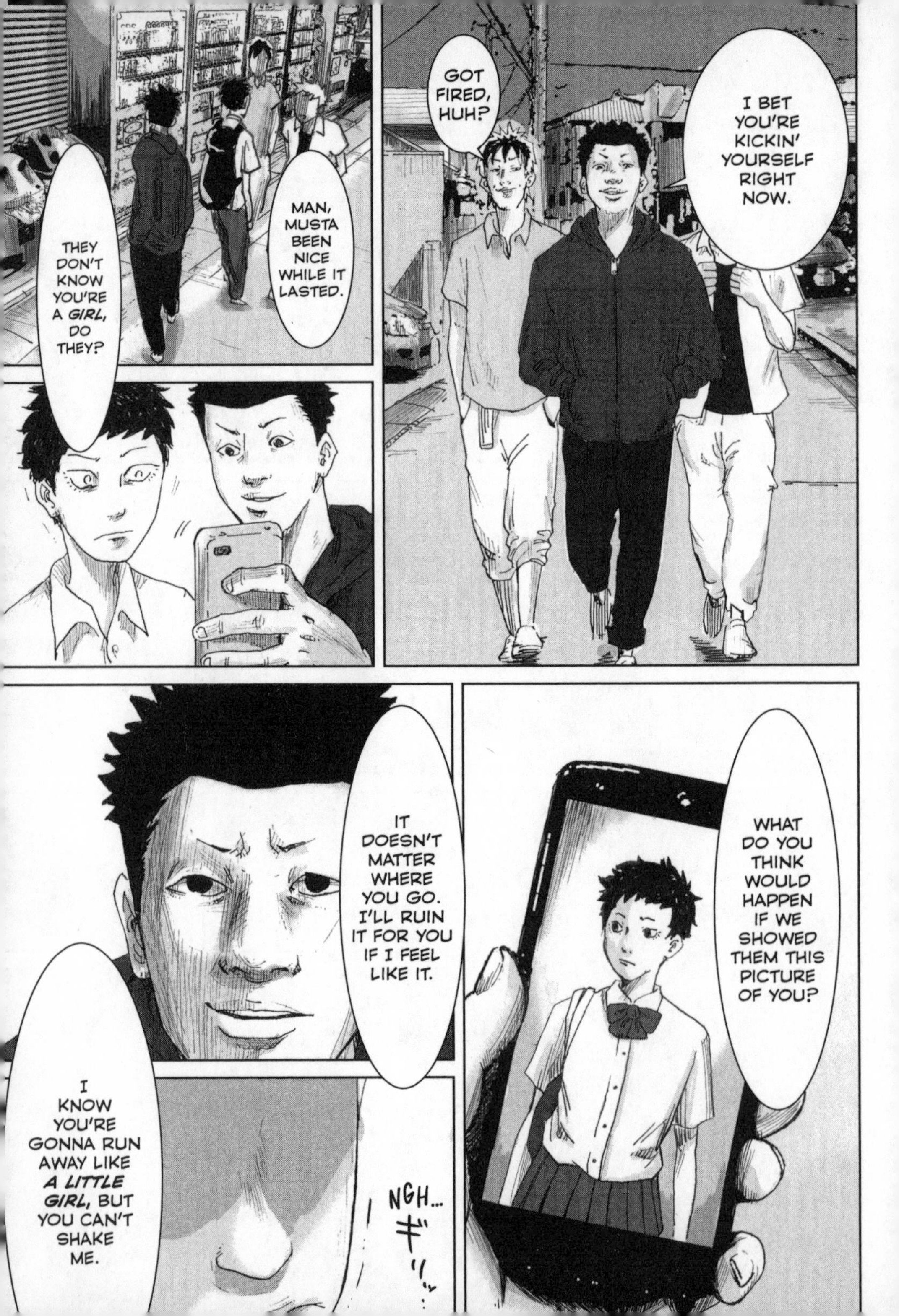
I BET YOU'RE KICKIN' YOURSELF RIGHT NOW.
GOT FIRED, HUH?
MAN, MUSTA BEEN NICE WHILE IT LASTED.
THEY DON'T KNOW YOU'RE A *GIRL*, DO THEY?
WHAT DO YOU THINK WOULD HAPPEN IF WE SHOWED THEM THIS PICTURE OF YOU?
IT DOESN'T MATTER WHERE YOU GO. I'LL RUIN IT FOR YOU IF I FEEL LIKE IT.
I KNOW YOU'RE GONNA RUN AWAY LIKE ***A LITTLE GIRL***, BUT YOU CAN'T SHAKE ME.
NGH...
ギ

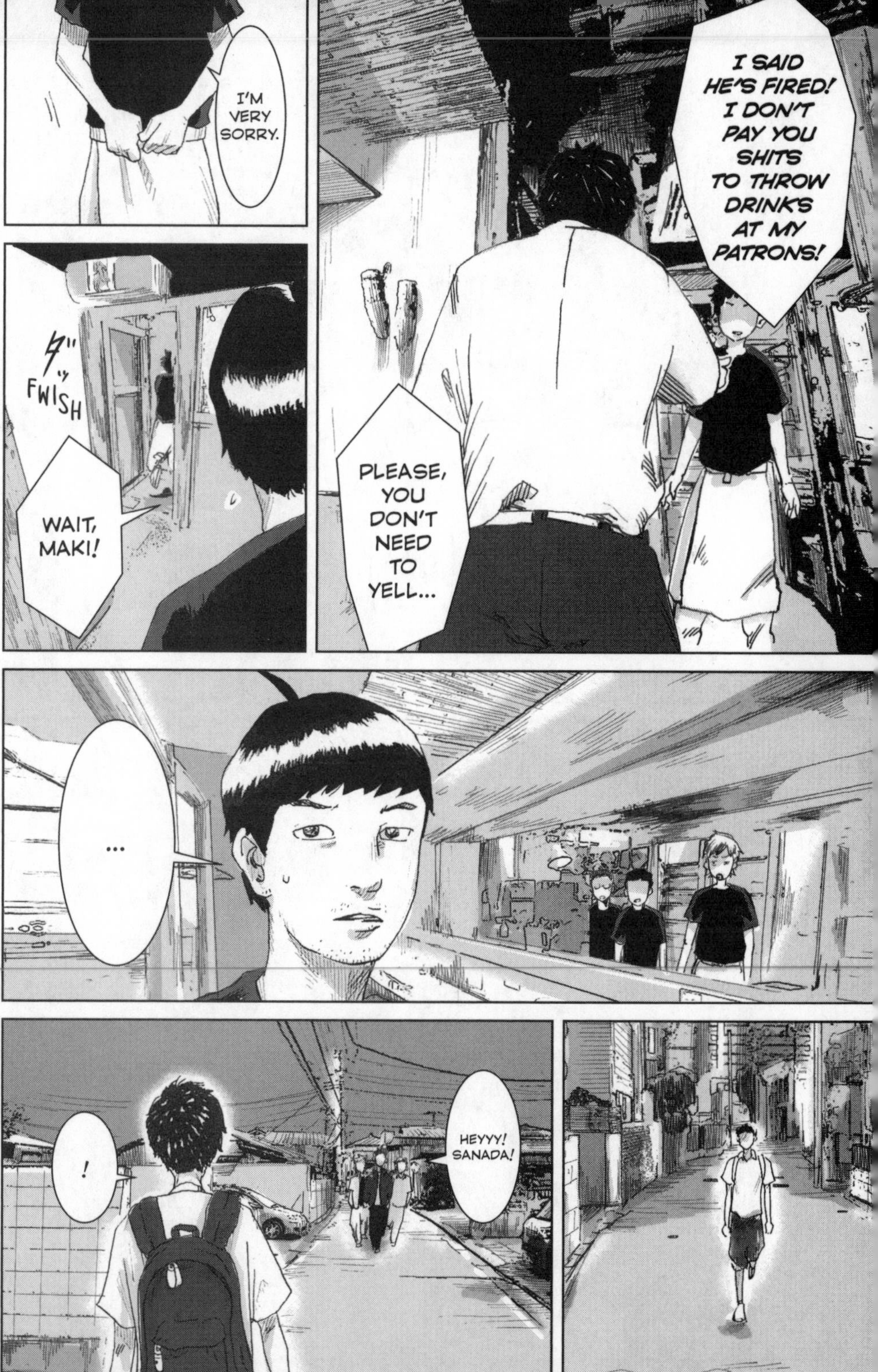
I SAID HE'S FIRED! I DON'T PAY YOU SHITS TO THROW DRINKS AT MY PATRONS!
PLEASE, YOU DON'T NEED TO YELL...
I'M VERY SORRY.
FWISH
WAIT, MAKI!
...
HEYYY! SANADA!
!

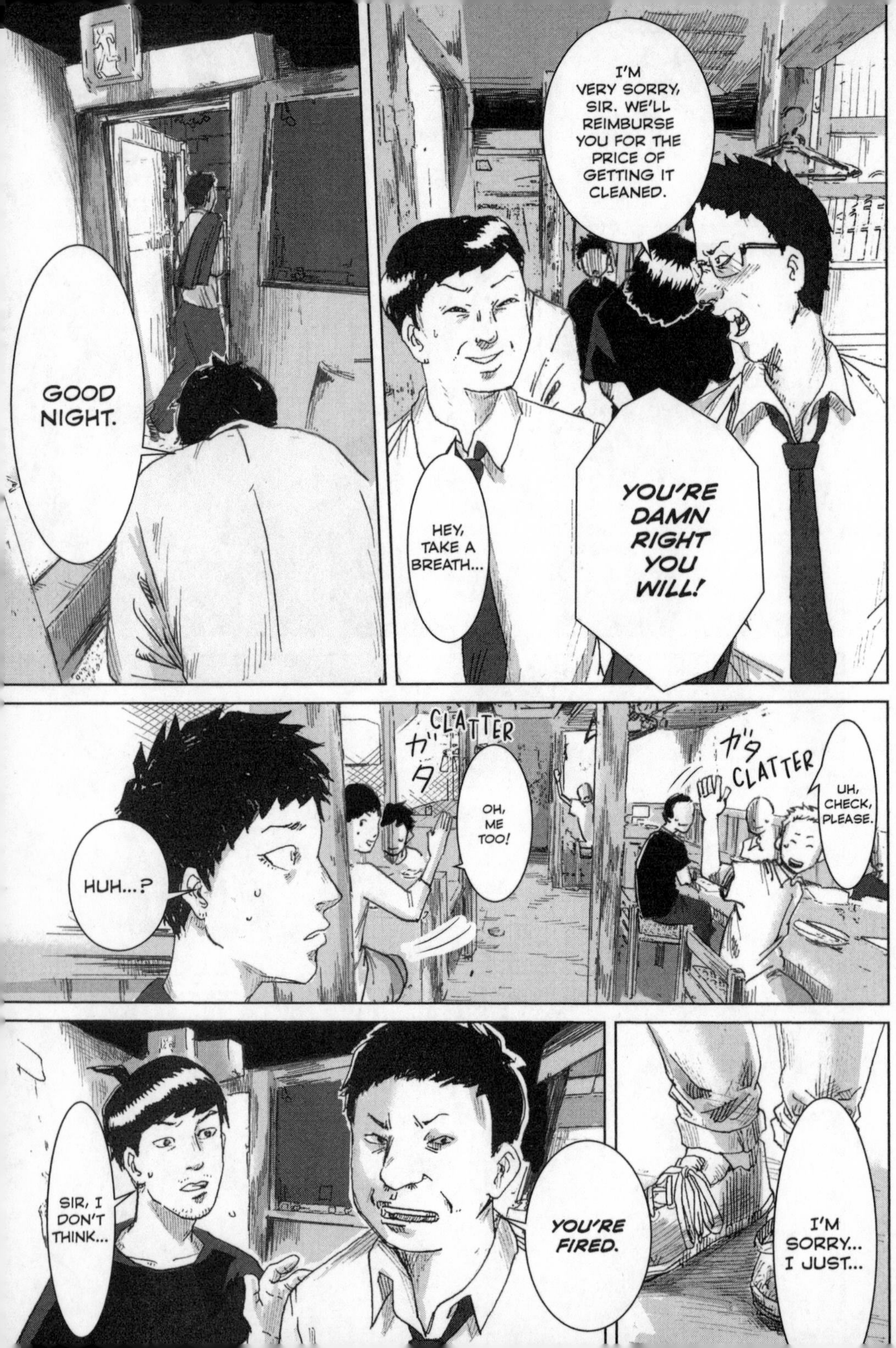
I'M VERY SORRY, SIR. WE'LL REIMBURSE YOU FOR THE PRICE OF GETTING IT CLEANED.
YOU'RE DAMN RIGHT YOU WILL!
HEY, TAKE A BREATH...
GOOD NIGHT.
UH, CHECK, PLEASE.
ガタ CLATTER
OH, ME TOO!
ガタ CLATTER
HUH...?
I'M SORRY... I JUST...
YOU'RE FIRED.
SIR, I DON'T THINK...

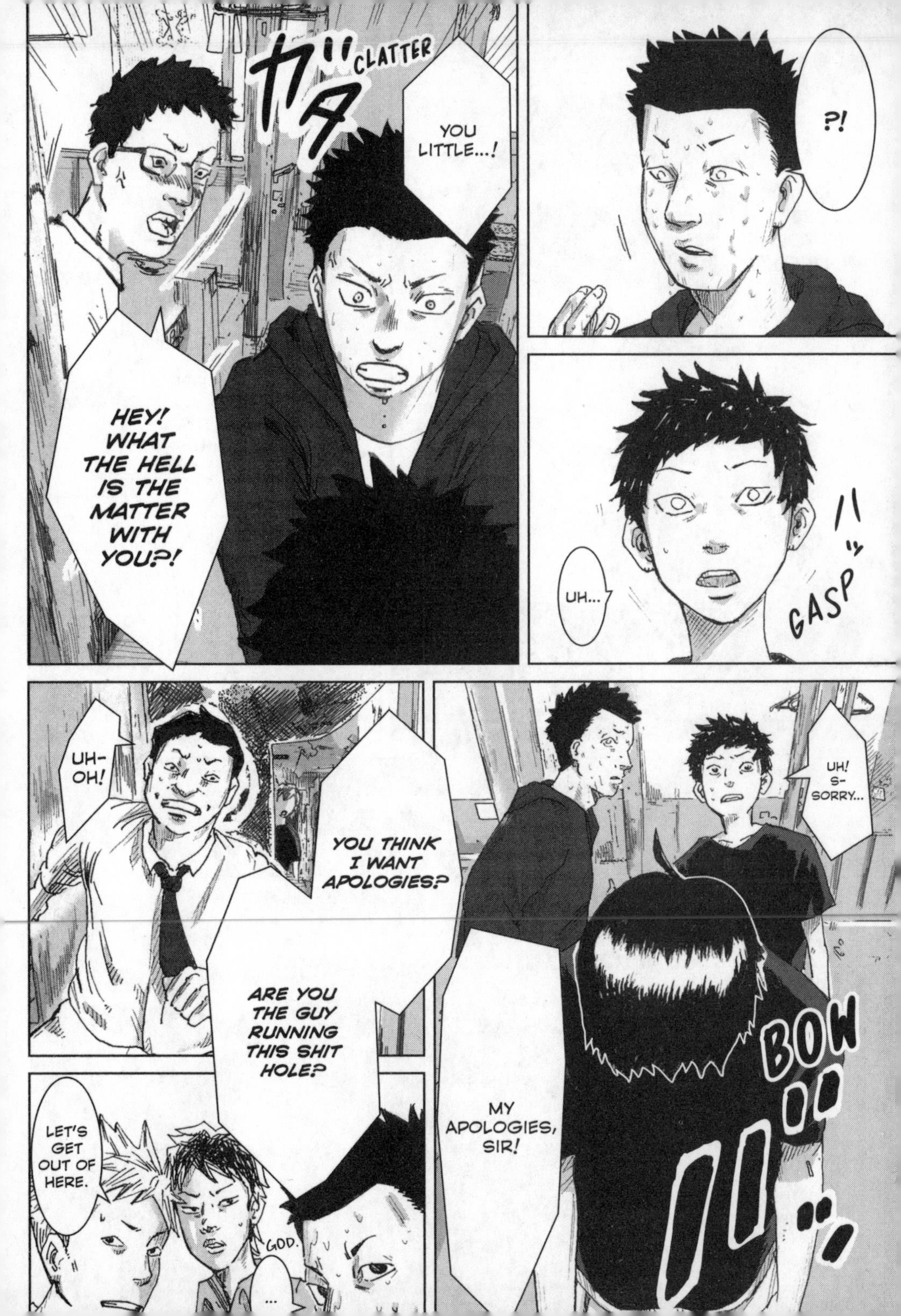

?!
UH...
ハッ
GASP
ガタ
CLATTER
YOU LITTLE...!
HEY! WHAT THE HELL IS THE MATTER WITH YOU?!
UH! S-SORRY...
MY APOLOGIES, SIR!
BOW
UH-OH!
YOU THINK I WANT APOLOGIES?
ARE YOU THE GUY RUNNING THIS SHIT HOLE?
LET'S GET OUT OF HERE.
GOD.
...

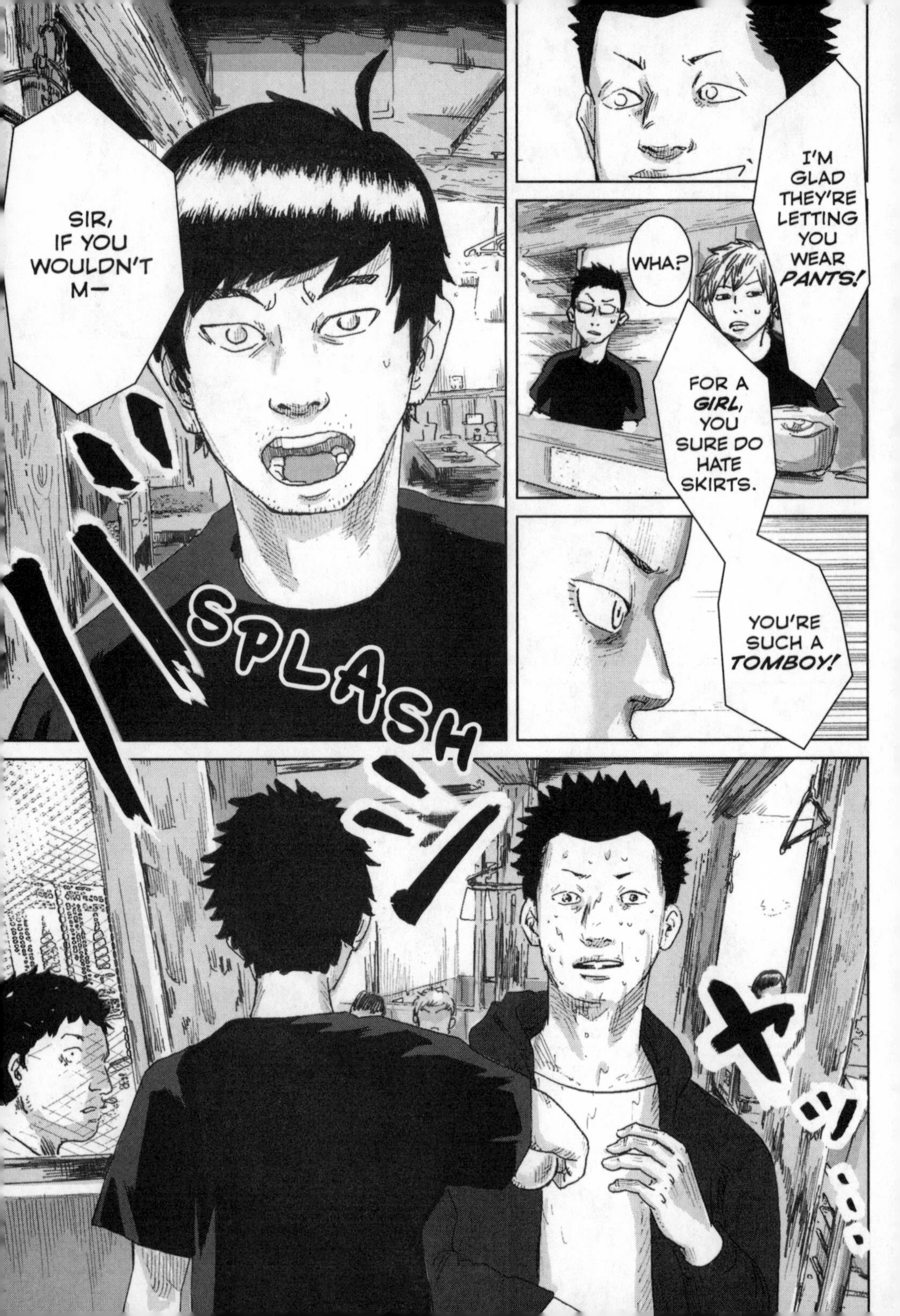
I'M GLAD THEY'RE LETTING YOU WEAR PANTS!
WHA?
FOR A GIRL, YOU SURE DO HATE SKIRTS.
YOU'RE SUCH A TOMBOY!
SIR, IF YOU WOULDN'T M—
SPLASH

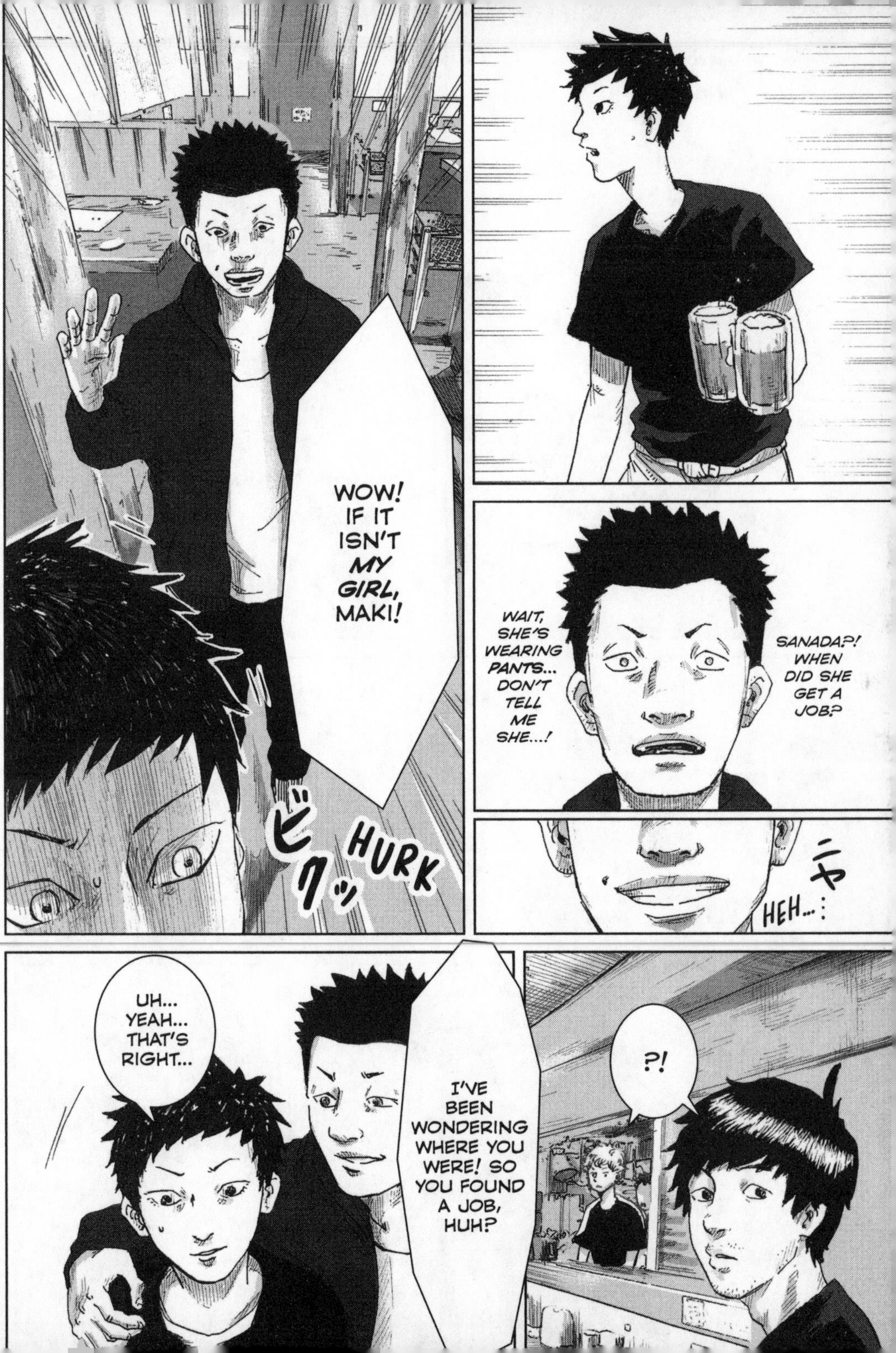
SANADA?! WHEN DID SHE GET A JOB?
WAIT, SHE'S WEARING PANTS... DON'T TELL ME SHE...!
ニヤ
HEH...
WOW! IF IT ISN'T MY GIRL, MAKI!
ビクッ
HURK
?!
I'VE BEEN WONDERING WHERE YOU WERE! SO YOU FOUND A JOB, HUH?
UH... YEAH... THAT'S RIGHT...

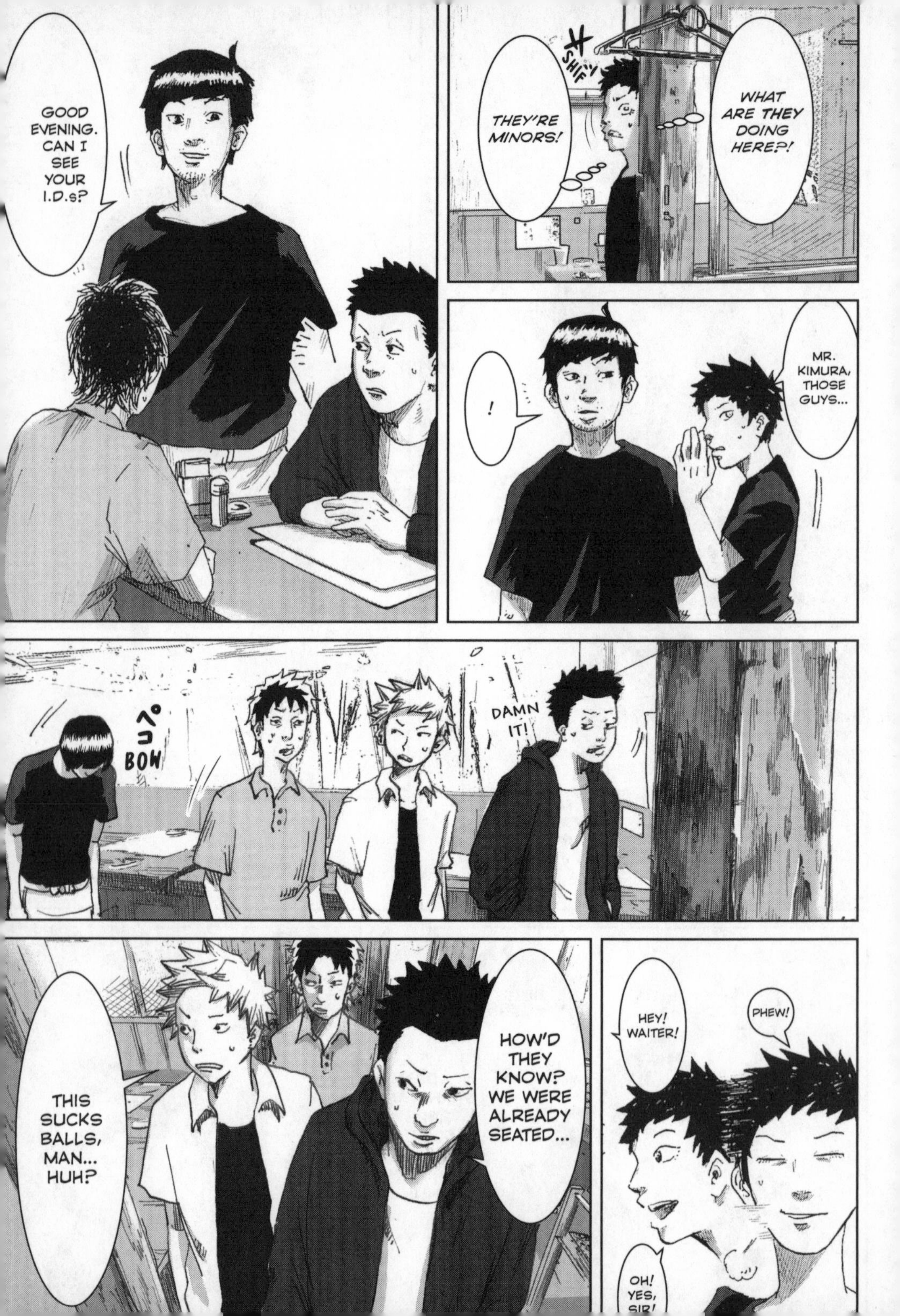
WHAT ARE THEY DOING HERE?!
SHIF
THEY'RE MINORS!
MR. KIMURA, THOSE GUYS...
!
GOOD EVENING. CAN I SEE YOUR I.D.s?
DAMN IT!
BOW
PHEW!
HEY! WAITER!
OH! YES, SIR!
HOW'D THEY KNOW? WE WERE ALREADY SEATED...
THIS SUCKS BALLS, MAN... HUH?

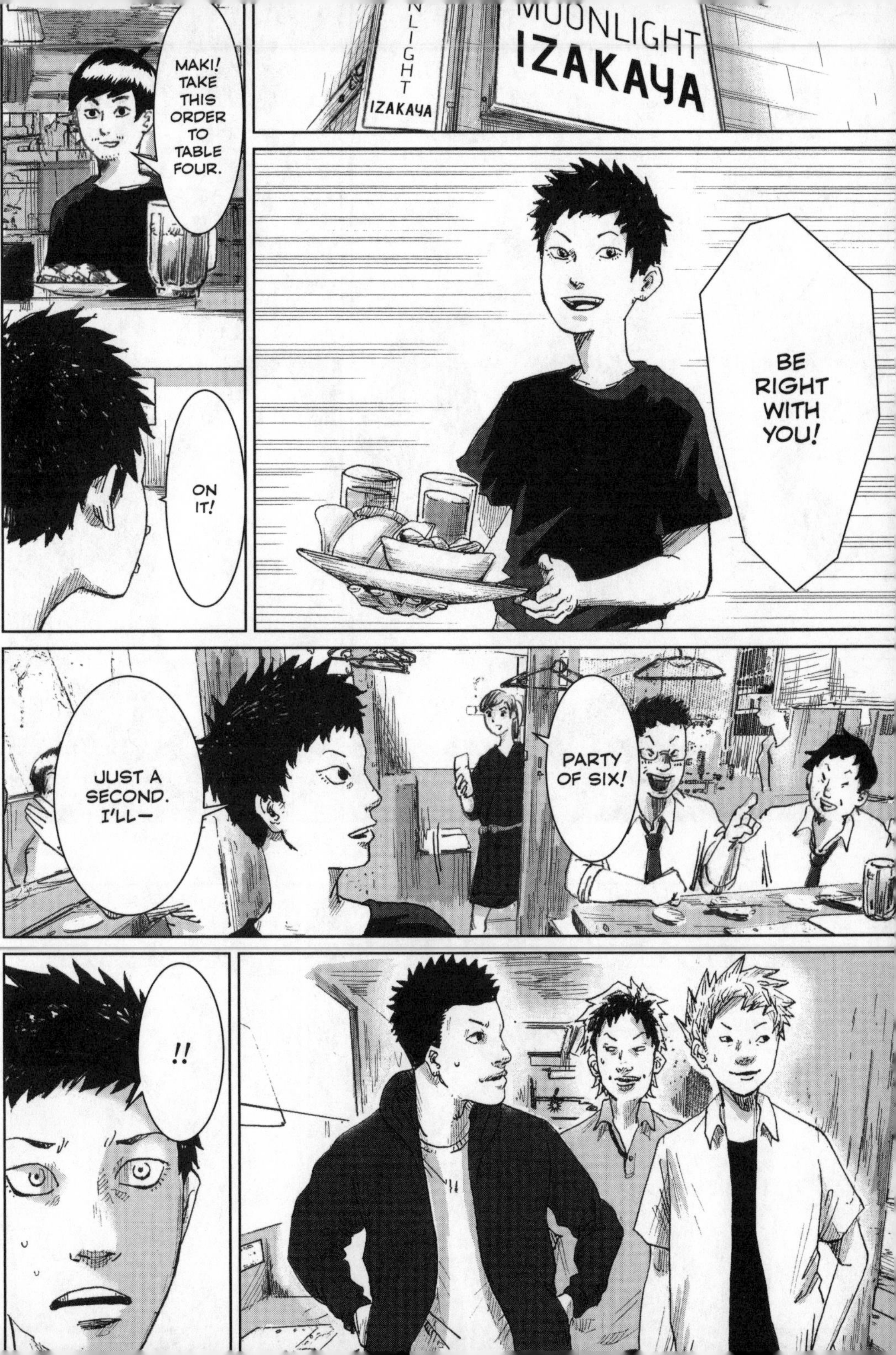
MOONLIGHT IZAKAYA
NLIGHT
IZAKAYA
MAKI! TAKE THIS ORDER TO TABLE FOUR.
BE RIGHT WITH YOU!
ON IT!
PARTY OF SIX!
JUST A SECOND. I'LL—
!!

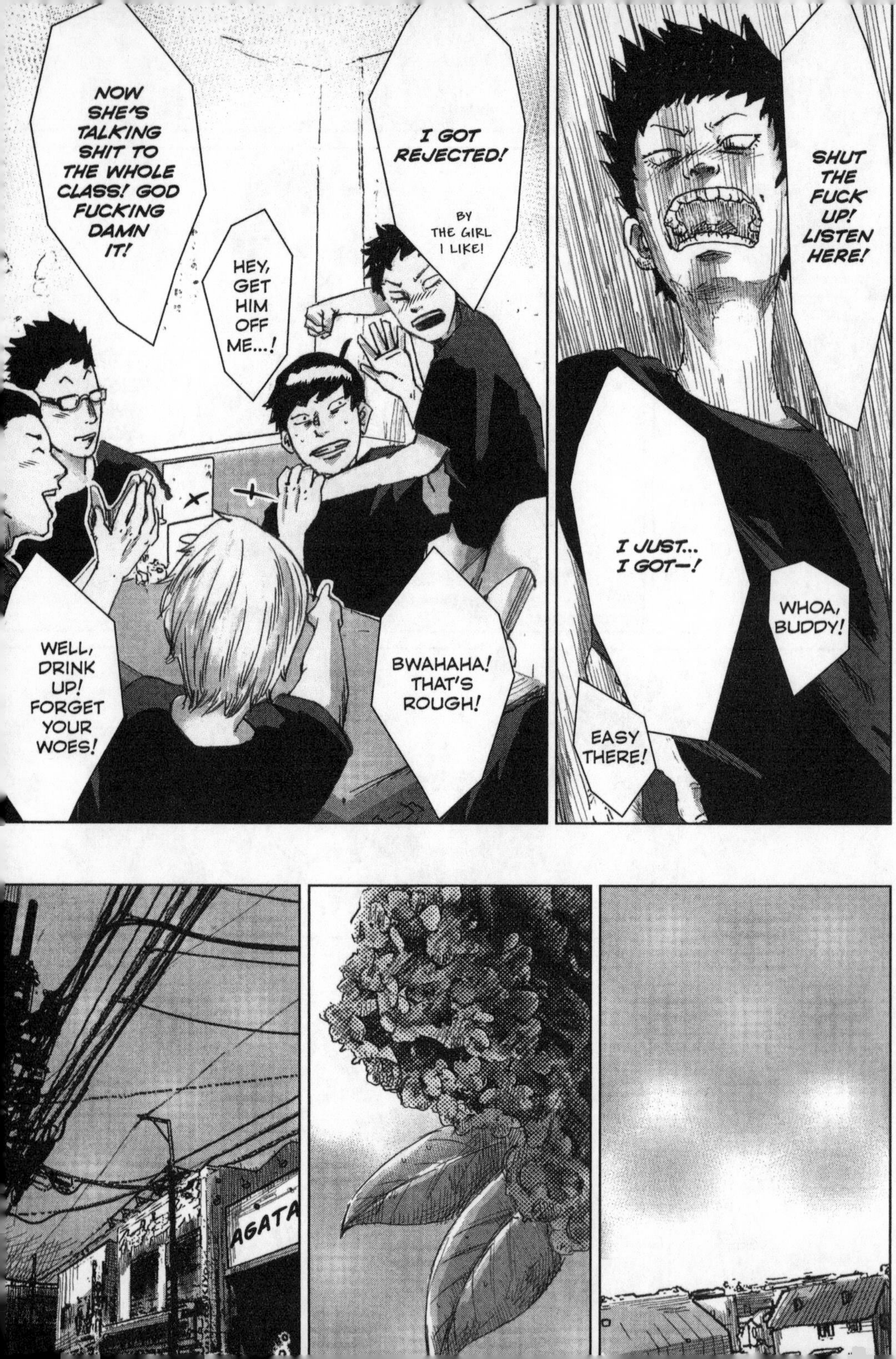
SHUT THE FUCK UP! LISTEN HERE!
I JUST... I GOT—!
WHOA, BUDDY!
EASY THERE!
I GOT REJECTED!
BY THE GIRL I LIKE!
NOW SHE'S TALKING SHIT TO THE WHOLE CLASS! GOD FUCKING DAMN IT!
HEY, GET HIM OFF ME...!
BWAHAHA! THAT'S ROUGH!
WELL, DRINK UP! FORGET YOUR WOES!
AGATA

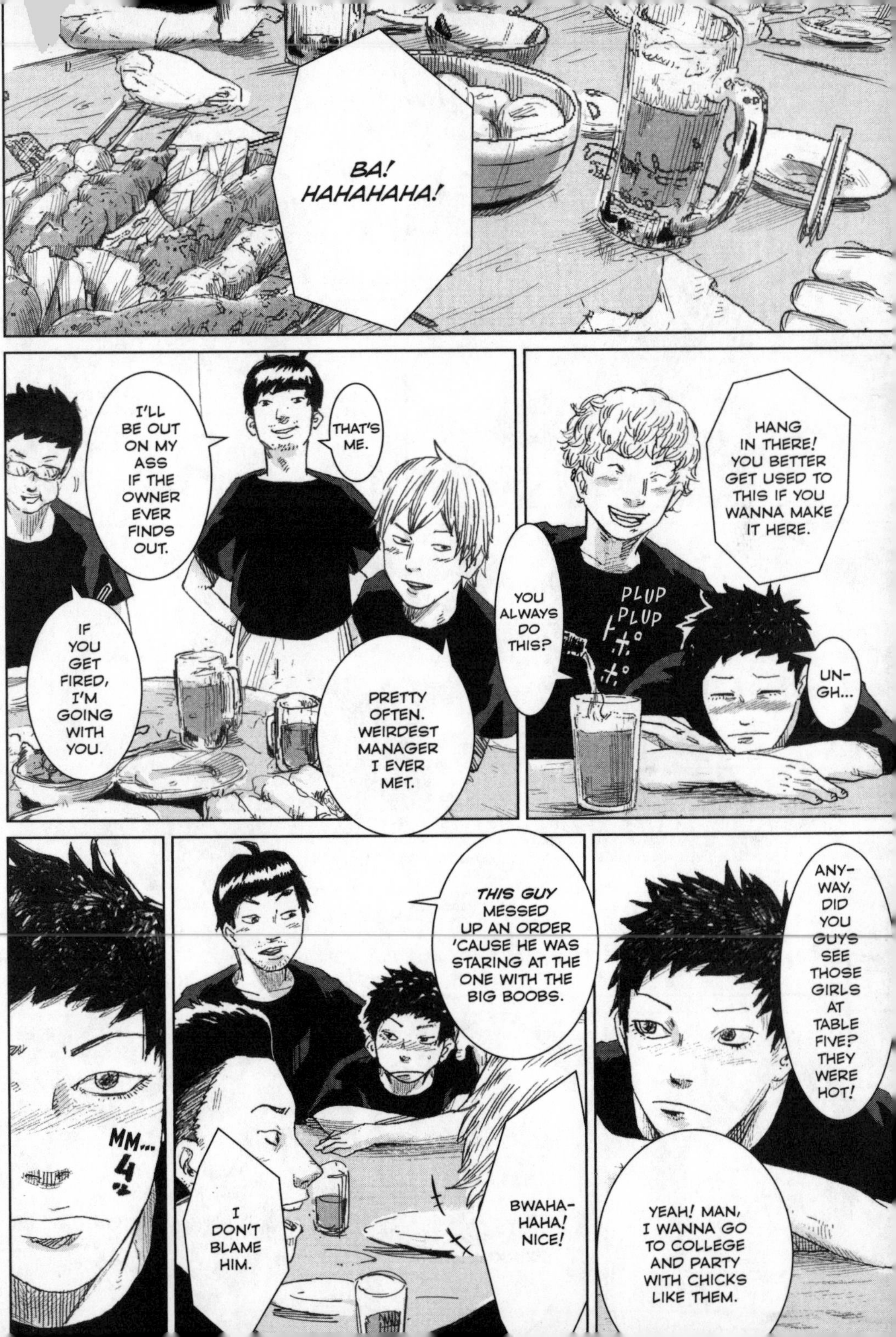
BA! HAHAHAHA!
HANG IN THERE! YOU BETTER GET USED TO THIS IF YOU WANNA MAKE IT HERE.
YOU ALWAYS DO THIS?
PLUP PLUP
UN-GH...
PRETTY OFTEN. WEIRDEST MANAGER I EVER MET.
THAT'S ME.
I'LL BE OUT ON MY ASS IF THE OWNER EVER FINDS OUT.
IF YOU GET FIRED, I'M GOING WITH YOU.
ANY-WAY, DID YOU GUYS SEE THOSE GIRLS AT TABLE FIVE? THEY WERE HOT!
YEAH! MAN, I WANNA GO TO COLLEGE AND PARTY WITH CHICKS LIKE THEM.
THIS GUY MESSED UP AN ORDER 'CAUSE HE WAS STARING AT THE ONE WITH THE BIG BOOBS.
BWAHA-HAHA! NICE!
I DON'T BLAME HIM.
MM...

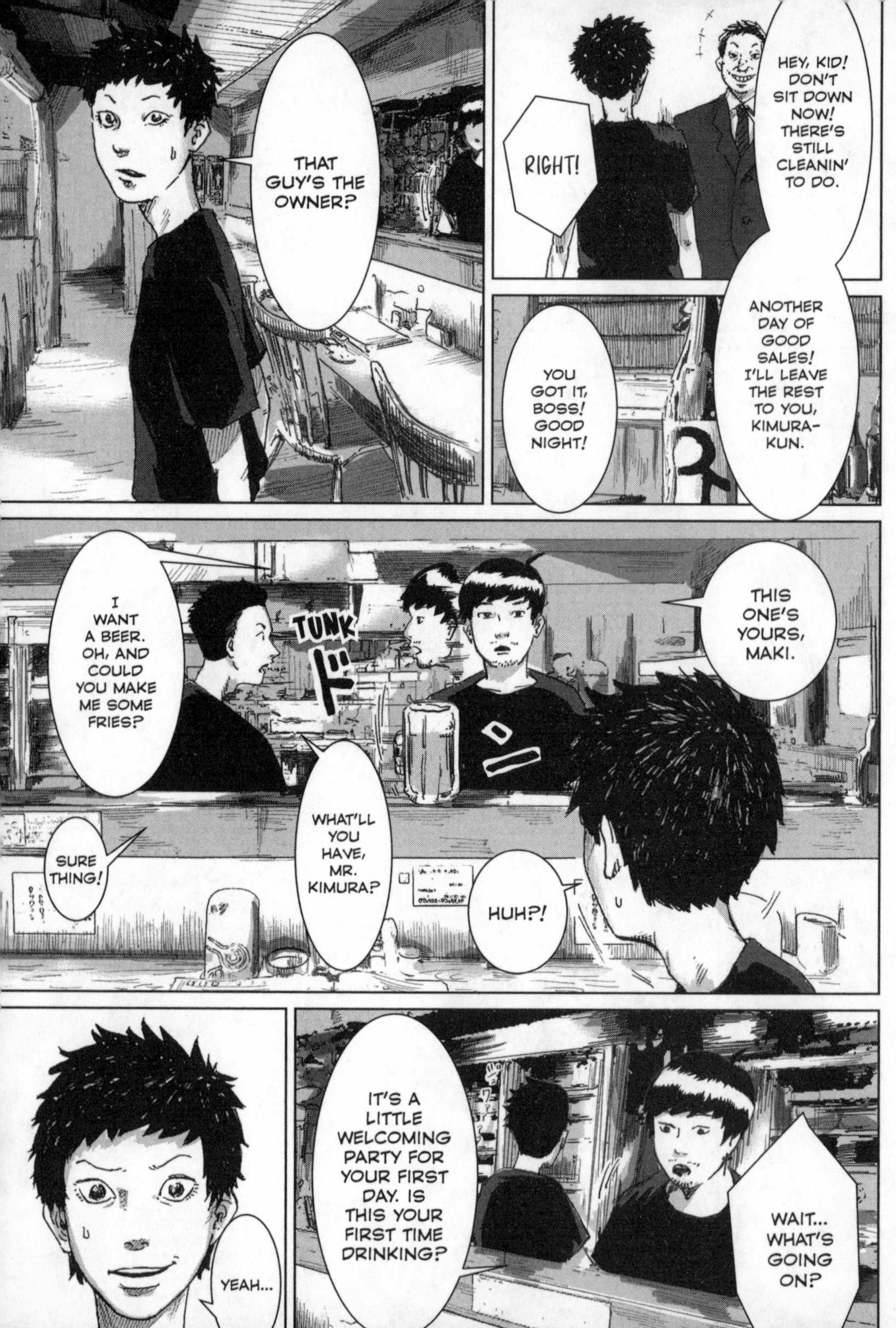
HEY, KID! DON'T SIT DOWN NOW! THERE'S STILL CLEANIN' TO DO.
RIGHT!
ANOTHER DAY OF GOOD SALES! I'LL LEAVE THE REST TO YOU, KIMURA-KUN.
YOU GOT IT, BOSS! GOOD NIGHT!
THAT GUY'S THE OWNER?
THIS ONE'S YOURS, MAKI.
I WANT A BEER. OH, AND COULD YOU MAKE ME SOME FRIES?
TUNK
WHAT'LL YOU HAVE, MR. KIMURA?
HUH?!
SURE THING!
WAIT... WHAT'S GOING ON?
IT'S A LITTLE WELCOMING PARTY FOR YOUR FIRST DAY. IS THIS YOUR FIRST TIME DRINKING?
YEAH...

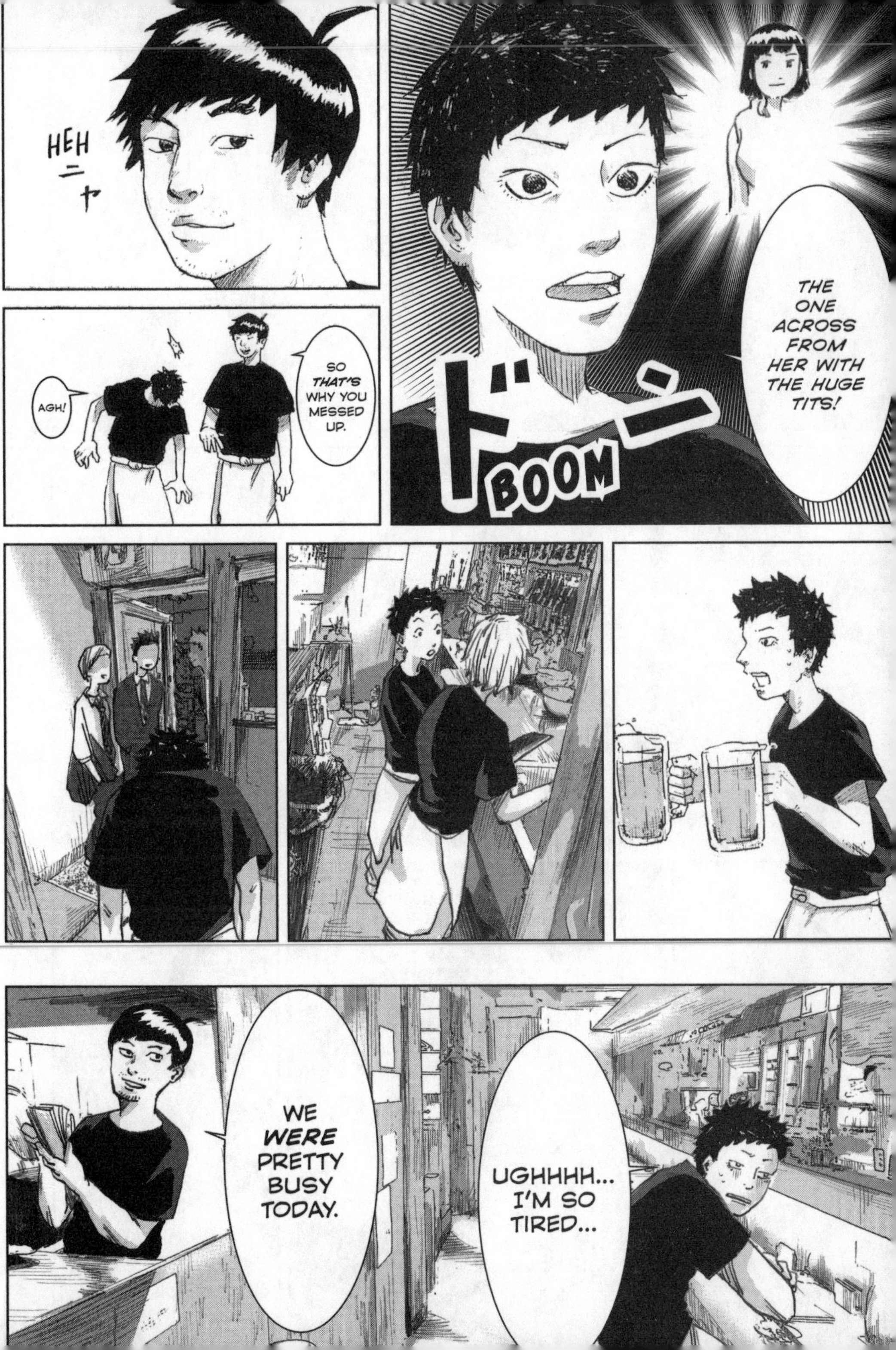
THE ONE ACROSS FROM HER WITH THE HUGE TITS!
ドーン
BOOM
HEH
ニヤ
SO *THAT'S* WHY YOU MESSED UP.
AGH!
UGHHHH... I'M SO TIRED...
WE *WERE* PRETTY BUSY TODAY.

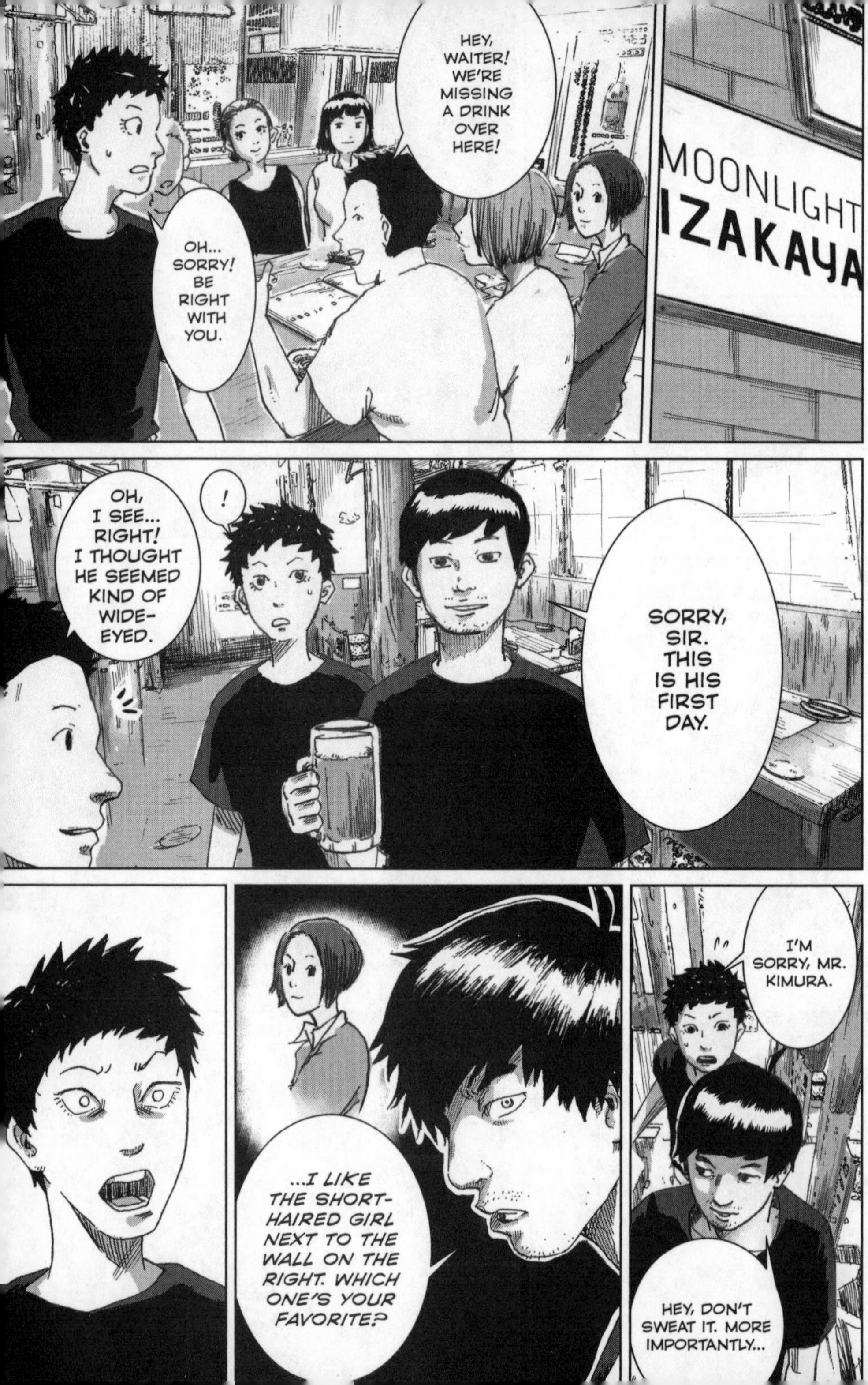
MOONLIGHT IZAKAYA
HEY, WAITER! WE'RE MISSING A DRINK OVER HERE!
OH... SORRY! BE RIGHT WITH YOU.
SORRY, SIR. THIS IS HIS FIRST DAY.
!
OH, I SEE... RIGHT! I THOUGHT HE SEEMED KIND OF WIDE-EYED.
I'M SORRY, MR. KIMURA.
HEY, DON'T SWEAT IT. MORE IMPORTANTLY...
...I LIKE THE SHORT-HAIRED GIRL NEXT TO THE WALL ON THE RIGHT. WHICH ONE'S YOUR FAVORITE?

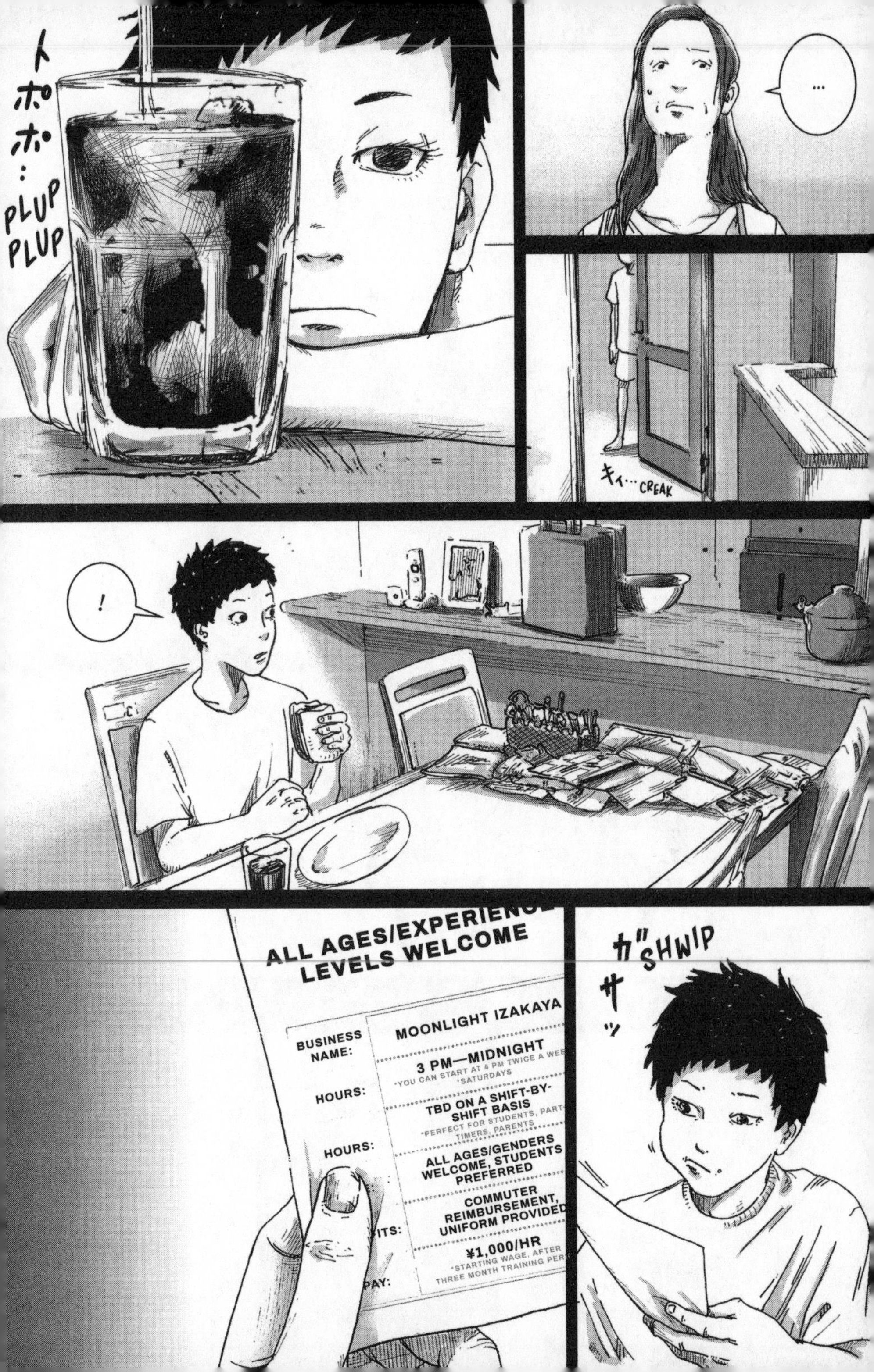
...
キィ… CREAK
トポポ… PLUP PLUP
!
ガサッ SHWIP
ALL AGES/EXPERIENCE LEVELS WELCOME
BUSINESS NAME:
MOONLIGHT IZAKAYA
HOURS:
3 PM—MIDNIGHT
*YOU CAN START AT 4 PM TWICE A WEE
*SATURDAYS
HOURS:
TBD ON A SHIFT-BY-SHIFT BASIS
*PERFECT FOR STUDENTS, PART-TIMERS, PARENTS
ALL AGES/GENDERS WELCOME, STUDENTS PREFERRED
COMMUTER REIMBURSEMENT, UNIFORM PROVIDED
ITS:
¥1,000/HR
*STARTING WAGE, AFTER THREE MONTH TRAINING PER
PAY:

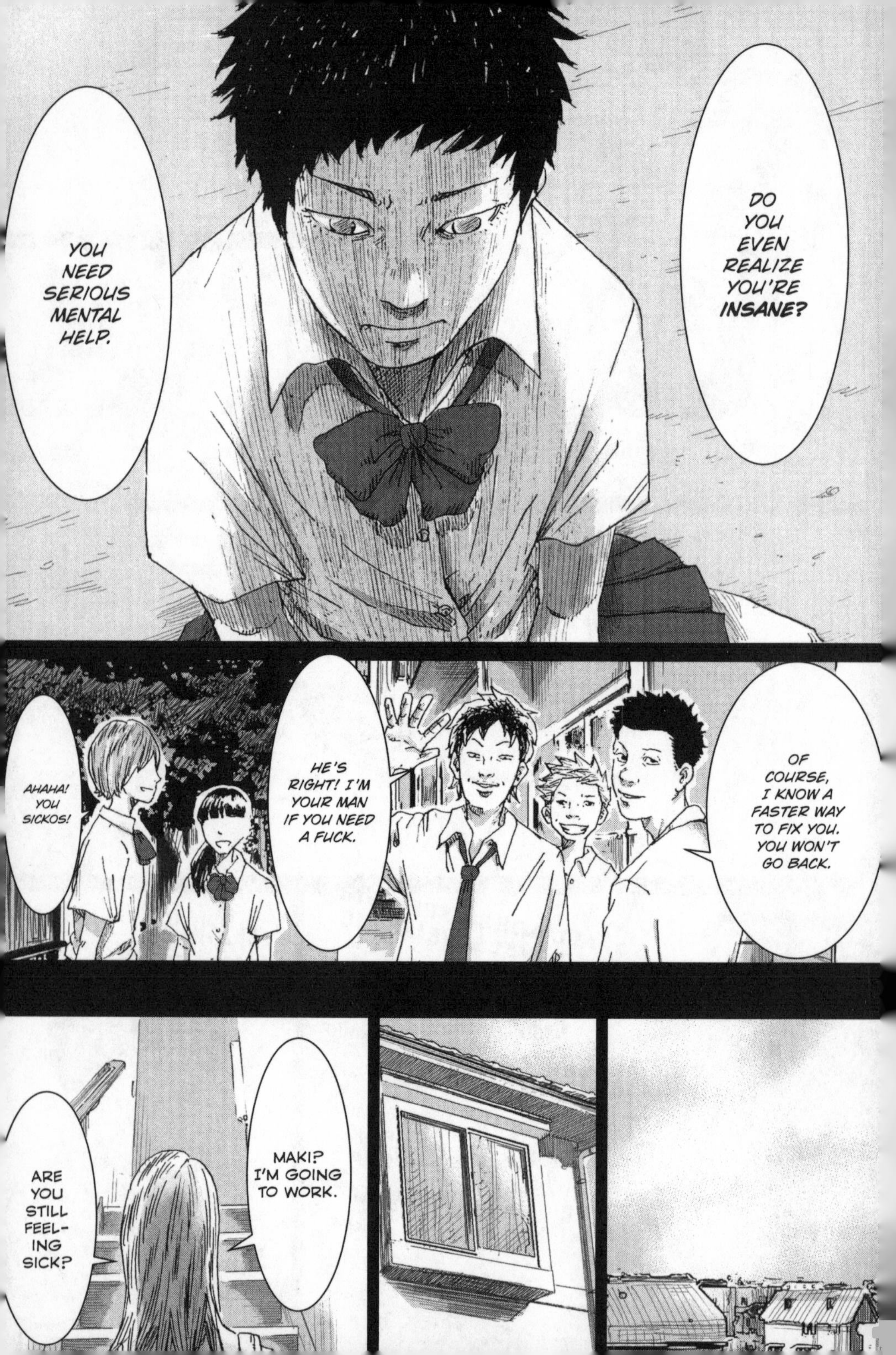
DO YOU EVEN REALIZE YOU'RE INSANE?
YOU NEED SERIOUS MENTAL HELP.
OF COURSE, I KNOW A FASTER WAY TO FIX YOU. YOU WON'T GO BACK.
HE'S RIGHT! I'M YOUR MAN IF YOU NEED A FUCK.
AHAHA! YOU SICKOS!
MAKI? I'M GOING TO WORK.
ARE YOU STILL FEEL-ING SICK?

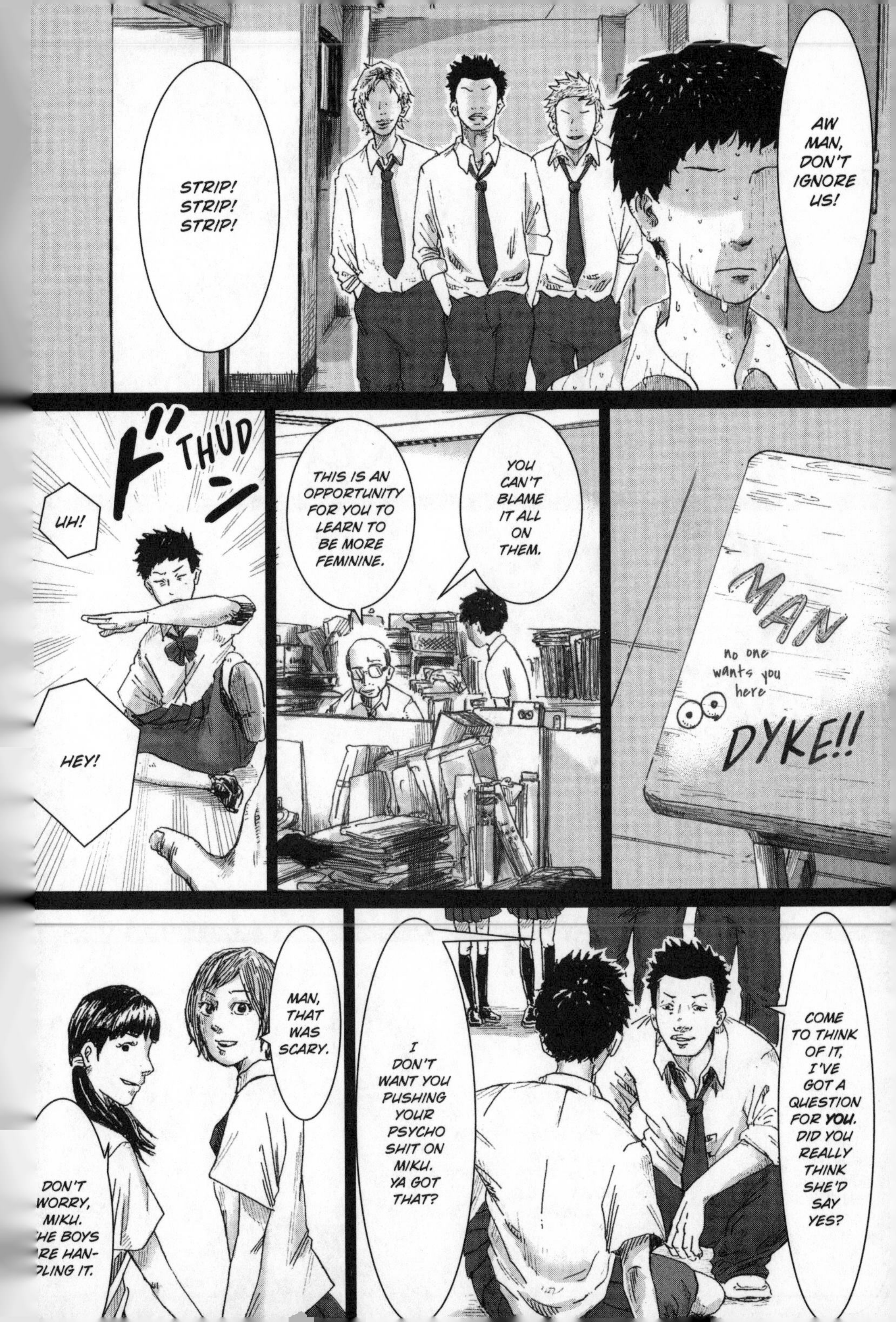
AW MAN, DON'T IGNORE US!
STRIP! STRIP! STRIP!
MAN
no one wants you here
DYKE!!
YOU CAN'T BLAME IT ALL ON THEM.
THIS IS AN OPPORTUNITY FOR YOU TO LEARN TO BE MORE FEMININE.
ドン
THUD
UH!
HEY!
COME TO THINK OF IT, I'VE GOT A QUESTION FOR **YOU**. DID YOU REALLY THINK SHE'D SAY YES?
I DON'T WANT YOU PUSHING YOUR PSYCHO SHIT ON MIKU. YA GOT THAT?
MAN, THAT WAS SCARY.
DON'T WORRY, MIKU. HE BOYS RE HAN-DLING IT.

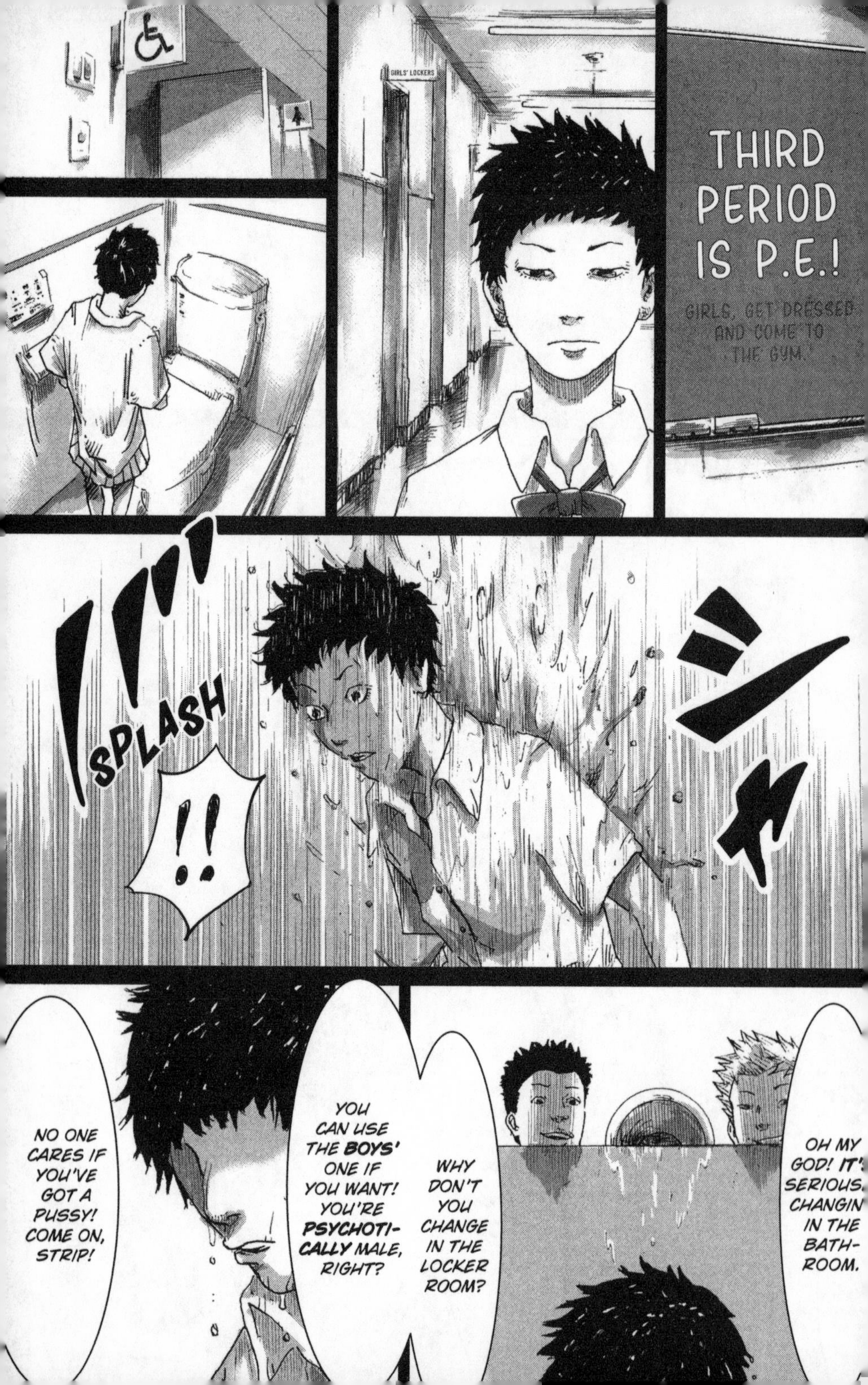
THIRD PERIOD IS P.E.!
GIRLS, GET DRESSED AND COME TO THE GYM.
GIRLS' LOCKERS
SPLASH
!!
OH MY GOD! IT'S SERIOUS. CHANGIN IN THE BATH-ROOM.
WHY DON'T YOU CHANGE IN THE LOCKER ROOM?
YOU CAN USE THE BOYS' ONE IF YOU WANT! YOU'RE PSYCHOTI-CALLY MALE, RIGHT?
NO ONE CARES IF YOU'VE GOT A PUSSY! COME ON, STRIP!

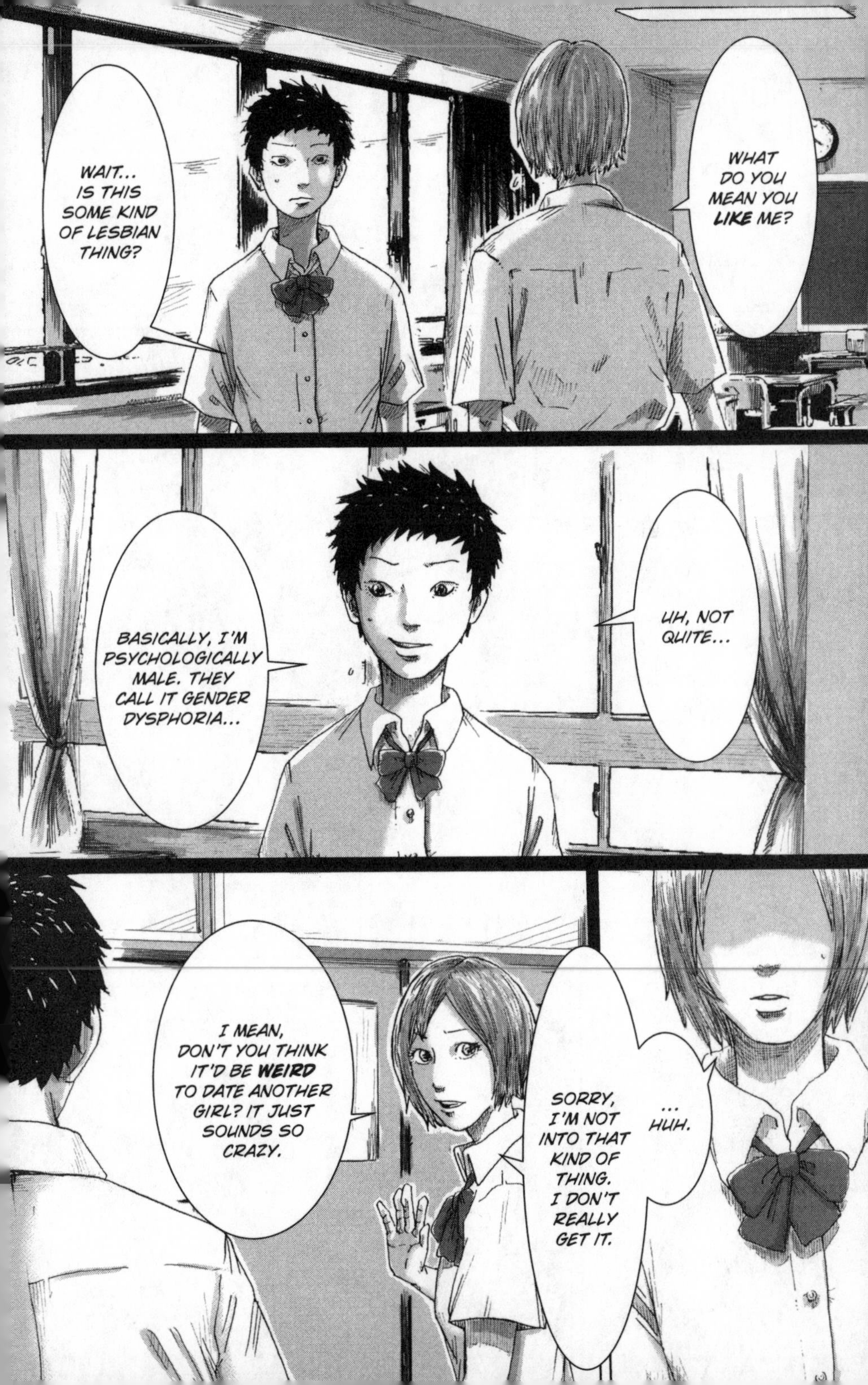
WHAT DO YOU MEAN YOU **LIKE** ME?
WAIT... IS THIS SOME KIND OF LESBIAN THING?
UH, NOT QUITE...
BASICALLY, I'M PSYCHOLOGICALLY MALE. THEY CALL IT GENDER DYSPHORIA...
... HUH.
SORRY, I'M NOT INTO THAT KIND OF THING. I DON'T REALLY GET IT.
I MEAN, DON'T YOU THINK IT'D BE **WEIRD** TO DATE ANOTHER GIRL? IT JUST SOUNDS SO CRAZY.

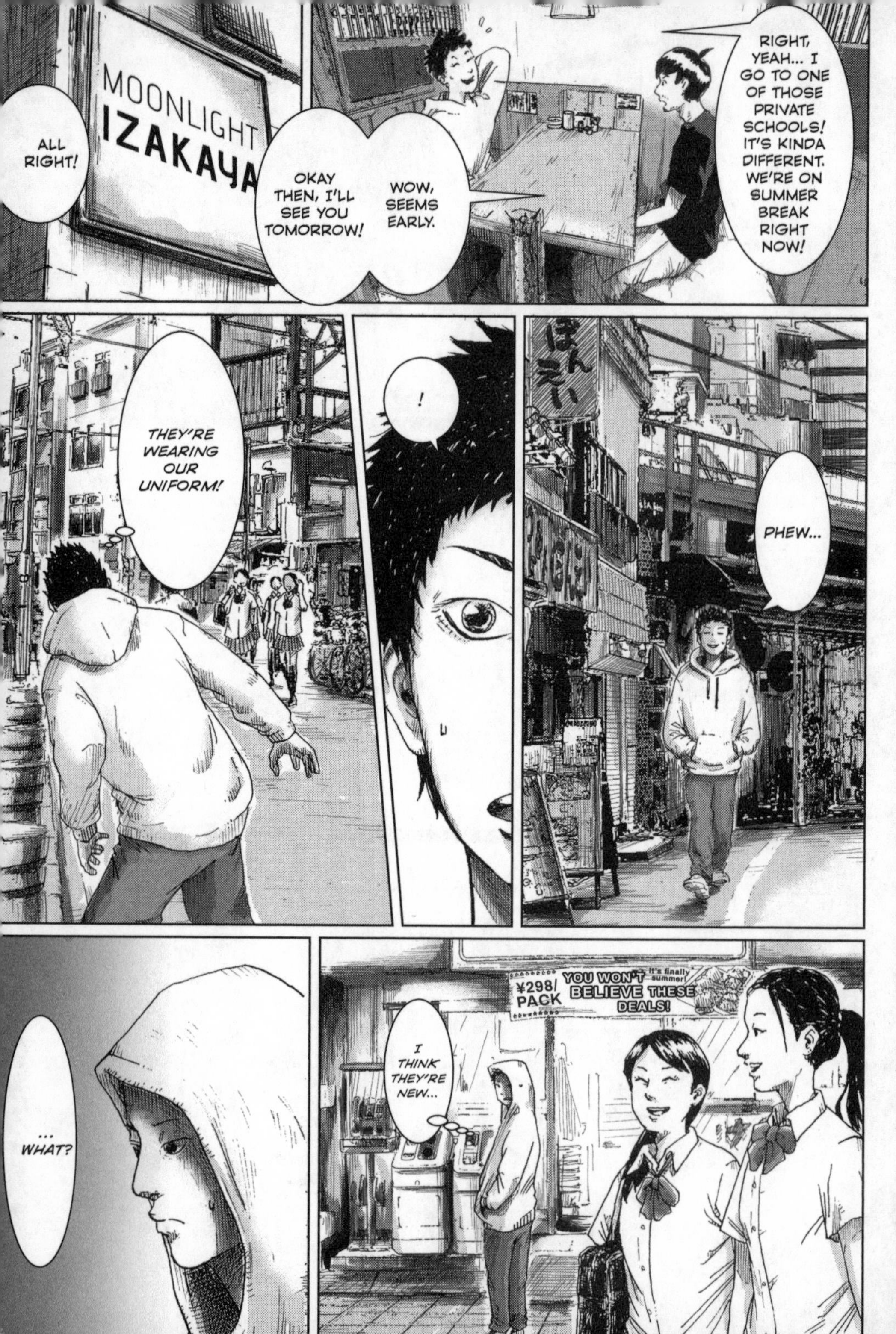
RIGHT, YEAH... I GO TO ONE OF THOSE PRIVATE SCHOOLS! IT'S KINDA DIFFERENT. WE'RE ON SUMMER BREAK RIGHT NOW!
WOW, SEEMS EARLY.
OKAY THEN, I'LL SEE YOU TOMORROW!
MOONLIGHT IZAKAYA
ALL RIGHT!
PHEW...
!
THEY'RE WEARING OUR UNIFORM!
¥298/ PACK
YOU WON'T BELIEVE THESE DEALS!
It's finally summer!
I THINK THEY'RE NEW...
... WHAT?

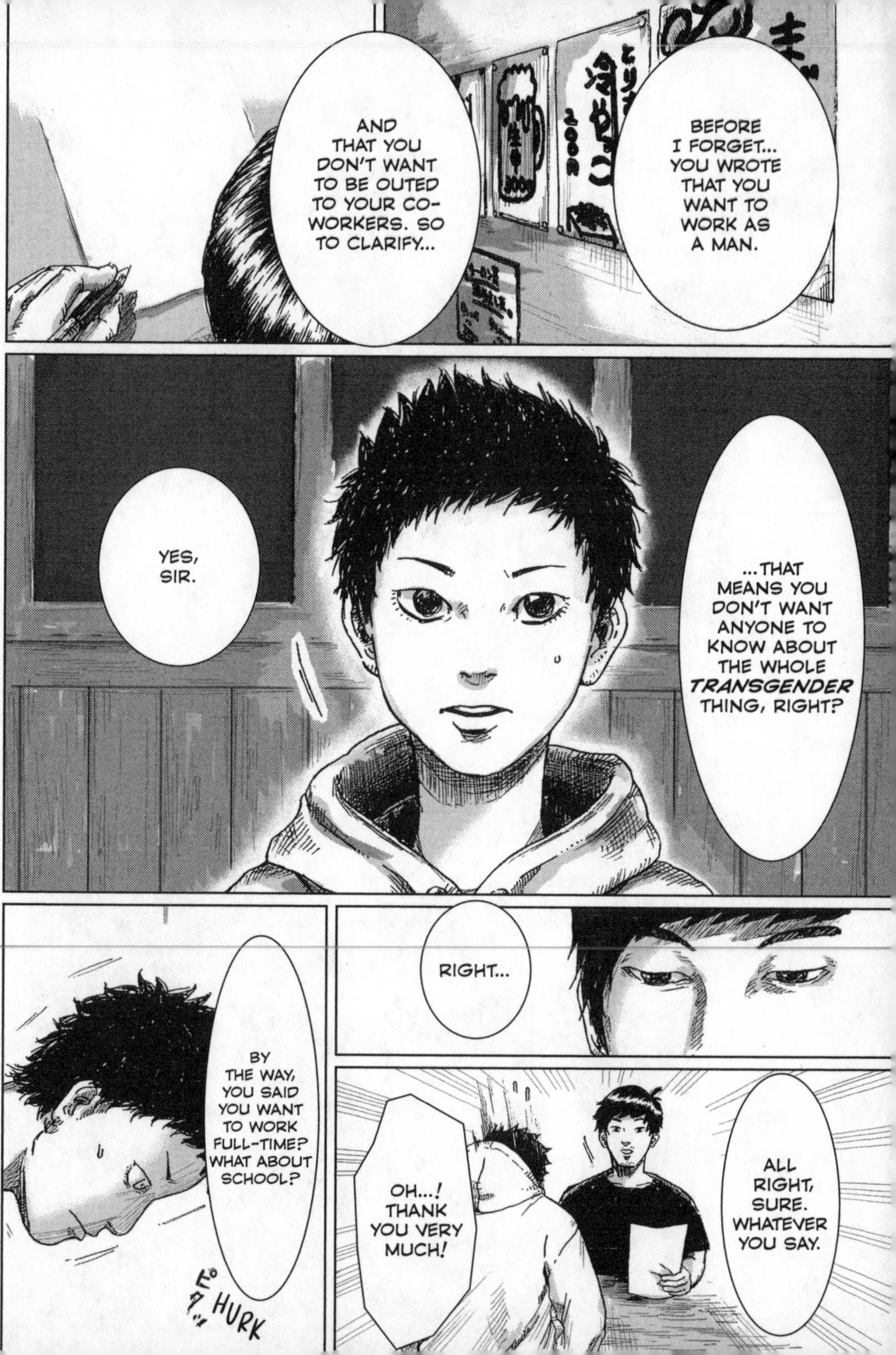
BEFORE I FORGET... YOU WROTE THAT YOU WANT TO WORK AS A MAN.
AND THAT YOU DON'T WANT TO BE OUTED TO YOUR CO-WORKERS. SO TO CLARIFY...
...THAT MEANS YOU DON'T WANT ANYONE TO KNOW ABOUT THE WHOLE TRANSGENDER THING, RIGHT?
YES, SIR.
RIGHT...
ALL RIGHT, SURE. WHATEVER YOU SAY.
OH...! THANK YOU VERY MUCH!
BY THE WAY, YOU SAID YOU WANT TO WORK FULL-TIME? WHAT ABOUT SCHOOL?
HURK

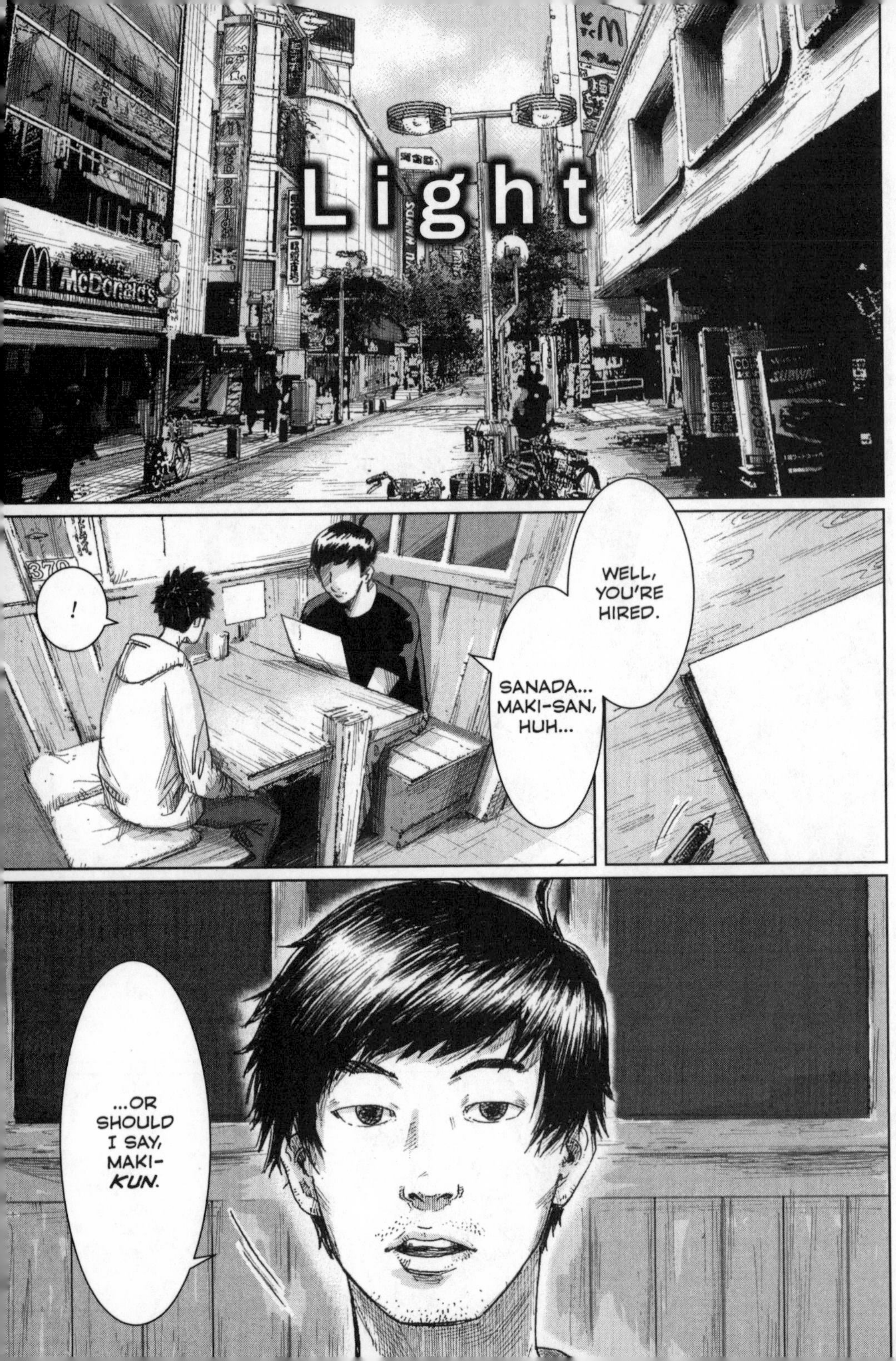
Light
McDonald's
WELL, YOU'RE HIRED.
SANADA... MAKI-SAN, HUH...
!
...OR SHOULD I SAY, MAKI-*KUN*.

Turn the page to read the bonus short story, *Light*—Keito Gaku's debut one-shot work and winner of the 77th Tetsuya Chiba Prize—which was later adapted into *Boys Run the Riot*.
[Content warning: Contains depictions of bullying, foul language, homophobia, misgendering, and transphobia]

BOYS RUN
ボーイズ・ラン・ザ・ライオット
THE RIOT

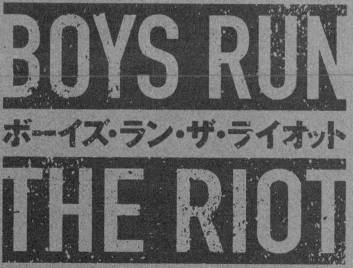

SPECIAL THANKS

INFO COLLABORATION / OUTFIT IDEAS

HEADGOONIE – Miki Ooyagi (Twitter/Instagram: @headgoonie)

PHOTO COLLABORATION

ART IN GALLERY

STAFF

Igarashi
Ryuusei Terada
Taiga Miyahara

SPECIAL VOLUME DESIGN

fake graphics – Akito Sumiyoshi

EDITORS

Hidemi Shiraki
Haruhito Uwai

SPECIAL VOLUME EDITORS

Tomohiro Ebitani
The Young Magazine editorial team

Thank you from the bottom of my heart
to everyone who supported the writing and publishing
of *Boys Run the Riot*, and to all my readers who
continued to love my work until the end.

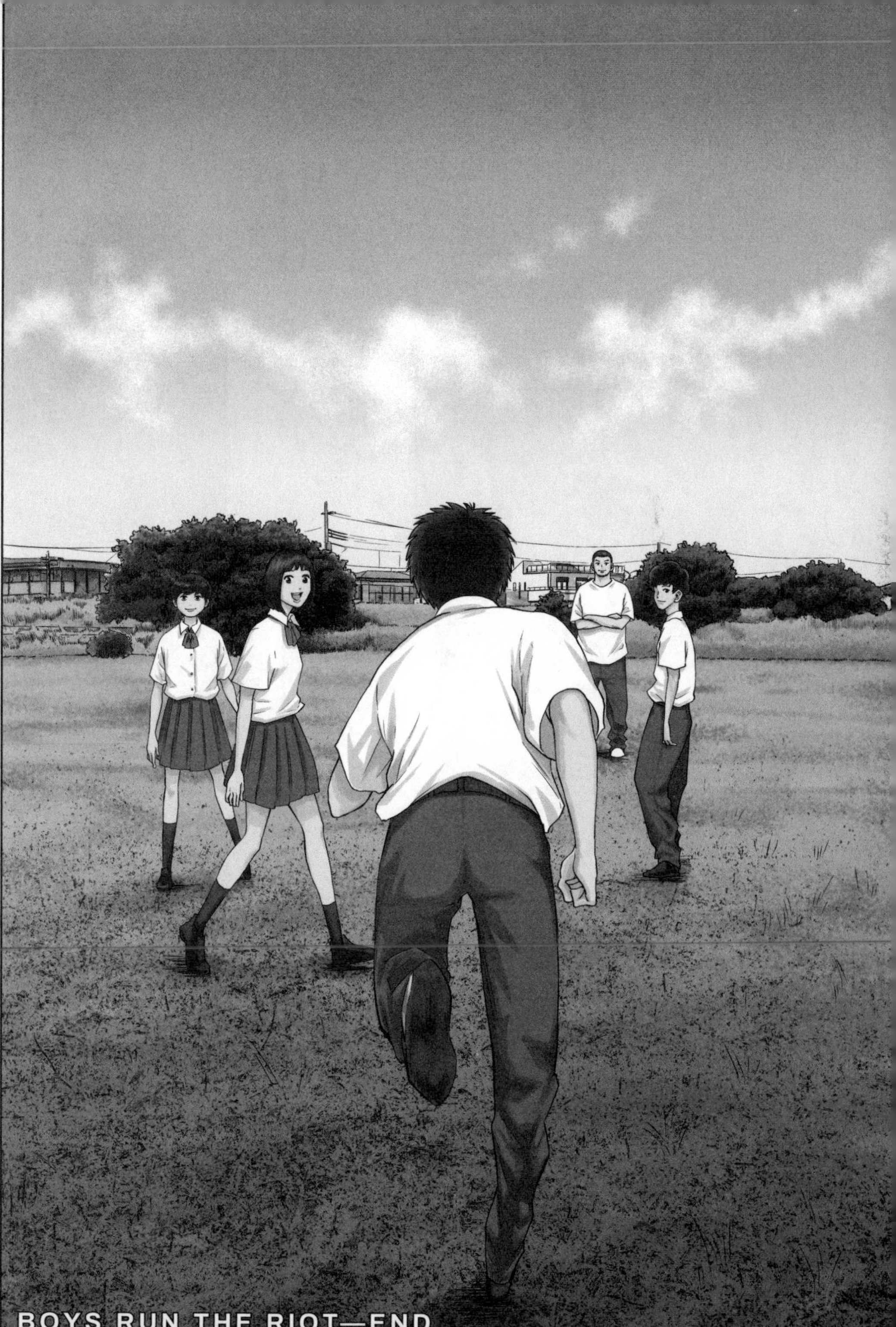

BOYS RUN THE RIOT—END

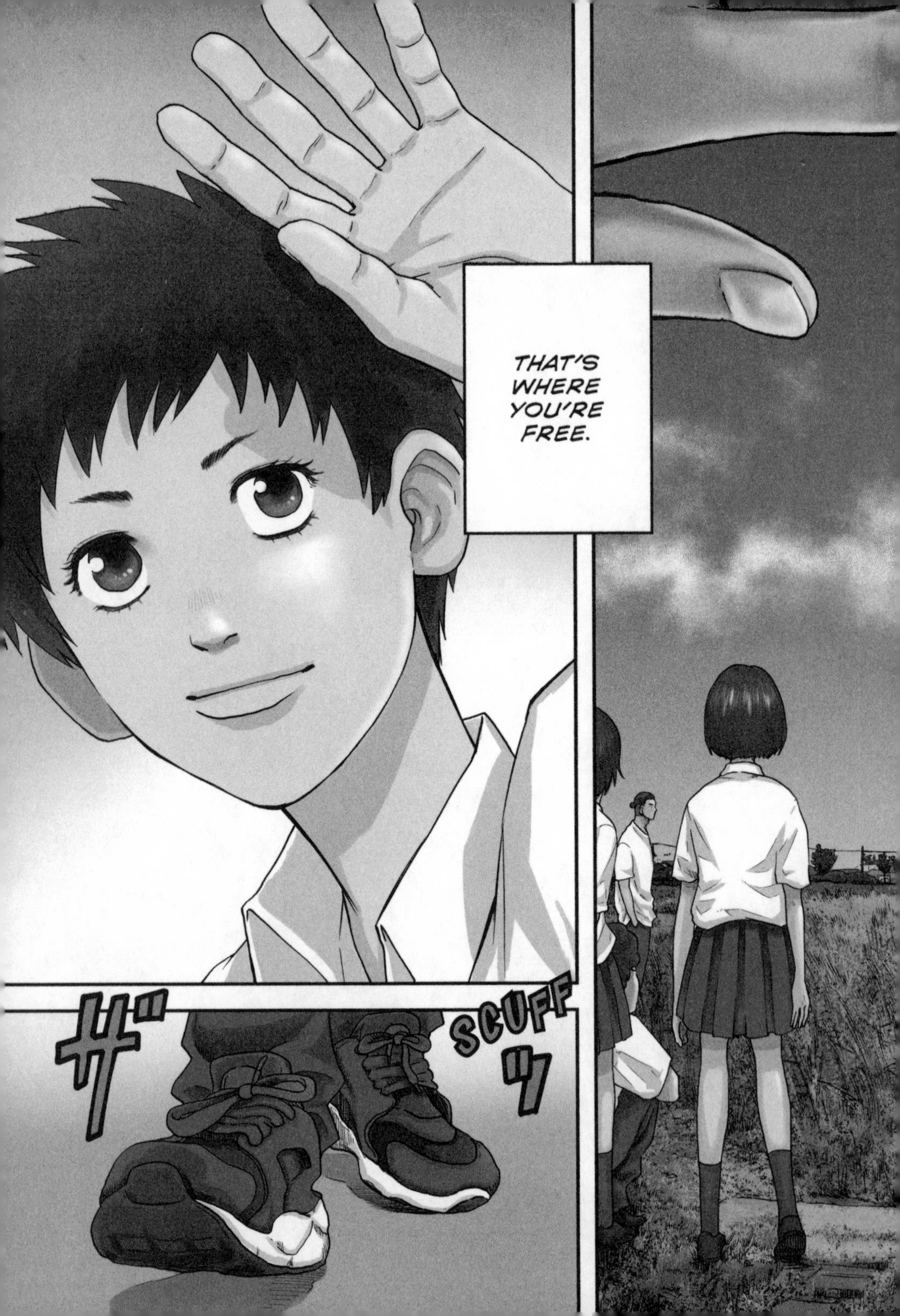
THAT'S WHERE YOU'RE FREE.
SCUFF
ザッ

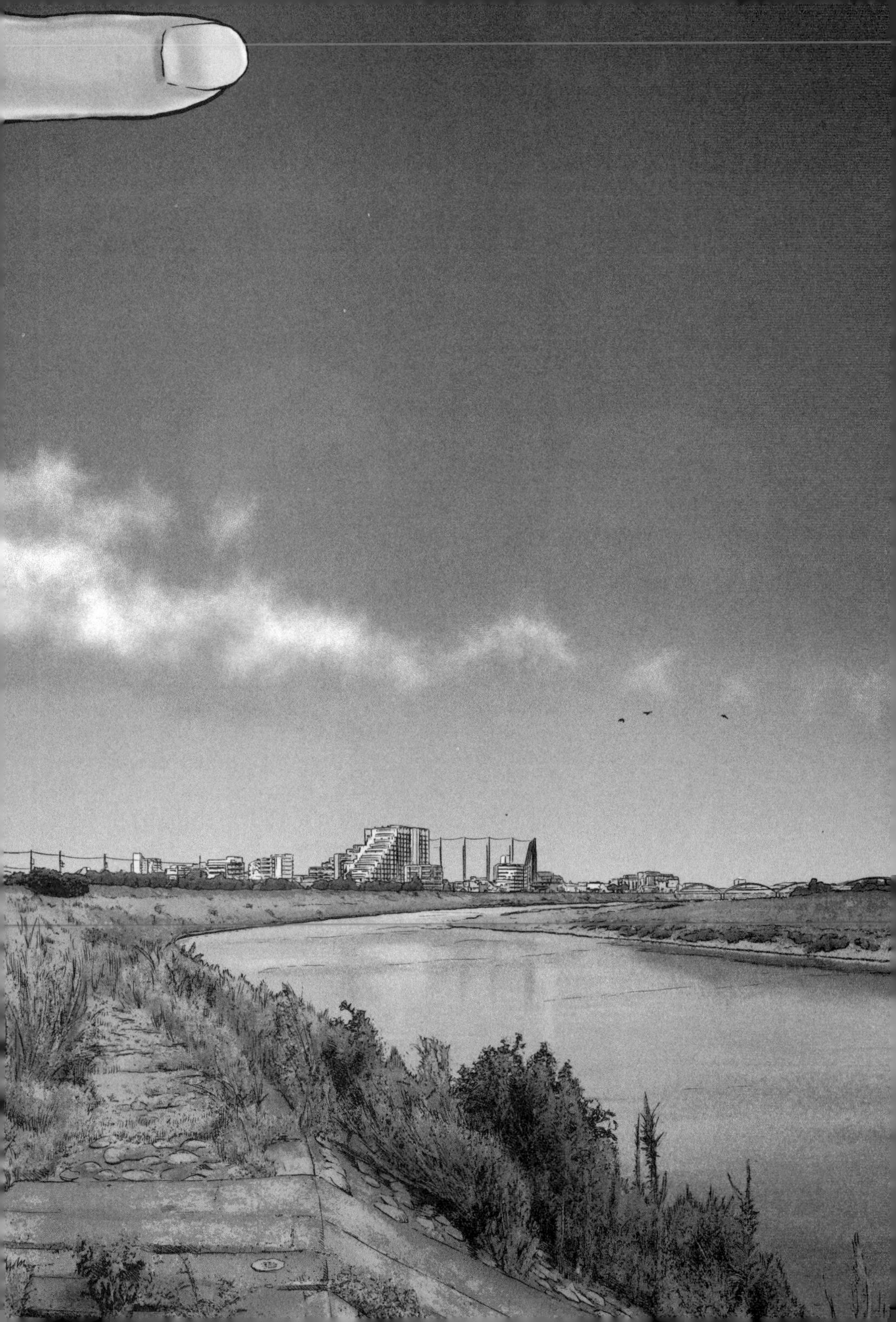

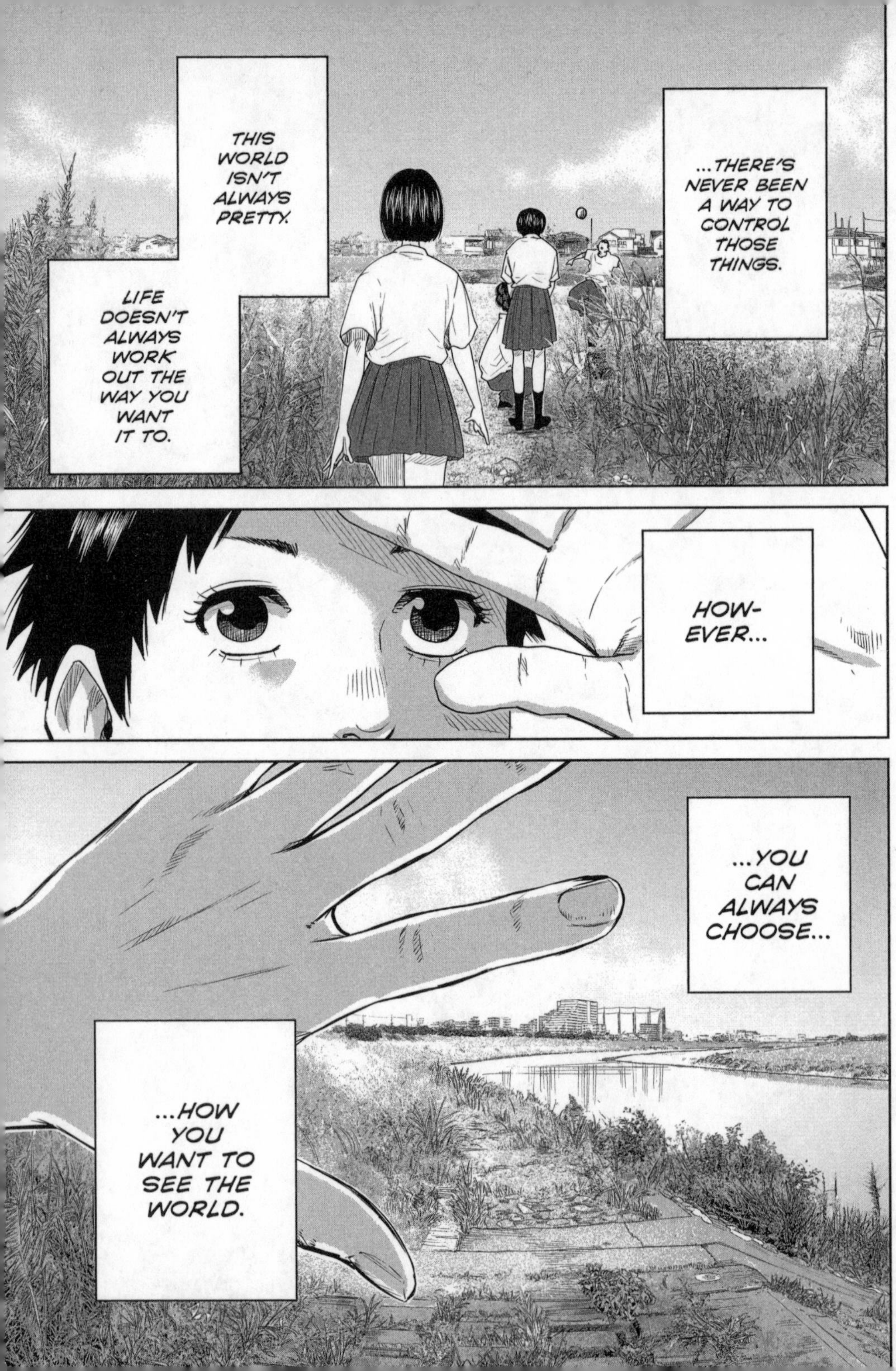
THIS WORLD ISN'T ALWAYS PRETTY.
LIFE DOESN'T ALWAYS WORK OUT THE WAY YOU WANT IT TO.
...THERE'S NEVER BEEN A WAY TO CONTROL THOSE THINGS.
HOW-EVER...
...YOU CAN ALWAYS CHOOSE...
...HOW YOU WANT TO SEE THE WORLD.

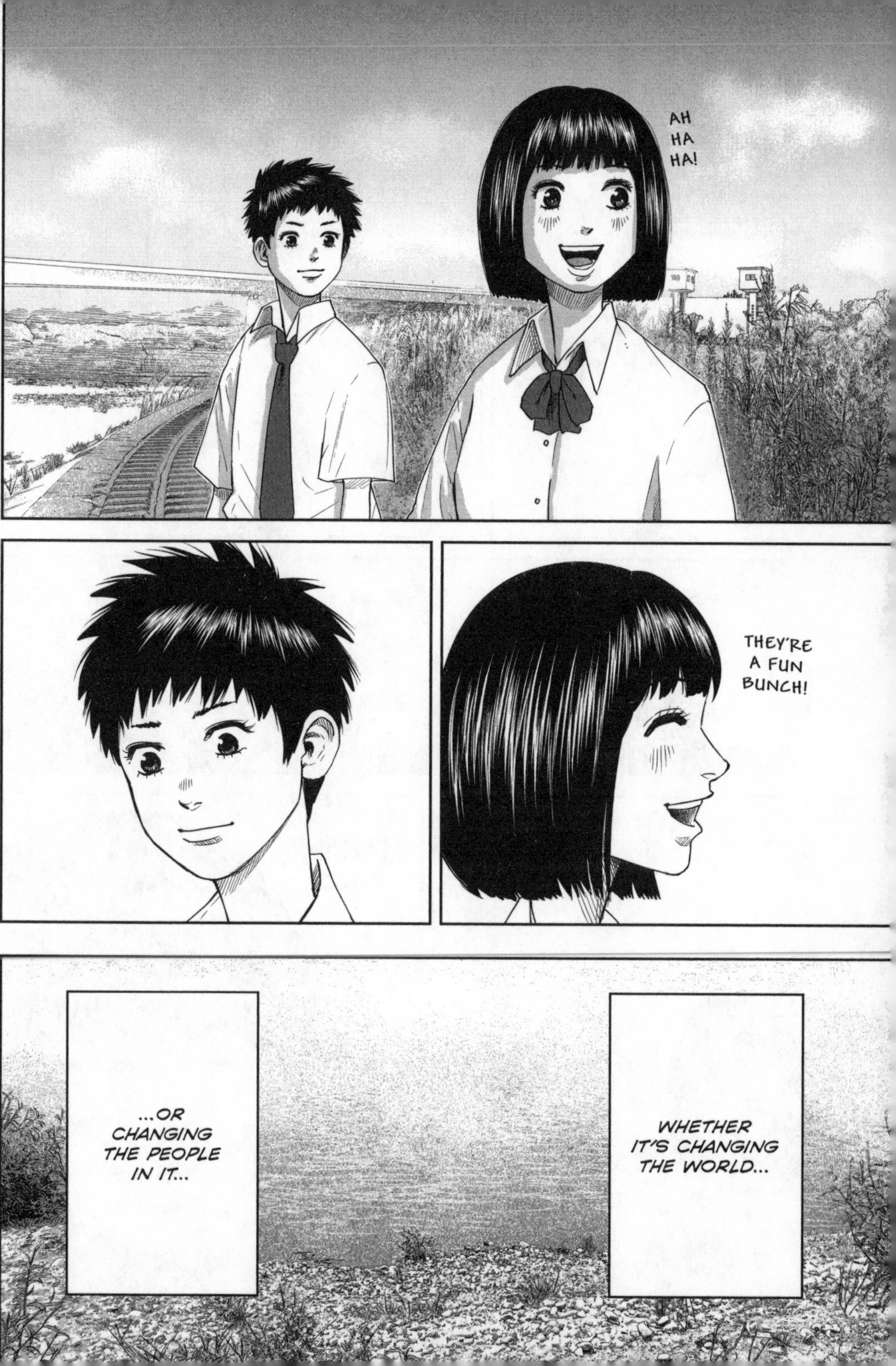
AH HA HA!
THEY'RE A FUN BUNCH!
WHETHER IT'S CHANGING THE WORLD...
...OR CHANGING THE PEOPLE IN IT...

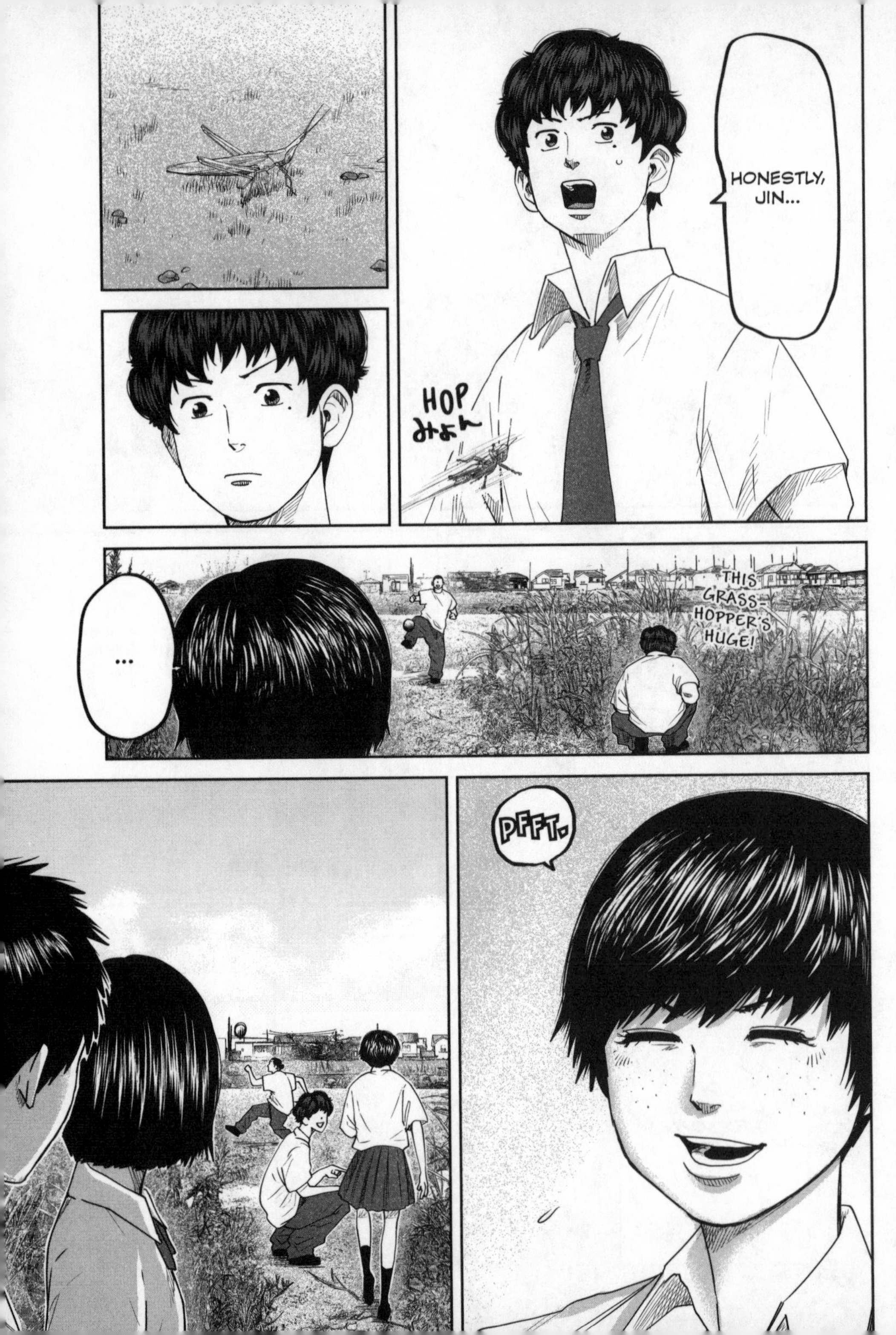
HONESTLY, JIN...
HOP
みょん
THIS GRASS-HOPPER'S HUGE!
...
PFFT.

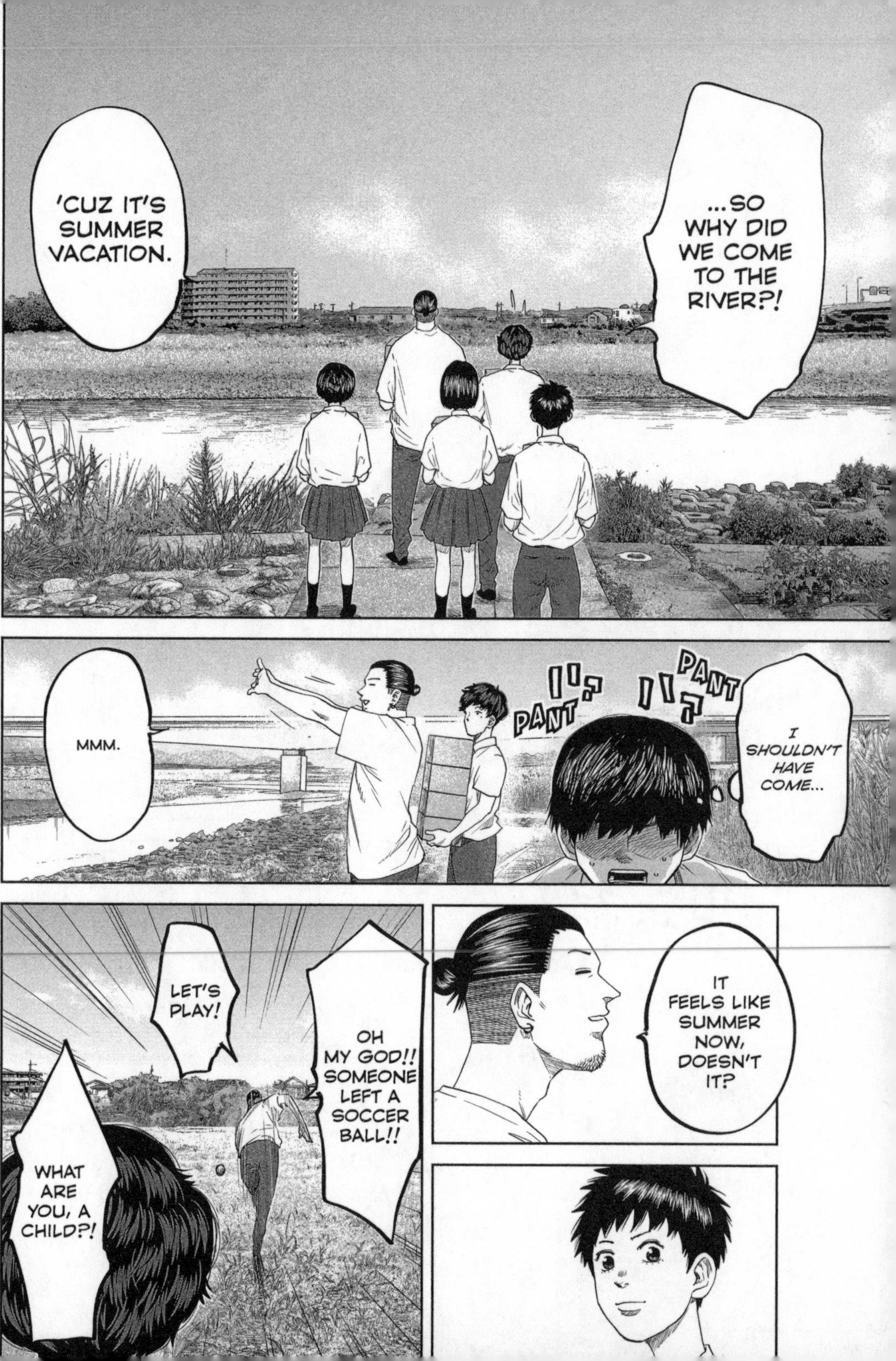
...SO WHY DID WE COME TO THE RIVER?!
'CUZ IT'S SUMMER VACATION.
PANT PANT
I SHOULDN'T HAVE COME...
MMM.
IT FEELS LIKE SUMMER NOW, DOESN'T IT?
OH MY GOD!! SOMEONE LEFT A SOCCER BALL!!
LET'S PLAY!
WHAT ARE YOU, A CHILD?!

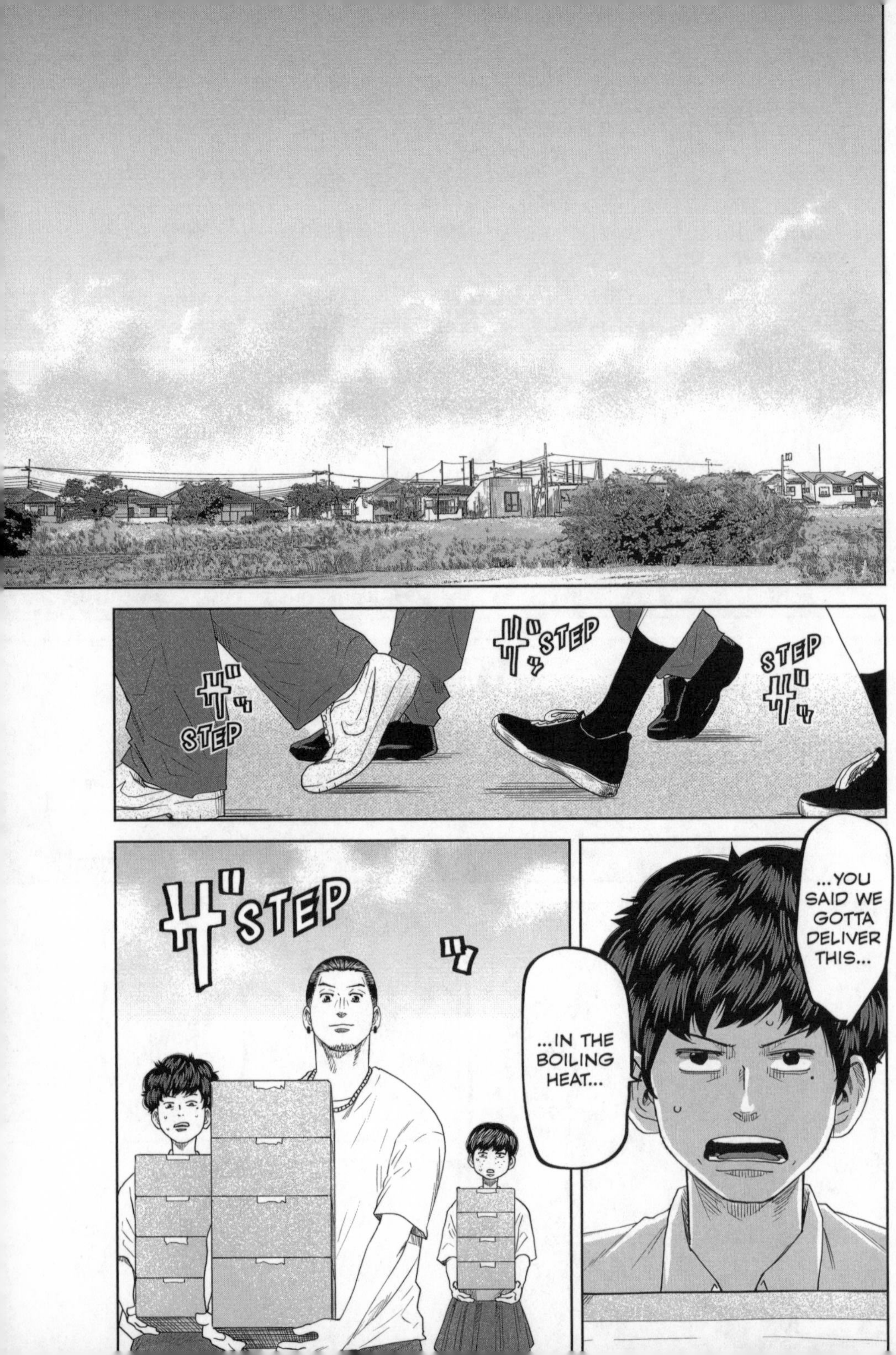
STEP ザッ
ザッ STEP
ザッ STEP
...YOU SAID WE GOTTA DELIVER THIS...
...IN THE BOILING HEAT...
ザッ STEP

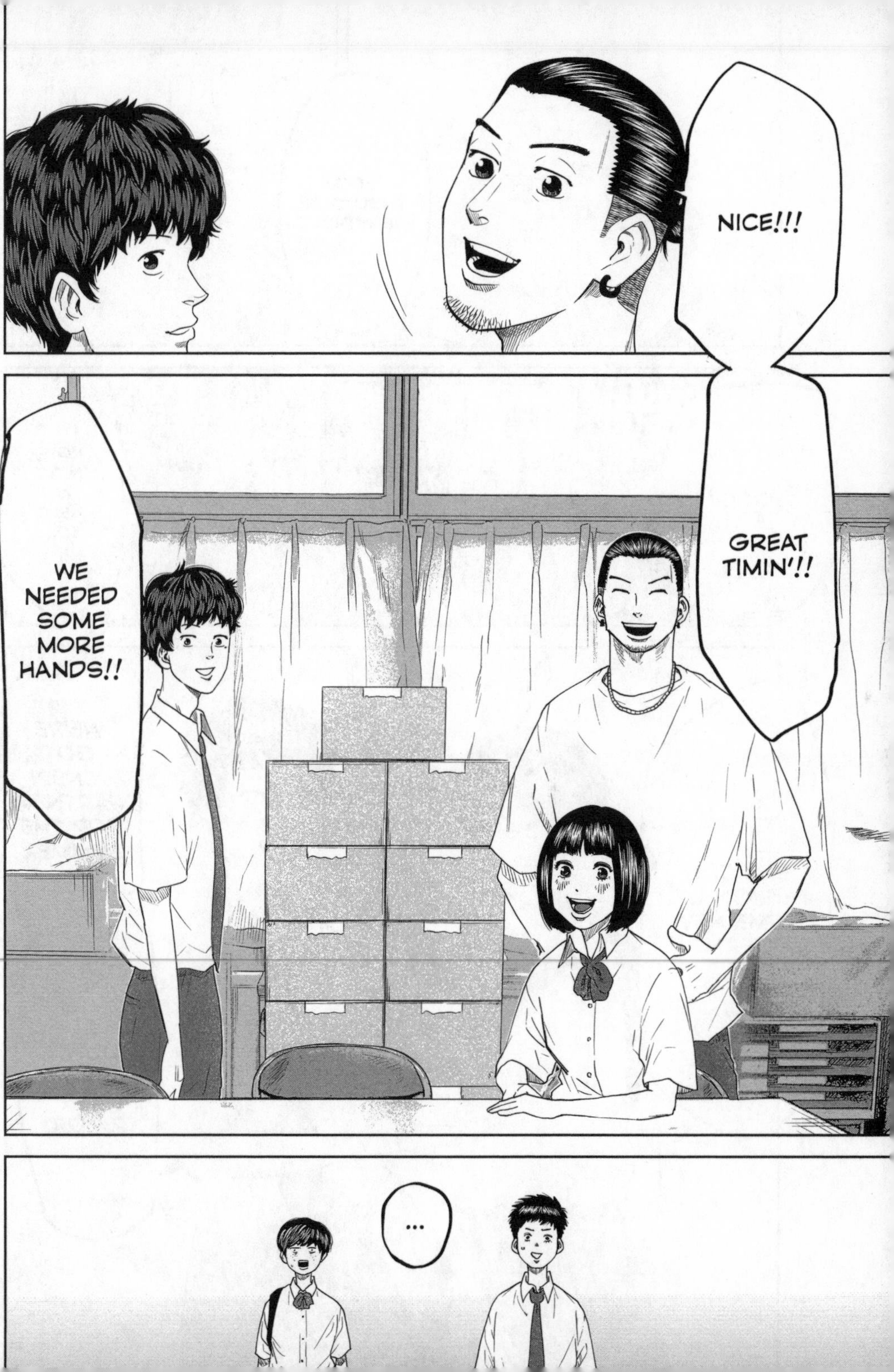
NICE!!! GREAT TIMIN'!!
WE NEEDED SOME MORE HANDS!!
...

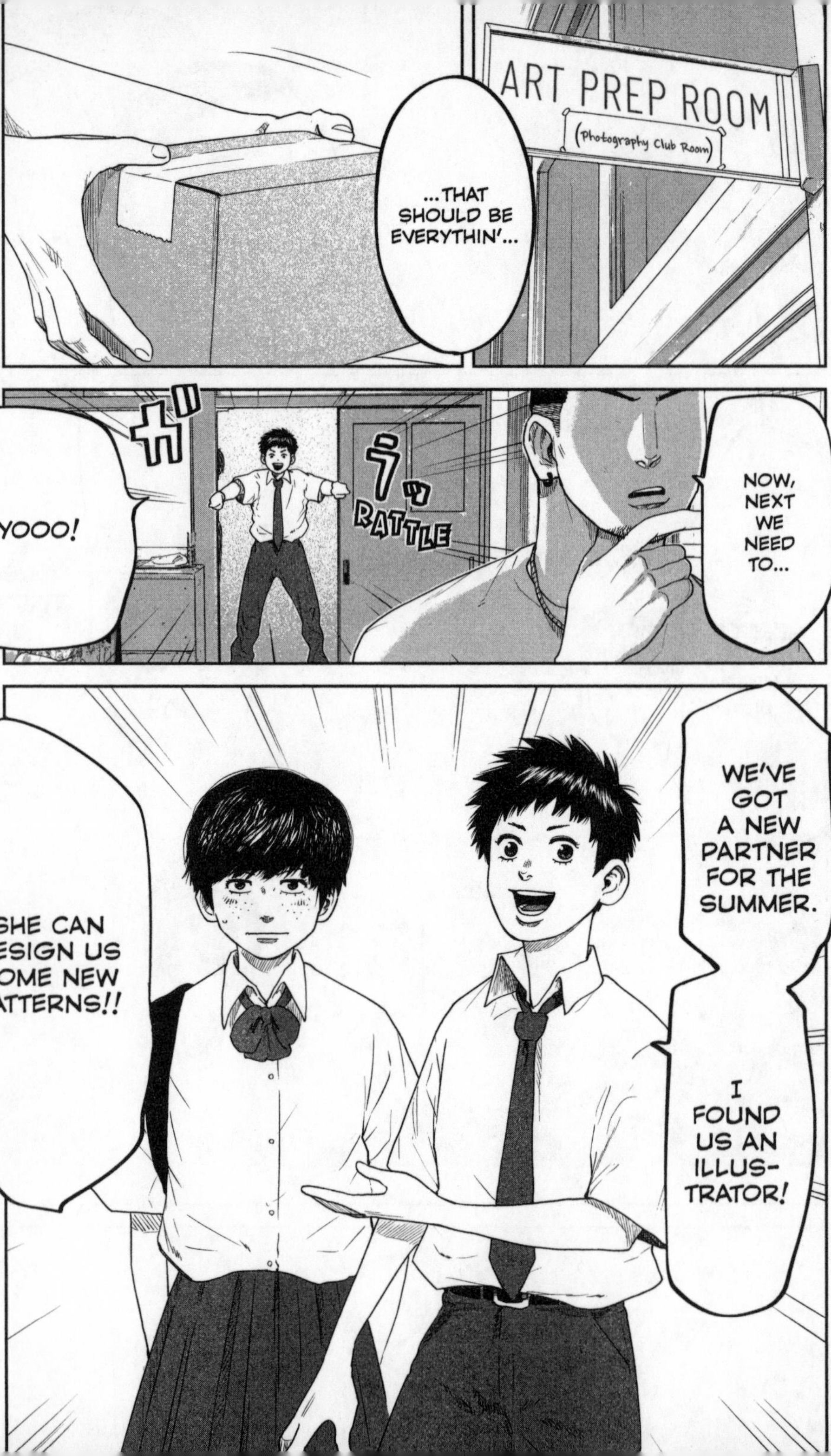
ART PREP ROOM
(Photography Club Room)
...THAT SHOULD BE EVERYTHIN'...
NOW, NEXT WE NEED TO...
ガラッ
RATTLE
YOOO!
WE'VE GOT A NEW PARTNER FOR THE SUMMER.
I FOUND US AN ILLUS-TRATOR!
SHE CAN DESIGN US SOME NEW PATTERNS!!

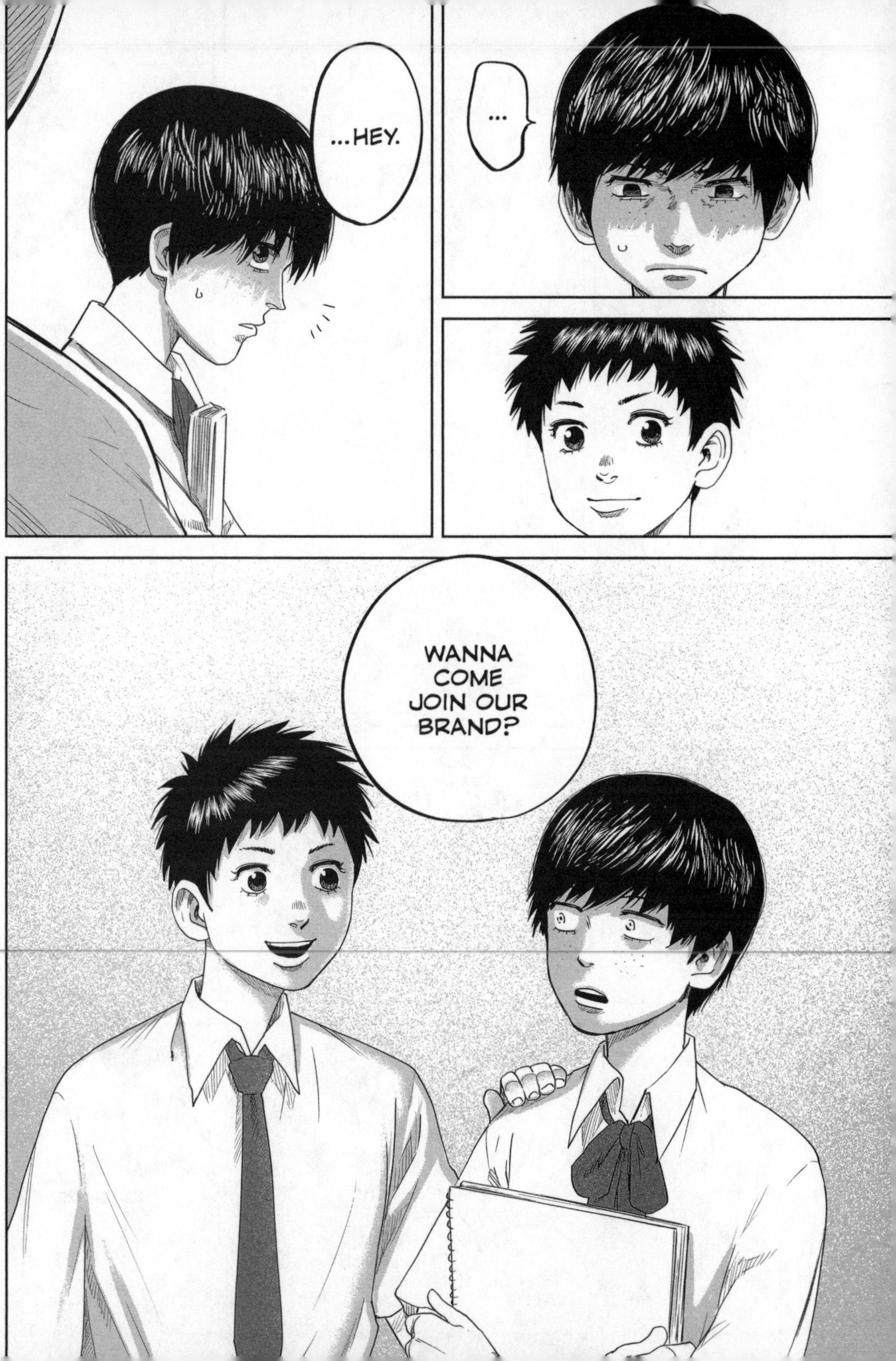
...
...HEY.
WANNA COME JOIN OUR BRAND?

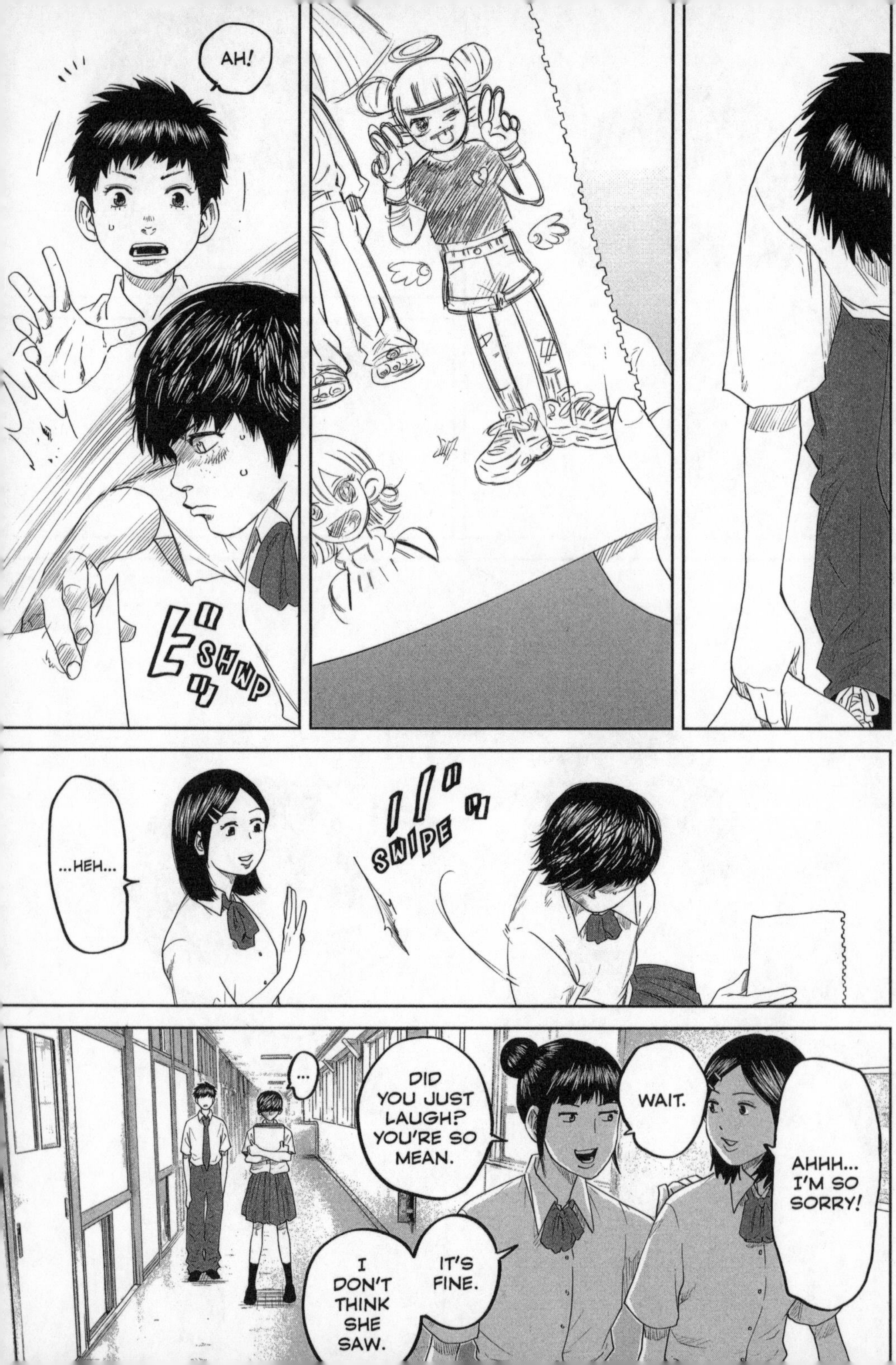
AH!
SHWP
SWIPE
...HEH...
AHHH... I'M SO SORRY!
WAIT.
DID YOU JUST LAUGH? YOU'RE SO MEAN.
...
IT'S FINE.
I DON'T THINK SHE SAW.

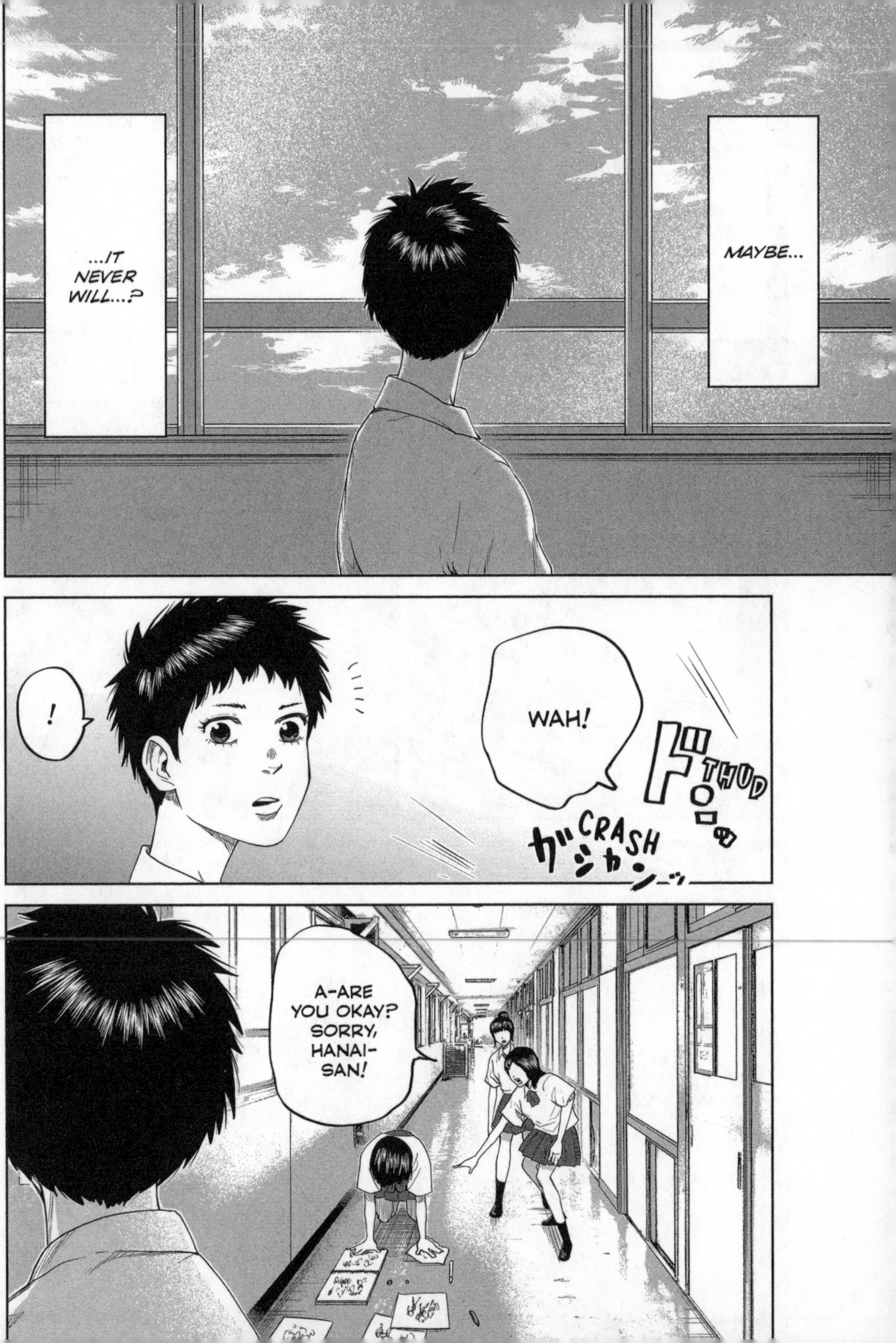
MAYBE...
...IT NEVER WILL...?
WAH!
THUD
CRASH
!
A-ARE YOU OKAY? SORRY, HANAI-SAN!

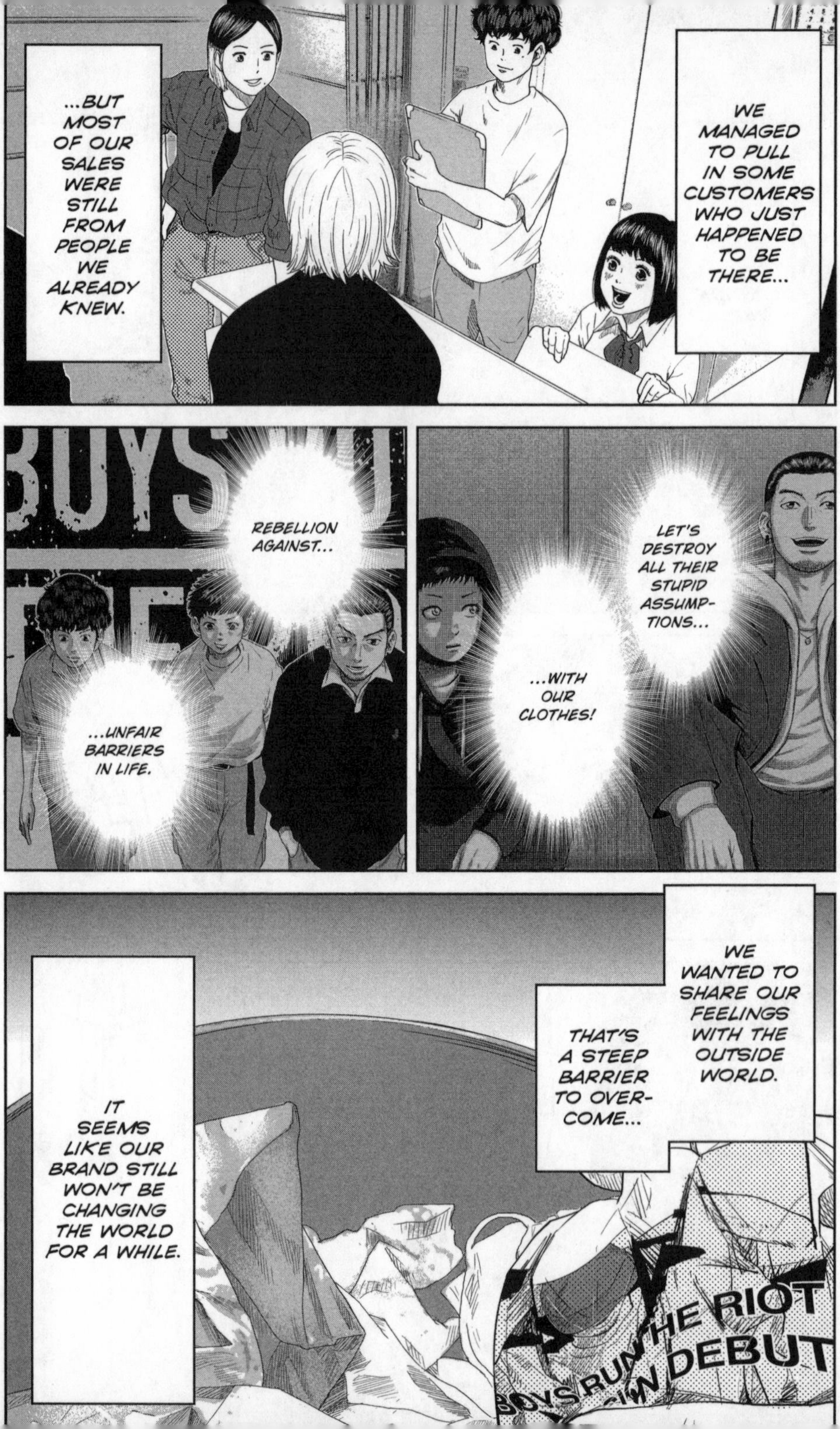
WE MANAGED TO PULL IN SOME CUSTOMERS WHO JUST HAPPENED TO BE THERE...
...BUT MOST OF OUR SALES WERE STILL FROM PEOPLE WE ALREADY KNEW.
LET'S DESTROY ALL THEIR STUPID ASSUMPTIONS...
...WITH OUR CLOTHES!
BOYS
REBELLION AGAINST...
...UNFAIR BARRIERS IN LIFE.
WE WANTED TO SHARE OUR FEELINGS WITH THE OUTSIDE WORLD.
THAT'S A STEEP BARRIER TO OVERCOME...
IT SEEMS LIKE OUR BRAND STILL WON'T BE CHANGING THE WORLD FOR A WHILE.
BOYS RUN THE RIOT
DEBUT

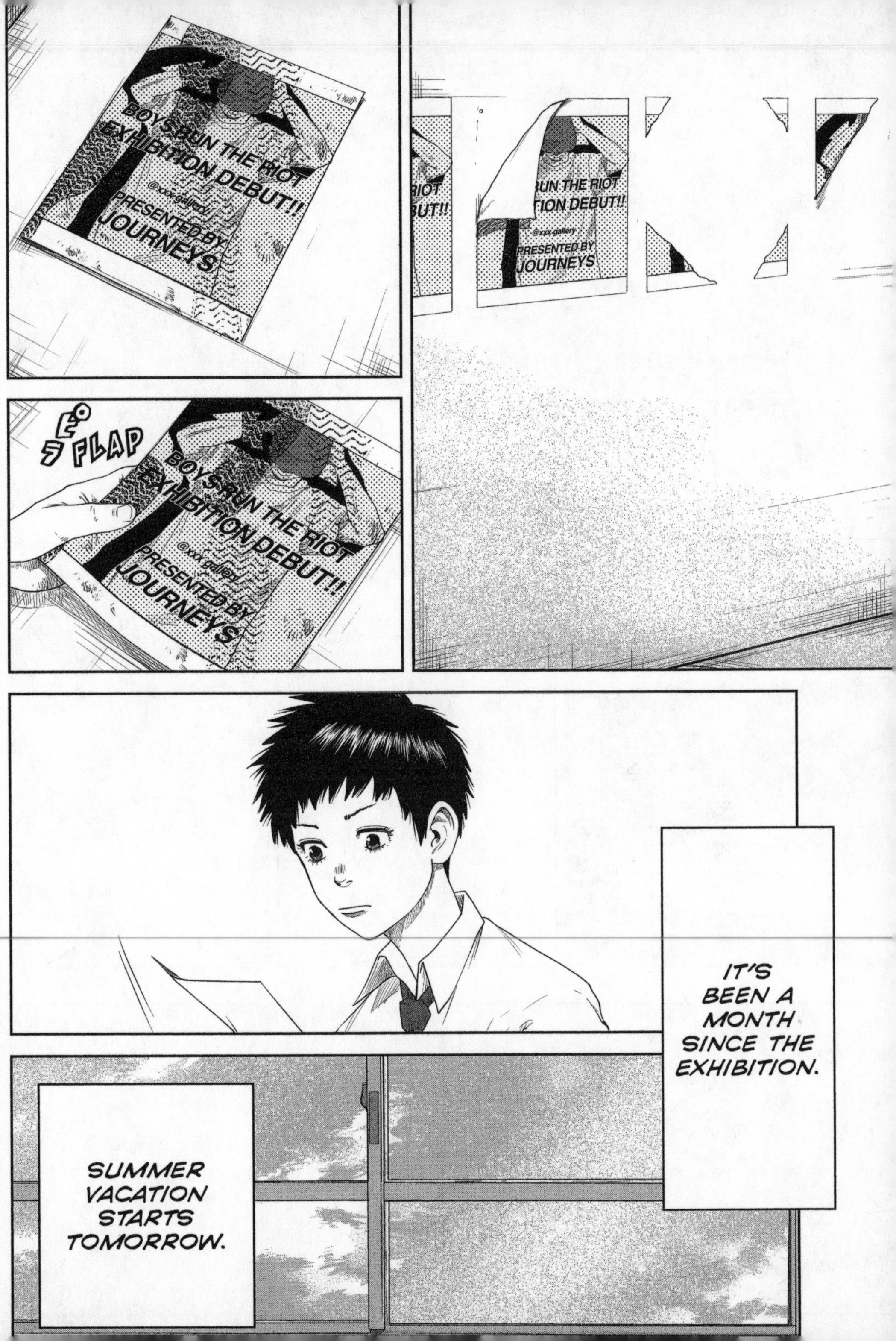
RUN THE RIOT
TION DEBUT!!
@xxx.gallery
PRESENTED BY
JOURNEYS
BOYS RUN THE RIOT
EXHIBITION DEBUT!!
@xxx.gallery
PRESENTED BY
JOURNEYS
FLAP
BOYS RUN THE RIOT
EXHIBITION DEBUT!!
@xxx.gallery
PRESENTED BY
JOURNEYS
IT'S BEEN A MONTH SINCE THE EXHIBITION.
SUMMER VACATION STARTS TOMORROW.

Final Chap. Freedom

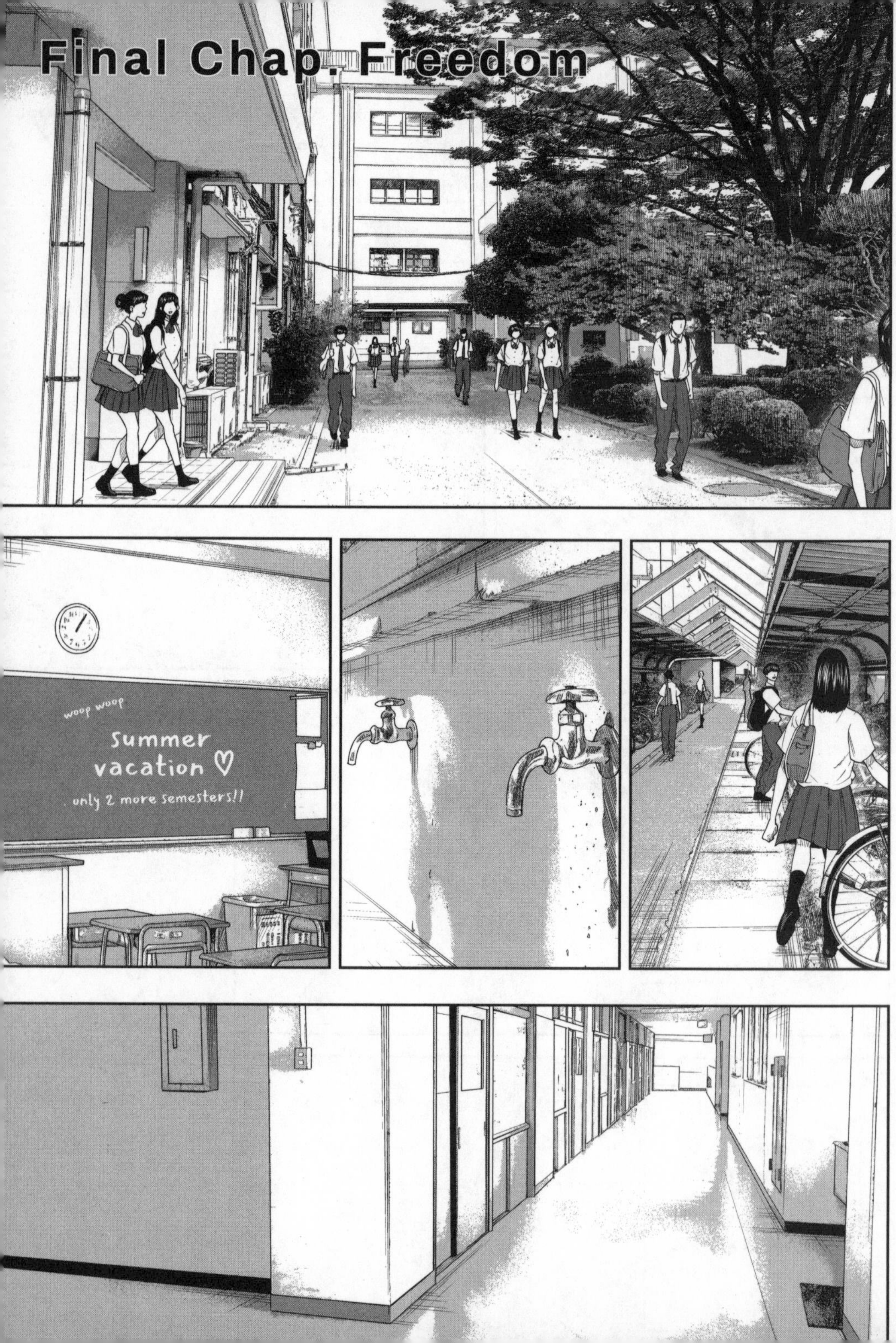
woop woop
summer vacation ♡
only 2 more semesters!!

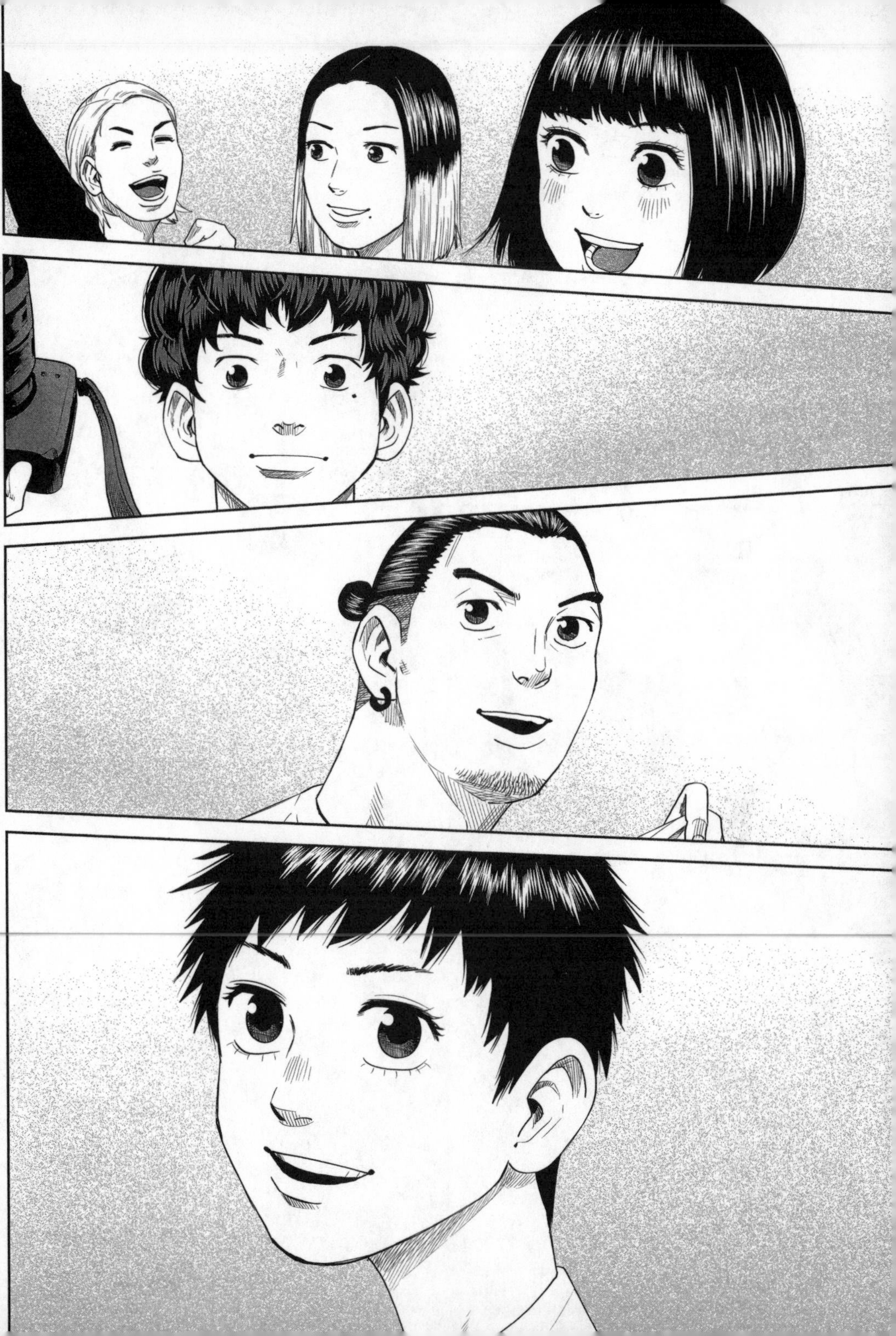

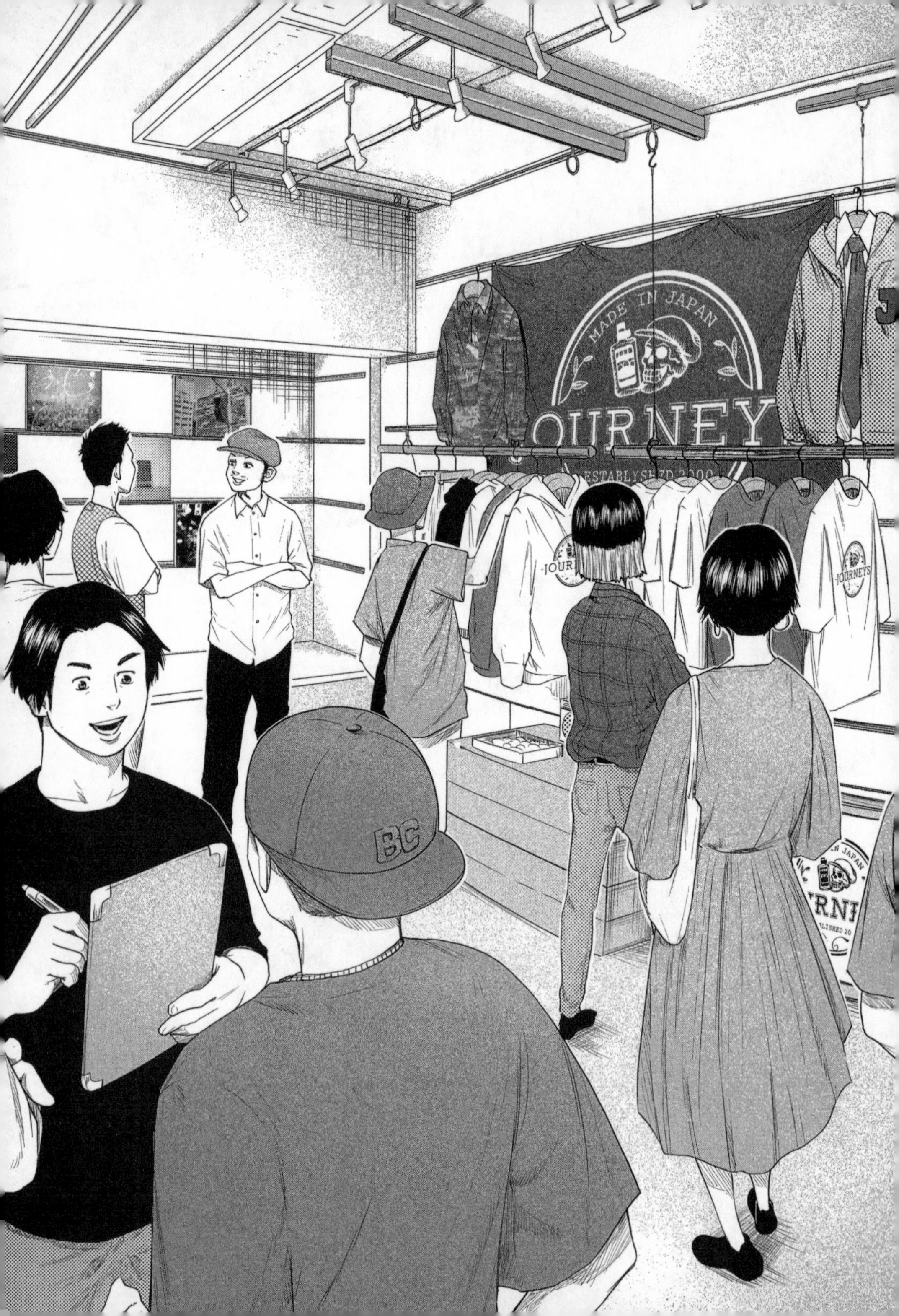

MADE IN JAPAN
JOURNEYS
BC

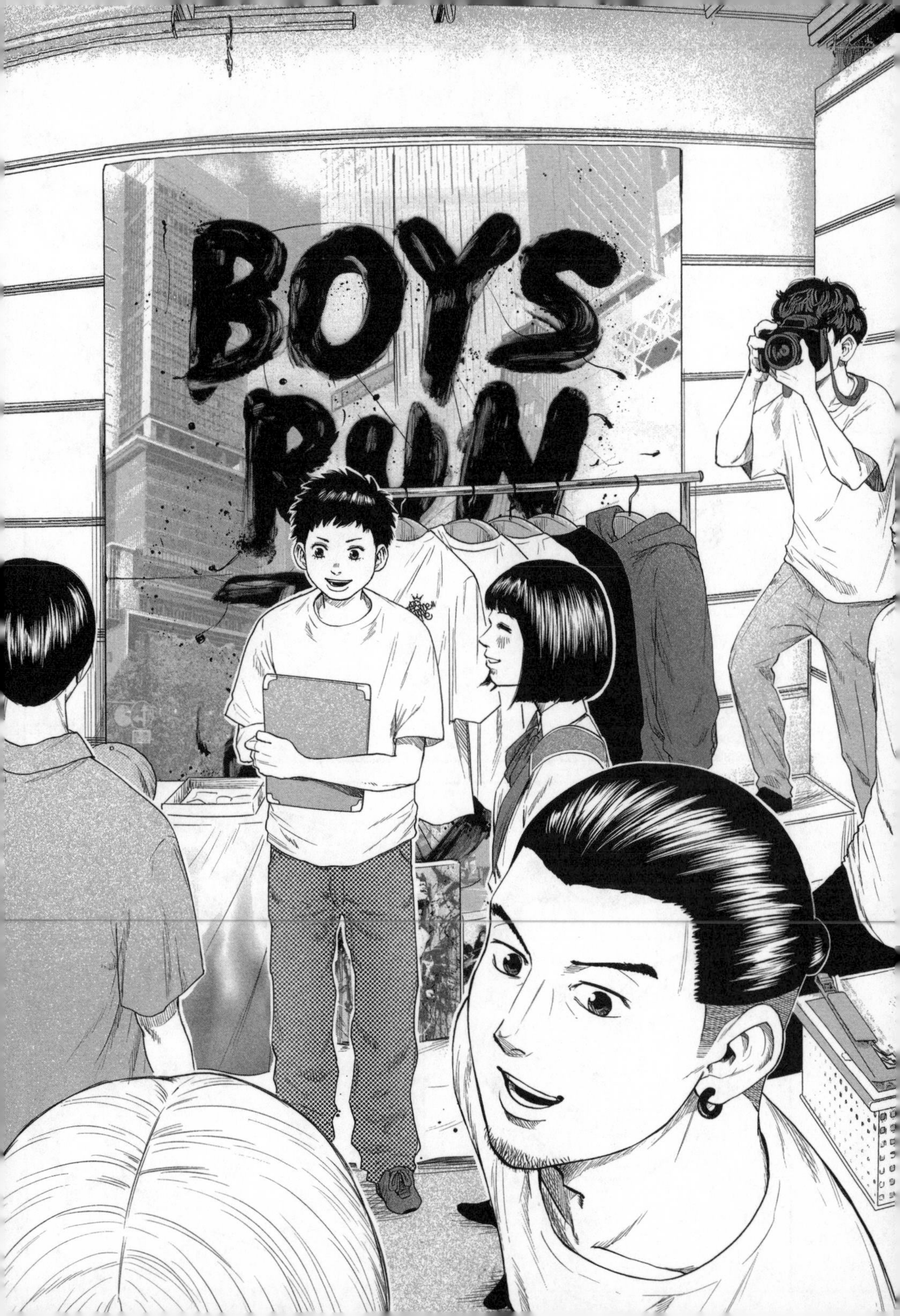
BOYS

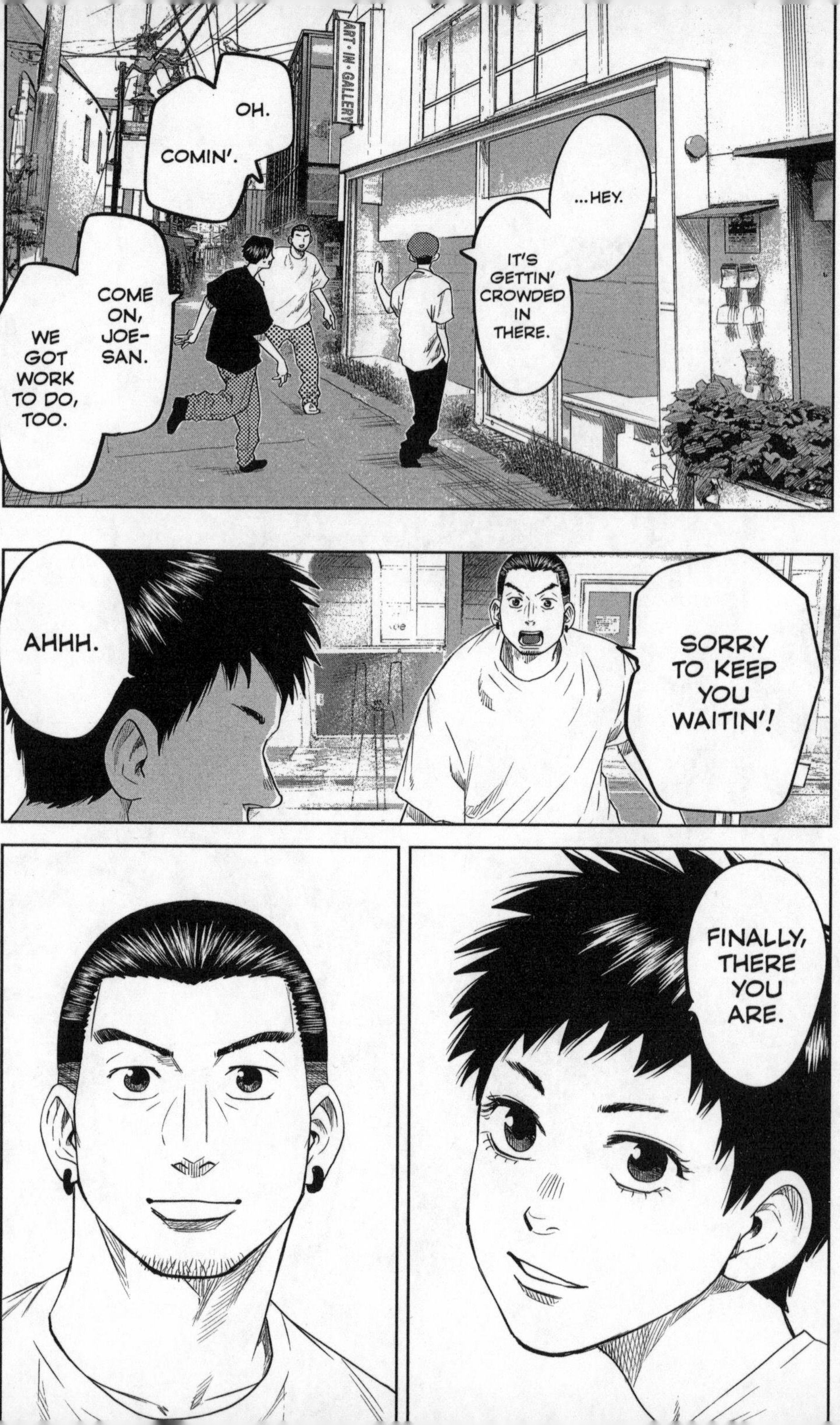
ART · IN · GALLERY
...HEY.
IT'S GETTIN' CROWDED IN THERE.
OH.
COMIN'.
COME ON, JOE-SAN.
WE GOT WORK TO DO, TOO.
SORRY TO KEEP YOU WAITIN'!
AHHH.
FINALLY, THERE YOU ARE.

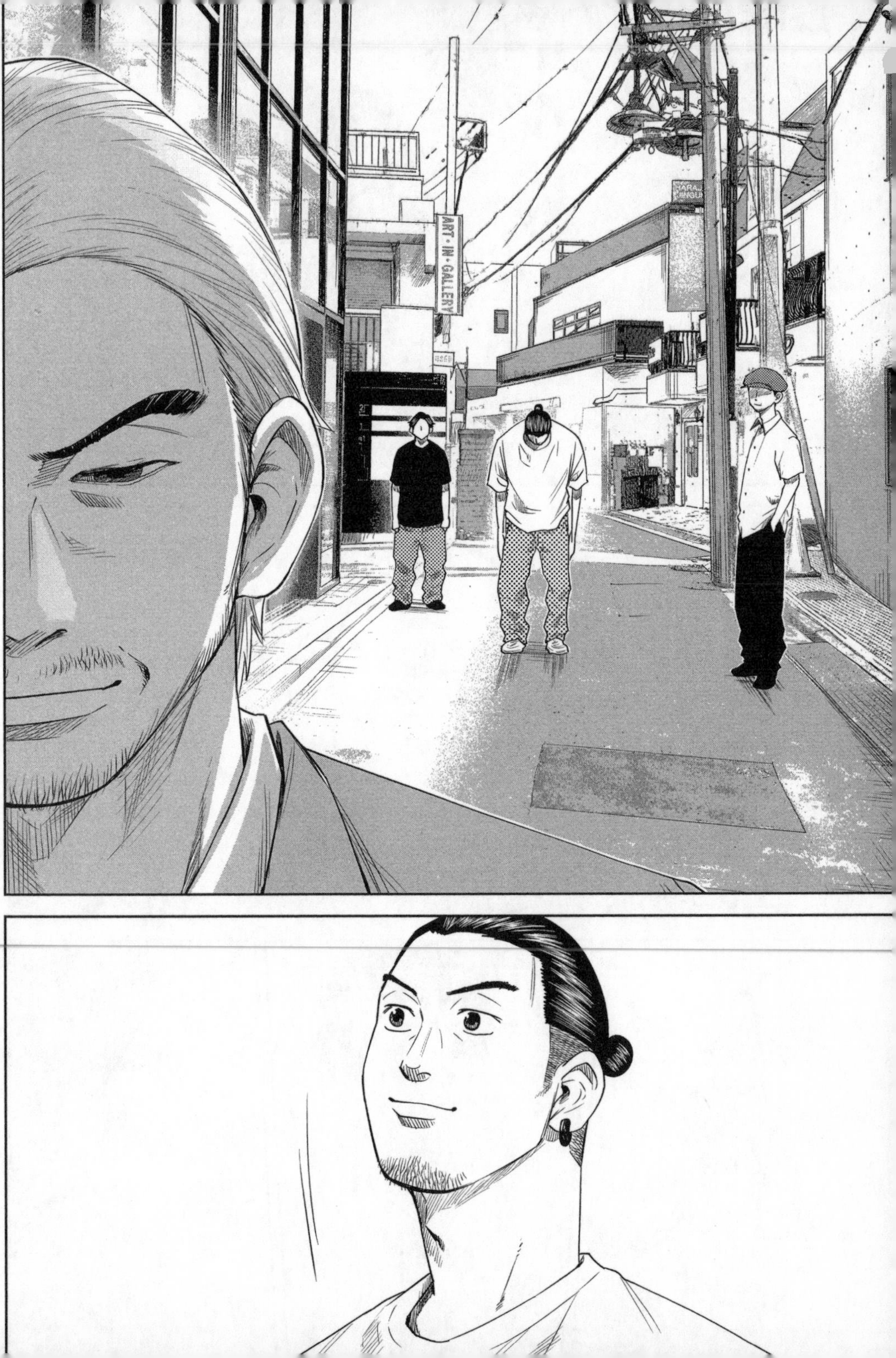
ART·IN·GALLERY

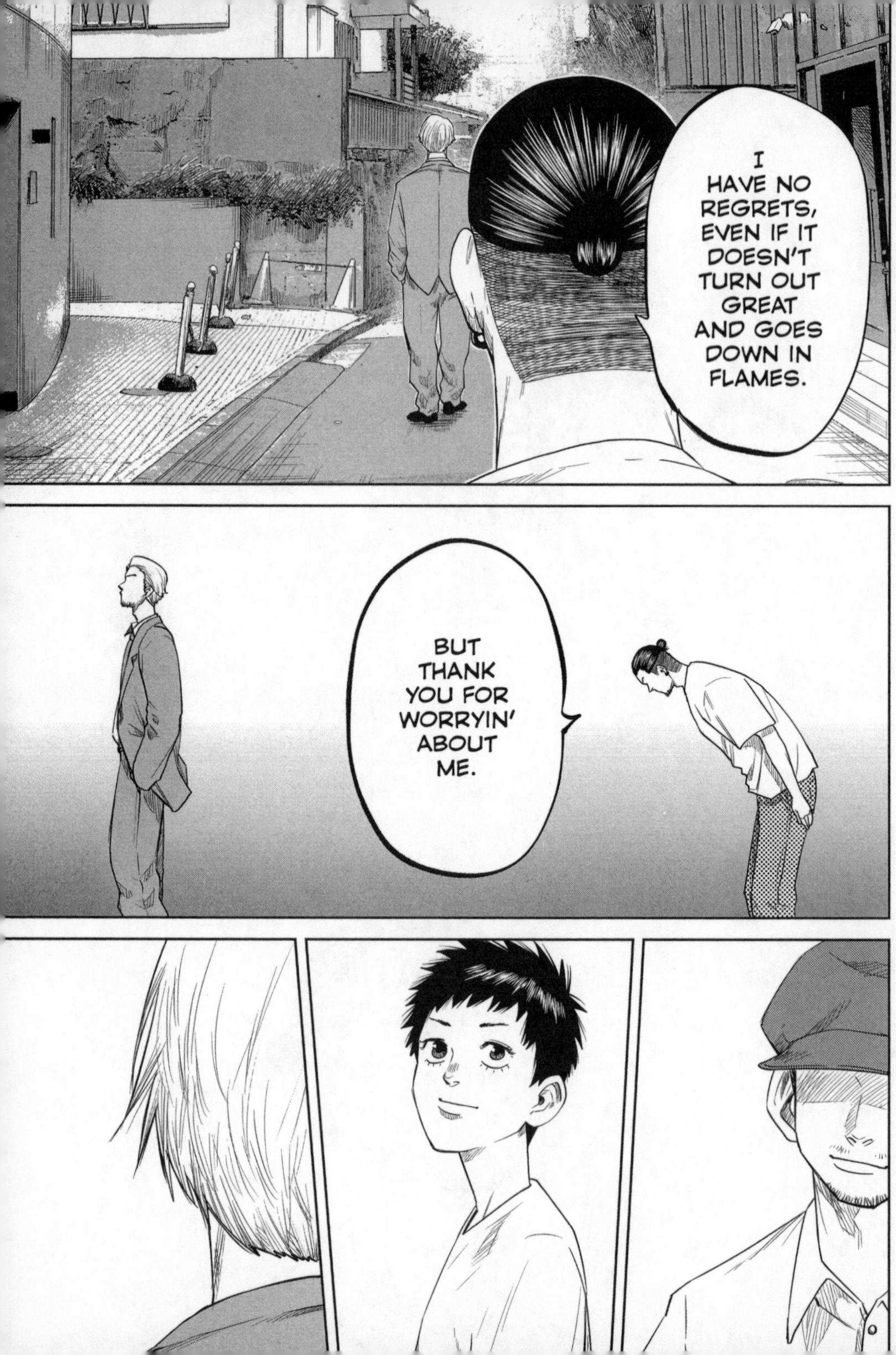
I HAVE NO REGRETS, EVEN IF IT DOESN'T TURN OUT GREAT AND GOES DOWN IN FLAMES.
BUT THANK YOU FOR WORRYIN' ABOUT ME.

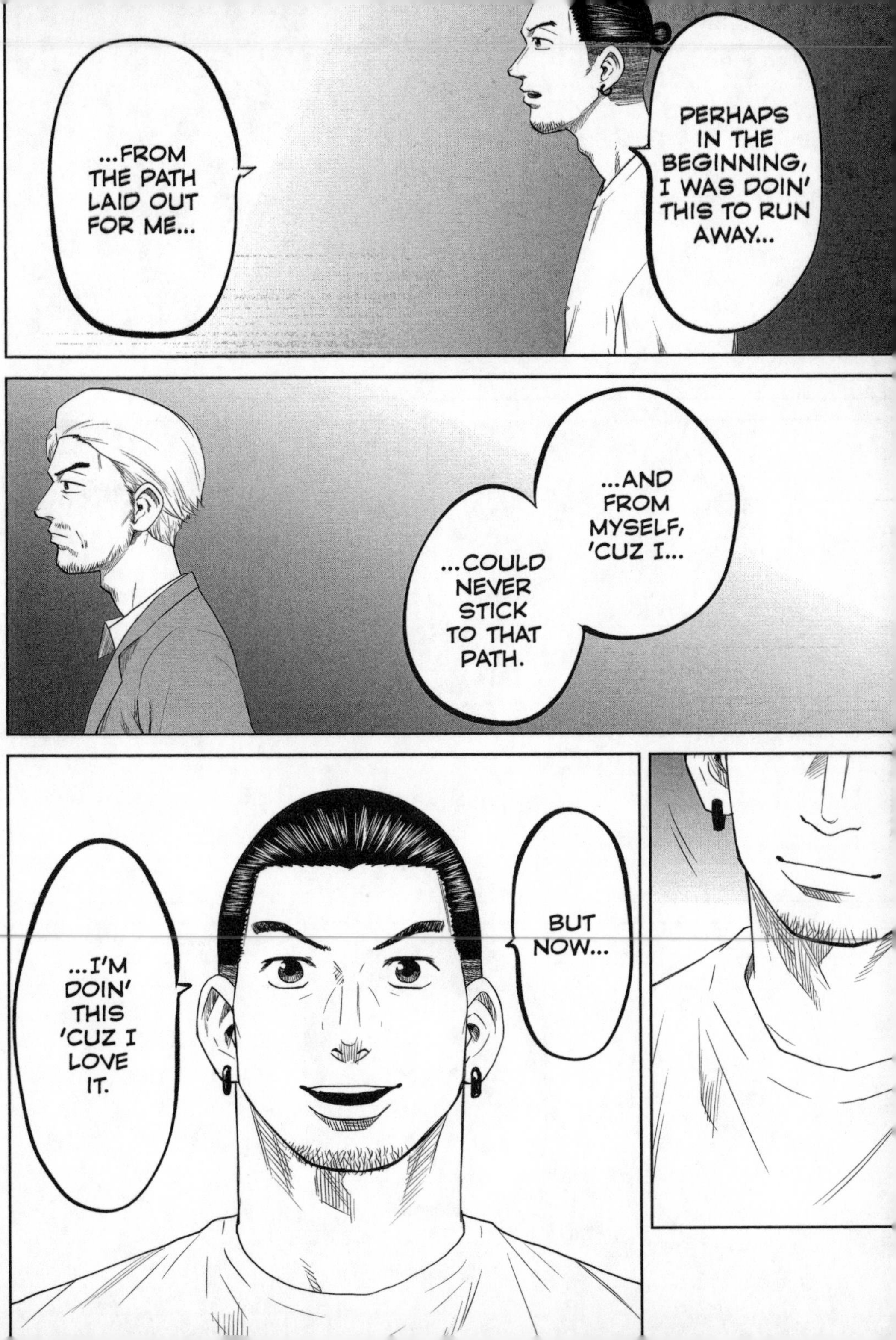
PERHAPS IN THE BEGINNING, I WAS DOIN' THIS TO RUN AWAY...
...FROM THE PATH LAID OUT FOR ME...
...AND FROM MYSELF, 'CUZ I...
...COULD NEVER STICK TO THAT PATH.
BUT NOW...
...I'M DOIN' THIS 'CUZ I LOVE IT.

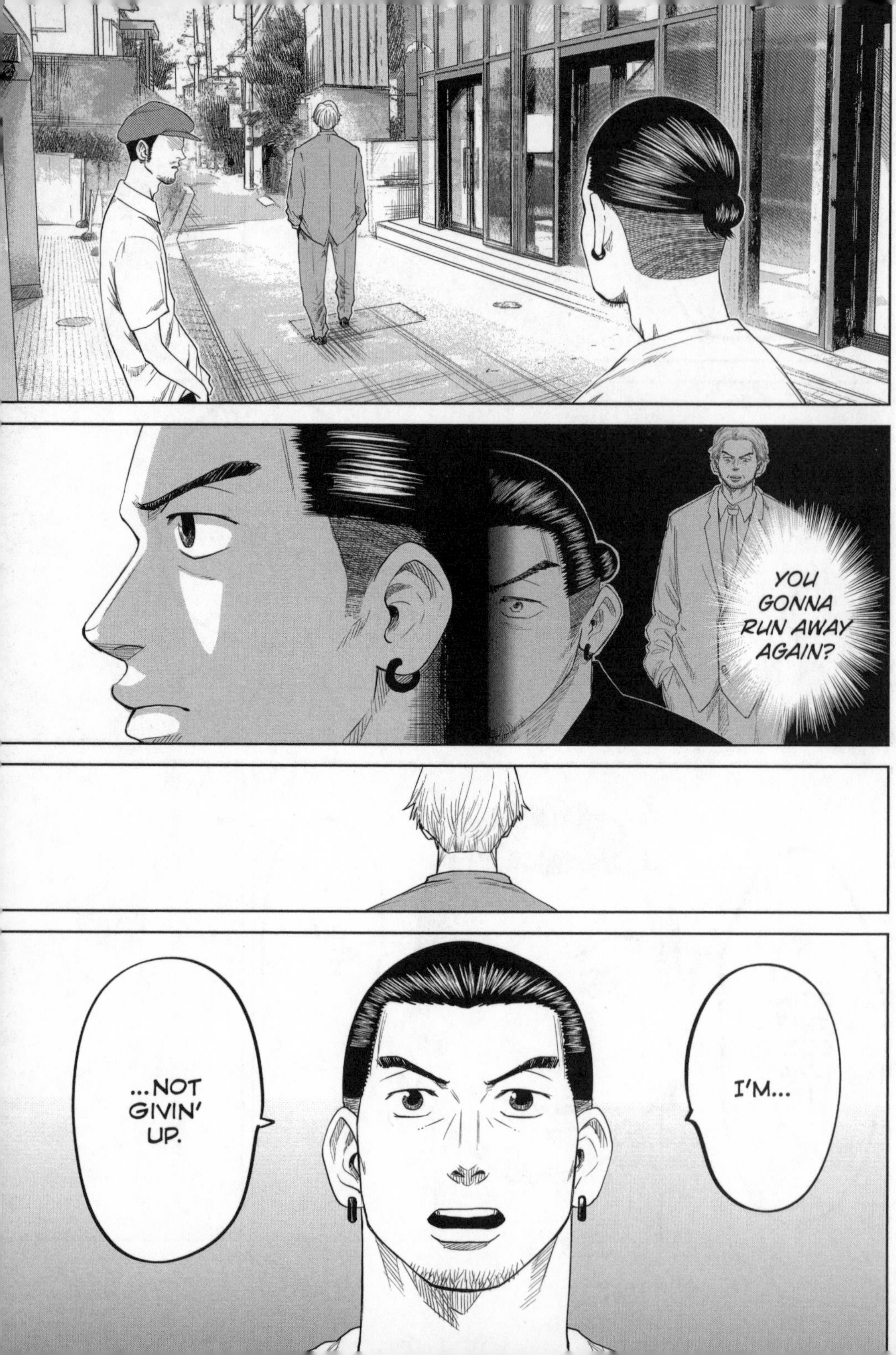
YOU GONNA RUN AWAY AGAIN?
I'M...
...NOT GIVIN' UP.

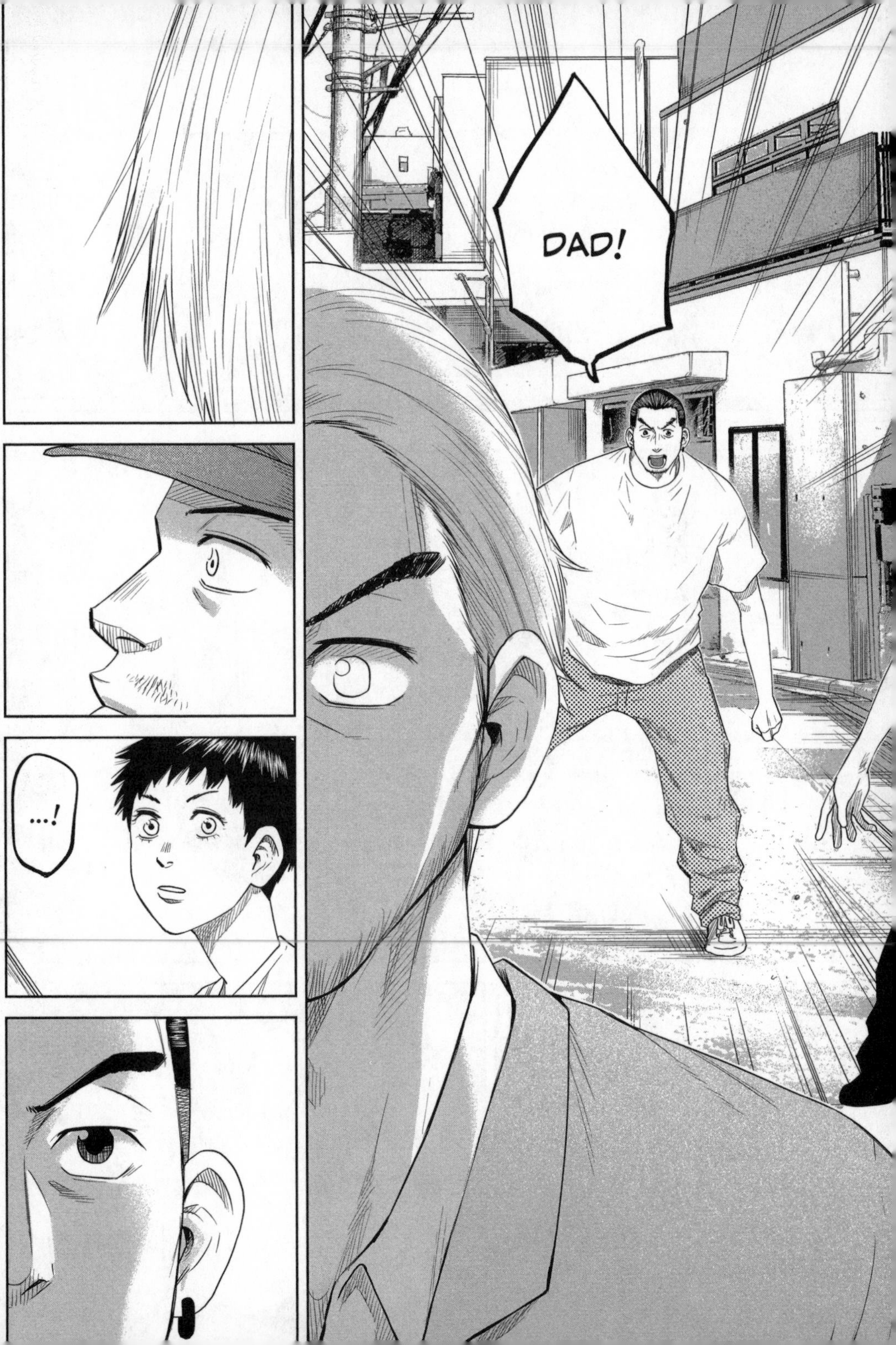
DAD!
...!

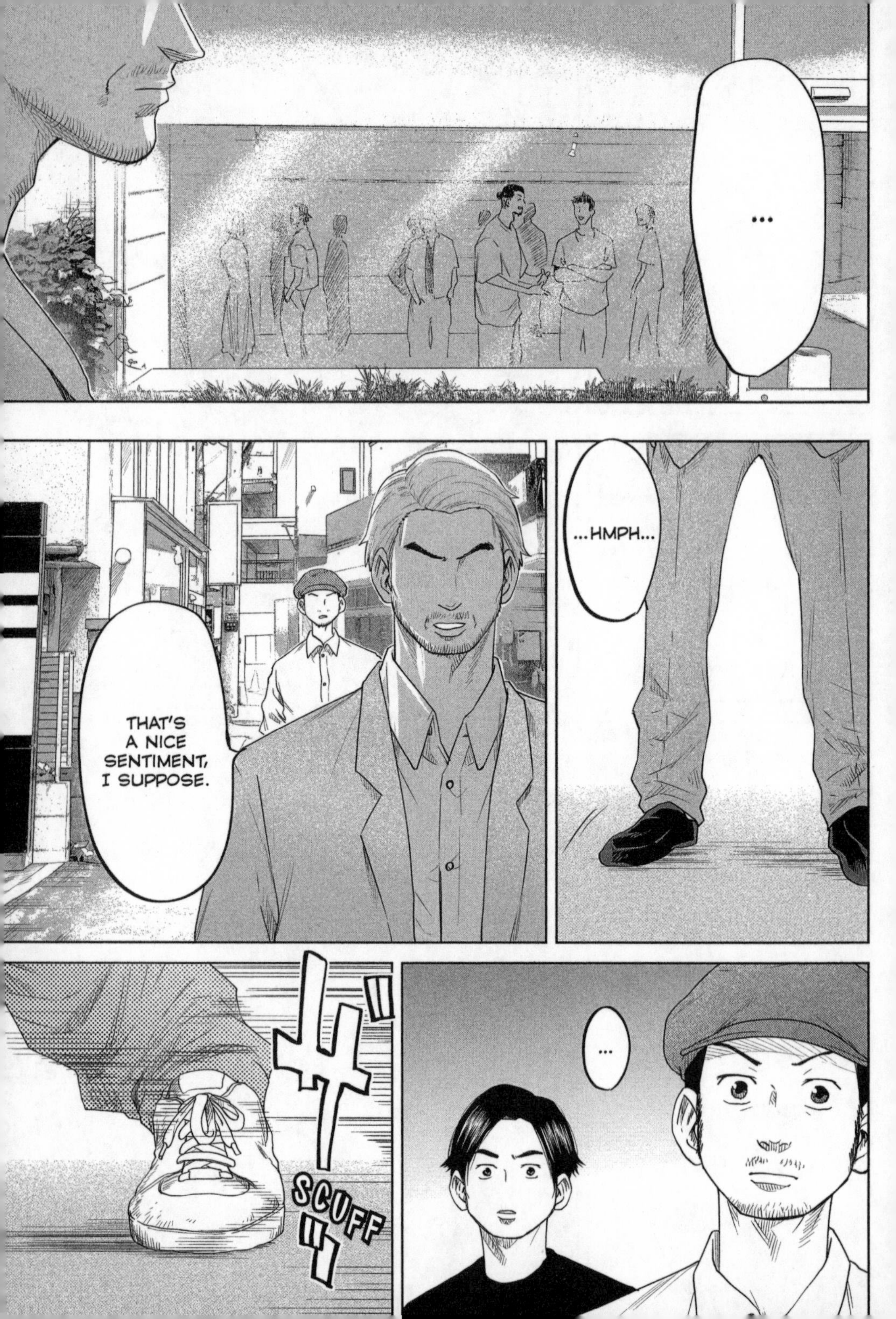
...
...HMPH...
THAT'S A NICE SENTIMENT, I SUPPOSE.
...
SCUFF

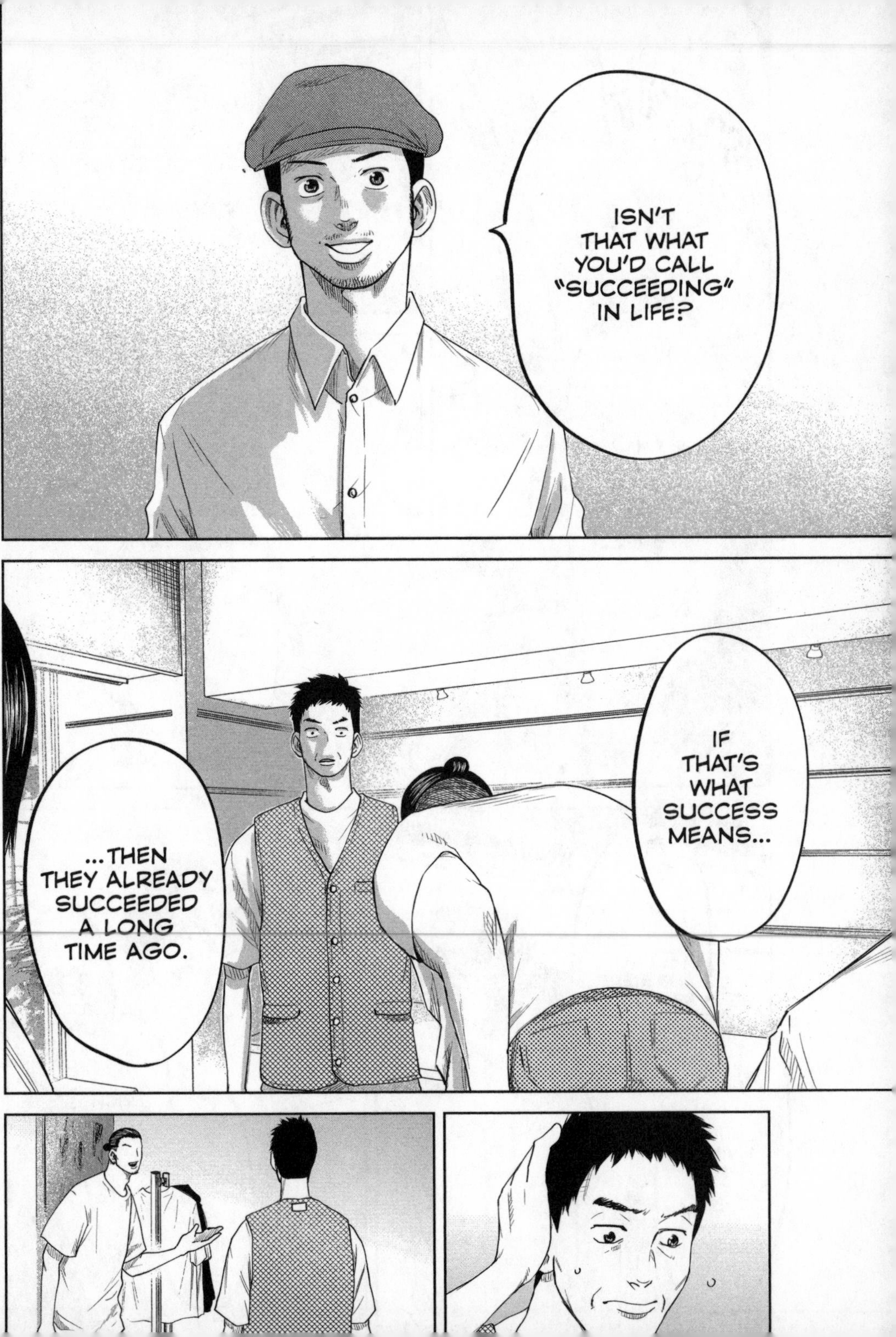
ISN'T THAT WHAT YOU'D CALL "SUCCEEDING" IN LIFE?
IF THAT'S WHAT SUCCESS MEANS...
...THEN THEY ALREADY SUCCEEDED A LONG TIME AGO.

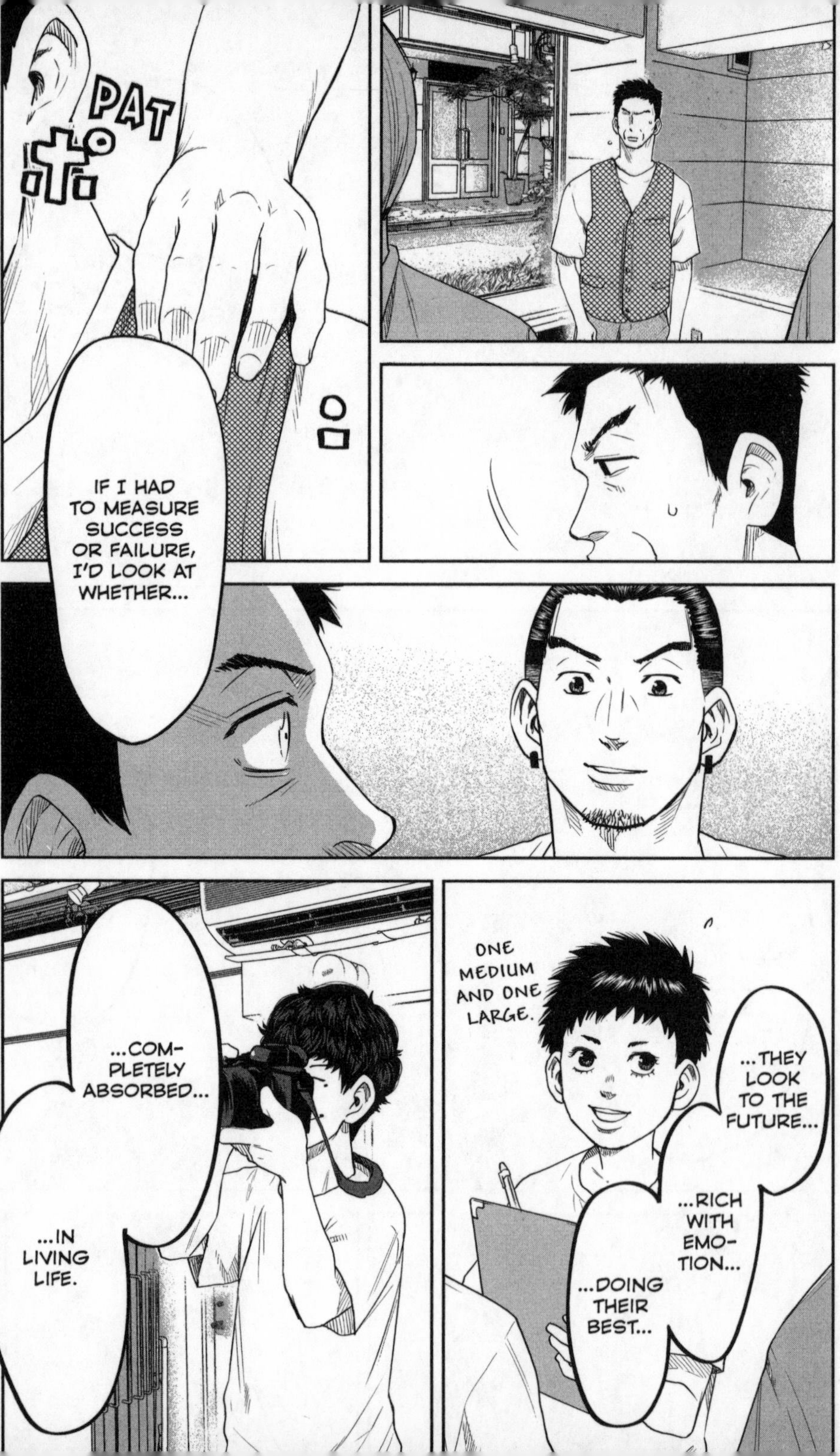
PAT
IF I HAD TO MEASURE SUCCESS OR FAILURE, I'D LOOK AT WHETHER...
ONE MEDIUM AND ONE LARGE.
...THEY LOOK TO THE FUTURE...
...RICH WITH EMO-TION...
...DOING THEIR BEST...
...COM-PLETELY ABSORBED...
...IN LIVING LIFE.

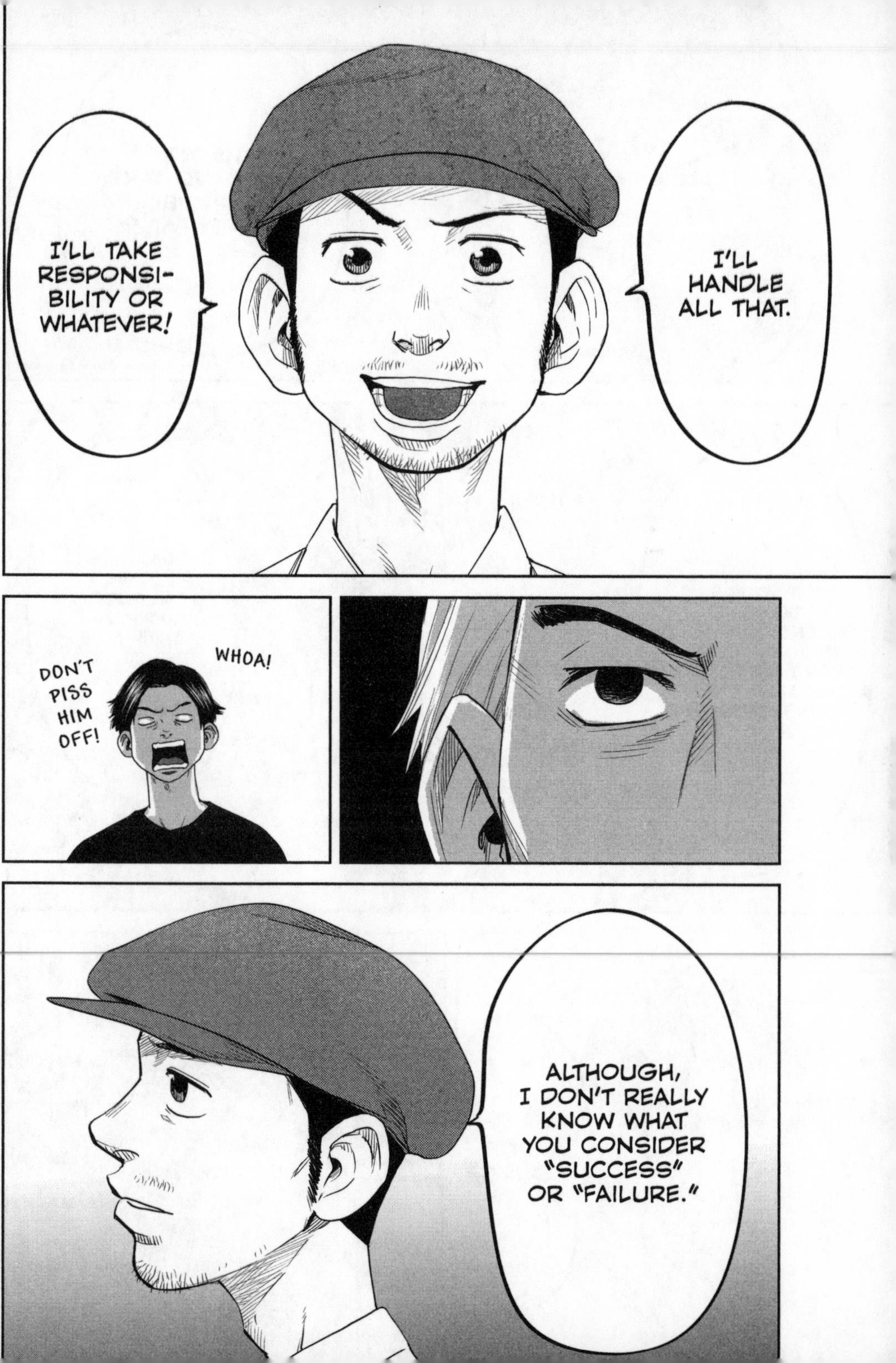
I'LL HANDLE ALL THAT.
I'LL TAKE RESPONSI-BILITY OR WHATEVER!
WHOA!
DON'T PISS HIM OFF!
ALTHOUGH, I DON'T REALLY KNOW WHAT YOU CONSIDER "SUCCESS" OR "FAILURE."

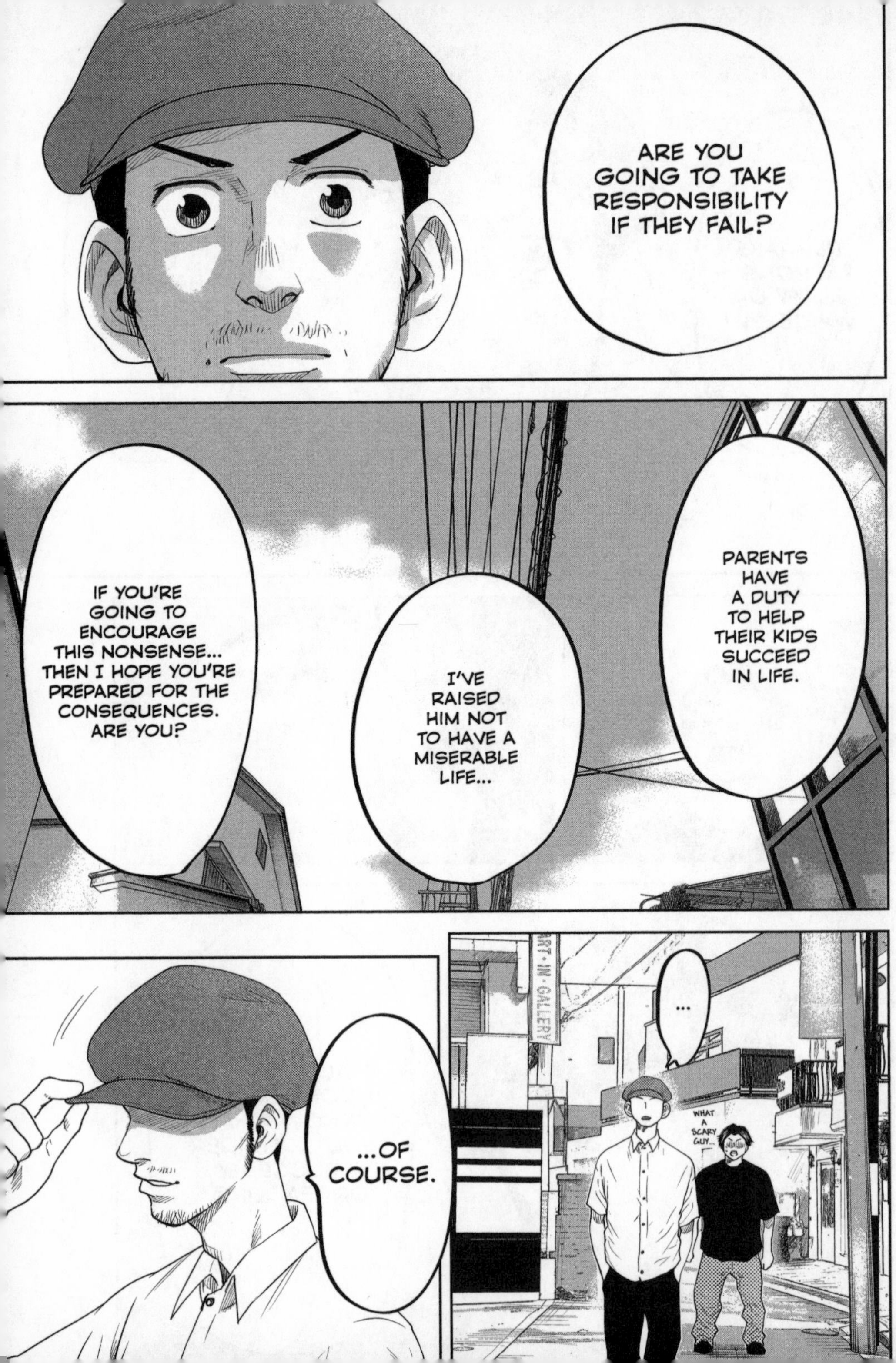
ARE YOU GOING TO TAKE RESPONSIBILITY IF THEY FAIL?
PARENTS HAVE A DUTY TO HELP THEIR KIDS SUCCEED IN LIFE.
I'VE RAISED HIM NOT TO HAVE A MISERABLE LIFE...
IF YOU'RE GOING TO ENCOURAGE THIS NONSENSE... THEN I HOPE YOU'RE PREPARED FOR THE CONSEQUENCES. ARE YOU?
ART·IN·GALLERY
...
WHAT A SCARY GUY...
...OF COURSE.

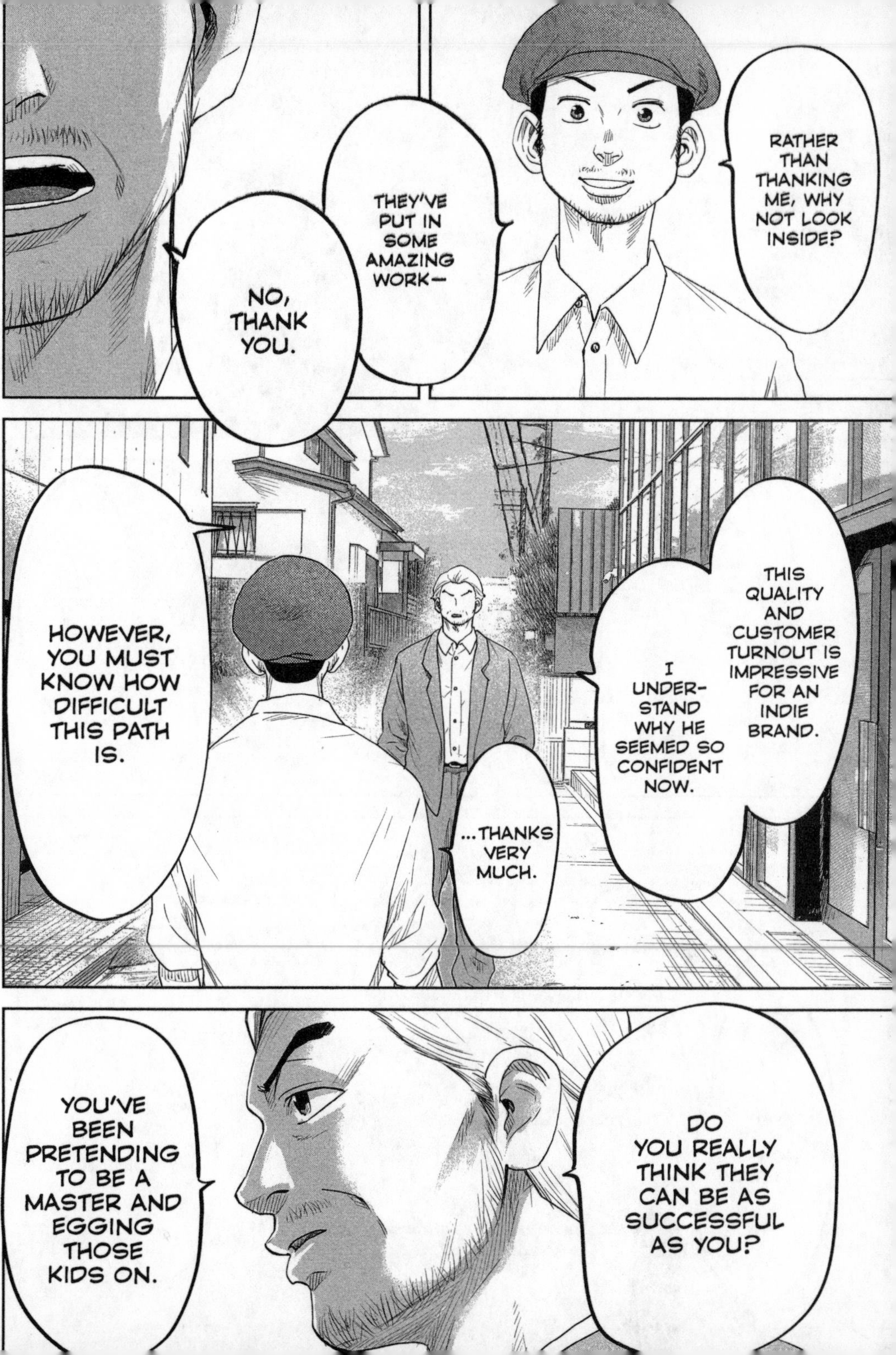
RATHER THAN THANKING ME, WHY NOT LOOK INSIDE?
THEY'VE PUT IN SOME AMAZING WORK—
NO, THANK YOU.
THIS QUALITY AND CUSTOMER TURNOUT IS IMPRESSIVE FOR AN INDIE BRAND.
I UNDER-STAND WHY HE SEEMED SO CONFIDENT NOW.
...THANKS VERY MUCH.
HOWEVER, YOU MUST KNOW HOW DIFFICULT THIS PATH IS.
DO YOU REALLY THINK THEY CAN BE AS SUCCESSFUL AS YOU?
YOU'VE BEEN PRETENDING TO BE A MASTER AND EGGING THOSE KIDS ON.

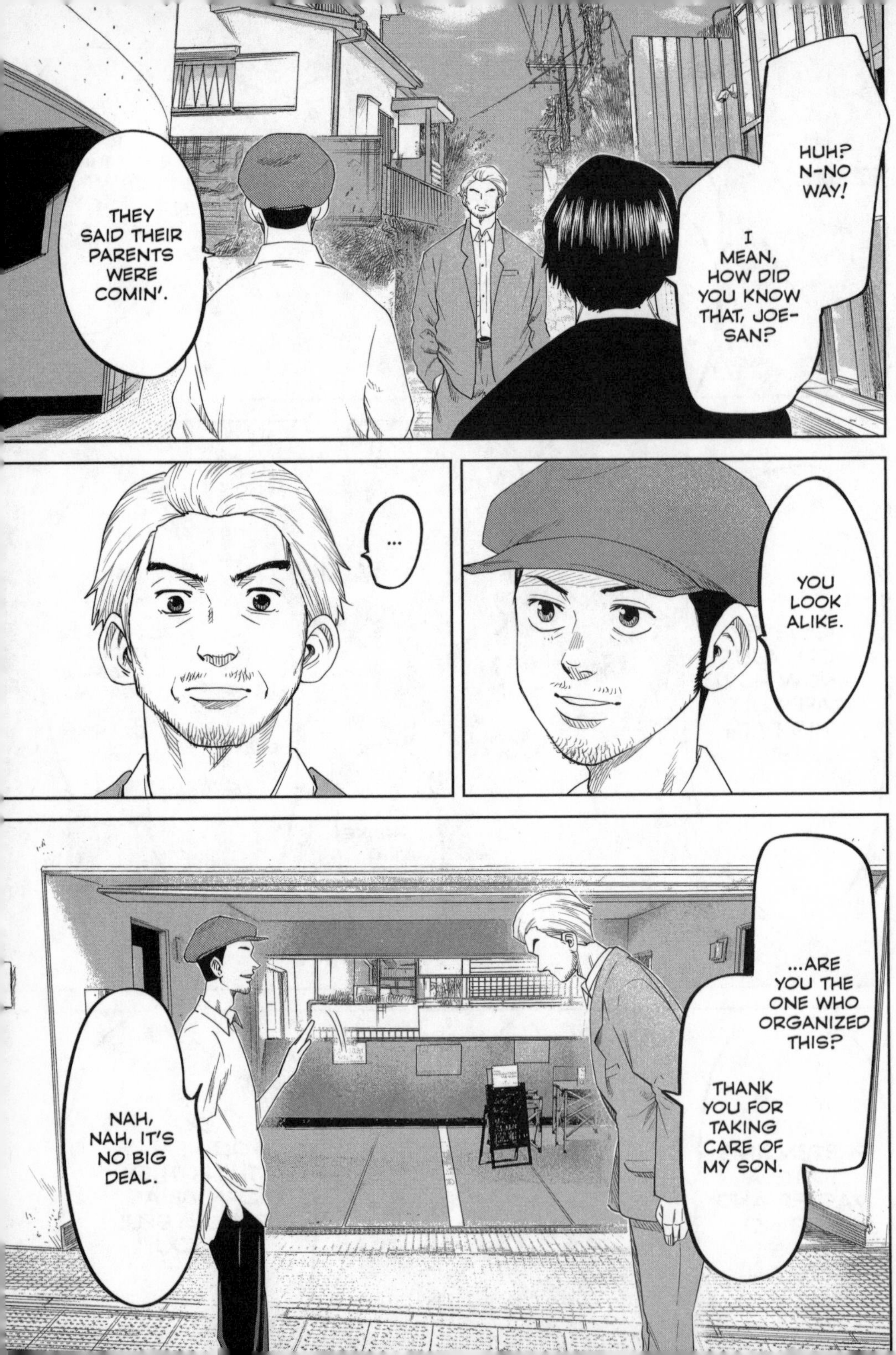
HUH? N-NO WAY!
I MEAN, HOW DID YOU KNOW THAT, JOE-SAN?
THEY SAID THEIR PARENTS WERE COMIN'.
YOU LOOK ALIKE.
...
...ARE YOU THE ONE WHO ORGANIZED THIS?
THANK YOU FOR TAKING CARE OF MY SON.
NAH, NAH, IT'S NO BIG DEAL.

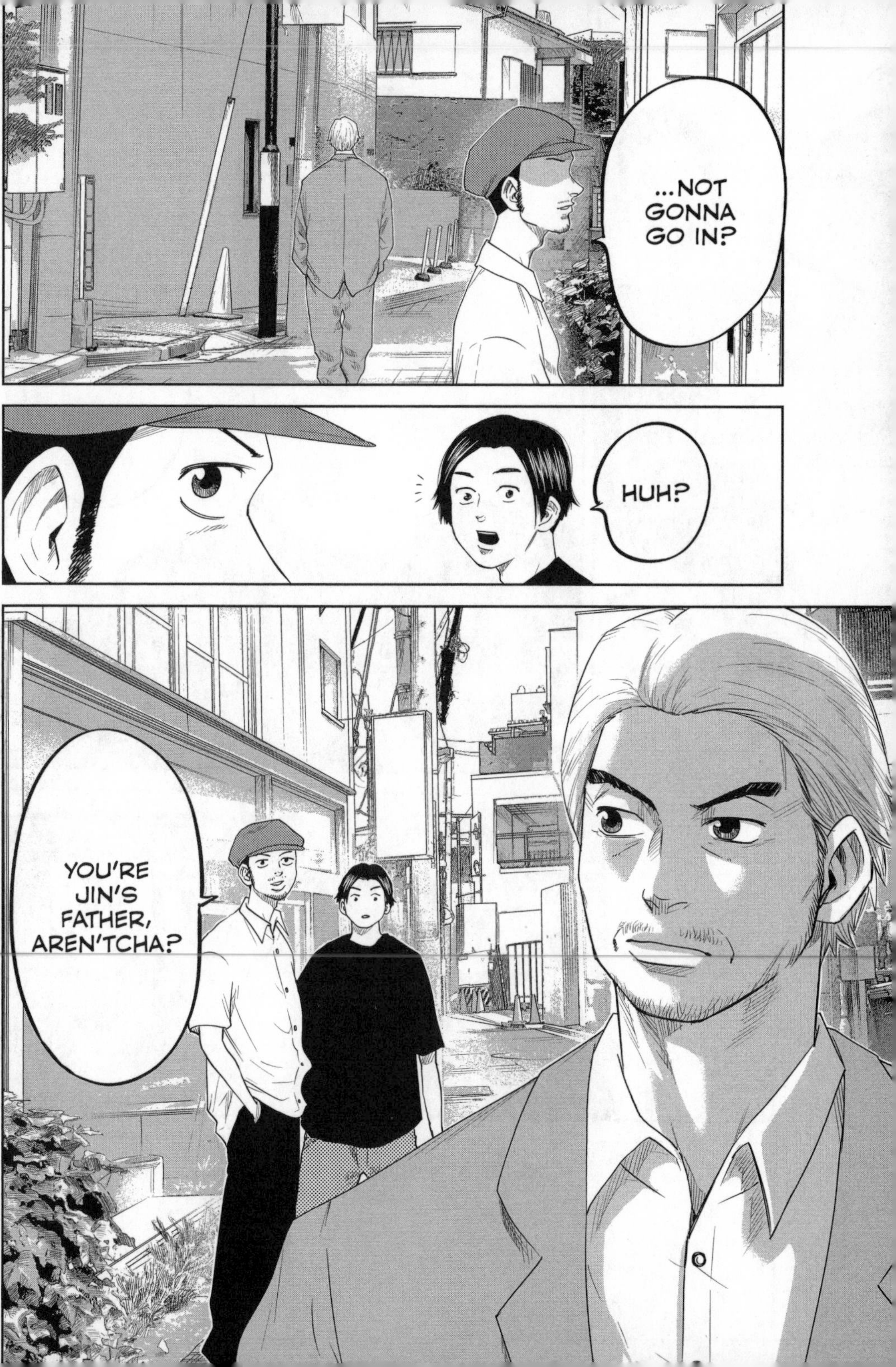
...NOT GONNA GO IN?
HUH?
YOU'RE JIN'S FATHER, AREN'TCHA?

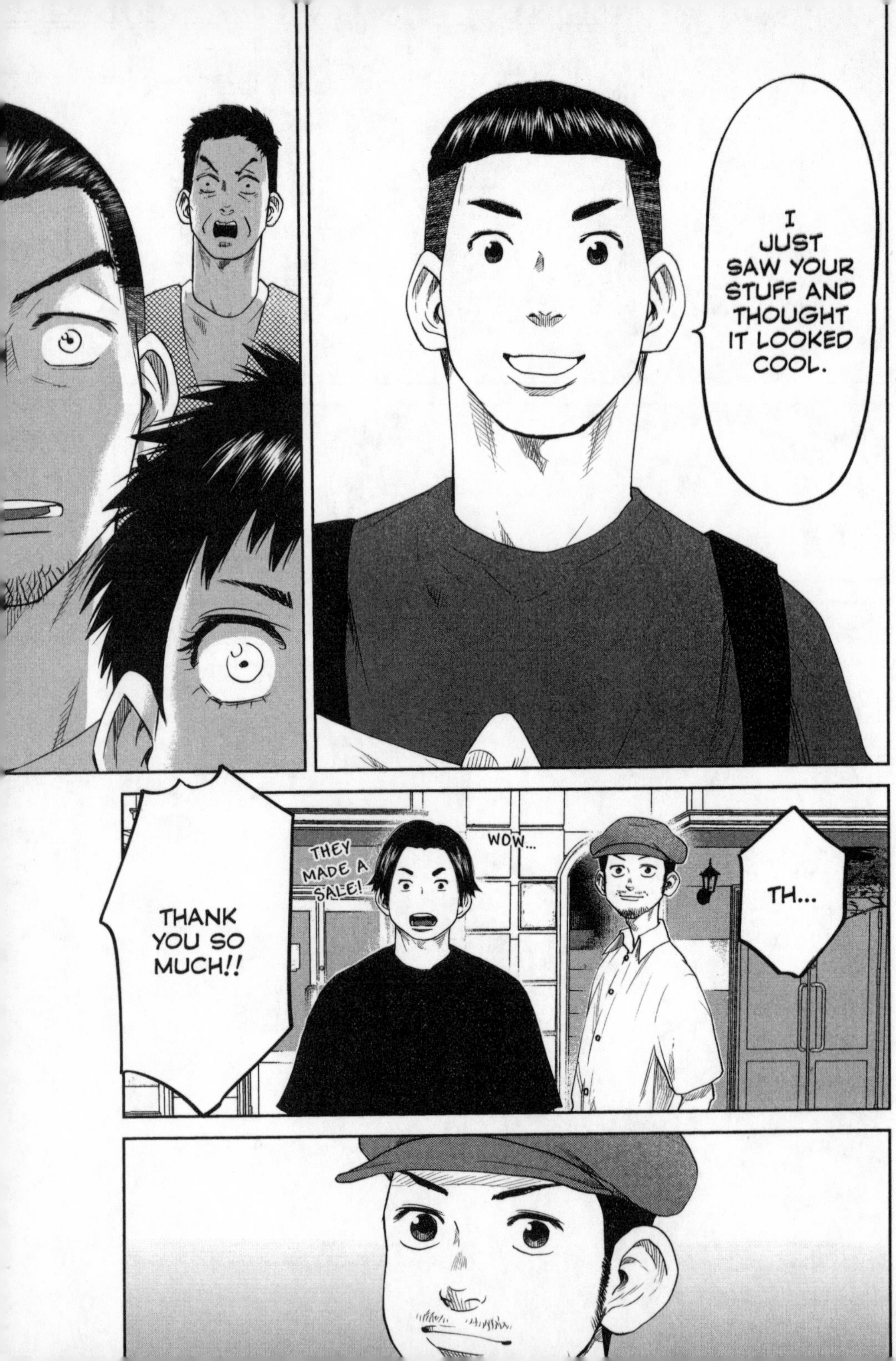
I JUST SAW YOUR STUFF AND THOUGHT IT LOOKED COOL.
TH...
WOW...
THEY MADE A SALE!
THANK YOU SO MUCH!!

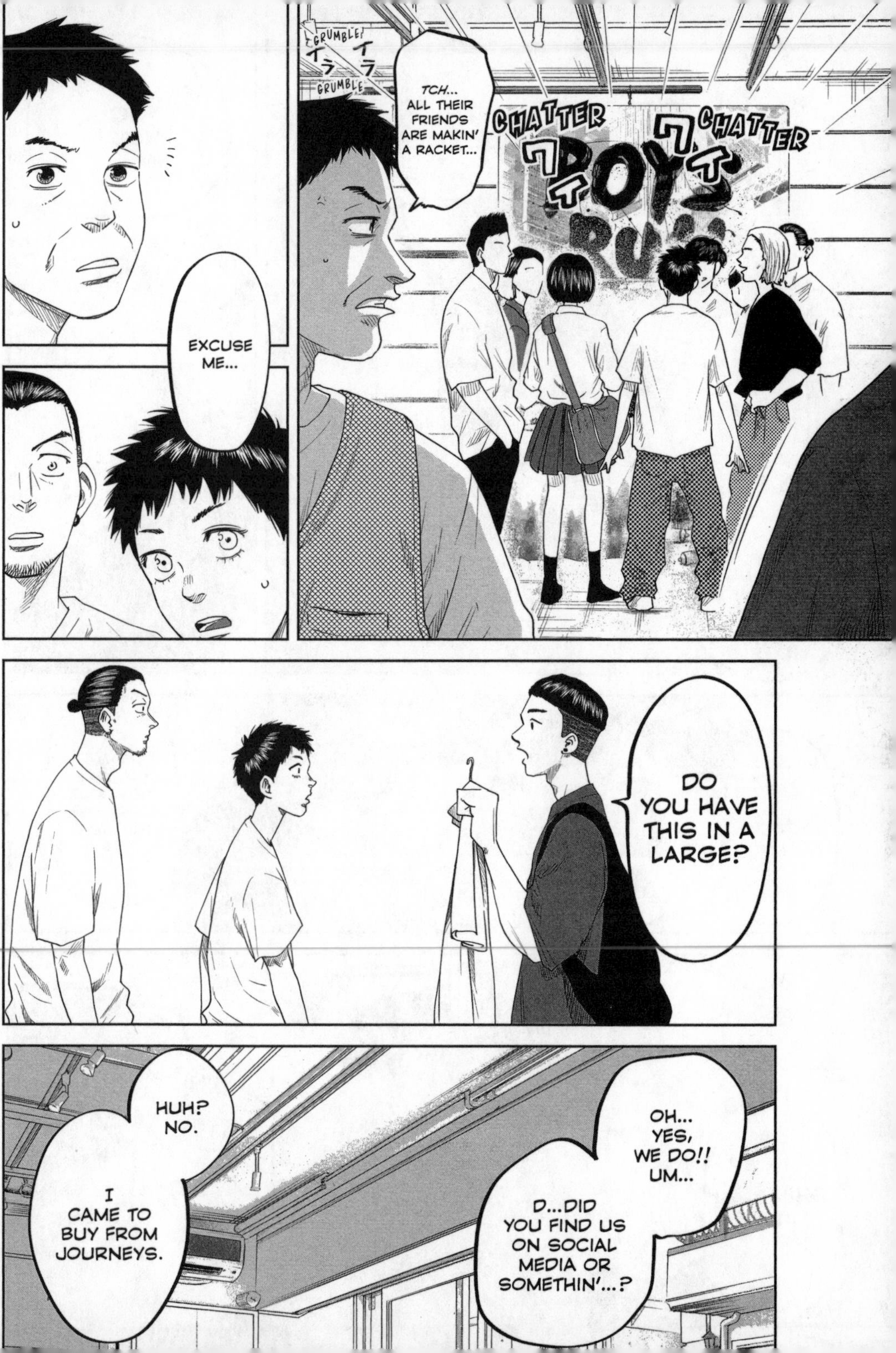
GRUMBLE
イラ
イラ
GRUMBLE
TCH... ALL THEIR FRIENDS ARE MAKIN' A RACKET...
CHATTER
ワイ
ワイ
CHATTER
EXCUSE ME...
DO YOU HAVE THIS IN A LARGE?
OH... YES, WE DO!! UM...
D...DID YOU FIND US ON SOCIAL MEDIA OR SOMETHIN'...?
HUH? NO.
I CAME TO BUY FROM JOURNEYS.

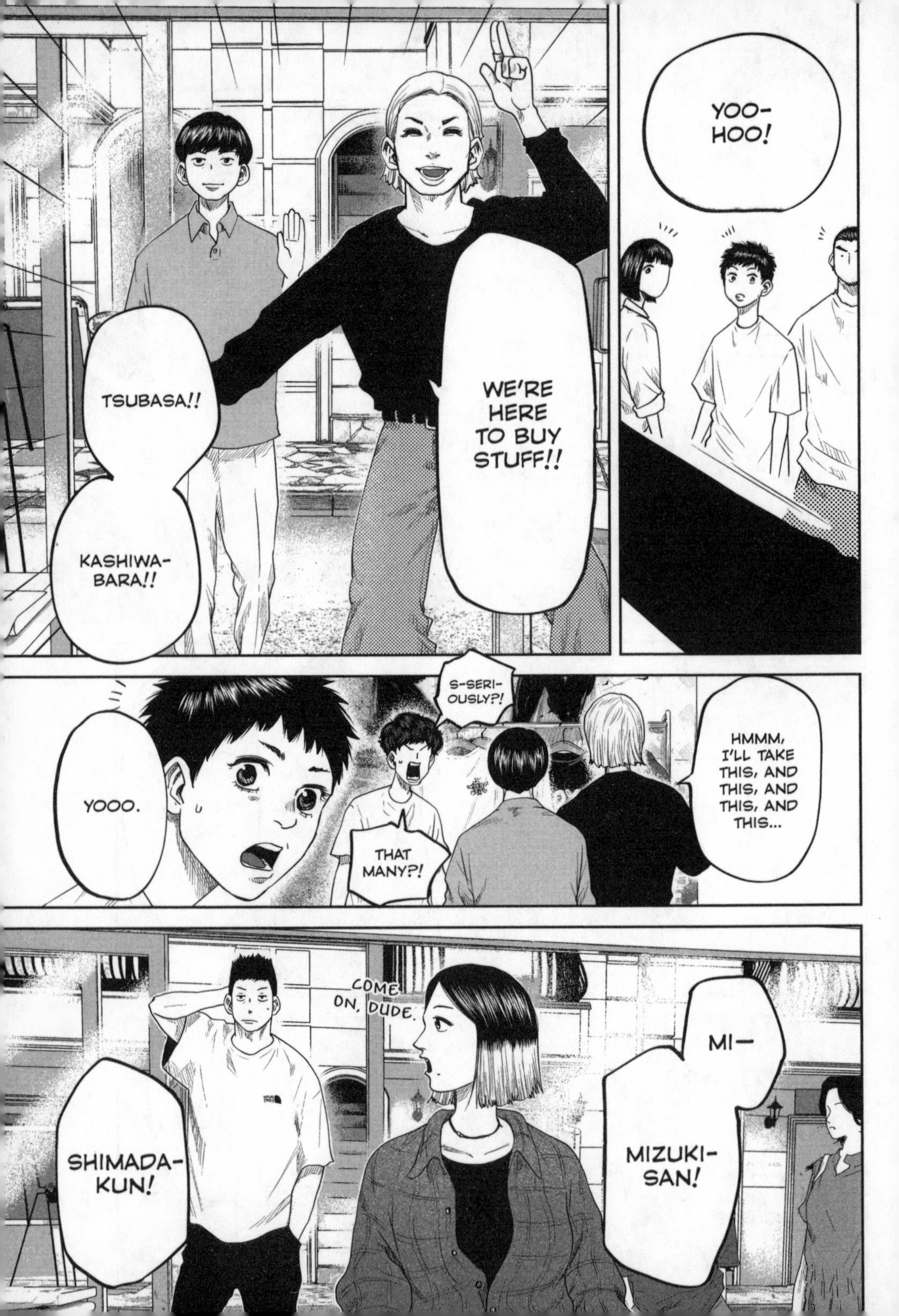
YOO-HOO!
WE'RE HERE TO BUY STUFF!!
TSUBASA!!
KASHIWA-BARA!!
HMMM, I'LL TAKE THIS, AND THIS, AND THIS, AND THIS...
S-SERI-OUSLY?!
THAT MANY?!
YOOO.
MI—
MIZUKI-SAN!
COME ON, DUDE.
SHIMADA-KUN!

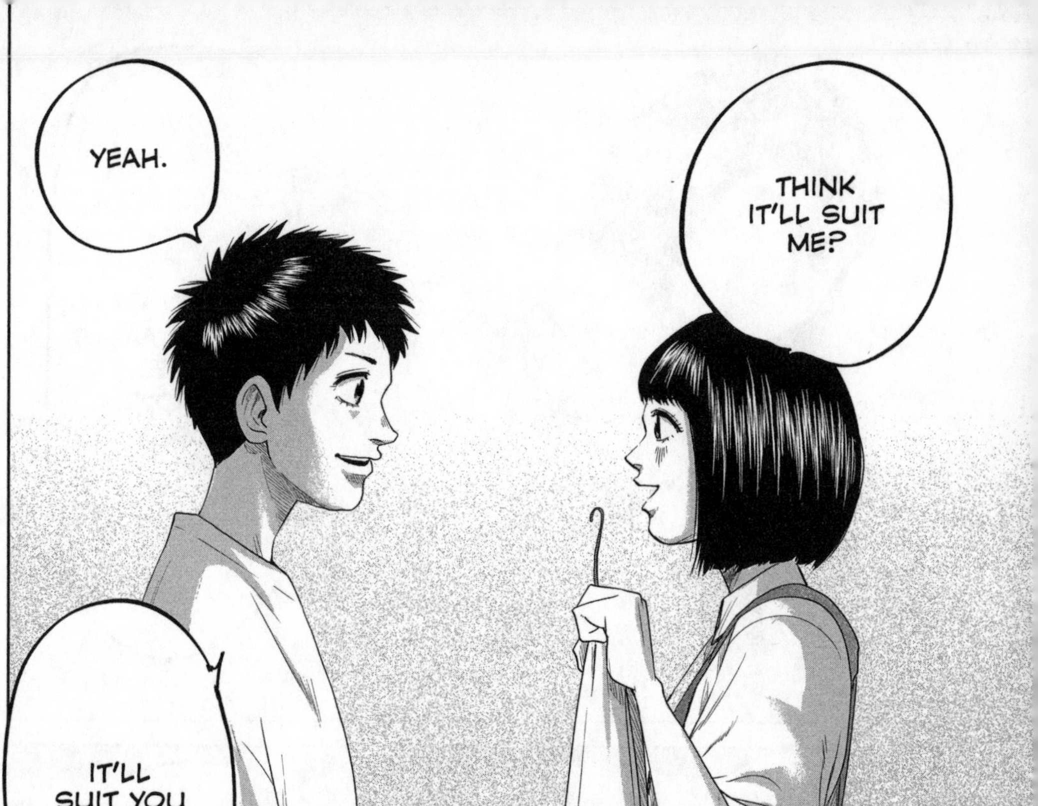
THINK IT'LL SUIT ME?
YEAH.
IT'LL SUIT YOU PERFECTLY!!

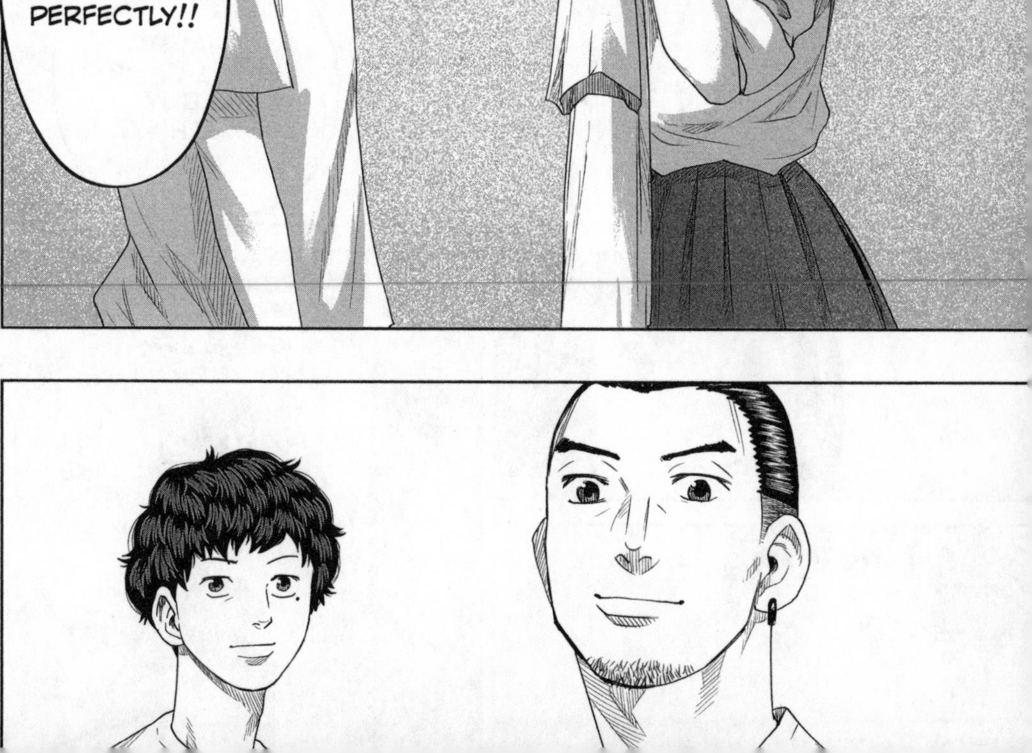

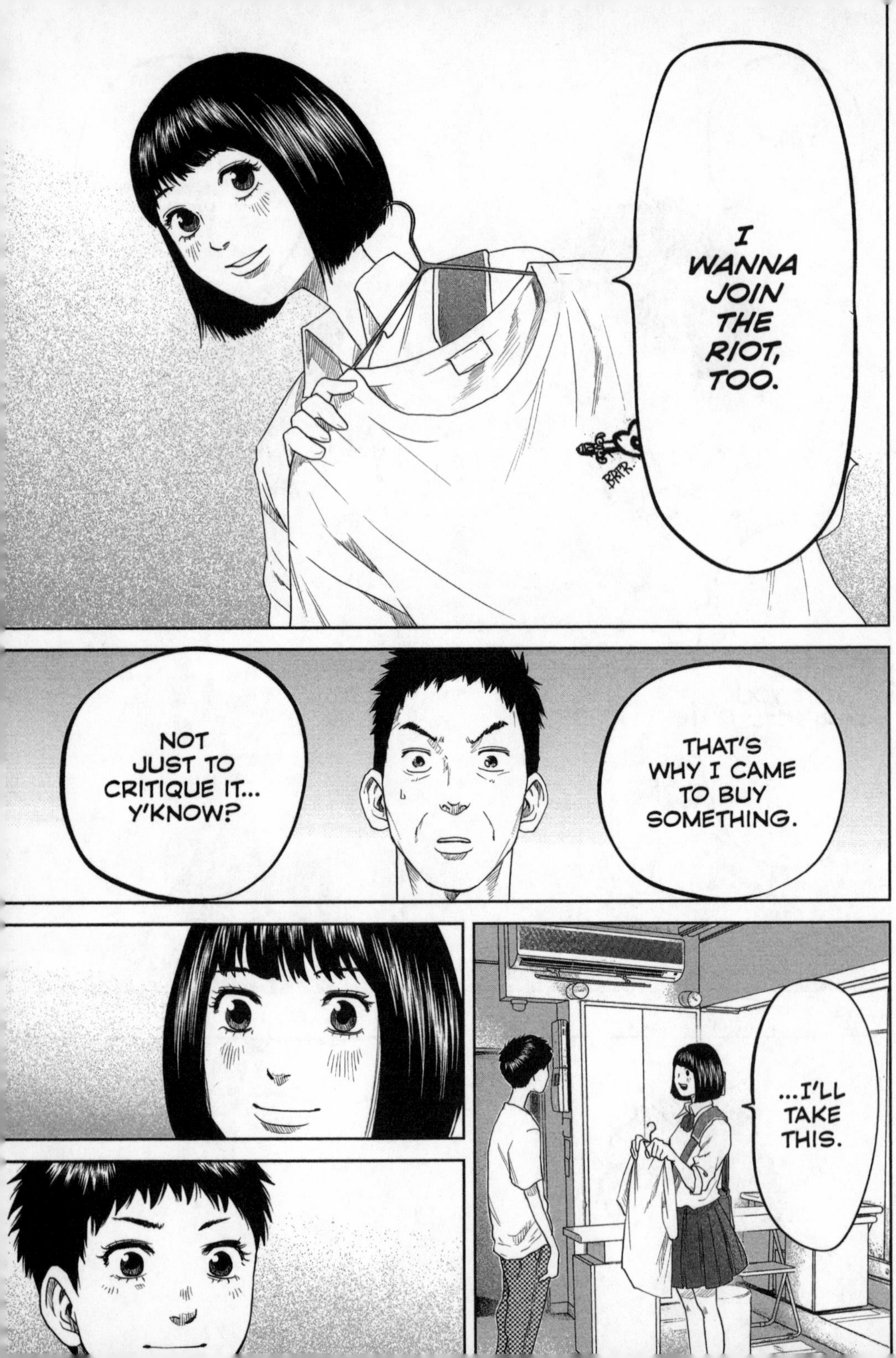
I WANNA JOIN THE RIOT, TOO.
THAT'S WHY I CAME TO BUY SOMETHING.
NOT JUST TO CRITIQUE IT... Y'KNOW?
...I'LL TAKE THIS.

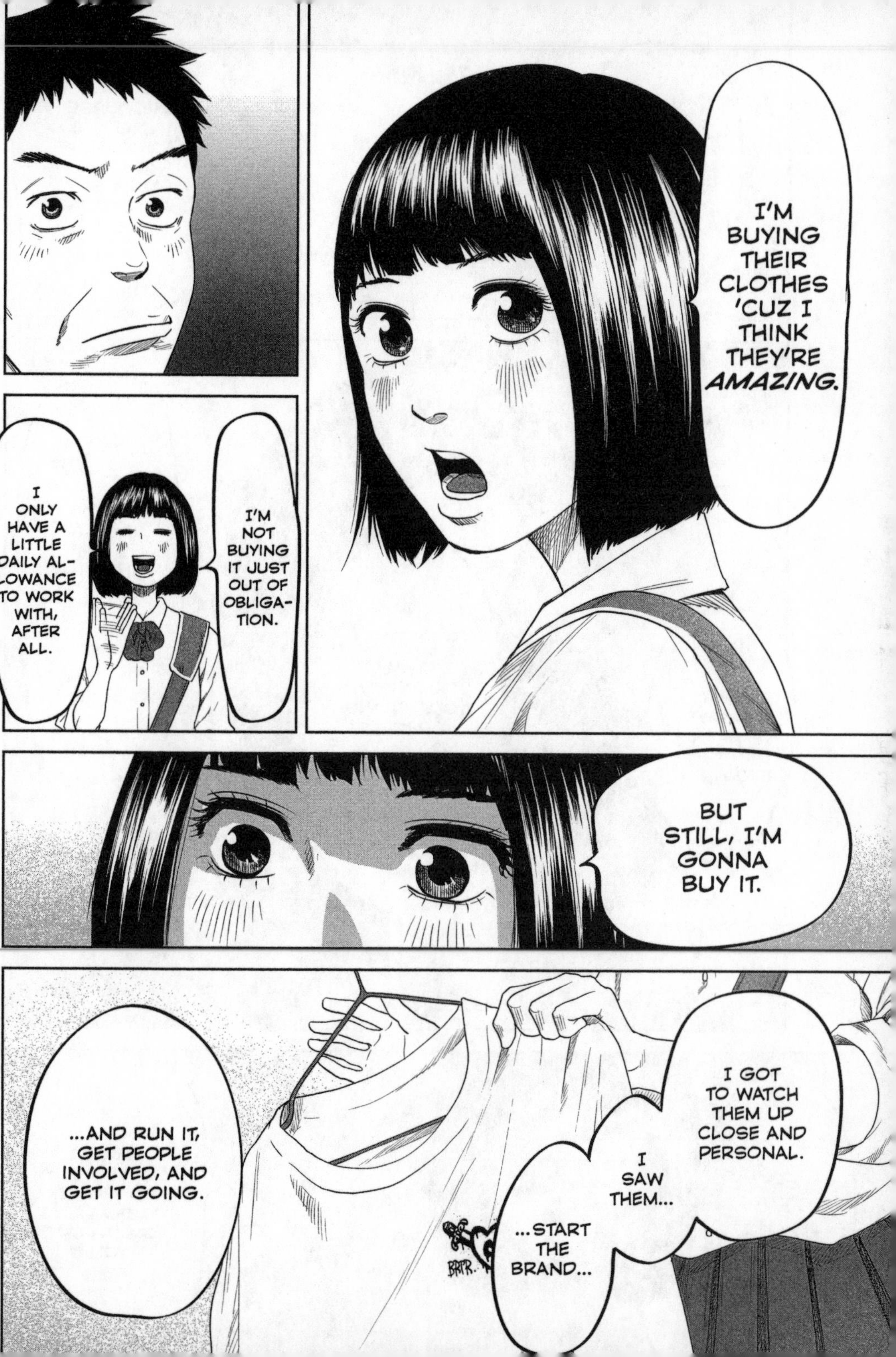
I'M BUYING THEIR CLOTHES 'CUZ I THINK THEY'RE *AMAZING.*
I'M NOT BUYING IT JUST OUT OF OBLIGATION.
I ONLY HAVE A LITTLE DAILY ALLOWANCE TO WORK WITH, AFTER ALL.
BUT STILL, I'M GONNA BUY IT.
I GOT TO WATCH THEM UP CLOSE AND PERSONAL.
I SAW THEM...
...START THE BRAND...
...AND RUN IT, GET PEOPLE INVOLVED, AND GET IT GOING.

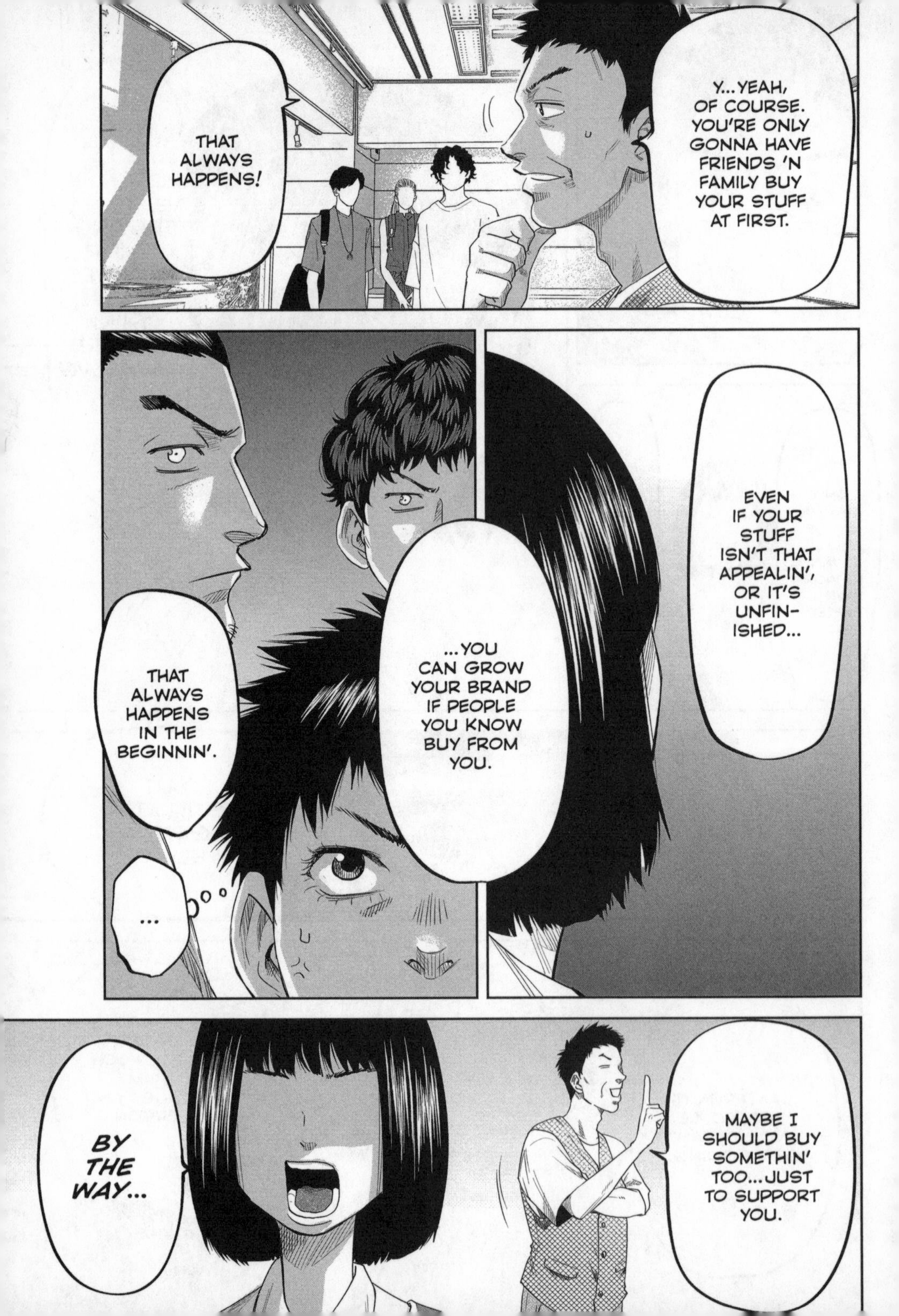
Y...YEAH, OF COURSE. YOU'RE ONLY GONNA HAVE FRIENDS 'N FAMILY BUY YOUR STUFF AT FIRST.
THAT ALWAYS HAPPENS!
EVEN IF YOUR STUFF ISN'T THAT APPEALIN', OR IT'S UNFIN-ISHED...
...YOU CAN GROW YOUR BRAND IF PEOPLE YOU KNOW BUY FROM YOU.
THAT ALWAYS HAPPENS IN THE BEGINNIN'.
...
MAYBE I SHOULD BUY SOMETHIN' TOO...JUST TO SUPPORT YOU.
BY THE WAY...

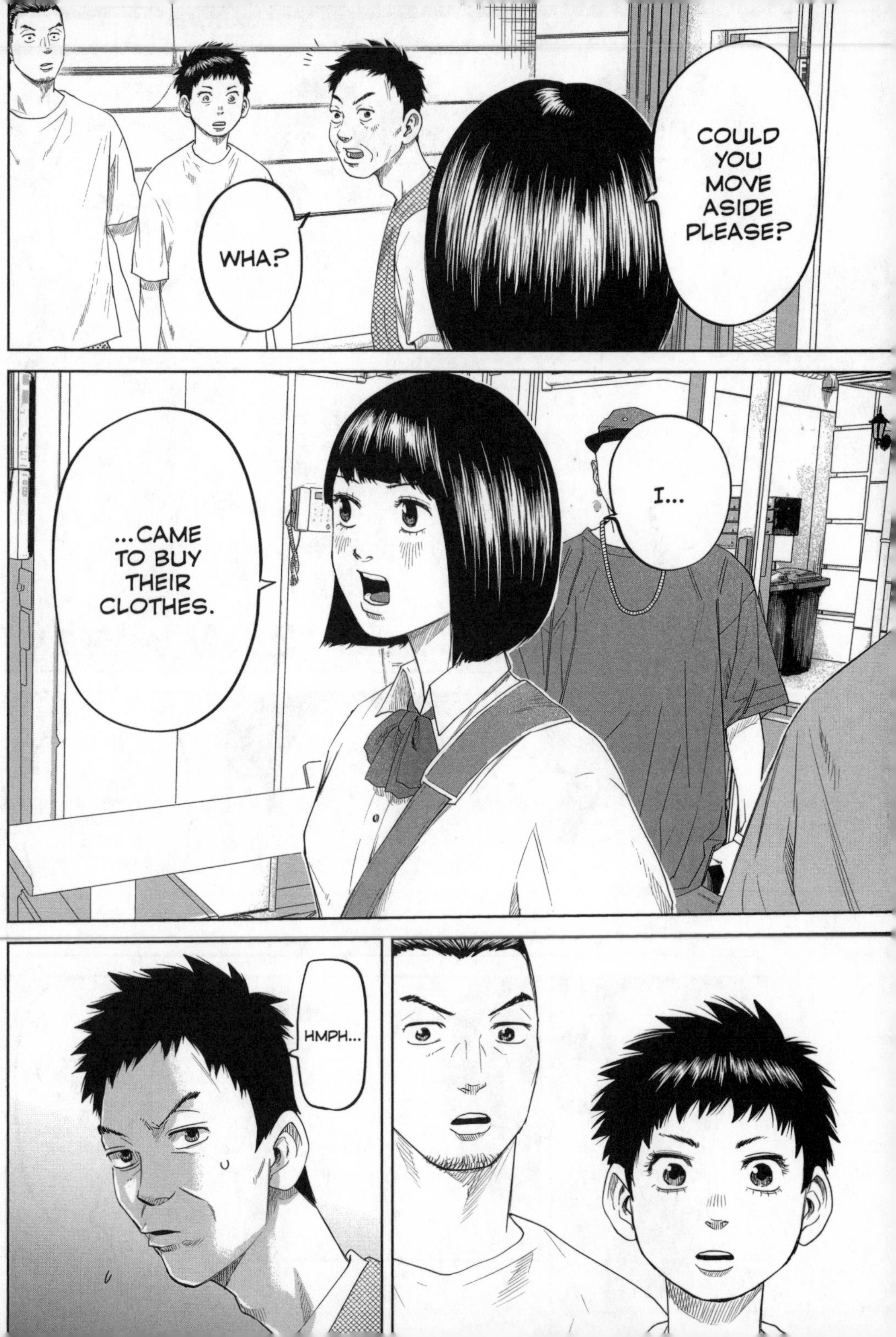
COULD YOU MOVE ASIDE PLEASE?
WHA?
I...
...CAME TO BUY THEIR CLOTHES.
HMPH...

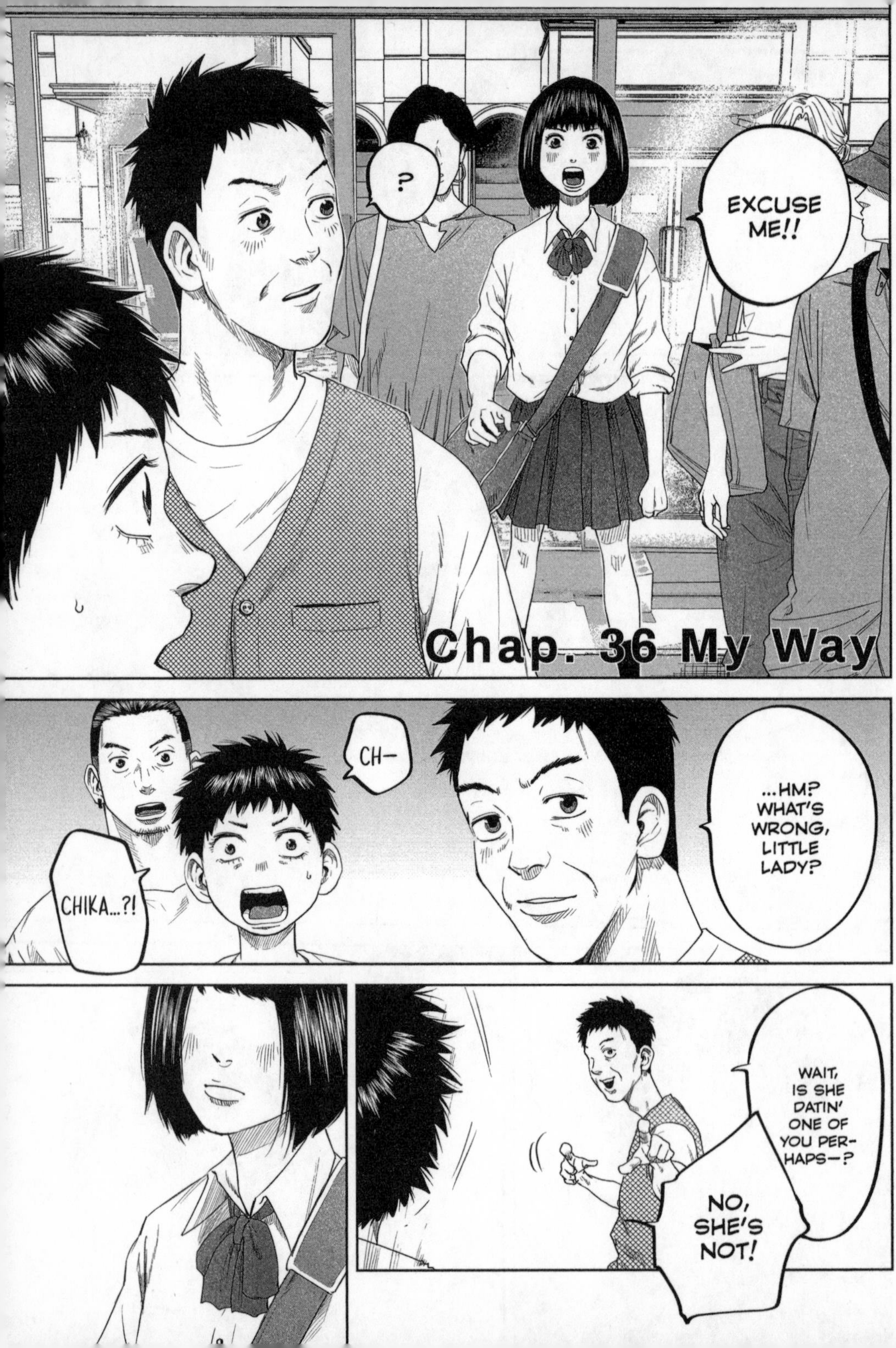
EXCUSE ME!!
?
Chap. 36 My Way
...HM? WHAT'S WRONG, LITTLE LADY?
CH-
CHIKA...?!
WAIT, IS SHE DATIN' ONE OF YOU PER-HAPS—?
NO, SHE'S NOT!

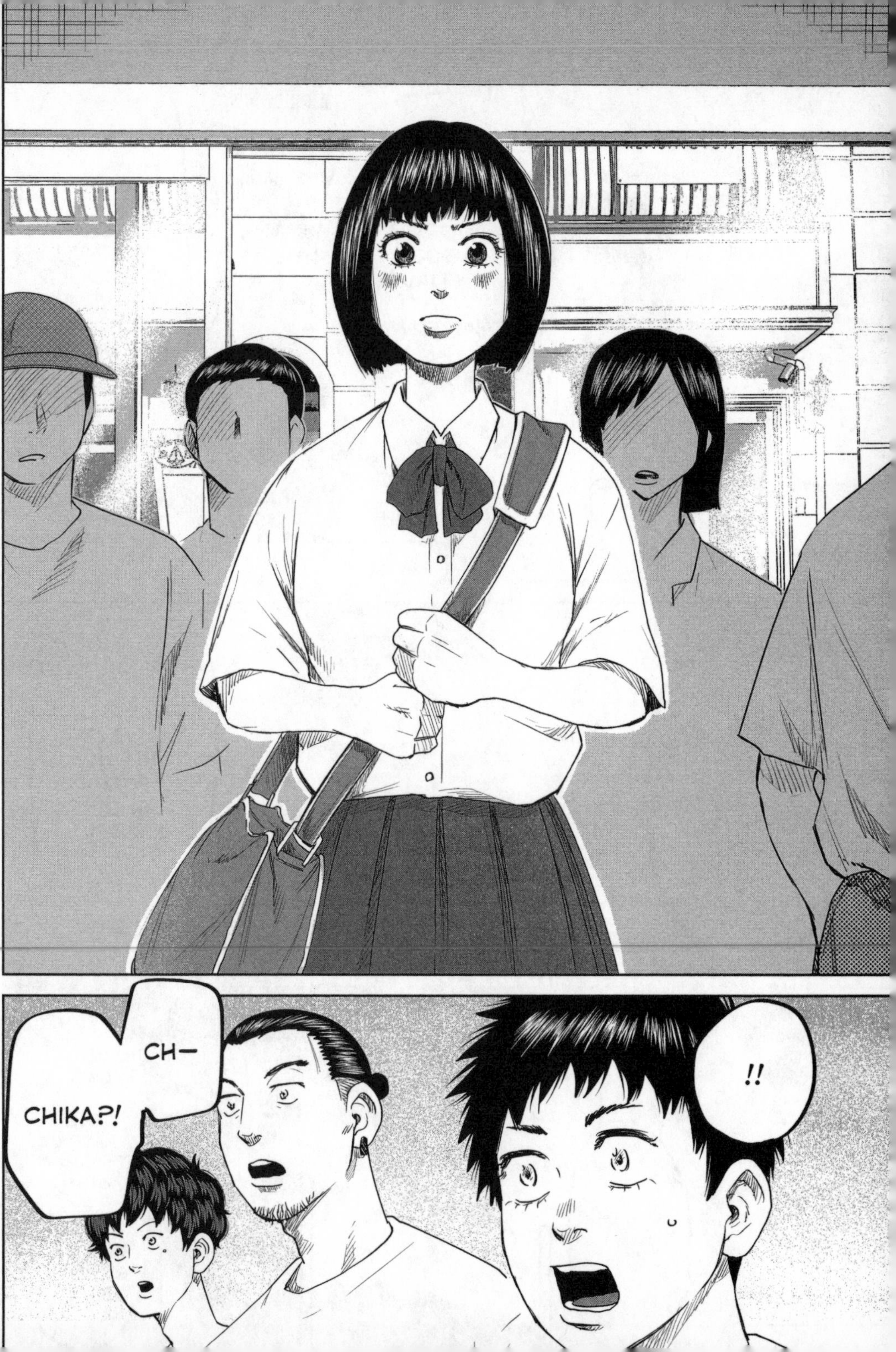
!!
CH— CHIKA?!

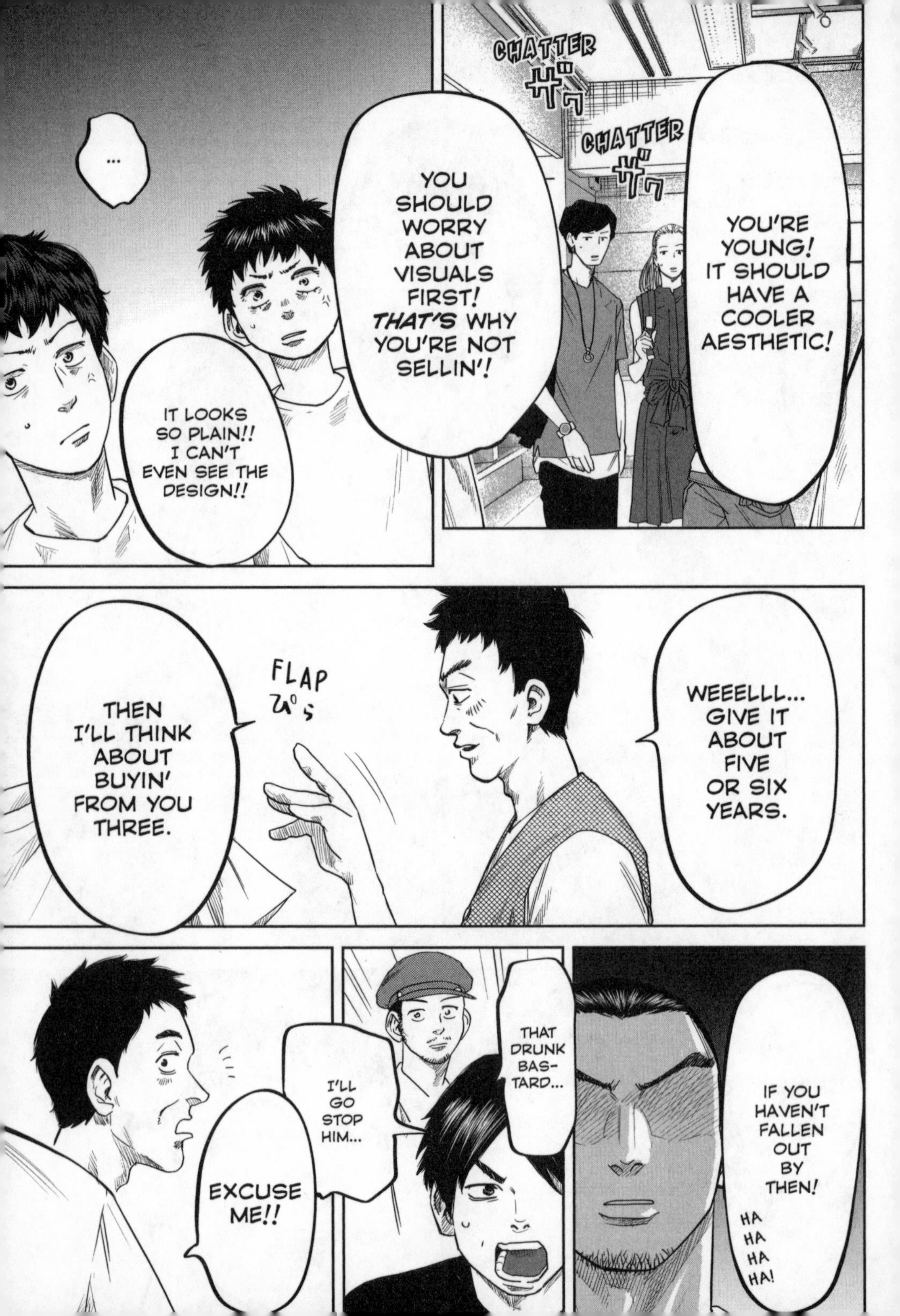
CHATTER
ザワ
CHATTER
ザワ
YOU'RE YOUNG! IT SHOULD HAVE A COOLER AESTHETIC!
YOU SHOULD WORRY ABOUT VISUALS FIRST! *THAT'S* WHY YOU'RE NOT SELLIN'!
IT LOOKS SO PLAIN!! I CAN'T EVEN SEE THE DESIGN!!
...
WEEELLL... GIVE IT ABOUT FIVE OR SIX YEARS.
FLAP
ぴら
THEN I'LL THINK ABOUT BUYIN' FROM YOU THREE.
IF YOU HAVEN'T FALLEN OUT BY THEN!
HA HA HA HA!
THAT DRUNK BAS-TARD...
I'LL GO STOP HIM...
EXCUSE ME!!

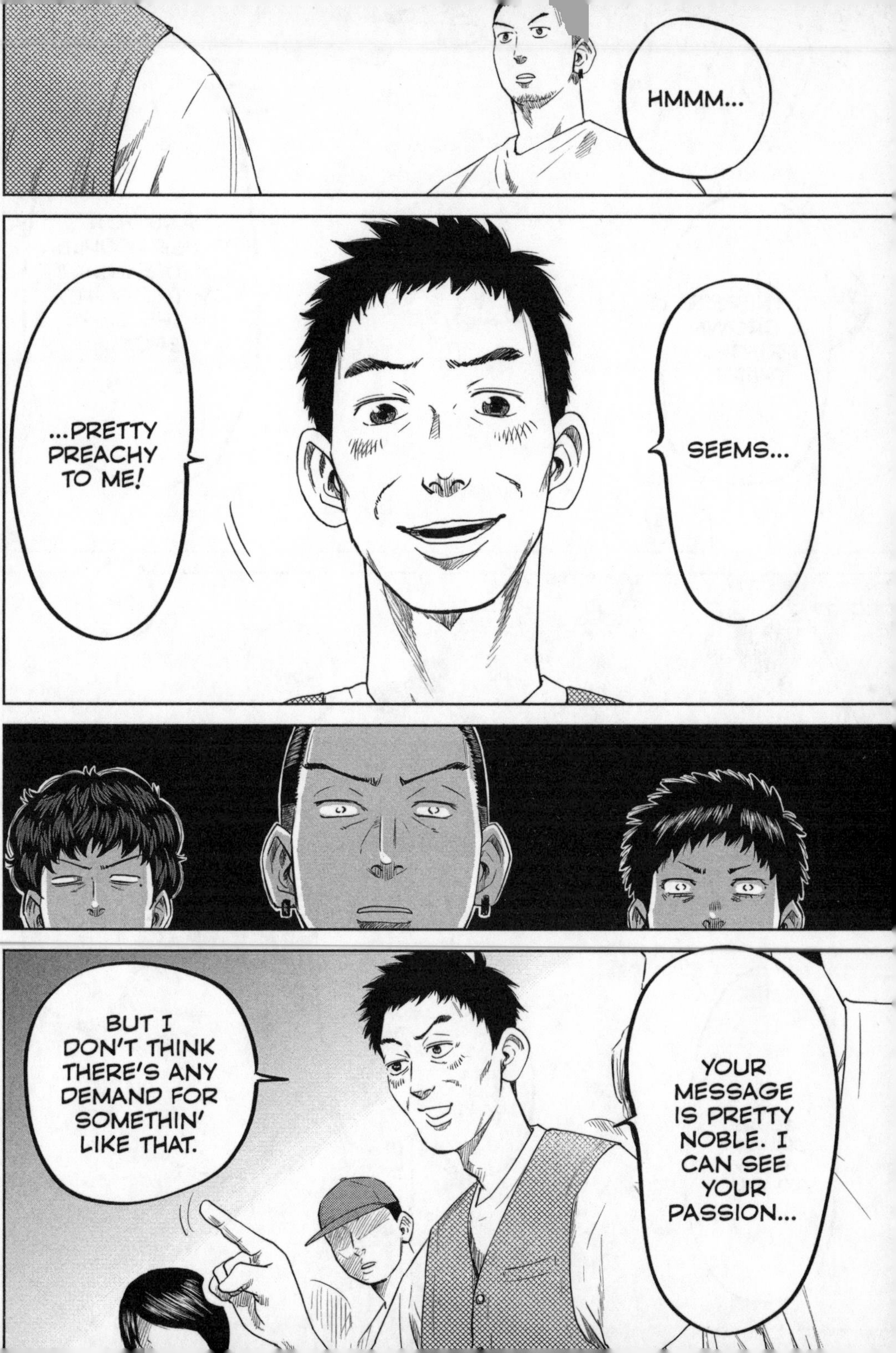
HMMM...
SEEMS...
...PRETTY PREACHY TO ME!
YOUR MESSAGE IS PRETTY NOBLE. I CAN SEE YOUR PASSION...
BUT I DON'T THINK THERE'S ANY DEMAND FOR SOMETHIN' LIKE THAT.

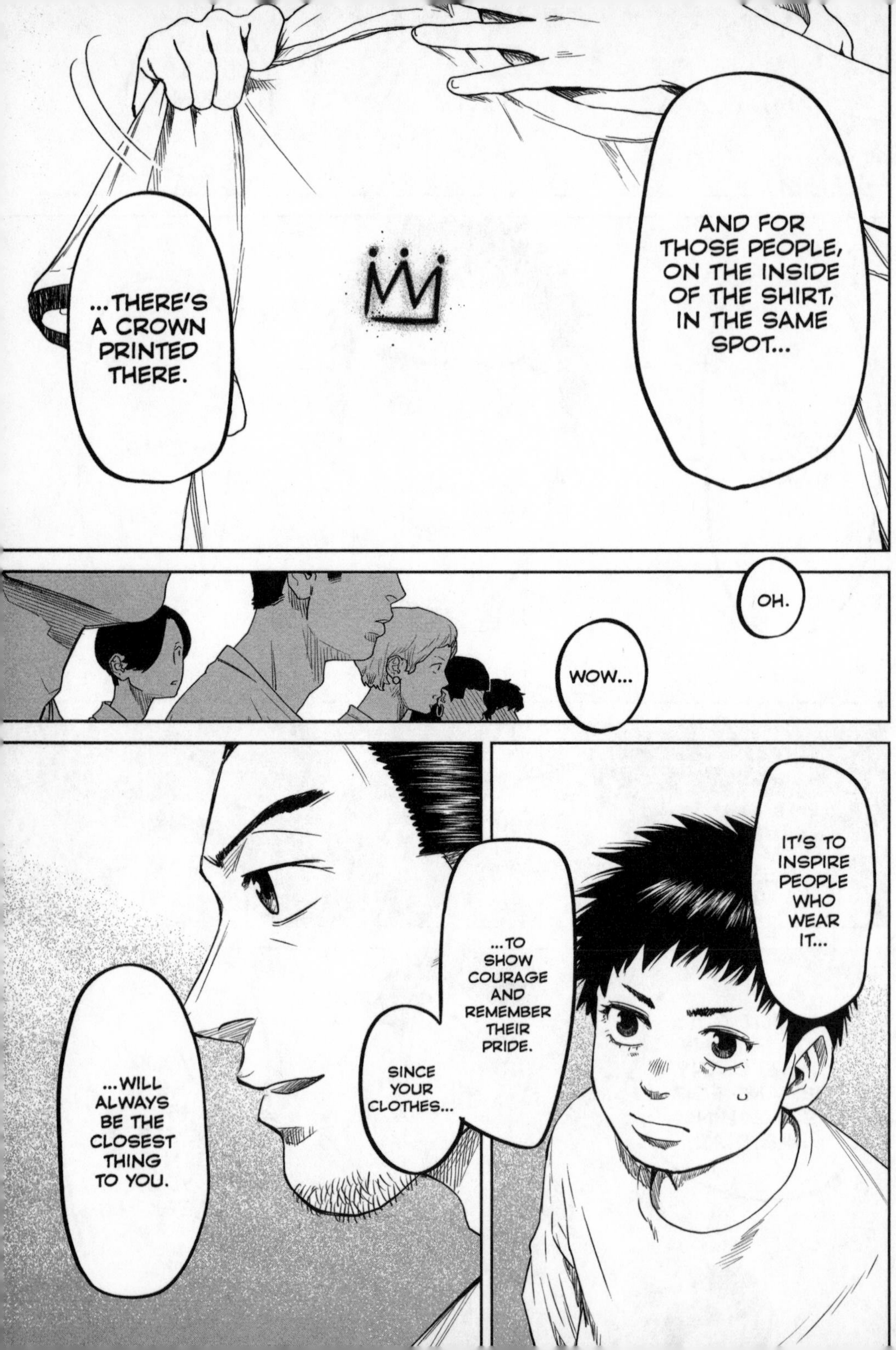
AND FOR THOSE PEOPLE, ON THE INSIDE OF THE SHIRT, IN THE SAME SPOT...
...THERE'S A CROWN PRINTED THERE.
OH.
WOW...
IT'S TO INSPIRE PEOPLE WHO WEAR IT...
...TO SHOW COURAGE AND REMEMBER THEIR PRIDE.
SINCE YOUR CLOTHES...
...WILL ALWAYS BE THE CLOSEST THING TO YOU.

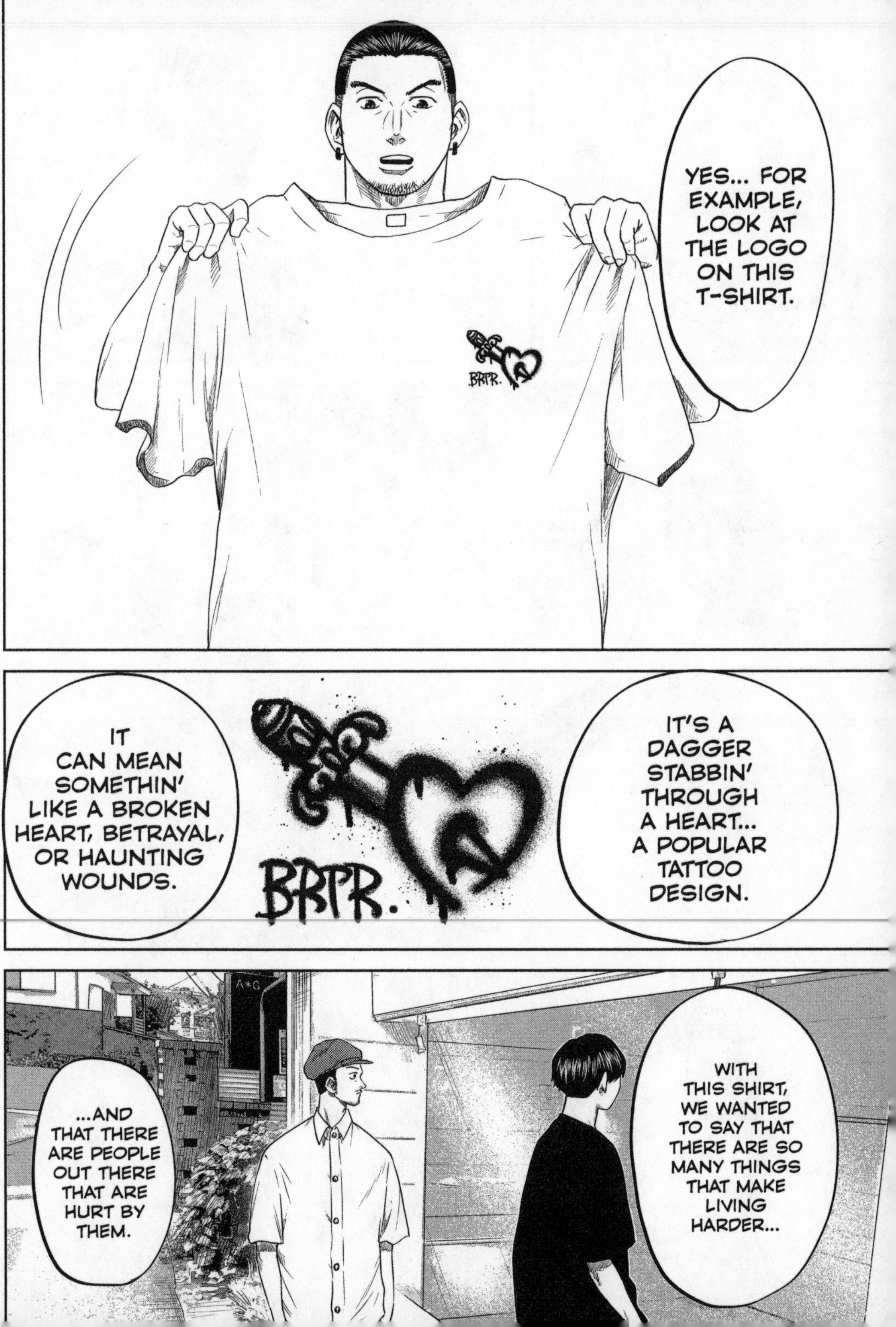
YES... FOR EXAMPLE, LOOK AT THE LOGO ON THIS T-SHIRT.
BRPR.
IT'S A DAGGER STABBIN' THROUGH A HEART... A POPULAR TATTOO DESIGN.
BRPR.
IT CAN MEAN SOMETHIN' LIKE A BROKEN HEART, BETRAYAL, OR HAUNTING WOUNDS.
A*G
WITH THIS SHIRT, WE WANTED TO SAY THAT THERE ARE SO MANY THINGS THAT MAKE LIVING HARDER...
...AND THAT THERE ARE PEOPLE OUT THERE THAT ARE HURT BY THEM.

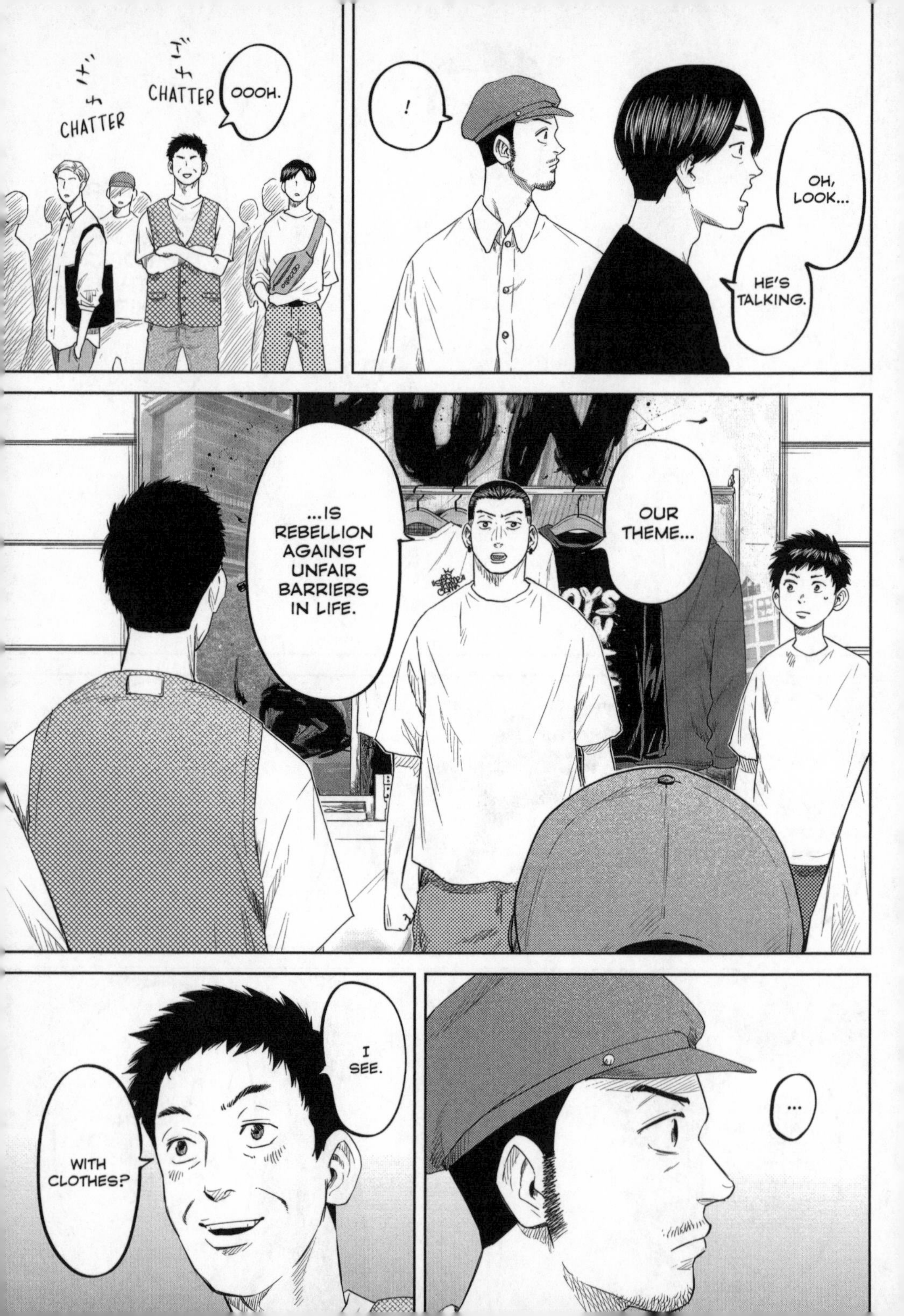
OH, LOOK...
HE'S TALKING.
!
OOOH.
CHATTER
CHATTER
OUR THEME...
...IS REBELLION AGAINST UNFAIR BARRIERS IN LIFE.
...
I SEE.
WITH CLOTHES?

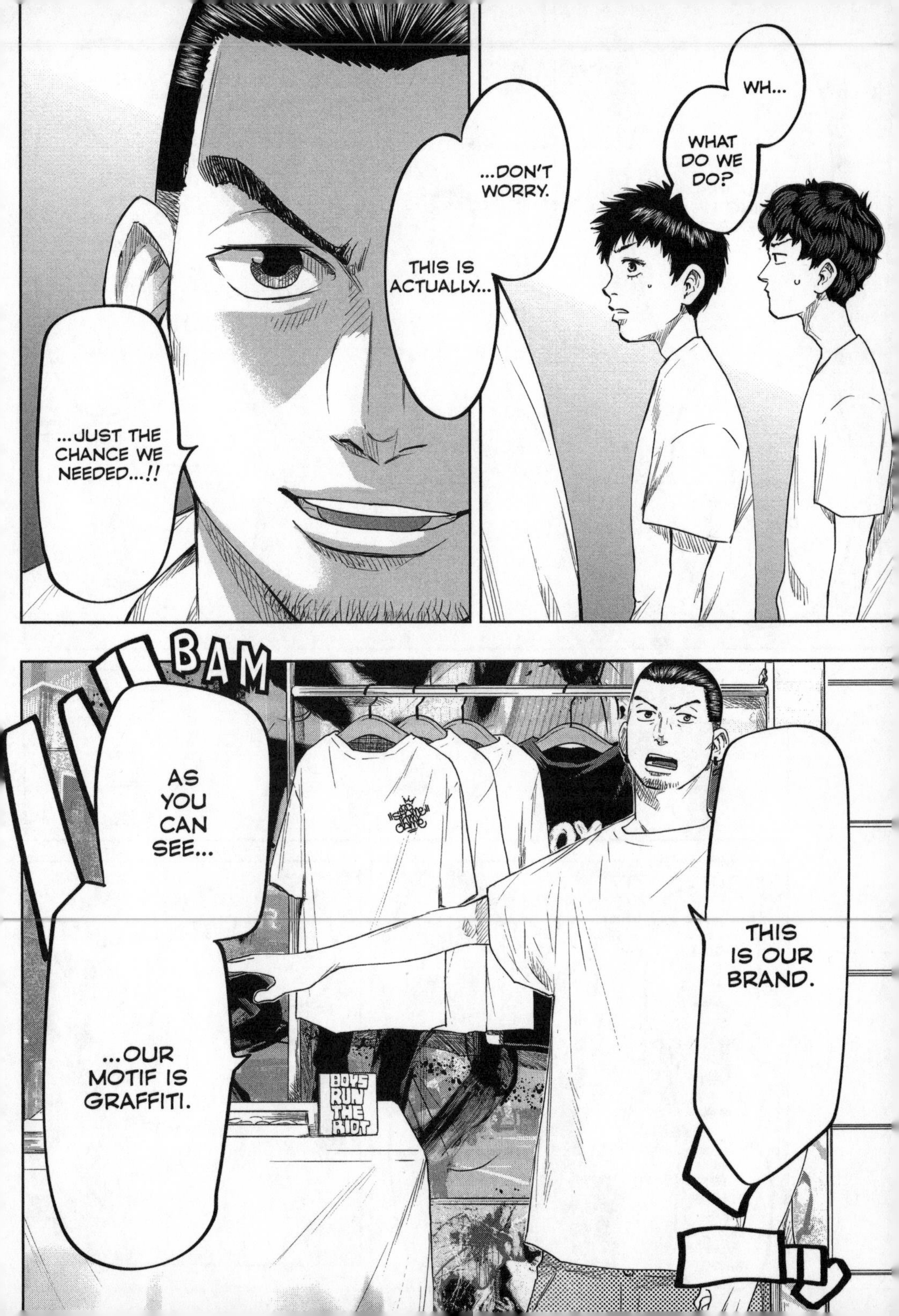
WH...
WHAT DO WE DO?
...DON'T WORRY.
THIS IS ACTUALLY...
...JUST THE CHANCE WE NEEDED...!!
BAM
THIS IS OUR BRAND.
AS YOU CAN SEE...
...OUR MOTIF IS GRAFFITI.
BOYS RUN THE RIOT

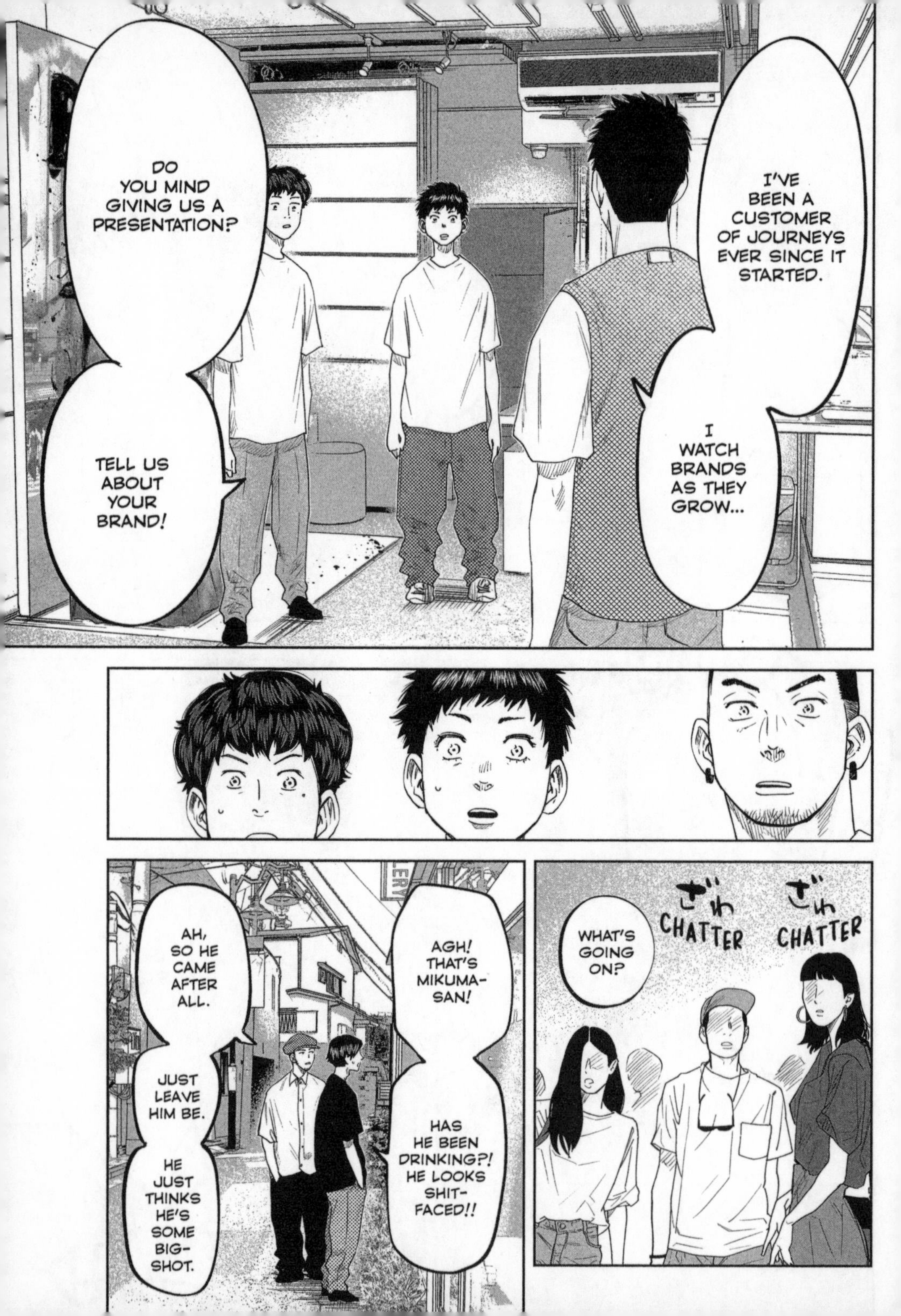
I'VE BEEN A CUSTOMER OF JOURNEYS EVER SINCE IT STARTED.
I WATCH BRANDS AS THEY GROW...
DO YOU MIND GIVING US A PRESENTATION?
TELL US ABOUT YOUR BRAND!
ざわ CHATTER
ざわ CHATTER
WHAT'S GOING ON?
AGH! THAT'S MIKUMA-SAN!
HAS HE BEEN DRINKING?! HE LOOKS SHIT-FACED!!
AH, SO HE CAME AFTER ALL.
JUST LEAVE HIM BE.
HE JUST THINKS HE'S SOME BIG-SHOT.

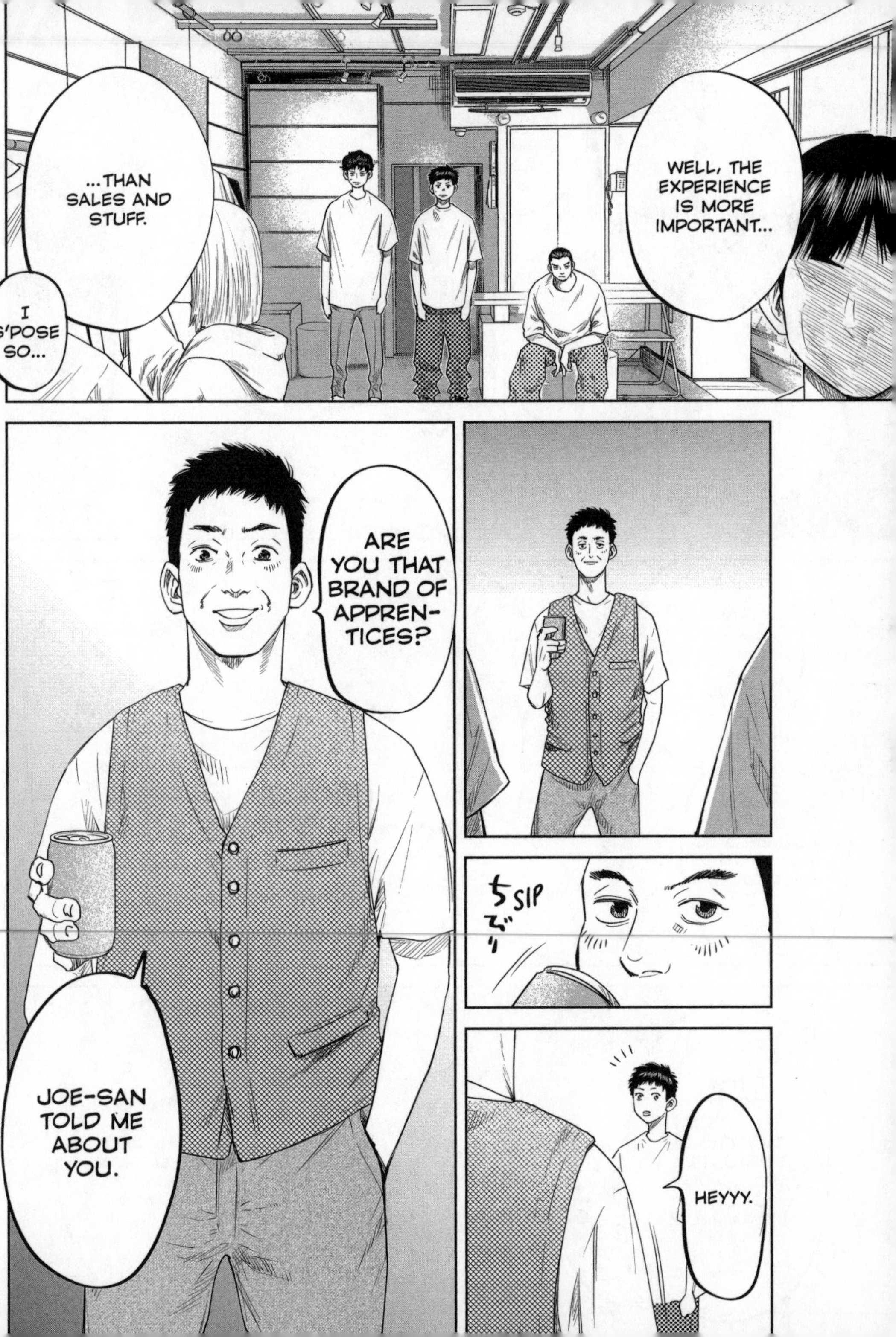
WELL, THE EXPERIENCE IS MORE IMPORTANT...
...THAN SALES AND STUFF.
I S'POSE SO...
SIP
HEYYY.
ARE YOU THAT BRAND OF APPREN-TICES?
JOE-SAN TOLD ME ABOUT YOU.

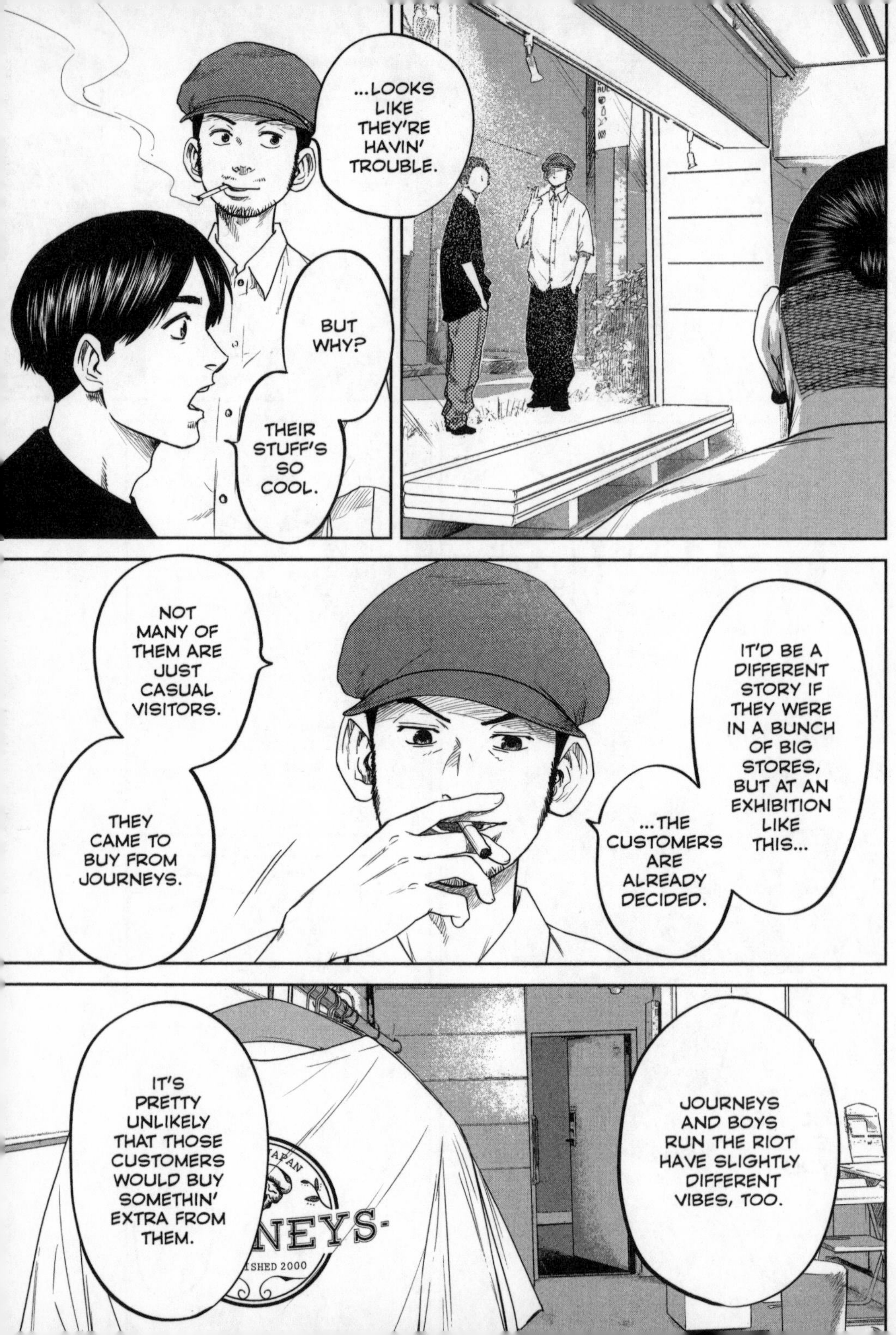
...LOOKS LIKE THEY'RE HAVIN' TROUBLE.
BUT WHY?
THEIR STUFF'S SO COOL.
IT'D BE A DIFFERENT STORY IF THEY WERE IN A BUNCH OF BIG STORES, BUT AT AN EXHIBITION LIKE THIS...
...THE CUSTOMERS ARE ALREADY DECIDED.
NOT MANY OF THEM ARE JUST CASUAL VISITORS.
THEY CAME TO BUY FROM JOURNEYS.
JOURNEYS AND BOYS RUN THE RIOT HAVE SLIGHTLY DIFFERENT VIBES, TOO.
IT'S PRETTY UNLIKELY THAT THOSE CUSTOMERS WOULD BUY SOMETHIN' EXTRA FROM THEM.

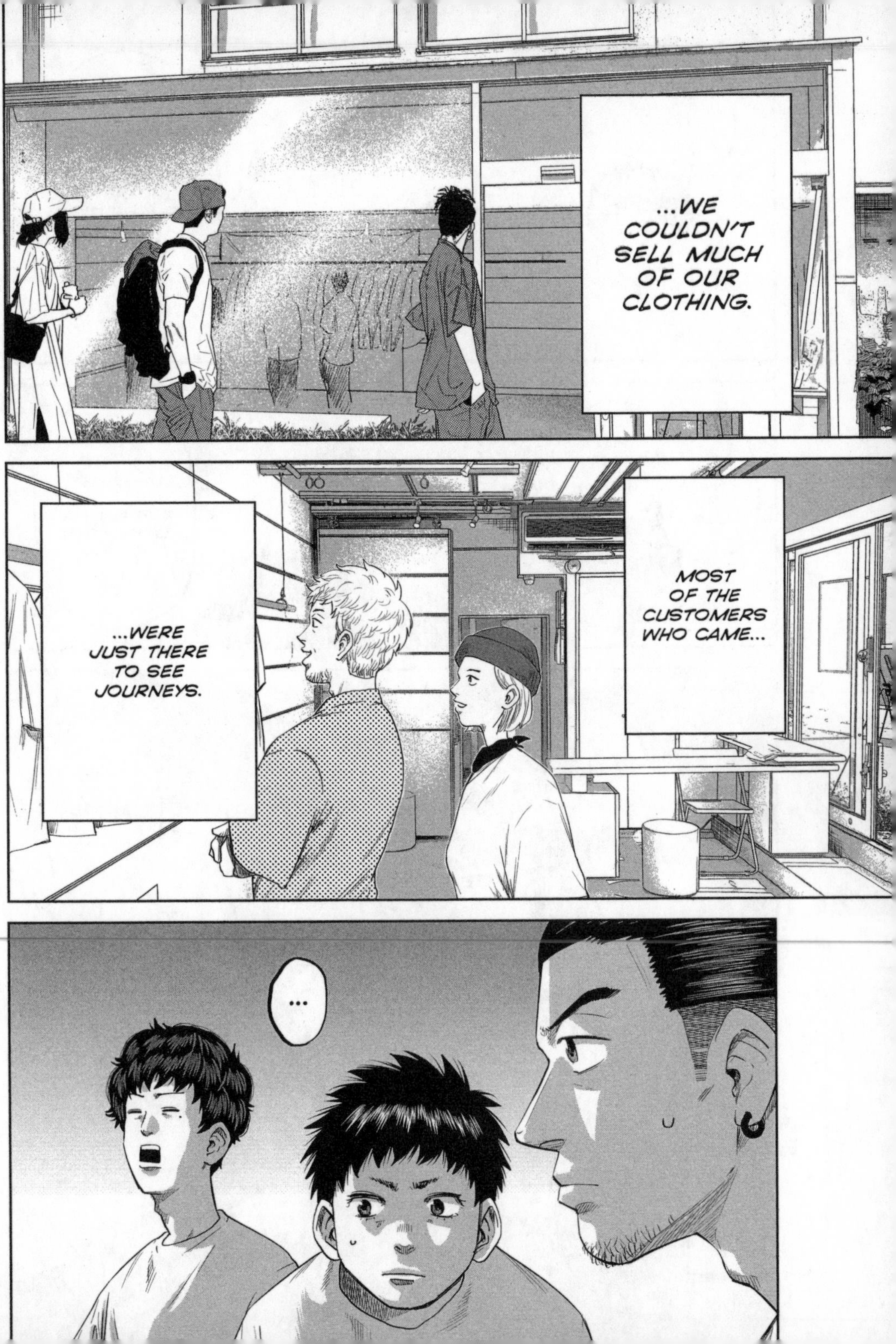
...WE COULDN'T SELL MUCH OF OUR CLOTHING.
MOST OF THE CUSTOMERS WHO CAME...
...WERE JUST THERE TO SEE JOURNEYS.
...

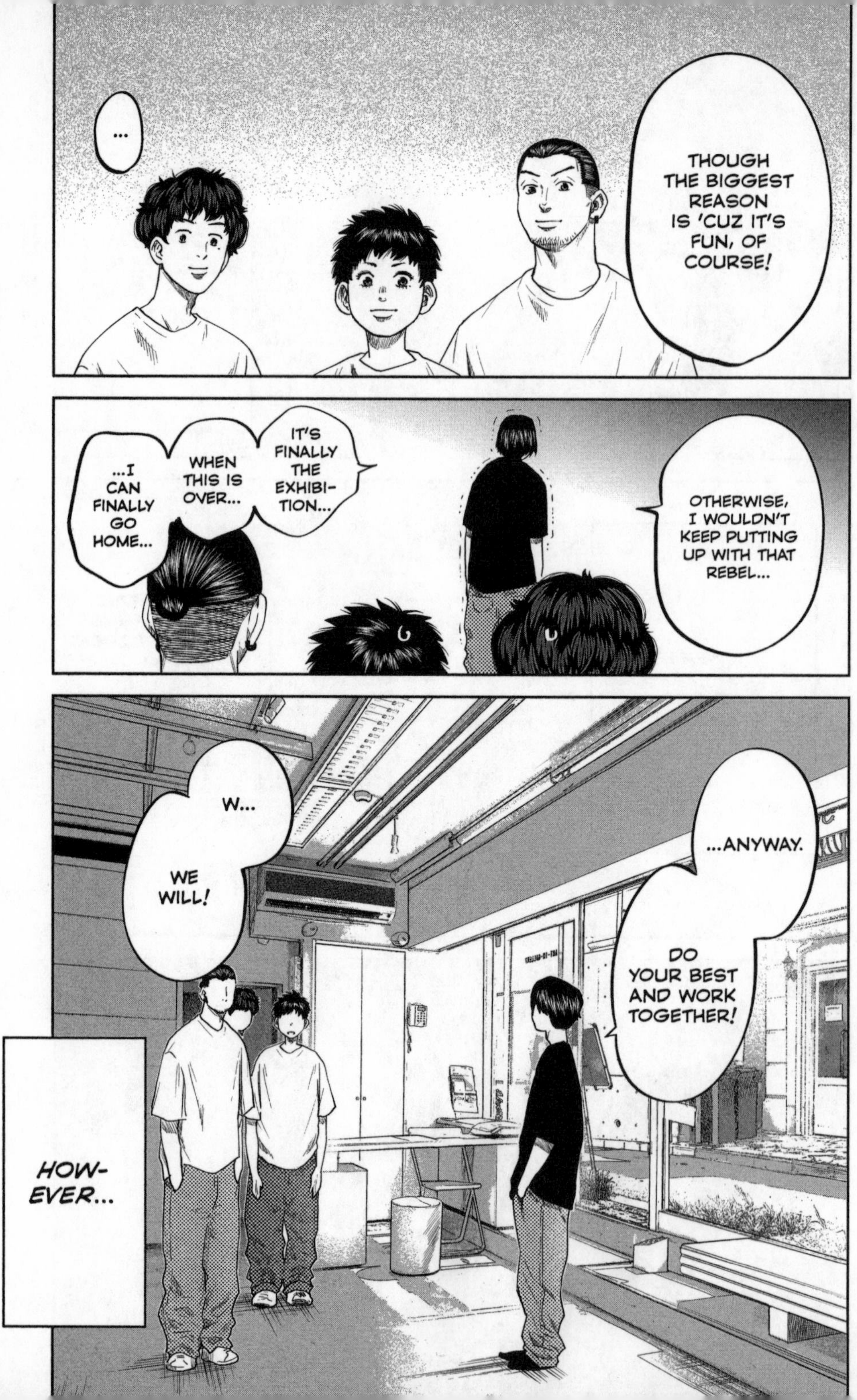
THOUGH THE BIGGEST REASON IS 'CUZ IT'S FUN, OF COURSE!
...
OTHERWISE, I WOULDN'T KEEP PUTTING UP WITH THAT REBEL...
IT'S FINALLY THE EXHIBITION...
WHEN THIS IS OVER...
...I CAN FINALLY GO HOME...
...ANYWAY.
DO YOUR BEST AND WORK TOGETHER!
W...
WE WILL!
HOW-EVER...

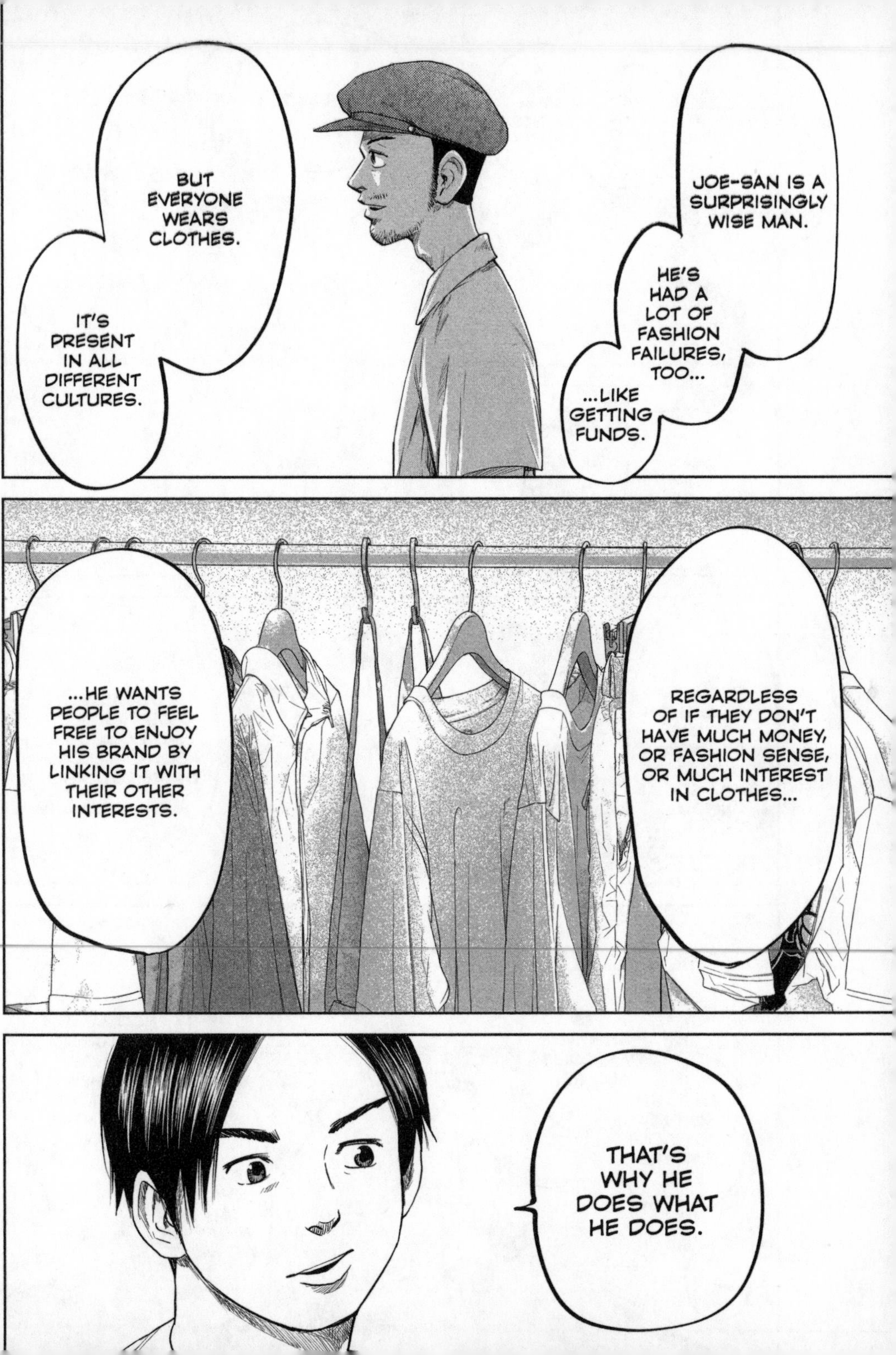
JOE-SAN IS A SURPRISINGLY WISE MAN.
HE'S HAD A LOT OF FASHION FAILURES, TOO...
...LIKE GETTING FUNDS.
BUT EVERYONE WEARS CLOTHES.
IT'S PRESENT IN ALL DIFFERENT CULTURES.
REGARDLESS OF IF THEY DON'T HAVE MUCH MONEY, OR FASHION SENSE, OR MUCH INTEREST IN CLOTHES...
...HE WANTS PEOPLE TO FEEL FREE TO ENJOY HIS BRAND BY LINKING IT WITH THEIR OTHER INTERESTS.
THAT'S WHY HE DOES WHAT HE DOES.

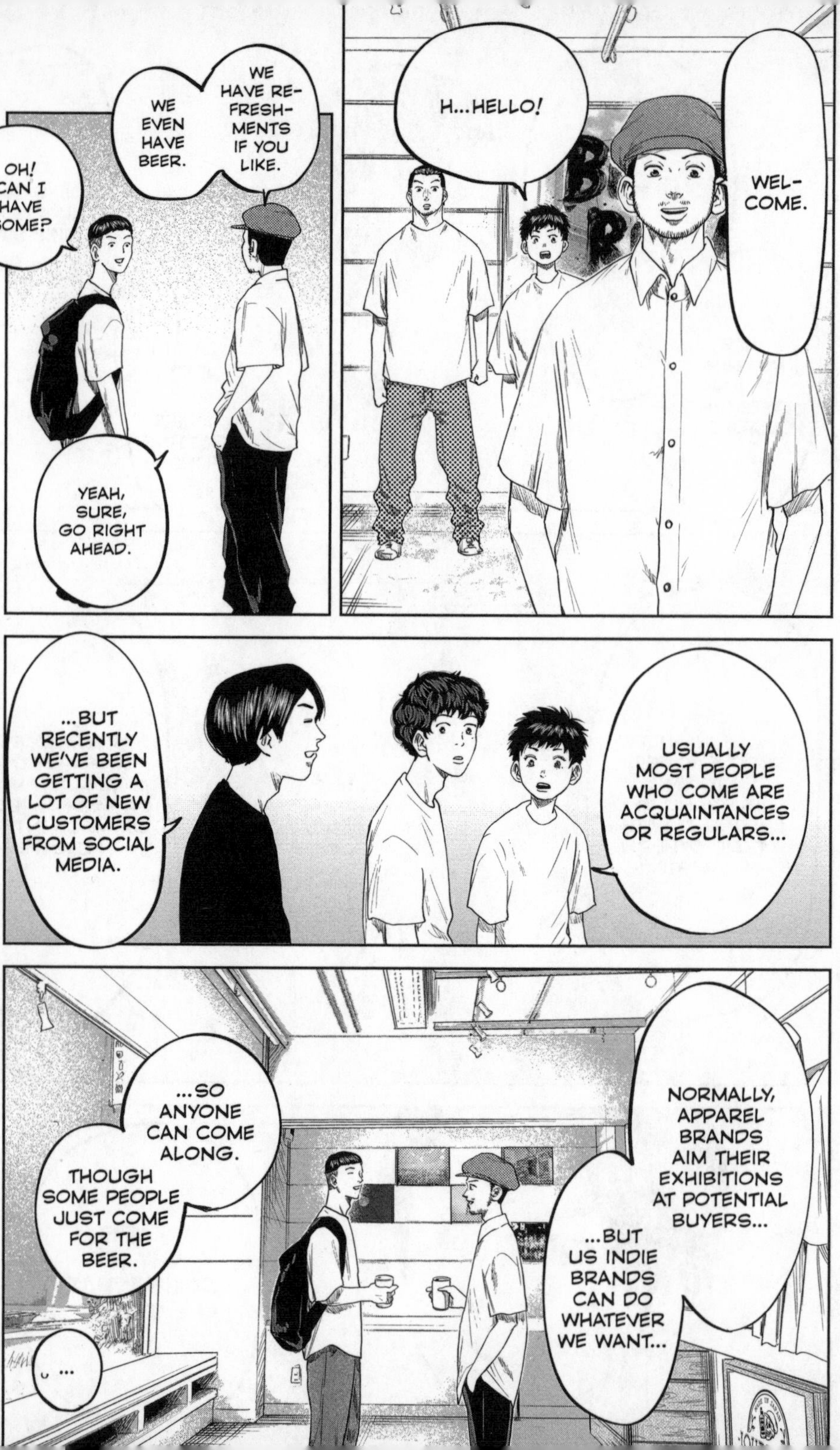
WEL-COME.
H...HELLO!
WE HAVE RE-FRESH-MENTS IF YOU LIKE.
WE EVEN HAVE BEER.
OH! CAN I HAVE SOME?
YEAH, SURE, GO RIGHT AHEAD.
USUALLY MOST PEOPLE WHO COME ARE ACQUAINTANCES OR REGULARS...
...BUT RECENTLY WE'VE BEEN GETTING A LOT OF NEW CUSTOMERS FROM SOCIAL MEDIA.
NORMALLY, APPAREL BRANDS AIM THEIR EXHIBITIONS AT POTENTIAL BUYERS...
...BUT US INDIE BRANDS CAN DO WHATEVER WE WANT...
...SO ANYONE CAN COME ALONG.
THOUGH SOME PEOPLE JUST COME FOR THE BEER.
...

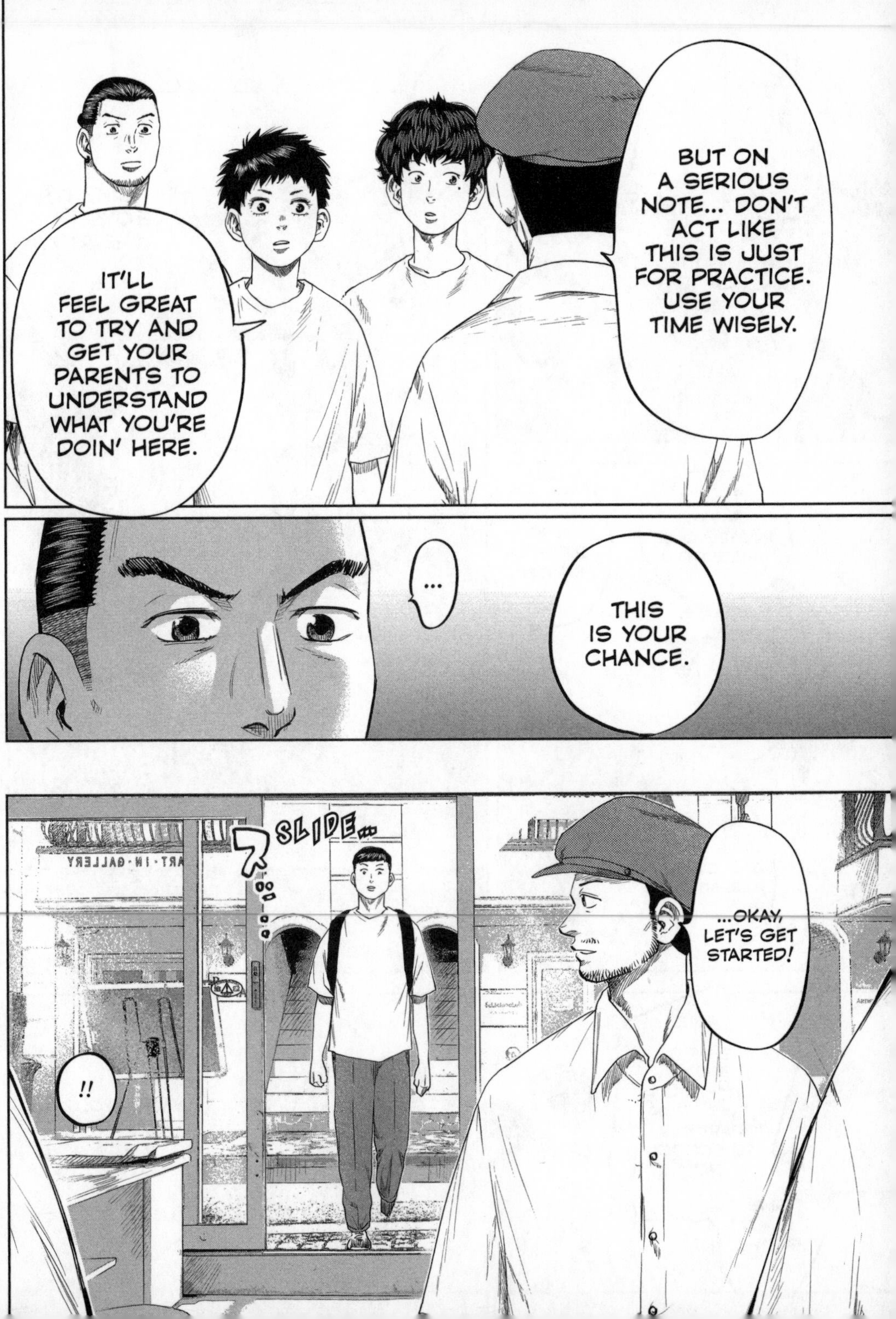
BUT ON A SERIOUS NOTE... DON'T ACT LIKE THIS IS JUST FOR PRACTICE. USE YOUR TIME WISELY.
IT'LL FEEL GREAT TO TRY AND GET YOUR PARENTS TO UNDERSTAND WHAT YOU'RE DOIN' HERE.
THIS IS YOUR CHANCE.
...
...OKAY, LET'S GET STARTED!
SLIDE...
ART-IN-GALLERY
!!

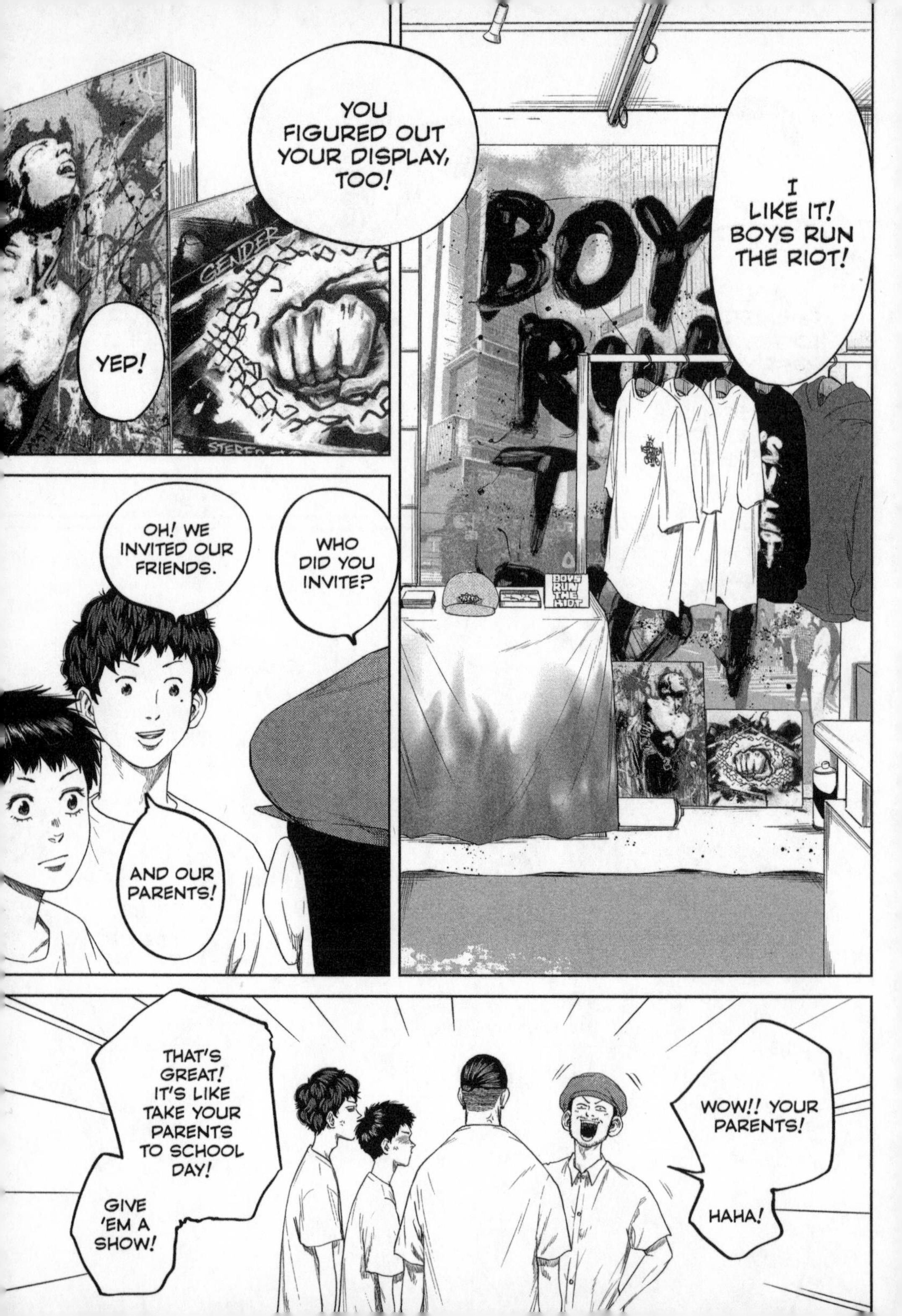
I LIKE IT! BOYS RUN THE RIOT!
BOYS RUN THE RIOT
YOU FIGURED OUT YOUR DISPLAY, TOO!
YEP!
WHO DID YOU INVITE?
OH! WE INVITED OUR FRIENDS.
AND OUR PARENTS!
WOW!! YOUR PARENTS!
HAHA!
THAT'S GREAT! IT'S LIKE TAKE YOUR PARENTS TO SCHOOL DAY!
GIVE 'EM A SHOW!

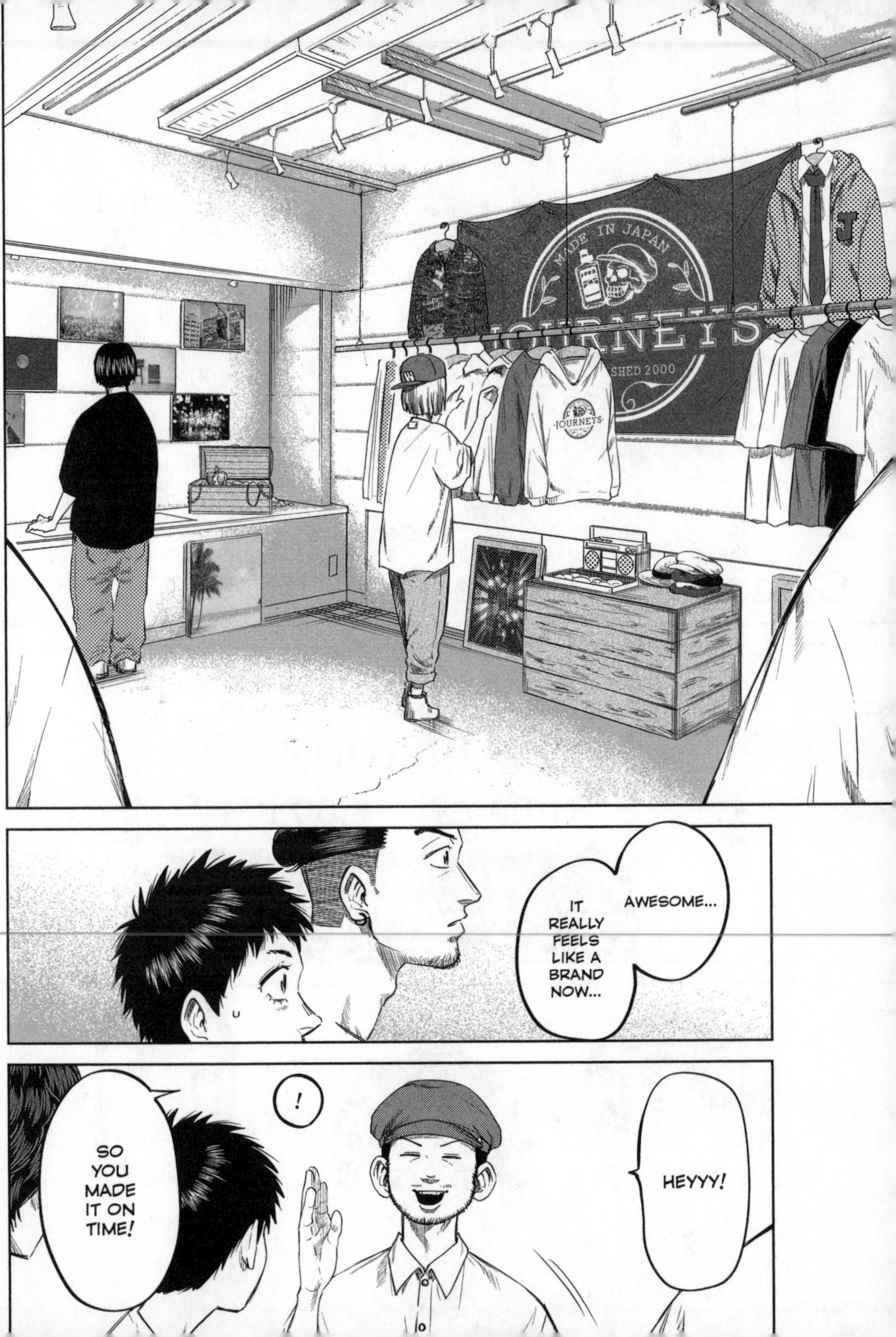
MADE IN JAPAN
JOURNEYS
JOURNEYS
AWESOME...
IT REALLY FEELS LIKE A BRAND NOW...
HEYYY!
!
SO YOU MADE IT ON TIME!

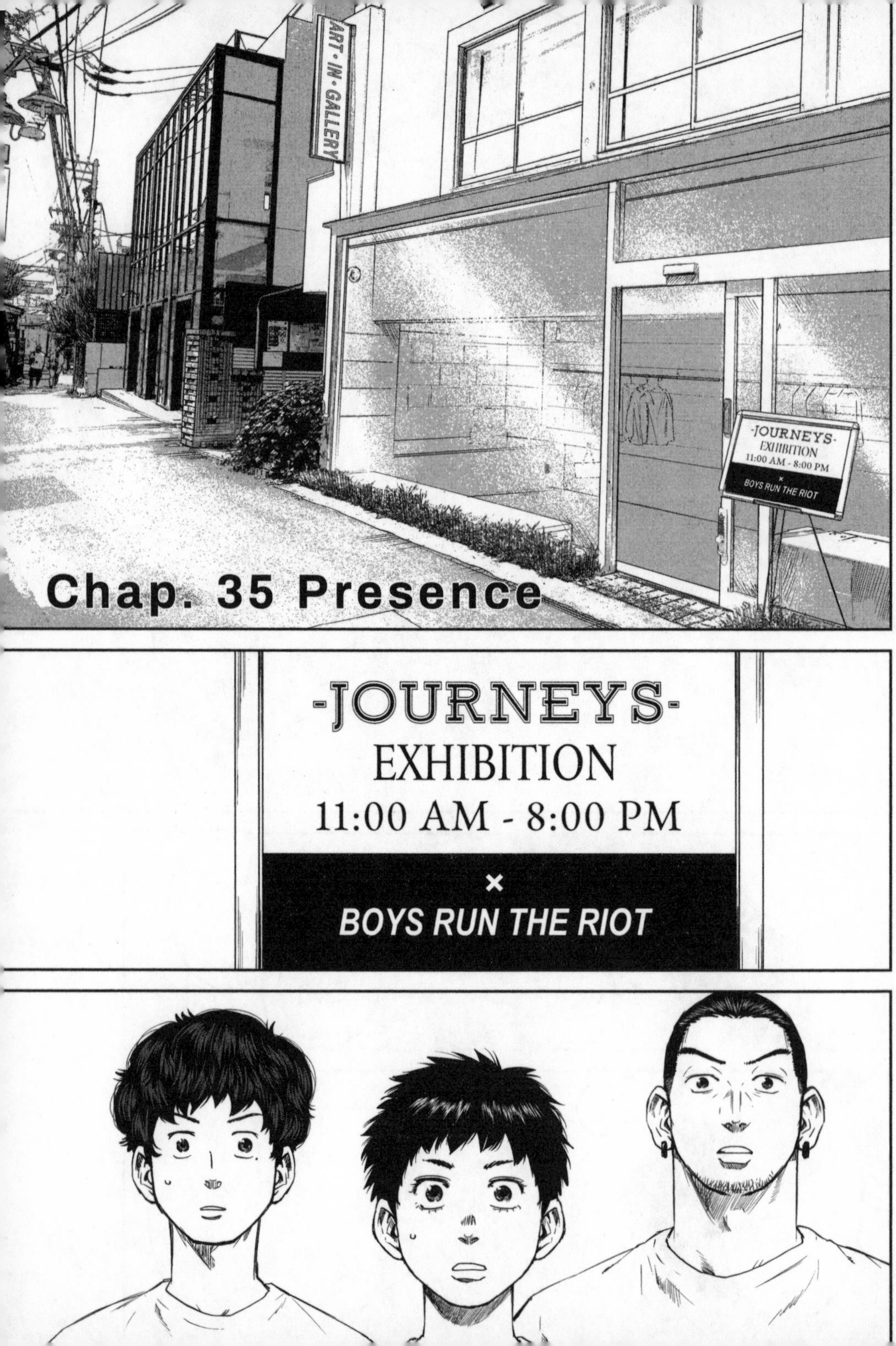
ART·IN·GALLERY
-JOURNEYS-
EXHIBITION
11:00 AM - 8:00 PM
×
BOYS RUN THE RIOT
Chap. 35 Presence
-JOURNEYS-
EXHIBITION
11:00 AM - 8:00 PM
×
BOYS RUN THE RIOT

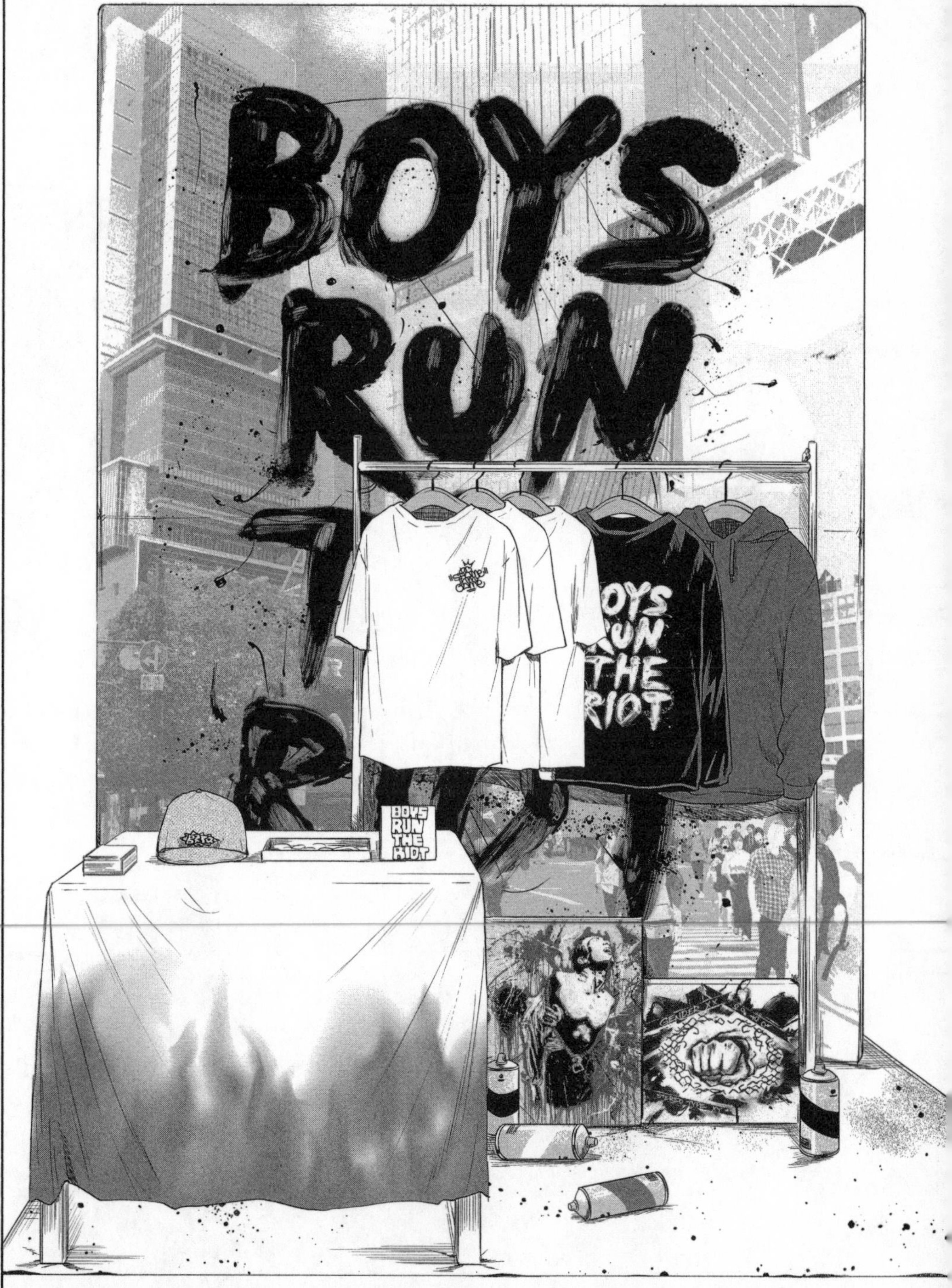
BOYS RUN
BOYS RUN THE RIOT
BOYS RUN THE RIOT

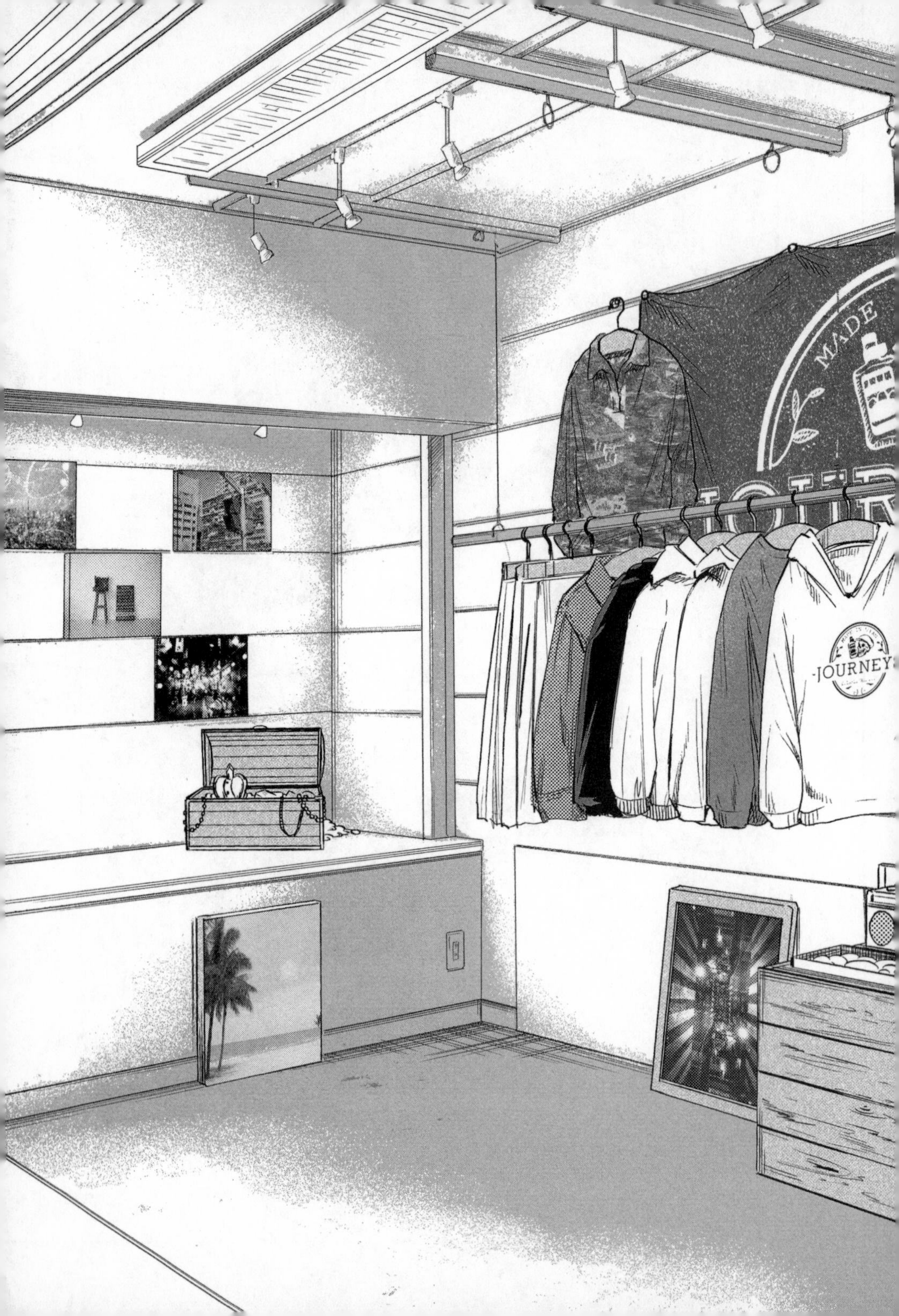
MADE
JOURNEYS

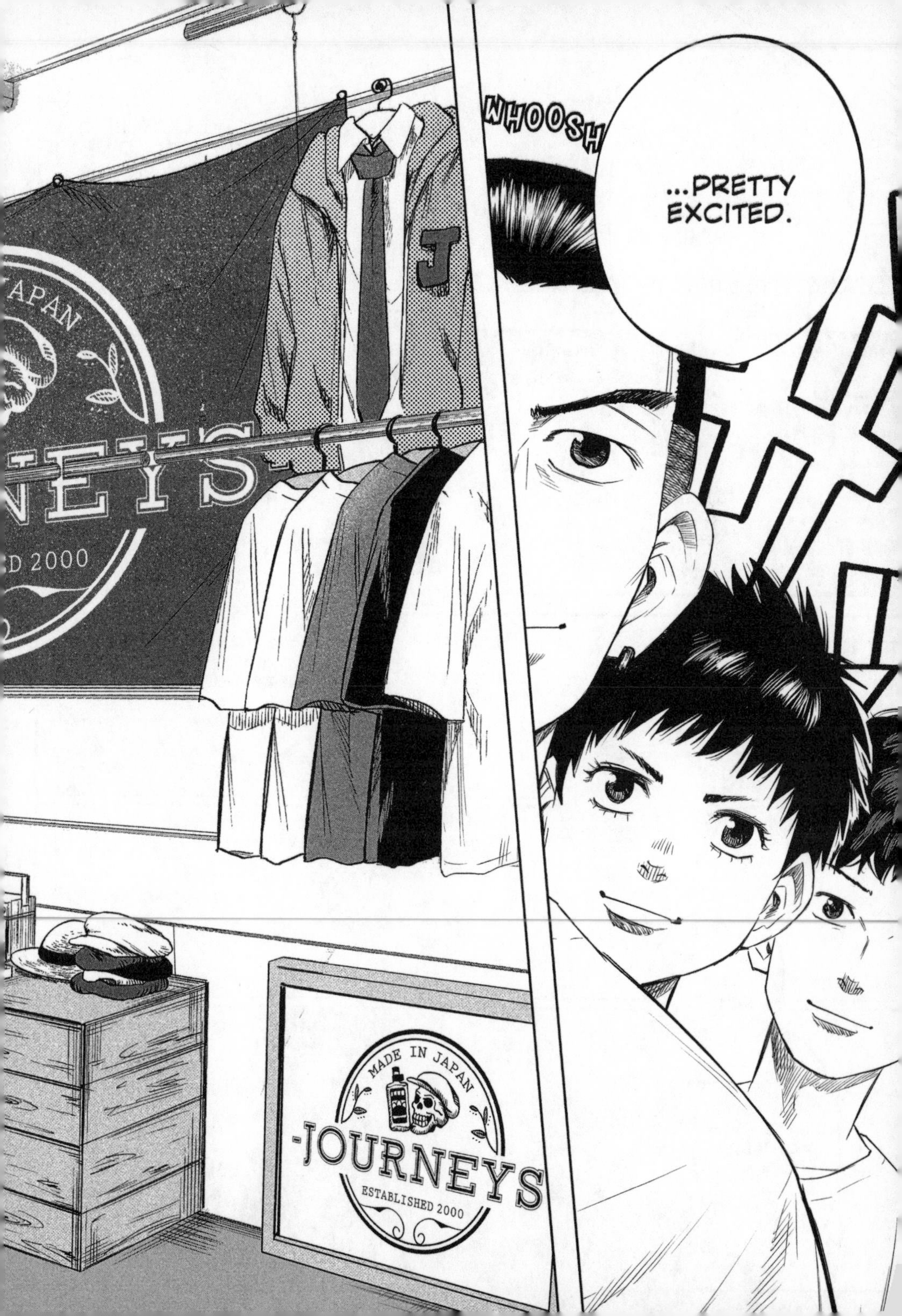
WHOOSH
...PRETTY EXCITED.
MADE IN JAPAN
JOURNEYS
ESTABLISHED 2000

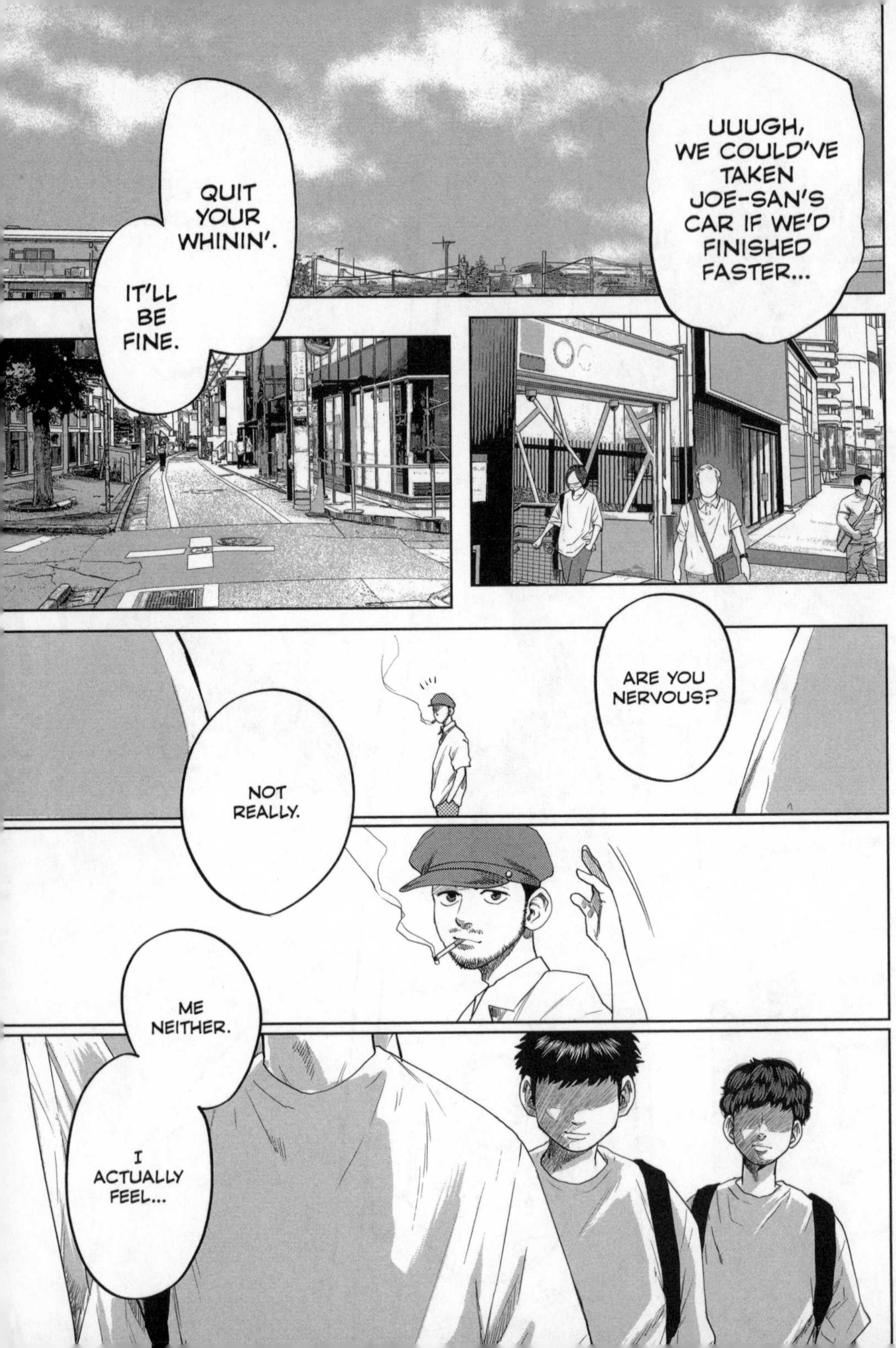
UUUGH, WE COULD'VE TAKEN JOE-SAN'S CAR IF WE'D FINISHED FASTER...
QUIT YOUR WHININ'.
IT'LL BE FINE.
ARE YOU NERVOUS?
NOT REALLY.
ME NEITHER.
I ACTUALLY FEEL...

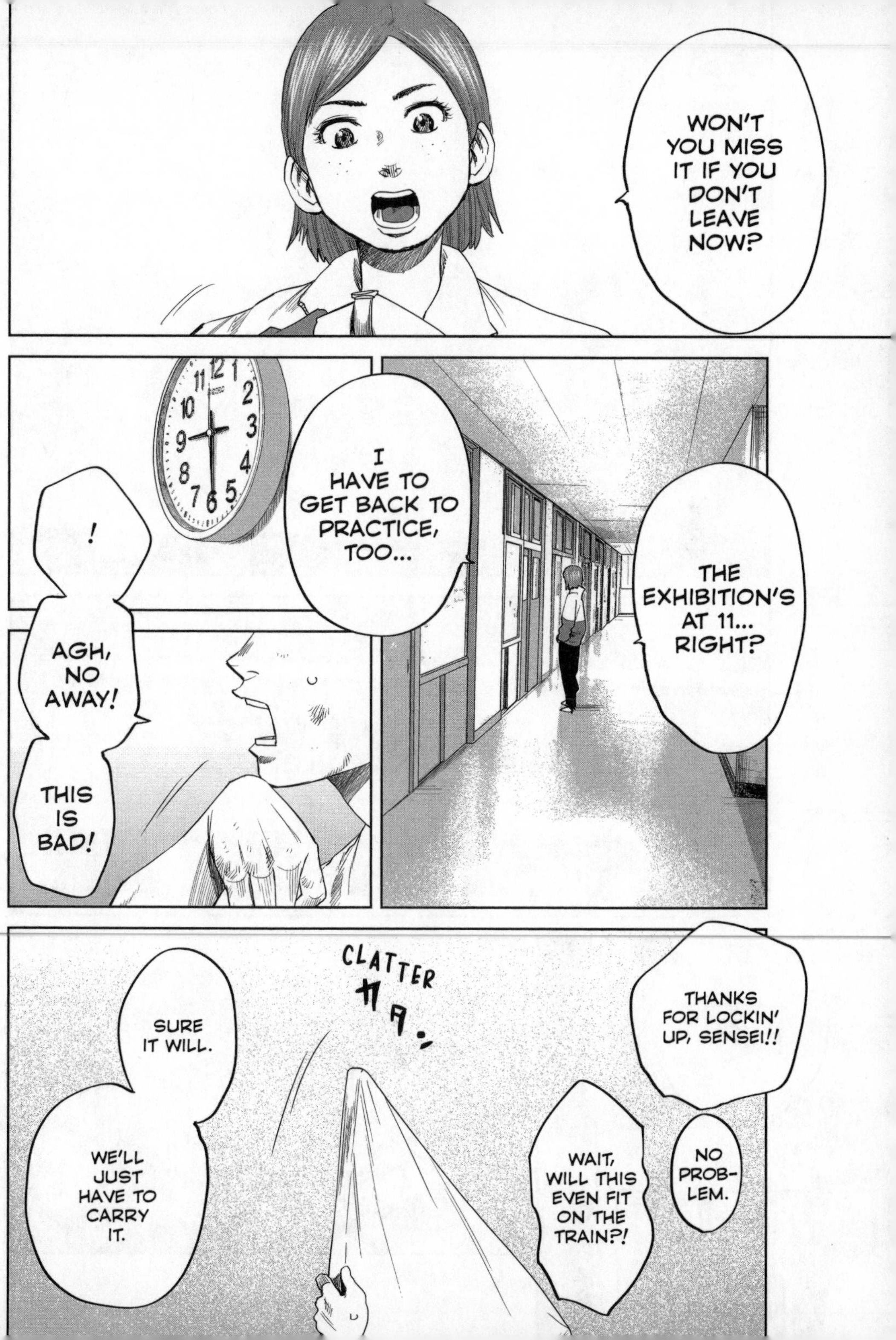
WON'T YOU MISS IT IF YOU DON'T LEAVE NOW?
THE EXHIBITION'S AT 11... RIGHT?
I HAVE TO GET BACK TO PRACTICE, TOO...
!
AGH, NO AWAY!
THIS IS BAD!
THANKS FOR LOCKIN' UP, SENSEI!!
NO PROB-LEM.
WAIT, WILL THIS EVEN FIT ON THE TRAIN?!
CLATTER
カタ
SURE IT WILL.
WE'LL JUST HAVE TO CARRY IT.

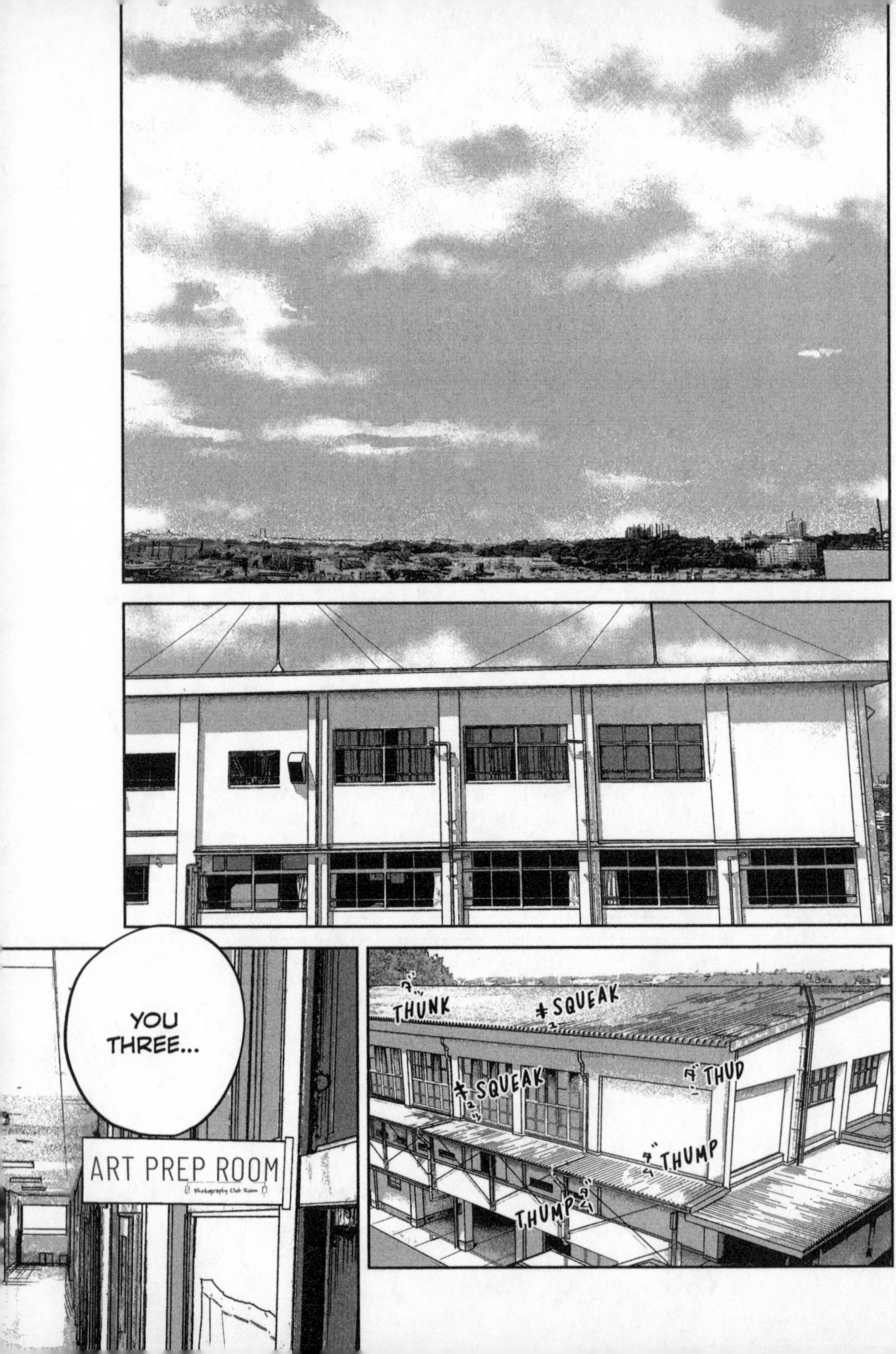
THUNK
SQUEAK
SQUEAK
THUD
THUMP
THUMP
YOU THREE...
ART PREP ROOM
Photography Club Room

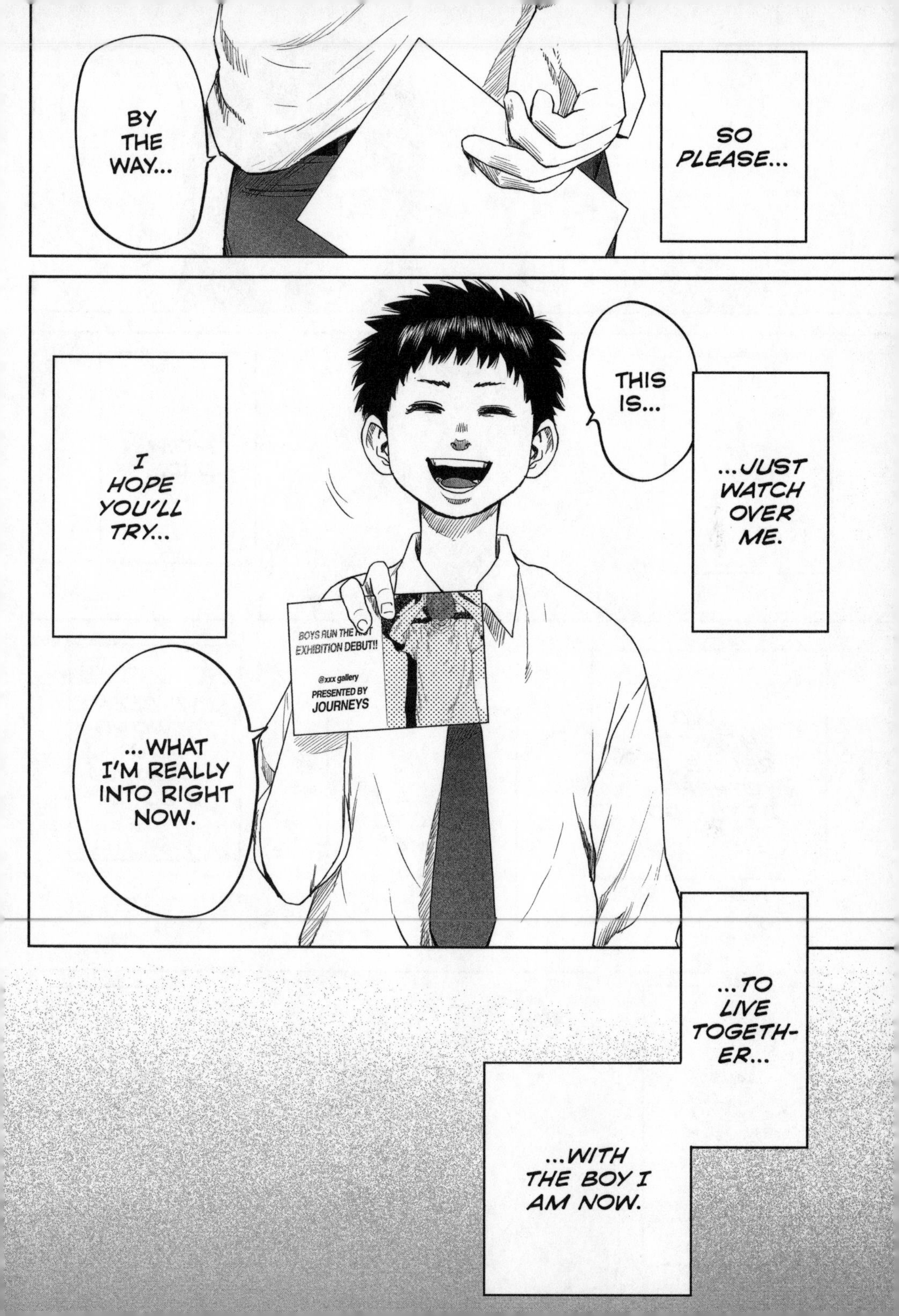
SO PLEASE...
BY THE WAY...
...JUST WATCH OVER ME.
THIS IS...
I HOPE YOU'LL TRY...
BOYS RUN THE
EXHIBITION DEBUT!!
@xxx gallery
PRESENTED BY
JOURNEYS
...WHAT I'M REALLY INTO RIGHT NOW.
...TO LIVE TOGETH-ER...
...WITH THE BOY I AM NOW.

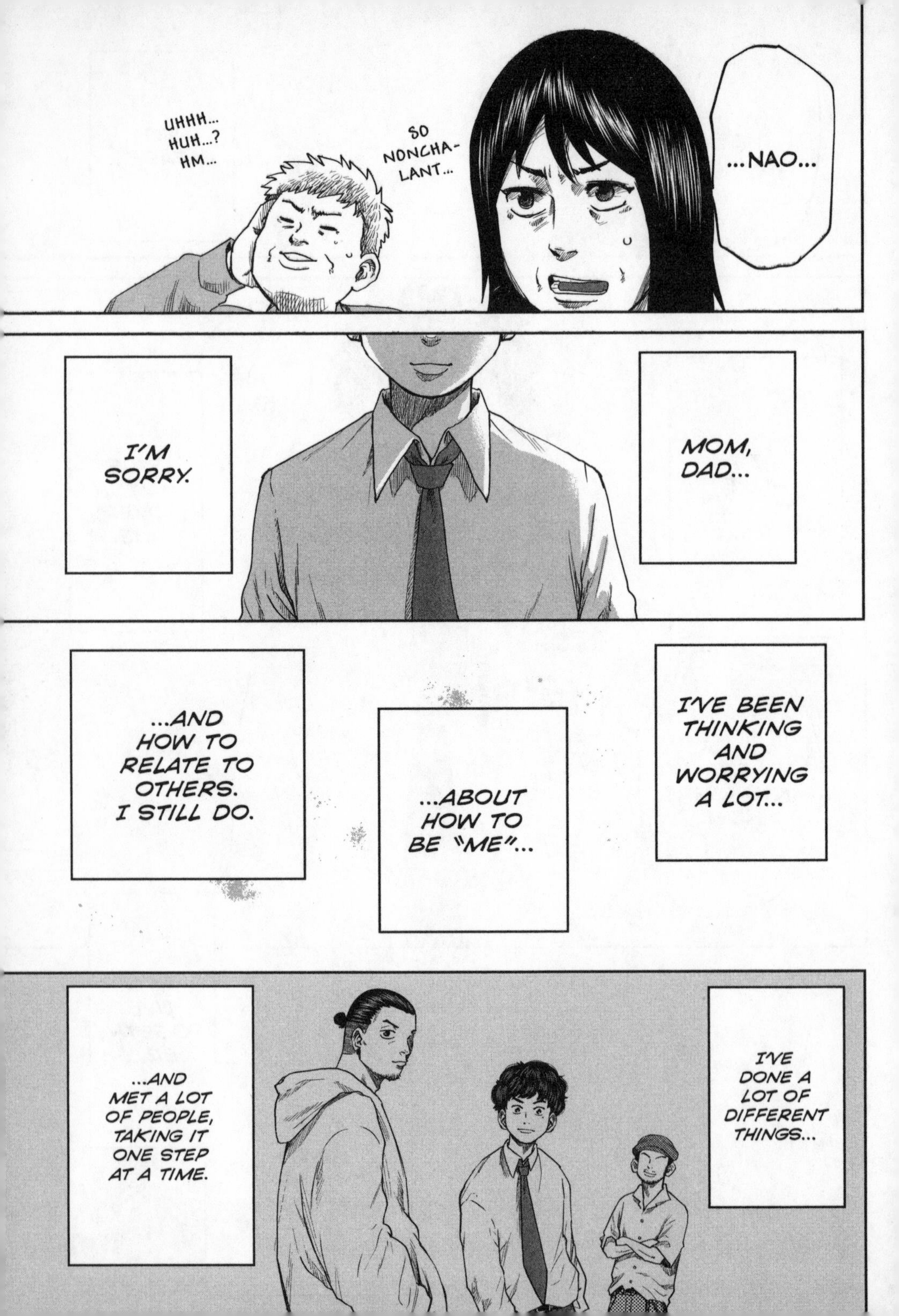
...NAO...
SO NONCHA-LANT...
UHHH... HUH...? HM...
MOM, DAD...
I'M SORRY.
I'VE BEEN THINKING AND WORRYING A LOT...
...ABOUT HOW TO BE "ME"...
...AND HOW TO RELATE TO OTHERS. I STILL DO.
I'VE DONE A LOT OF DIFFERENT THINGS...
...AND MET A LOT OF PEOPLE, TAKING IT ONE STEP AT A TIME.

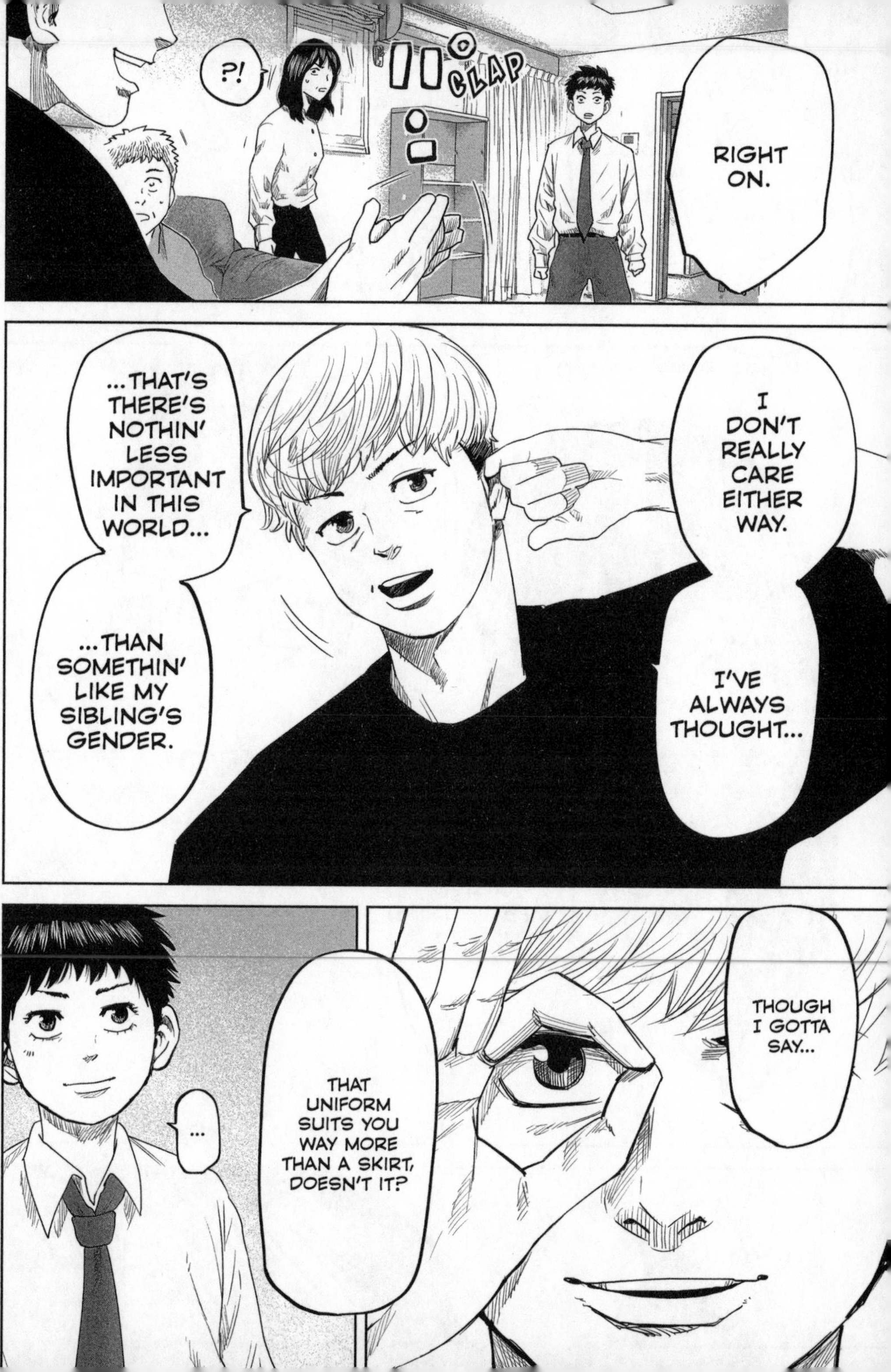
RIGHT ON.
CLAP
?!
I DON'T REALLY CARE EITHER WAY.
I'VE ALWAYS THOUGHT...
...THAT'S THERE'S NOTHIN' LESS IMPORTANT IN THIS WORLD...
...THAN SOMETHIN' LIKE MY SIBLING'S GENDER.
THOUGH I GOTTA SAY...
THAT UNIFORM SUITS YOU WAY MORE THAN A SKIRT, DOESN'T IT?
...

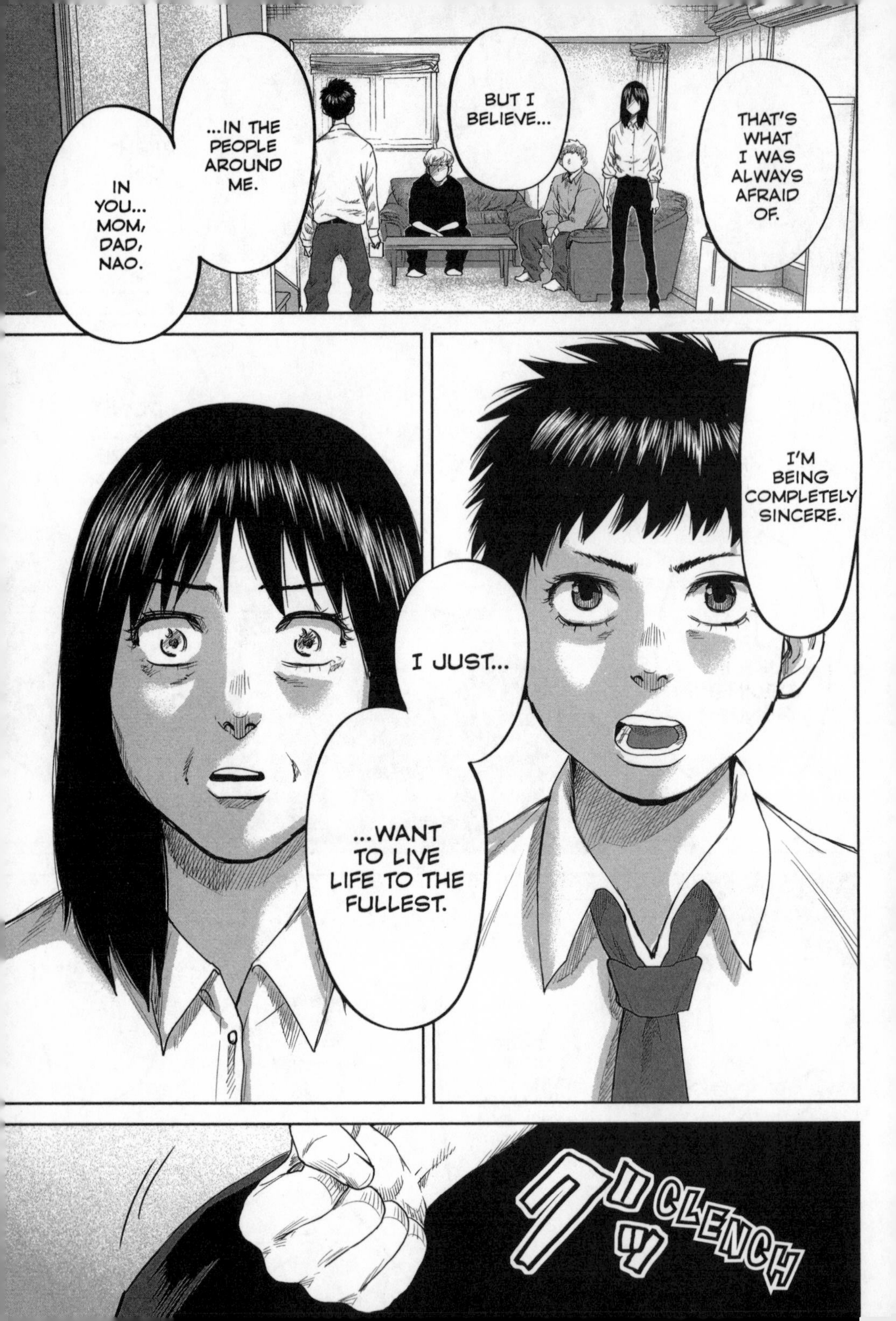
THAT'S WHAT I WAS ALWAYS AFRAID OF.
BUT I BELIEVE...
...IN THE PEOPLE AROUND ME.
IN YOU... MOM, DAD, NAO.
I'M BEING COMPLETELY SINCERE.
I JUST...
...WANT TO LIVE LIFE TO THE FULLEST.
クッ
CLENCH

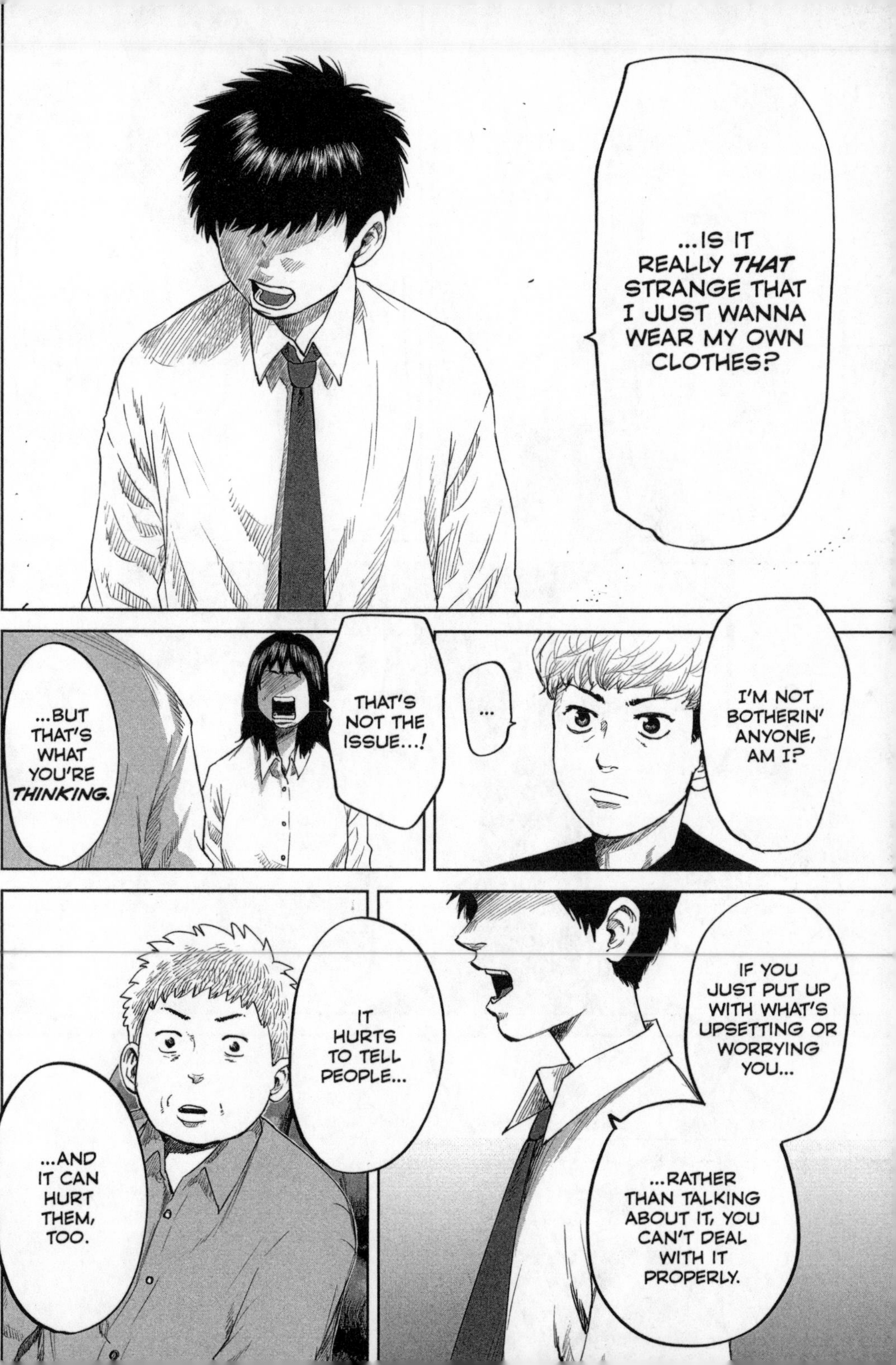
...IS IT REALLY *THAT* STRANGE THAT I JUST WANNA WEAR MY OWN CLOTHES?
I'M NOT BOTHERIN' ANYONE, AM I?
...
THAT'S NOT THE ISSUE...!
...BUT THAT'S WHAT YOU'RE *THINKING.*
IF YOU JUST PUT UP WITH WHAT'S UPSETTING OR WORRYING YOU...
...RATHER THAN TALKING ABOUT IT, YOU CAN'T DEAL WITH IT PROPERLY.
IT HURTS TO TELL PEOPLE...
...AND IT CAN HURT THEM, TOO.

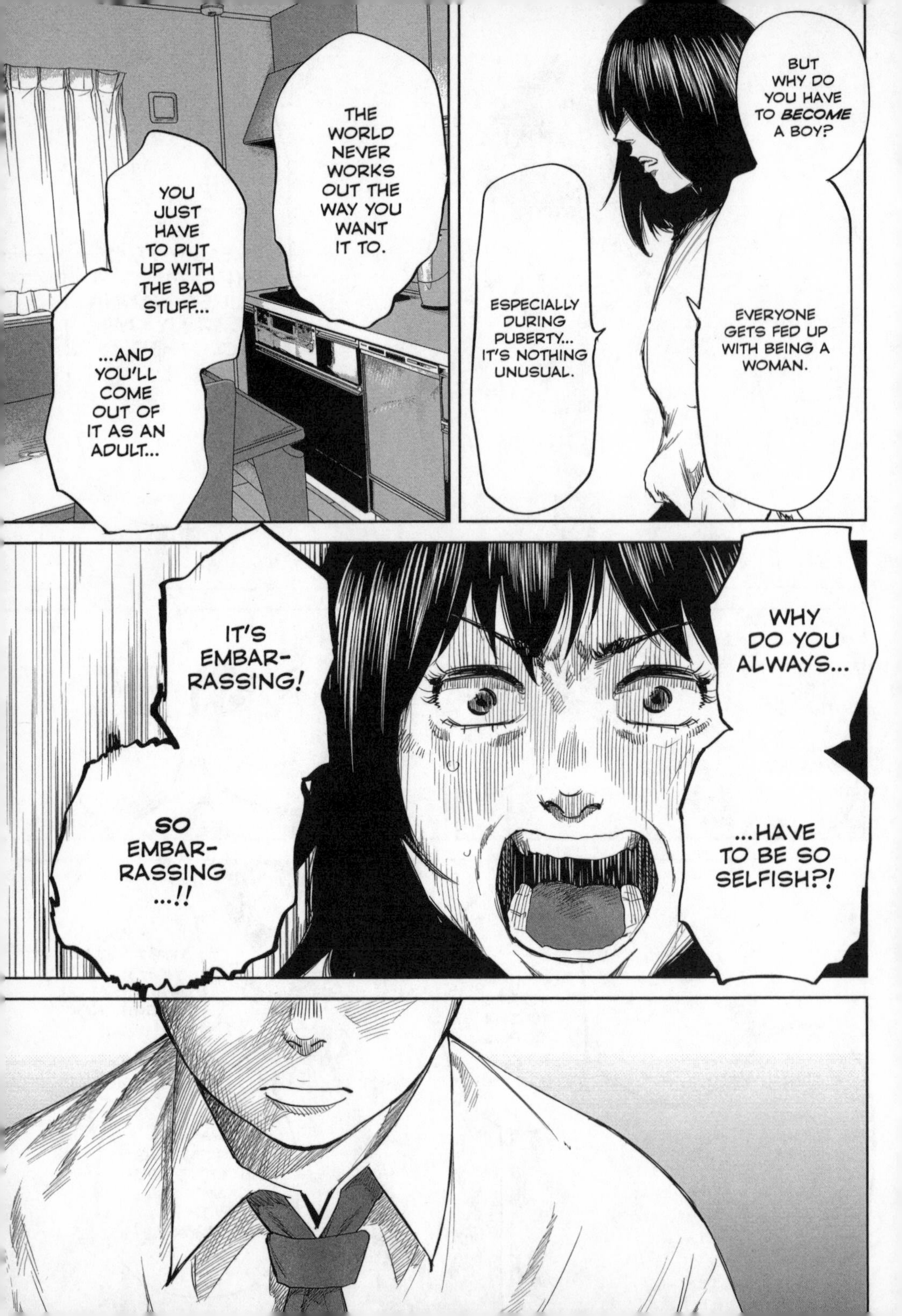
BUT WHY DO YOU HAVE TO *BECOME* A BOY?
EVERYONE GETS FED UP WITH BEING A WOMAN.
ESPECIALLY DURING PUBERTY... IT'S NOTHING UNUSUAL.
THE WORLD NEVER WORKS OUT THE WAY YOU WANT IT TO.
YOU JUST HAVE TO PUT UP WITH THE BAD STUFF...
...AND YOU'LL COME OUT OF IT AS AN ADULT...
WHY DO YOU ALWAYS...
...HAVE TO BE SO SELFISH?!
IT'S EMBAR-RASSING!
SO EMBAR-RASSING...!!

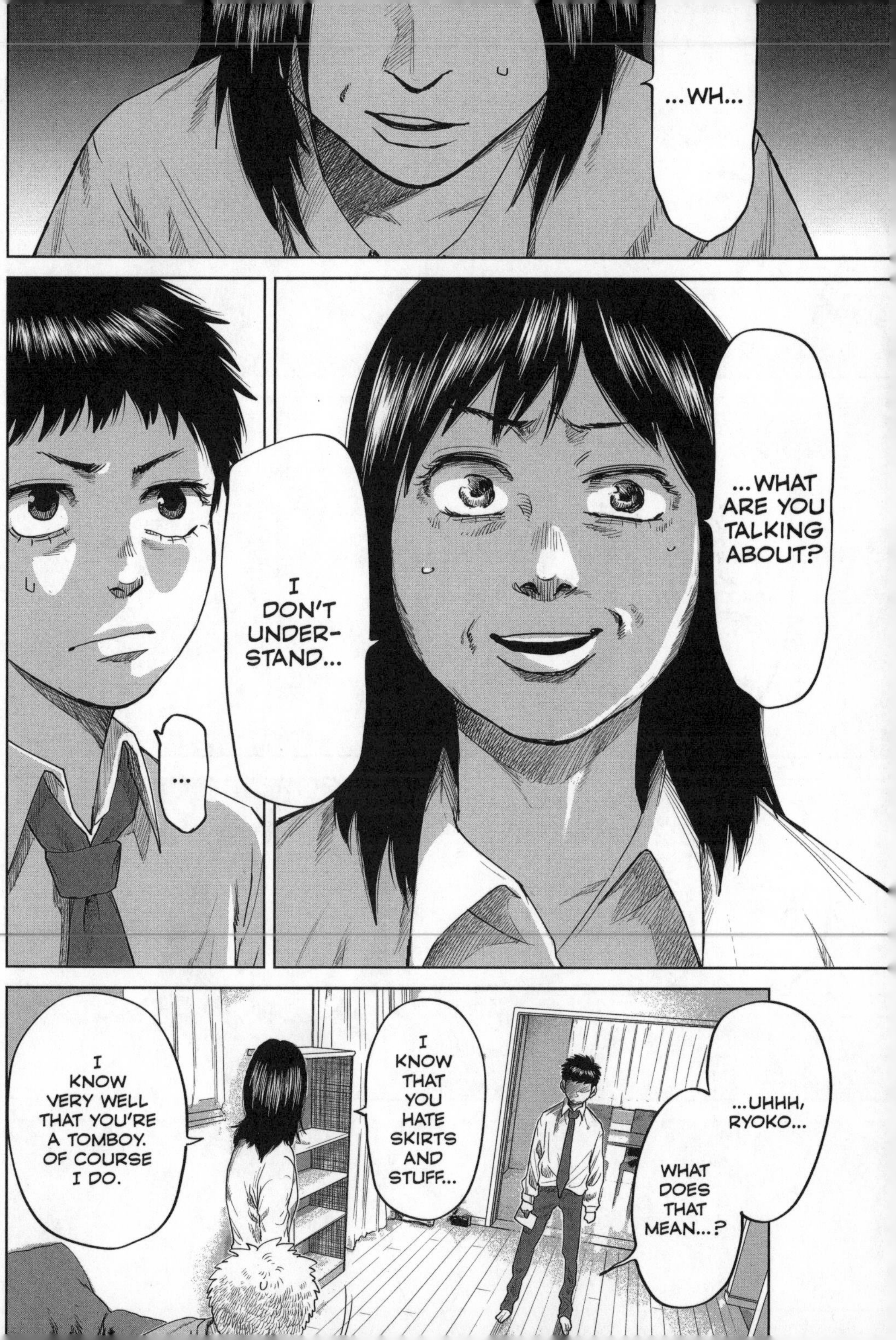
...WH...
...WHAT ARE YOU TALKING ABOUT?
I DON'T UNDER-STAND...
...
...UHHH, RYOKO...
WHAT DOES THAT MEAN...?
I KNOW THAT YOU HATE SKIRTS AND STUFF...
I KNOW VERY WELL THAT YOU'RE A TOMBOY. OF COURSE I DO.

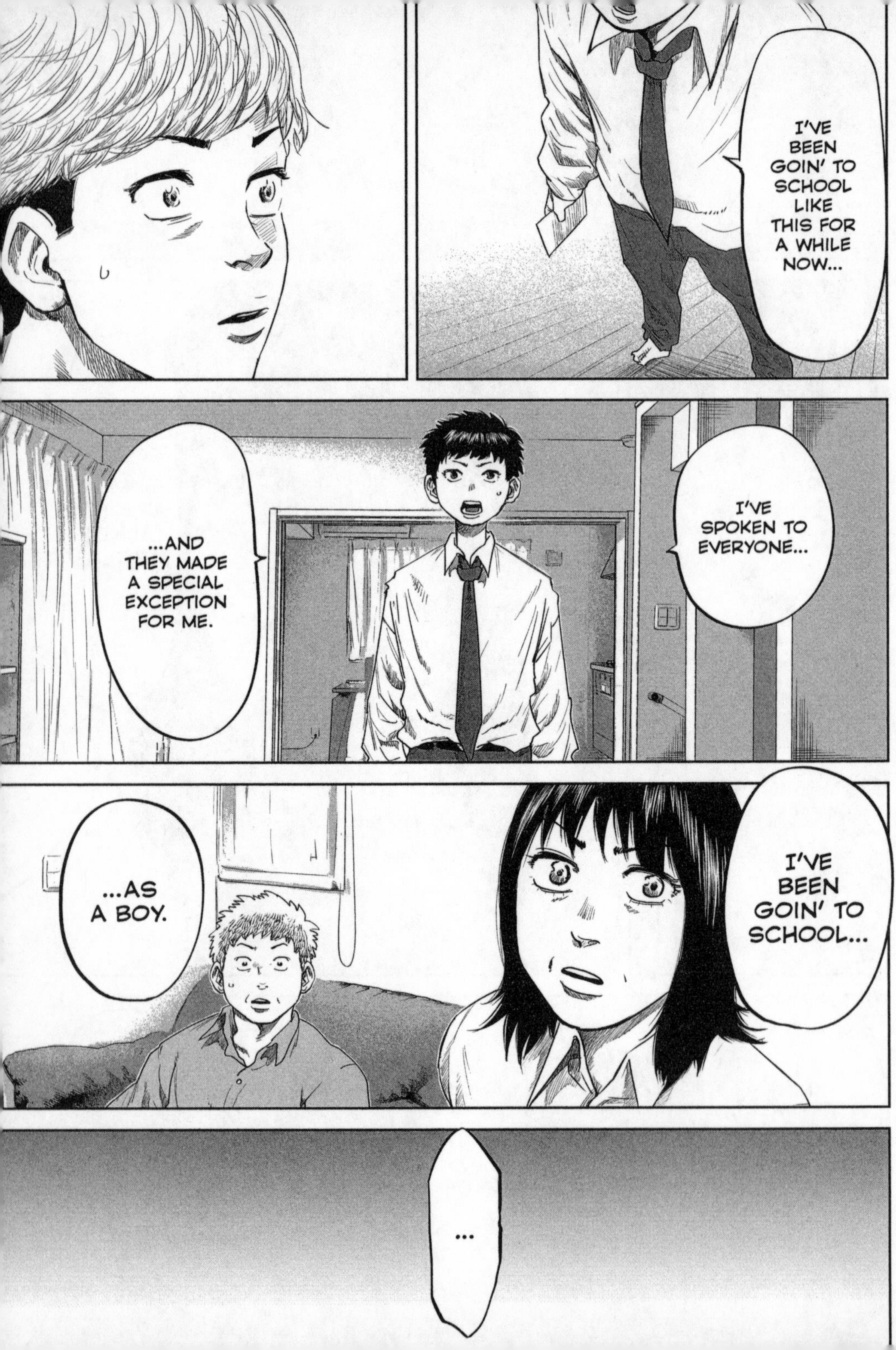
I'VE BEEN GOIN' TO SCHOOL LIKE THIS FOR A WHILE NOW...
I'VE SPOKEN TO EVERYONE...
...AND THEY MADE A SPECIAL EXCEPTION FOR ME.
I'VE BEEN GOIN' TO SCHOOL...
...AS A BOY.
...

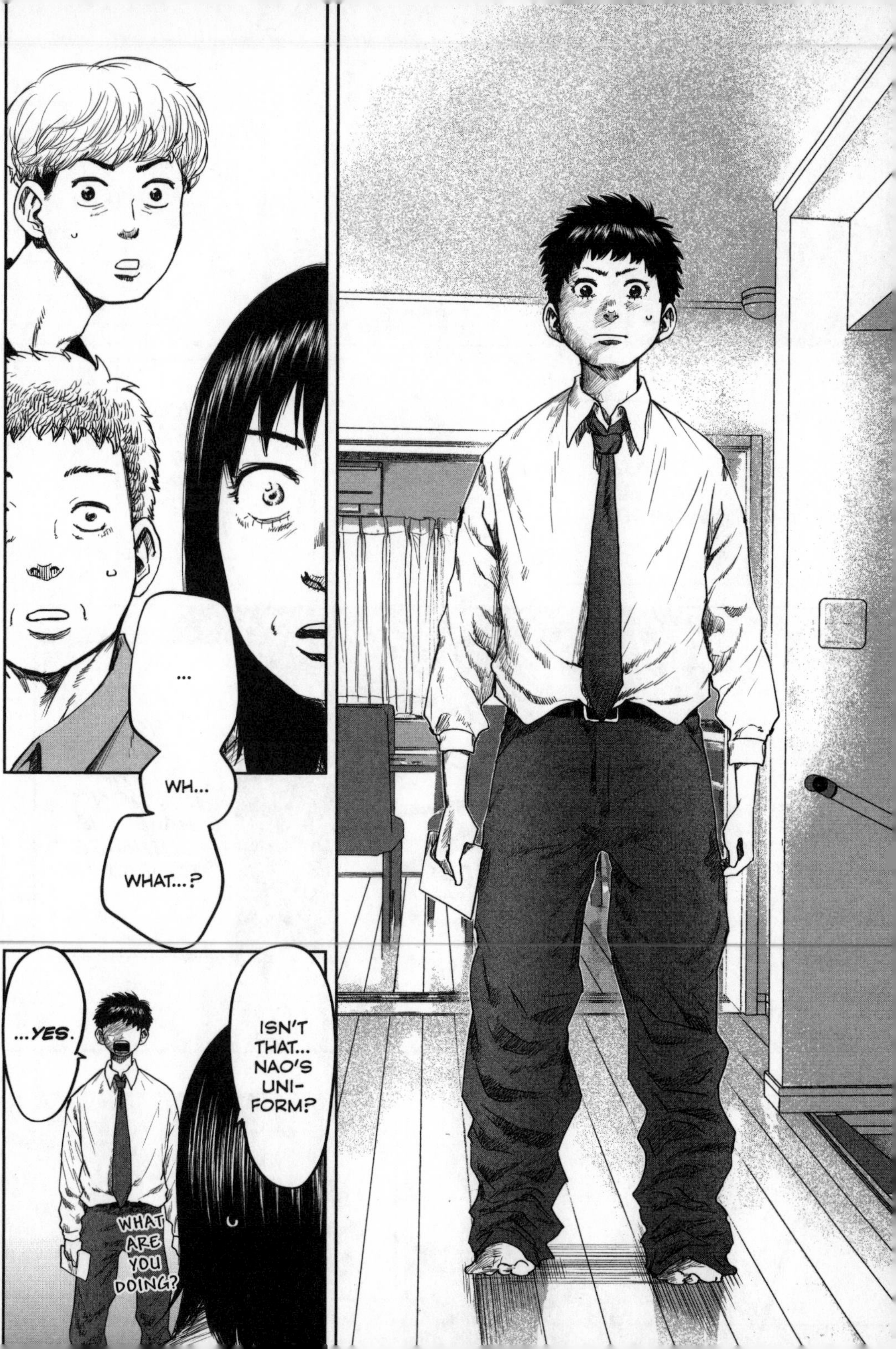
...
WH... WHAT...?
ISN'T THAT... NAO'S UNI-FORM?
...YES.
WHAT ARE YOU DOING?

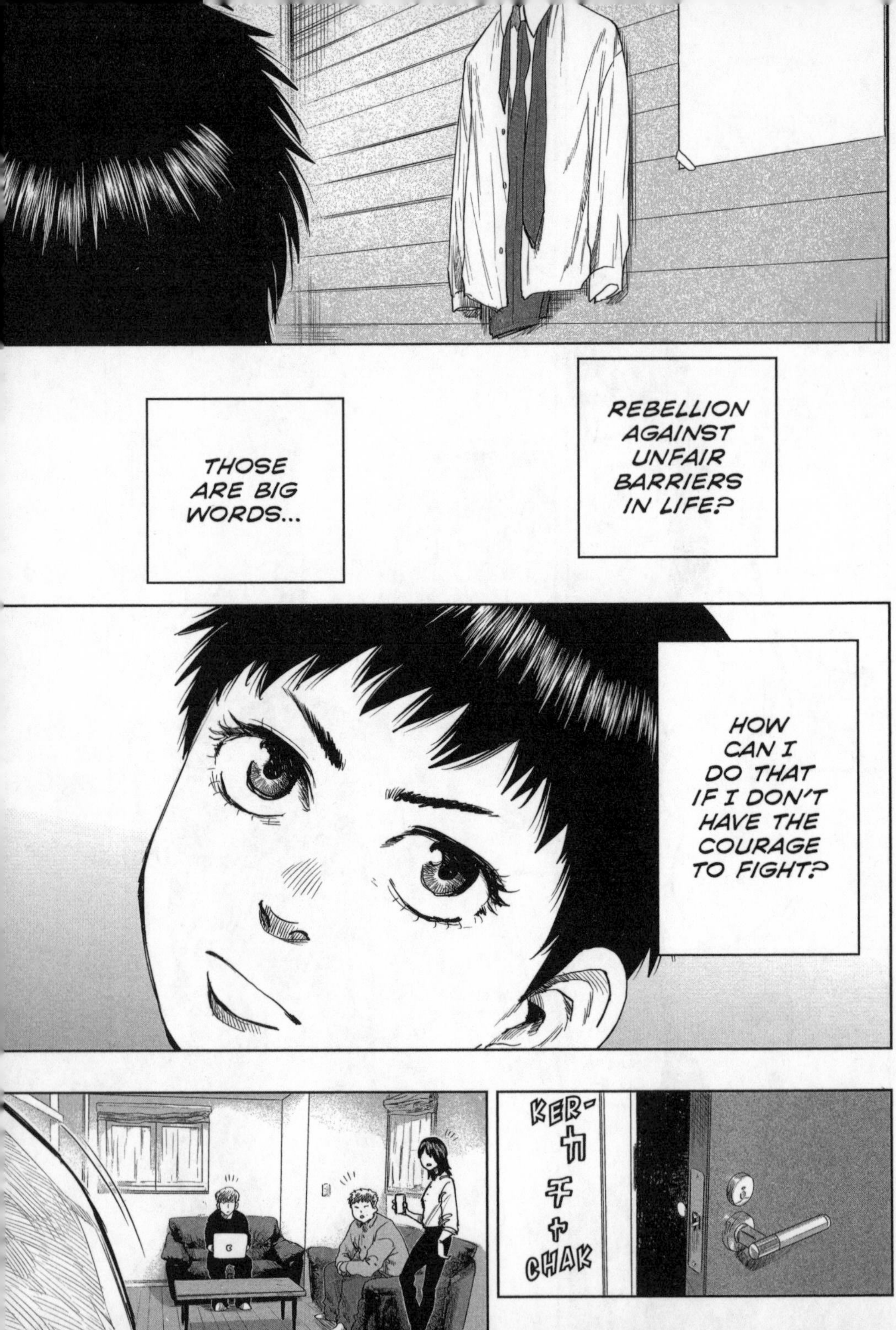
REBELLION AGAINST UNFAIR BARRIERS IN LIFE?
THOSE ARE BIG WORDS...
HOW CAN I DO THAT IF I DON'T HAVE THE COURAGE TO FIGHT?
KER-CHAK
カチャ

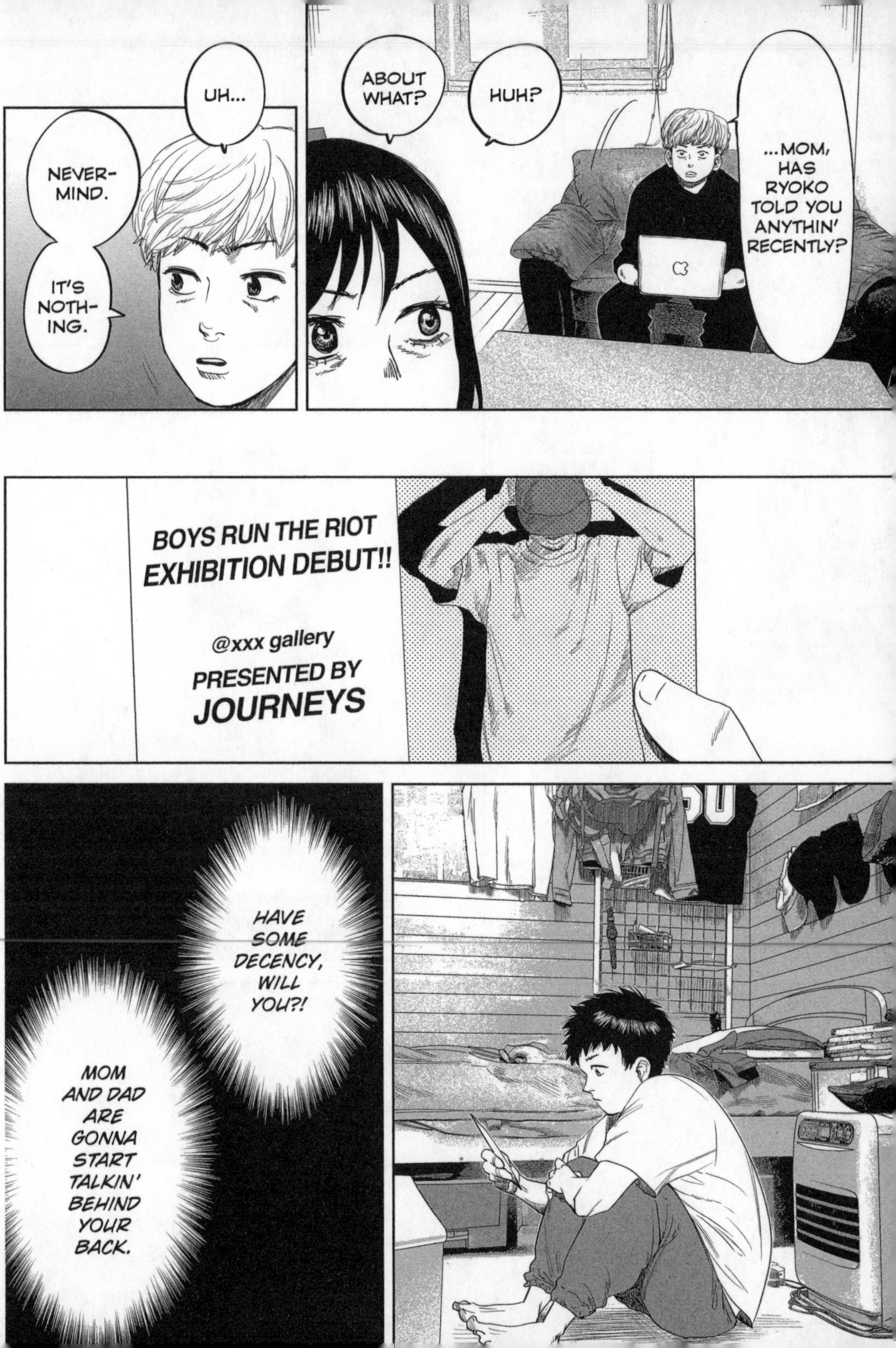
...MOM, HAS RYOKO TOLD YOU ANYTHIN' RECENTLY?
HUH?
ABOUT WHAT?
UH...
NEVERMIND.
IT'S NOTHING.
BOYS RUN THE RIOT EXHIBITION DEBUT!!
@xxx gallery
PRESENTED BY JOURNEYS
HAVE SOME DECENCY, WILL YOU?!
MOM AND DAD ARE GONNA START TALKIN' BEHIND YOUR BACK.

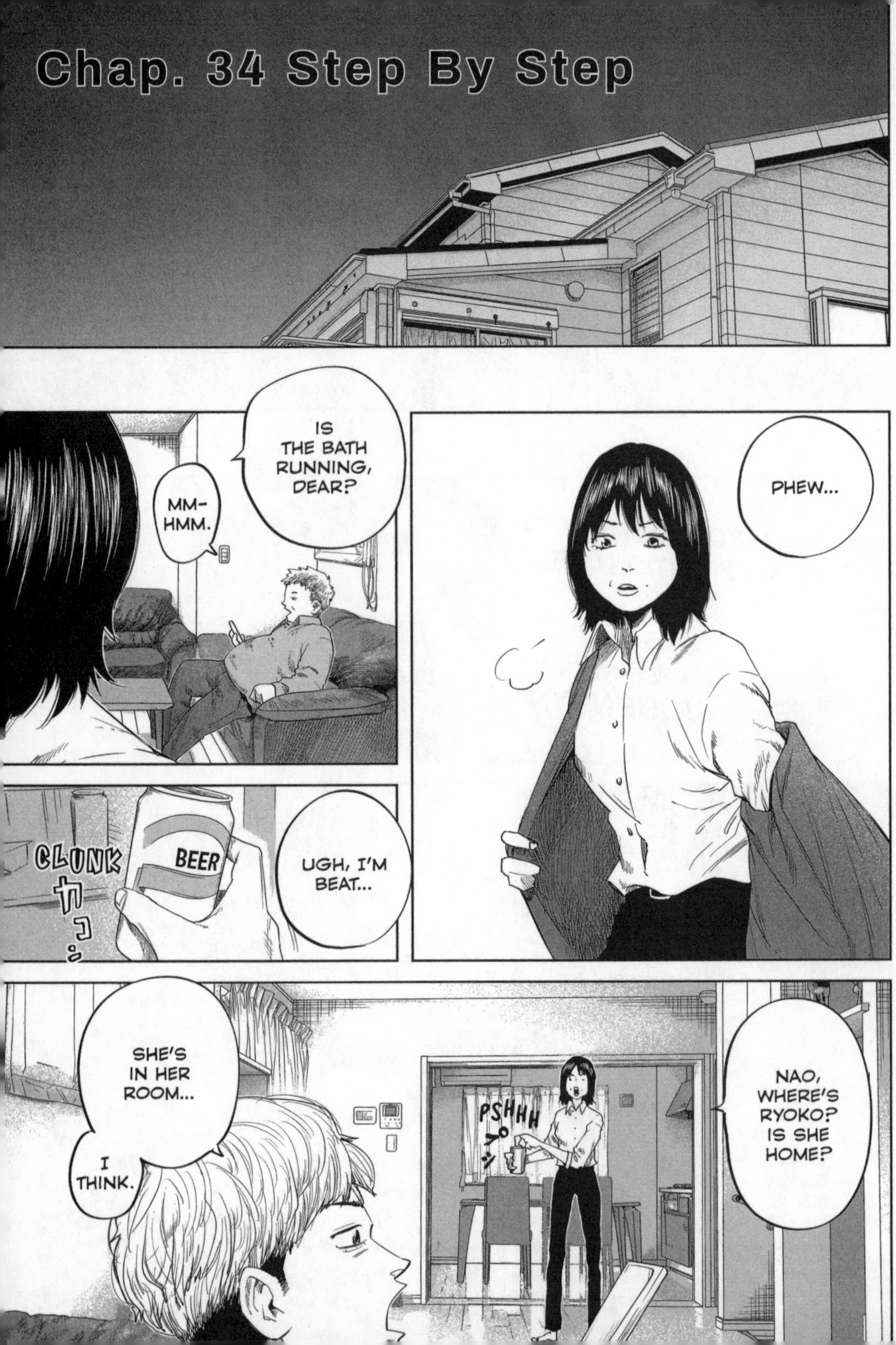
Chap. 34 Step By Step
PHEW...
IS THE BATH RUNNING, DEAR?
MM-HMM.
UGH, I'M BEAT...
BEER
CLUNK
カコッ
NAO, WHERE'S RYOKO? IS SHE HOME?
PSHHH
プシッ
SHE'S IN HER ROOM...
I THINK.

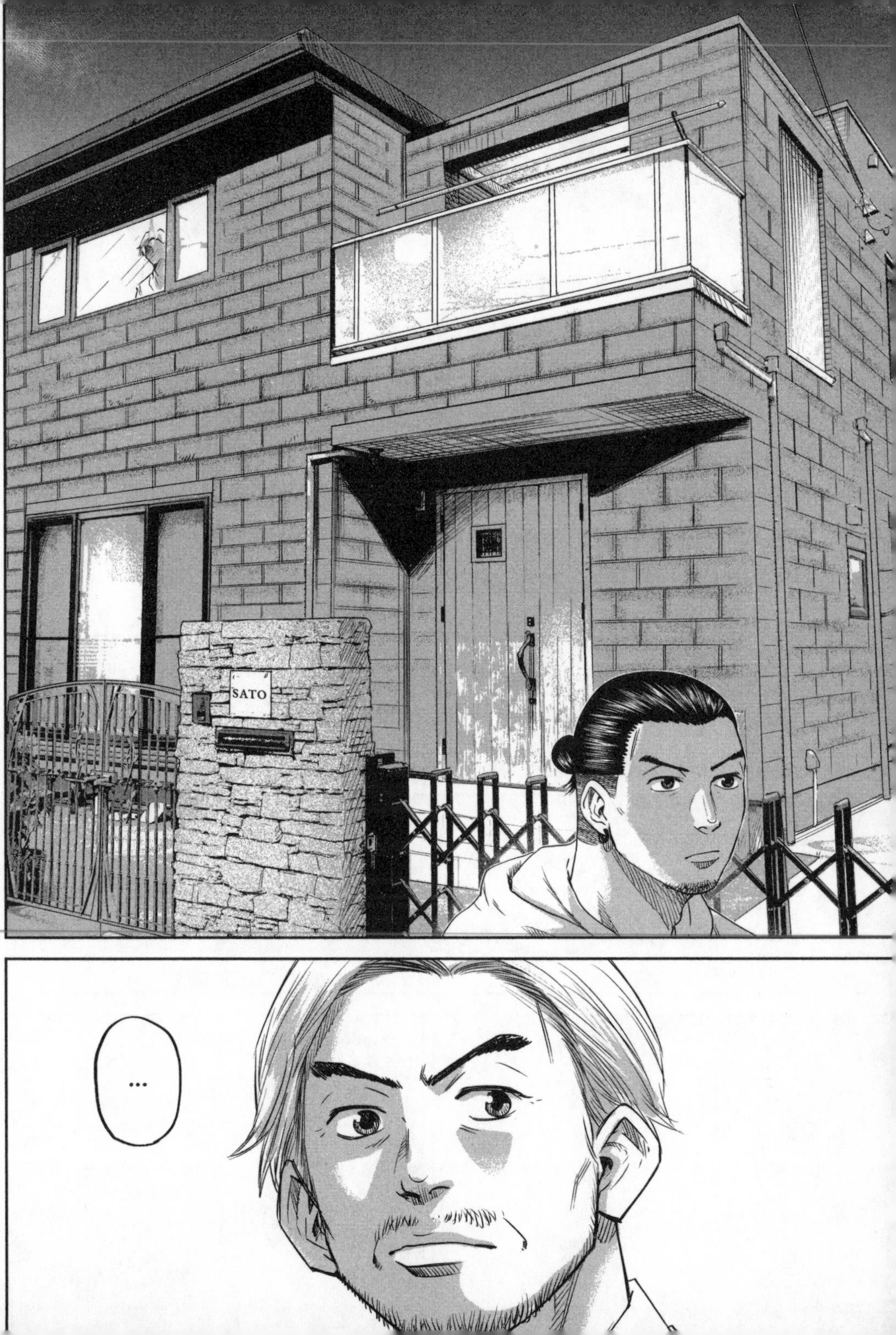
SATO
...

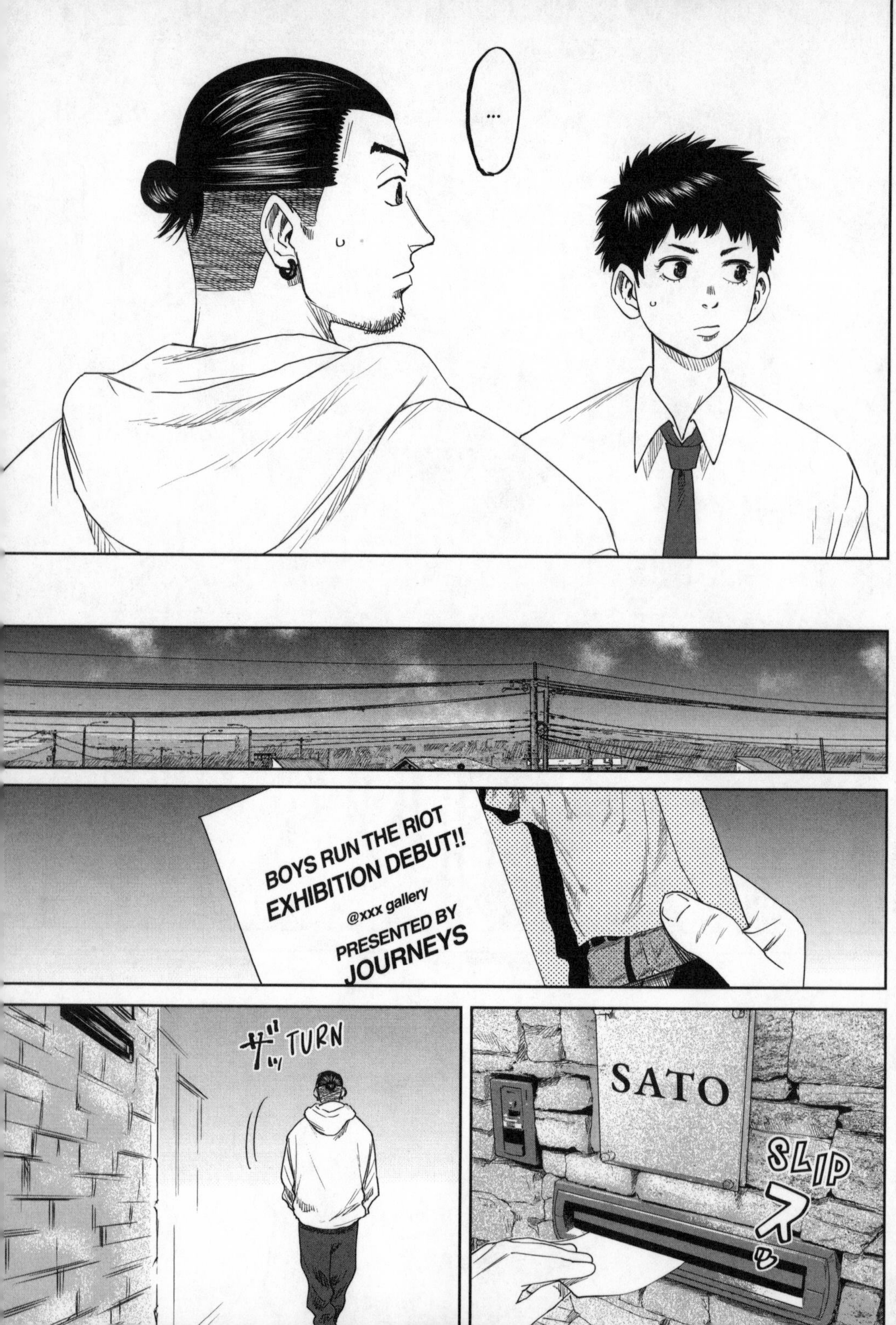
...
BOYS RUN THE RIOT
EXHIBITION DEBUT!!
@xxx gallery
PRESENTED BY
JOURNEYS
SATO
SLIP
ス
ザッ TURN

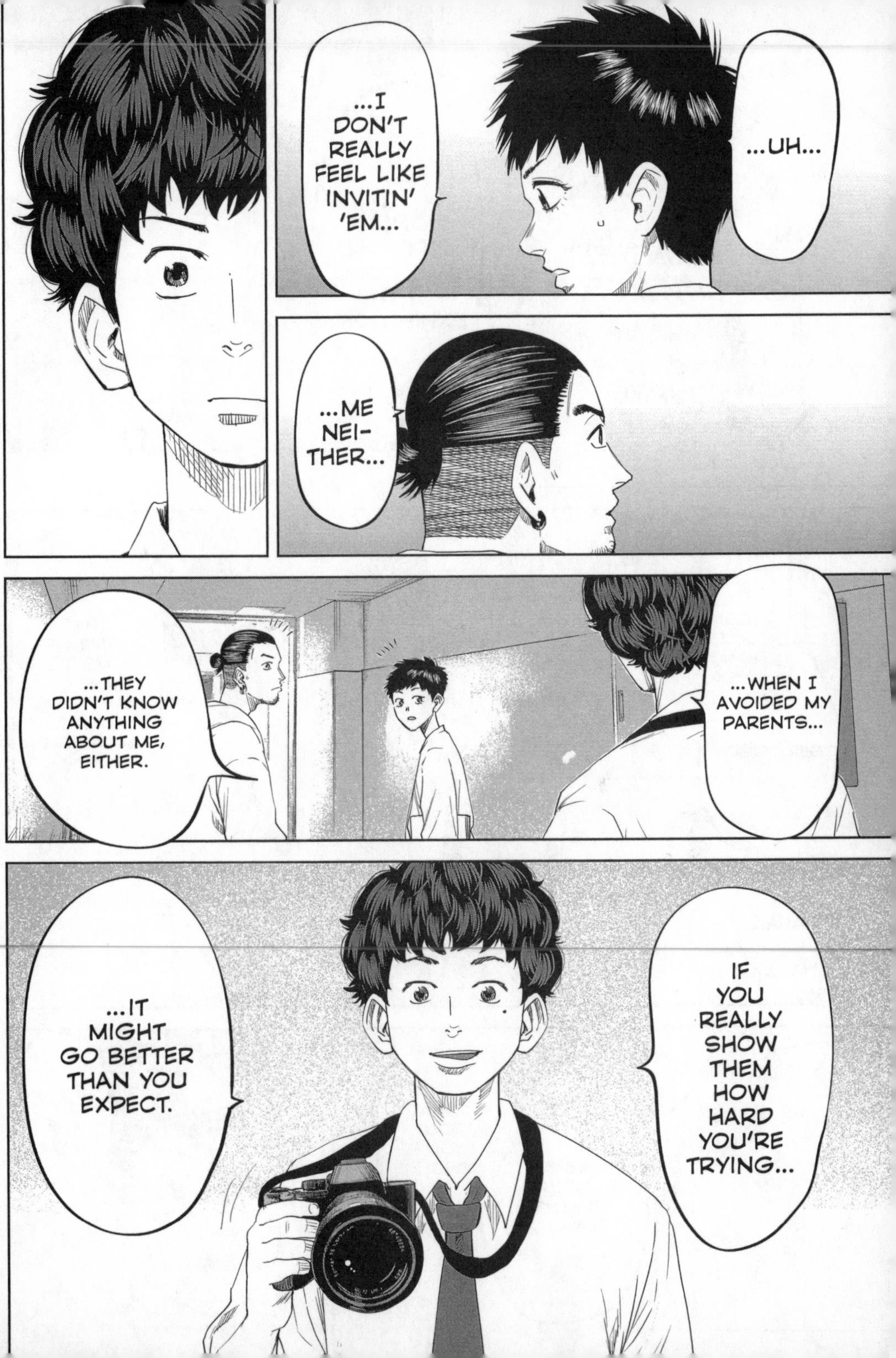
...UH...
...I DON'T REALLY FEEL LIKE INVITIN' 'EM...
...ME NEI-THER...
...WHEN I AVOIDED MY PARENTS...
...THEY DIDN'T KNOW ANYTHING ABOUT ME, EITHER.
IF YOU REALLY SHOW THEM HOW HARD YOU'RE TRYING...
...IT MIGHT GO BETTER THAN YOU EXPECT.

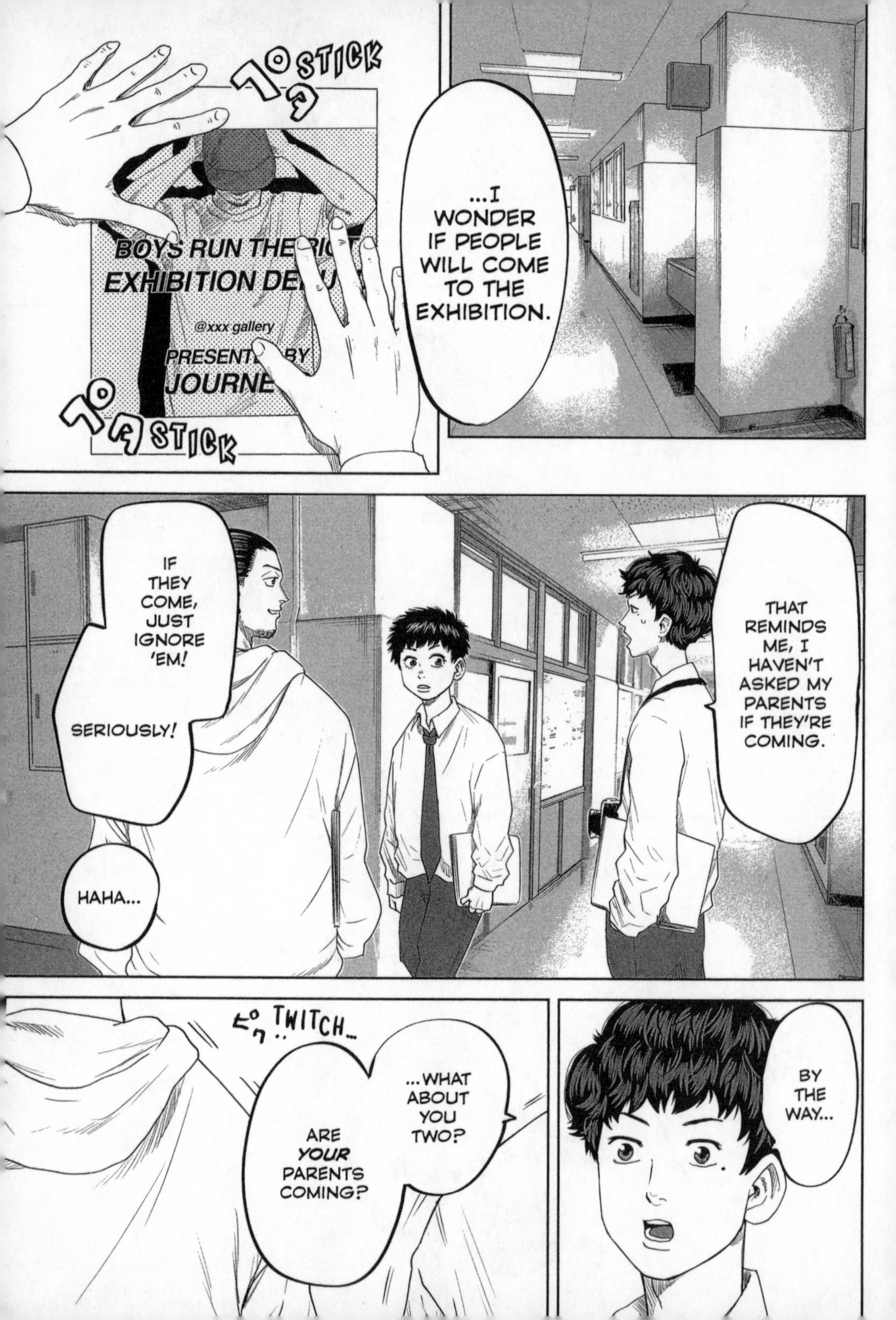
...I WONDER IF PEOPLE WILL COME TO THE EXHIBITION.
STICK
@xxx gallery
STICK
THAT REMINDS ME, I HAVEN'T ASKED MY PARENTS IF THEY'RE COMING.
IF THEY COME, JUST IGNORE 'EM!
SERIOUSLY!
HAHA...
BY THE WAY...
TWITCH...
...WHAT ABOUT YOU TWO?
ARE *YOUR* PARENTS COMING?

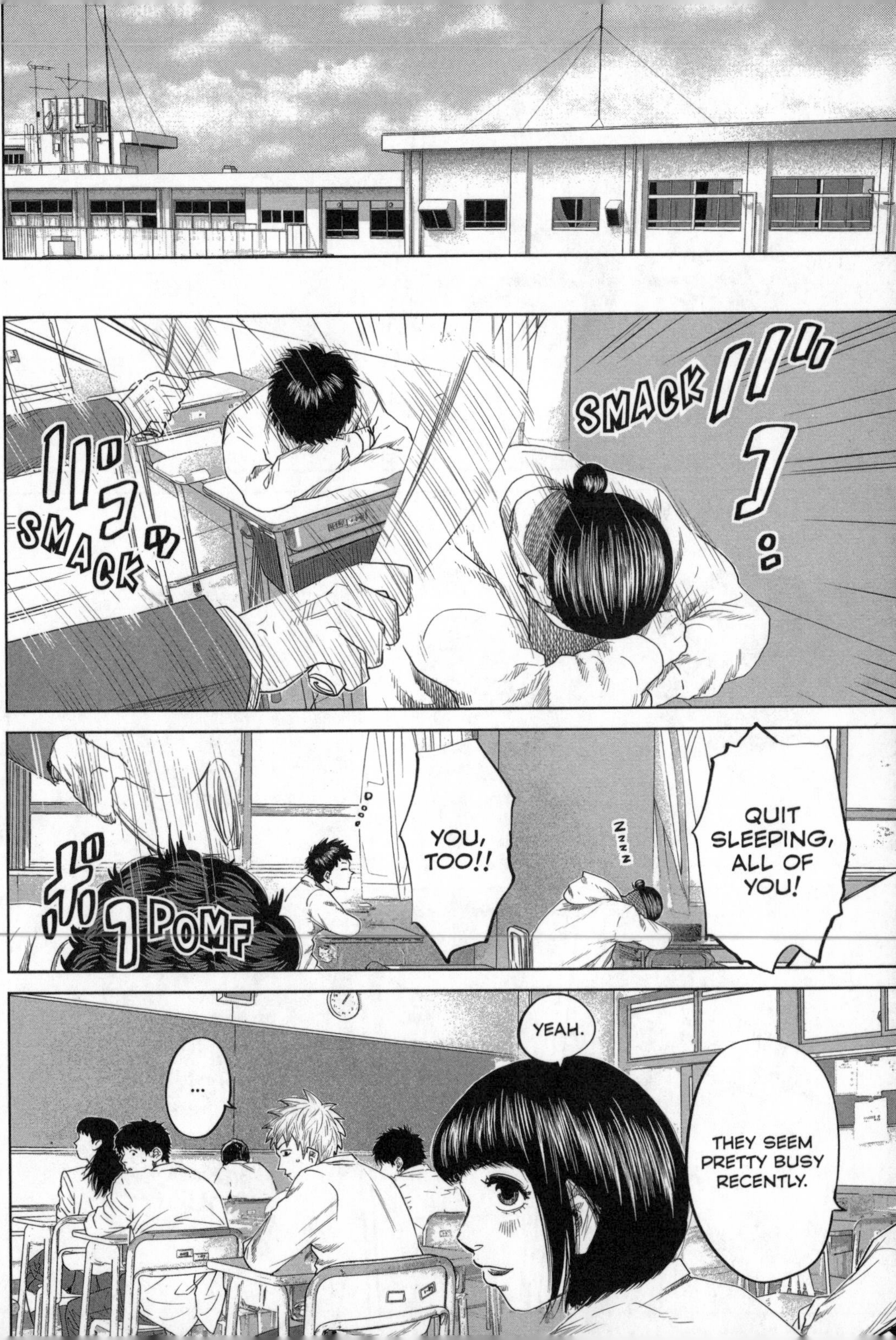
SMACK
SMACK
QUIT SLEEPING, ALL OF YOU!
ZZZZ
YOU, TOO!!
POMF
THEY SEEM PRETTY BUSY RECENTLY.
YEAH.
...

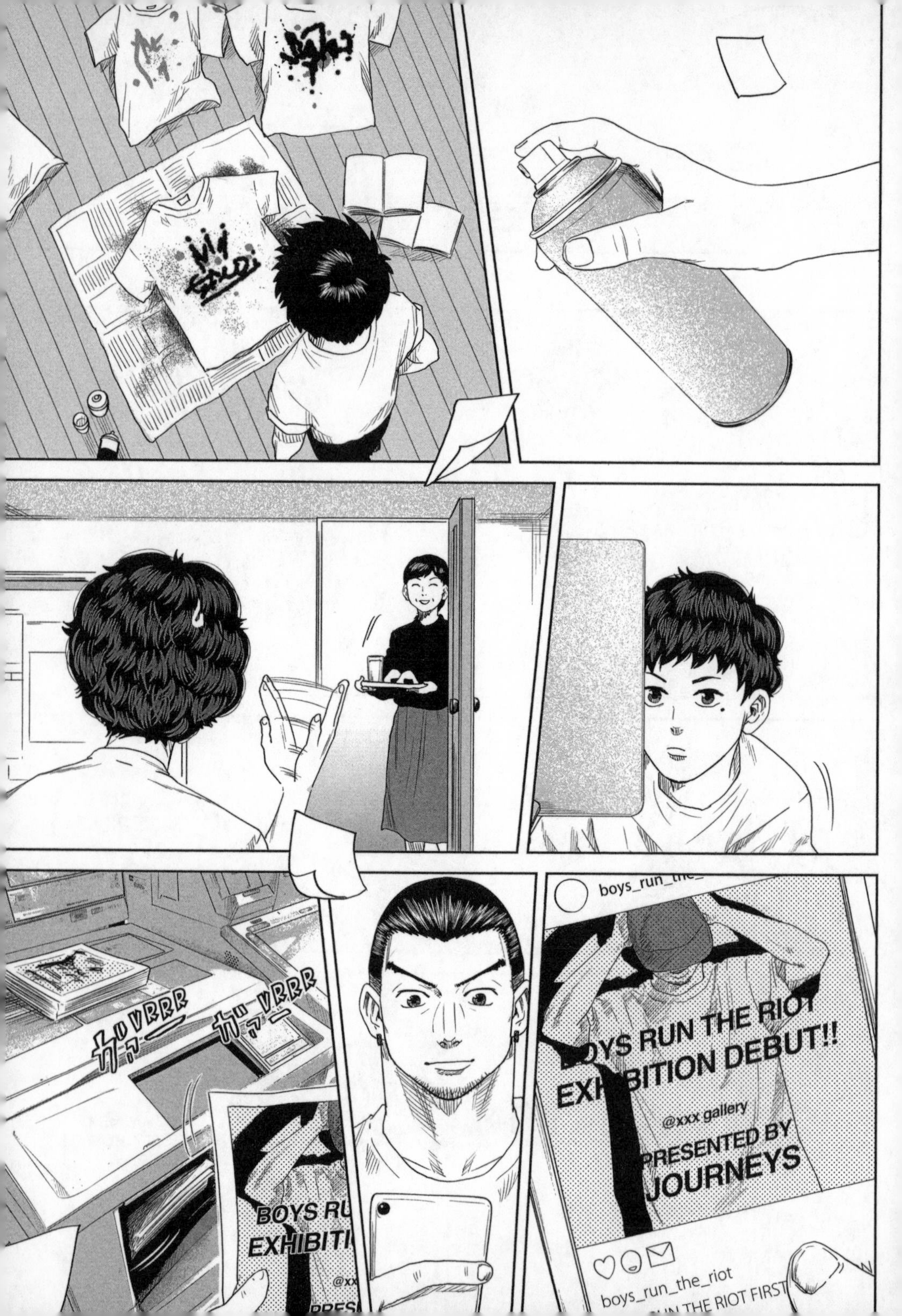
boys_run_the_
BOYS RUN THE RIOT
EXHIBITION DEBUT!!
@xxx gallery
PRESENTED BY
JOURNEYS
boys_run_the_riot
UN THE RIOT FIRST
BOYS RU
EXHIBITI
ガァー VRRR
ガァー VRRR

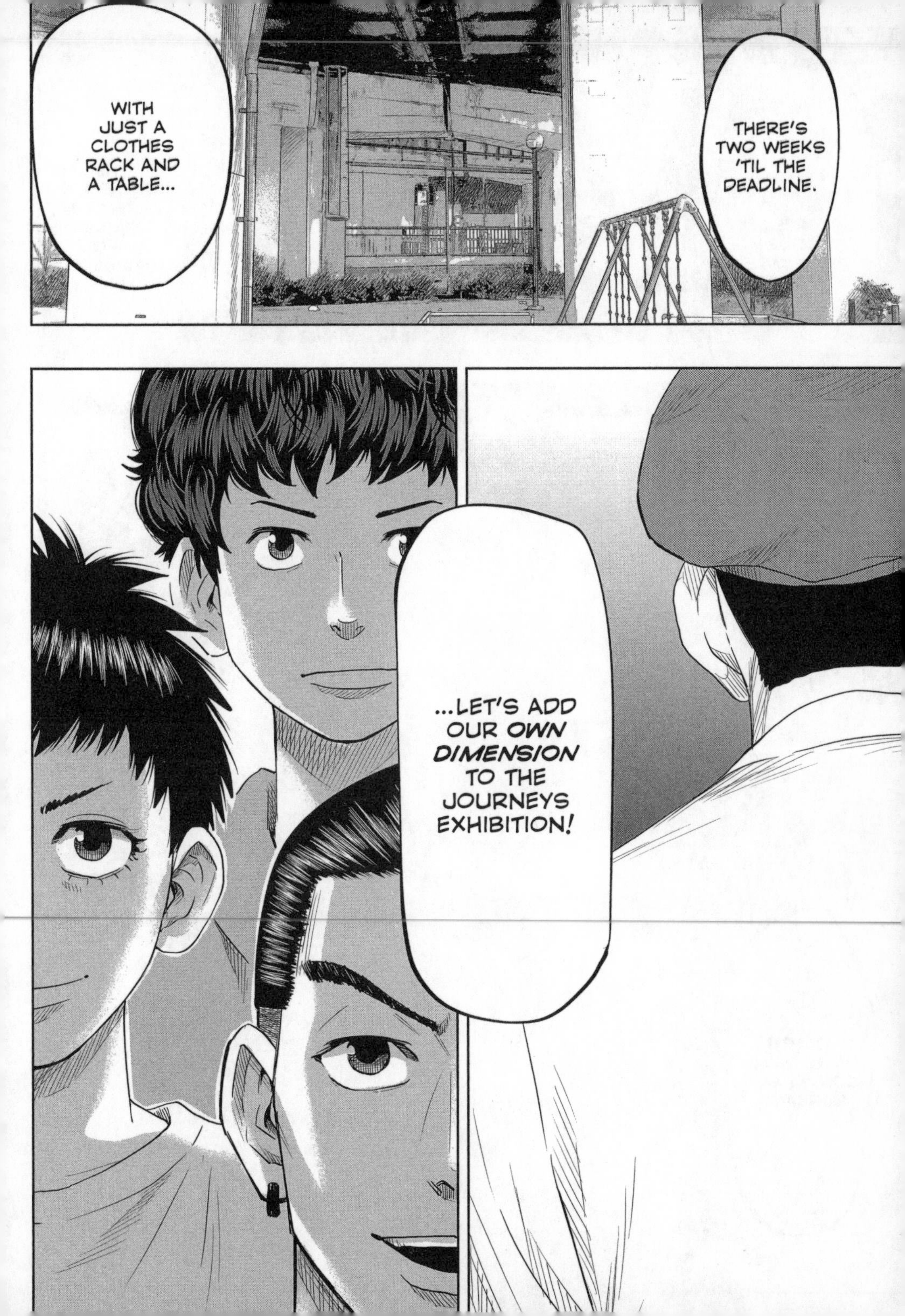
THERE'S TWO WEEKS 'TIL THE DEADLINE.
WITH JUST A CLOTHES RACK AND A TABLE...
...LET'S ADD OUR *OWN DIMENSION* TO THE JOURNEYS EXHIBITION!

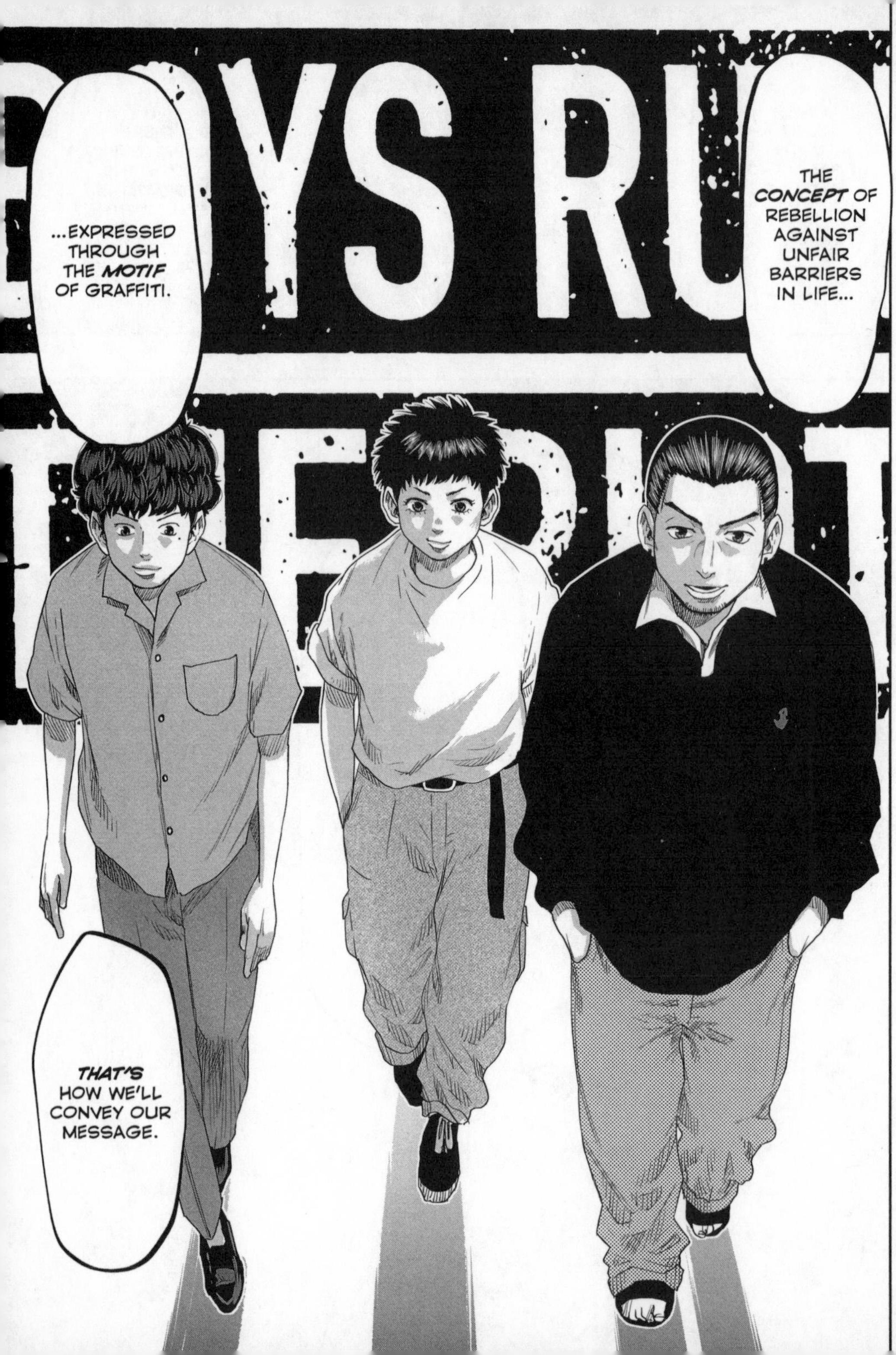
THE CONCEPT OF REBELLION AGAINST UNFAIR BARRIERS IN LIFE...
...EXPRESSED THROUGH THE MOTIF OF GRAFFITI.
THAT'S HOW WE'LL CONVEY OUR MESSAGE.

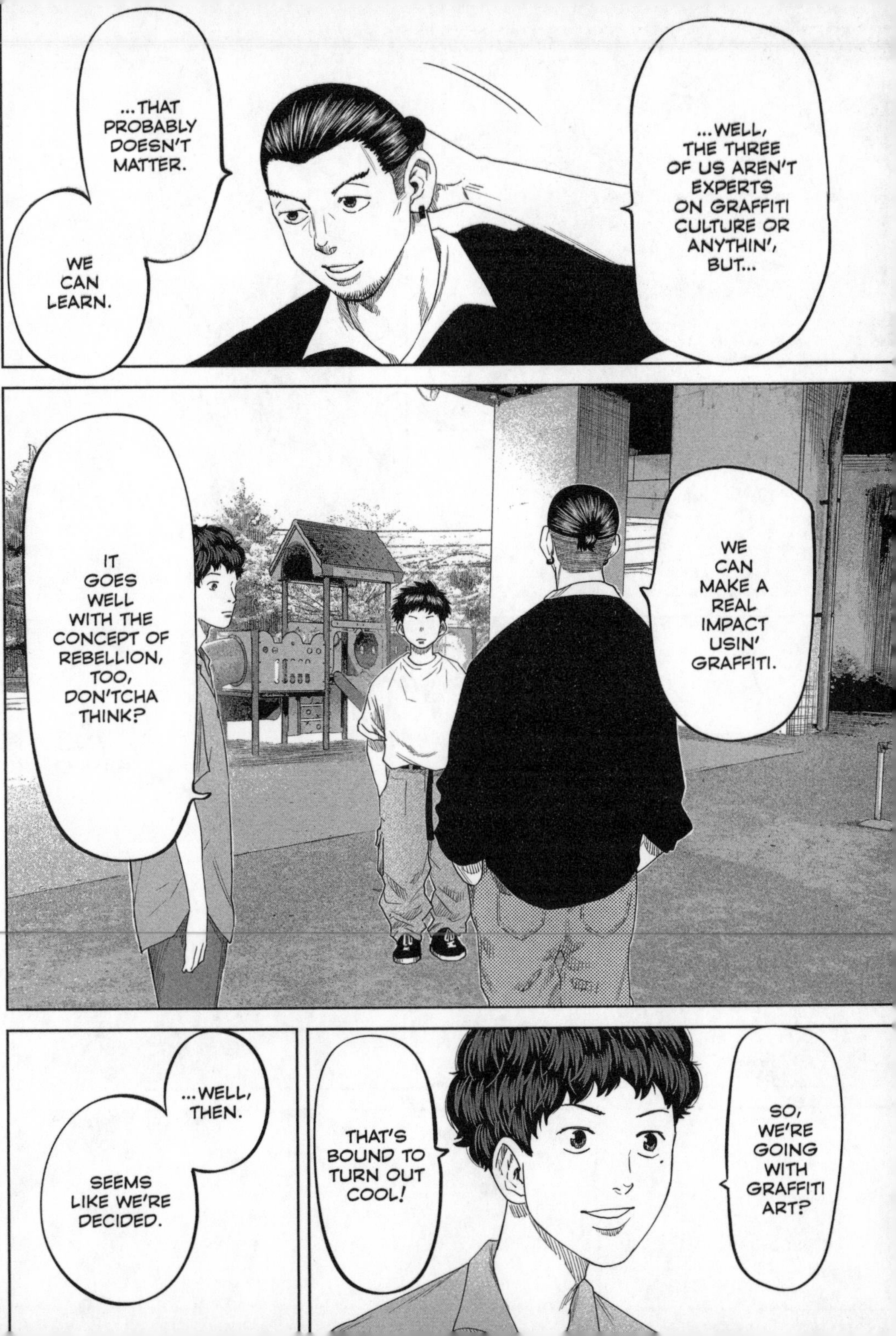
...WELL, THE THREE OF US AREN'T EXPERTS ON GRAFFITI CULTURE OR ANYTHIN', BUT...
...THAT PROBABLY DOESN'T MATTER.
WE CAN LEARN.
WE CAN MAKE A REAL IMPACT USIN' GRAFFITI.
IT GOES WELL WITH THE CONCEPT OF REBELLION, TOO, DON'TCHA THINK?
SO, WE'RE GOING WITH GRAFFITI ART?
THAT'S BOUND TO TURN OUT COOL!
...WELL, THEN.
SEEMS LIKE WE'RE DECIDED.

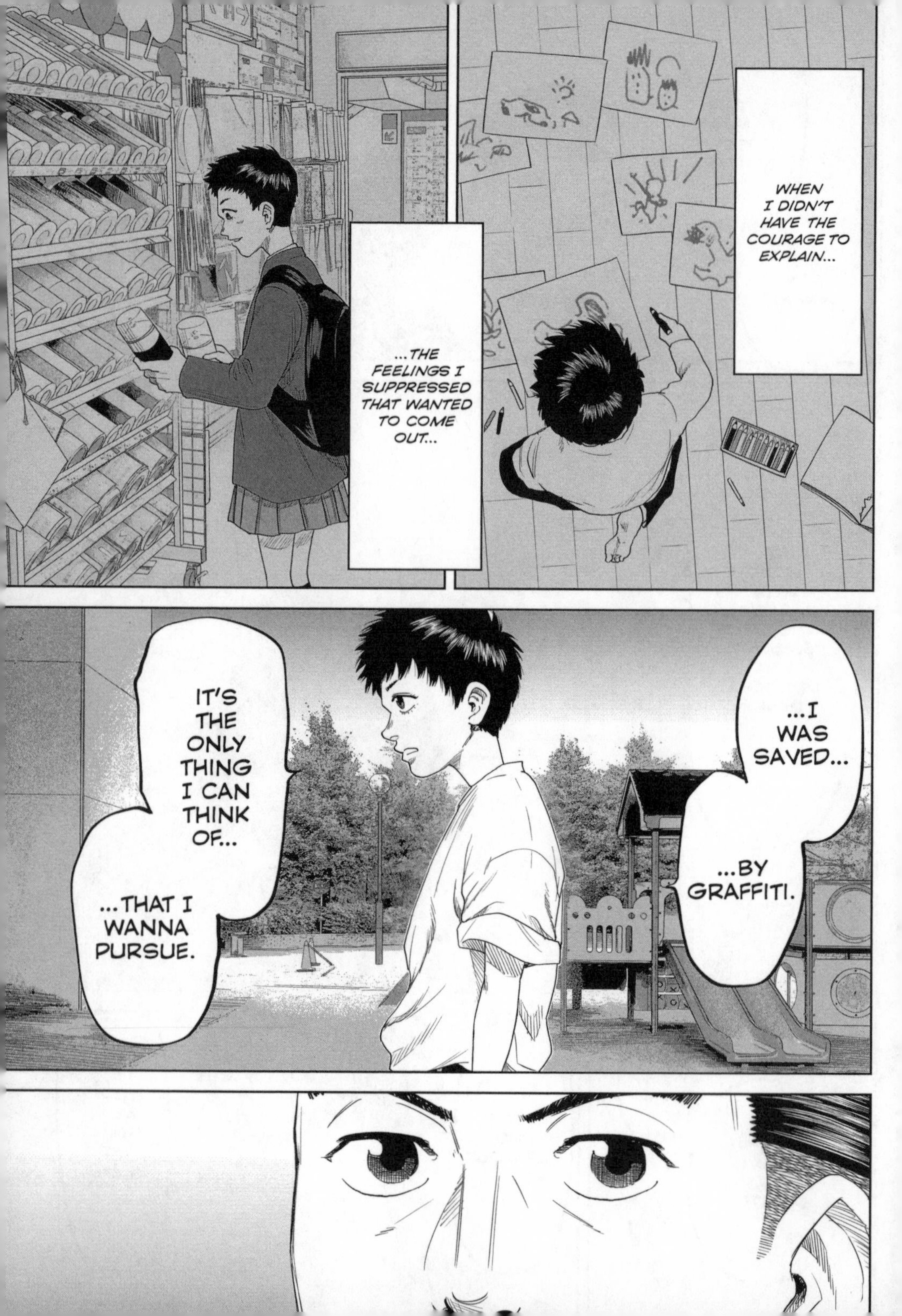
WHEN I DIDN'T HAVE THE COURAGE TO EXPLAIN...
...THE FEELINGS I SUPPRESSED THAT WANTED TO COME OUT...
...I WAS SAVED...
...BY GRAFFITI.
IT'S THE ONLY THING I CAN THINK OF...
...THAT I WANNA PURSUE.

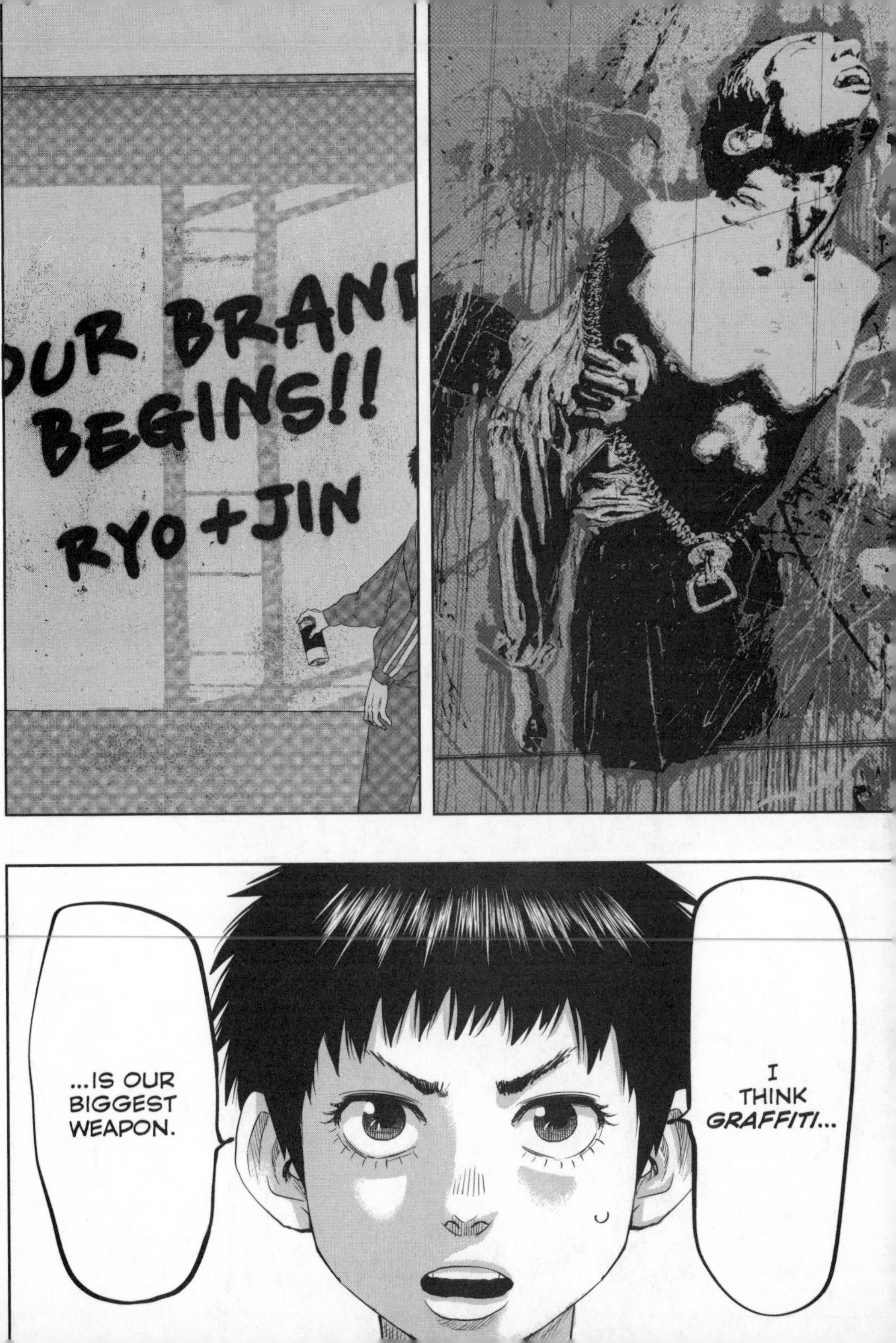
OUR BRAND BEGINS!! RYO+JIN
I THINK *GRAFFITI*...
...IS OUR BIGGEST WEAPON.

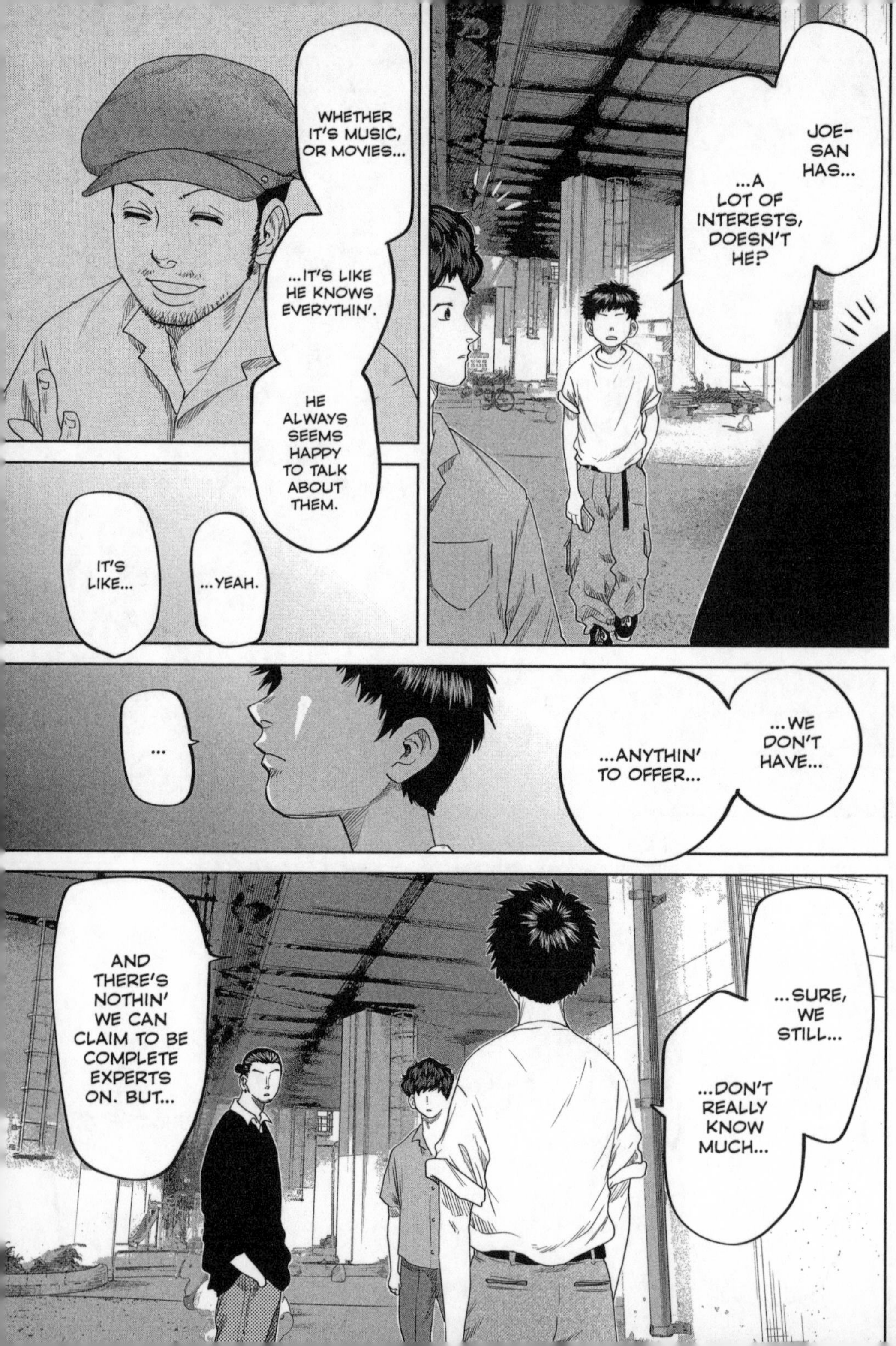
JOE-SAN HAS...
...A LOT OF INTERESTS, DOESN'T HE?
WHETHER IT'S MUSIC, OR MOVIES...
...IT'S LIKE HE KNOWS EVERYTHIN'.
HE ALWAYS SEEMS HAPPY TO TALK ABOUT THEM.
...YEAH.
IT'S LIKE...
...WE DON'T HAVE...
...ANYTHIN' TO OFFER...
...
...SURE, WE STILL...
...DON'T REALLY KNOW MUCH...
AND THERE'S NOTHIN' WE CAN CLAIM TO BE COMPLETE EXPERTS ON. BUT...

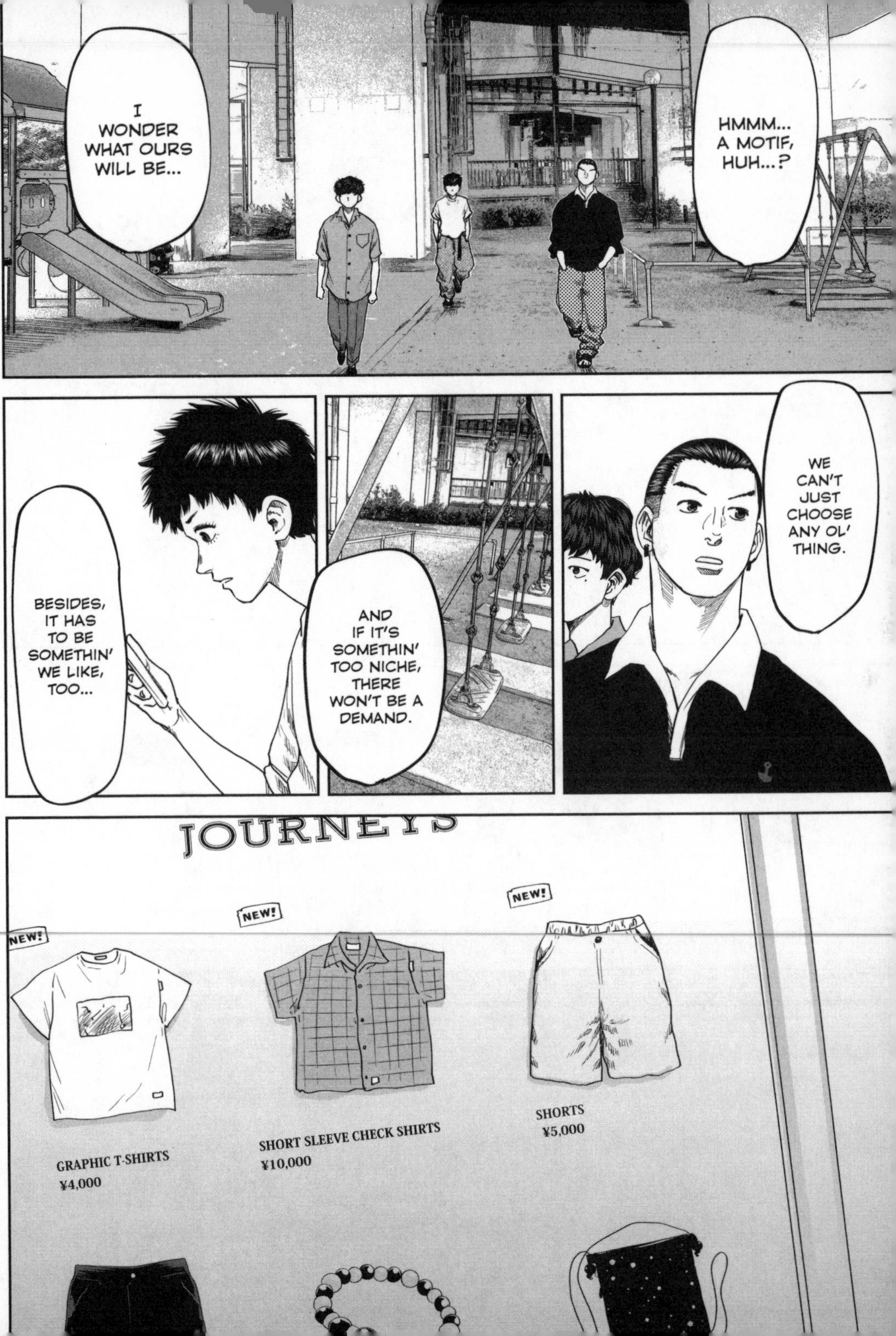
HMMM... A MOTIF, HUH...?
I WONDER WHAT OURS WILL BE...
WE CAN'T JUST CHOOSE ANY OL' THING.
AND IF IT'S SOMETHIN' TOO NICHE, THERE WON'T BE A DEMAND.
BESIDES, IT HAS TO BE SOMETHIN' WE LIKE, TOO...
JOURNEYS
NEW!
NEW!
NEW!
SHORTS
¥5,000
SHORT SLEEVE CHECK SHIRTS
¥10,000
GRAPHIC T-SHIRTS
¥4,000

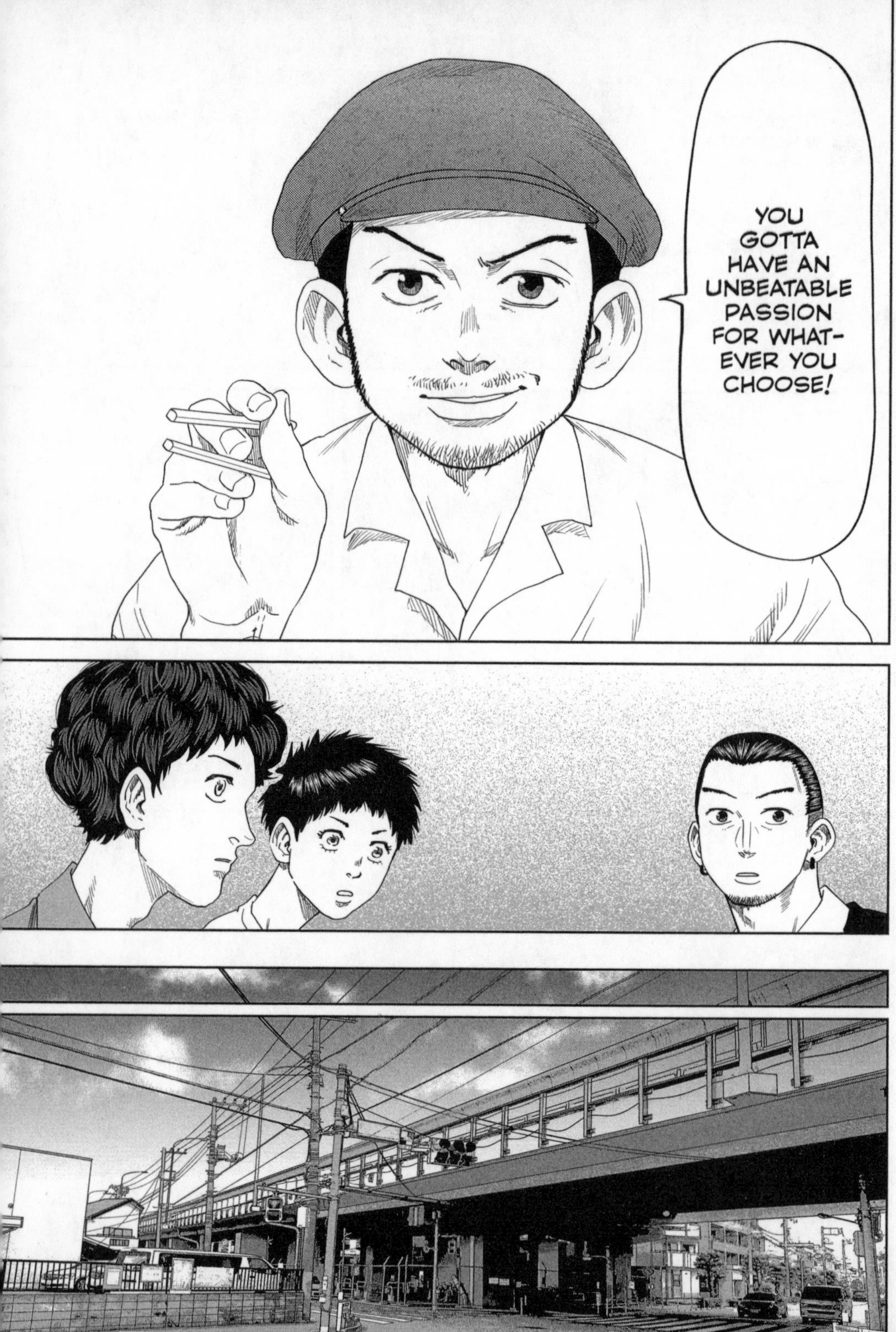
YOU GOTTA HAVE AN UNBEATABLE PASSION FOR WHAT-EVER YOU CHOOSE!

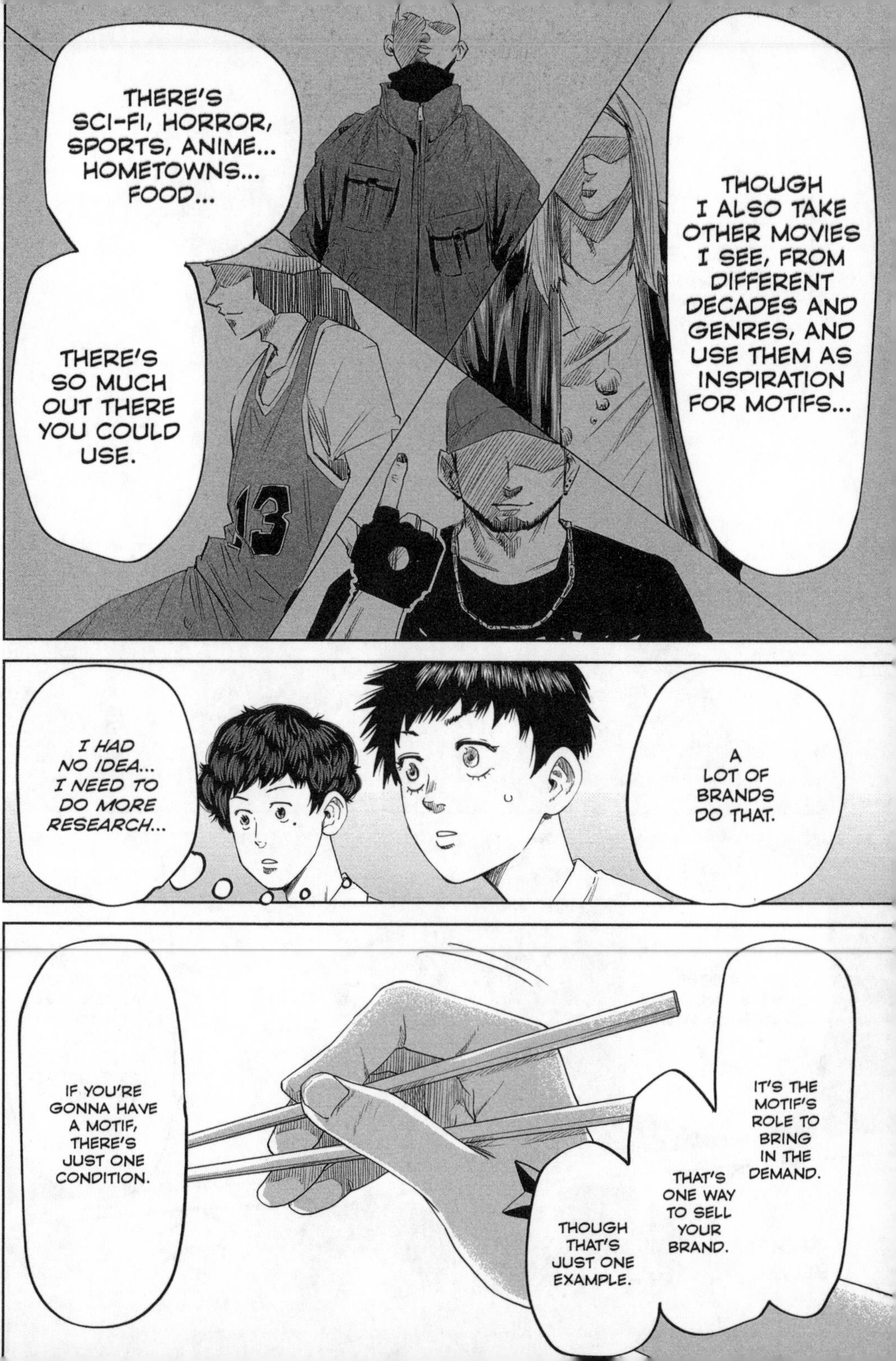
THOUGH I ALSO TAKE OTHER MOVIES I SEE, FROM DIFFERENT DECADES AND GENRES, AND USE THEM AS INSPIRATION FOR MOTIFS...
THERE'S SCI-FI, HORROR, SPORTS, ANIME... HOMETOWNS... FOOD...
THERE'S SO MUCH OUT THERE YOU COULD USE.
13
A LOT OF BRANDS DO THAT.
I HAD NO IDEA... I NEED TO DO MORE RESEARCH...
IT'S THE MOTIF'S ROLE TO BRING IN THE DEMAND.
THAT'S ONE WAY TO SELL YOUR BRAND.
THOUGH THAT'S JUST ONE EXAMPLE.
IF YOU'RE GONNA HAVE A MOTIF, THERE'S JUST ONE CONDITION.

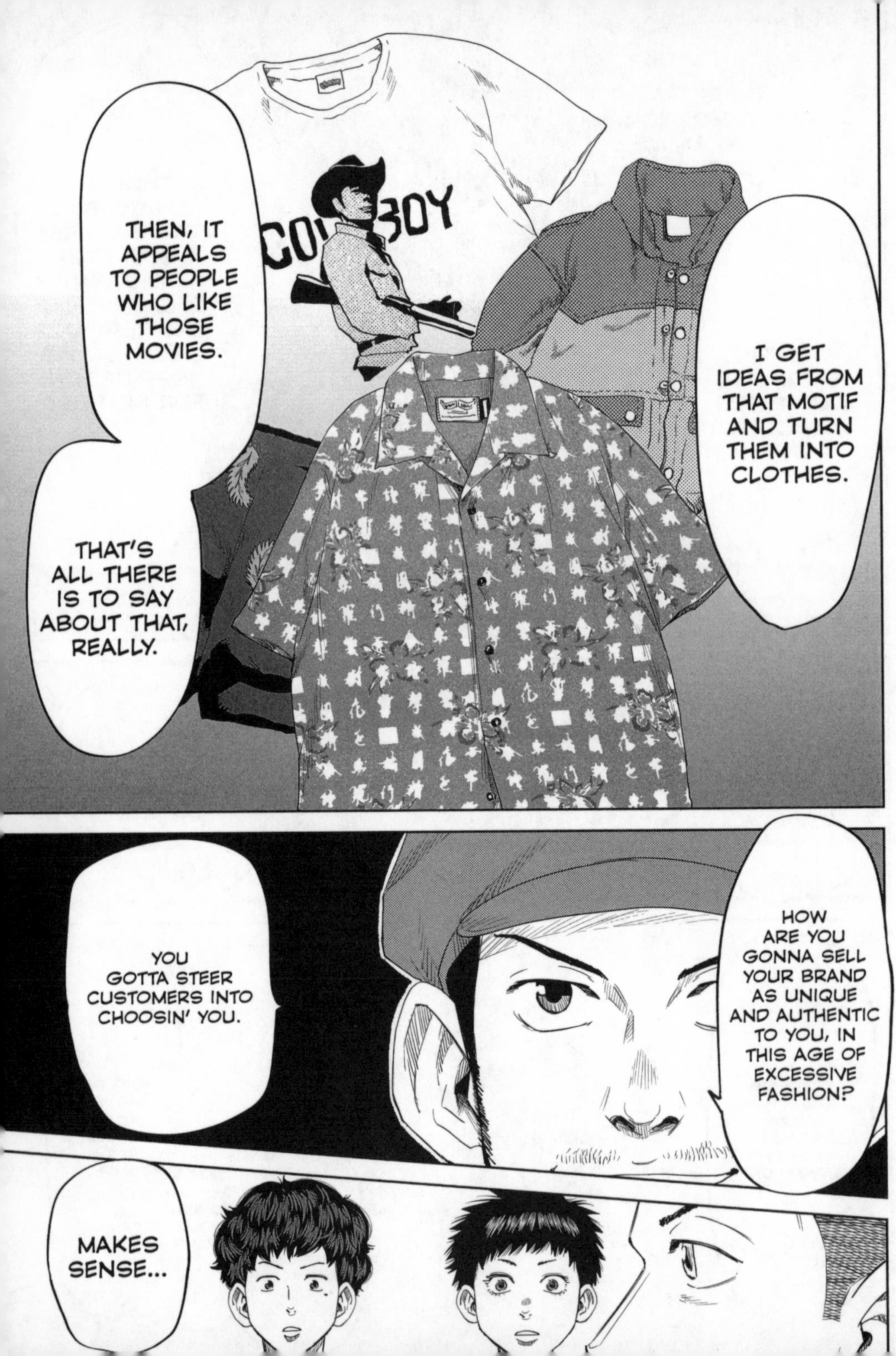
I GET IDEAS FROM THAT MOTIF AND TURN THEM INTO CLOTHES.
THEN, IT APPEALS TO PEOPLE WHO LIKE THOSE MOVIES.
THAT'S ALL THERE IS TO SAY ABOUT THAT, REALLY.
HOW ARE YOU GONNA SELL YOUR BRAND AS UNIQUE AND AUTHENTIC TO YOU, IN THIS AGE OF EXCESSIVE FASHION?
YOU GOTTA STEER CUSTOMERS INTO CHOOSIN' YOU.
MAKES SENSE...

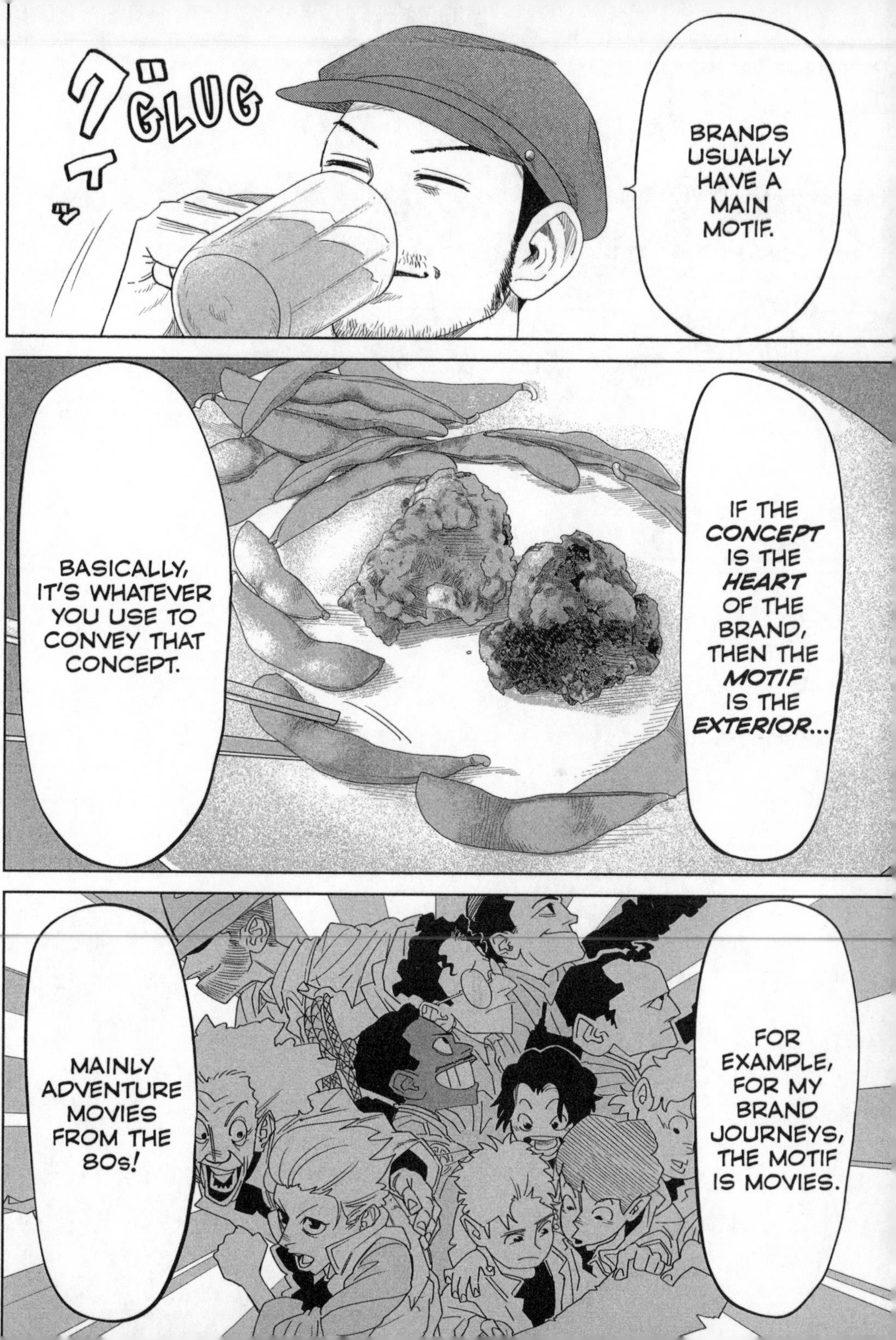
GLUG
BRANDS USUALLY HAVE A MAIN MOTIF.
IF THE CONCEPT IS THE HEART OF THE BRAND, THEN THE MOTIF IS THE EXTERIOR...
BASICALLY, IT'S WHATEVER YOU USE TO CONVEY THAT CONCEPT.
FOR EXAMPLE, FOR MY BRAND JOURNEYS, THE MOTIF IS MOVIES.
MAINLY ADVENTURE MOVIES FROM THE 80s!

Chap. 33 Motif

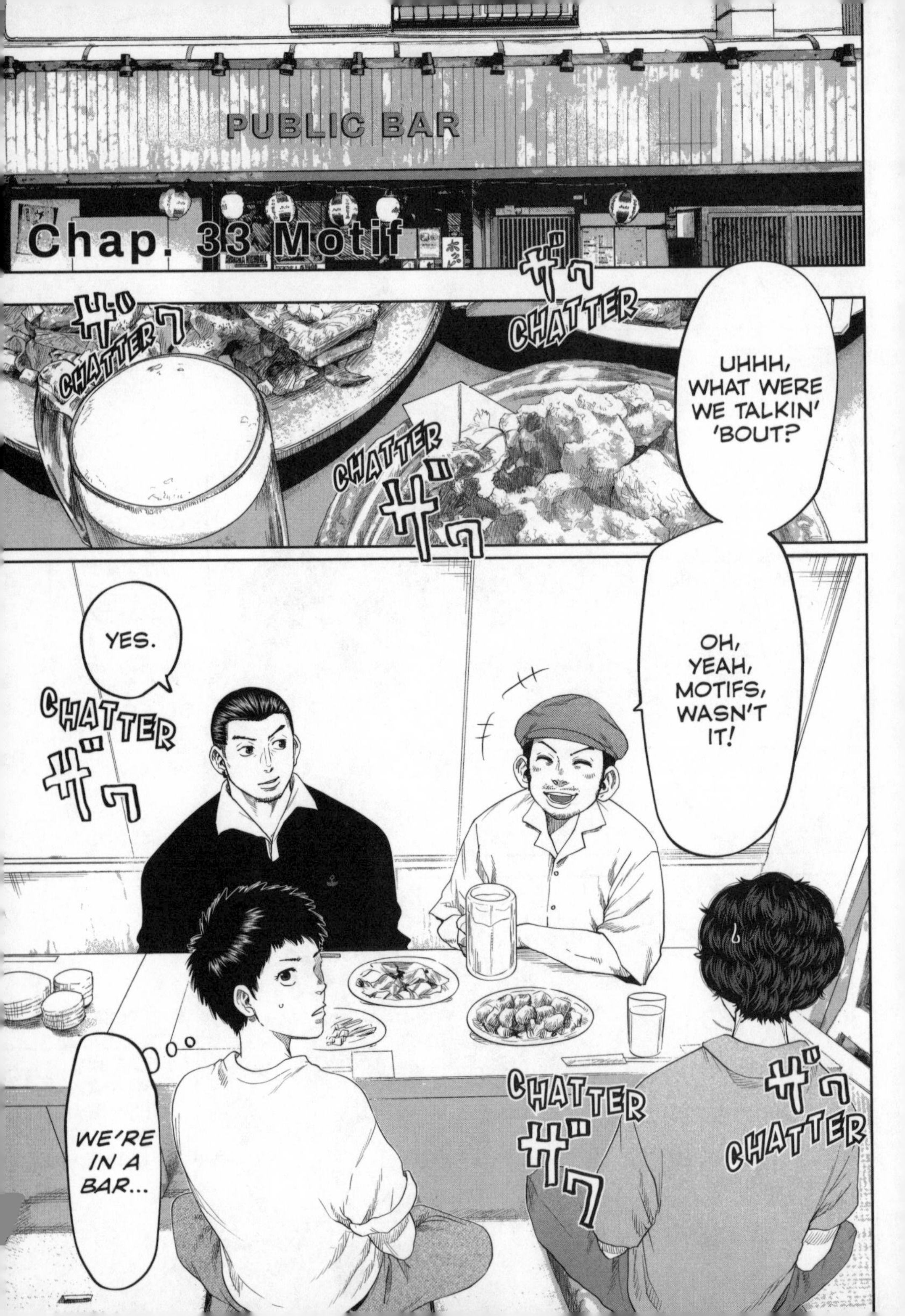
PUBLIC BAR
UHHH, WHAT WERE WE TALKIN' 'BOUT?
CHATTER
CHATTER
CHATTER
OH, YEAH, MOTIFS, WASN'T IT!
YES.
CHATTER
CHATTER
CHATTER
WE'RE IN A BAR...

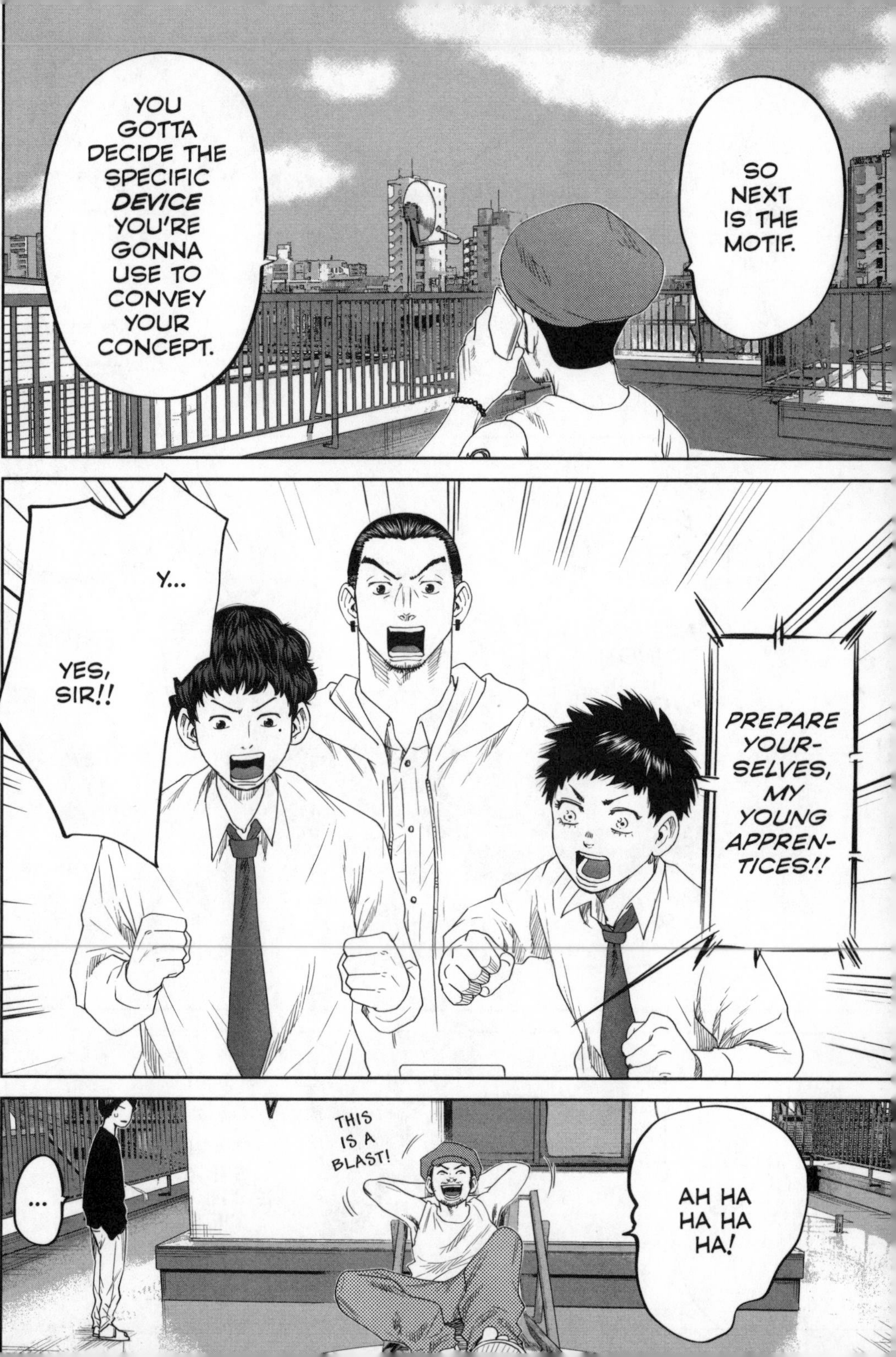
SO NEXT IS THE MOTIF.
YOU GOTTA DECIDE THE SPECIFIC *DEVICE* YOU'RE GONNA USE TO CONVEY YOUR CONCEPT.
PREPARE YOURSELVES, MY YOUNG APPRENTICES!!
Y...
YES, SIR!!
AH HA HA HA HA!
THIS IS A BLAST!
...

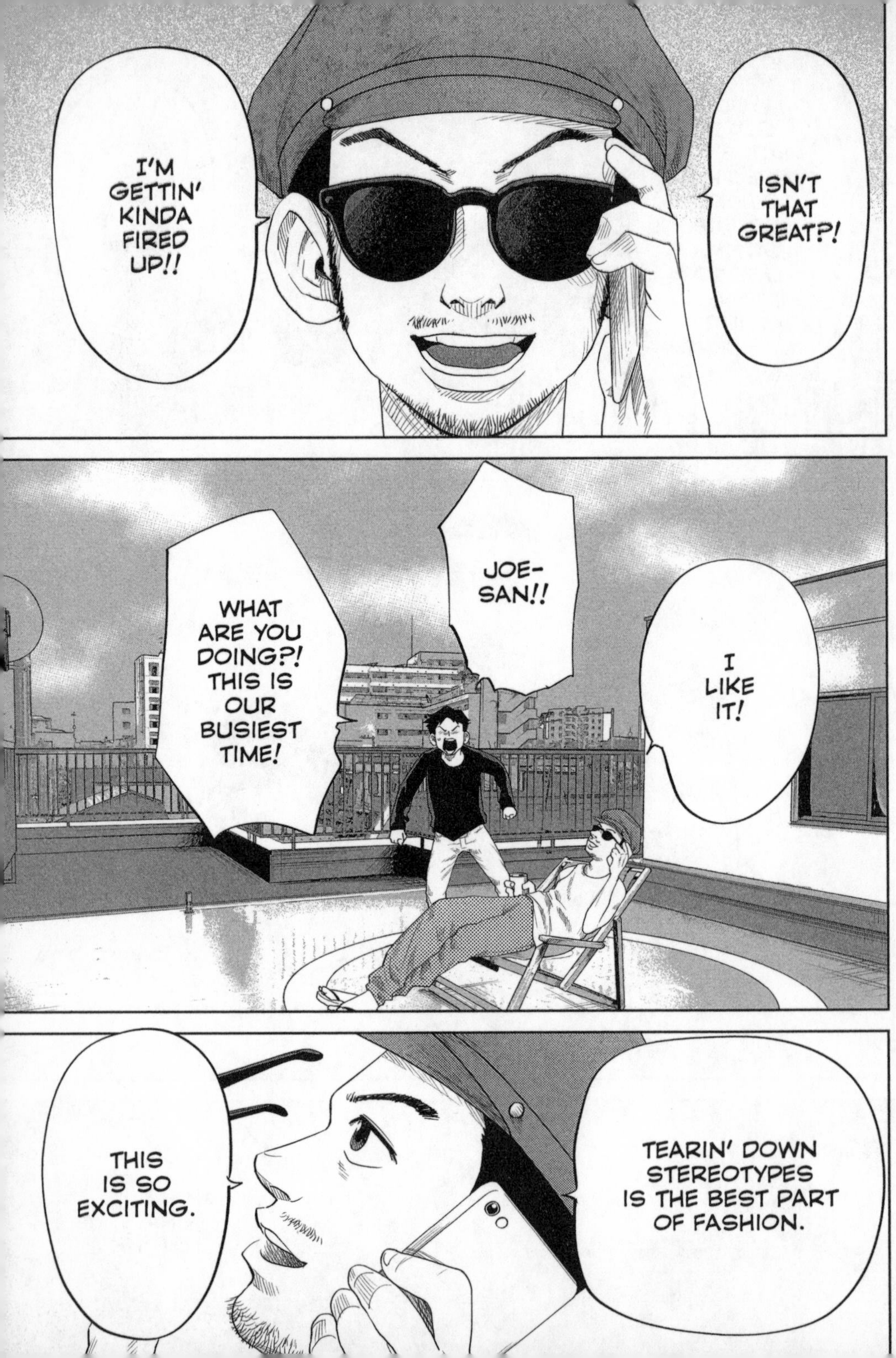
ISN'T THAT GREAT?!
I'M GETTIN' KINDA FIRED UP!!
I LIKE IT!
JOE-SAN!!
WHAT ARE YOU DOING?! THIS IS OUR BUSIEST TIME!
TEARIN' DOWN STEREOTYPES IS THE BEST PART OF FASHION.
THIS IS SO EXCITING.

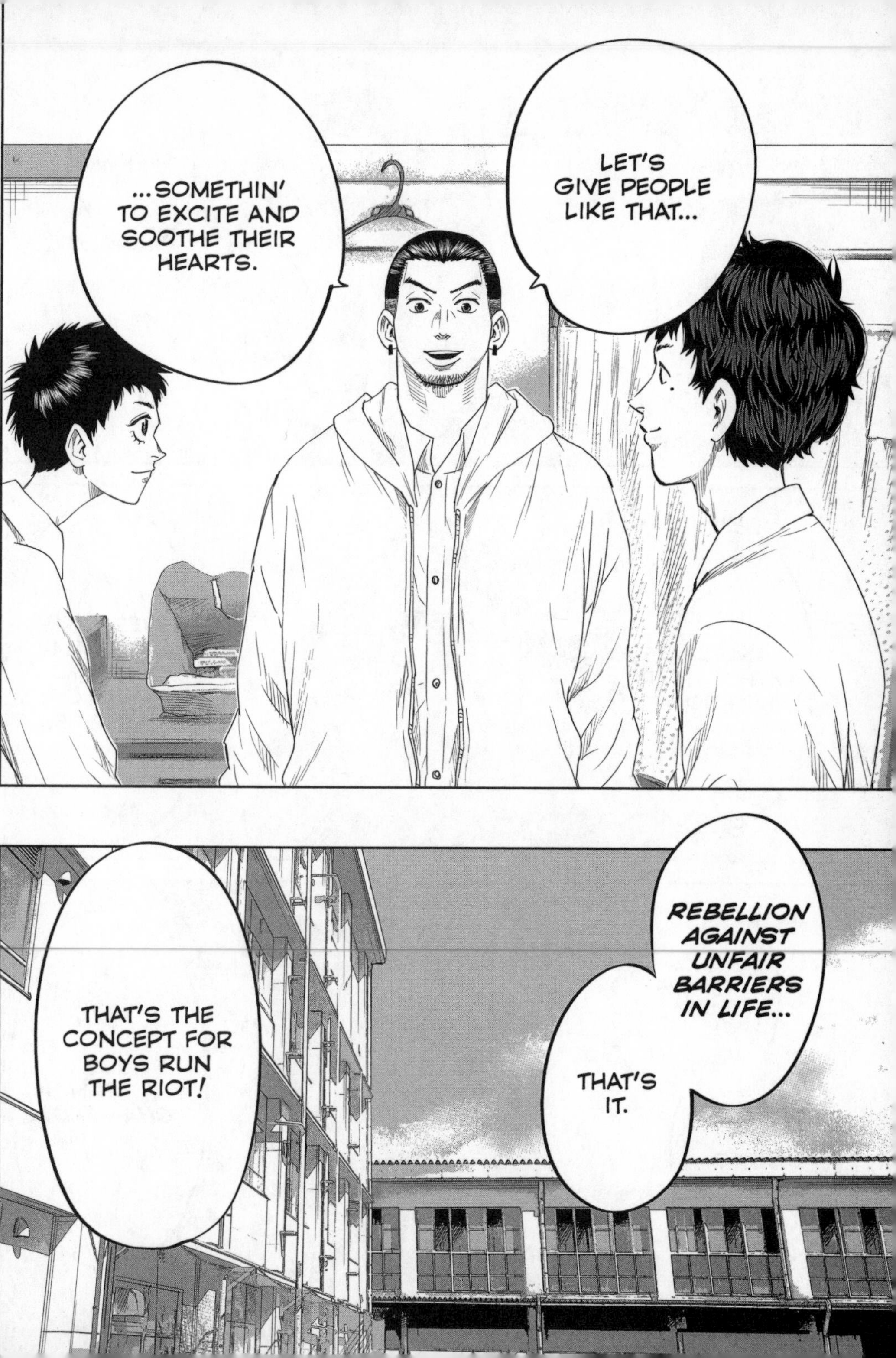
LET'S GIVE PEOPLE LIKE THAT...
...SOMETHIN' TO EXCITE AND SOOTHE THEIR HEARTS.
REBELLION AGAINST UNFAIR BARRIERS IN LIFE...
THAT'S IT.
THAT'S THE CONCEPT FOR BOYS RUN THE RIOT!

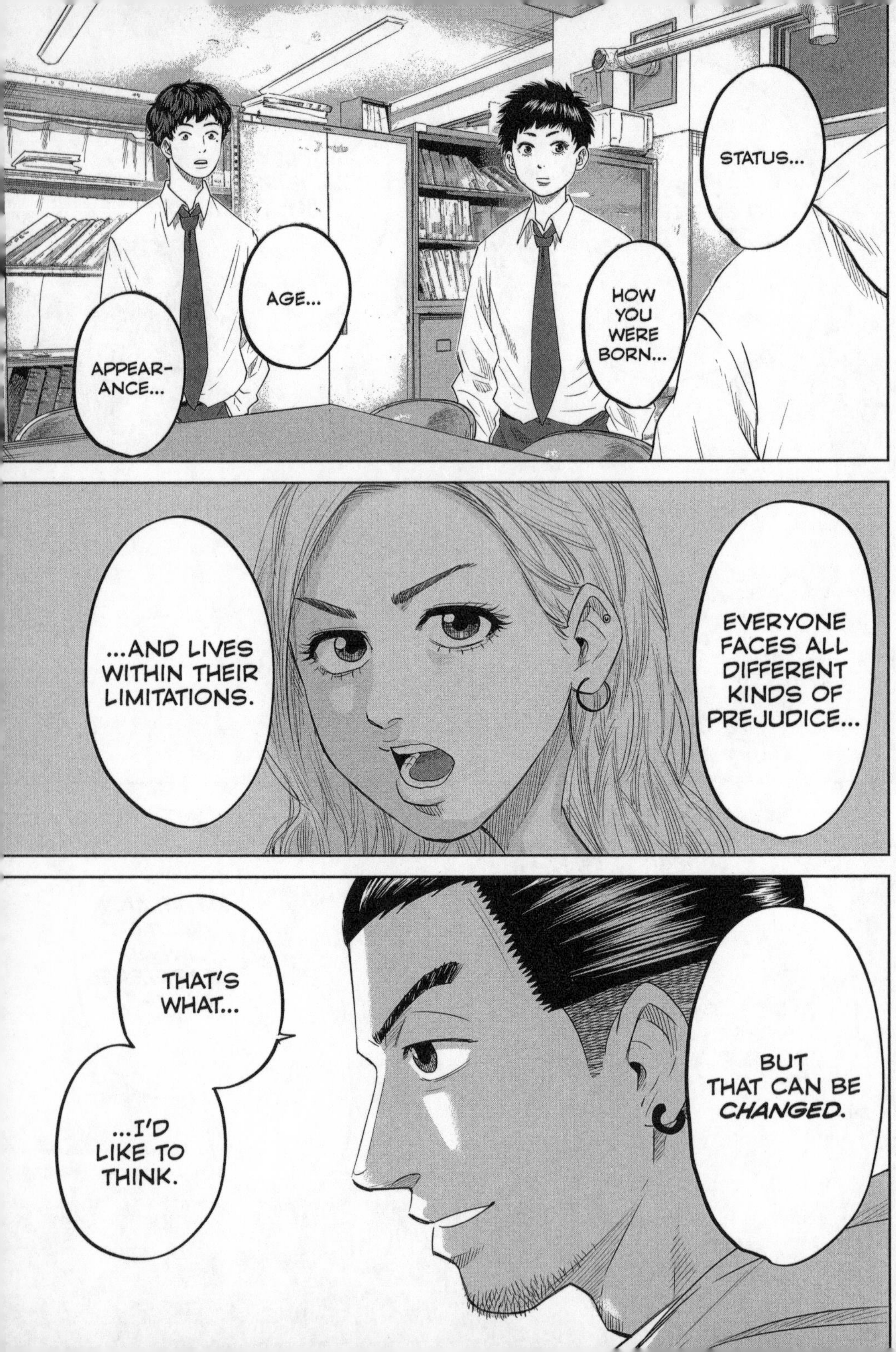
STATUS...
HOW YOU WERE BORN...
AGE...
APPEARANCE...
EVERYONE FACES ALL DIFFERENT KINDS OF PREJUDICE...
...AND LIVES WITHIN THEIR LIMITATIONS.
BUT THAT CAN BE *CHANGED*.
THAT'S WHAT...
...I'D LIKE TO THINK.

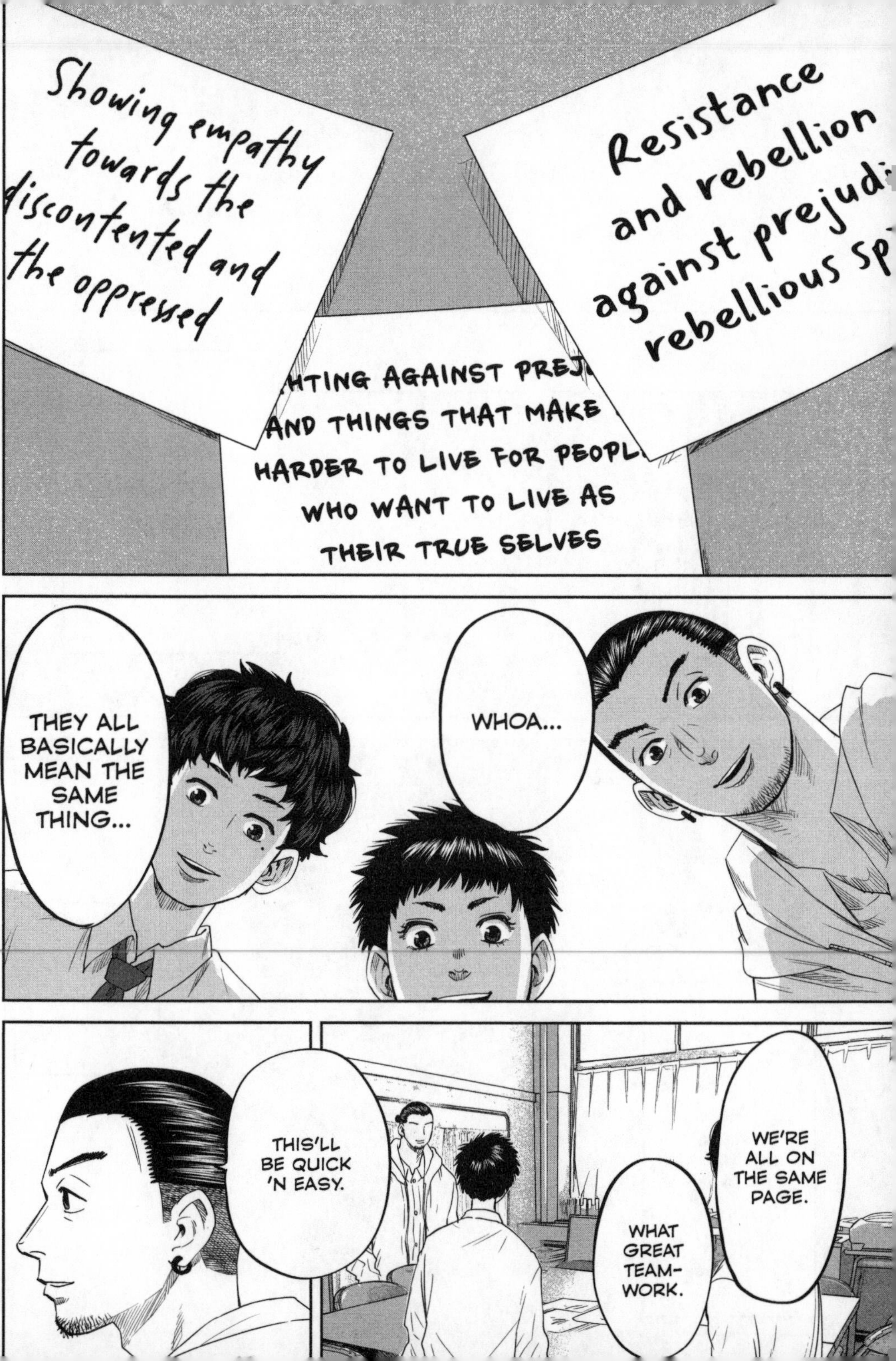
Resistance and rebellion against prejudi rebellious sp
Showing empathy towards the discontented and the oppressed
HTING AGAINST PREJ AND THINGS THAT MAKE HARDER TO LIVE FOR PEOPL WHO WANT TO LIVE AS THEIR TRUE SELVES
WHOA...
THEY ALL BASICALLY MEAN THE SAME THING...
WE'RE ALL ON THE SAME PAGE.
WHAT GREAT TEAM-WORK.
THIS'LL BE QUICK 'N EASY.

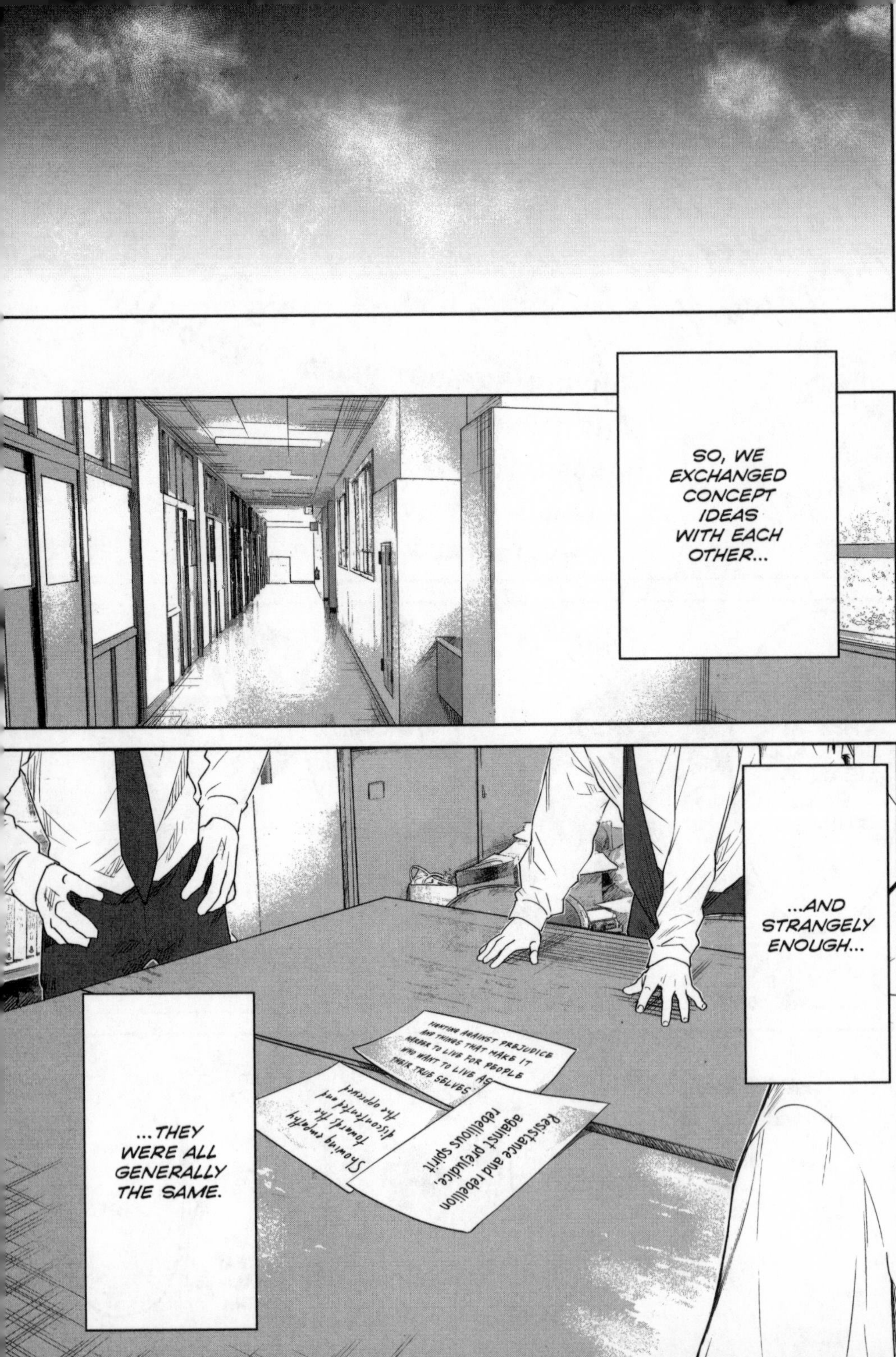
SO, WE EXCHANGED CONCEPT IDEAS WITH EACH OTHER...
...AND STRANGELY ENOUGH...
FIGHTING AGAINST PREJUDICE AND THINGS THAT MAKE IT HARDER TO LIVE FOR PEOPLE WHO WANT TO LIVE AS THEIR TRUE SELVES.
Resistance and rebellion against prejudice, rebellious spirit
Showing empathy towards the discontented and the oppressed
...THEY WERE ALL GENERALLY THE SAME.

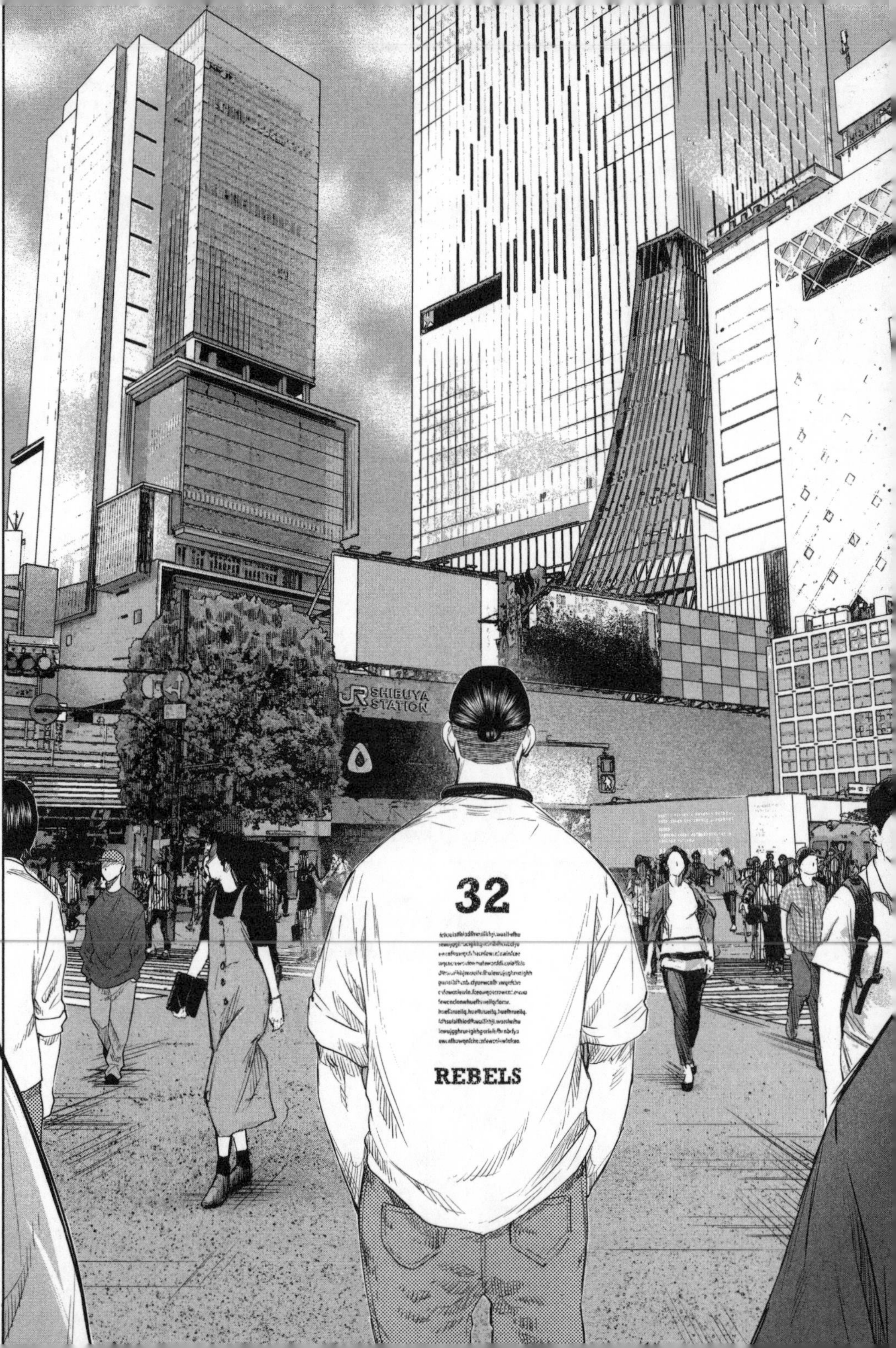
JR SHIBUYA STATION
32
REBELS

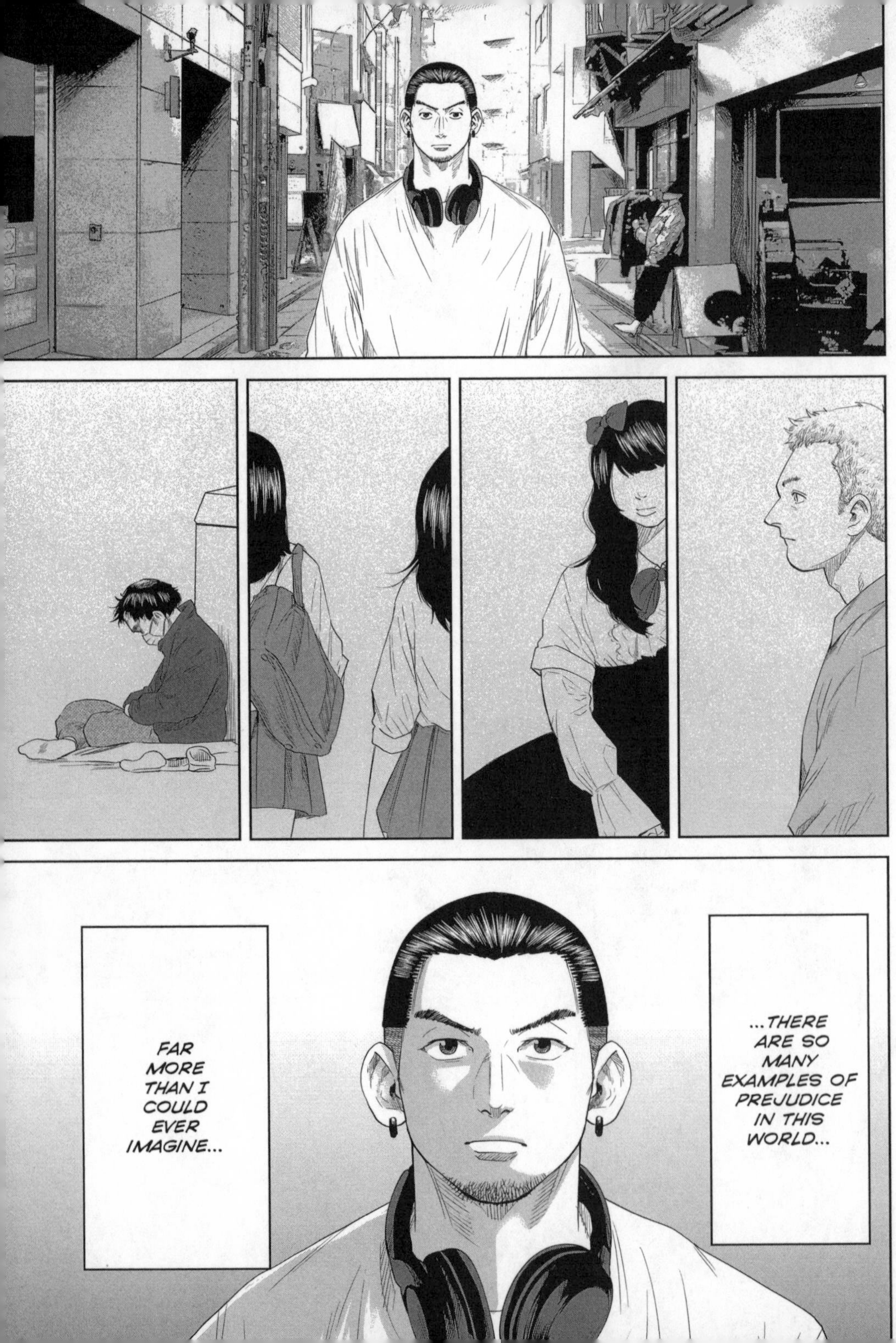
...THERE ARE SO MANY EXAMPLES OF PREJUDICE IN THIS WORLD...
FAR MORE THAN I COULD EVER IMAGINE...

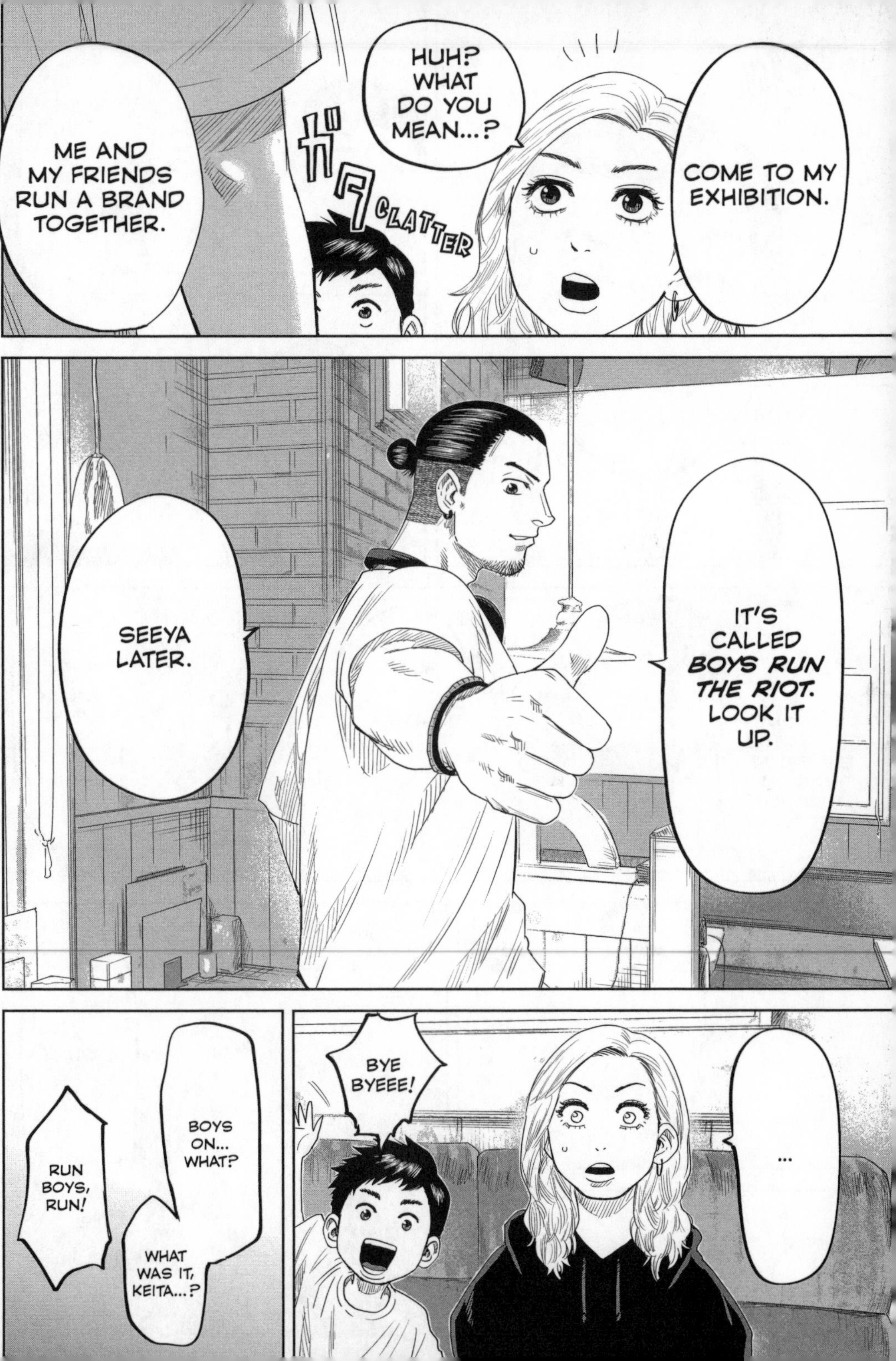
COME TO MY EXHIBITION.
HUH? WHAT DO YOU MEAN...?
ガラ CLATTER
ME AND MY FRIENDS RUN A BRAND TOGETHER.
IT'S CALLED *BOYS RUN THE RIOT*. LOOK IT UP.
SEEYA LATER.
...
BYE BYEEE!
BOYS ON... WHAT?
WHAT WAS IT, KEITA...?
RUN BOYS, RUN!

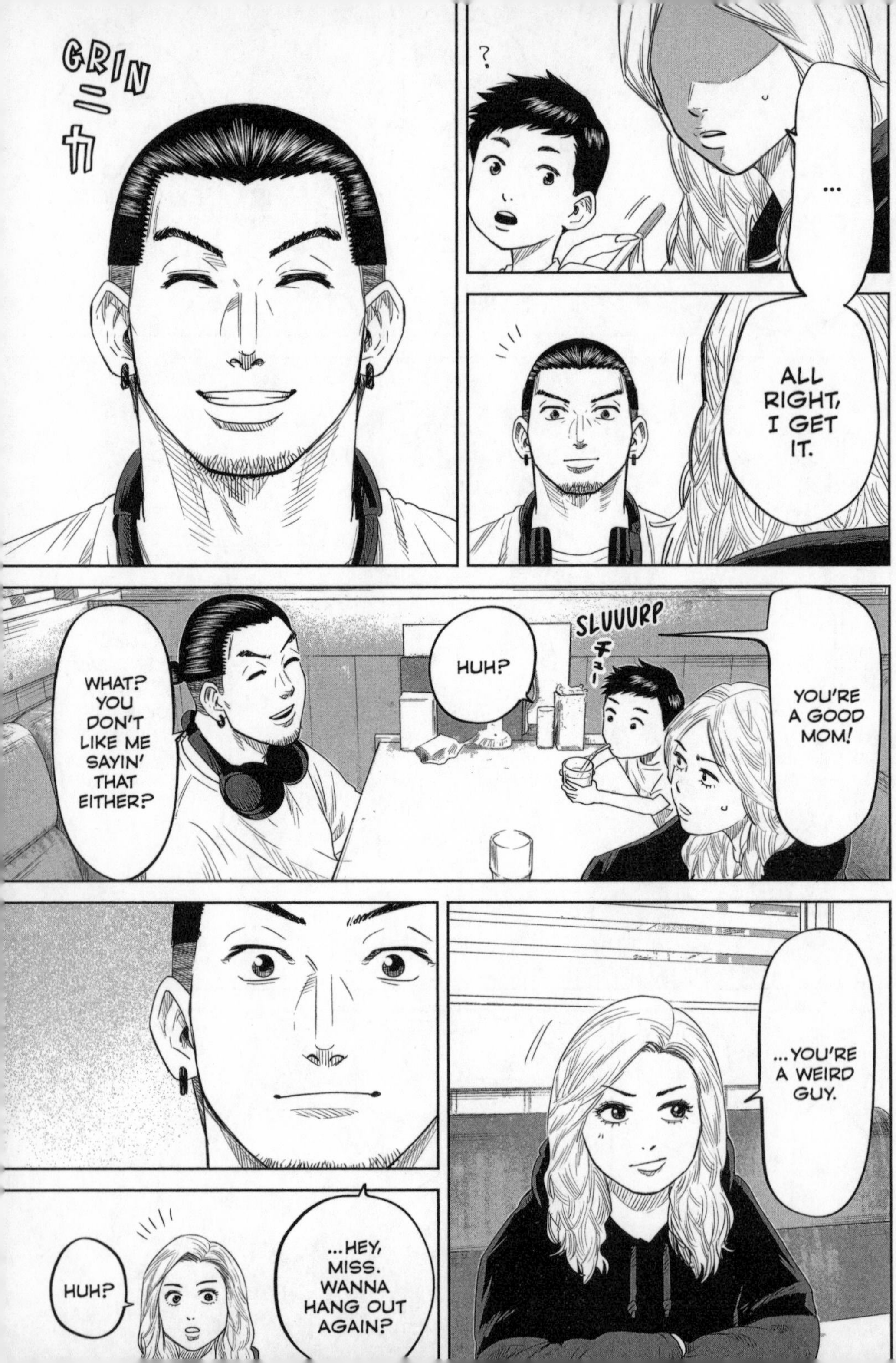
?
...
ALL RIGHT, I GET IT.
GRIN
ニカ
YOU'RE A GOOD MOM!
SLUUURP
チュー
HUH?
WHAT? YOU DON'T LIKE ME SAYIN' THAT EITHER?
...YOU'RE A WEIRD GUY.
...HEY, MISS. WANNA HANG OUT AGAIN?
HUH?

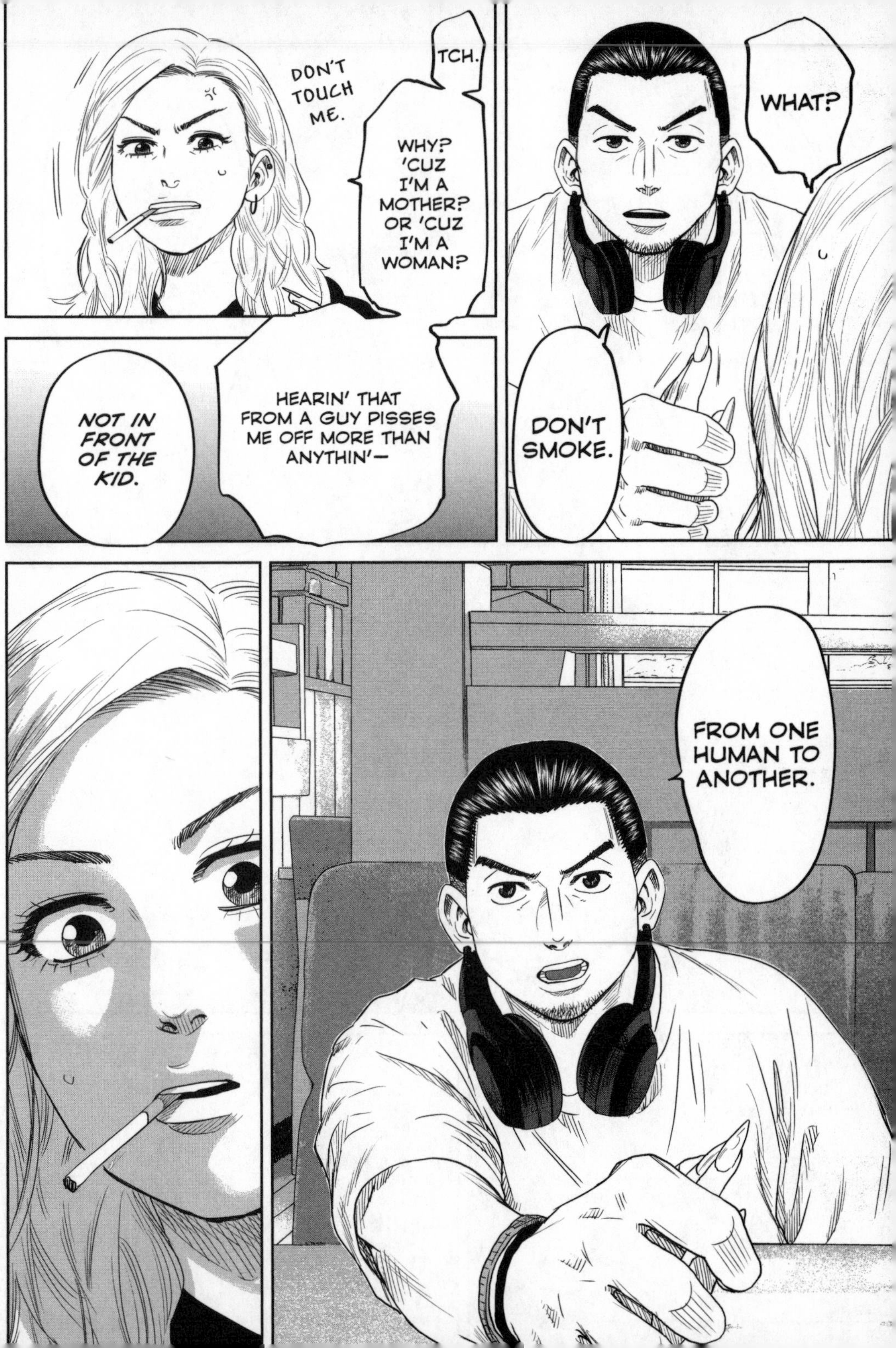
WHAT?
TCH.
DON'T TOUCH ME.
WHY? 'CUZ I'M A MOTHER? OR 'CUZ I'M A WOMAN?
DON'T SMOKE.
HEARIN' THAT FROM A GUY PISSES ME OFF MORE THAN ANYTHIN'—
NOT IN FRONT OF THE KID.
FROM ONE HUMAN TO ANOTHER.

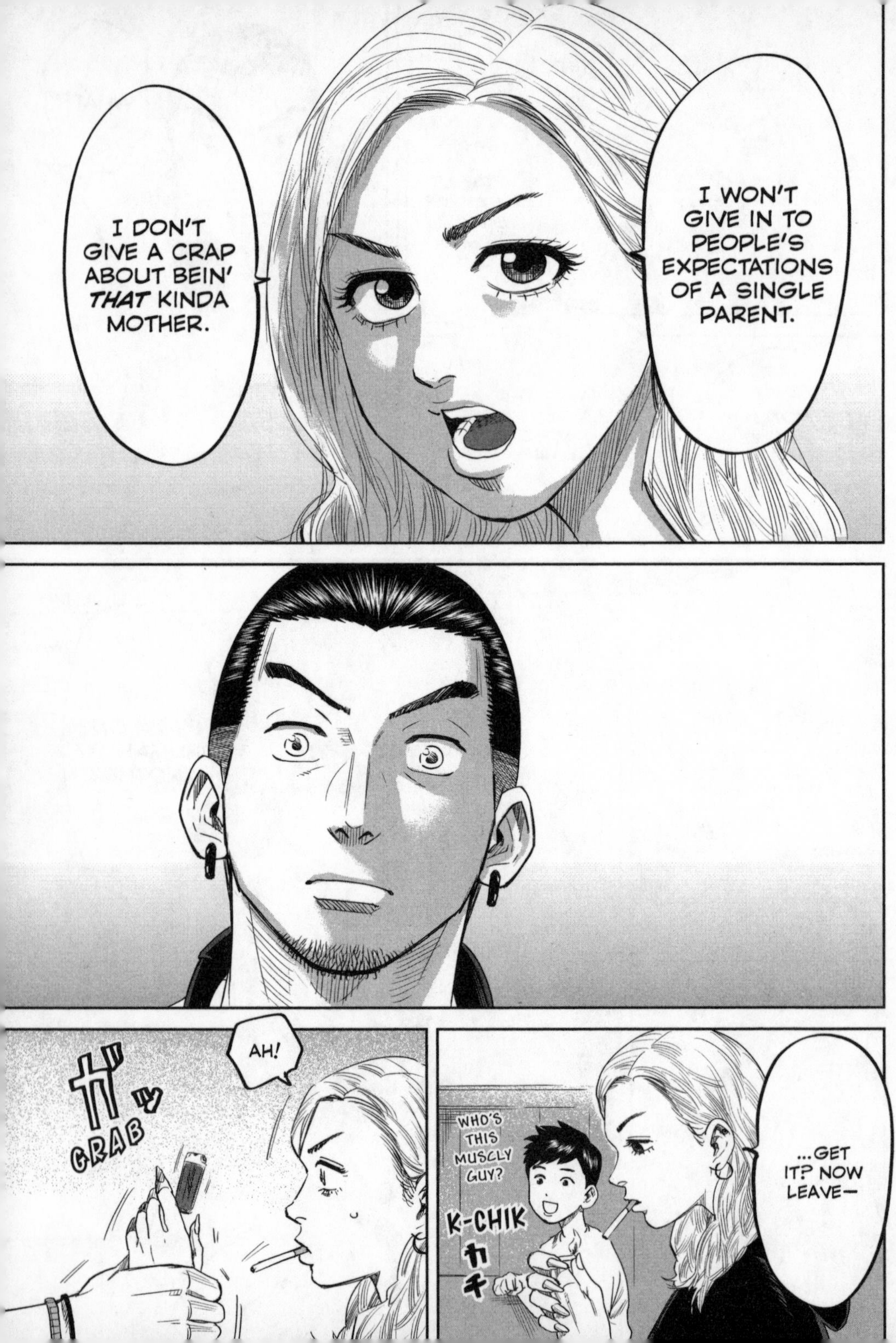
I WON'T GIVE IN TO PEOPLE'S EXPECTATIONS OF A SINGLE PARENT.
I DON'T GIVE A CRAP ABOUT BEIN' *THAT* KINDA MOTHER.
...GET IT? NOW LEAVE—
WHO'S THIS MUSCLY GUY?
K-CHIK
カチ
AH!
ガッ
GRAB

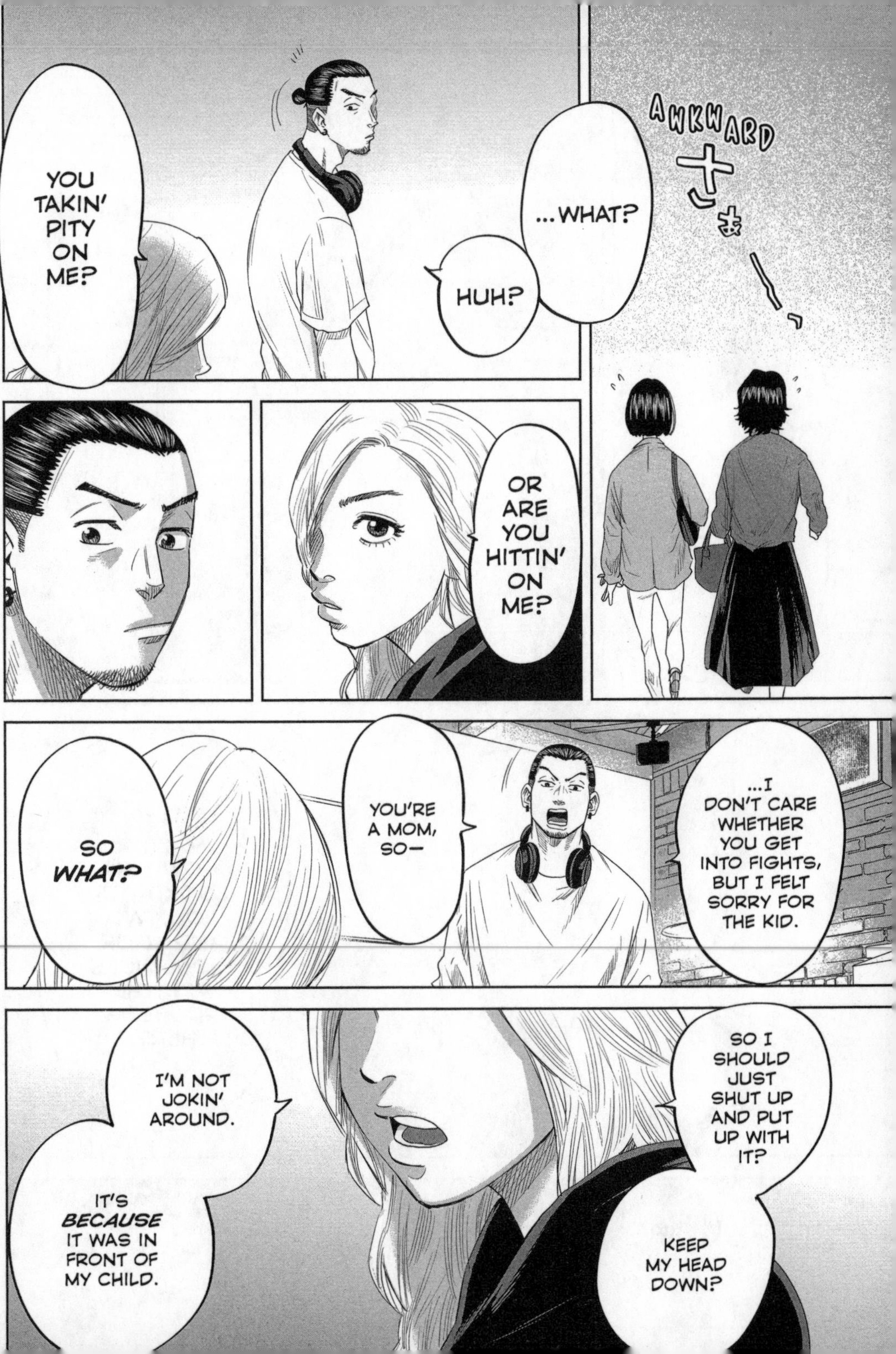
AWKWARD
...WHAT?
YOU TAKIN' PITY ON ME?
HUH?
OR ARE YOU HITTIN' ON ME?
...I DON'T CARE WHETHER YOU GET INTO FIGHTS, BUT I FELT SORRY FOR THE KID.
YOU'RE A MOM, SO—
SO *WHAT?*
SO I SHOULD JUST SHUT UP AND PUT UP WITH IT?
KEEP MY HEAD DOWN?
I'M NOT JOKIN' AROUND.
IT'S *BECAUSE* IT WAS IN FRONT OF MY CHILD.

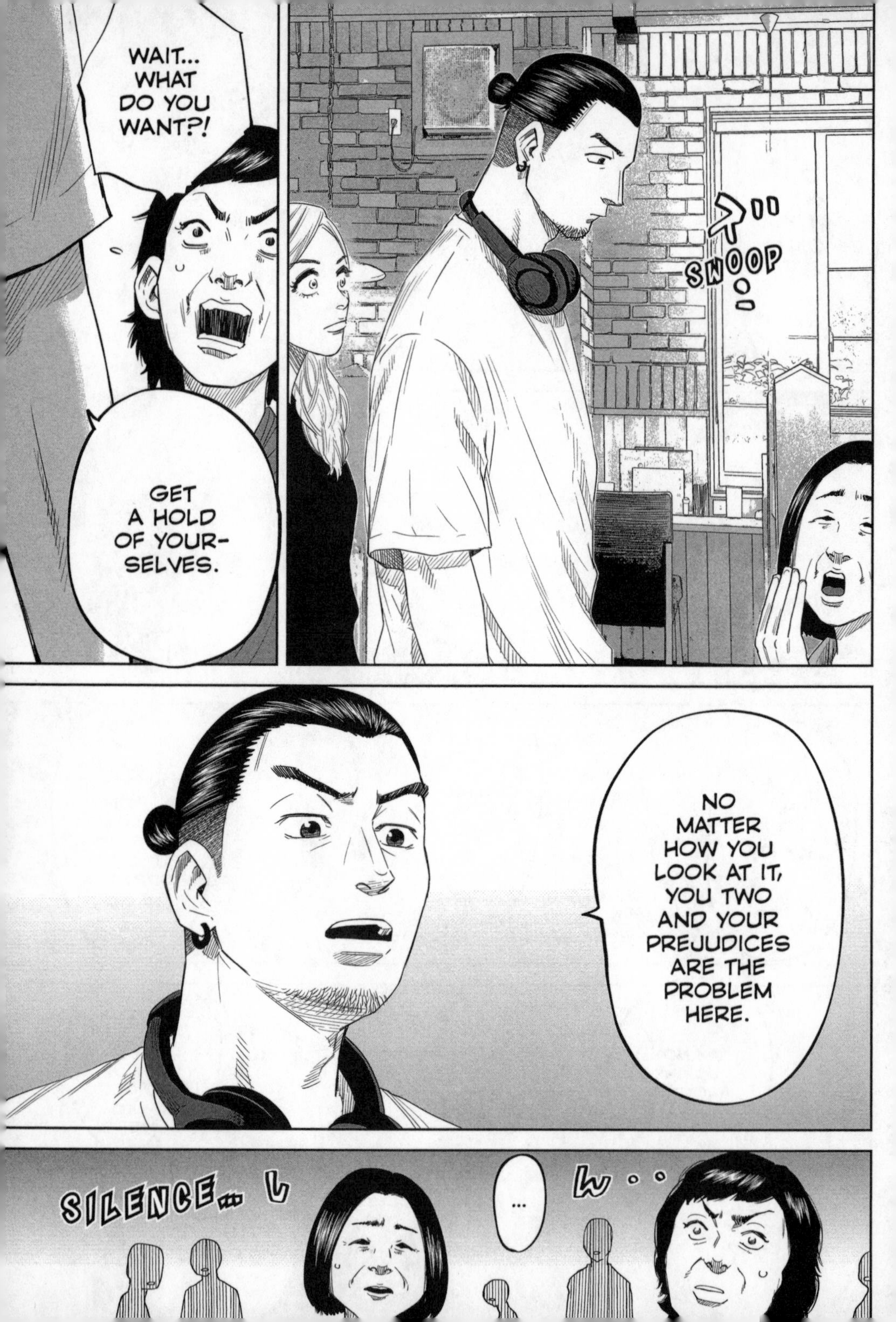
SWOOP
WAIT... WHAT DO YOU WANT?!
GET A HOLD OF YOUR-SELVES.
NO MATTER HOW YOU LOOK AT IT, YOU TWO AND YOUR PREJUDICES ARE THE PROBLEM HERE.
...
SILENCE...

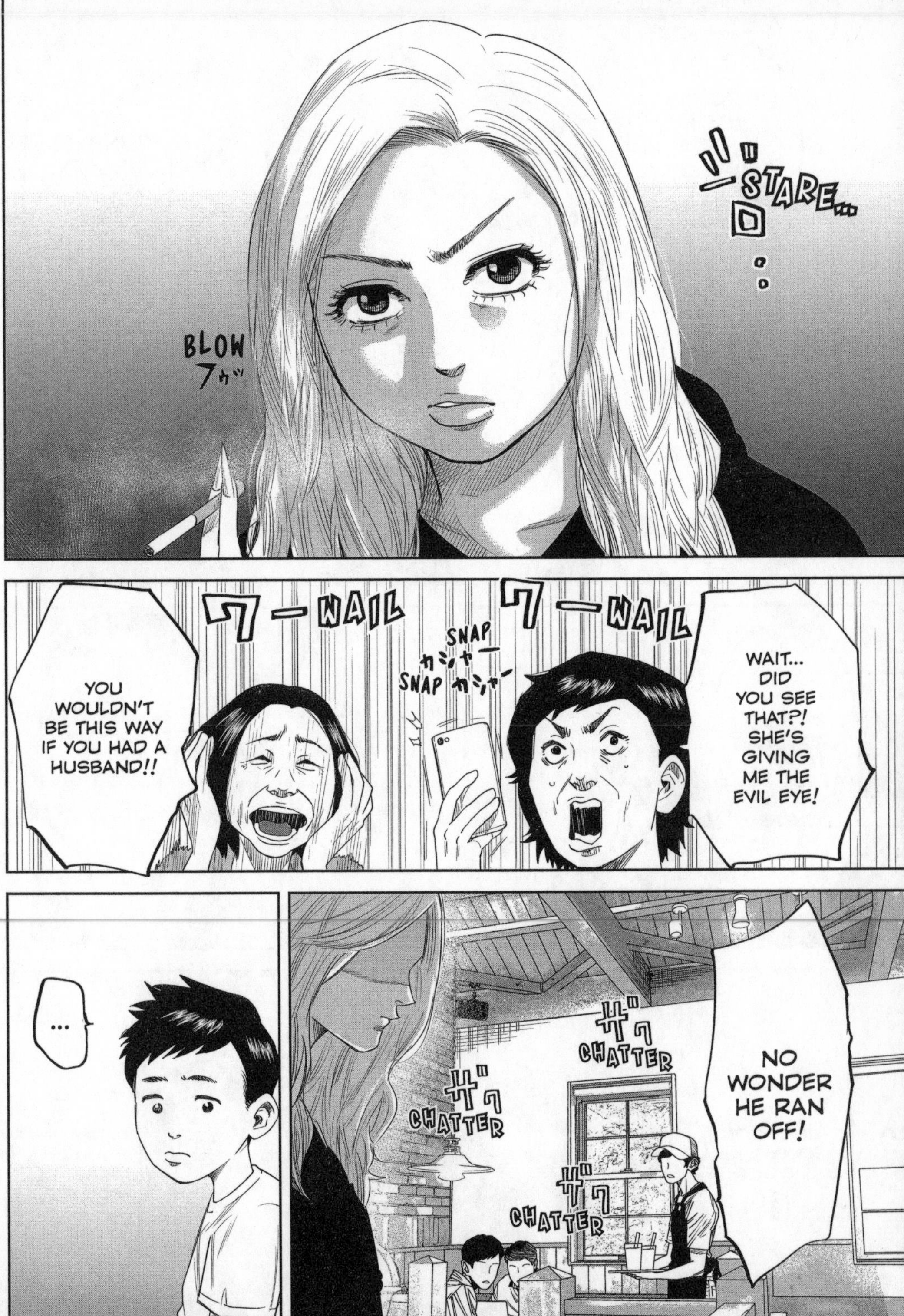
STARE...
BLOW
WAIT... DID YOU SEE THAT?! SHE'S GIVING ME THE EVIL EYE!
WAIL
SNAP
SNAP
WAIL
YOU WOULDN'T BE THIS WAY IF YOU HAD A HUSBAND!!
NO WONDER HE RAN OFF!
CHATTER
CHATTER
CHATTER
...

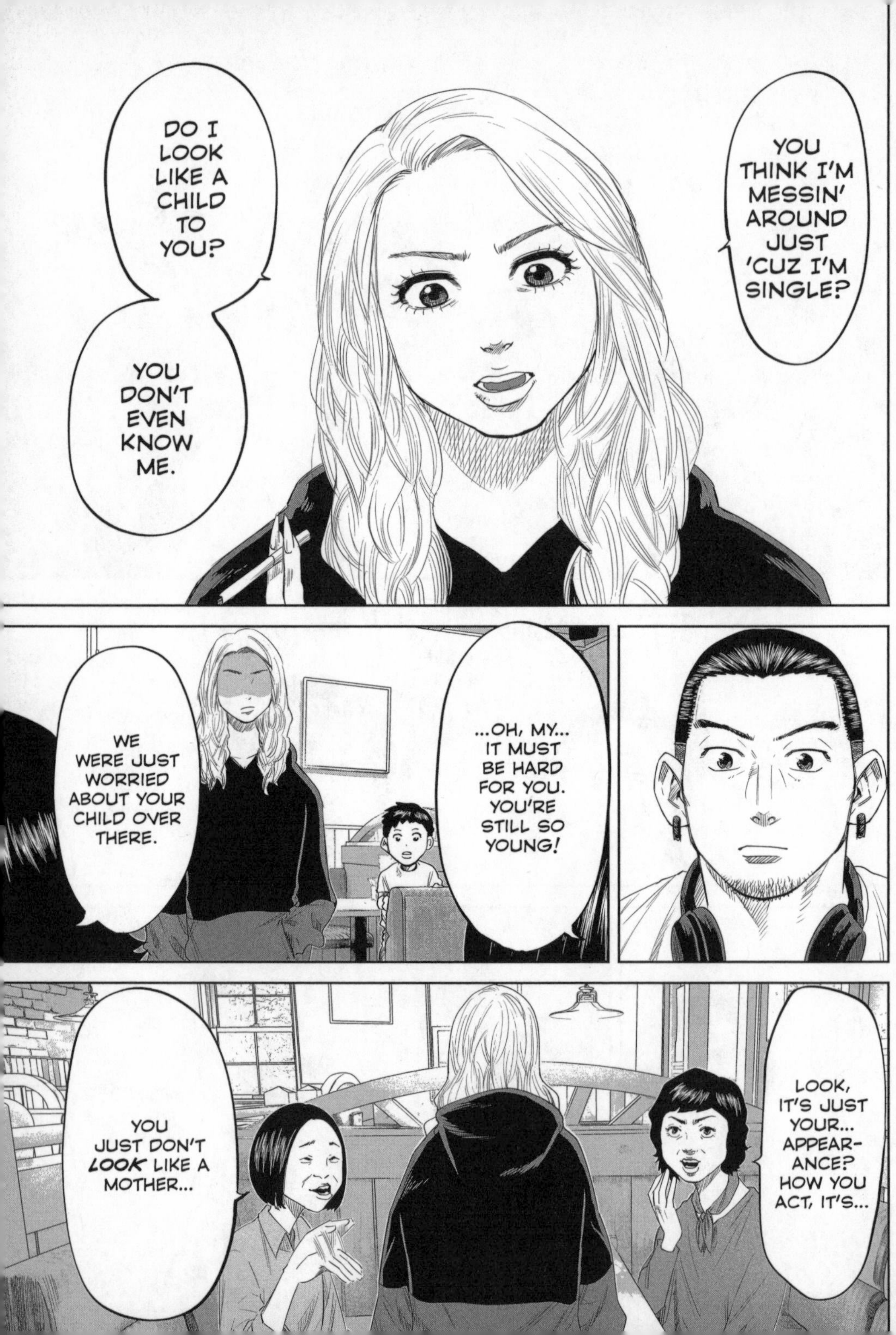
YOU THINK I'M MESSIN' AROUND JUST 'CUZ I'M SINGLE?
DO I LOOK LIKE A CHILD TO YOU?
YOU DON'T EVEN KNOW ME.
...OH, MY... IT MUST BE HARD FOR YOU. YOU'RE STILL SO YOUNG!
WE WERE JUST WORRIED ABOUT YOUR CHILD OVER THERE.
LOOK, IT'S JUST YOUR... APPEARANCE? HOW YOU ACT, IT'S...
YOU JUST DON'T *LOOK* LIKE A MOTHER...

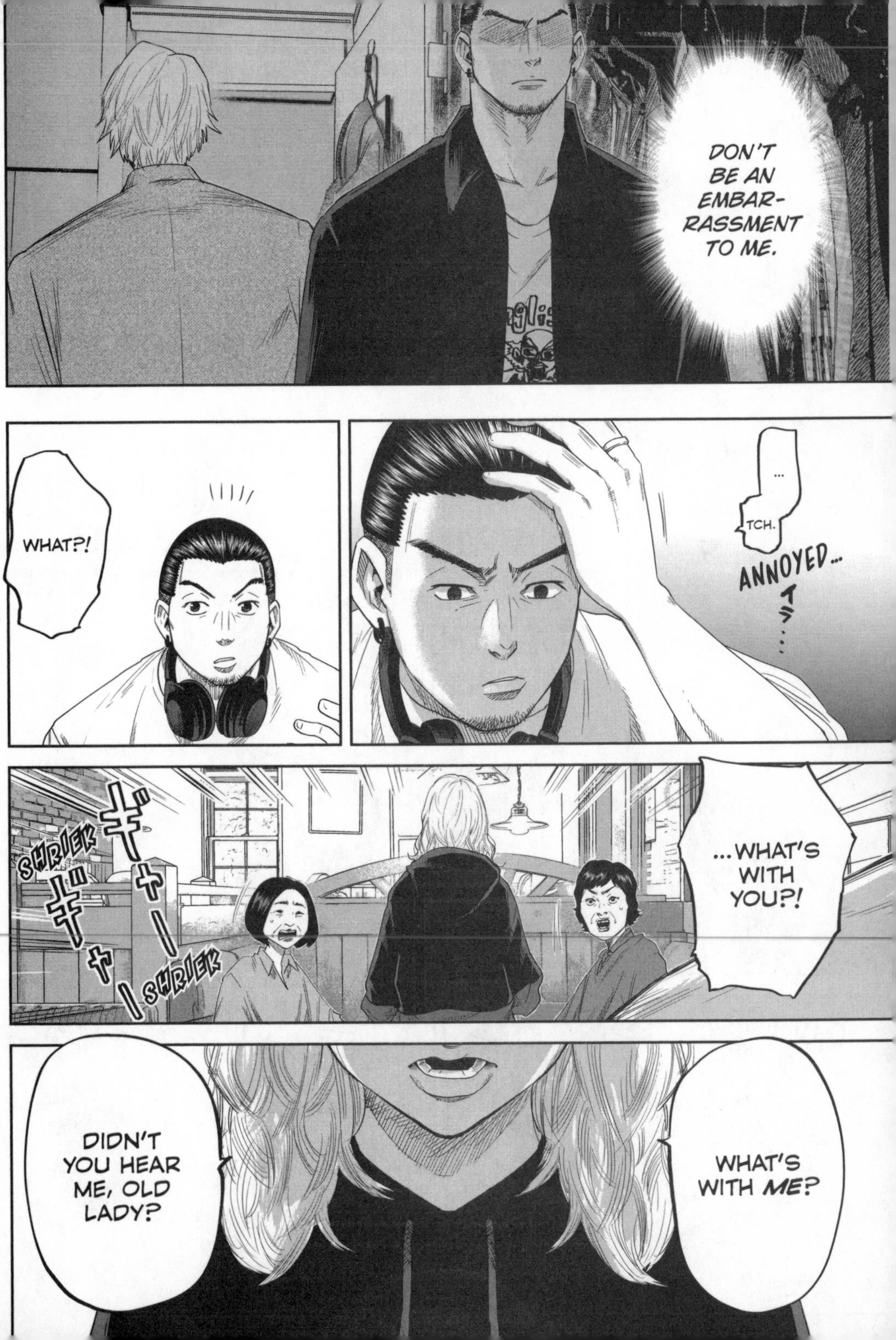
DON'T BE AN EMBARRASSMENT TO ME.
...
TCH.
ANNOYED...
イラ...
WHAT?!
...WHAT'S WITH YOU?!
ギャー
SHRIEK
ギャー
SHRIEK
WHAT'S WITH *ME*?
DIDN'T YOU HEAR ME, OLD LADY?

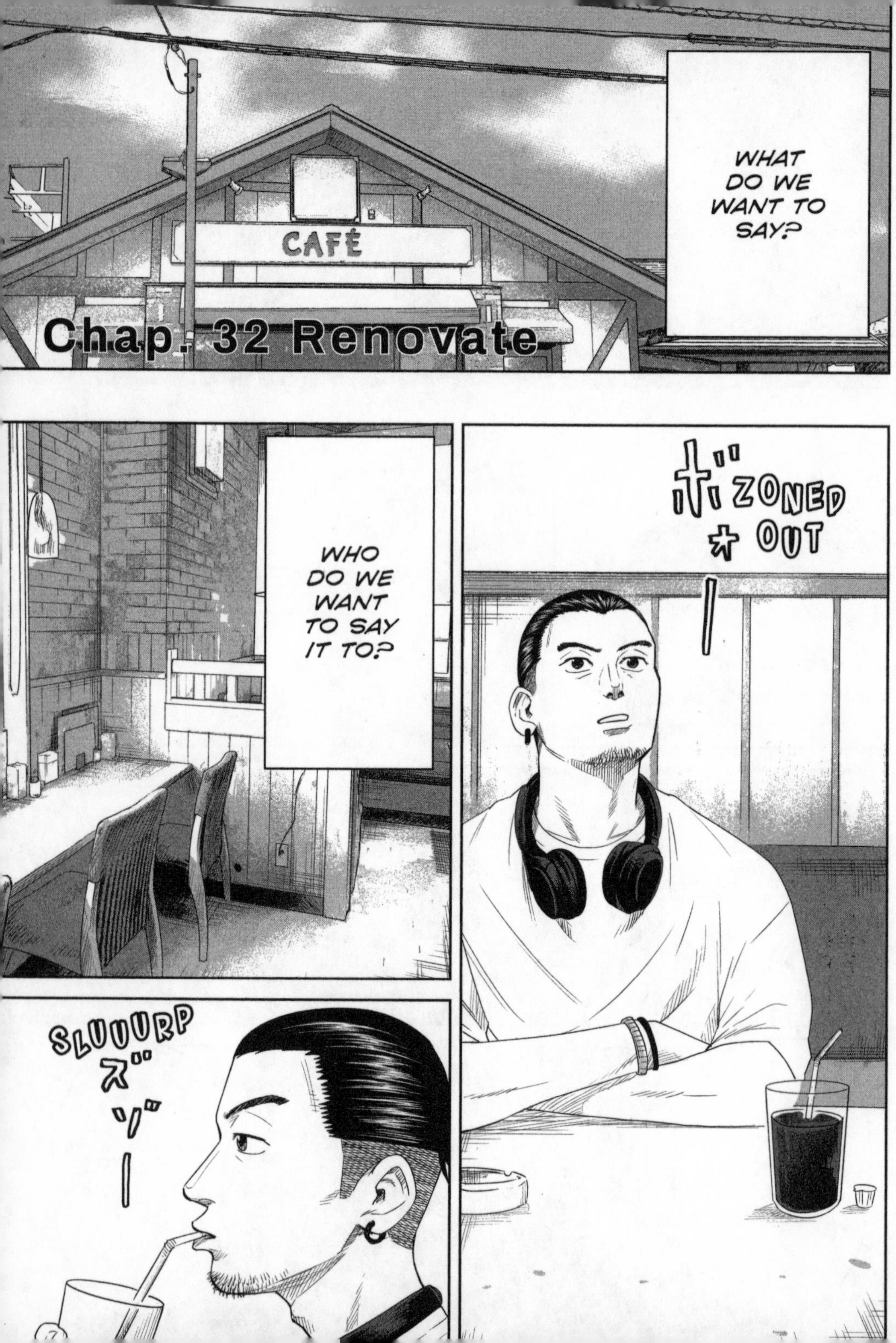

WHAT DO WE WANT TO SAY?
CAFÉ
Chap. 32 Renovate
ZONED OUT
WHO DO WE WANT TO SAY IT TO?
SLUUURP

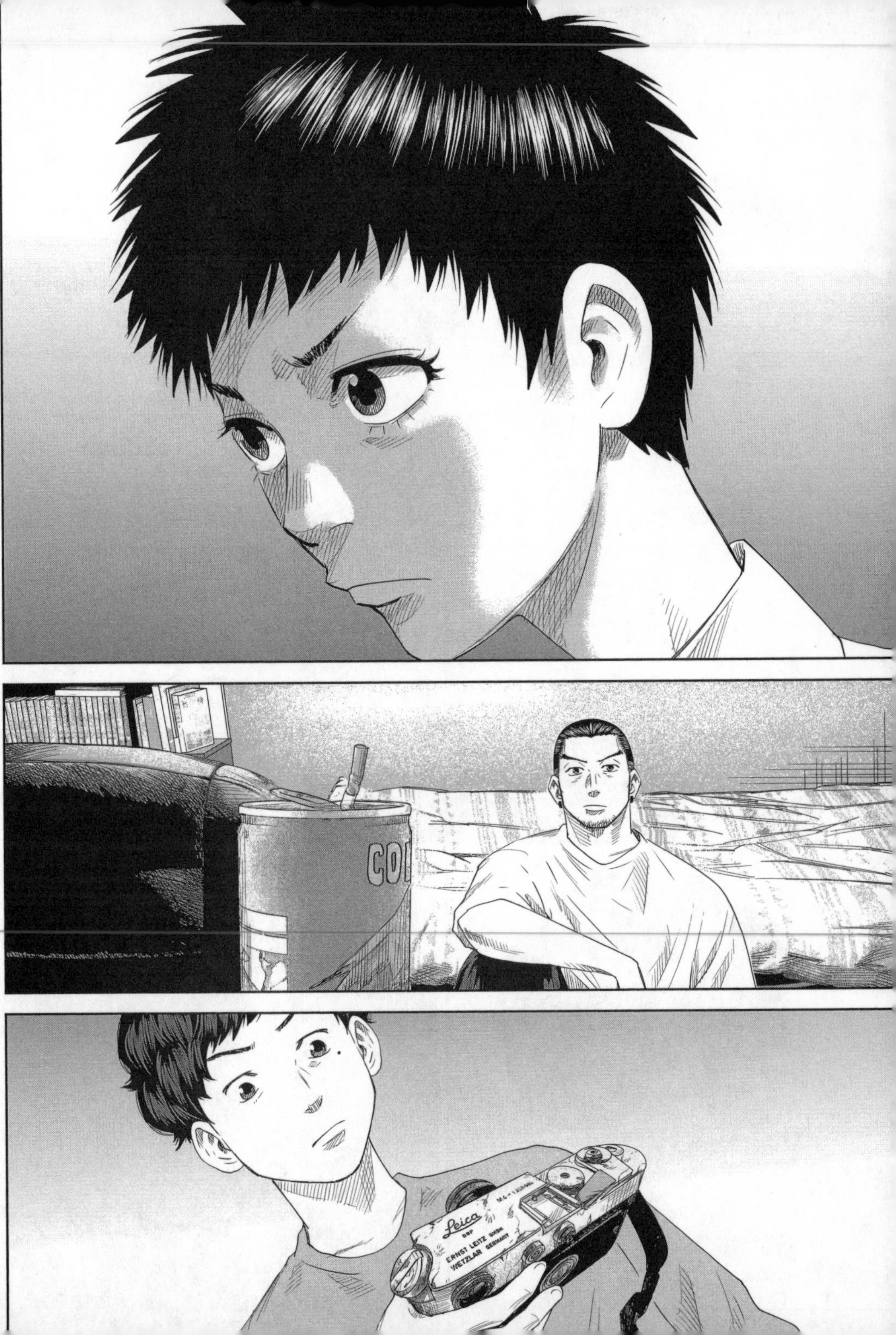
Leica
ERNST LEITZ GMBH
WETZLAR GERMANY

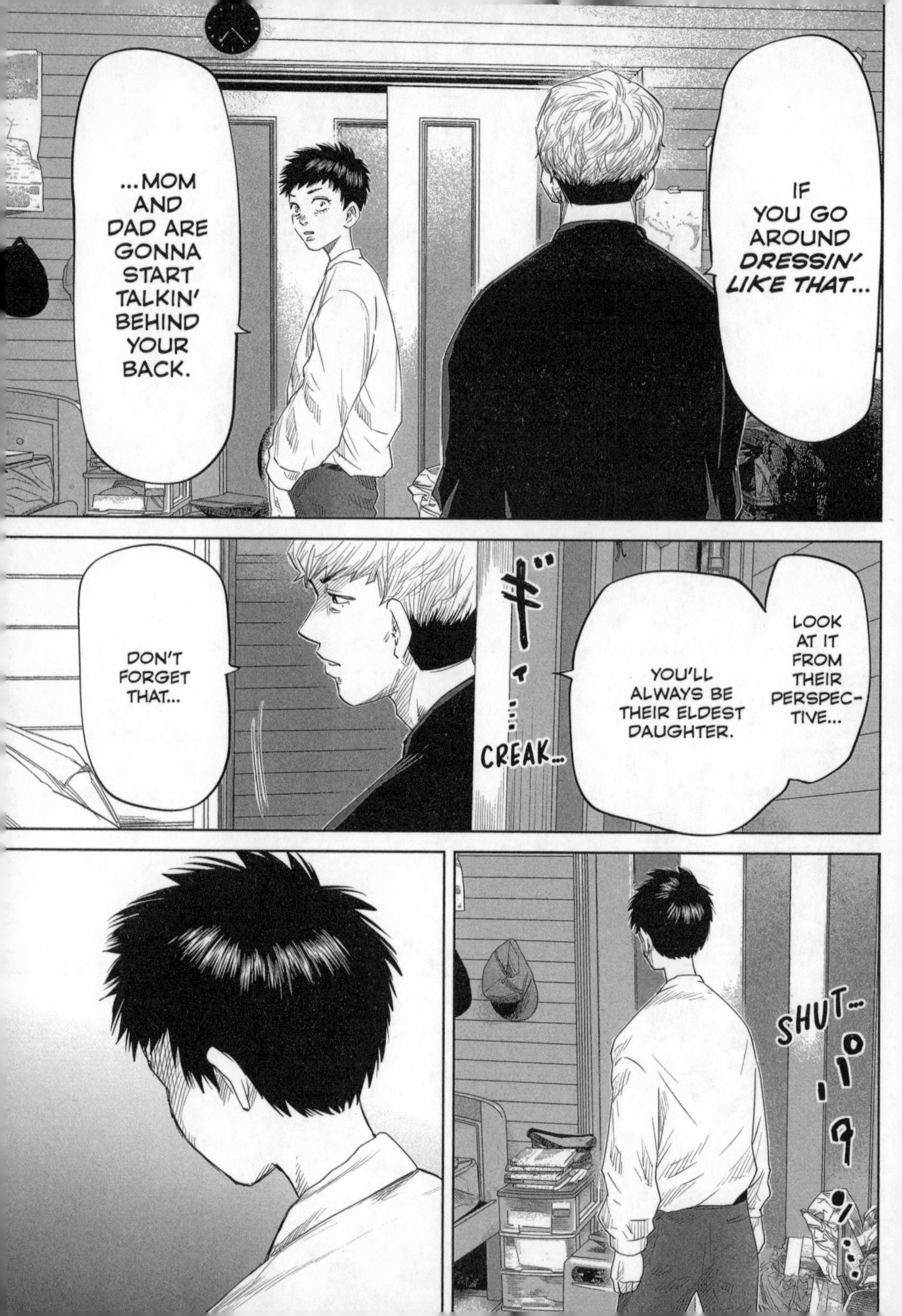
IF YOU GO AROUND DRESSIN' LIKE THAT...
...MOM AND DAD ARE GONNA START TALKIN' BEHIND YOUR BACK.
LOOK AT IT FROM THEIR PERSPEC-TIVE...
YOU'LL ALWAYS BE THEIR ELDEST DAUGHTER.
CREAK...
DON'T FORGET THAT...
SHUT...

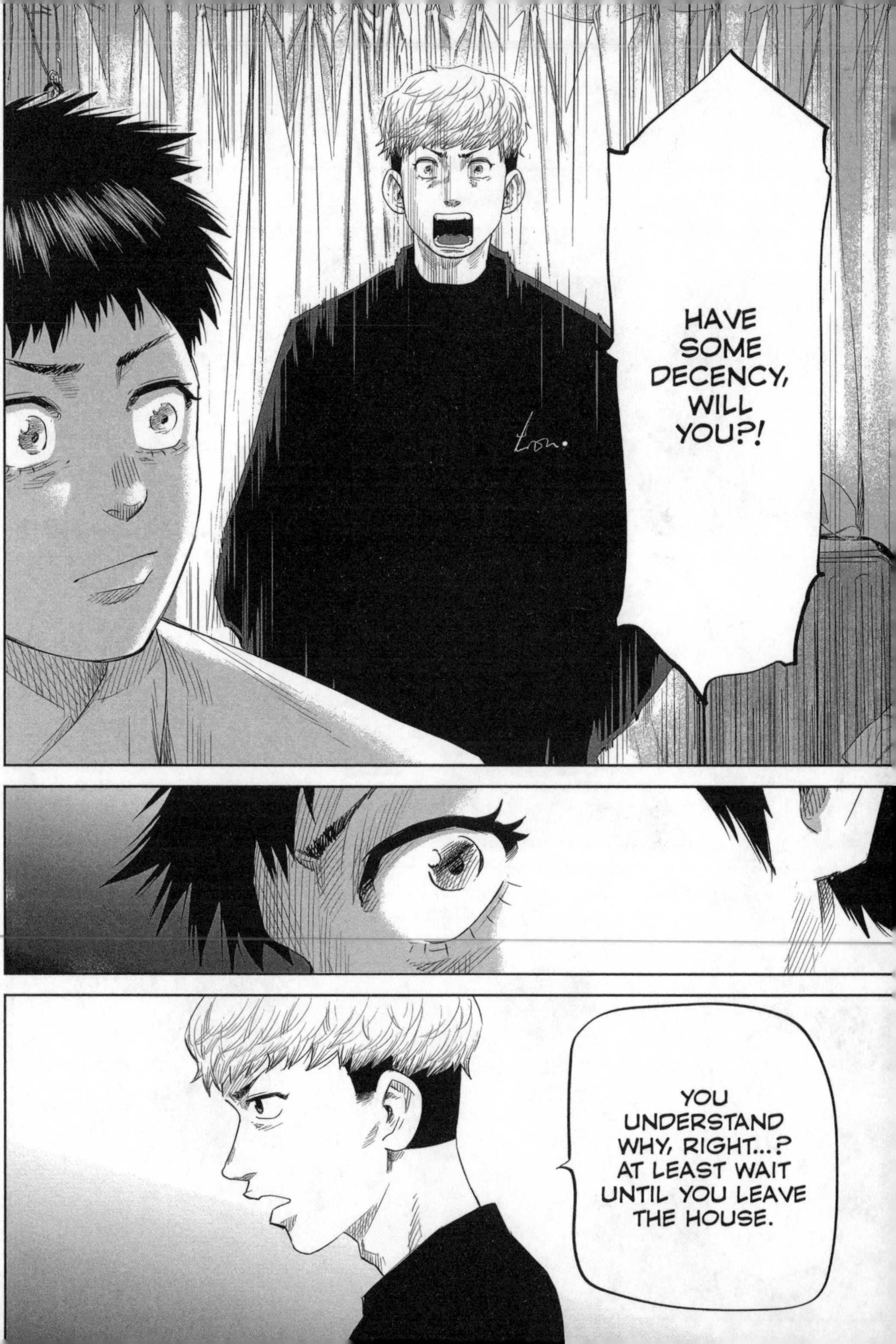
HAVE SOME DECENCY, WILL YOU?!
YOU UNDERSTAND WHY, RIGHT...? AT LEAST WAIT UNTIL YOU LEAVE THE HOUSE.

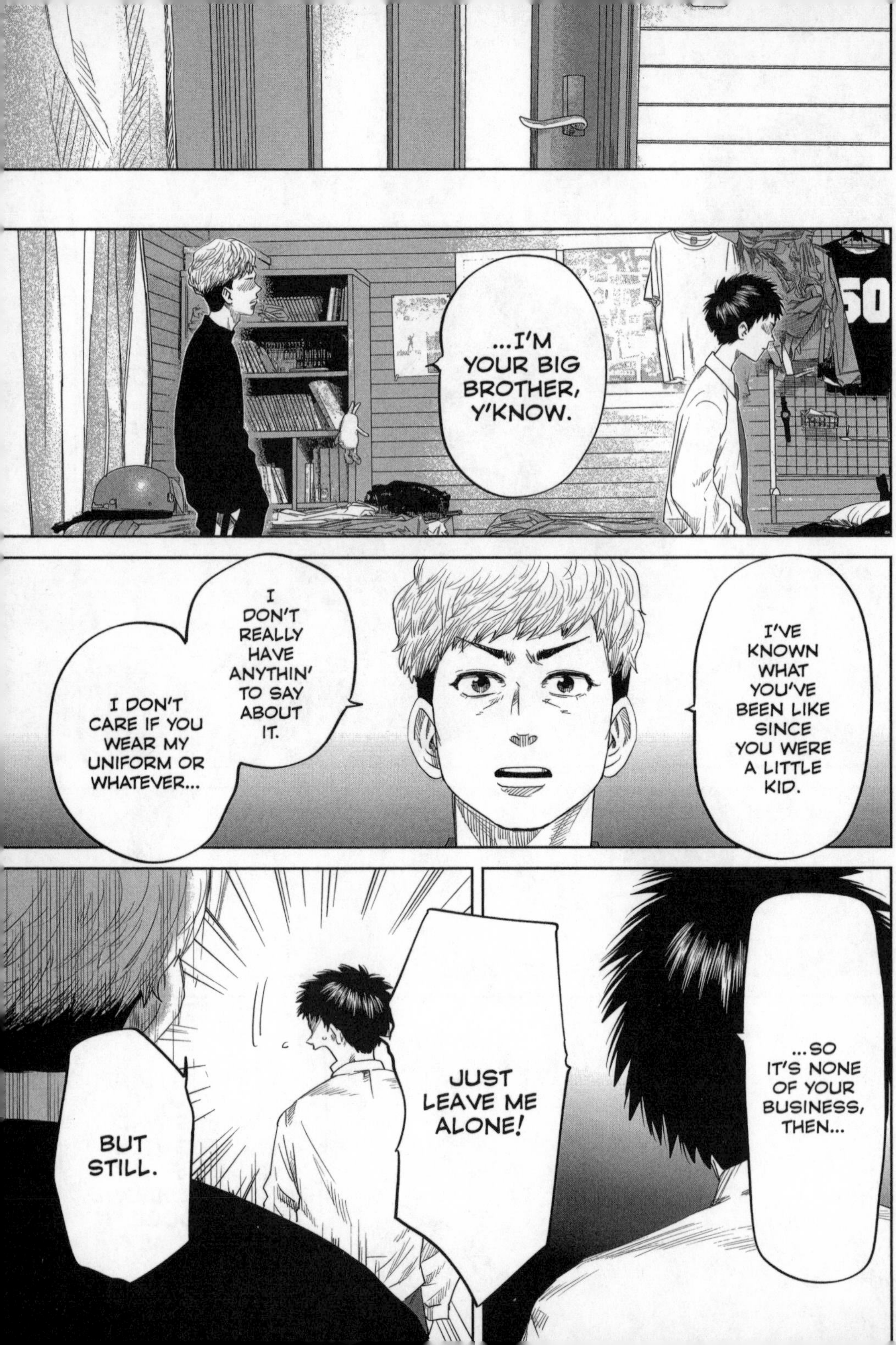
...I'M YOUR BIG BROTHER, Y'KNOW.
I'VE KNOWN WHAT YOU'VE BEEN LIKE SINCE YOU WERE A LITTLE KID.
I DON'T REALLY HAVE ANYTHIN' TO SAY ABOUT IT.
I DON'T CARE IF YOU WEAR MY UNIFORM OR WHATEVER...
...SO IT'S NONE OF YOUR BUSINESS, THEN...
JUST LEAVE ME ALONE!
BUT STILL.

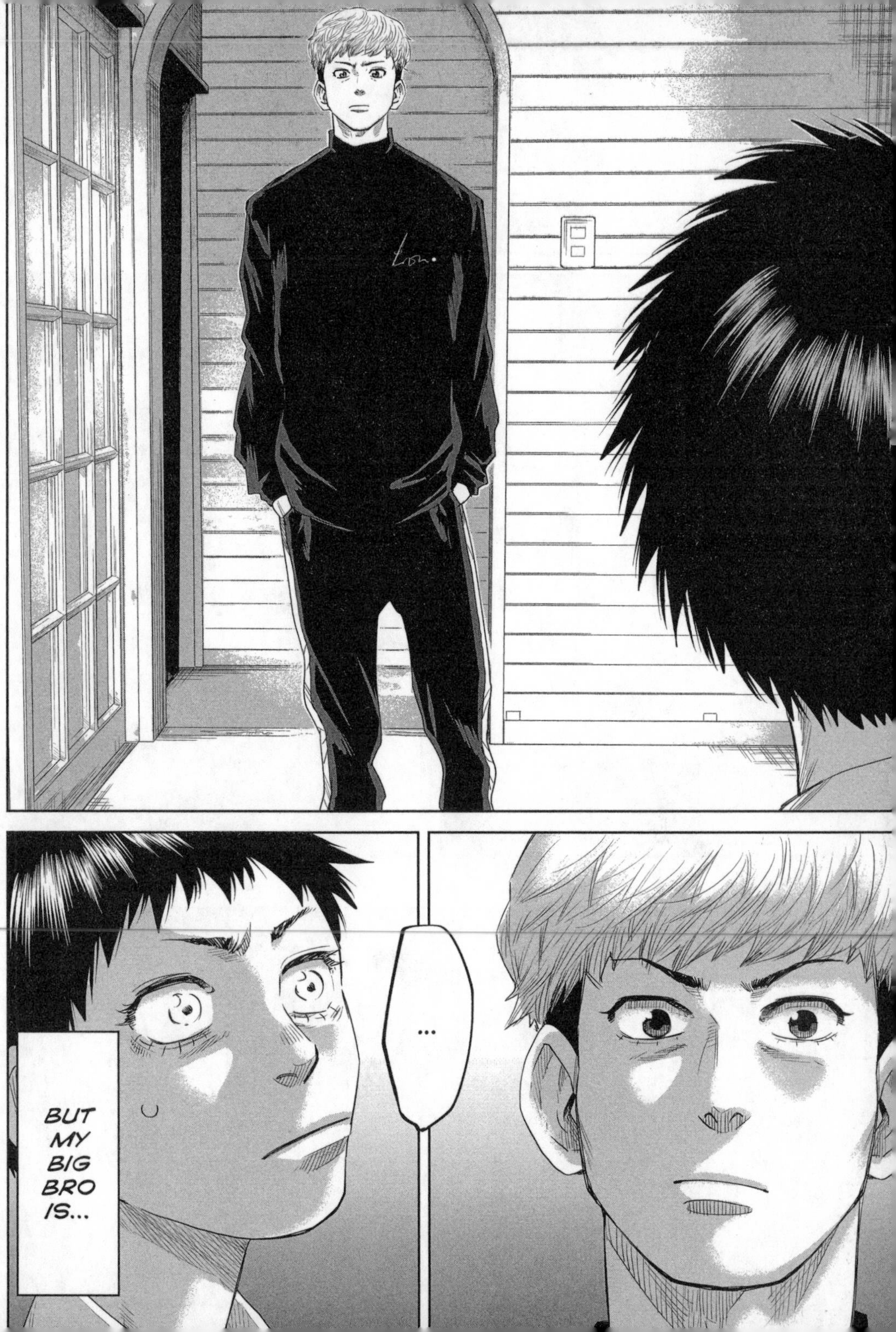
...
BUT MY BIG BRO IS...

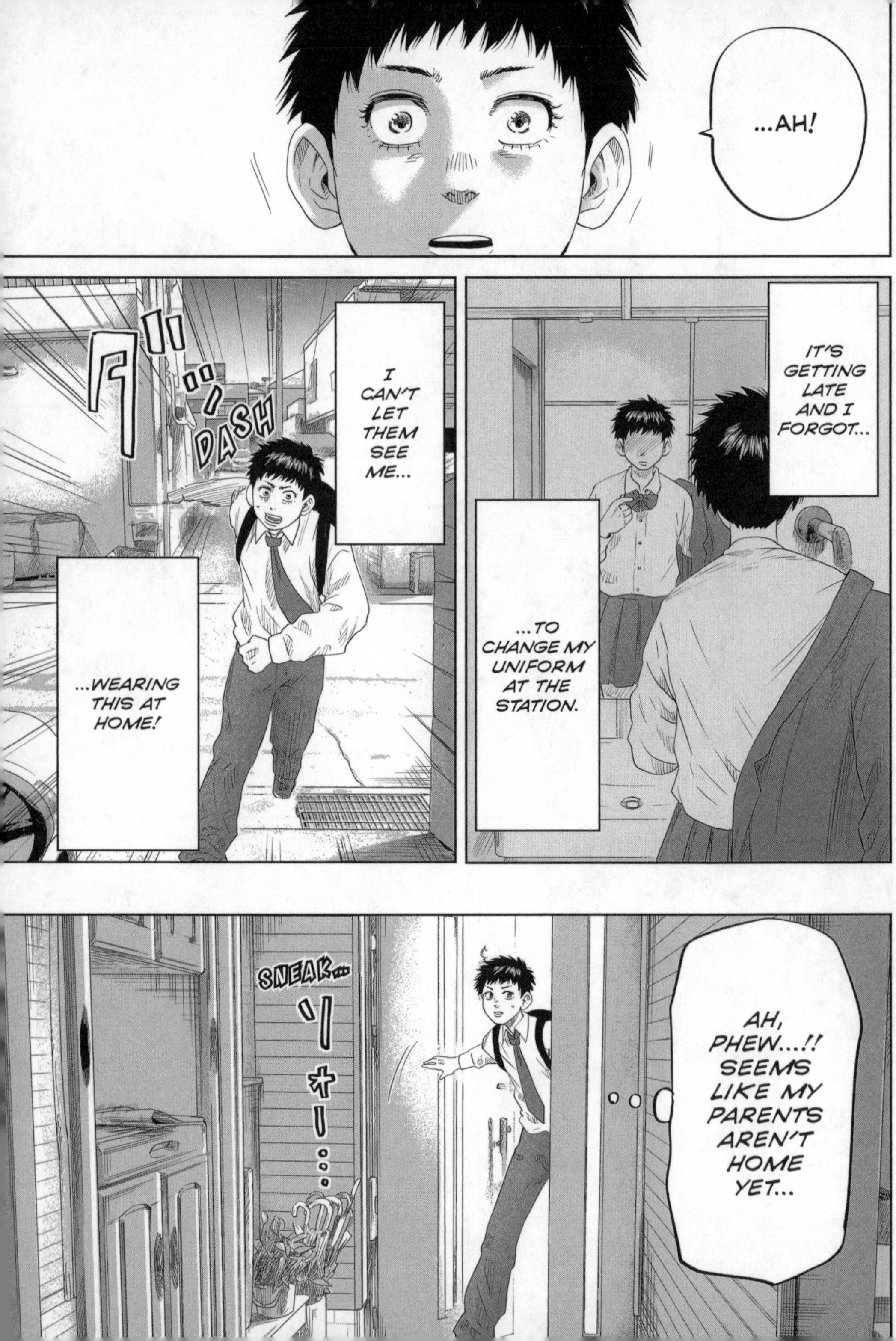
...AH!
IT'S GETTING LATE AND I FORGOT...
...TO CHANGE MY UNIFORM AT THE STATION.
DASH
I CAN'T LET THEM SEE ME...
...WEARING THIS AT HOME!
AH, PHEW...!! SEEMS LIKE MY PARENTS AREN'T HOME YET...
SNEAK...

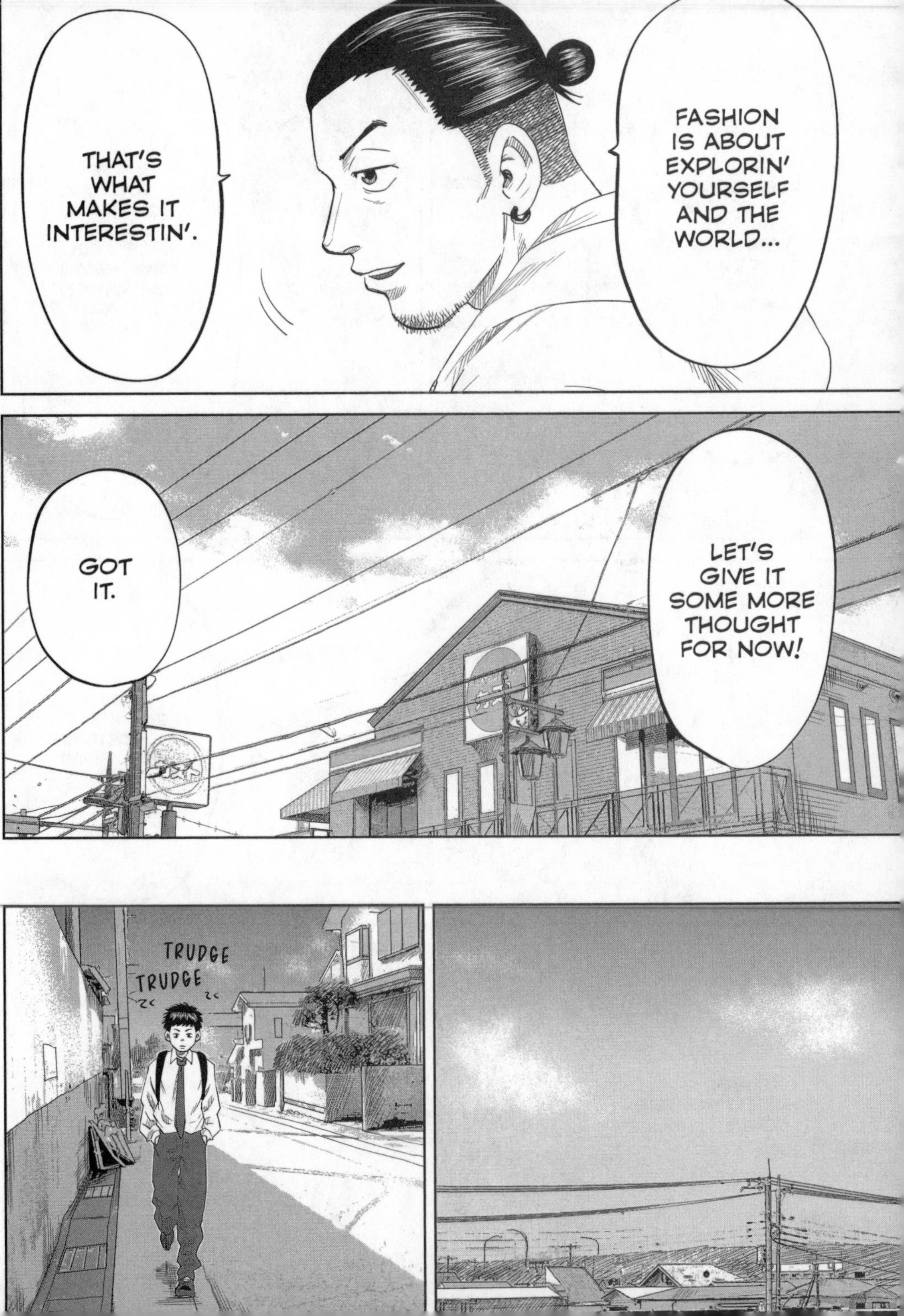
FASHION IS ABOUT EXPLORIN' YOURSELF AND THE WORLD...
THAT'S WHAT MAKES IT INTERESTIN'.
LET'S GIVE IT SOME MORE THOUGHT FOR NOW!
GOT IT.
TRUDGE
TRUDGE

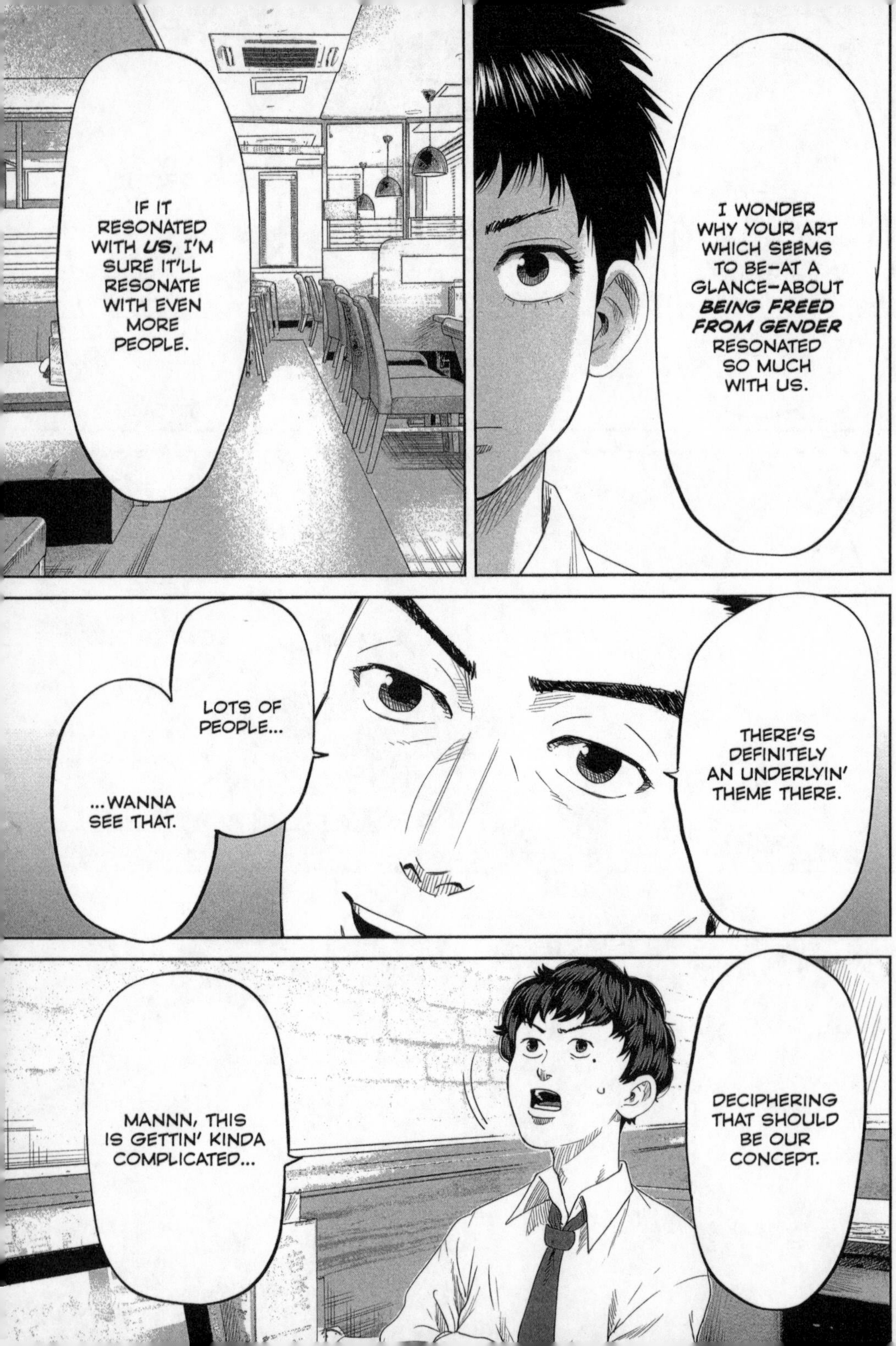
I WONDER WHY YOUR ART WHICH SEEMS TO BE—AT A GLANCE—ABOUT *BEING FREED FROM GENDER* RESONATED SO MUCH WITH US.
IF IT RESONATED WITH *US*, I'M SURE IT'LL RESONATE WITH EVEN MORE PEOPLE.
THERE'S DEFINITELY AN UNDERLYIN' THEME THERE.
LOTS OF PEOPLE...
...WANNA SEE THAT.
DECIPHERING THAT SHOULD BE OUR CONCEPT.
MANNN, THIS IS GETTIN' KINDA COMPLICATED...

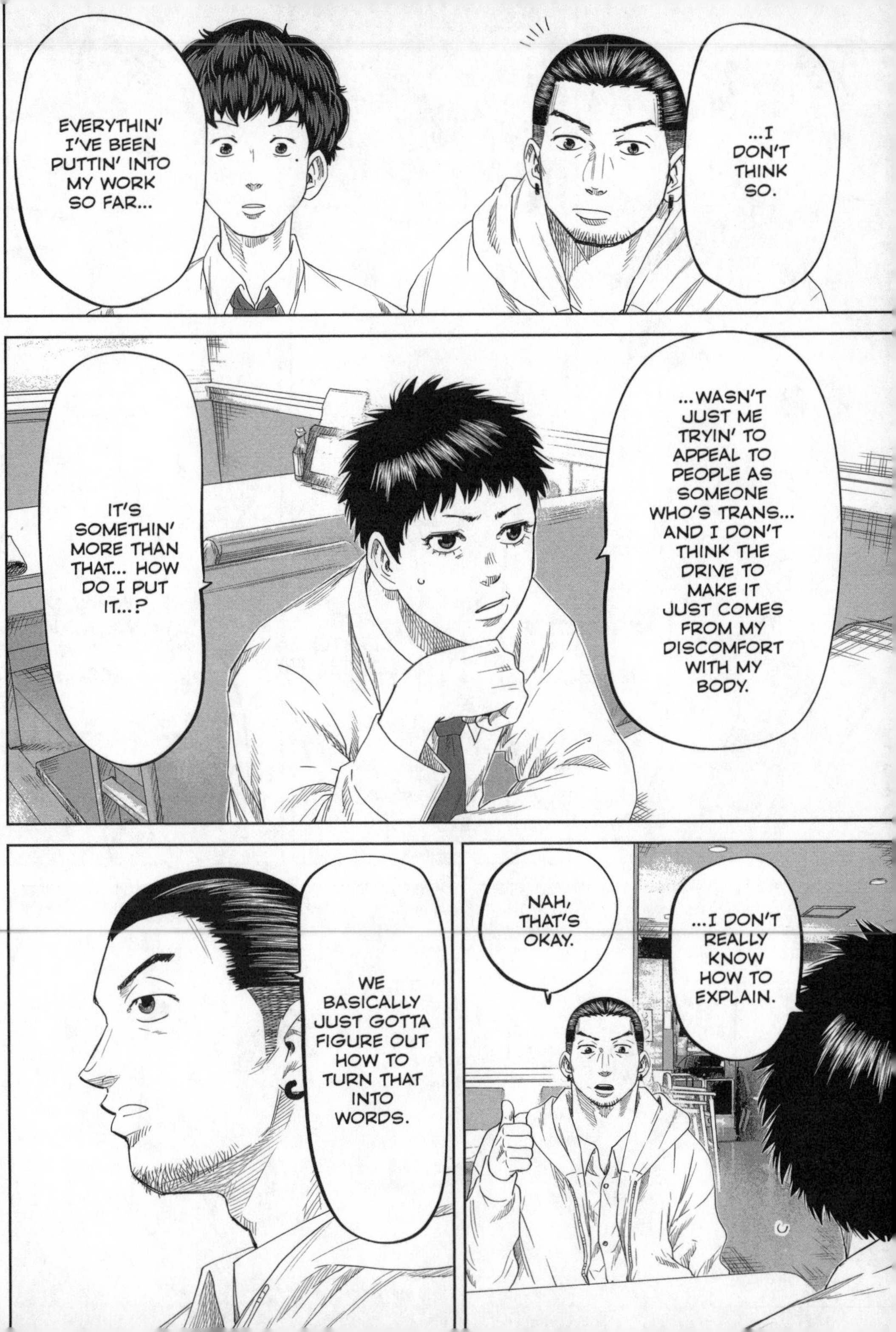
...I DON'T THINK SO.
EVERYTHIN' I'VE BEEN PUTTIN' INTO MY WORK SO FAR...
...WASN'T JUST ME TRYIN' TO APPEAL TO PEOPLE AS SOMEONE WHO'S TRANS... AND I DON'T THINK THE DRIVE TO MAKE IT JUST COMES FROM MY DISCOMFORT WITH MY BODY.
IT'S SOMETHIN' MORE THAN THAT... HOW DO I PUT IT...?
...I DON'T REALLY KNOW HOW TO EXPLAIN.
NAH, THAT'S OKAY.
WE BASICALLY JUST GOTTA FIGURE OUT HOW TO TURN THAT INTO WORDS.

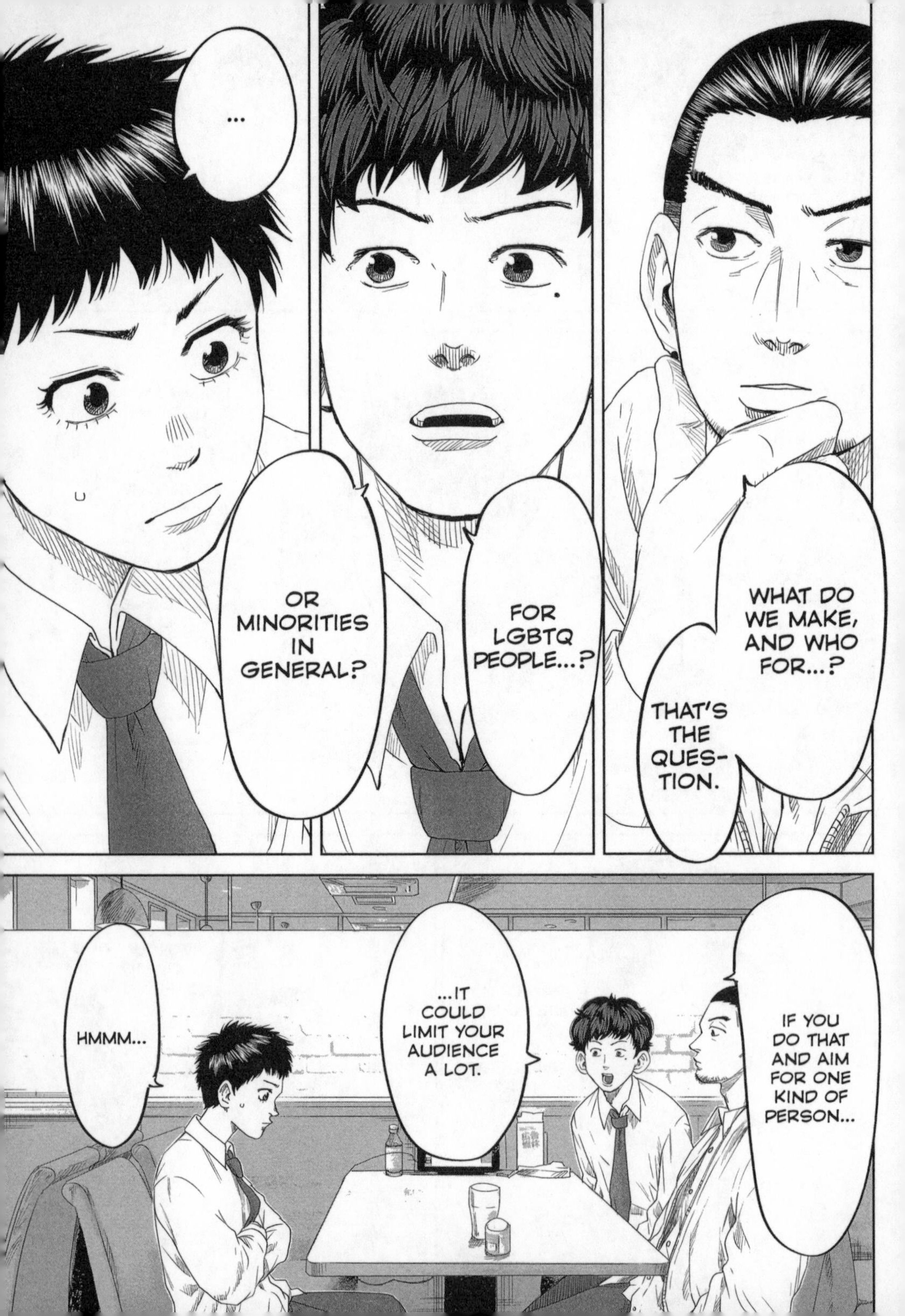
WHAT DO WE MAKE, AND WHO FOR...?
THAT'S THE QUES-TION.
FOR LGBTQ PEOPLE...?
...
OR MINORITIES IN GENERAL?
IF YOU DO THAT AND AIM FOR ONE KIND OF PERSON...
...IT COULD LIMIT YOUR AUDIENCE A LOT.
HMMM...

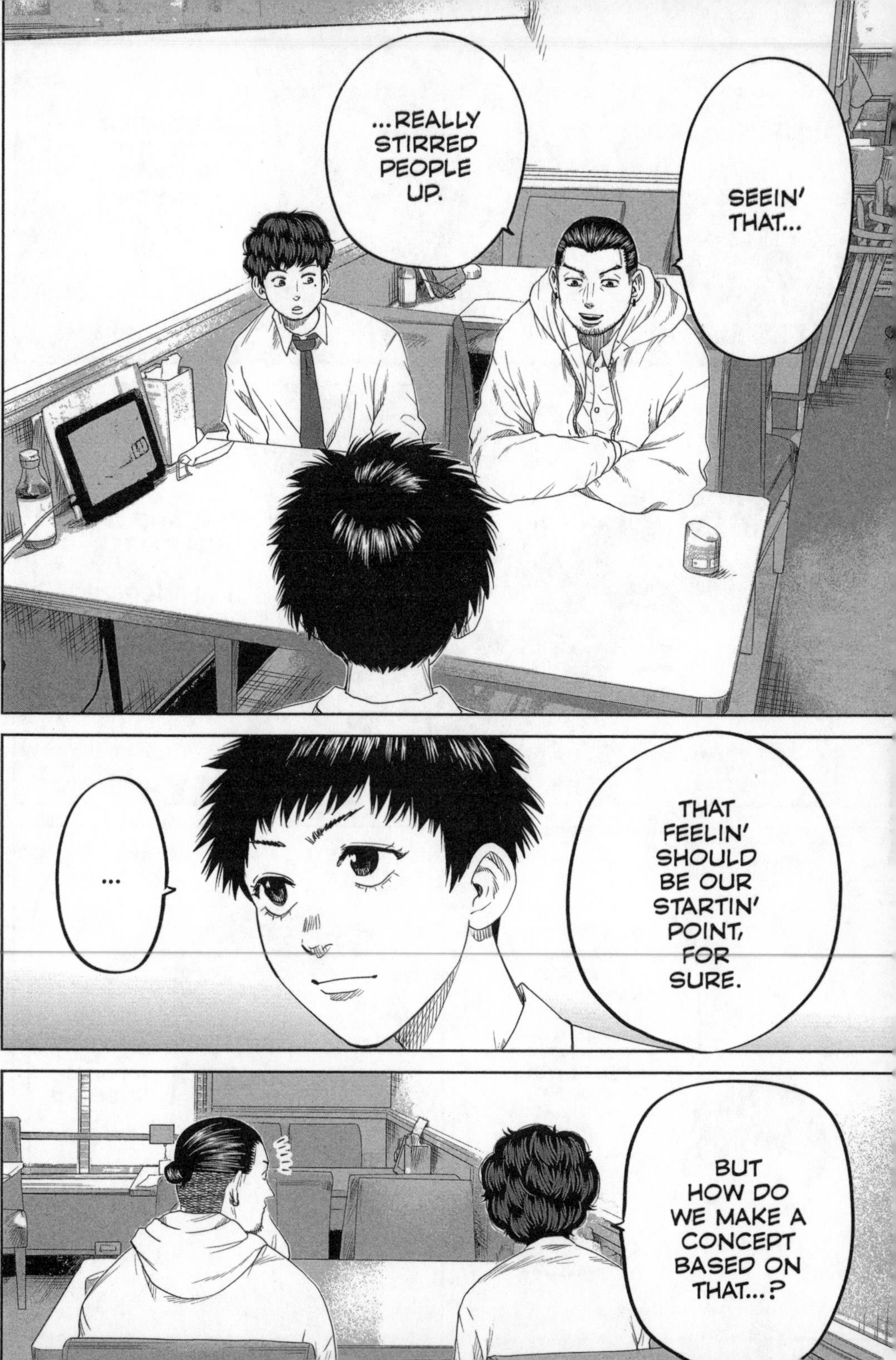
...REALLY STIRRED PEOPLE UP.
SEEIN' THAT...
THAT FEELIN' SHOULD BE OUR STARTIN' POINT, FOR SURE.
...
BUT HOW DO WE MAKE A CONCEPT BASED ON THAT...?

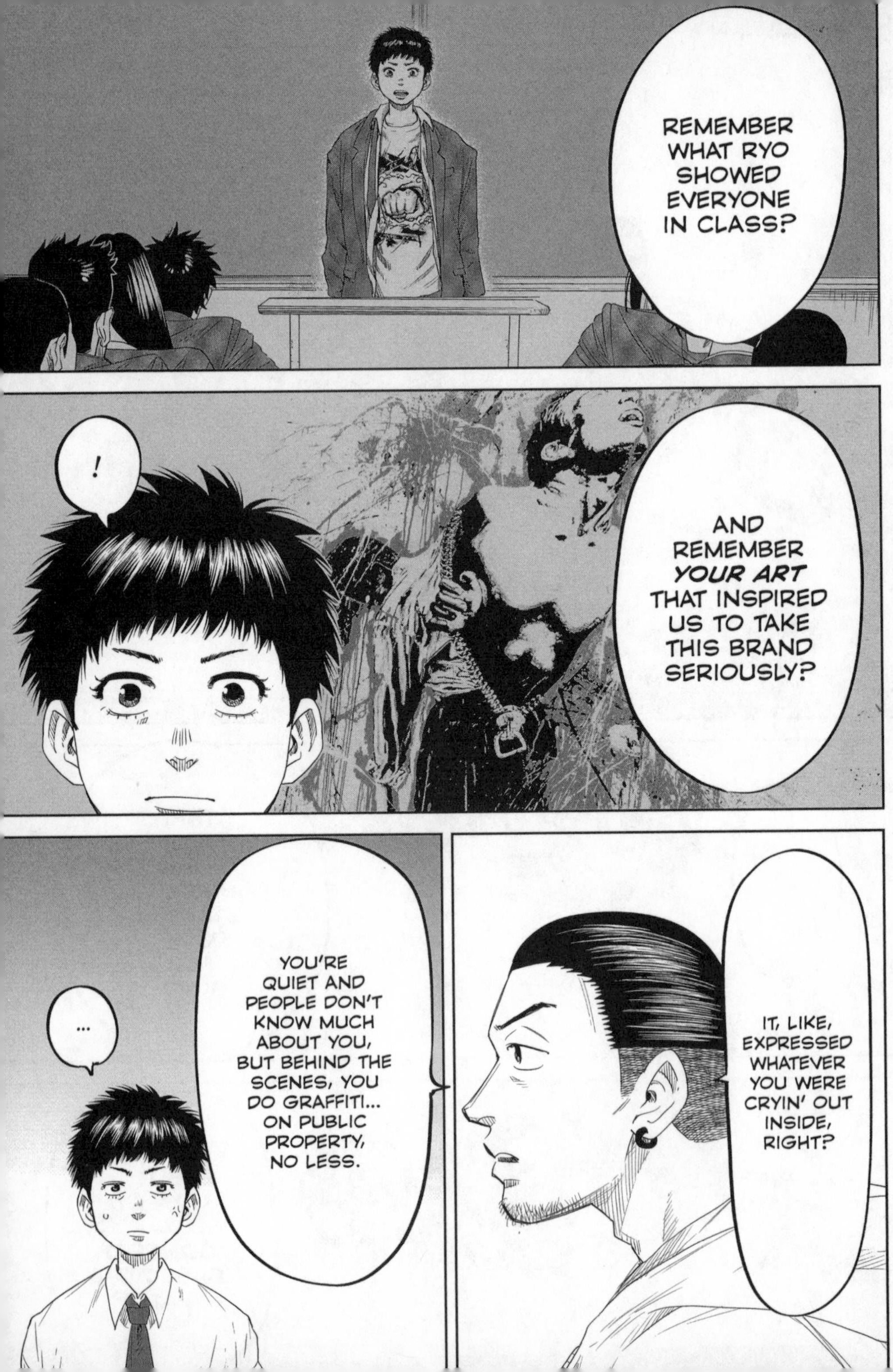
REMEMBER WHAT RYO SHOWED EVERYONE IN CLASS?
AND REMEMBER *YOUR ART* THAT INSPIRED US TO TAKE THIS BRAND SERIOUSLY?
!
IT, LIKE, EXPRESSED WHATEVER YOU WERE CRYIN' OUT INSIDE, RIGHT?
YOU'RE QUIET AND PEOPLE DON'T KNOW MUCH ABOUT YOU, BUT BEHIND THE SCENES, YOU DO GRAFFITI... ON PUBLIC PROPERTY, NO LESS.
...

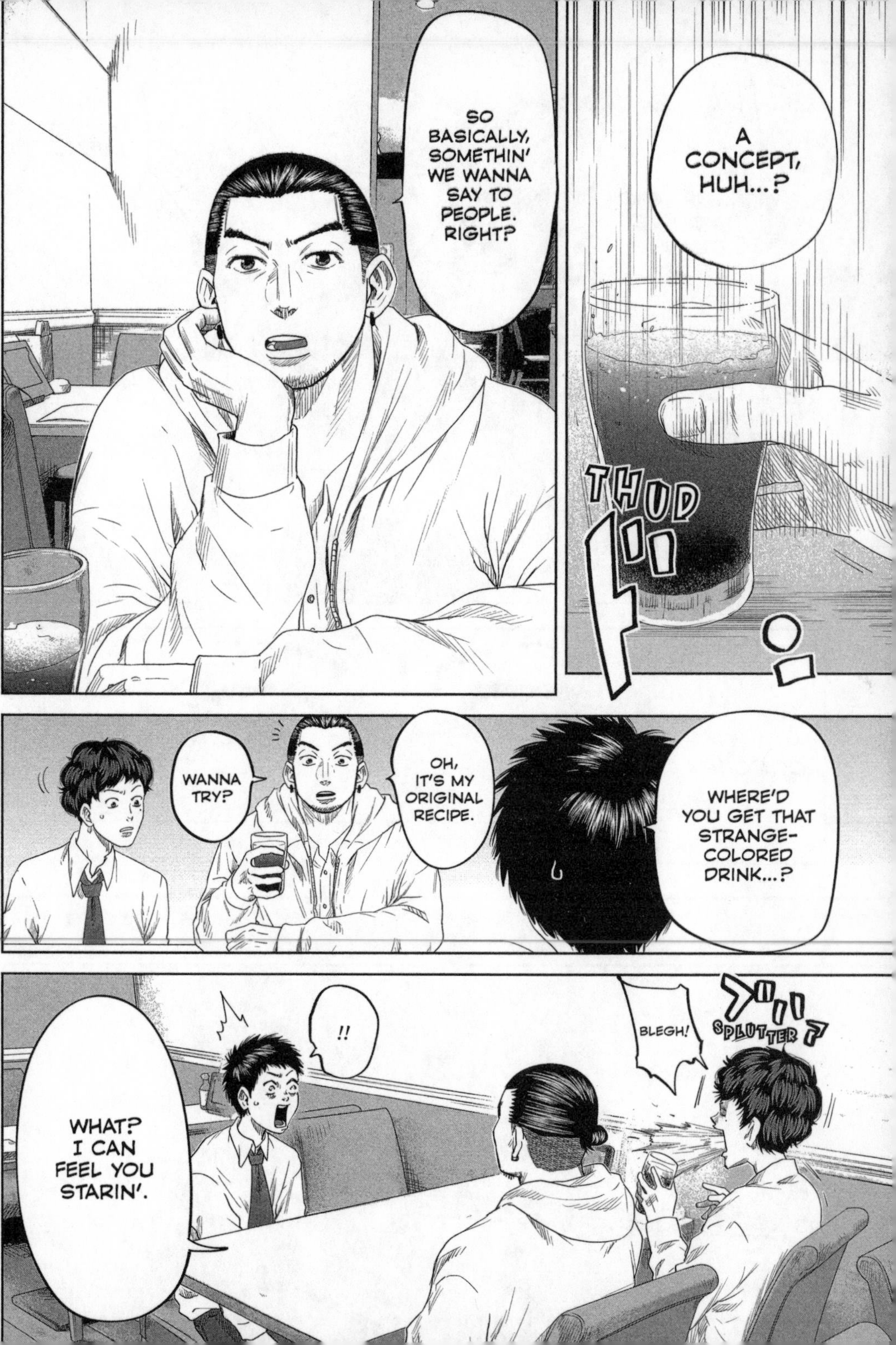
A CONCEPT, HUH...?
THUD
SO BASICALLY, SOMETHIN' WE WANNA SAY TO PEOPLE. RIGHT?
WHERE'D YOU GET THAT STRANGE-COLORED DRINK...?
OH, IT'S MY ORIGINAL RECIPE.
WANNA TRY?
SPLUTTER
BLEGH!
!!
WHAT? I CAN FEEL YOU STARIN'.

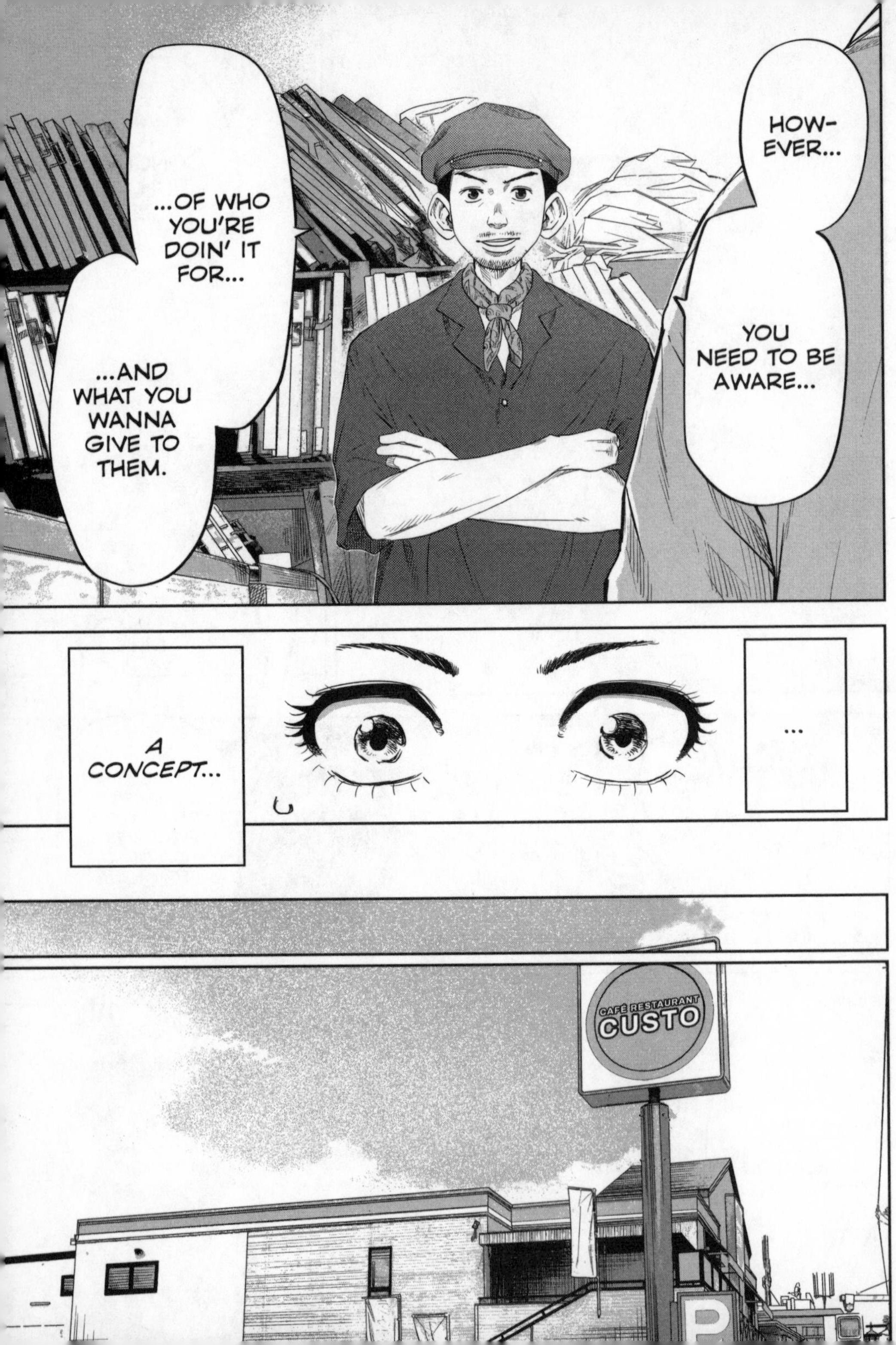
HOW-EVER...
YOU NEED TO BE AWARE...
...OF WHO YOU'RE DOIN' IT FOR...
...AND WHAT YOU WANNA GIVE TO THEM.
...
A CONCEPT...
CAFÉ RESTAURANT
CUSTO
P

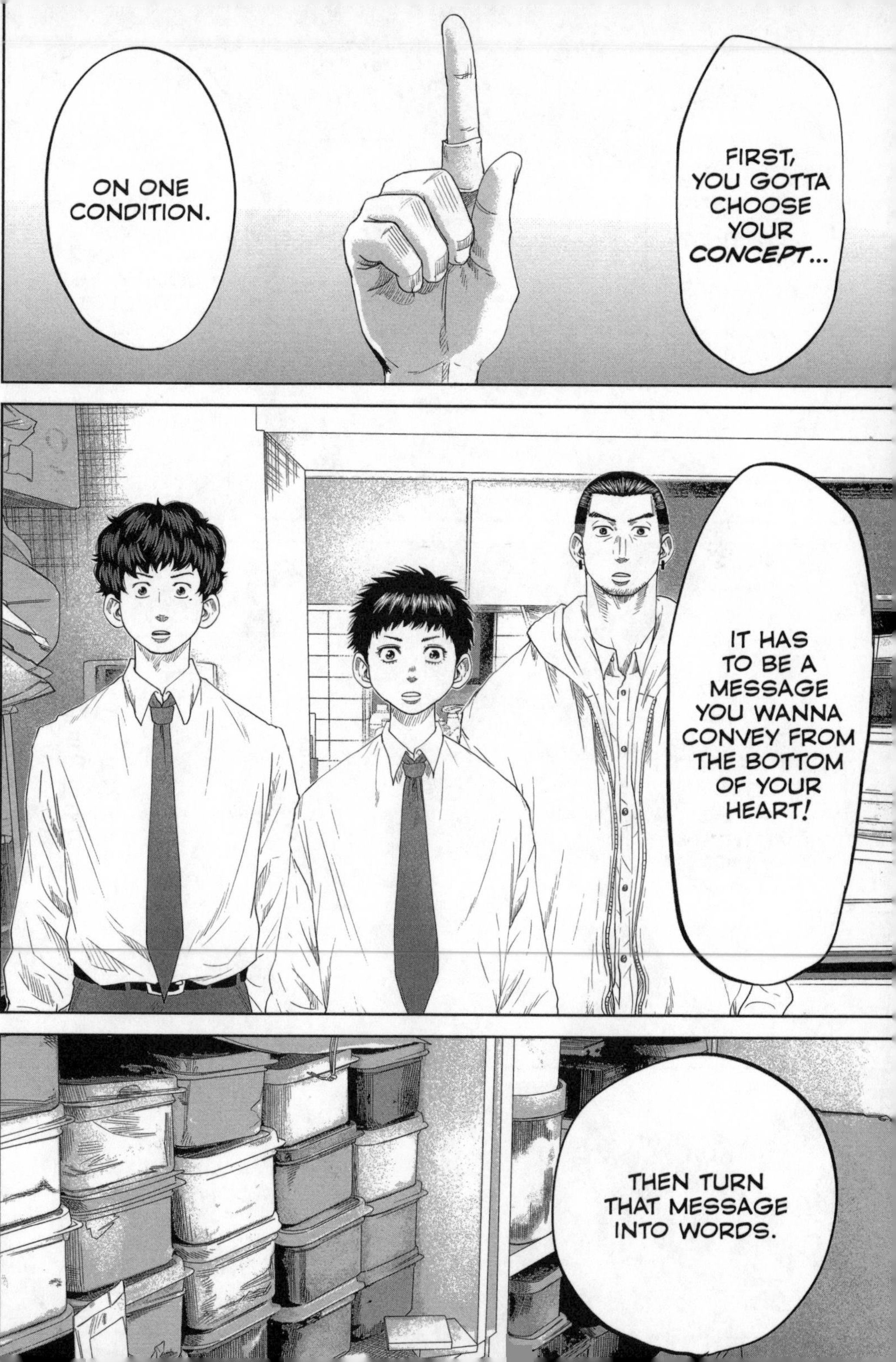
ON ONE CONDITION.
FIRST, YOU GOTTA CHOOSE YOUR *CONCEPT*...
IT HAS TO BE A MESSAGE YOU WANNA CONVEY FROM THE BOTTOM OF YOUR HEART!
THEN TURN THAT MESSAGE INTO WORDS.

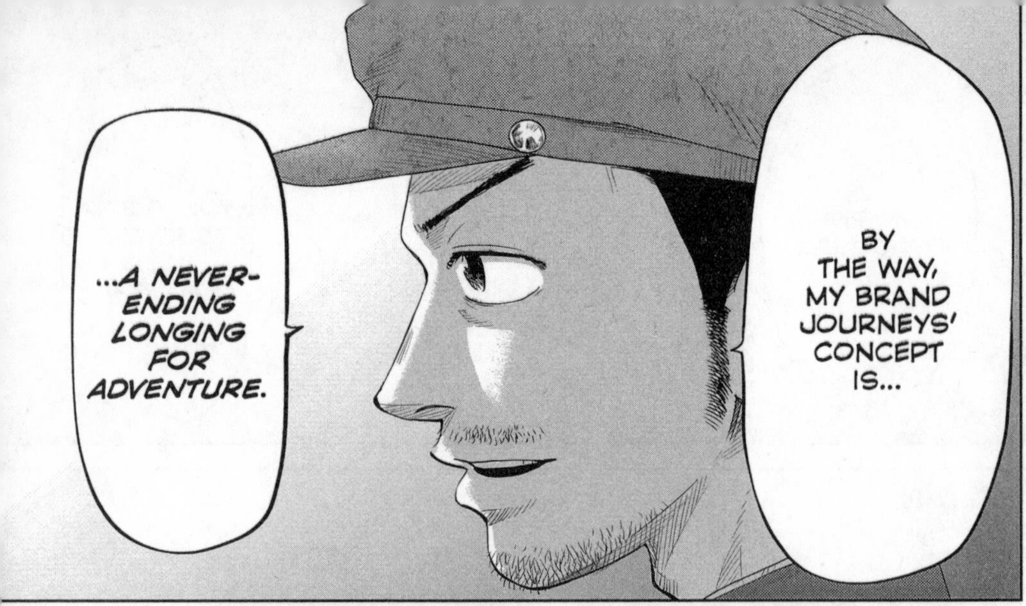
BY THE WAY, MY BRAND JOURNEYS' CONCEPT IS...
...A NEVER-ENDING LONGING FOR ADVENTURE.

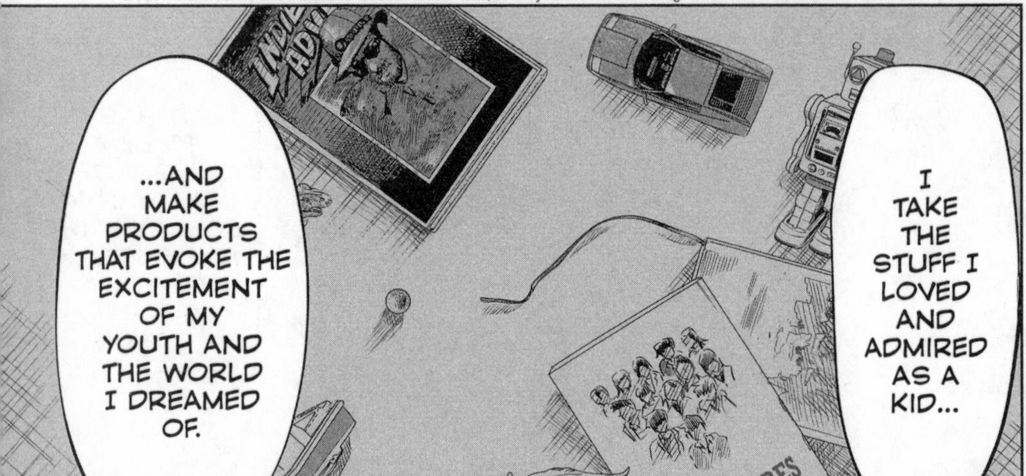
I TAKE THE STUFF I LOVED AND ADMIRED AS A KID...
...AND MAKE PRODUCTS THAT EVOKE THE EXCITEMENT OF MY YOUTH AND THE WORLD I DREAMED OF.
ADVENTURES OF 13 KIDS

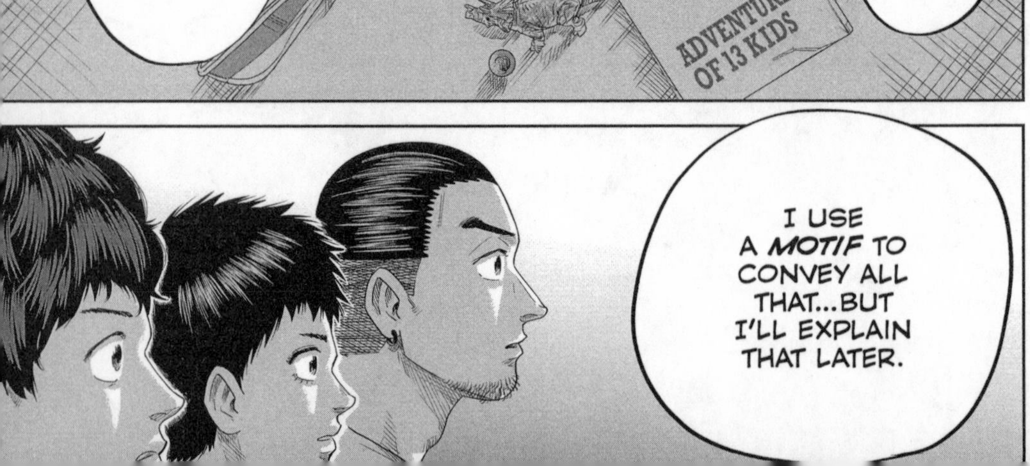
I USE A *MOTIF* TO CONVEY ALL THAT...BUT I'LL EXPLAIN THAT LATER.

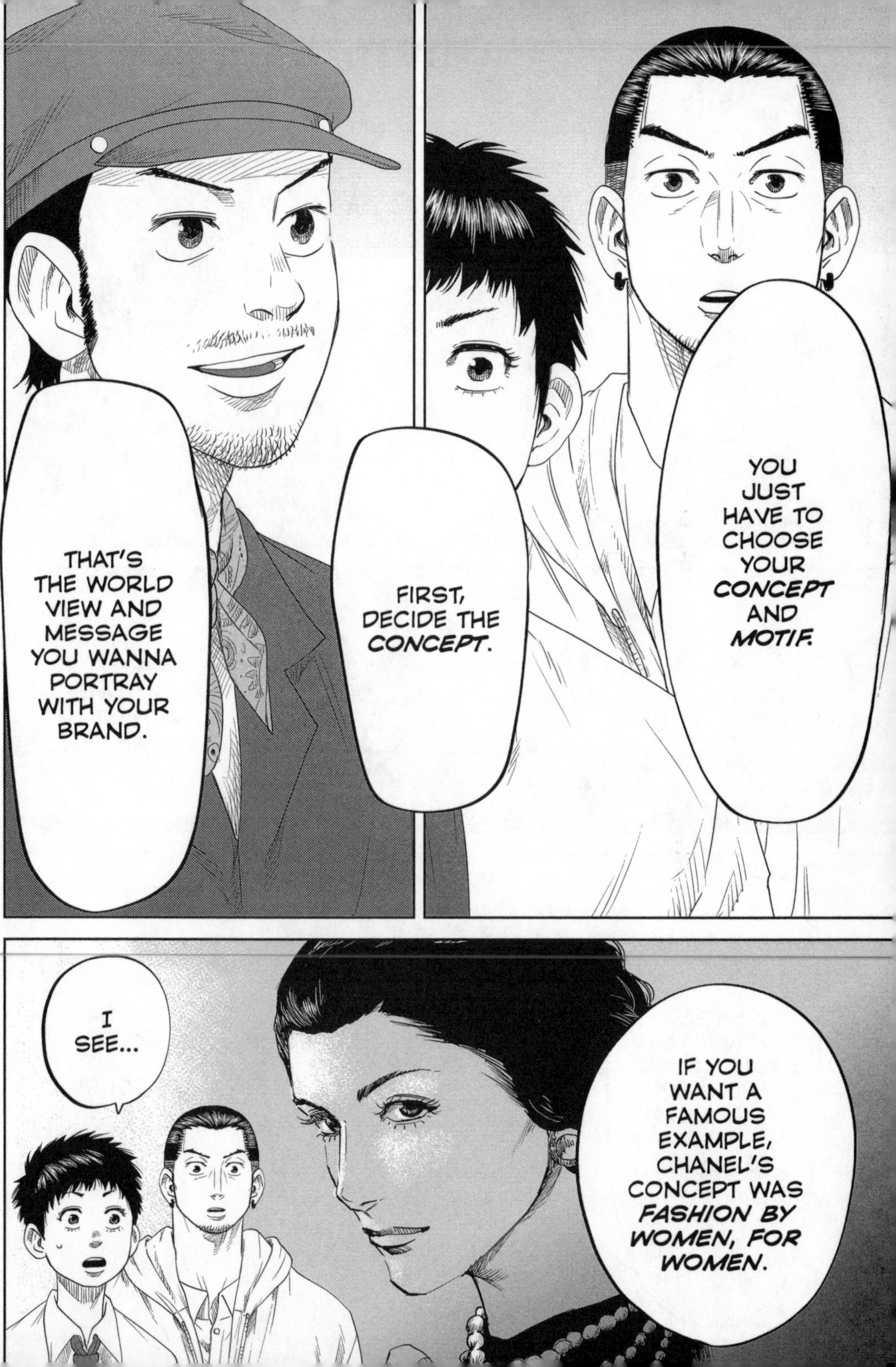
YOU JUST HAVE TO CHOOSE YOUR *CONCEPT* AND *MOTIF.*
FIRST, DECIDE THE *CONCEPT*.
THAT'S THE WORLD VIEW AND MESSAGE YOU WANNA PORTRAY WITH YOUR BRAND.
IF YOU WANT A FAMOUS EXAMPLE, CHANEL'S CONCEPT WAS *FASHION BY WOMEN, FOR WOMEN*.
I SEE...

Chap. 31 Concept

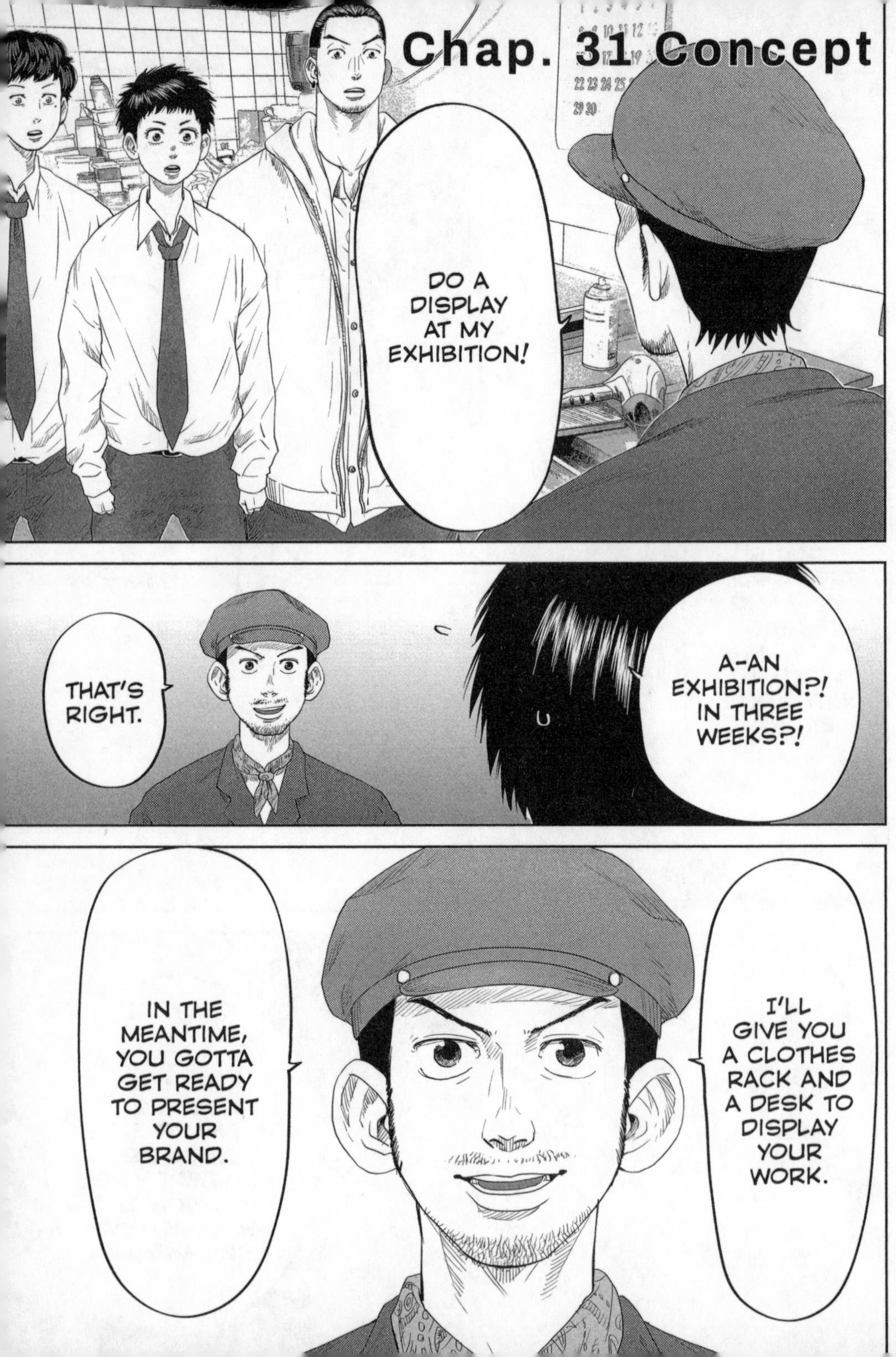
DO A DISPLAY AT MY EXHIBITION!
A-AN EXHIBITION?! IN THREE WEEKS?!
THAT'S RIGHT.
I'LL GIVE YOU A CLOTHES RACK AND A DESK TO DISPLAY YOUR WORK.
IN THE MEANTIME, YOU GOTTA GET READY TO PRESENT YOUR BRAND.

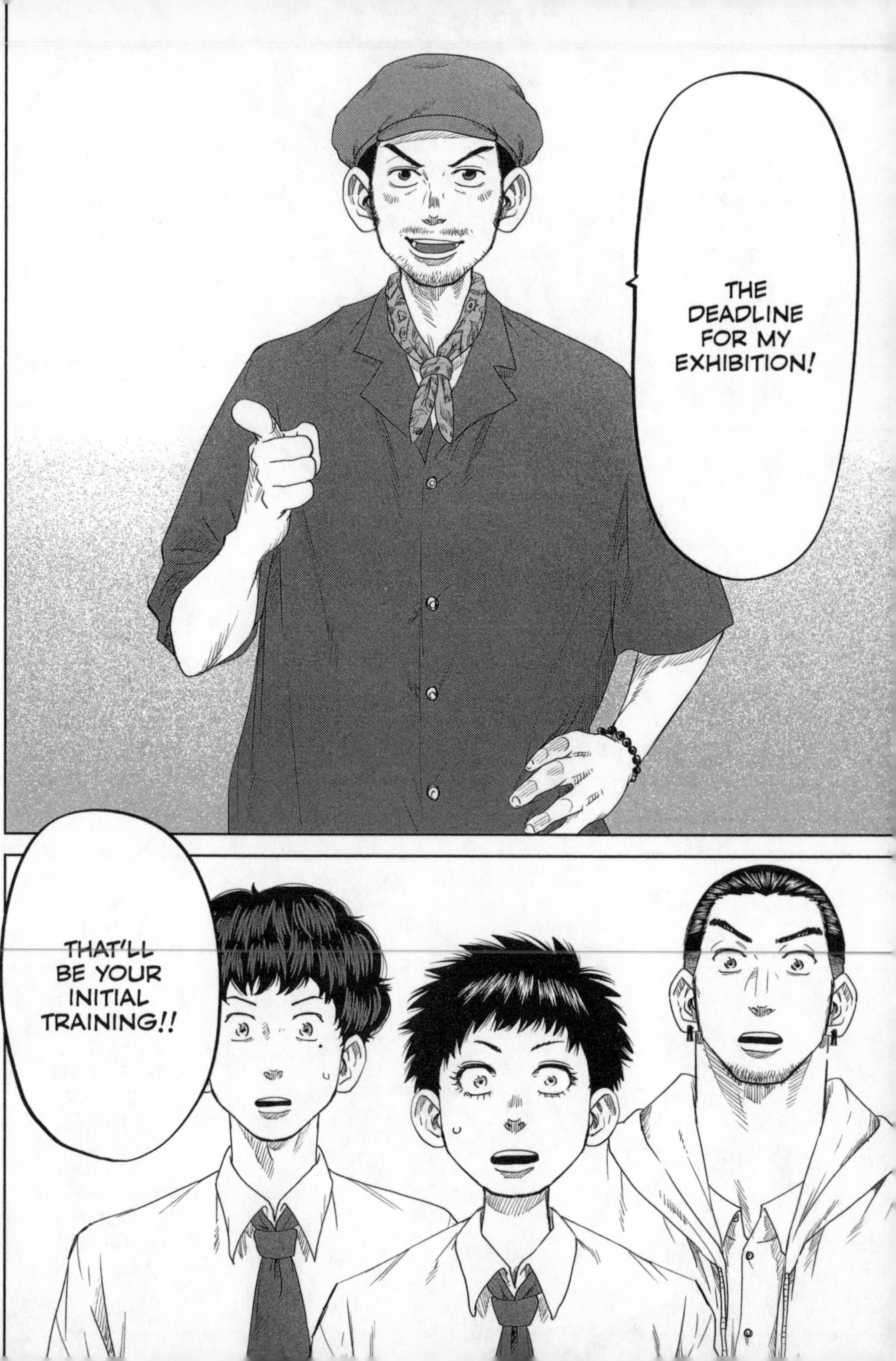
THE DEADLINE FOR MY EXHIBITION!
THAT'LL BE YOUR INITIAL TRAINING!!

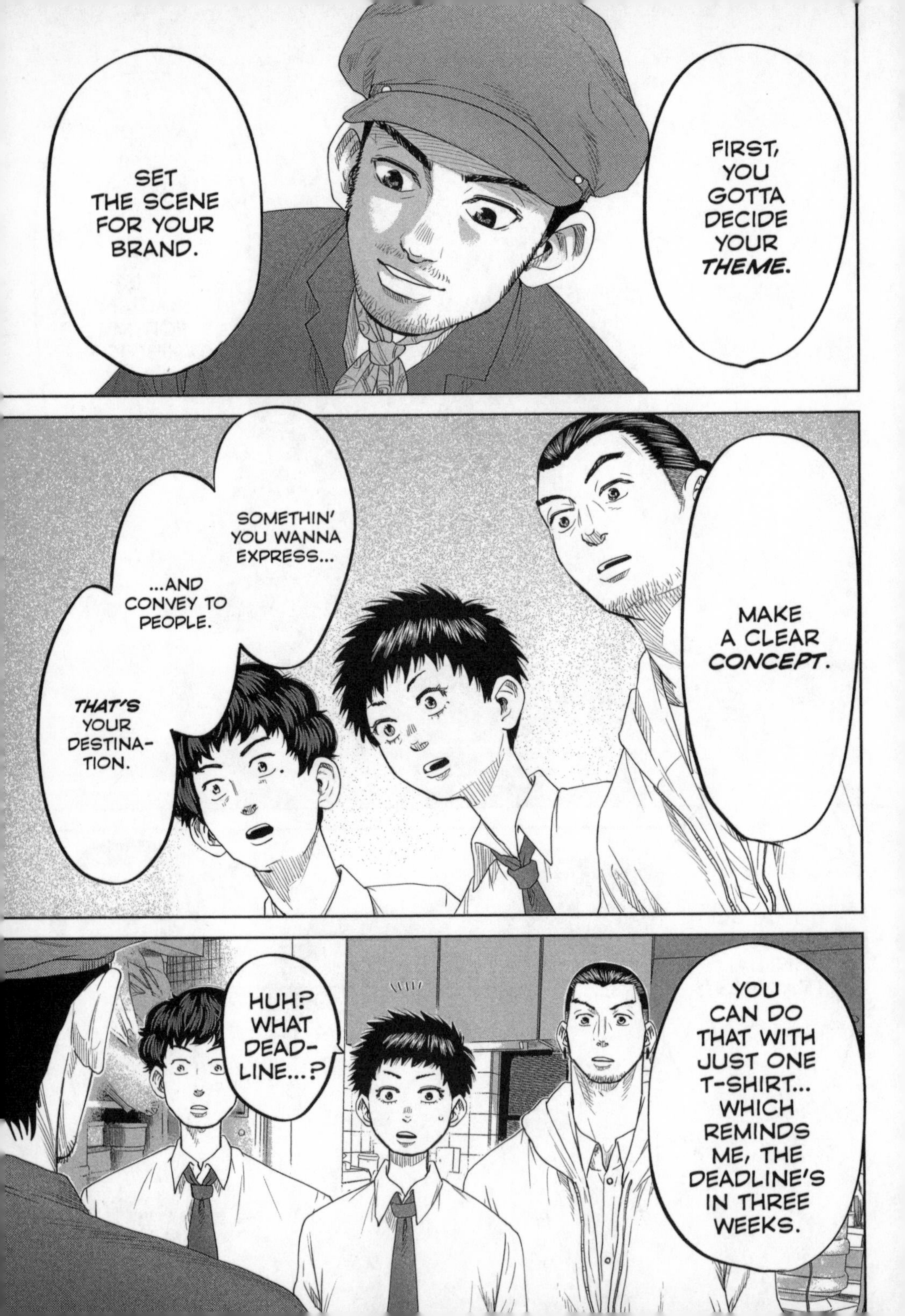
FIRST, YOU GOTTA DECIDE YOUR *THEME*.
SET THE SCENE FOR YOUR BRAND.
MAKE A CLEAR *CONCEPT*.
SOMETHIN' YOU WANNA EXPRESS...
...AND CONVEY TO PEOPLE.
THAT'S YOUR DESTINATION.
YOU CAN DO THAT WITH JUST ONE T-SHIRT... WHICH REMINDS ME, THE DEADLINE'S IN THREE WEEKS.
HUH? WHAT DEADLINE...?

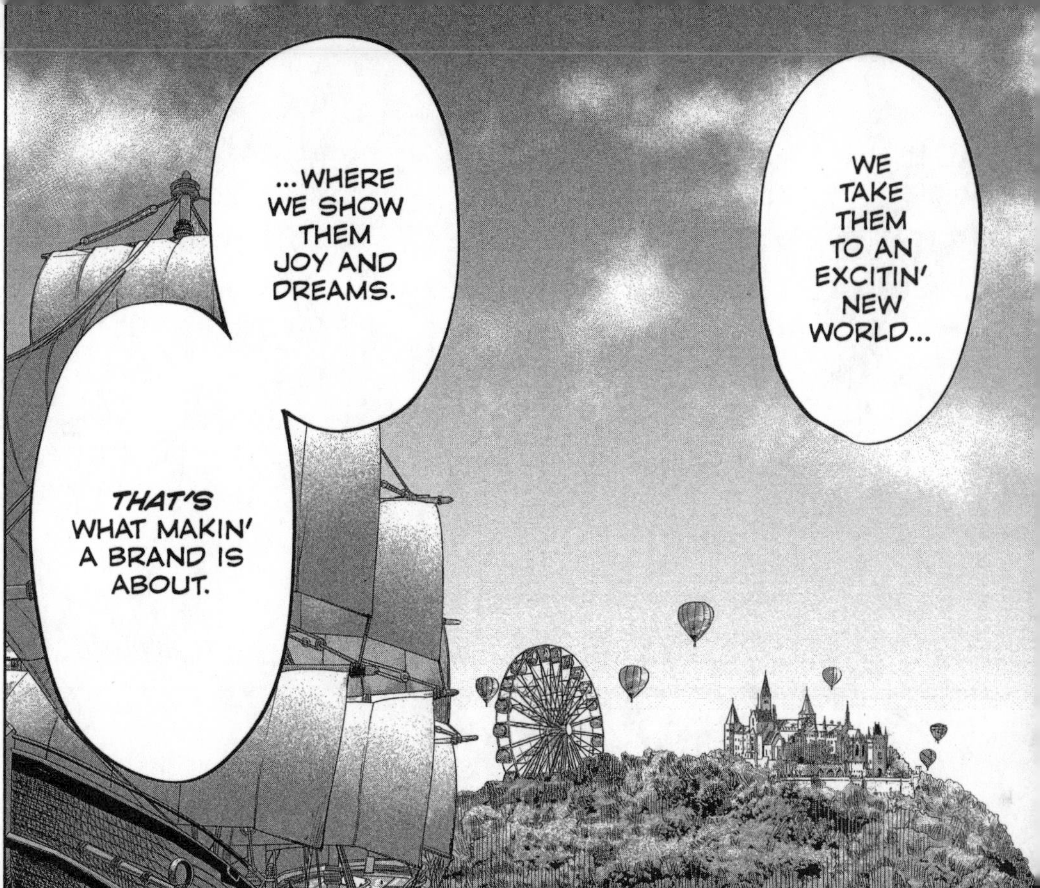
WE TAKE THEM TO AN EXCITIN' NEW WORLD...
...WHERE WE SHOW THEM JOY AND DREAMS.
THAT'S WHAT MAKIN' A BRAND IS ABOUT.
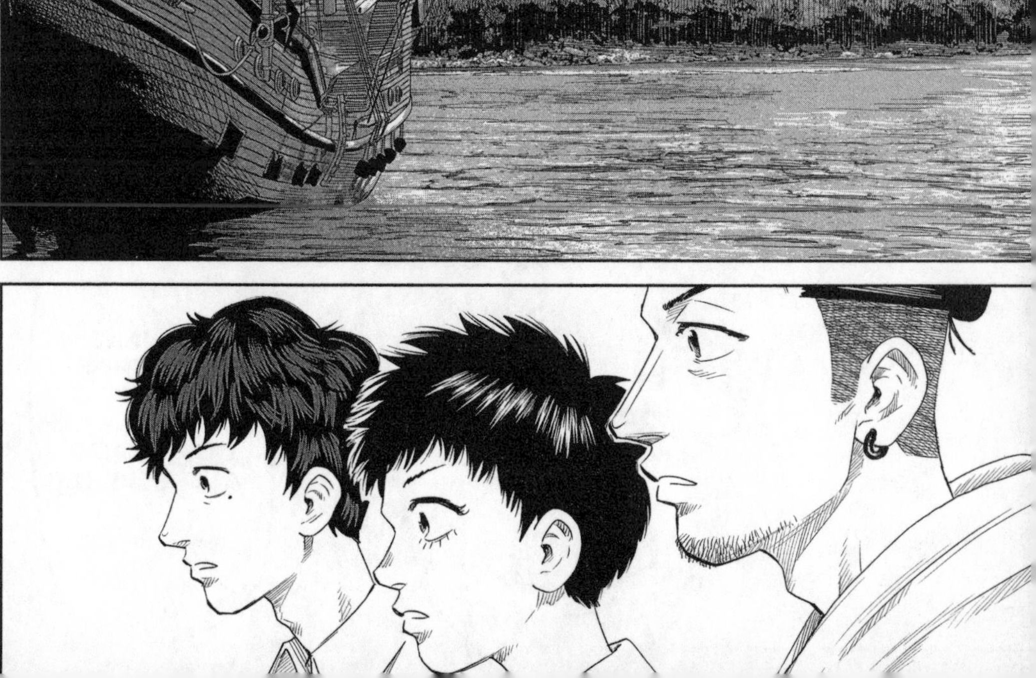

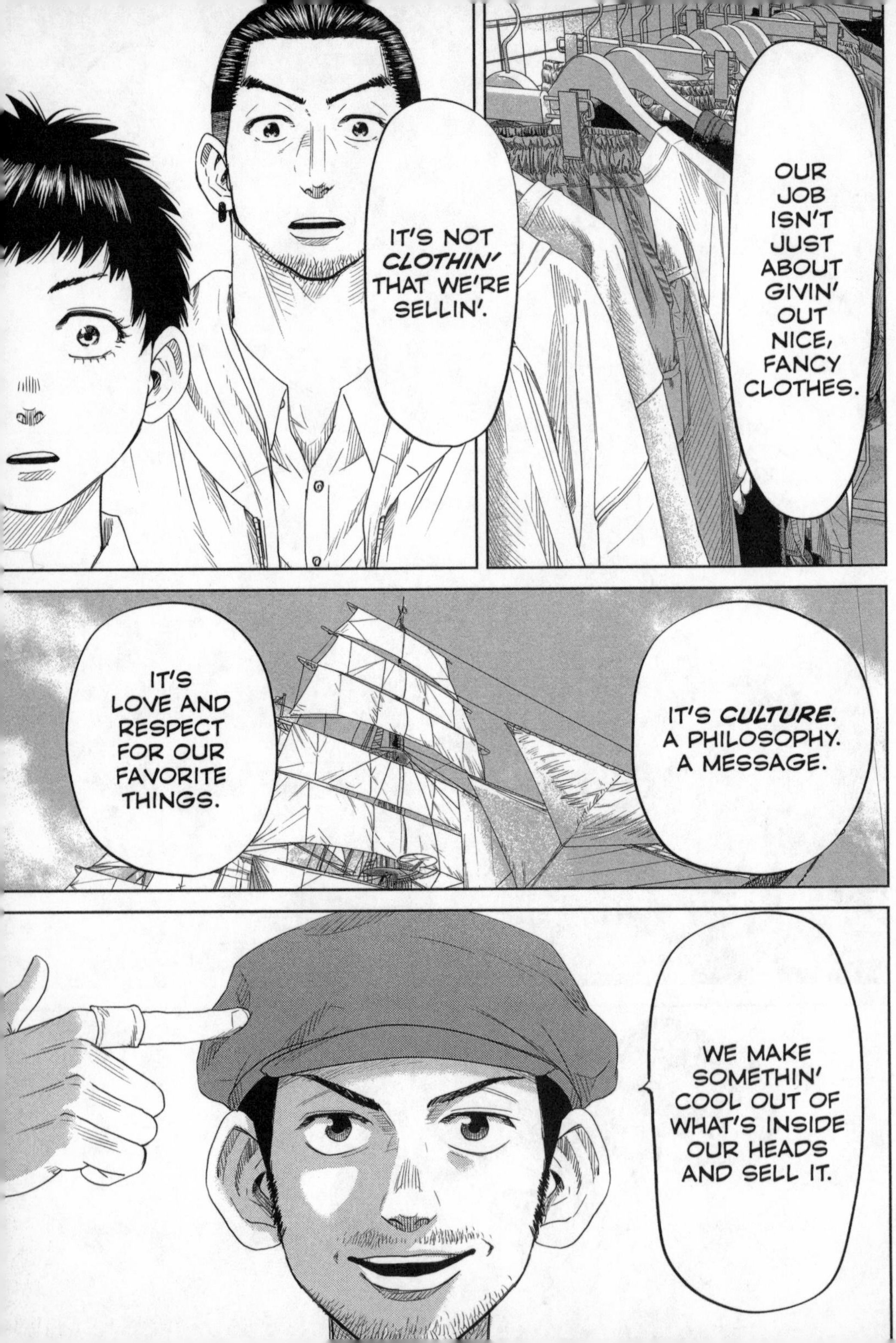
OUR JOB ISN'T JUST ABOUT GIVIN' OUT NICE, FANCY CLOTHES.
IT'S NOT CLOTHIN' THAT WE'RE SELLIN'.
IT'S CULTURE. A PHILOSOPHY. A MESSAGE.
IT'S LOVE AND RESPECT FOR OUR FAVORITE THINGS.
WE MAKE SOMETHIN' COOL OUT OF WHAT'S INSIDE OUR HEADS AND SELL IT.

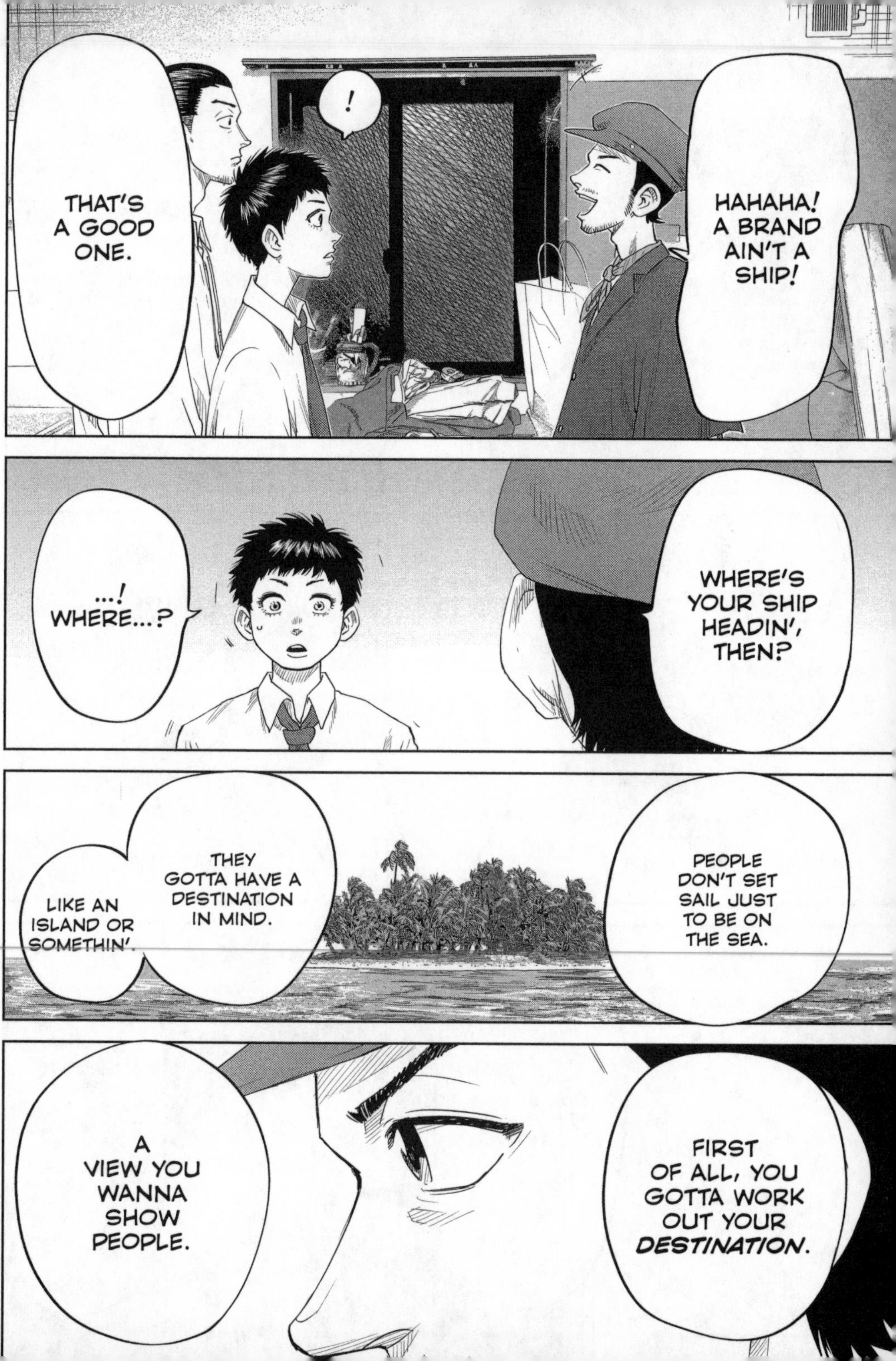
HAHAHA! A BRAND AIN'T A SHIP!
!
THAT'S A GOOD ONE.
WHERE'S YOUR SHIP HEADIN', THEN?
...! WHERE...?
PEOPLE DON'T SET SAIL JUST TO BE ON THE SEA.
THEY GOTTA HAVE A DESTINATION IN MIND.
LIKE AN ISLAND OR SOMETHIN'.
FIRST OF ALL, YOU GOTTA WORK OUT YOUR *DESTINATION*.
A VIEW YOU WANNA SHOW PEOPLE.

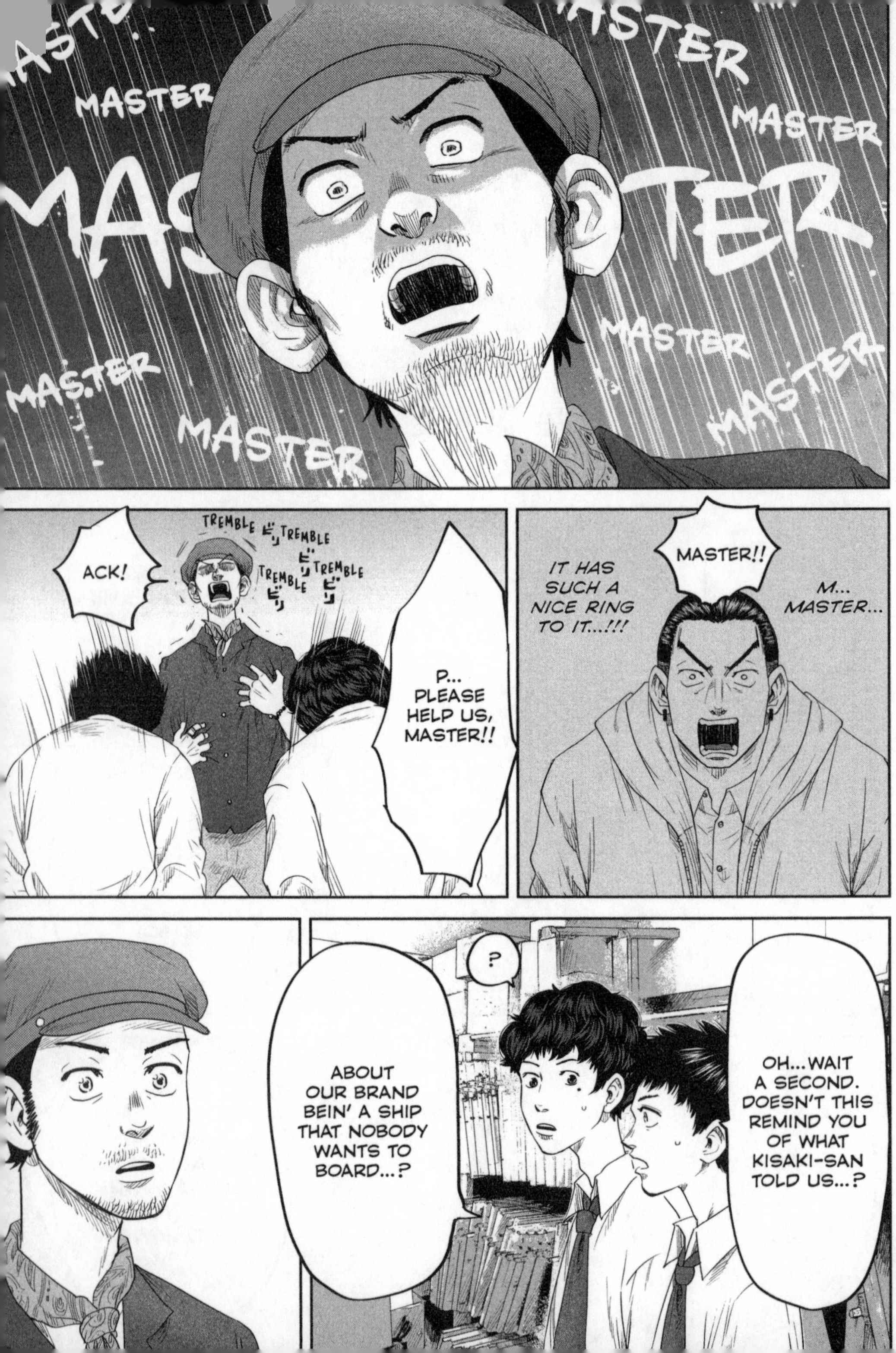
MASTER
MASTER
MASTER
MASTER
MASTER
MASTER
MASTER
MASTER
MASTER!!
M... MASTER...
IT HAS SUCH A NICE RING TO IT...!!!
P... PLEASE HELP US, MASTER!!
TREMBLE TREMBLE TREMBLE TREMBLE
ACK!
OH...WAIT A SECOND. DOESN'T THIS REMIND YOU OF WHAT KISAKI-SAN TOLD US...?
?
ABOUT OUR BRAND BEIN' A SHIP THAT NOBODY WANTS TO BOARD...?

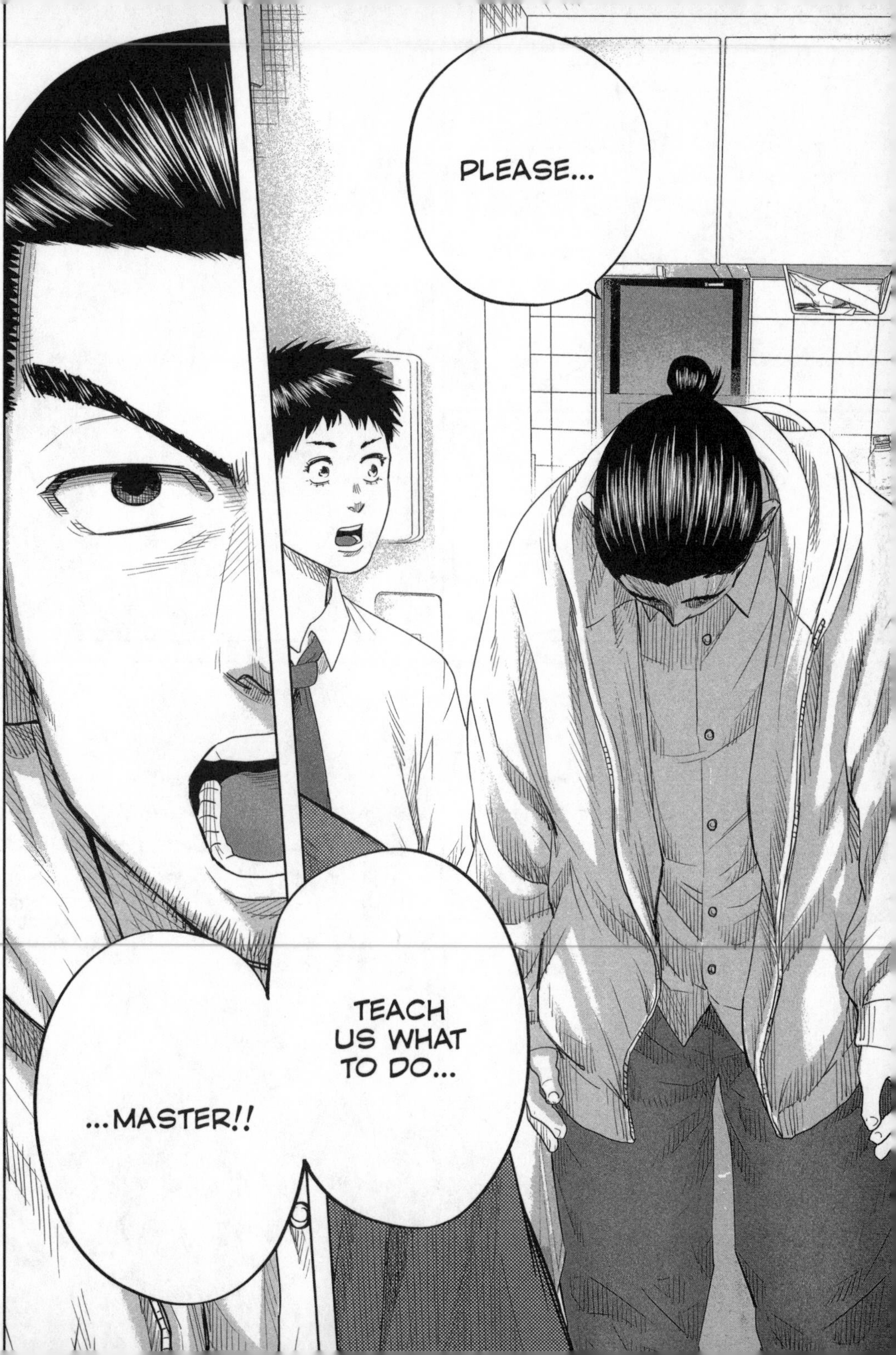
PLEASE...
TEACH US WHAT TO DO...
...MASTER!!

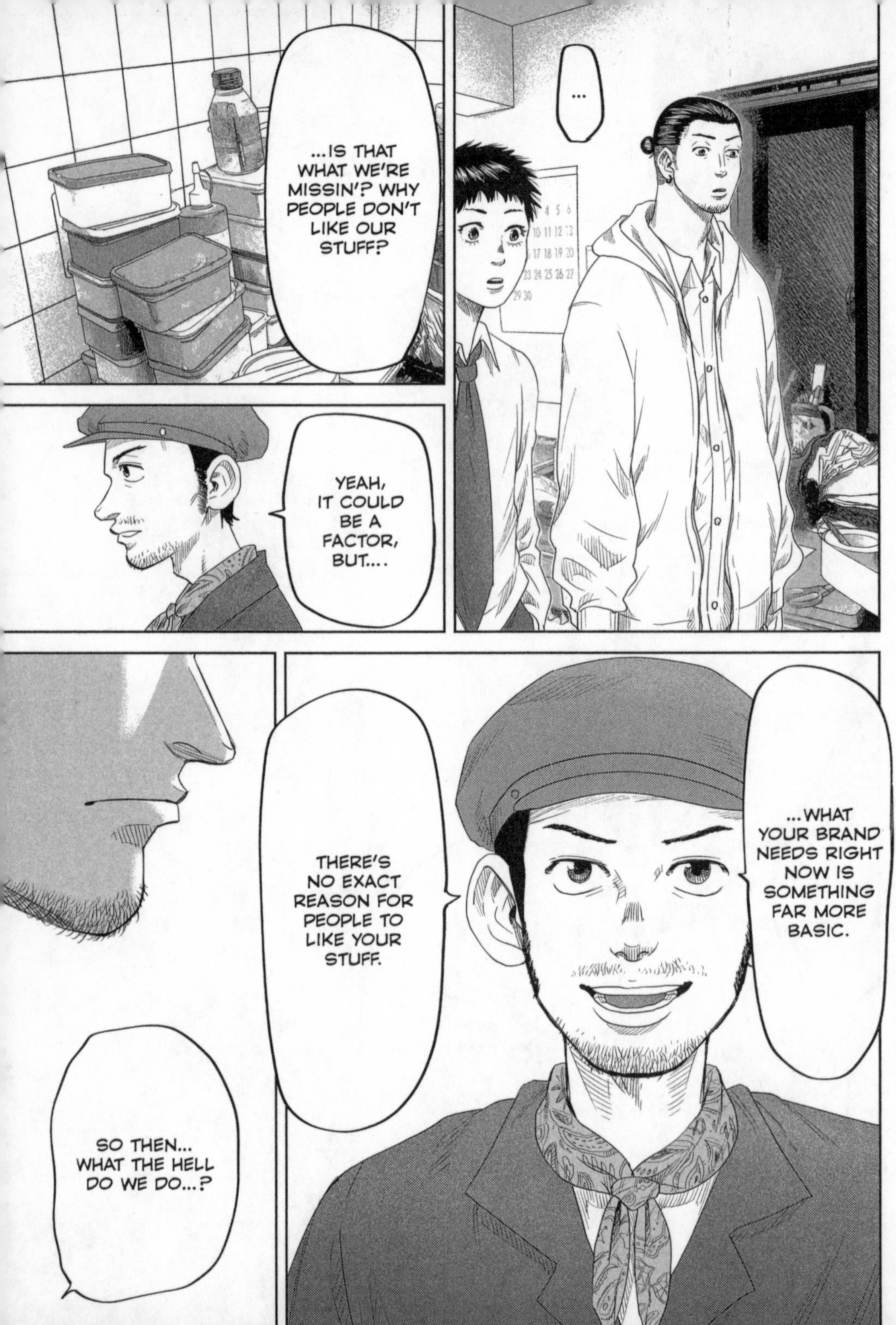
...
...IS THAT WHAT WE'RE MISSIN'? WHY PEOPLE DON'T LIKE OUR STUFF?
YEAH, IT COULD BE A FACTOR, BUT....
...WHAT YOUR BRAND NEEDS RIGHT NOW IS SOMETHING FAR MORE BASIC.
THERE'S NO EXACT REASON FOR PEOPLE TO LIKE YOUR STUFF.
SO THEN... WHAT THE HELL DO WE DO...?

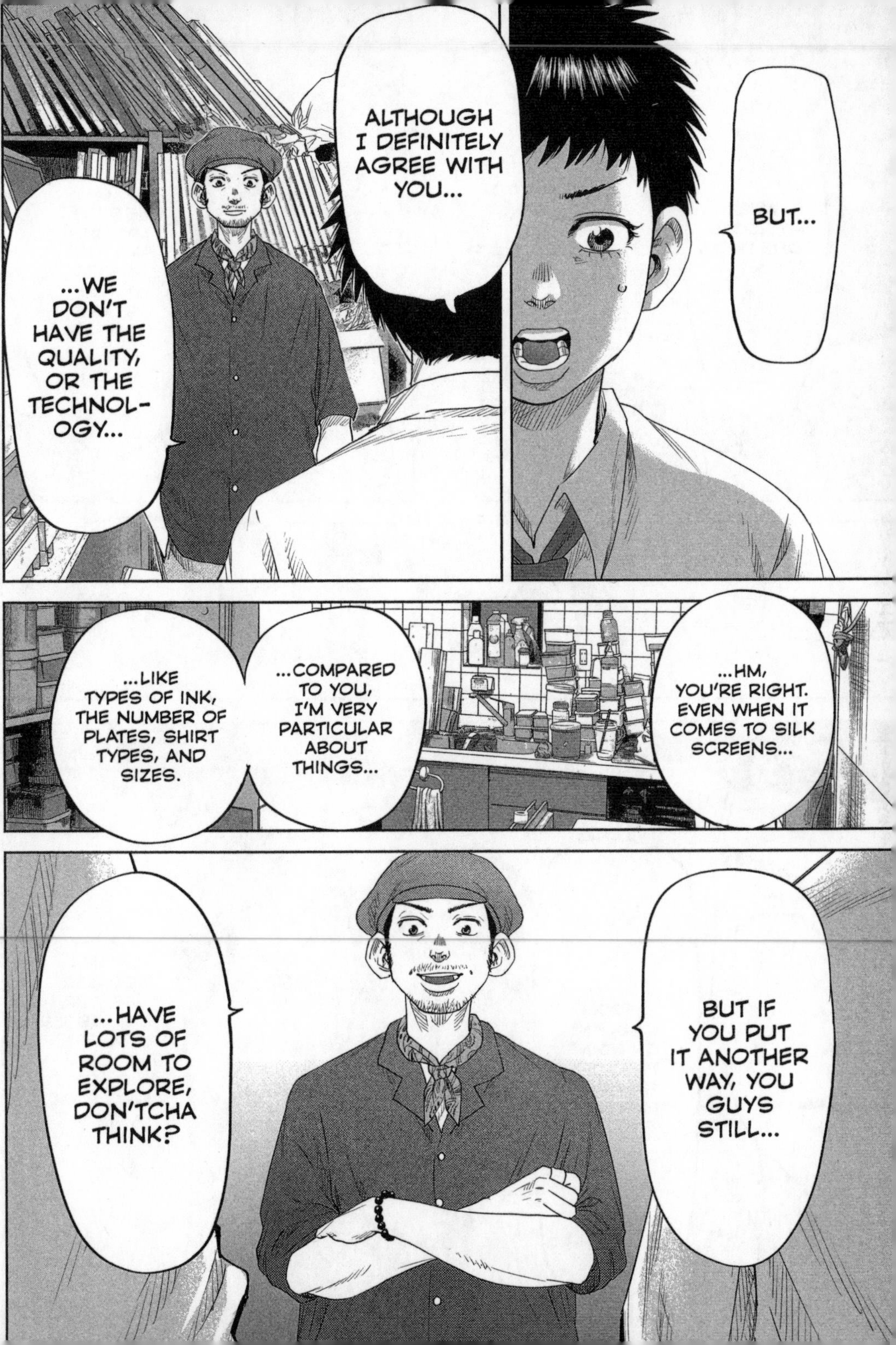
BUT...
ALTHOUGH I DEFINITELY AGREE WITH YOU...
...WE DON'T HAVE THE QUALITY, OR THE TECHNOLOGY...
...HM, YOU'RE RIGHT. EVEN WHEN IT COMES TO SILK SCREENS...
...COMPARED TO YOU, I'M VERY PARTICULAR ABOUT THINGS...
...LIKE TYPES OF INK, THE NUMBER OF PLATES, SHIRT TYPES, AND SIZES.
BUT IF YOU PUT IT ANOTHER WAY, YOU GUYS STILL...
...HAVE LOTS OF ROOM TO EXPLORE, DON'TCHA THINK?

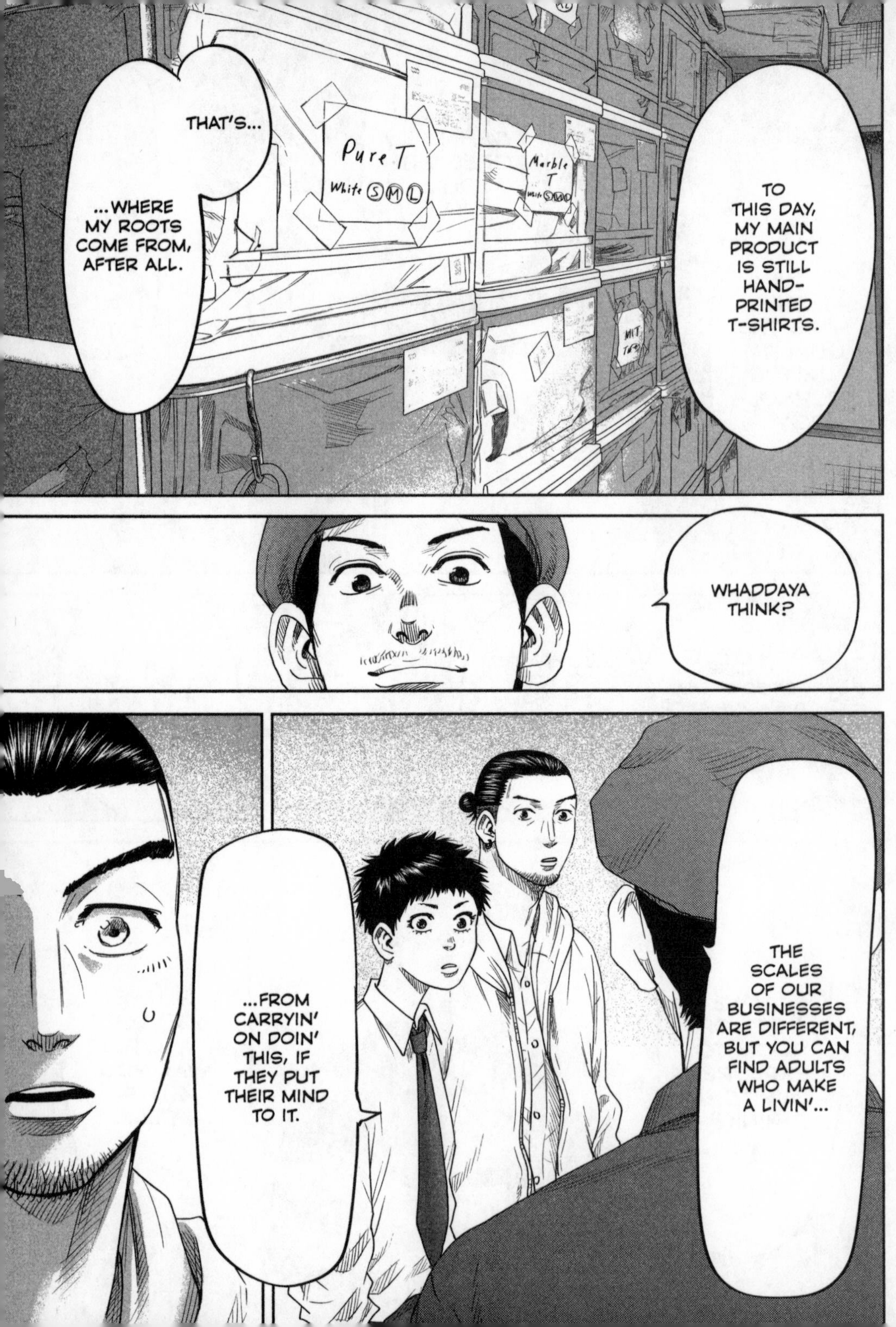
TO THIS DAY, MY MAIN PRODUCT IS STILL HAND-PRINTED T-SHIRTS.
Marble T
White SML
Pure T
White SML
THAT'S...
...WHERE MY ROOTS COME FROM, AFTER ALL.
WHADDAYA THINK?
THE SCALES OF OUR BUSINESSES ARE DIFFERENT, BUT YOU CAN FIND ADULTS WHO MAKE A LIVIN'...
...FROM CARRYIN' ON DOIN' THIS, IF THEY PUT THEIR MIND TO IT.

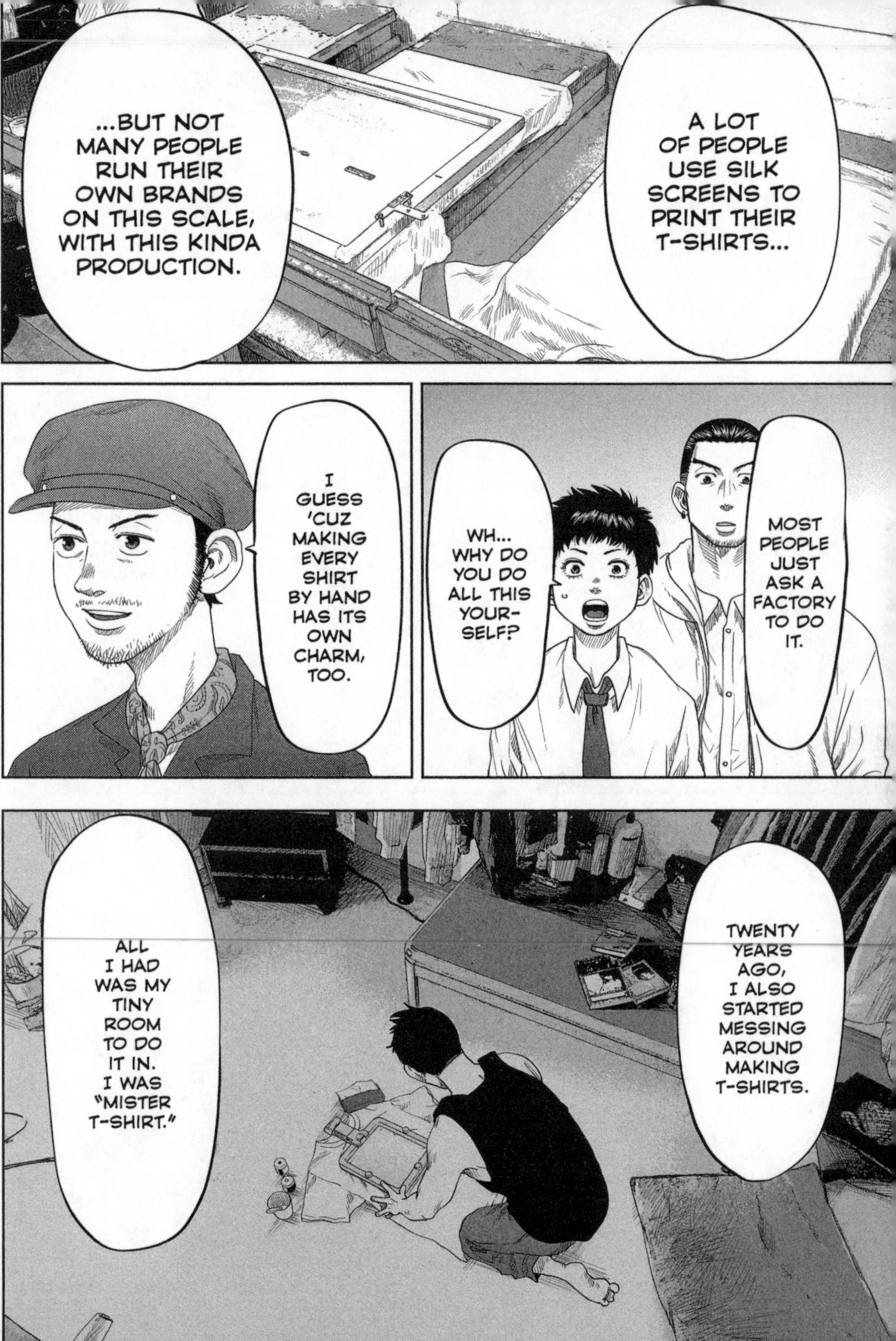
A LOT OF PEOPLE USE SILK SCREENS TO PRINT THEIR T-SHIRTS...
...BUT NOT MANY PEOPLE RUN THEIR OWN BRANDS ON THIS SCALE, WITH THIS KINDA PRODUCTION.
MOST PEOPLE JUST ASK A FACTORY TO DO IT.
WH... WHY DO YOU DO ALL THIS YOUR-SELF?
I GUESS 'CUZ MAKING EVERY SHIRT BY HAND HAS ITS OWN CHARM, TOO.
TWENTY YEARS AGO, I ALSO STARTED MESSING AROUND MAKING T-SHIRTS.
ALL I HAD WAS MY TINY ROOM TO DO IT IN. I WAS "MISTER T-SHIRT."

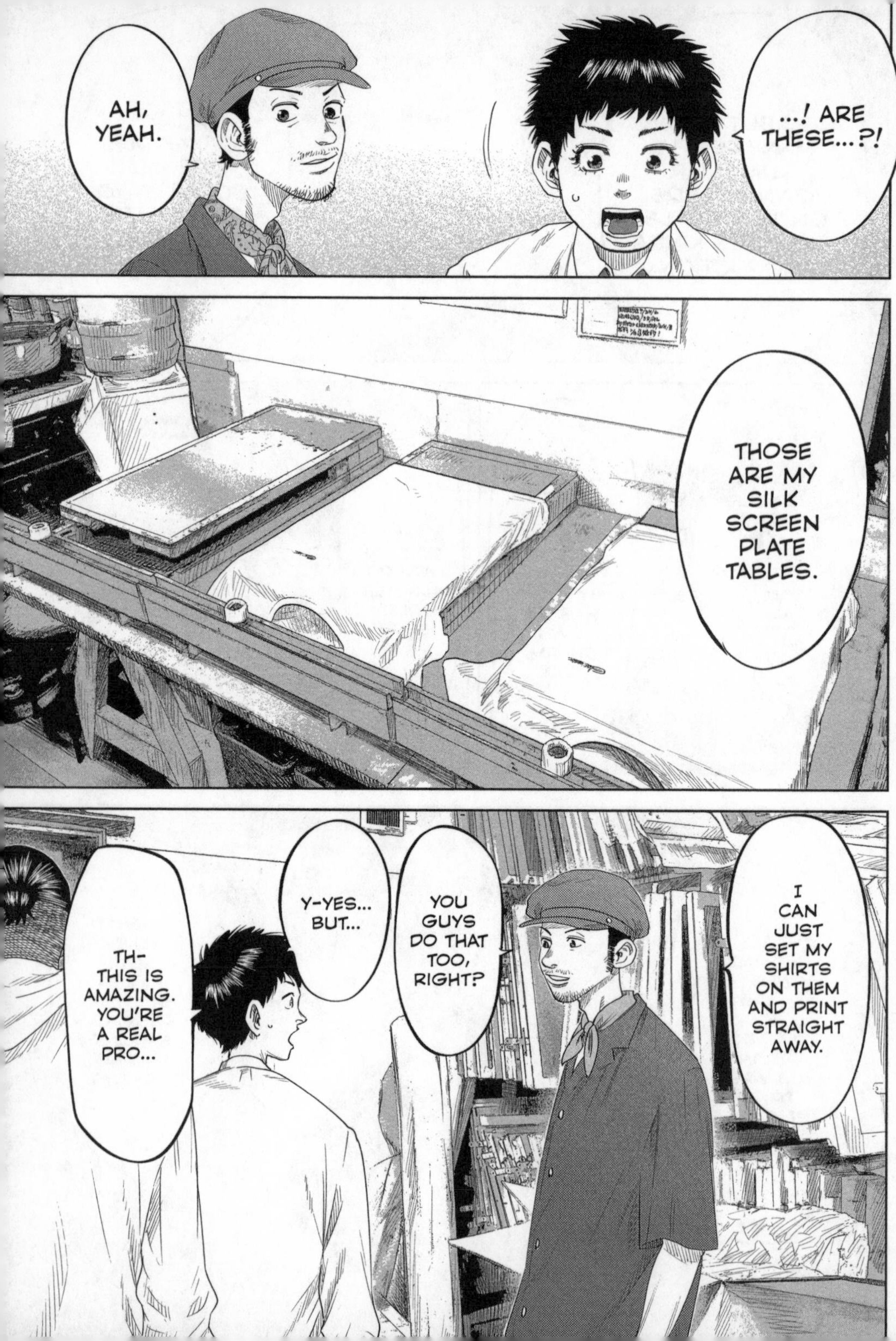
...! ARE THESE...?!
AH, YEAH.
THOSE ARE MY SILK SCREEN PLATE TABLES.
I CAN JUST SET MY SHIRTS ON THEM AND PRINT STRAIGHT AWAY.
YOU GUYS DO THAT TOO, RIGHT?
Y-YES... BUT...
TH- THIS IS AMAZING. YOU'RE A REAL PRO...

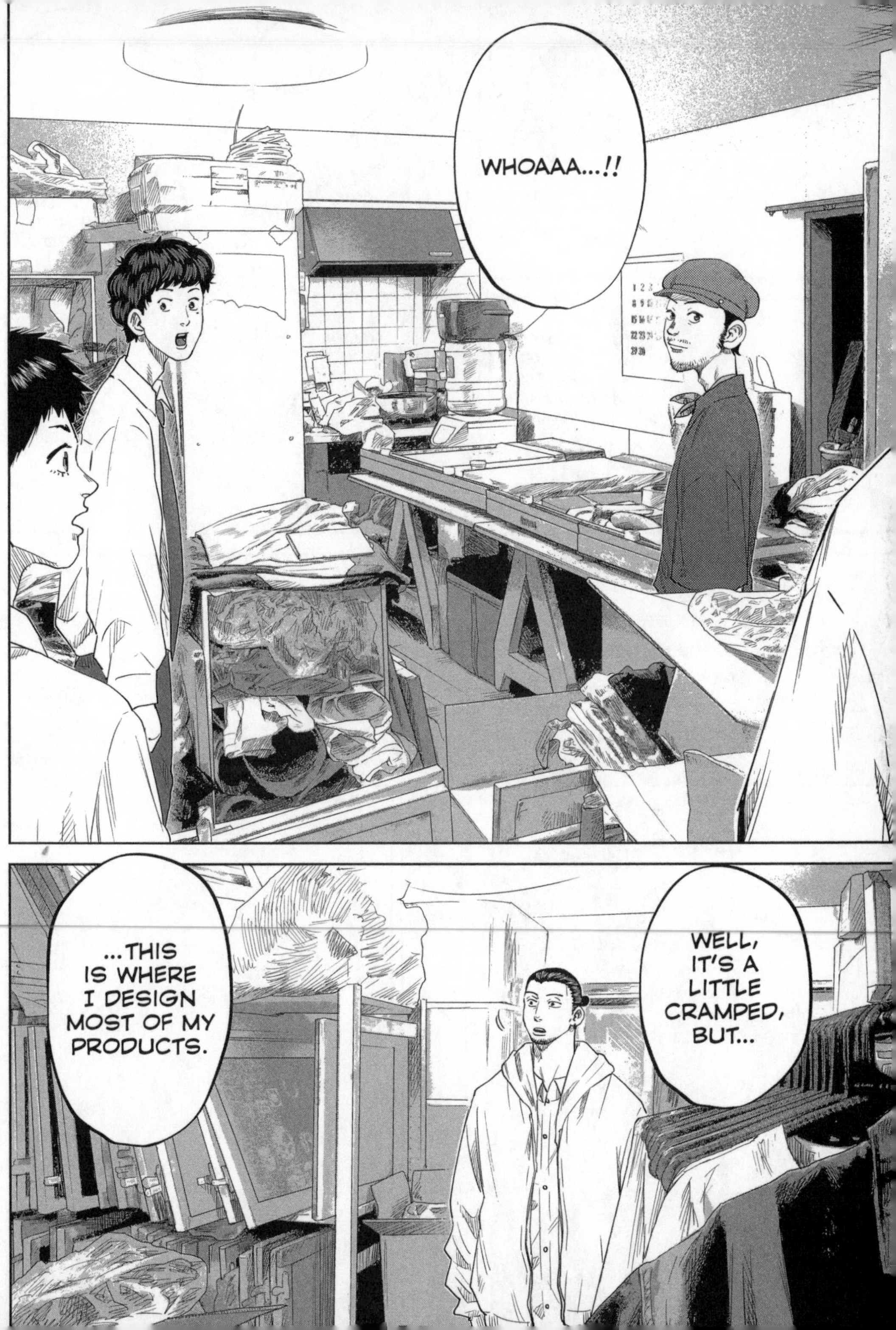
WHOAAA...!!
WELL, IT'S A LITTLE CRAMPED, BUT...
...THIS IS WHERE I DESIGN MOST OF MY PRODUCTS.

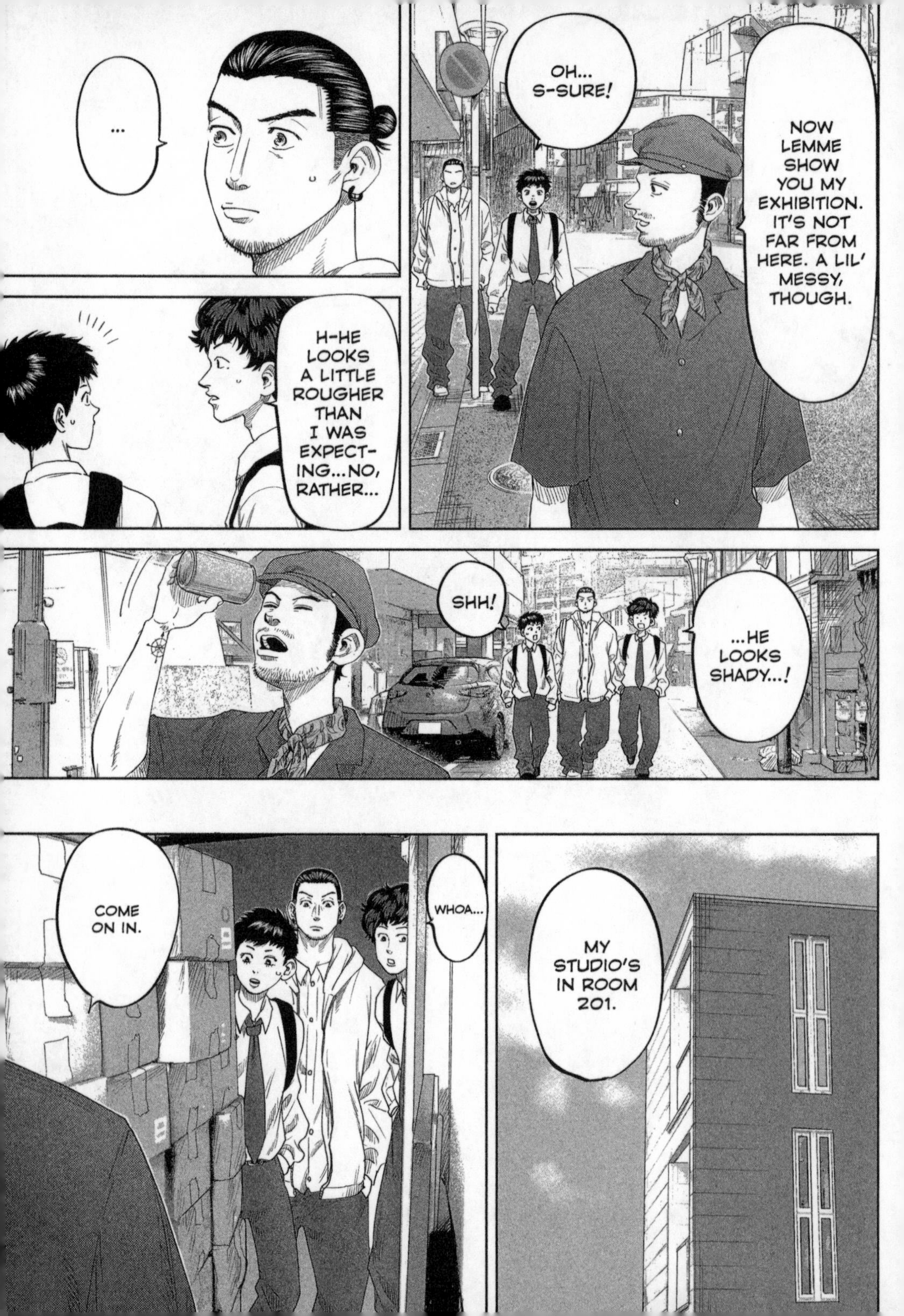
NOW LEMME SHOW YOU MY EXHIBITION. IT'S NOT FAR FROM HERE. A LIL' MESSY, THOUGH.
OH... S-SURE!
...
H-HE LOOKS A LITTLE ROUGHER THAN I WAS EXPECTING...NO, RATHER...
...HE LOOKS SHADY...!
SHH!
MY STUDIO'S IN ROOM 201.
WHOA...
COME ON IN.

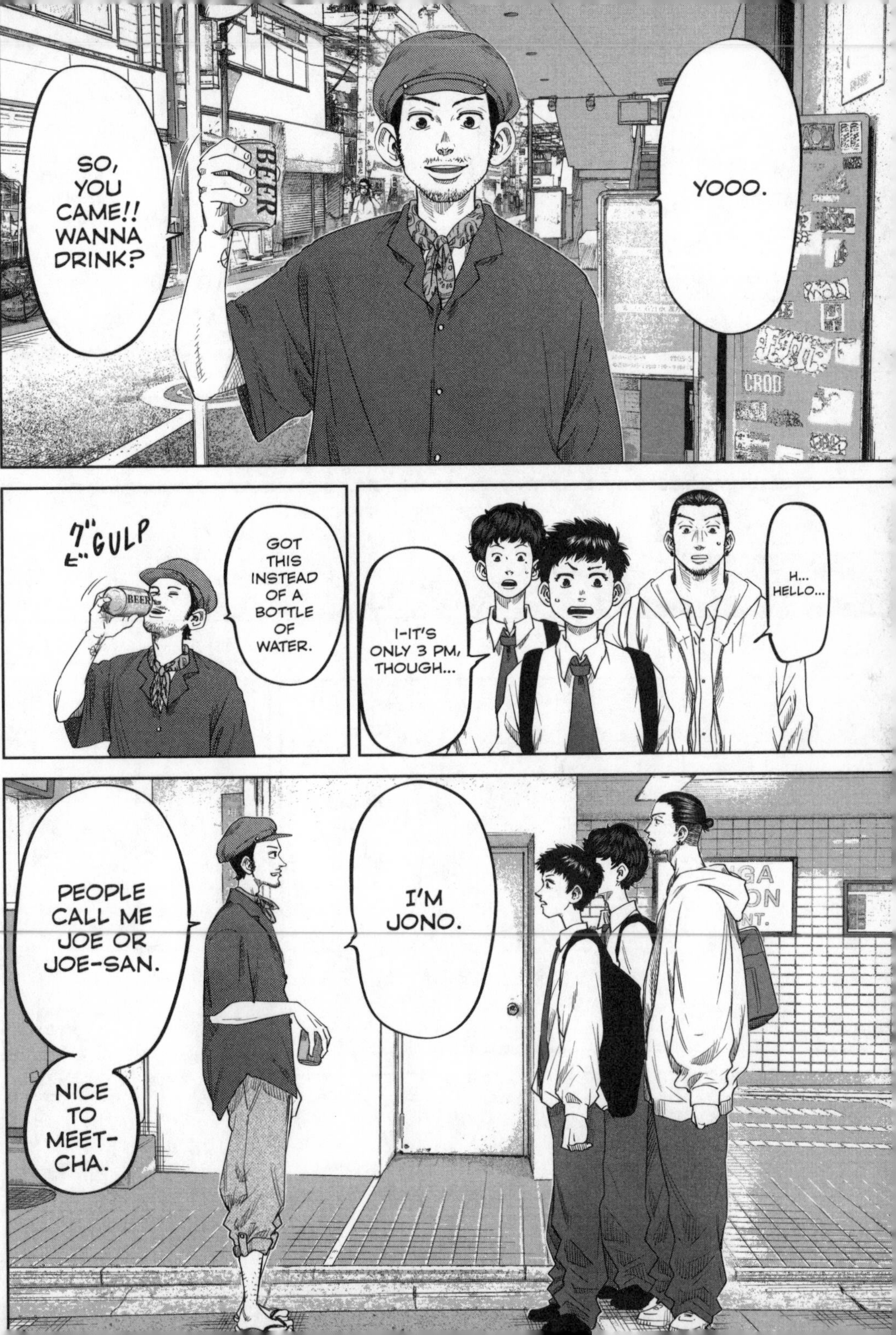
YOOO.
SO, YOU CAME!! WANNA DRINK?
H... HELLO...
I-IT'S ONLY 3 PM, THOUGH...
GOT THIS INSTEAD OF A BOTTLE OF WATER.
GULP
I'M JONO.
PEOPLE CALL ME JOE OR JOE-SAN.
NICE TO MEET-CHA.

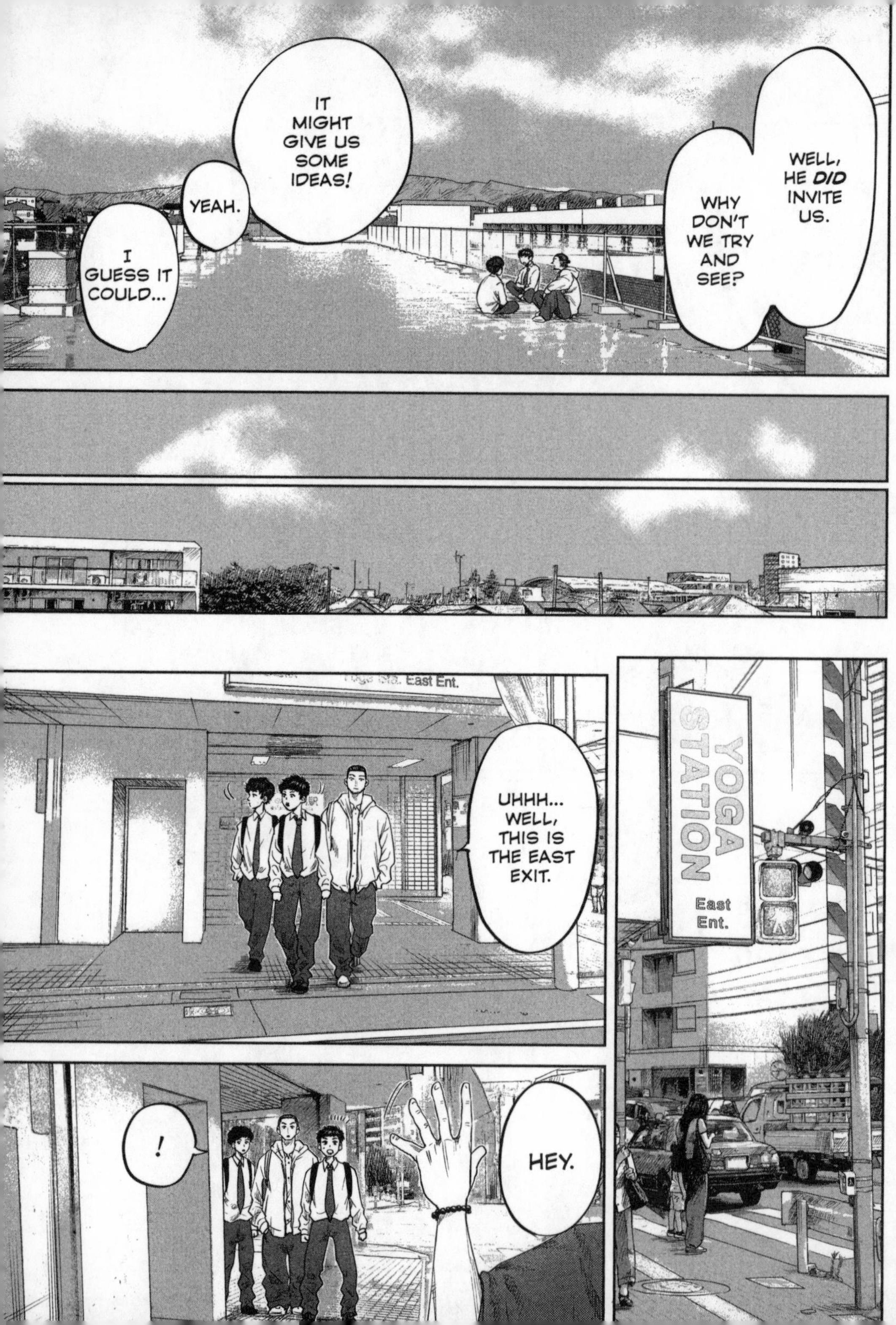
WELL, HE *DID* INVITE US.
WHY DON'T WE TRY AND SEE?
IT MIGHT GIVE US SOME IDEAS!
YEAH.
I GUESS IT COULD...
YOGA STATION
East Ent.
East Ent.
UHHH... WELL, THIS IS THE EAST EXIT.
HEY.
!

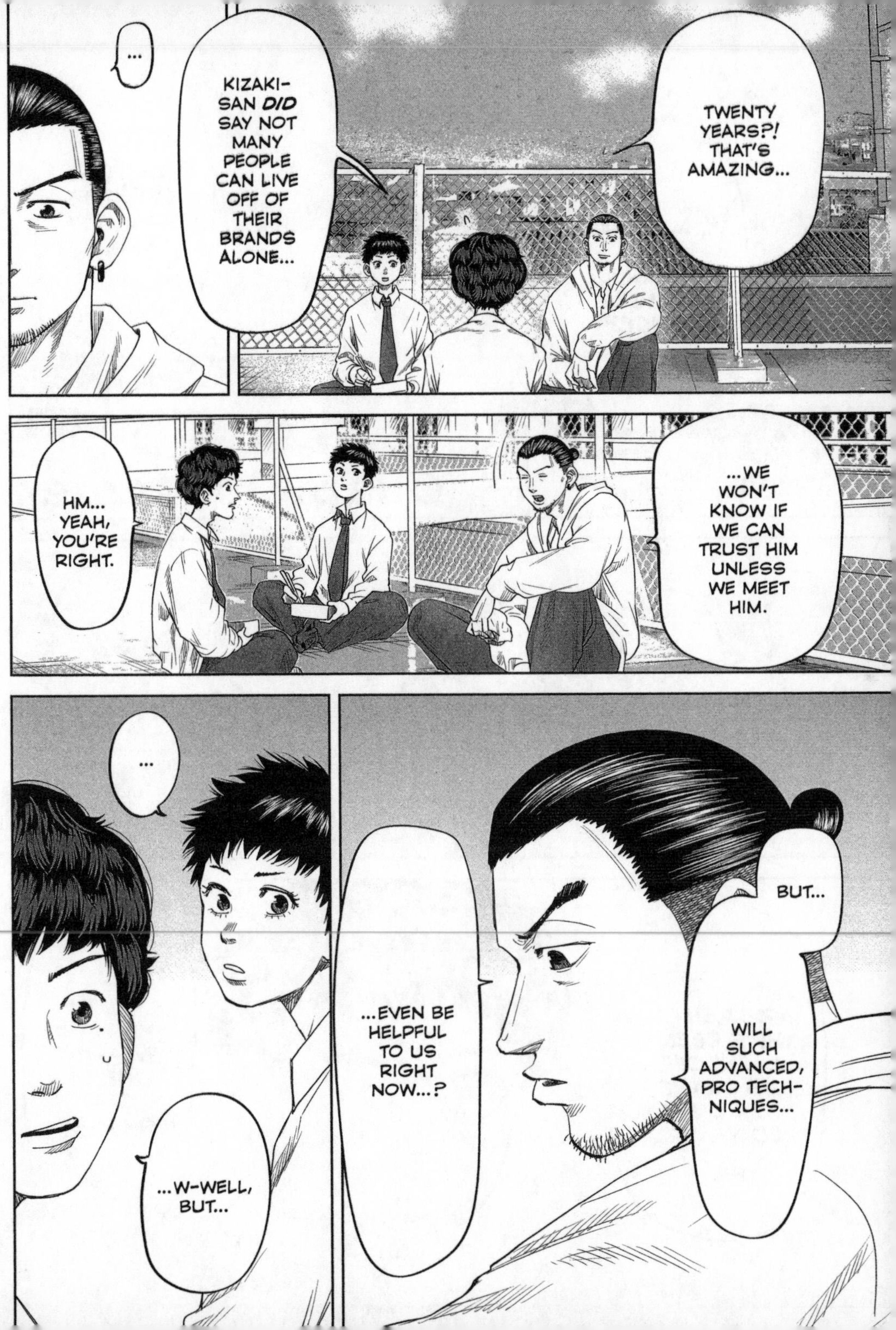
TWENTY YEARS?! THAT'S AMAZING...
KIZAKI-SAN *DID* SAY NOT MANY PEOPLE CAN LIVE OFF OF THEIR BRANDS ALONE...
...
...WE WON'T KNOW IF WE CAN TRUST HIM UNLESS WE MEET HIM.
HM... YEAH, YOU'RE RIGHT.
BUT...
WILL SUCH ADVANCED, PRO TECHNIQUES...
...EVEN BE HELPFUL TO US RIGHT NOW...?
...
...W-WELL, BUT...

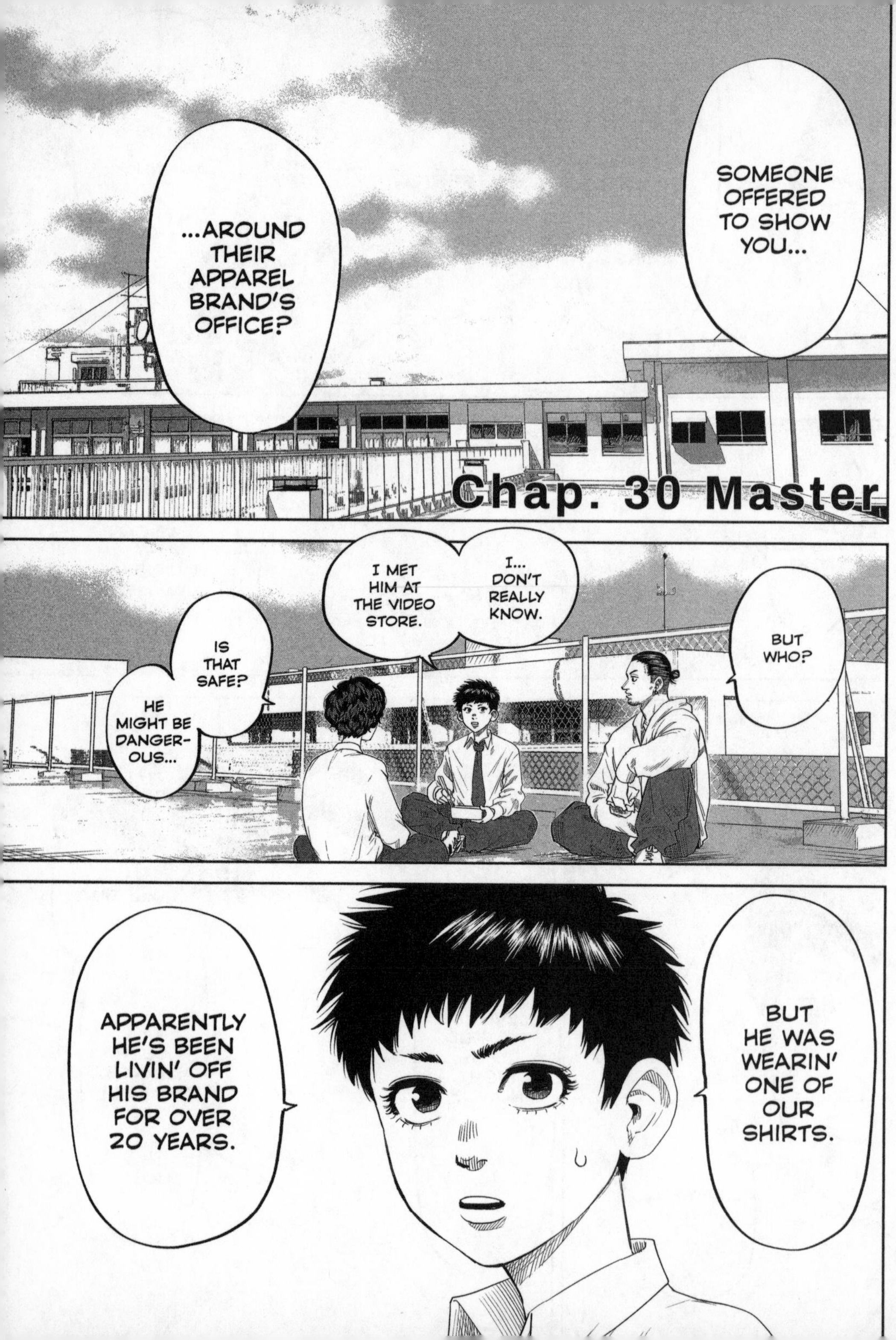
SOMEONE OFFERED TO SHOW YOU...
...AROUND THEIR APPAREL BRAND'S OFFICE?
Chap. 30 Master
BUT WHO?
I... DON'T REALLY KNOW.
I MET HIM AT THE VIDEO STORE.
IS THAT SAFE?
HE MIGHT BE DANGER-OUS...
BUT HE WAS WEARIN' ONE OF OUR SHIRTS.
APPARENTLY HE'S BEEN LIVIN' OFF HIS BRAND FOR OVER 20 YEARS.

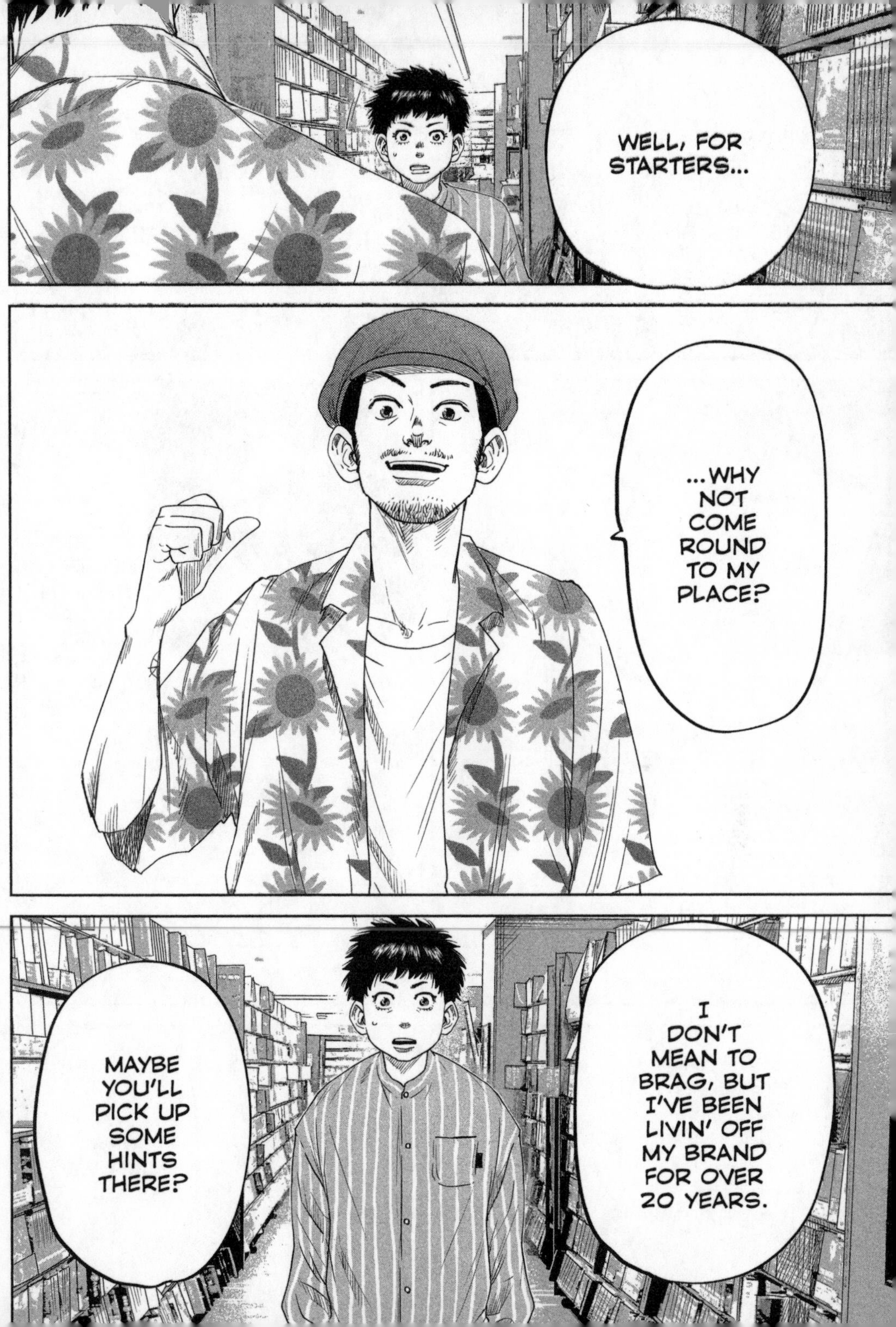
WELL, FOR STARTERS...
...WHY NOT COME ROUND TO MY PLACE?
I DON'T MEAN TO BRAG, BUT I'VE BEEN LIVIN' OFF MY BRAND FOR OVER 20 YEARS.
MAYBE YOU'LL PICK UP SOME HINTS THERE?

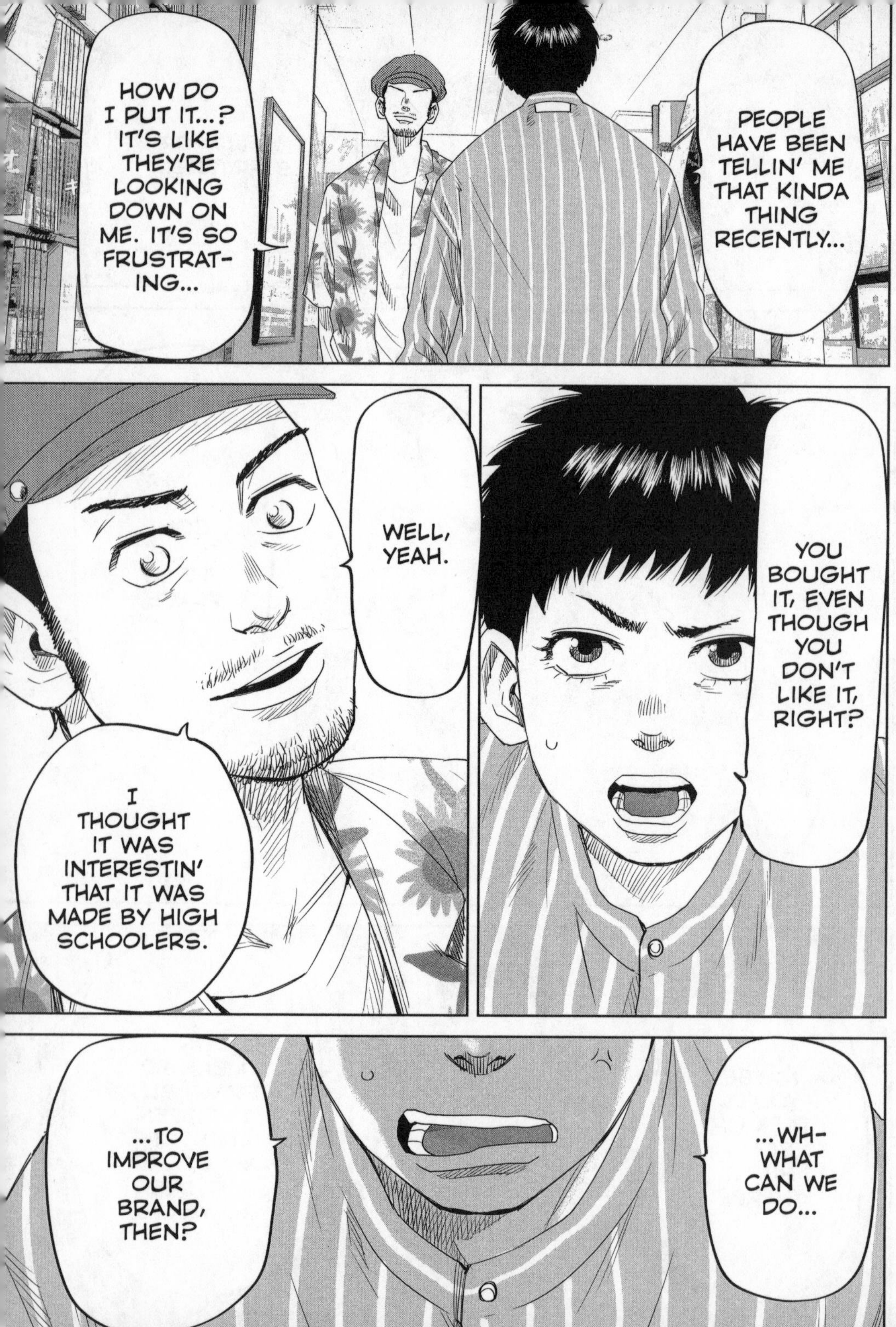
PEOPLE HAVE BEEN TELLIN' ME THAT KINDA THING RECENTLY...
HOW DO I PUT IT...? IT'S LIKE THEY'RE LOOKING DOWN ON ME. IT'S SO FRUSTRAT-ING...
YOU BOUGHT IT, EVEN THOUGH YOU DON'T LIKE IT, RIGHT?
WELL, YEAH.
I THOUGHT IT WAS INTERESTIN' THAT IT WAS MADE BY HIGH SCHOOLERS.
...WH-WHAT CAN WE DO...
...TO IMPROVE OUR BRAND, THEN?

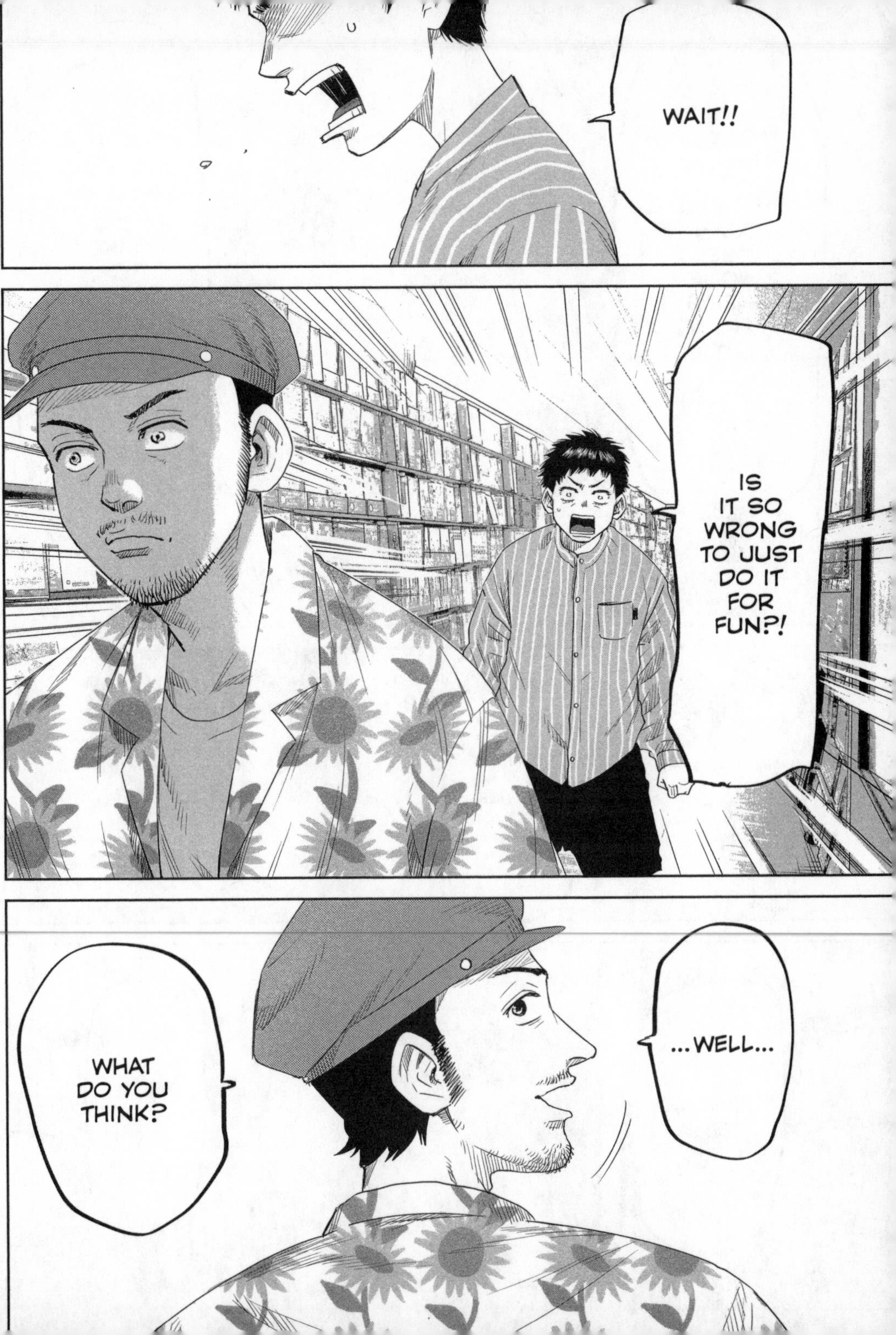
WAIT!!
IS IT SO WRONG TO JUST DO IT FOR FUN?!
...WELL...
WHAT DO YOU THINK?

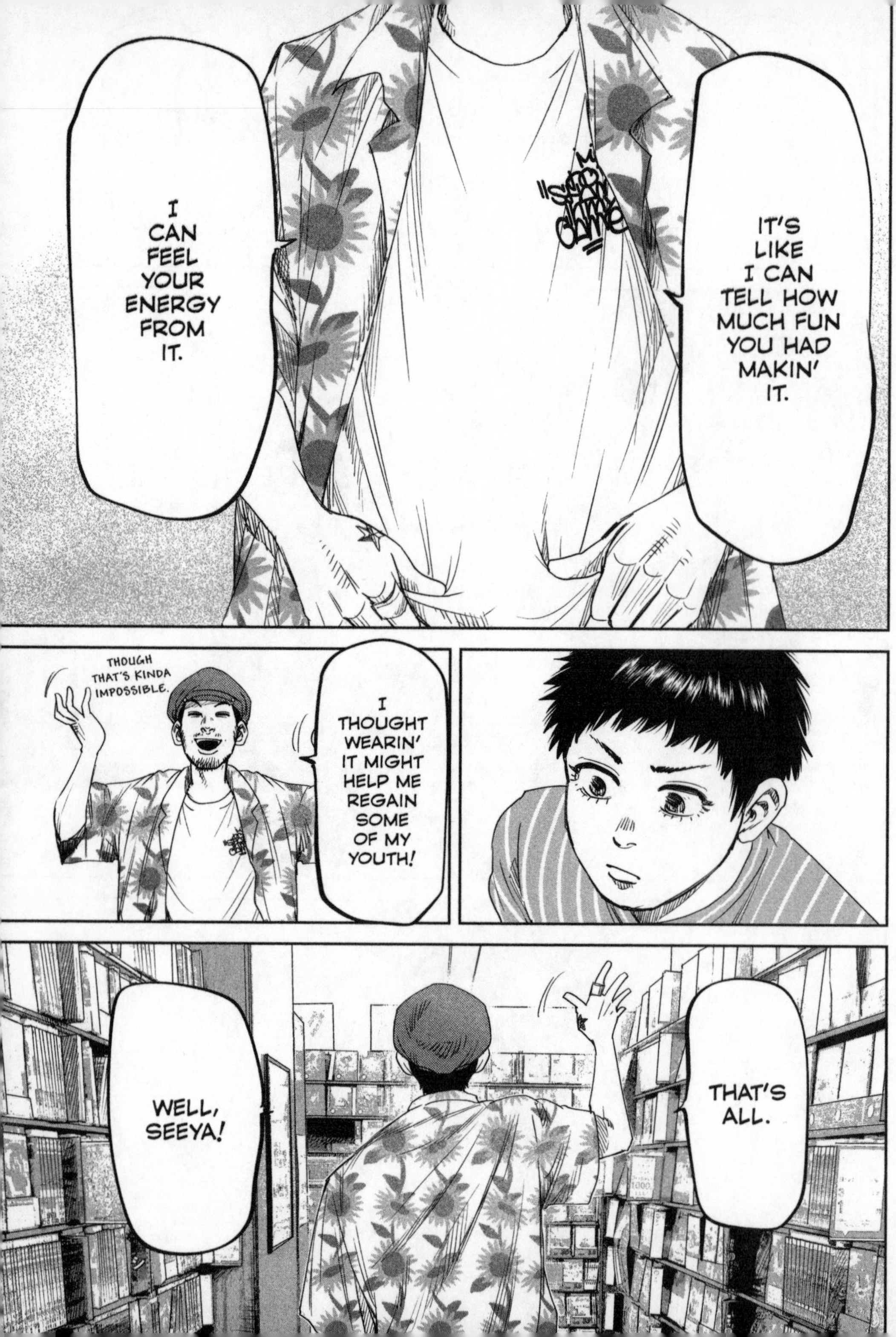
IT'S LIKE I CAN TELL HOW MUCH FUN YOU HAD MAKIN' IT.
I CAN FEEL YOUR ENERGY FROM IT.
I THOUGHT WEARIN' IT MIGHT HELP ME REGAIN SOME OF MY YOUTH!
THOUGH THAT'S KINDA IMPOSSIBLE.
THAT'S ALL.
WELL, SEEYA!

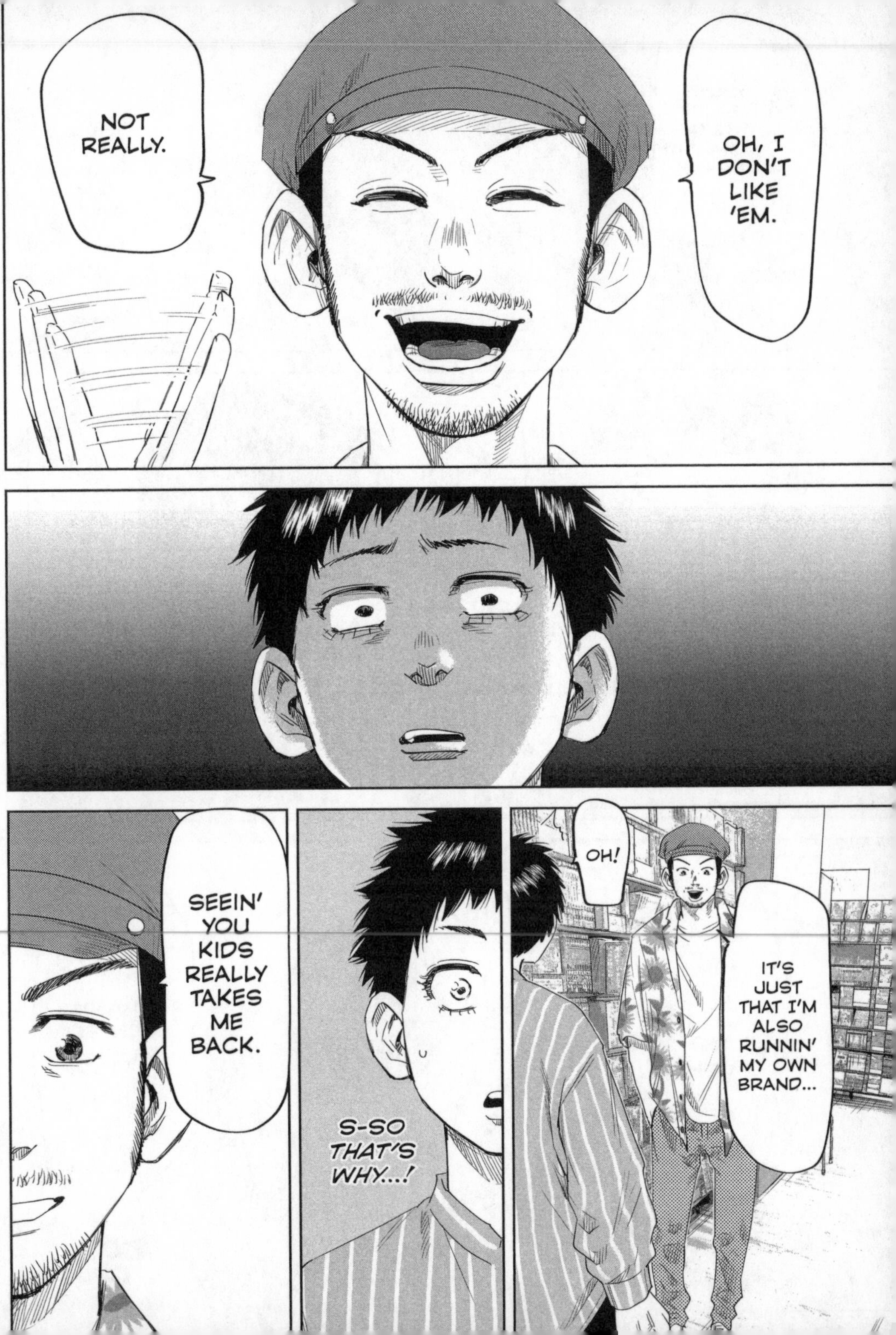
OH, I DON'T LIKE 'EM.
NOT REALLY.
OH!
IT'S JUST THAT I'M ALSO RUNNIN' MY OWN BRAND...
S-SO THAT'S WHY...!
SEEIN' YOU KIDS REALLY TAKES ME BACK.

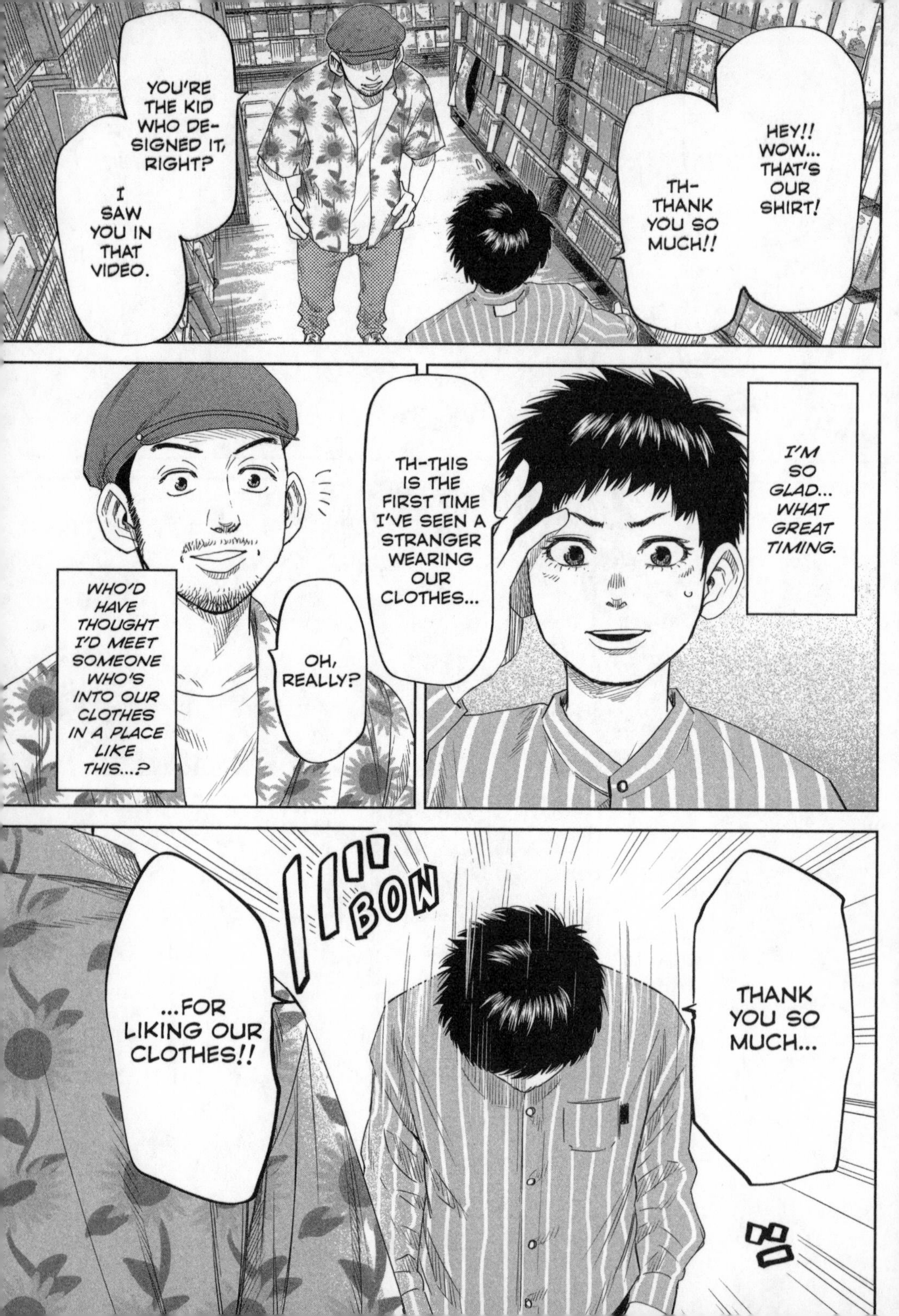
HEY!! WOW... THAT'S OUR SHIRT!
TH-THANK YOU SO MUCH!!
YOU'RE THE KID WHO DE-SIGNED IT, RIGHT?
I SAW YOU IN THAT VIDEO.
I'M SO GLAD... WHAT GREAT TIMING.
TH-THIS IS THE FIRST TIME I'VE SEEN A STRANGER WEARING OUR CLOTHES...
OH, REALLY?
WHO'D HAVE THOUGHT I'D MEET SOMEONE WHO'S INTO OUR CLOTHES IN A PLACE LIKE THIS...?
THANK YOU SO MUCH...
BOW
...FOR LIKING OUR CLOTHES!!

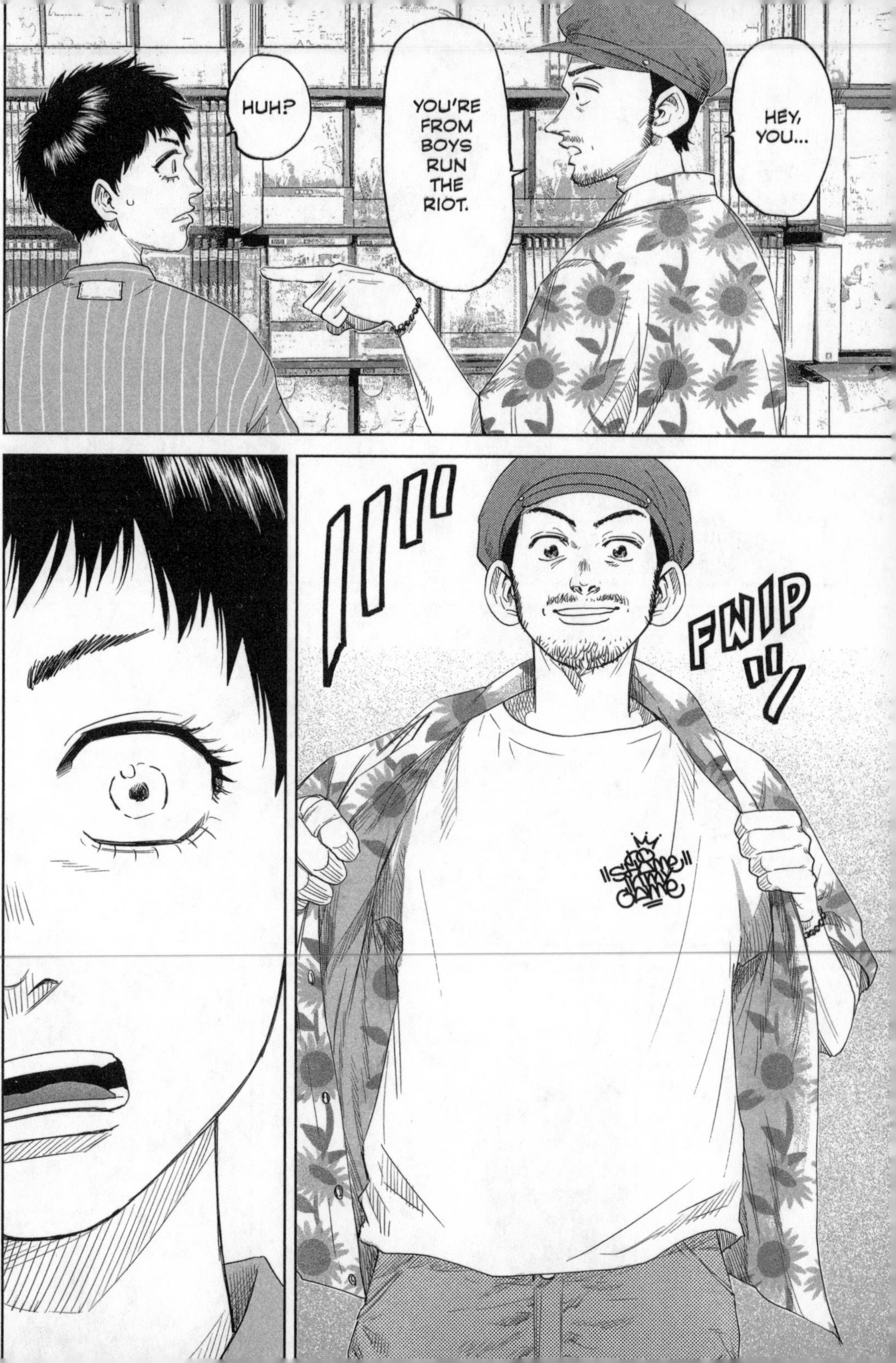
HEY, YOU...
YOU'RE FROM BOYS RUN THE RIOT.
HUH?
FWIP

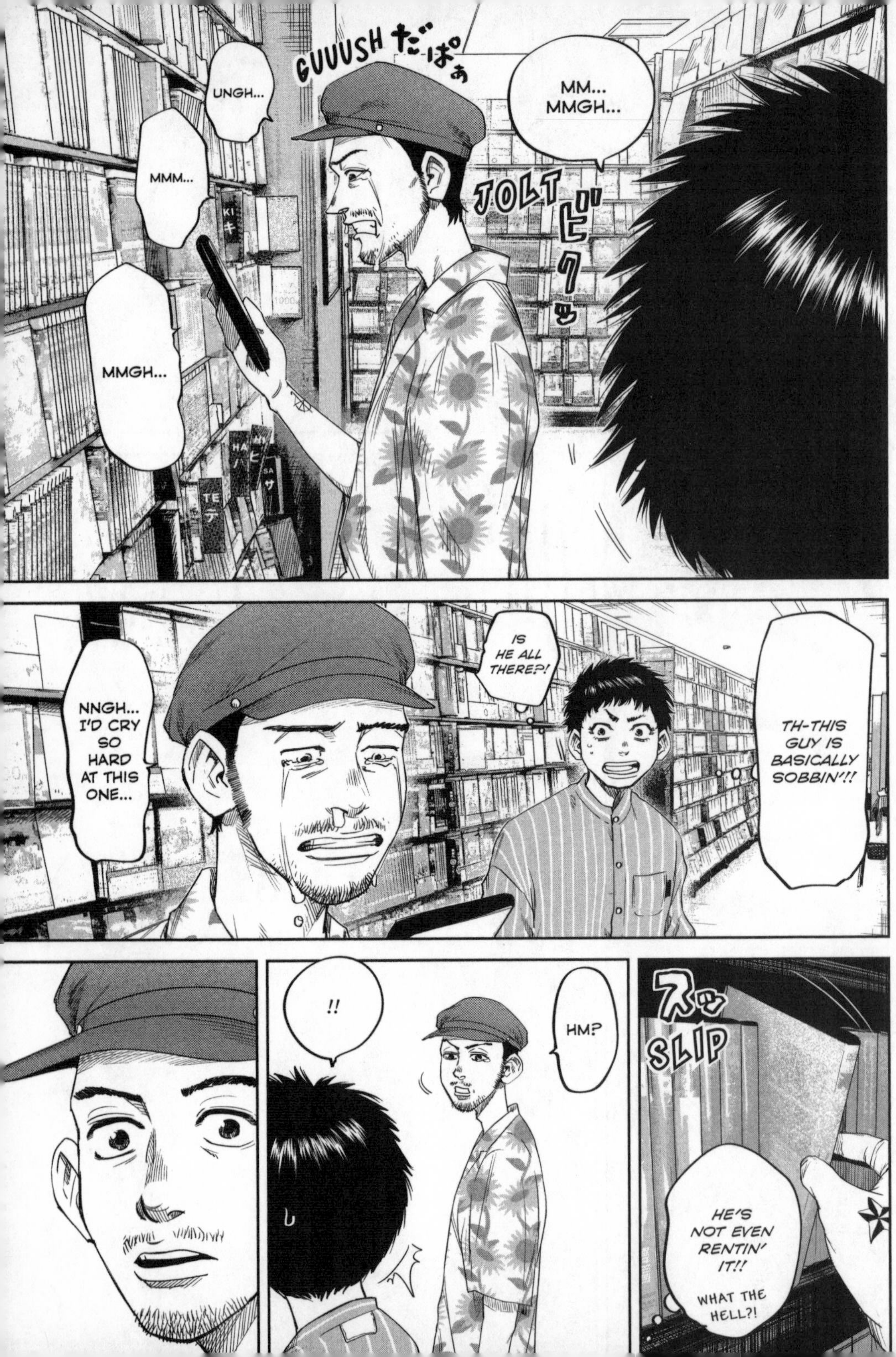
MM... MMGH...
JOLT ビクッ
GUUUSH だぱぁ
UNGH...
MMM...
MMGH...
TH-THIS GUY IS BASICALLY SOBBIN'!!
IS HE ALL THERE?!
NNGH... I'D CRY SO HARD AT THIS ONE...
スッ SLIP
HE'S NOT EVEN RENTIN' IT!!
WHAT THE HELL?!
HM?
!!

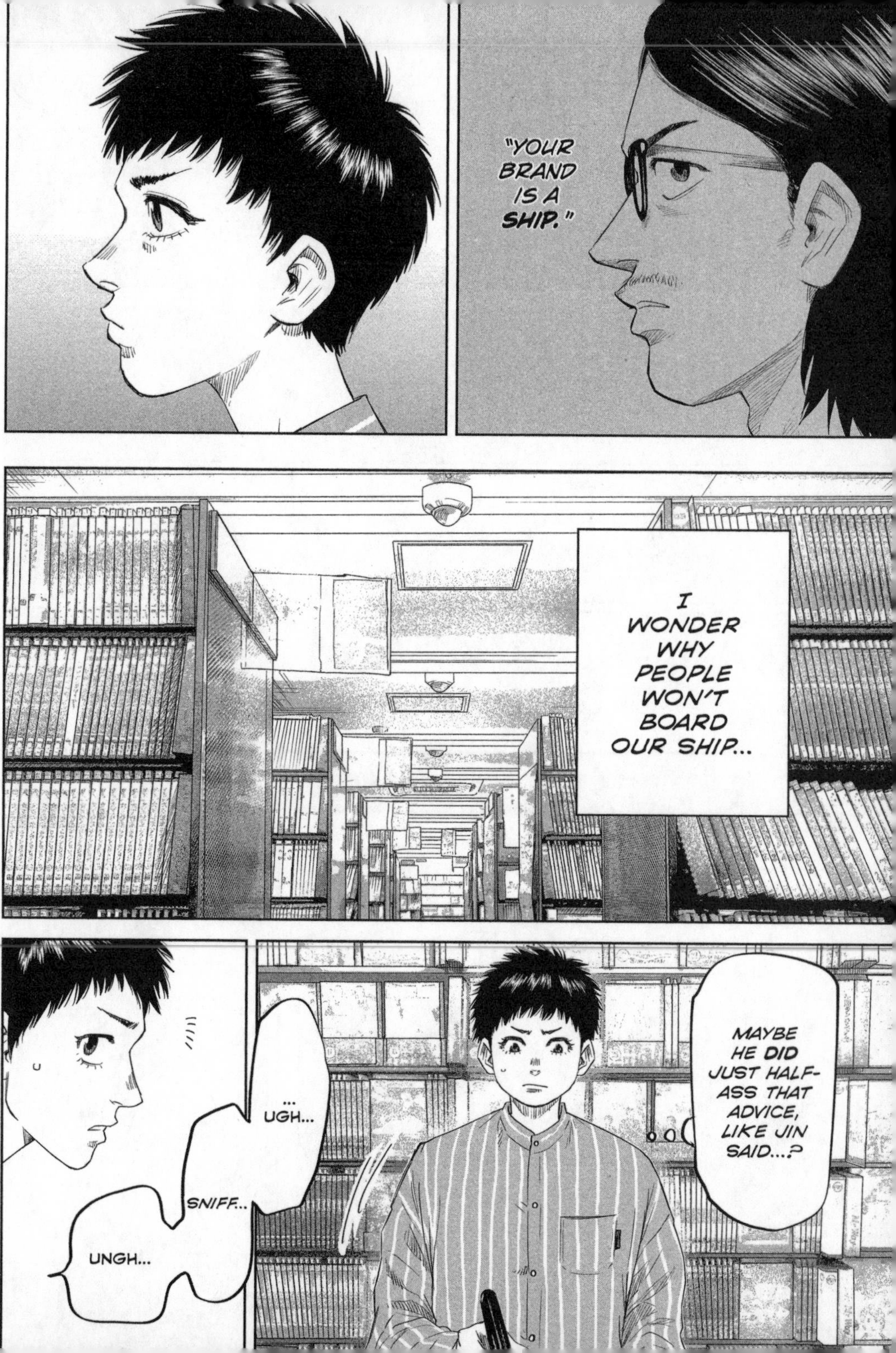
"YOUR BRAND IS A SHIP."
I WONDER WHY PEOPLE WON'T BOARD OUR SHIP...
MAYBE HE DID JUST HALF-ASS THAT ADVICE, LIKE JIN SAID...?
... UGH...
SNIFF...
UNGH...

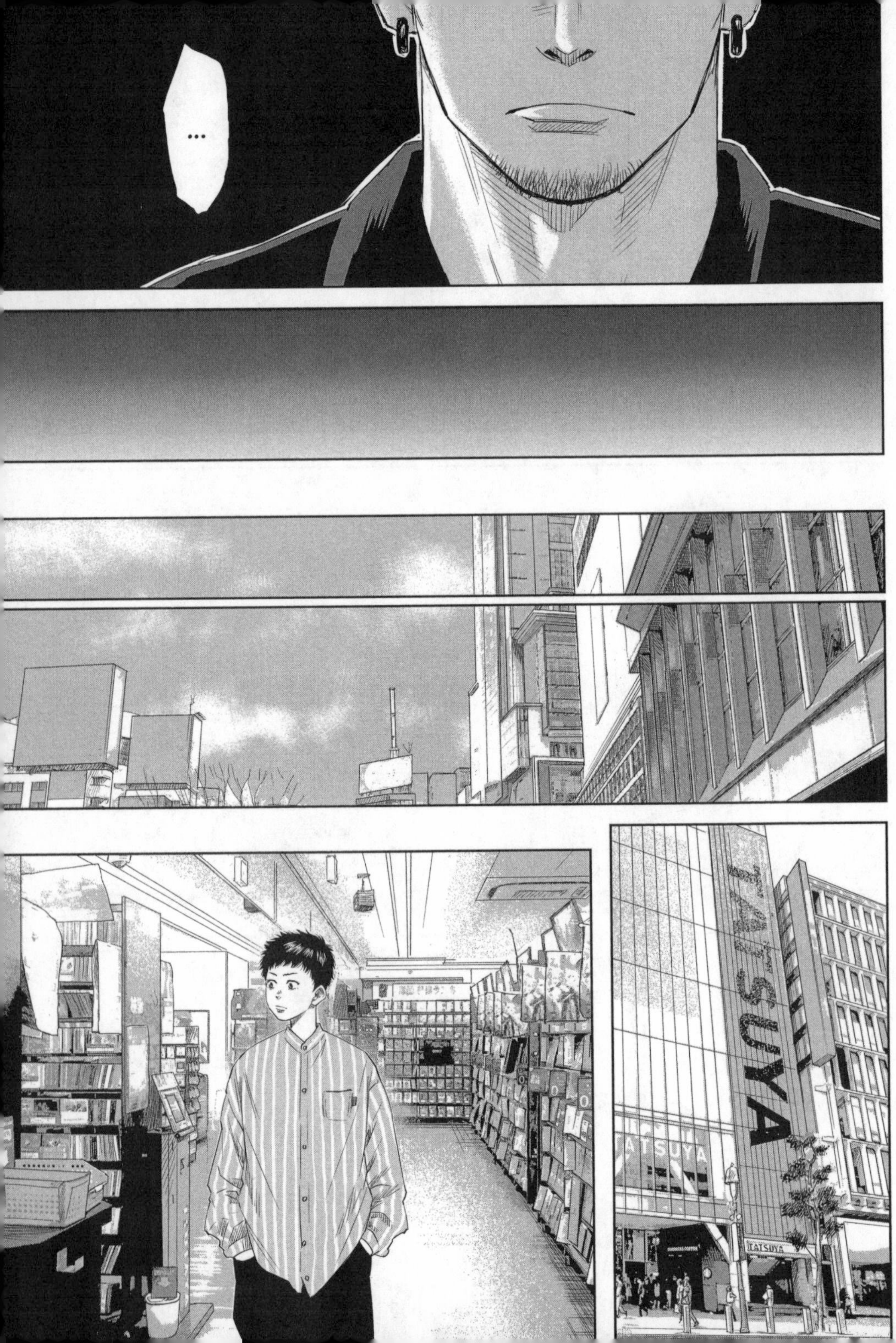
…
SUYA
TATSUYA
TATSUYA

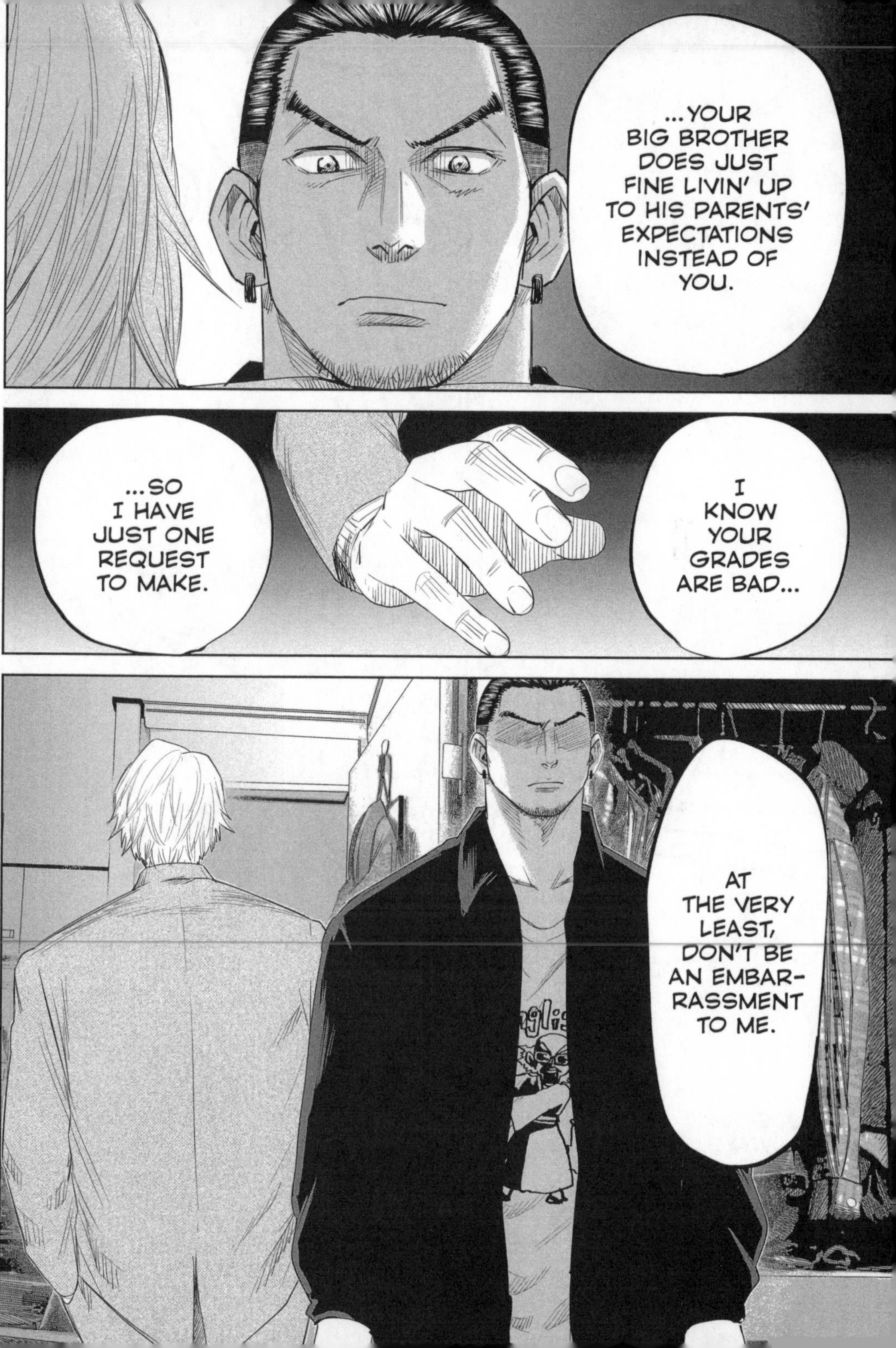
...YOUR BIG BROTHER DOES JUST FINE LIVIN' UP TO HIS PARENTS' EXPECTATIONS INSTEAD OF YOU.
I KNOW YOUR GRADES ARE BAD...
...SO I HAVE JUST ONE REQUEST TO MAKE.
AT THE VERY LEAST, DON'T BE AN EMBARRASSMENT TO ME.

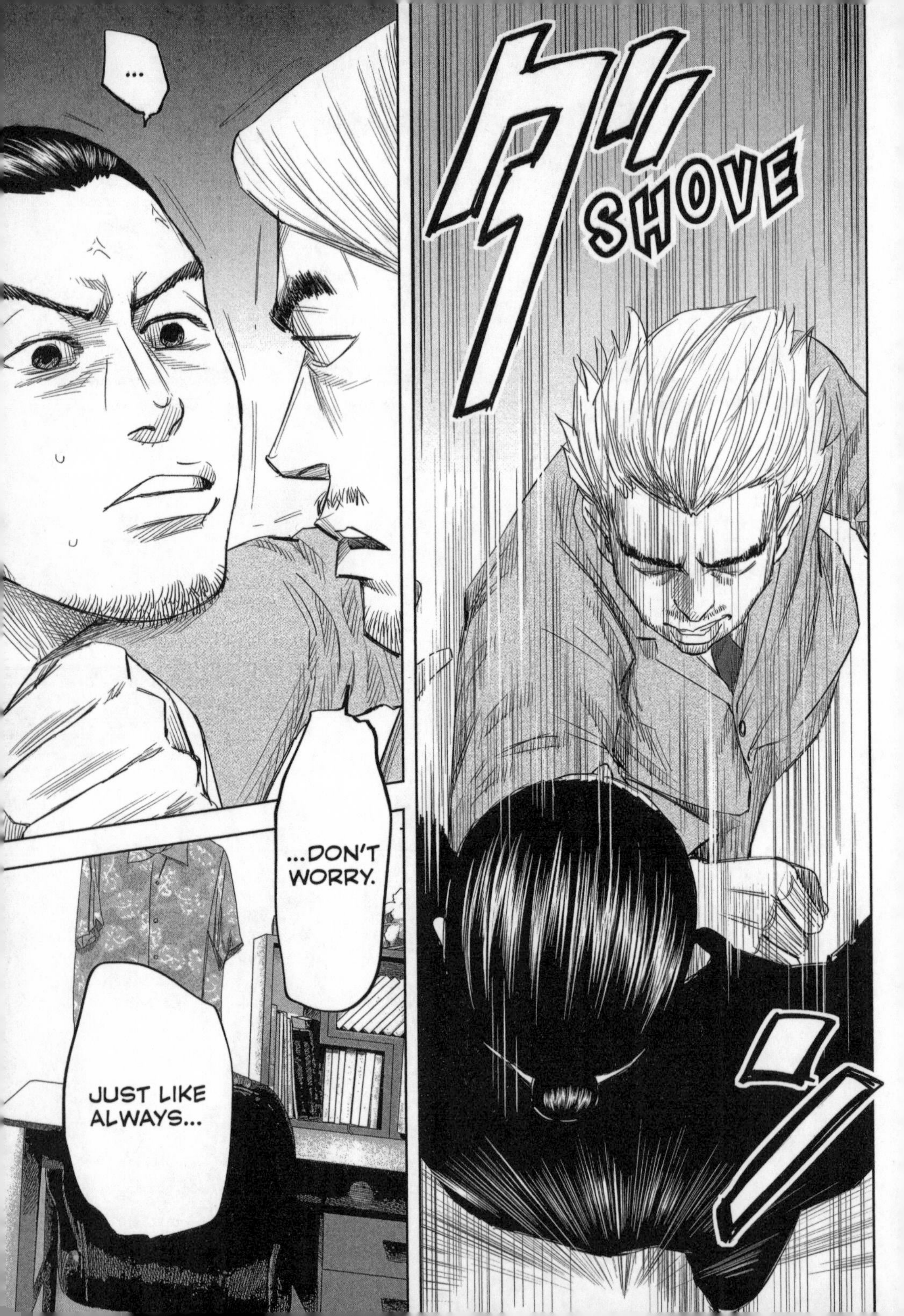
SHOVE
...
...DON'T WORRY.
JUST LIKE ALWAYS...

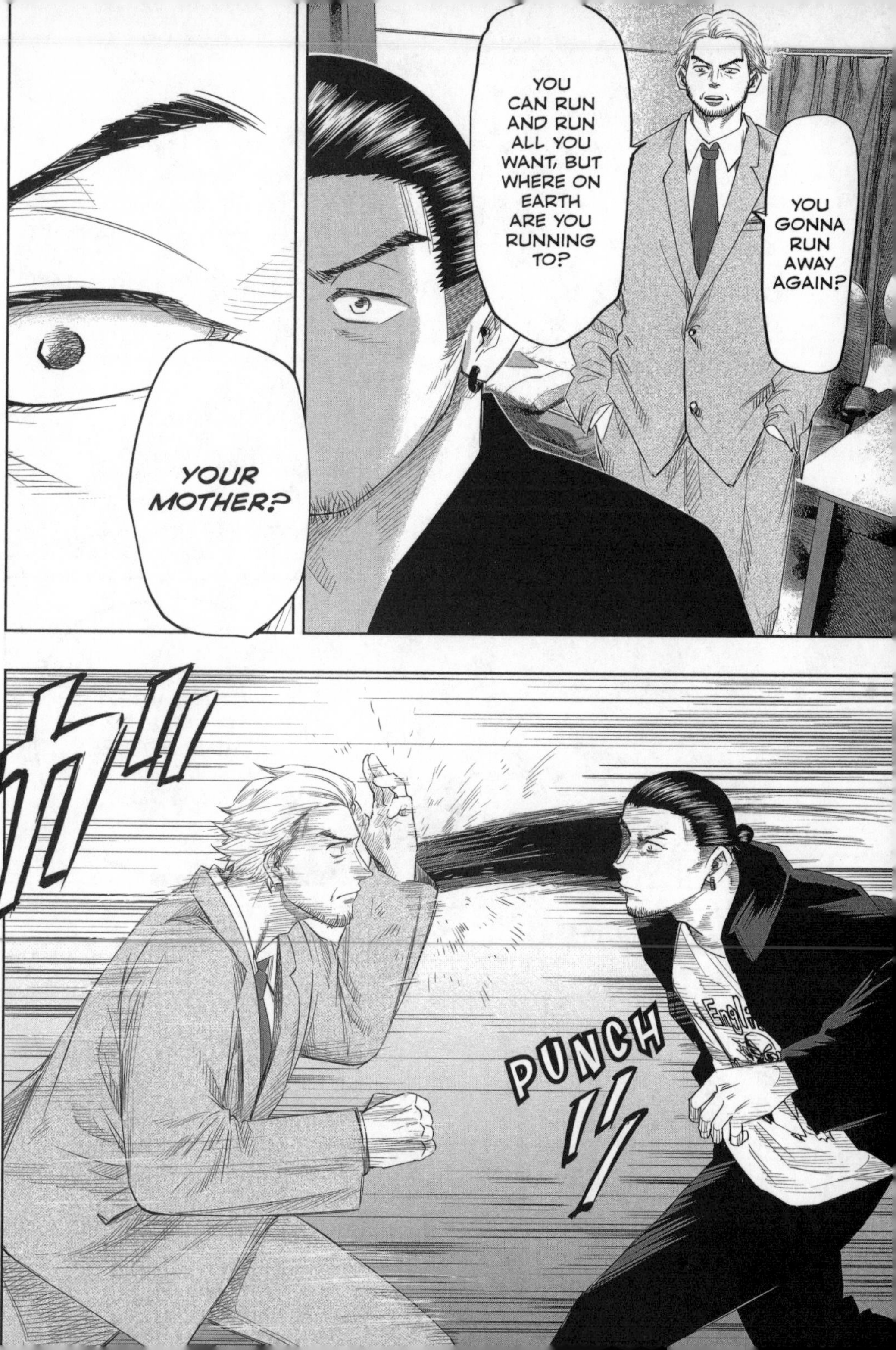
YOU GONNA RUN AWAY AGAIN?
YOU CAN RUN AND RUN ALL YOU WANT, BUT WHERE ON EARTH ARE YOU RUNNING TO?
YOUR MOTHER?
カッ
PUNCH!!

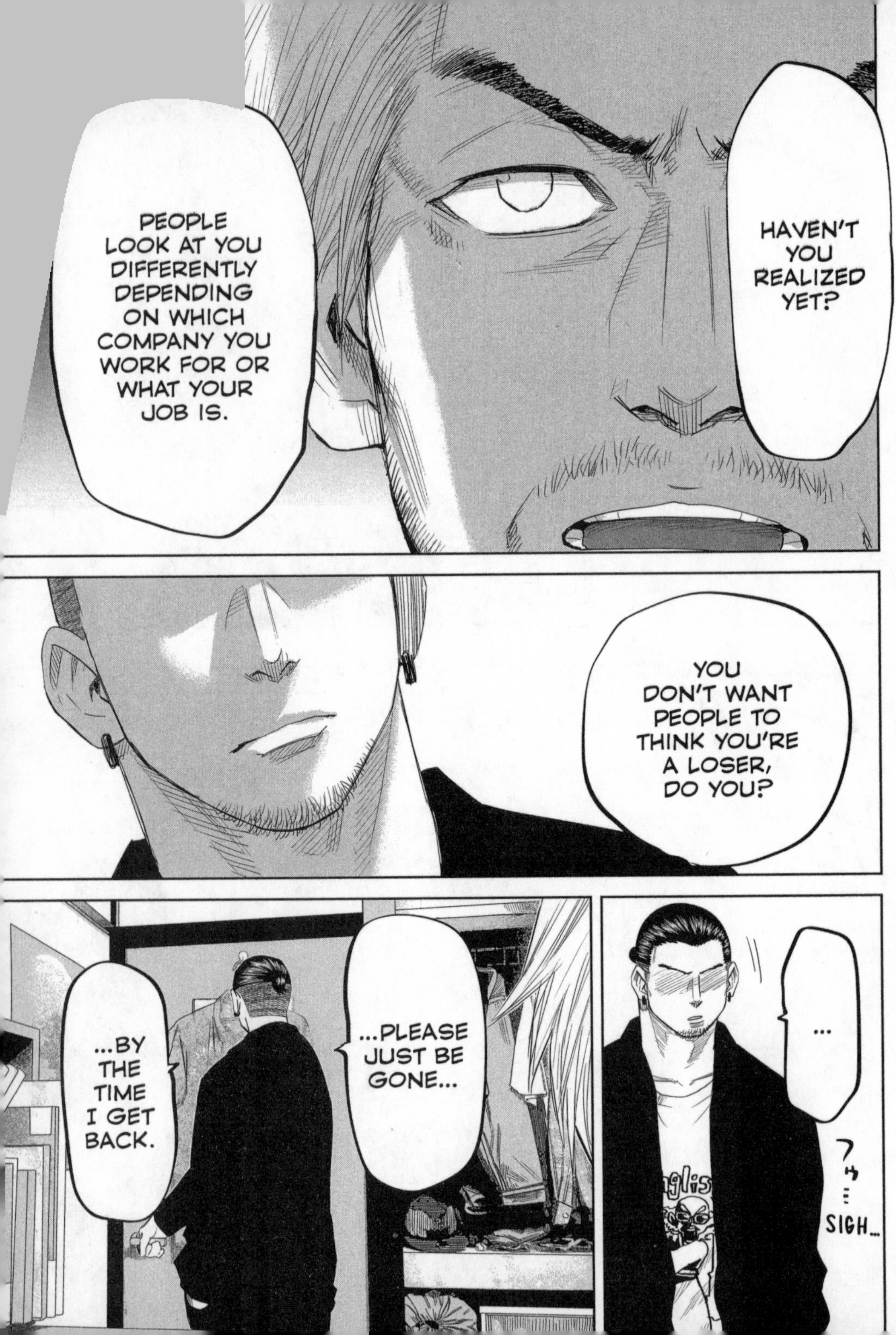
HAVEN'T YOU REALIZED YET?
PEOPLE LOOK AT YOU DIFFERENTLY DEPENDING ON WHICH COMPANY YOU WORK FOR OR WHAT YOUR JOB IS.
YOU DON'T WANT PEOPLE TO THINK YOU'RE A LOSER, DO YOU?
...
フゥ…
SIGH...
...PLEASE JUST BE GONE...
...BY THE TIME I GET BACK.

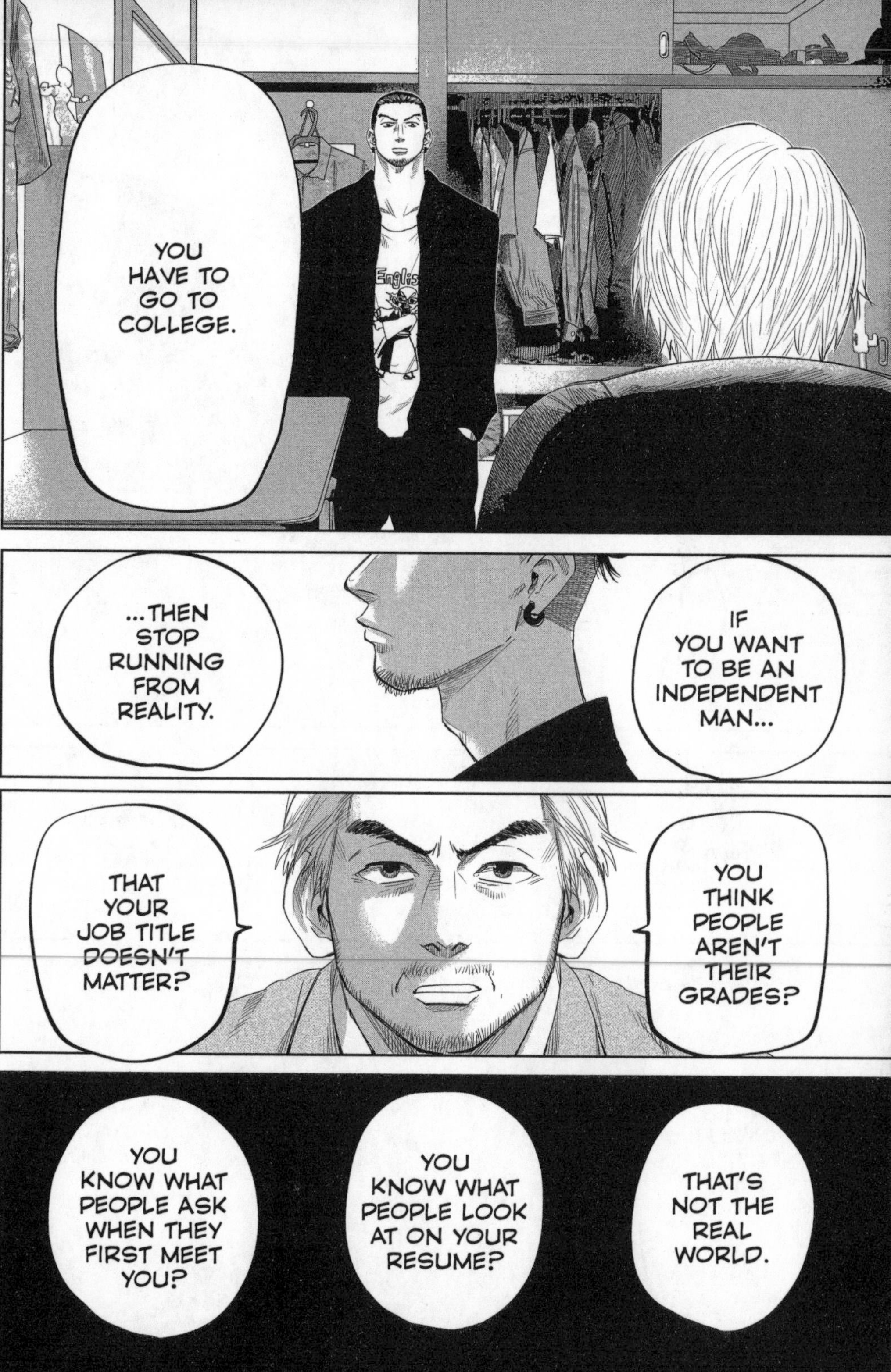
YOU HAVE TO GO TO COLLEGE.
IF YOU WANT TO BE AN INDEPENDENT MAN...
...THEN STOP RUNNING FROM REALITY.
YOU THINK PEOPLE AREN'T THEIR GRADES?
THAT YOUR JOB TITLE DOESN'T MATTER?
THAT'S NOT THE REAL WORLD.
YOU KNOW WHAT PEOPLE LOOK AT ON YOUR RESUME?
YOU KNOW WHAT PEOPLE ASK WHEN THEY FIRST MEET YOU?

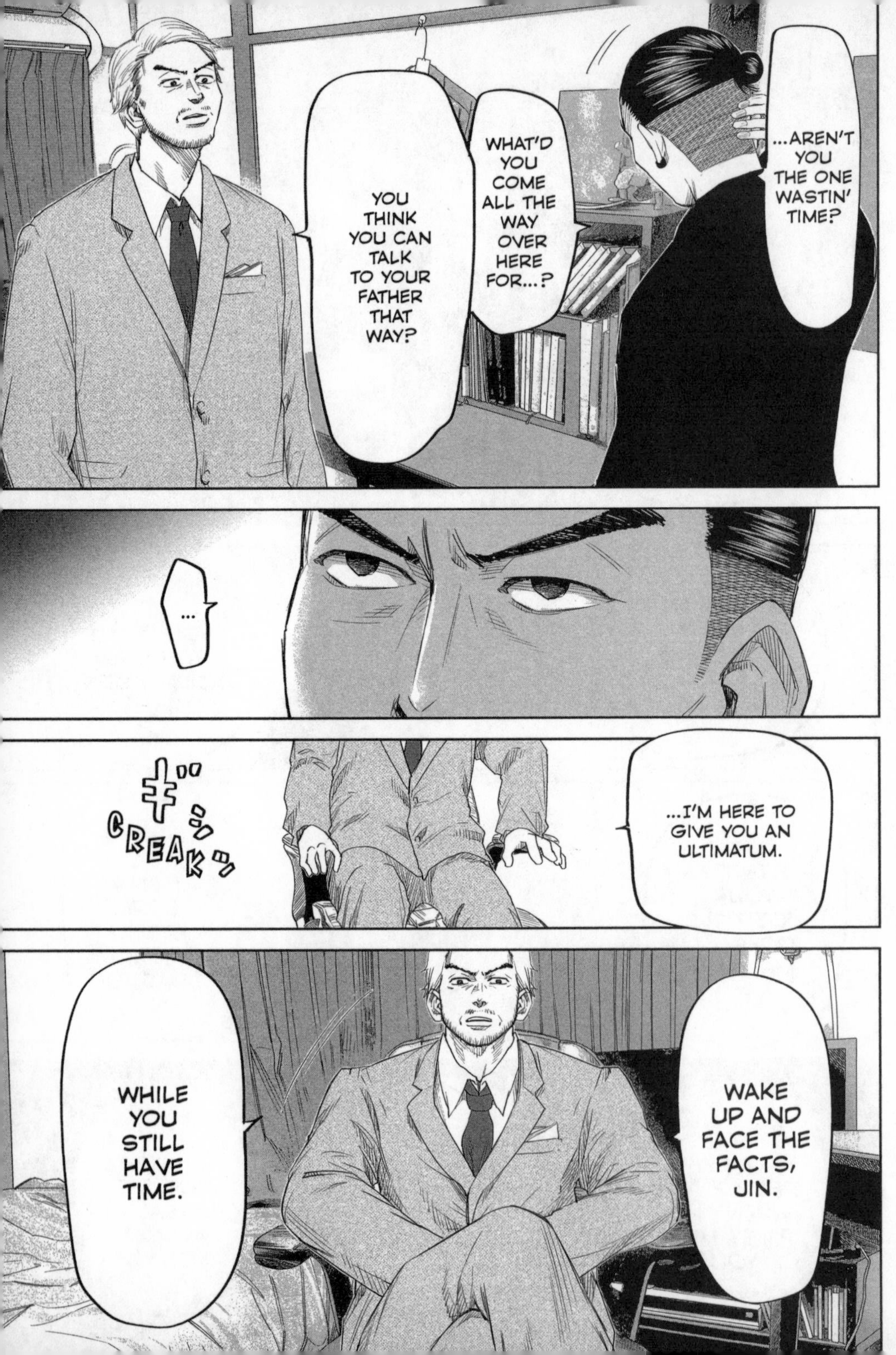
...AREN'T YOU THE ONE WASTIN' TIME?
WHAT'D YOU COME ALL THE WAY OVER HERE FOR...?
YOU THINK YOU CAN TALK TO YOUR FATHER THAT WAY?
...
...I'M HERE TO GIVE YOU AN ULTIMATUM.
CREAK
WAKE UP AND FACE THE FACTS, JIN.
WHILE YOU STILL HAVE TIME.

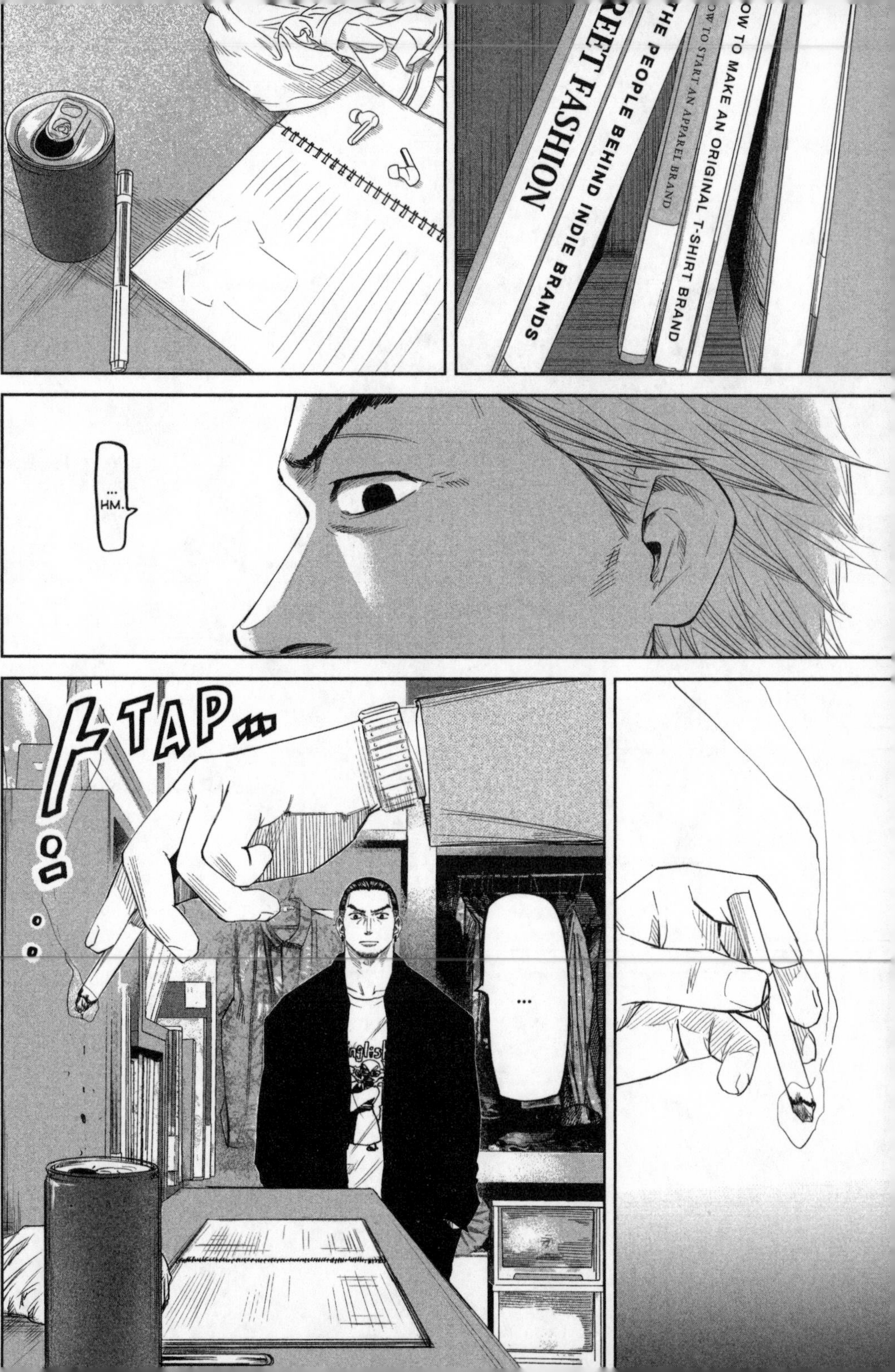
OW TO MAKE AN ORIGINAL T-SHIRT BRAND
OW TO START AN APPAREL BRAND
THE PEOPLE BEHIND INDIE BRANDS
REET FASHION
... HM.
TAP...
...

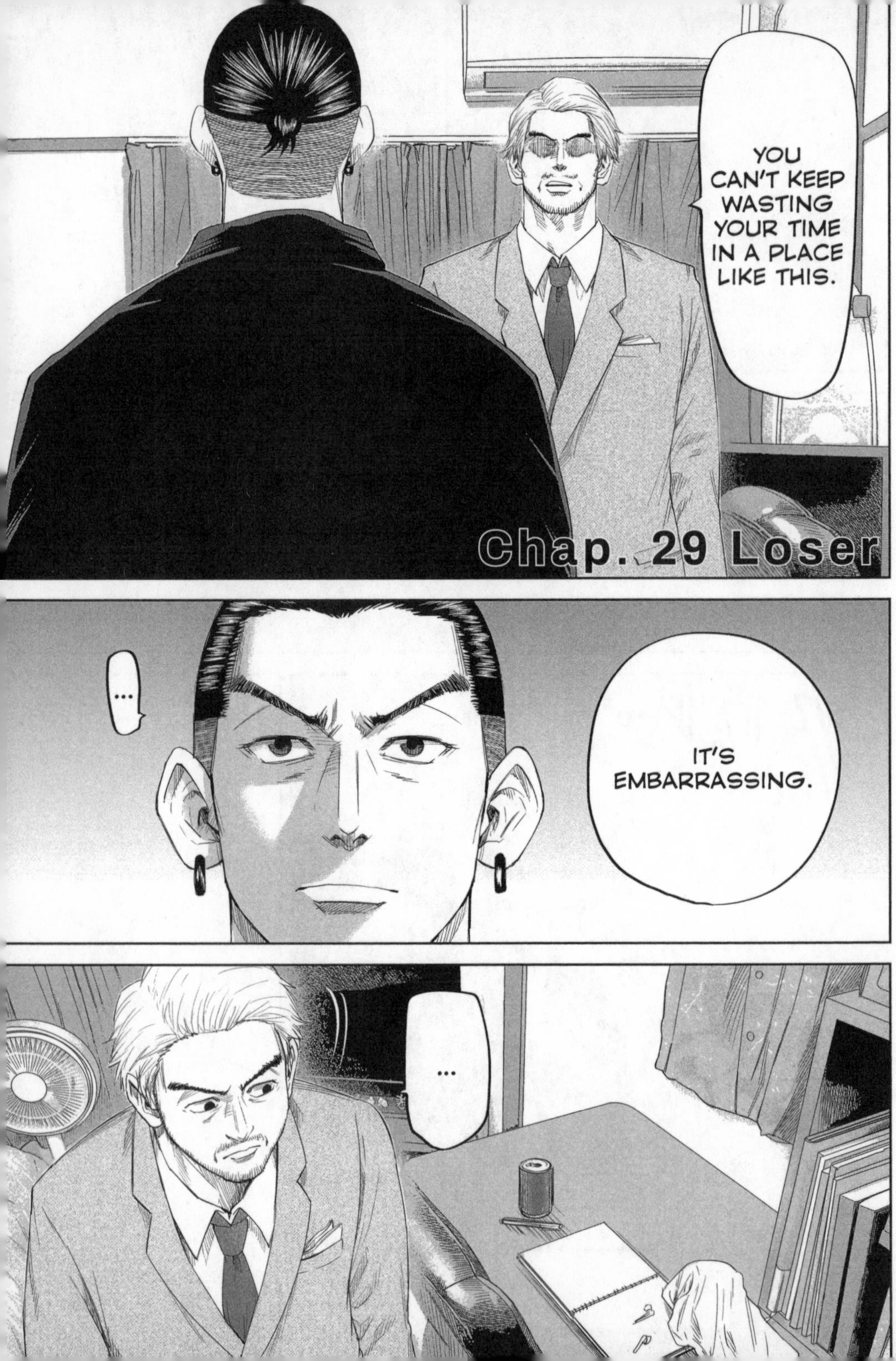
YOU CAN'T KEEP WASTING YOUR TIME IN A PLACE LIKE THIS.
Chap. 29 Loser
IT'S EMBARRASSING.
...
...

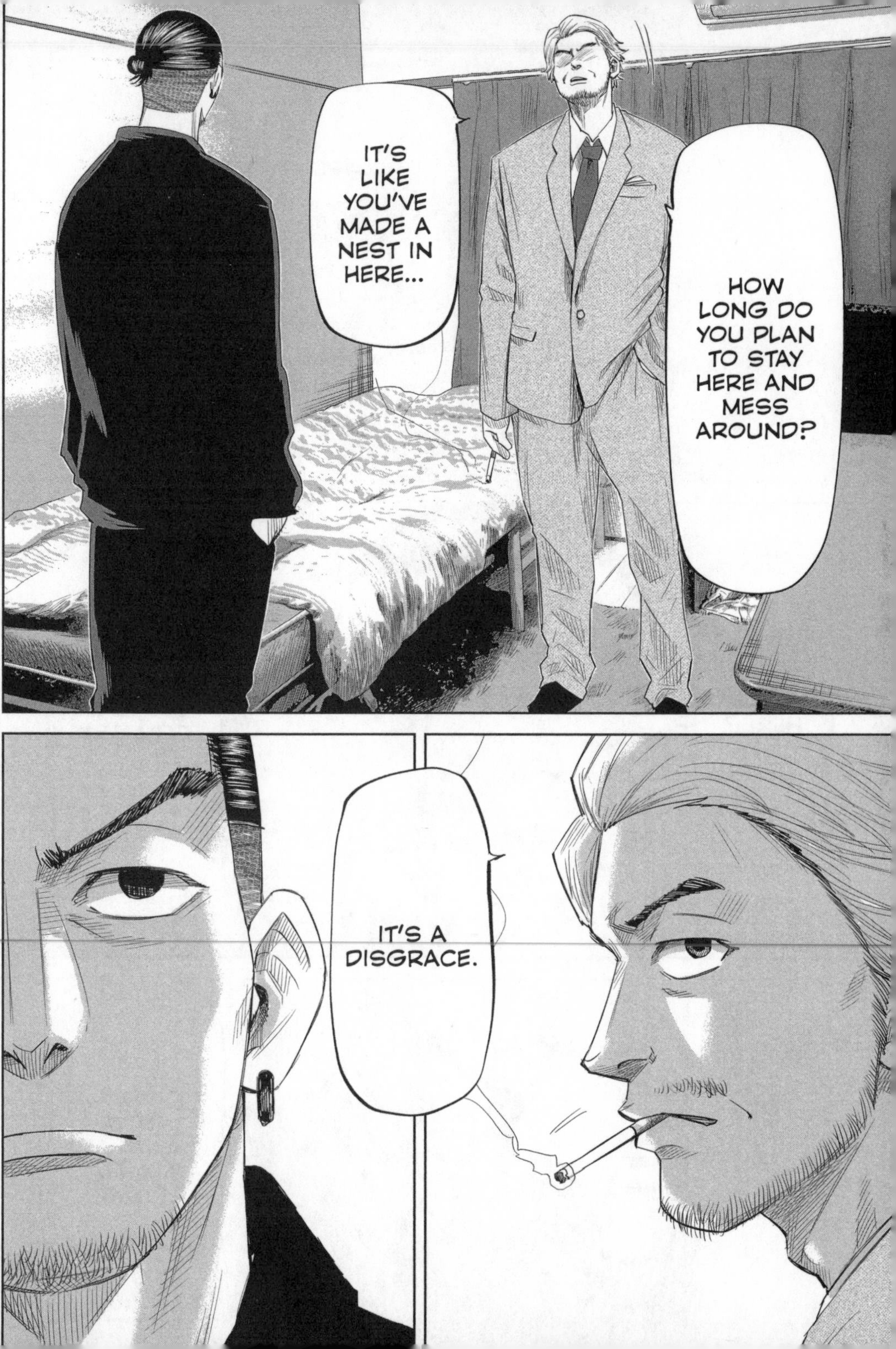
HOW LONG DO YOU PLAN TO STAY HERE AND MESS AROUND?
IT'S LIKE YOU'VE MADE A NEST IN HERE...
IT'S A DISGRACE.

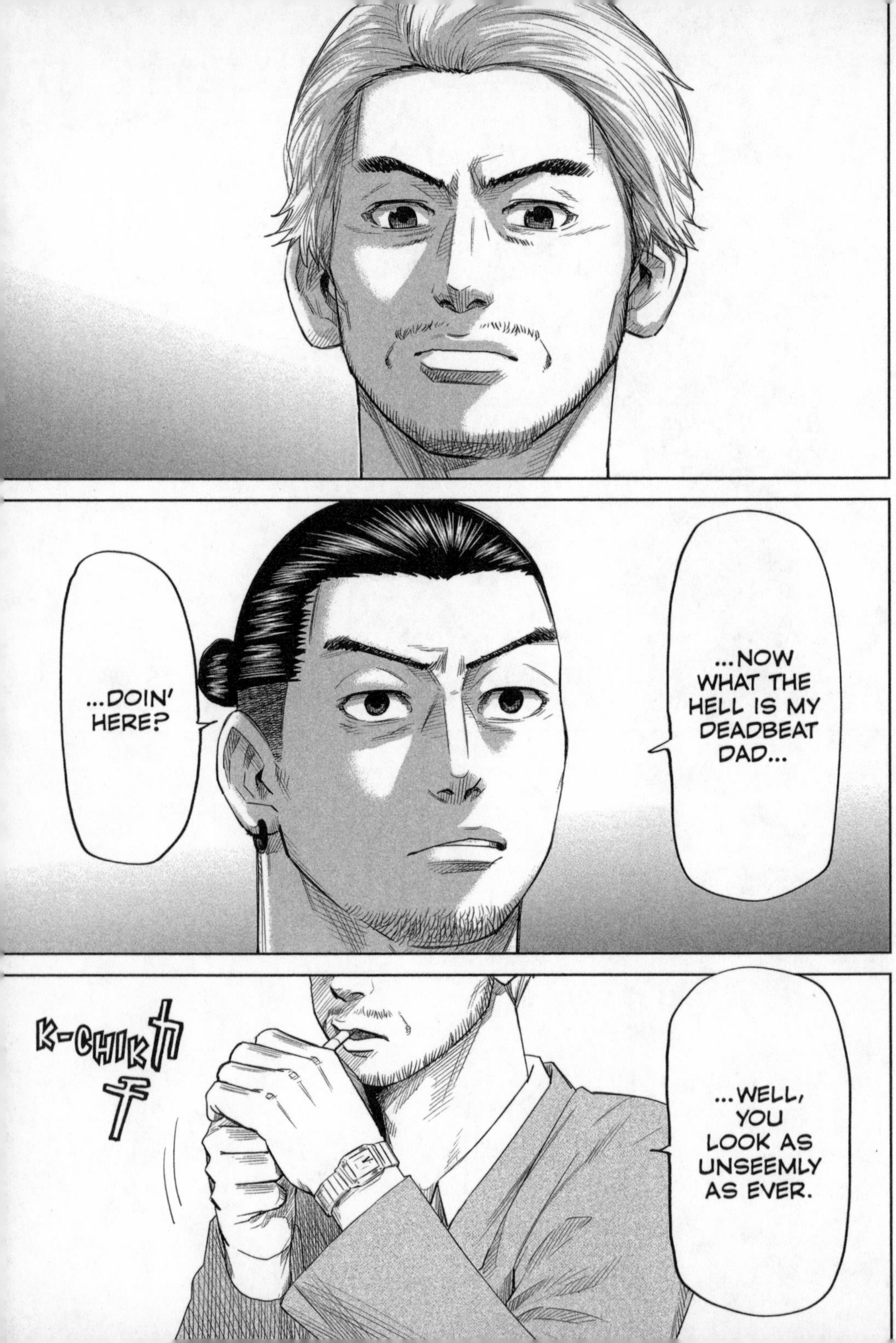
...NOW WHAT THE HELL IS MY DEADBEAT DAD...
...DOIN' HERE?
...WELL, YOU LOOK AS UNSEEMLY AS EVER.
K-CHIK

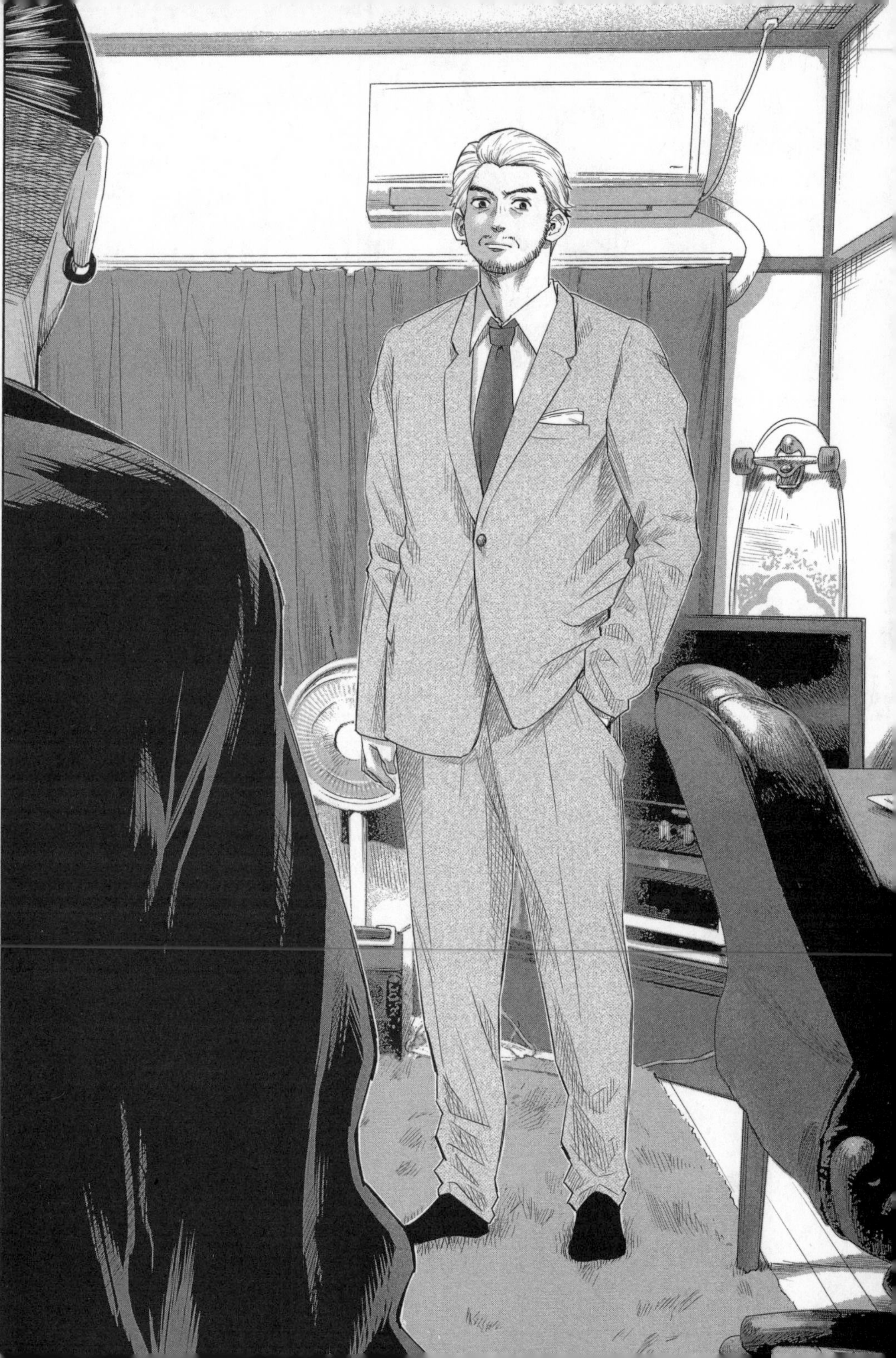

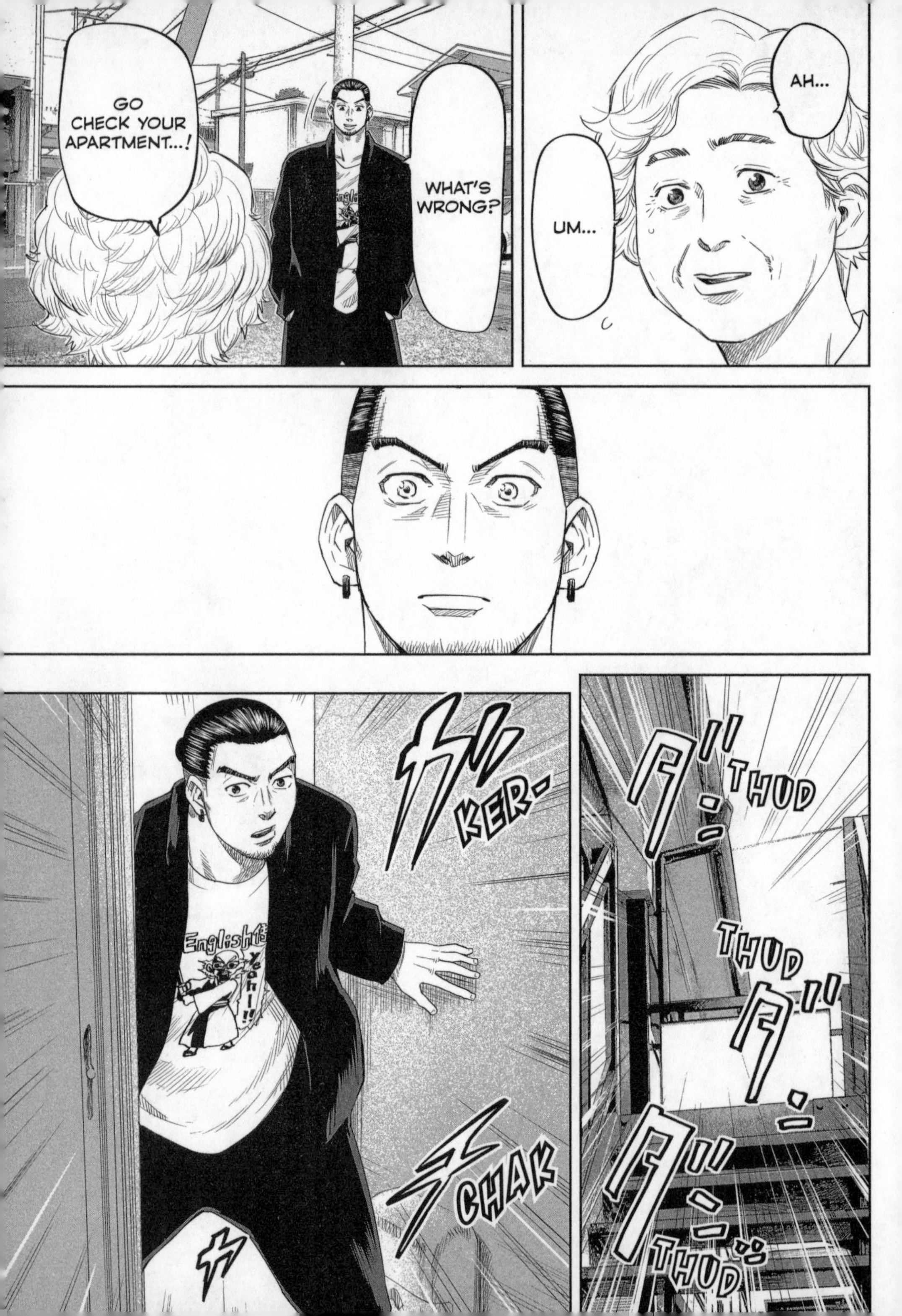
AH...
UM...
WHAT'S WRONG?
GO CHECK YOUR APARTMENT...!
THUD
THUD
THUD
KER-
CHAK

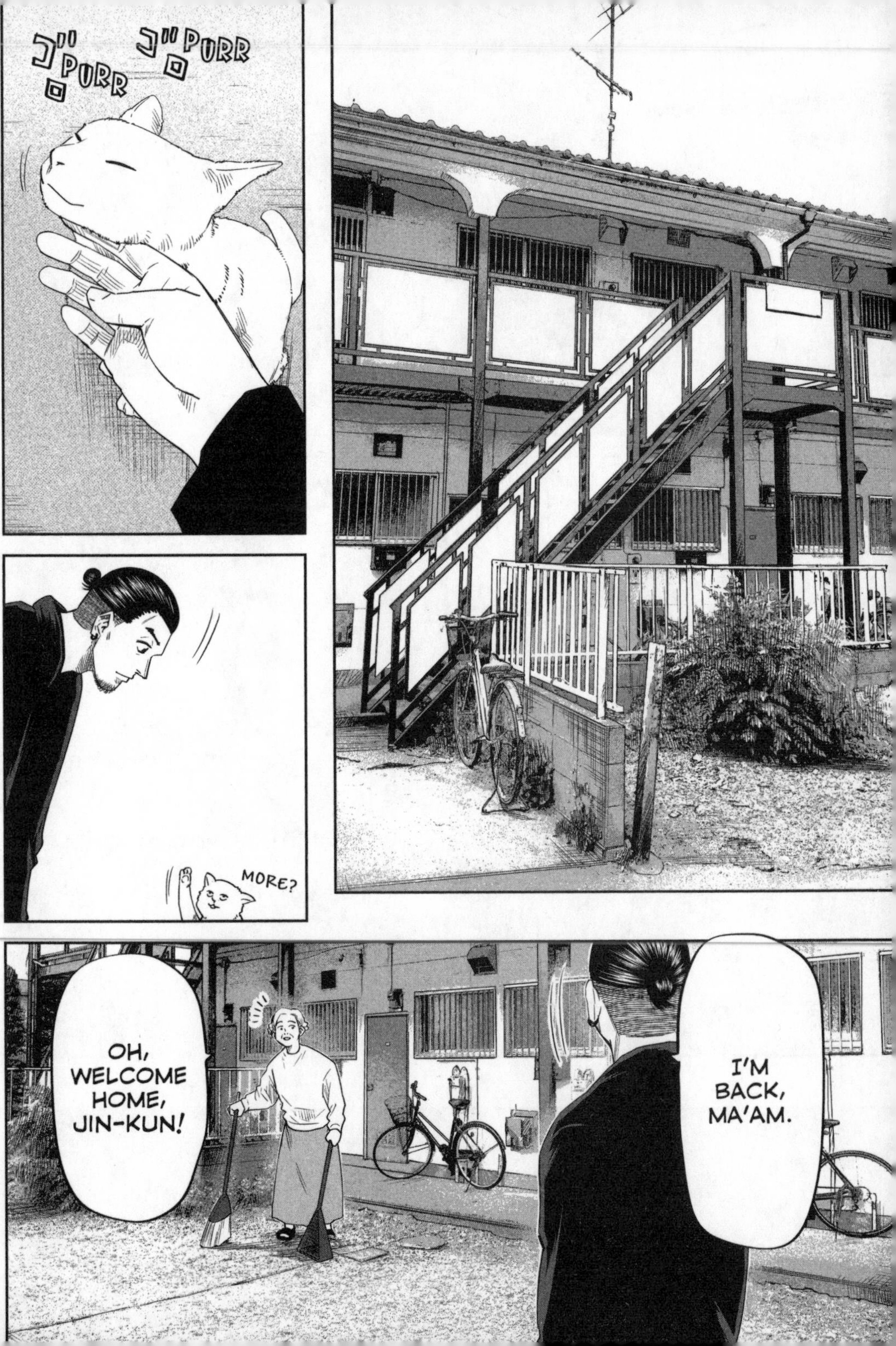
ゴロ PURR
ゴロ PURR
MORE?
I'M BACK, MA'AM.
OH, WELCOME HOME, JIN-KUN!

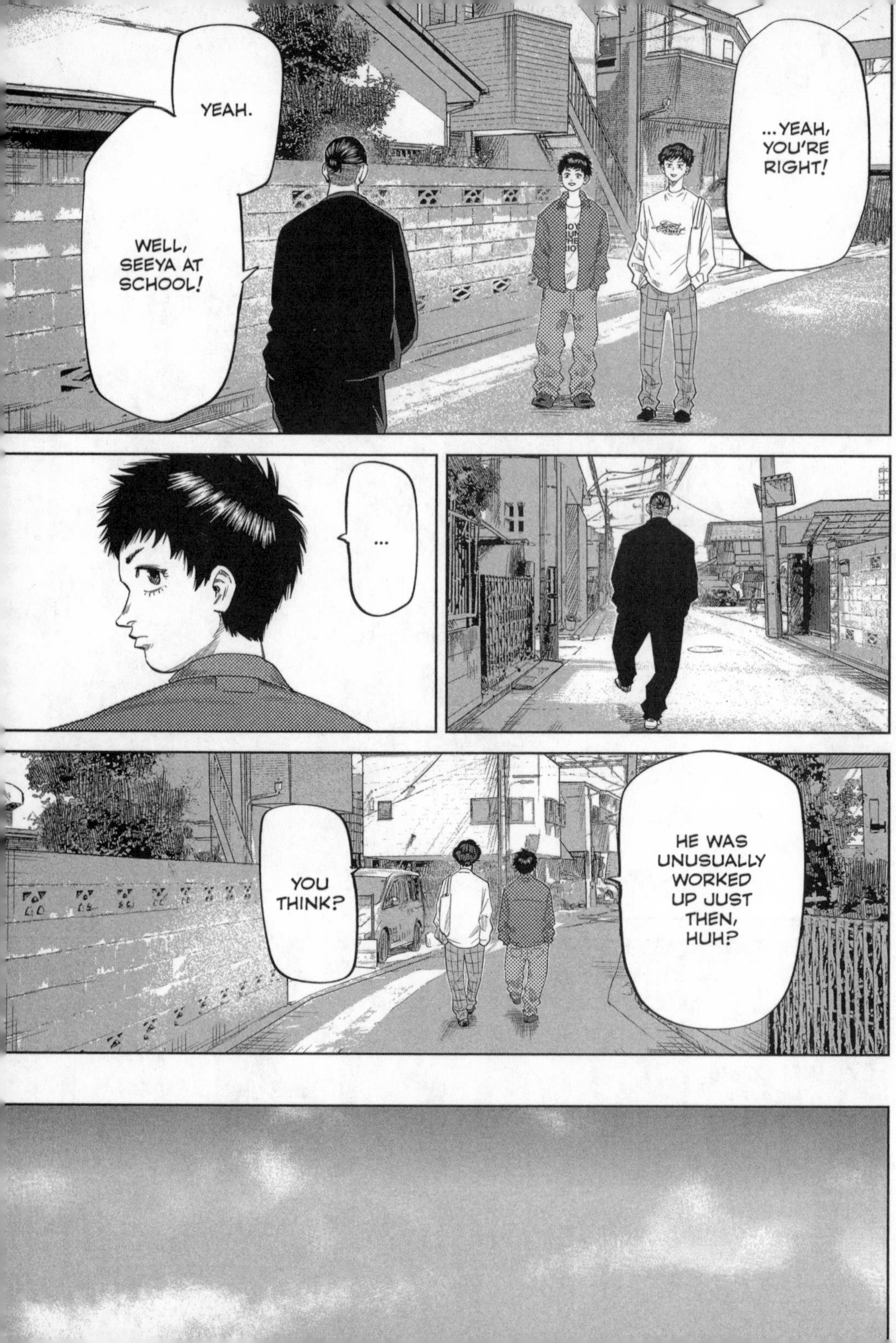
...YEAH, YOU'RE RIGHT!
YEAH.
WELL, SEEYA AT SCHOOL!
...
HE WAS UNUSUALLY WORKED UP JUST THEN, HUH?
YOU THINK?

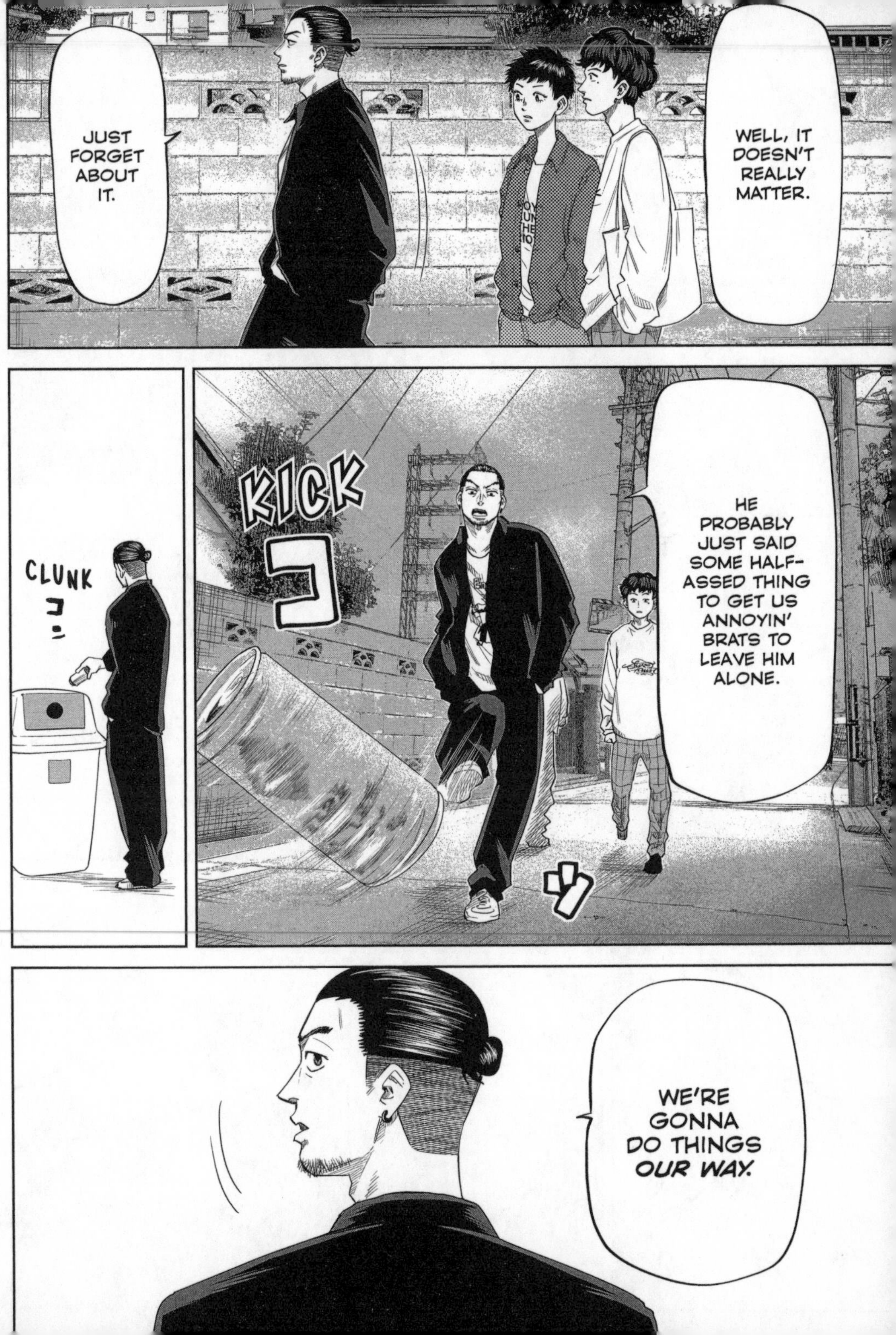
WELL, IT DOESN'T REALLY MATTER.
JUST FORGET ABOUT IT.
HE PROBABLY JUST SAID SOME HALF-ASSED THING TO GET US ANNOYIN' BRATS TO LEAVE HIM ALONE.
KICK
CLUNK
WE'RE GONNA DO THINGS *OUR WAY.*

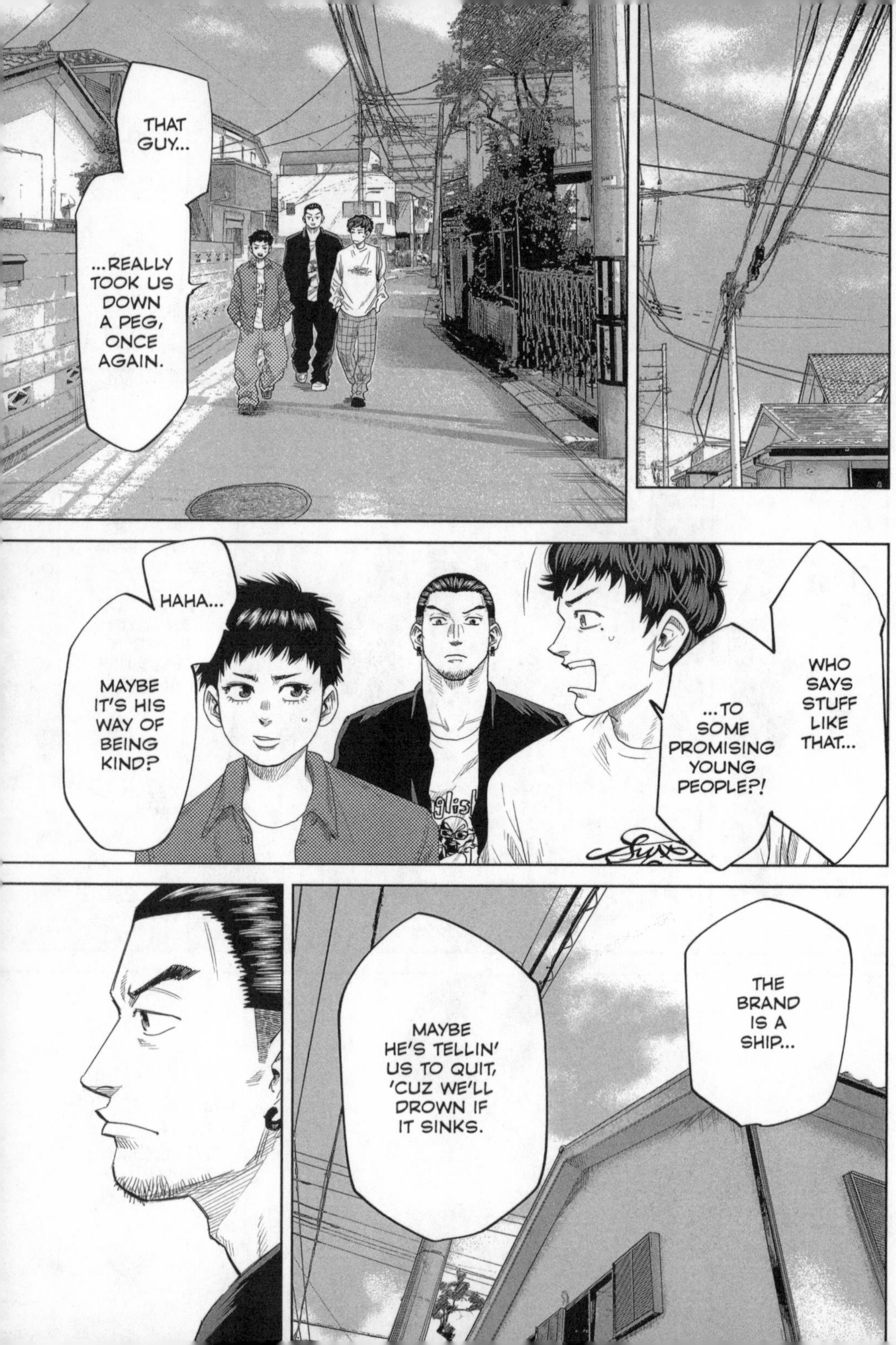
THAT GUY...
...REALLY TOOK US DOWN A PEG, ONCE AGAIN.
WHO SAYS STUFF LIKE THAT...
...TO SOME PROMISING YOUNG PEOPLE?!
HAHA...
MAYBE IT'S HIS WAY OF BEING KIND?
THE BRAND IS A SHIP...
MAYBE HE'S TELLIN' US TO QUIT, 'CUZ WE'LL DROWN IF IT SINKS.

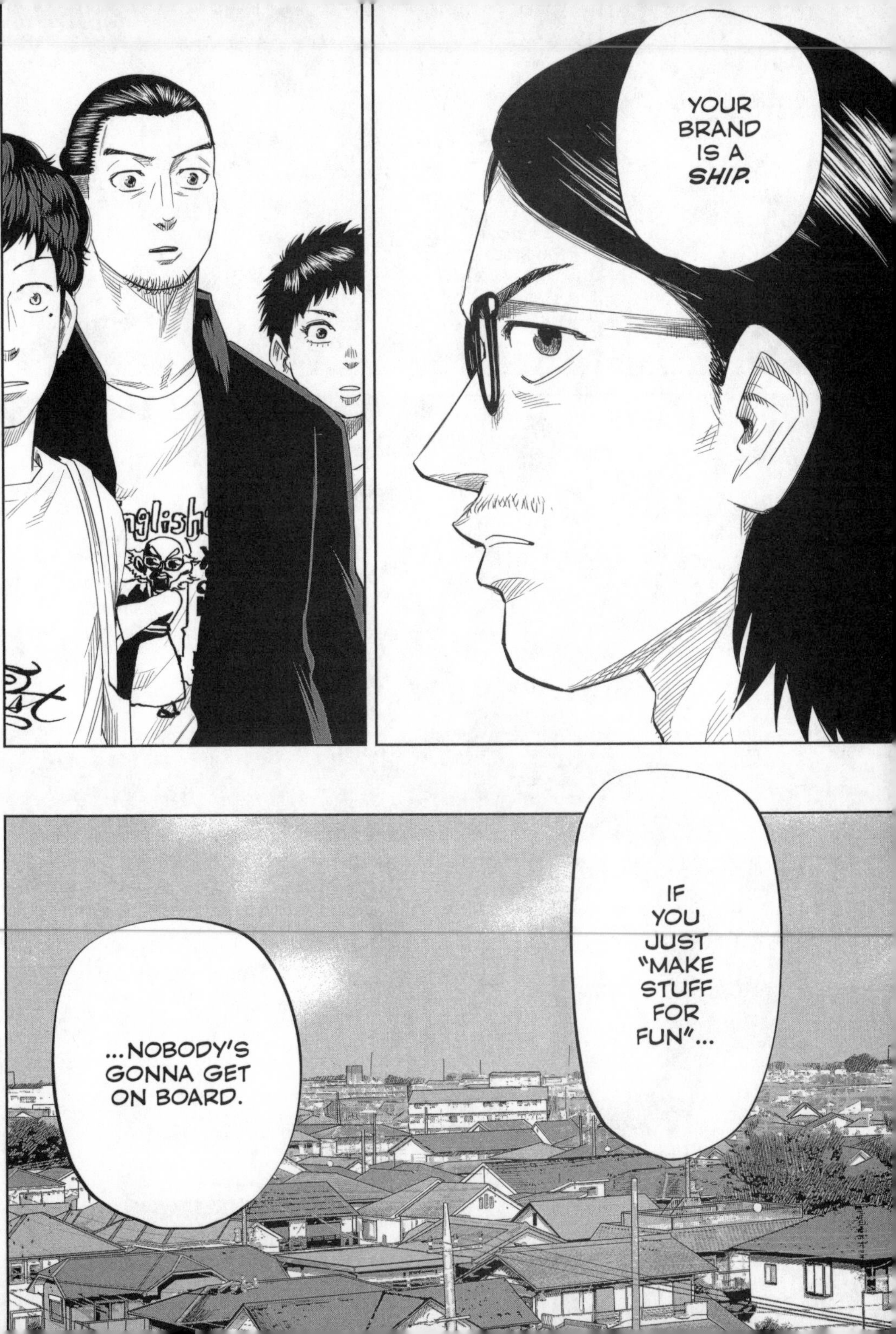
YOUR BRAND IS A SHIP.
IF YOU JUST "MAKE STUFF FOR FUN"...
...NOBODY'S GONNA GET ON BOARD.

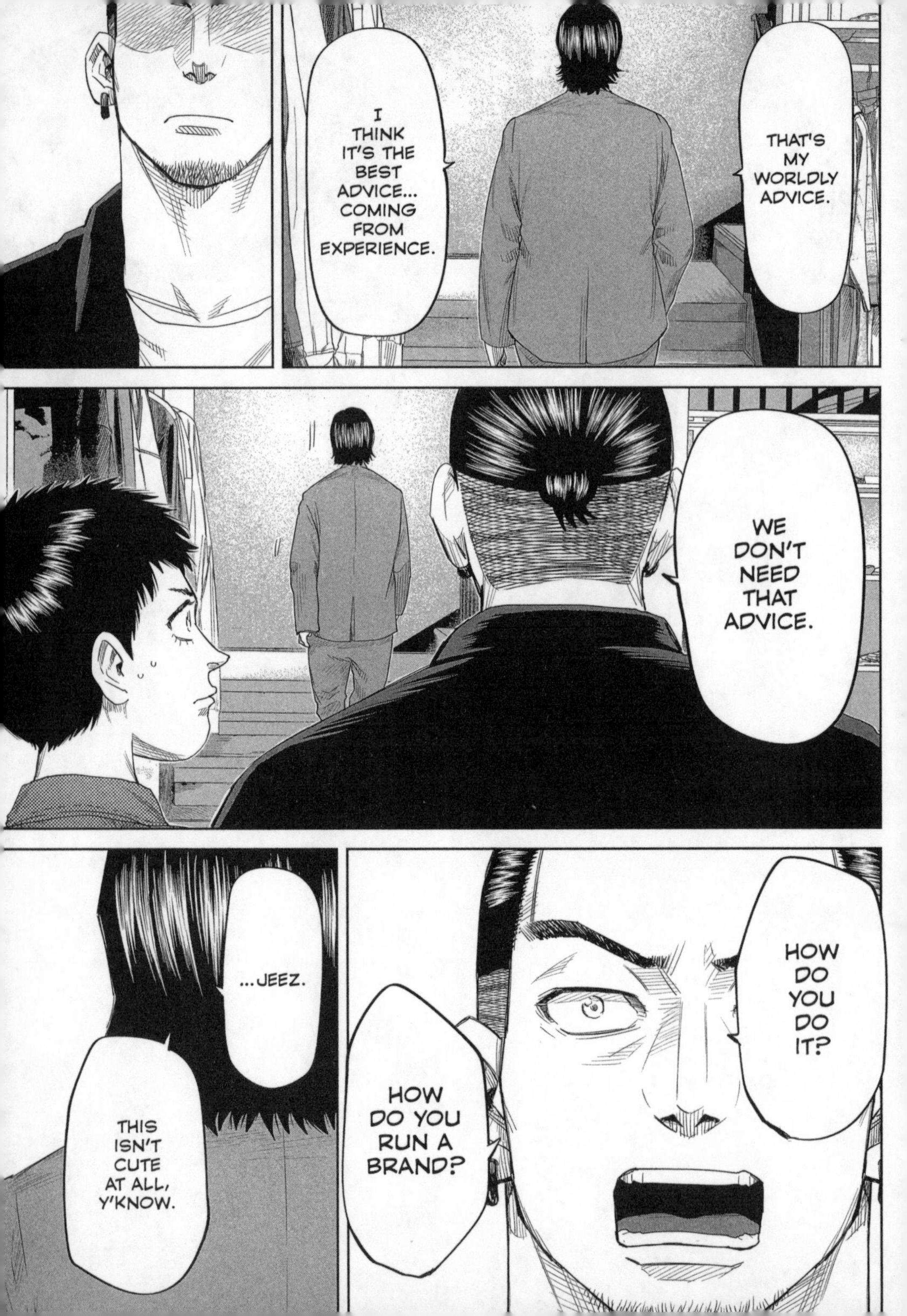
THAT'S MY WORLDLY ADVICE.
I THINK IT'S THE BEST ADVICE... COMING FROM EXPERIENCE.
WE DON'T NEED THAT ADVICE.
HOW DO YOU DO IT?
HOW DO YOU RUN A BRAND?
...JEEZ.
THIS ISN'T CUTE AT ALL, Y'KNOW.

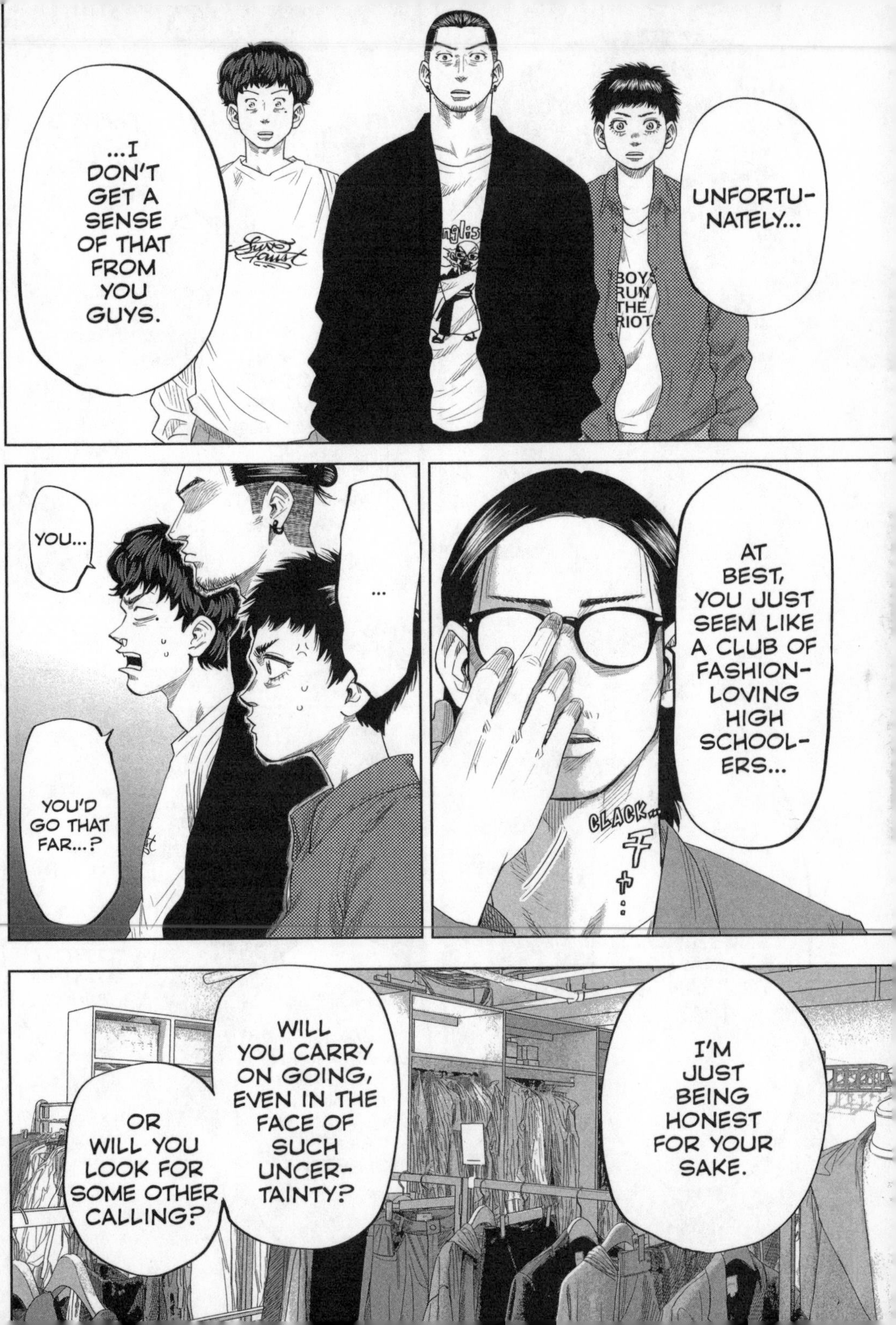
UNFORTUNATELY...
...I DON'T GET A SENSE OF THAT FROM YOU GUYS.
BOYS RUN THE RIOT
AT BEST, YOU JUST SEEM LIKE A CLUB OF FASHION-LOVING HIGH SCHOOLERS...
CLACK...
...
YOU...
YOU'D GO THAT FAR...?
I'M JUST BEING HONEST FOR YOUR SAKE.
WILL YOU CARRY ON GOING, EVEN IN THE FACE OF SUCH UNCERTAINTY?
OR WILL YOU LOOK FOR SOME OTHER CALLING?

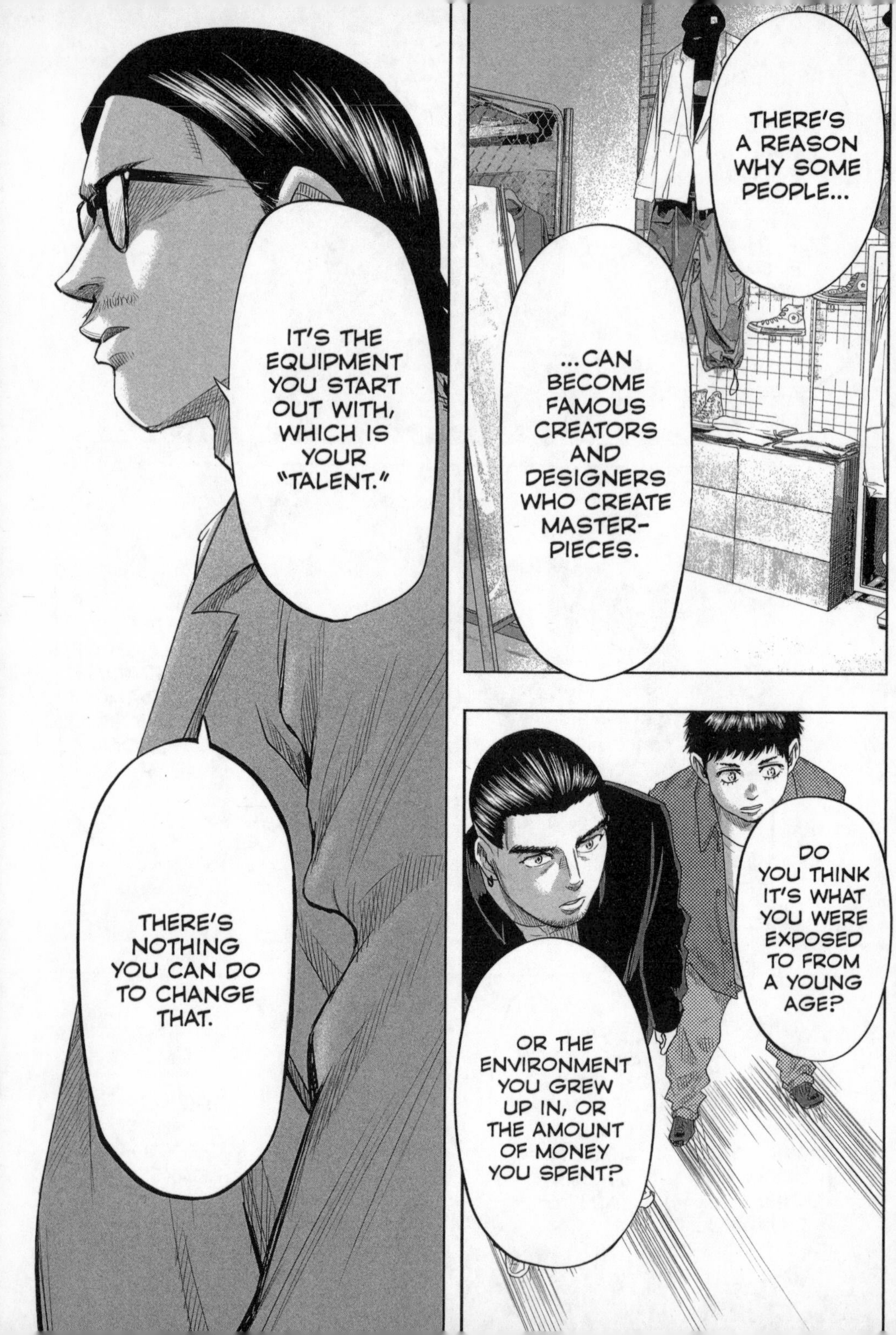
THERE'S A REASON WHY SOME PEOPLE...
...CAN BECOME FAMOUS CREATORS AND DESIGNERS WHO CREATE MASTER-PIECES.
DO YOU THINK IT'S WHAT YOU WERE EXPOSED TO FROM A YOUNG AGE?
OR THE ENVIRONMENT YOU GREW UP IN, OR THE AMOUNT OF MONEY YOU SPENT?
IT'S THE EQUIPMENT YOU START OUT WITH, WHICH IS YOUR "TALENT."
THERE'S NOTHING YOU CAN DO TO CHANGE THAT.

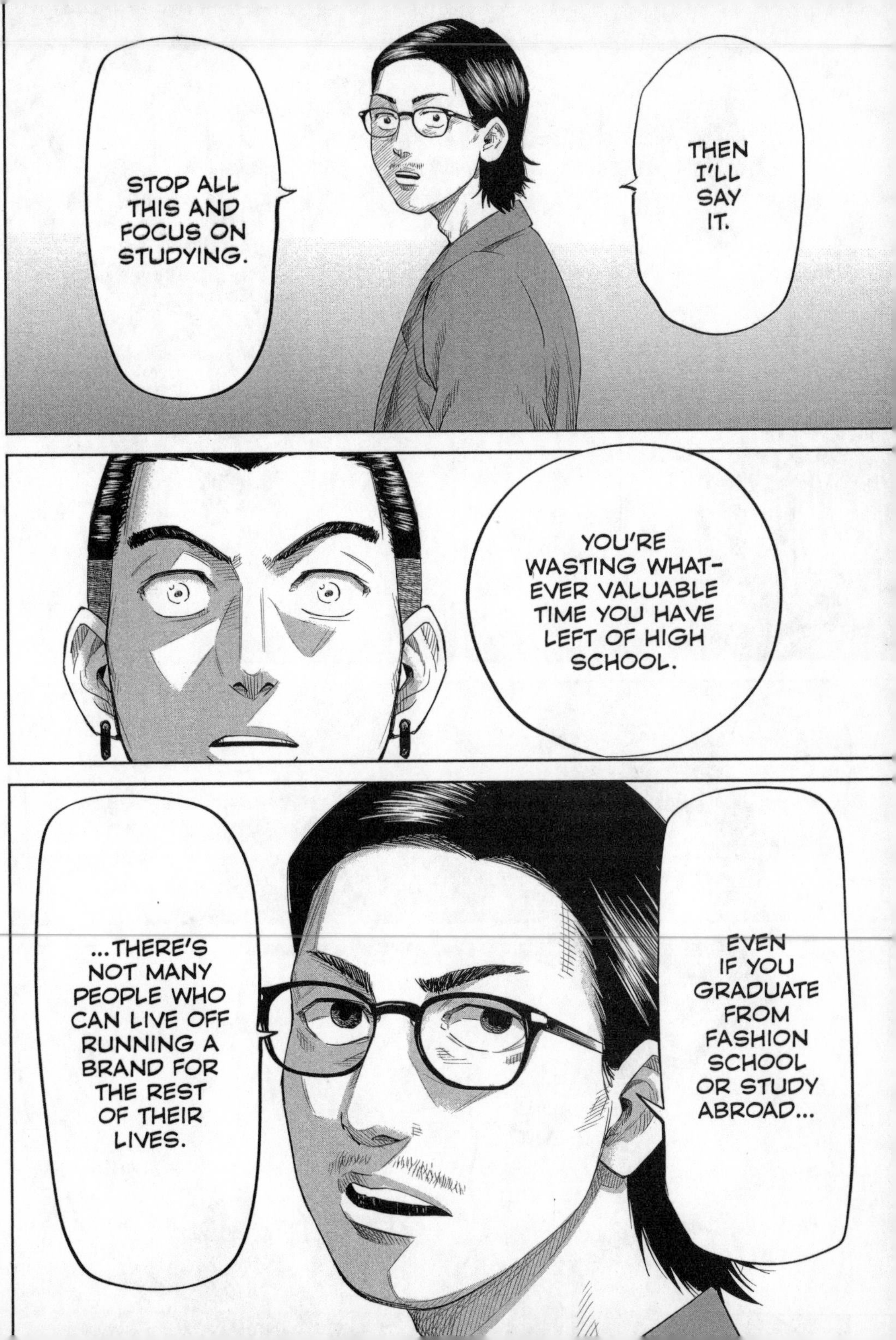
THEN I'LL SAY IT.
STOP ALL THIS AND FOCUS ON STUDYING.
YOU'RE WASTING WHAT-EVER VALUABLE TIME YOU HAVE LEFT OF HIGH SCHOOL.
EVEN IF YOU GRADUATE FROM FASHION SCHOOL OR STUDY ABROAD...
...THERE'S NOT MANY PEOPLE WHO CAN LIVE OFF RUNNING A BRAND FOR THE REST OF THEIR LIVES.

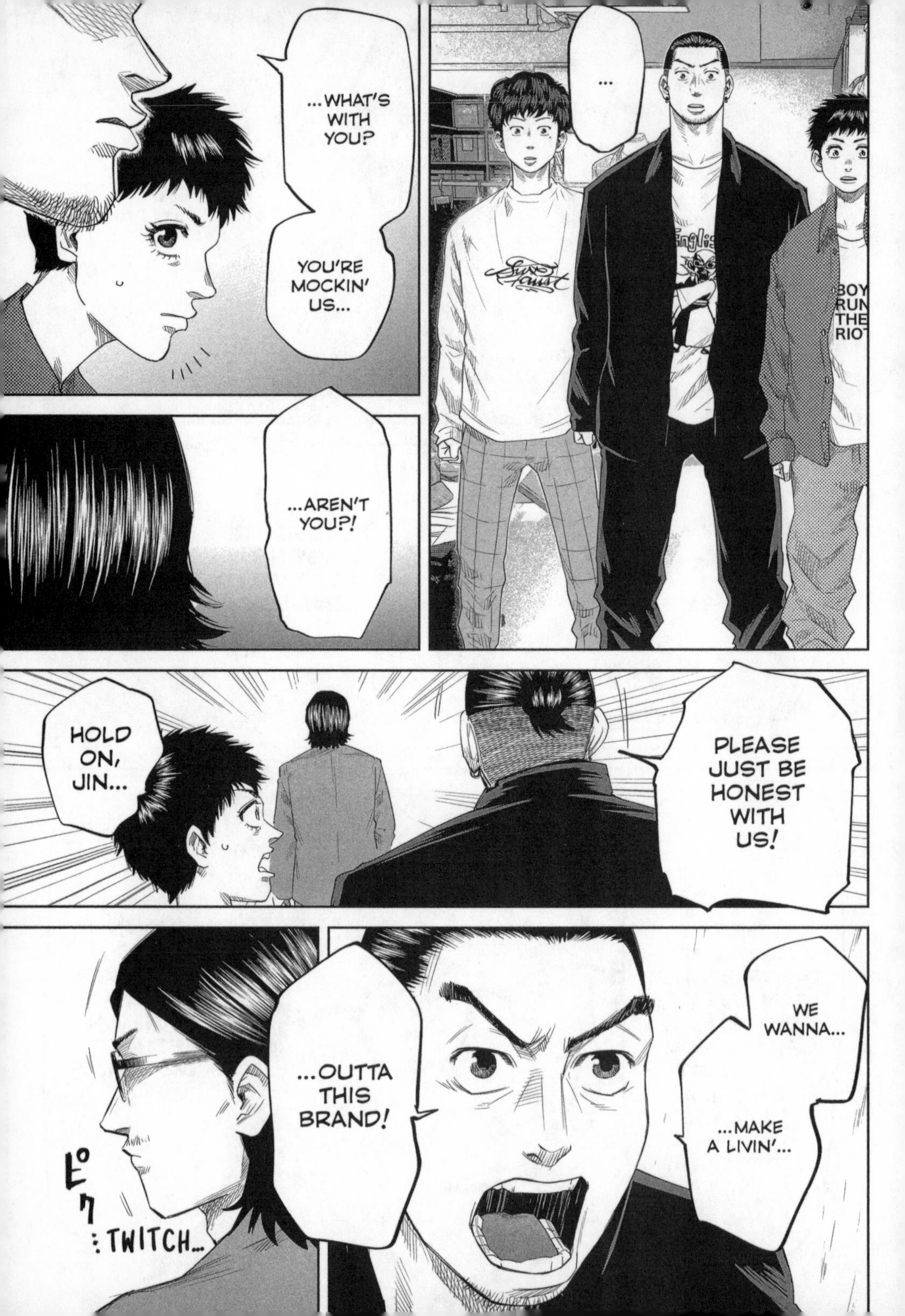
...
...WHAT'S WITH YOU?
YOU'RE MOCKIN' US...
...AREN'T YOU?!
PLEASE JUST BE HONEST WITH US!
HOLD ON, JIN...
WE WANNA...
...MAKE A LIVIN'...
...OUTTA THIS BRAND!
ピク
TWITCH...

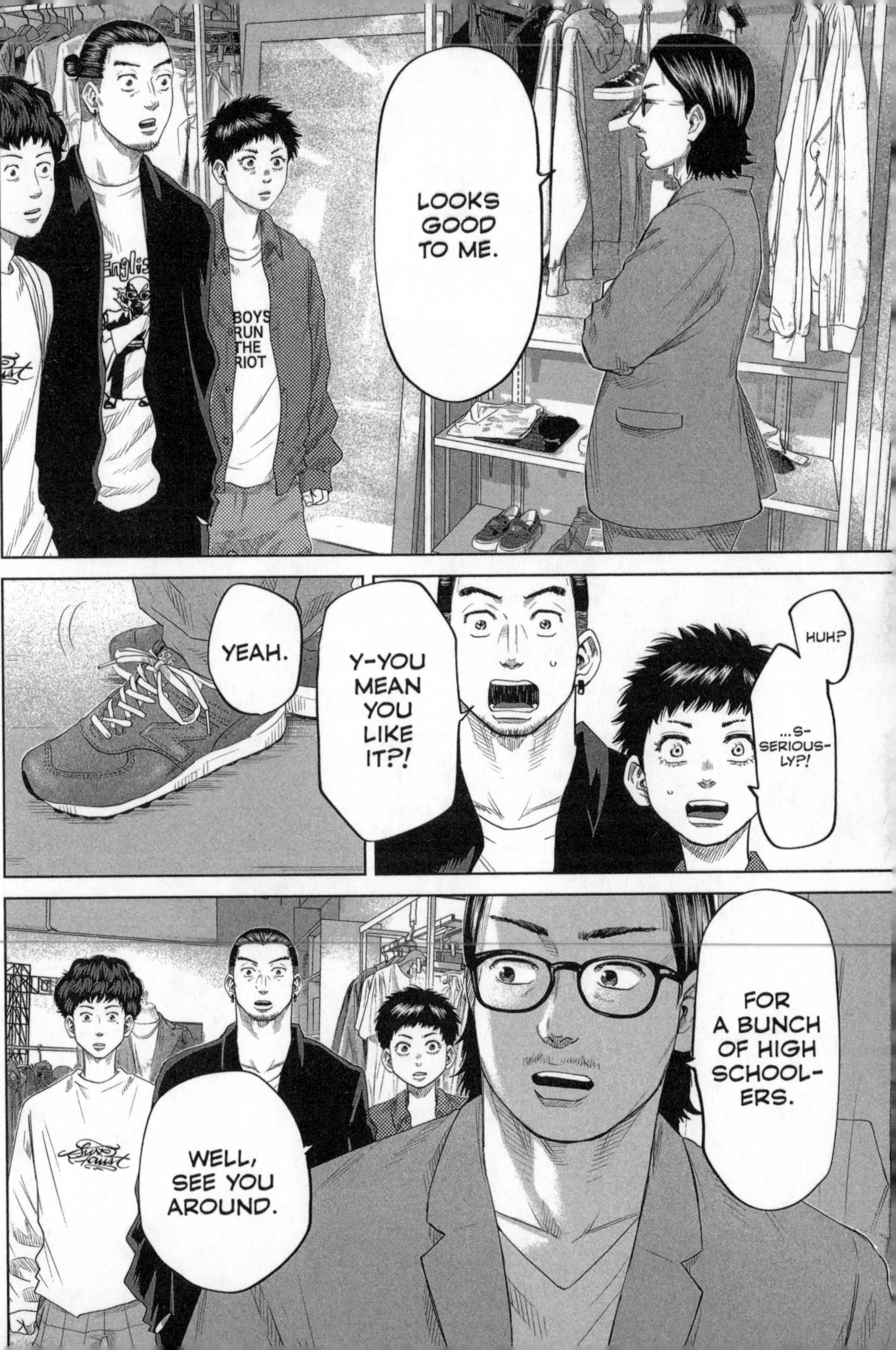
BOYS RUN THE RIOT
LOOKS GOOD TO ME.
HUH?
Y-YOU MEAN YOU LIKE IT?!
...S-SERIOUSLY?!
YEAH.
FOR A BUNCH OF HIGH SCHOOL-ERS.
WELL, SEE YOU AROUND.

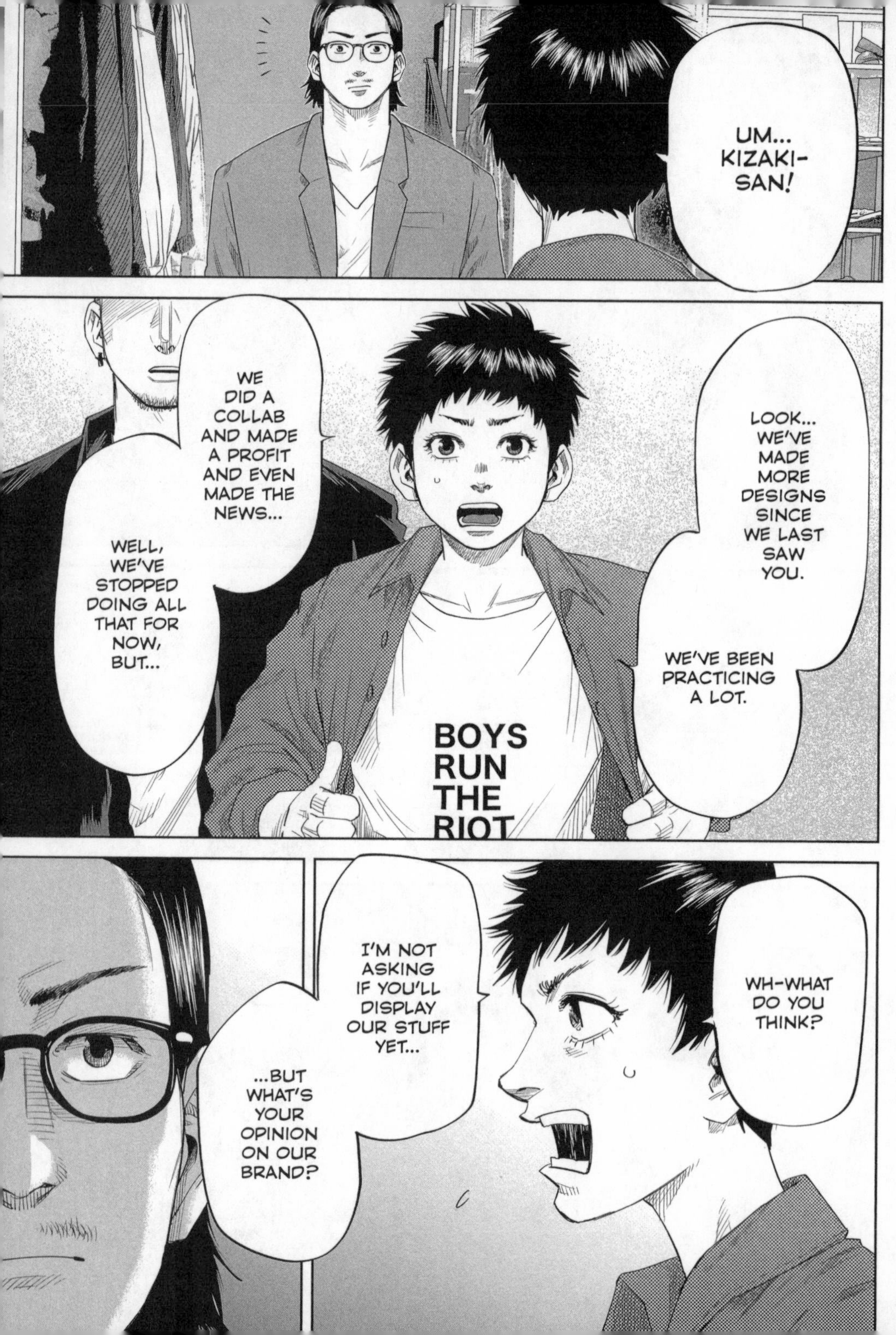
UM... KIZAKI-SAN!
LOOK... WE'VE MADE MORE DESIGNS SINCE WE LAST SAW YOU.
WE'VE BEEN PRACTICING A LOT.
BOYS RUN THE RIOT
WE DID A COLLAB AND MADE A PROFIT AND EVEN MADE THE NEWS...
WELL, WE'VE STOPPED DOING ALL THAT FOR NOW, BUT...
WH-WHAT DO YOU THINK?
I'M NOT ASKING IF YOU'LL DISPLAY OUR STUFF YET...
...BUT WHAT'S YOUR OPINION ON OUR BRAND?

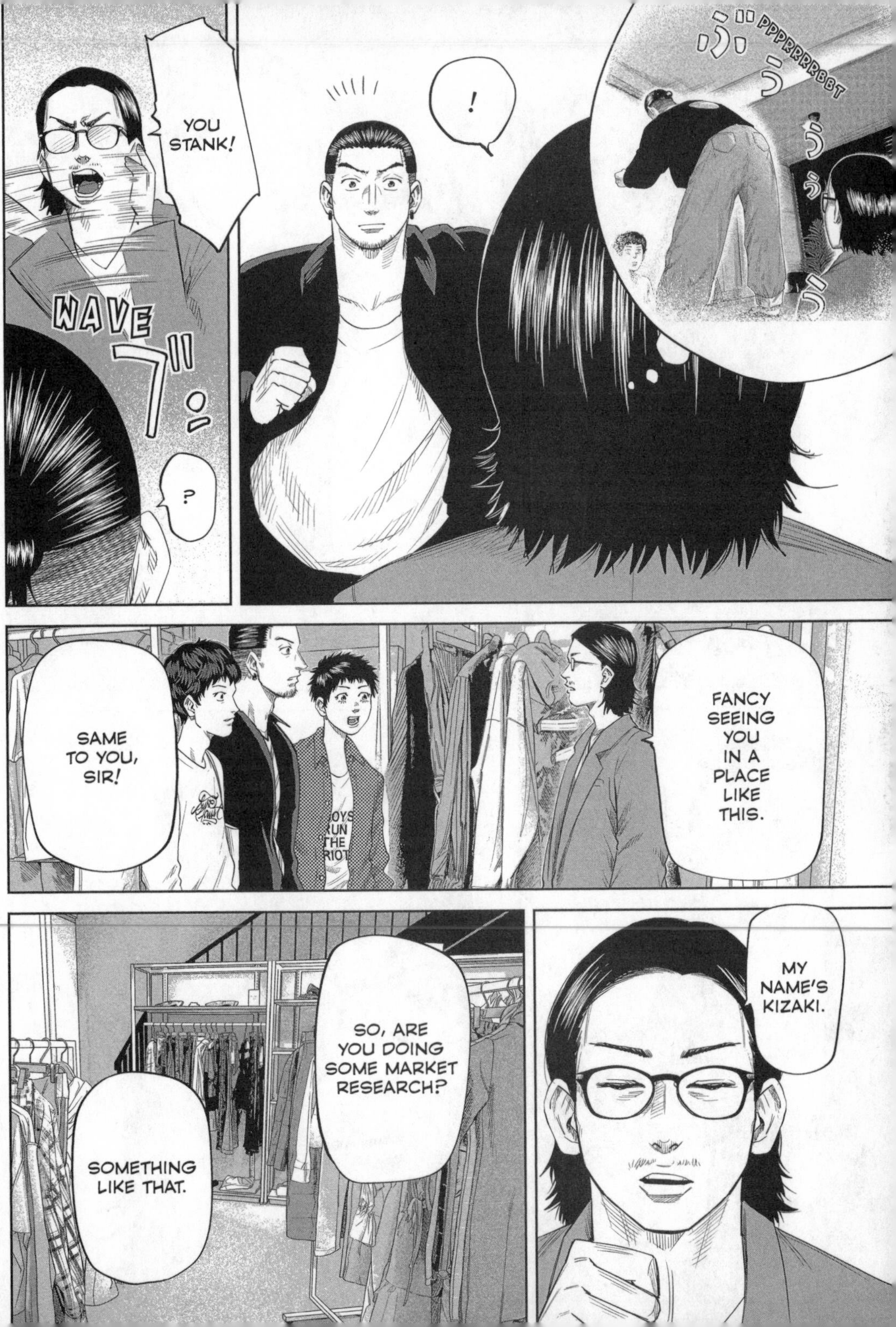
PPPRRRRRBBT
!
YOU STANK!
WAVE
?
FANCY SEEING YOU IN A PLACE LIKE THIS.
SAME TO YOU, SIR!
MY NAME'S KIZAKI.
SO, ARE YOU DOING SOME MARKET RESEARCH?
SOMETHING LIKE THAT.

Chap. 28 Gift

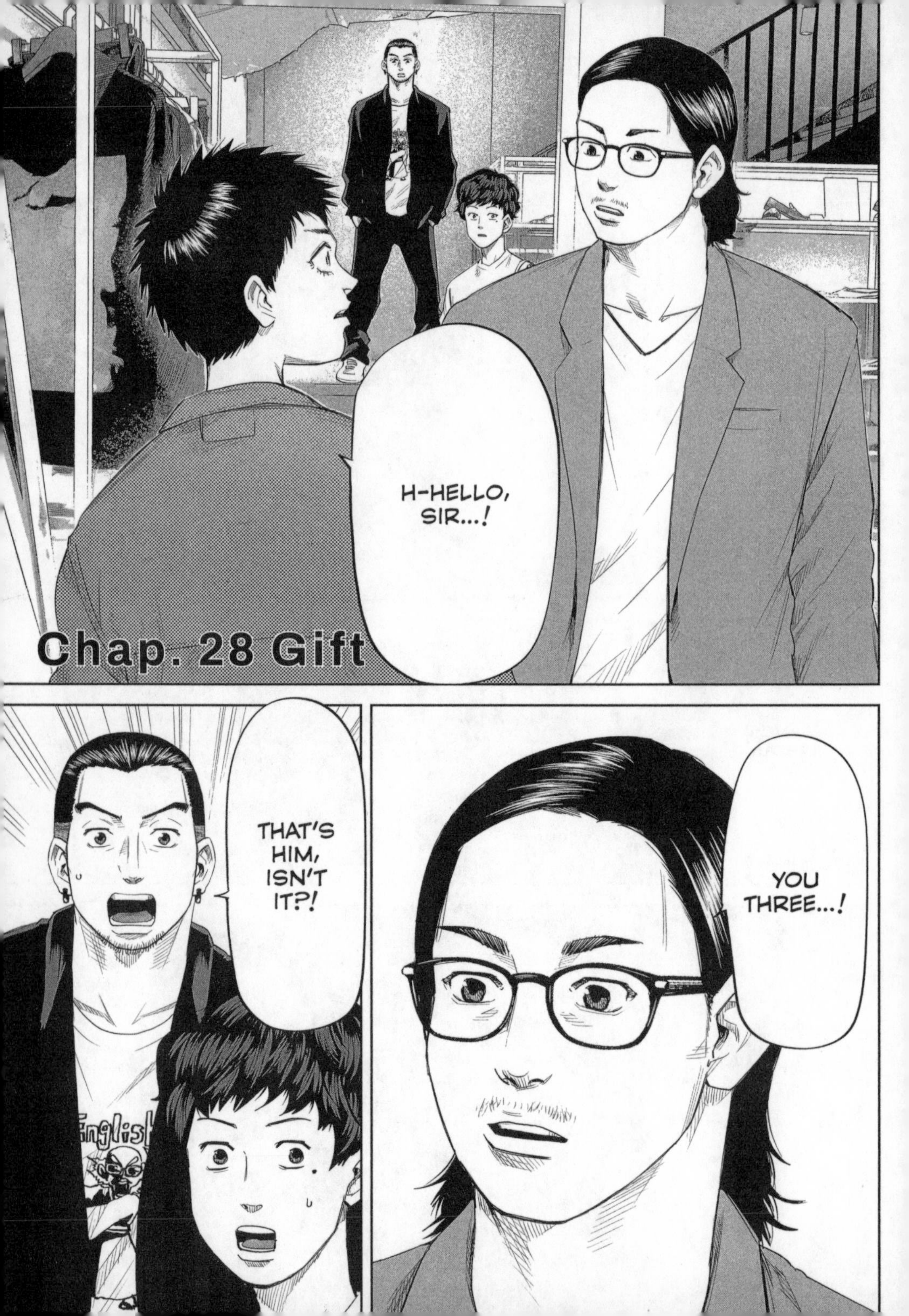
H-HELLO, SIR...!
YOU THREE...!
THAT'S HIM, ISN'T IT?!

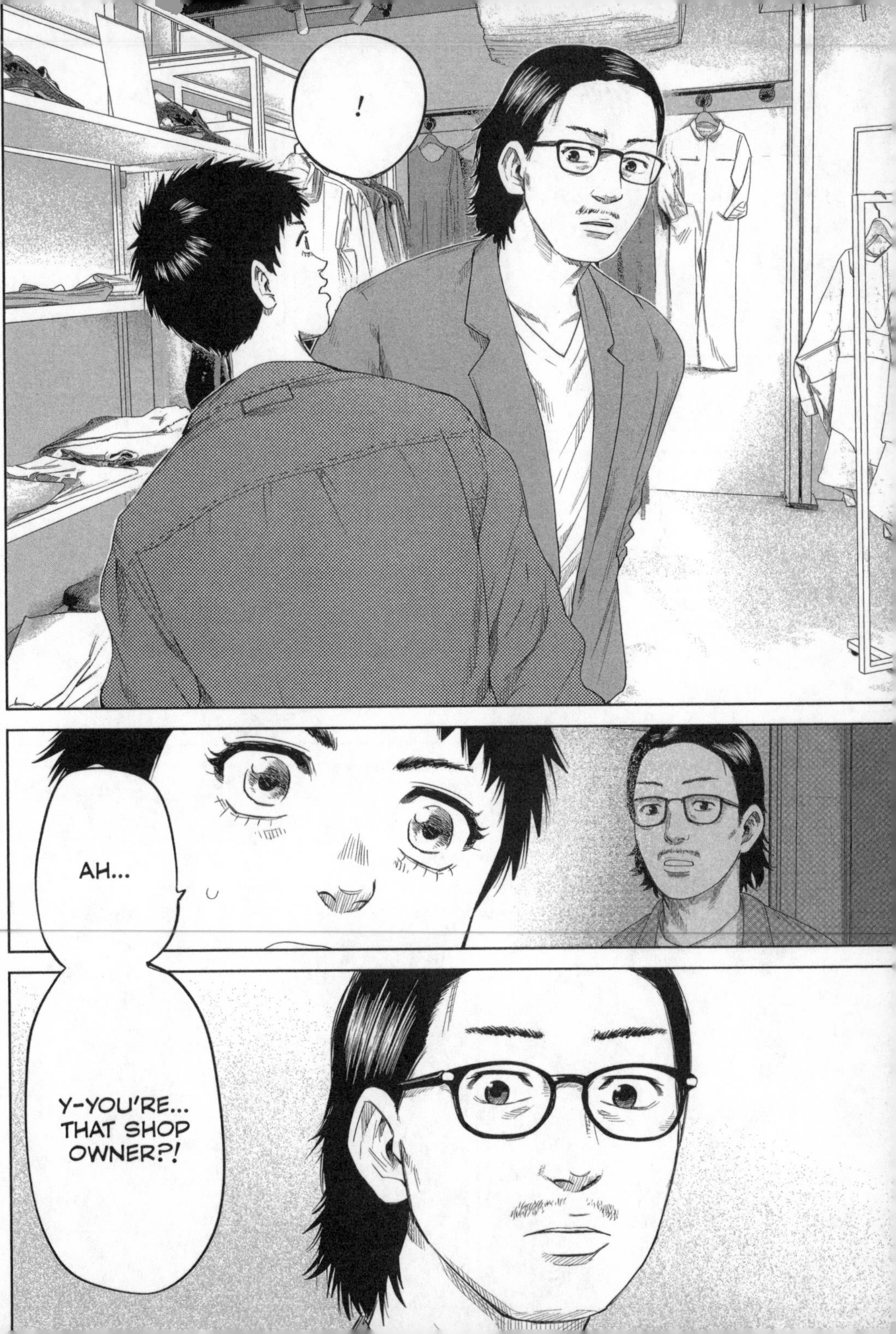
!
AH...
Y-YOU'RE... THAT SHOP OWNER?!

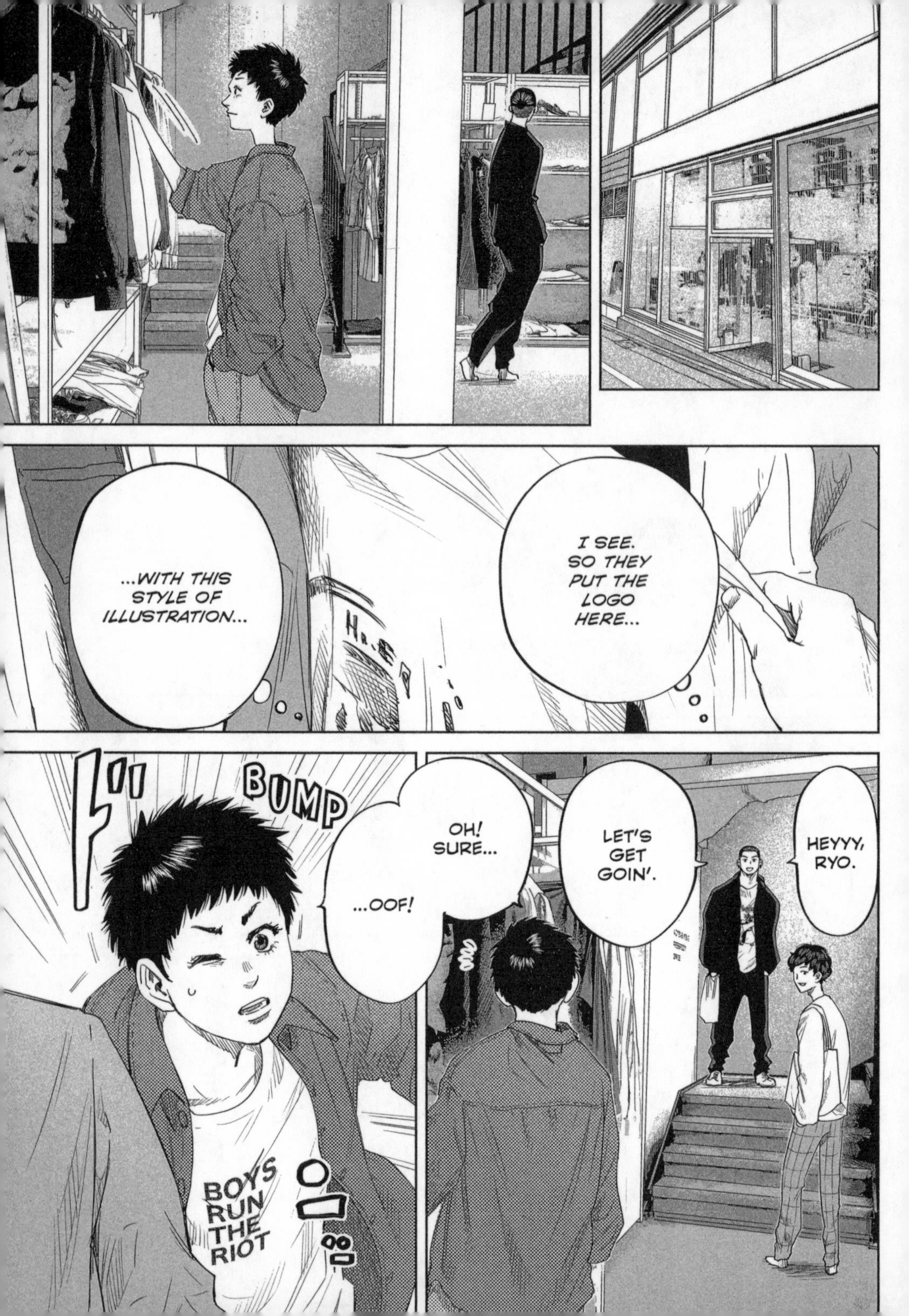
I SEE. SO THEY PUT THE LOGO HERE...
...WITH THIS STYLE OF ILLUSTRATION...
HEYYY, RYO.
LET'S GET GOIN'.
OH! SURE...
...OOF!
BUMP
BOYS RUN THE RIOT

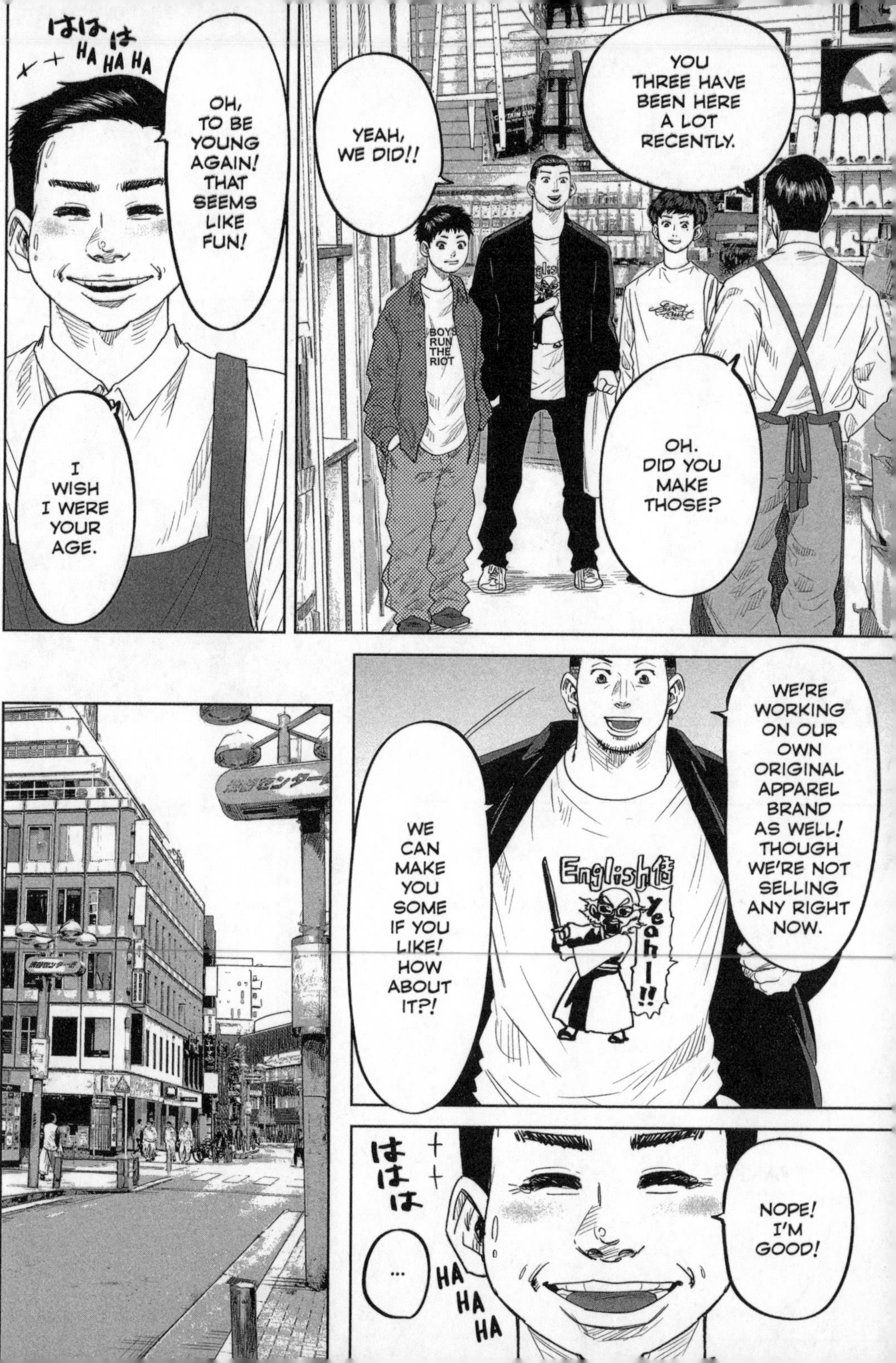

YOU THREE HAVE BEEN HERE A LOT RECENTLY.
YEAH, WE DID!!
OH. DID YOU MAKE THOSE?
BOYS RUN THE RIOT
ははは HA HA HA
OH, TO BE YOUNG AGAIN! THAT SEEMS LIKE FUN!
I WISH I WERE YOUR AGE.
WE'RE WORKING ON OUR OWN ORIGINAL APPAREL BRAND AS WELL! THOUGH WE'RE NOT SELLING ANY RIGHT NOW.
English侍
Yeah!!
WE CAN MAKE YOU SOME IF YOU LIKE! HOW ABOUT IT?!
NOPE! I'M GOOD!
ははは
HA HA HA
...

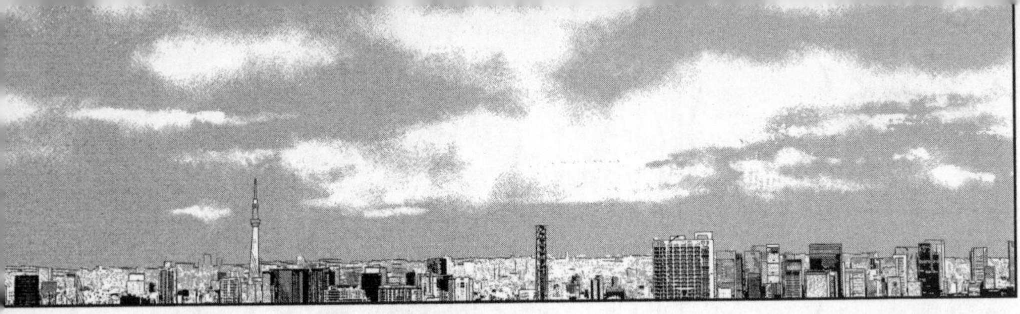

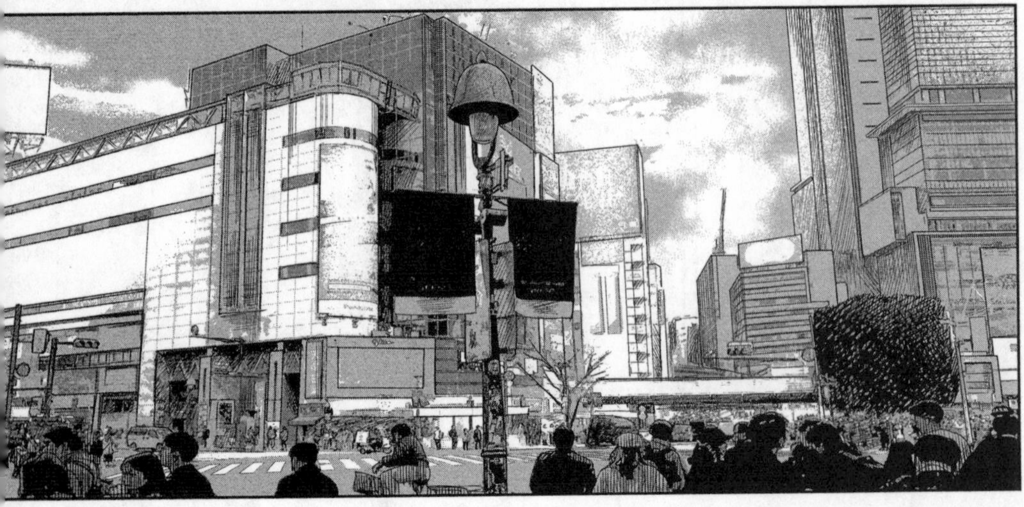

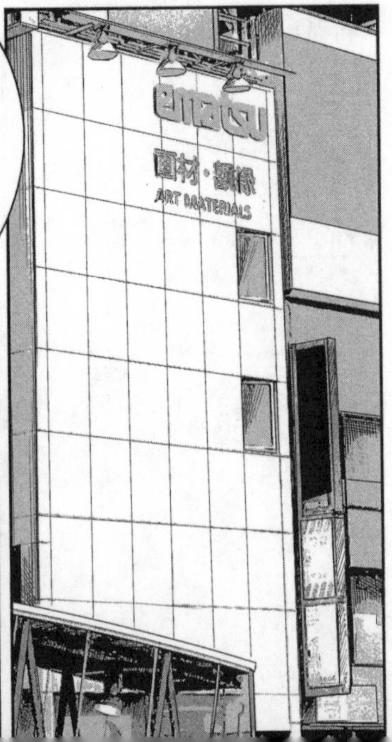
画材・額縁
ART MATERIALS

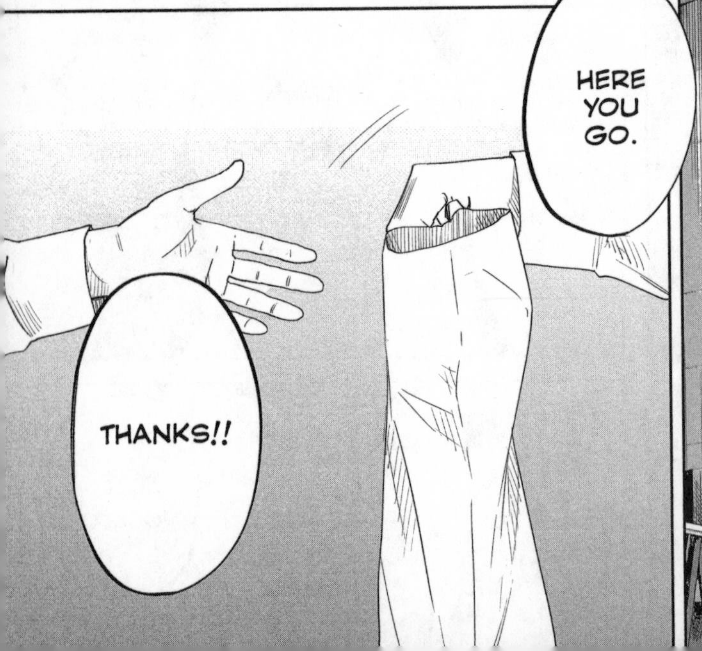
HERE YOU GO.
THANKS!!

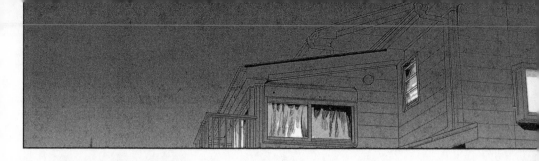

OH. I GUESS THIS IS IN FASHION RIGHT NOW.

HM-HM-HMMM...

HM-HMMM...

...

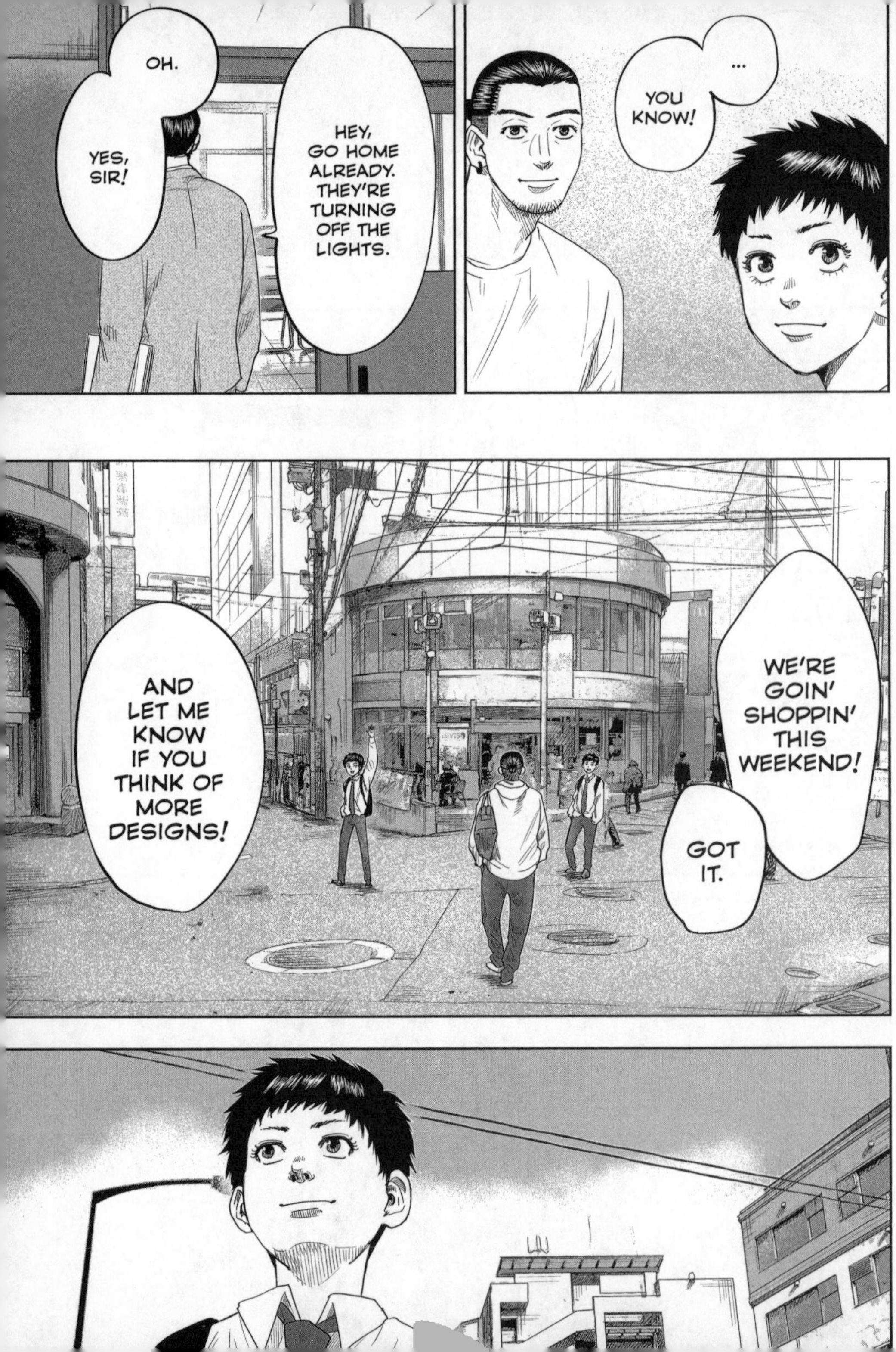
...
YOU KNOW!
HEY, GO HOME ALREADY. THEY'RE TURNING OFF THE LIGHTS.
OH.
YES, SIR!
WE'RE GOIN' SHOPPIN' THIS WEEKEND!
GOT IT.
AND LET ME KNOW IF YOU THINK OF MORE DESIGNS!

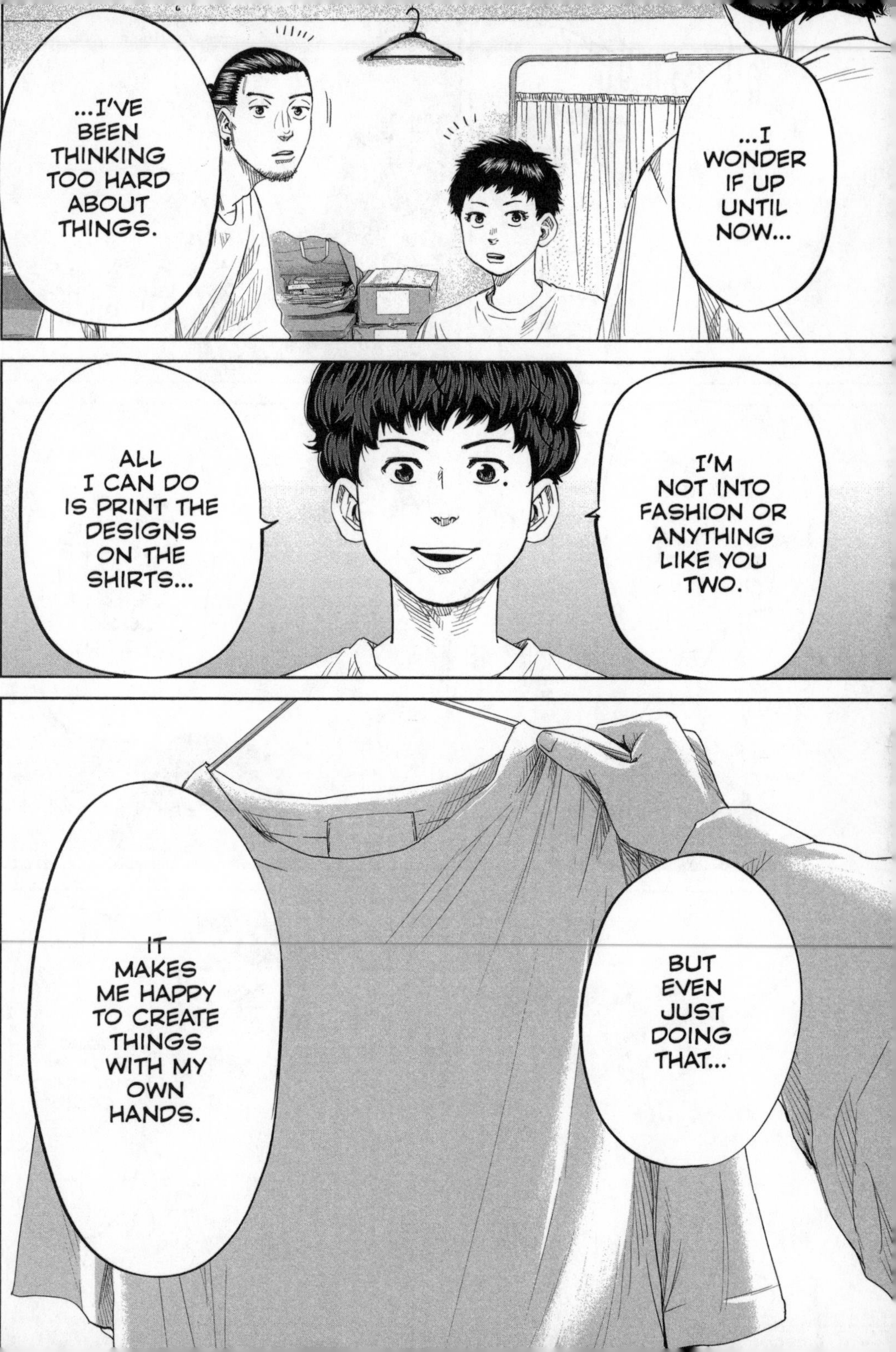
...I WONDER IF UP UNTIL NOW...
...I'VE BEEN THINKING TOO HARD ABOUT THINGS.
I'M NOT INTO FASHION OR ANYTHING LIKE YOU TWO.
ALL I CAN DO IS PRINT THE DESIGNS ON THE SHIRTS...
BUT EVEN JUST DOING THAT...
IT MAKES ME HAPPY TO CREATE THINGS WITH MY OWN HANDS.

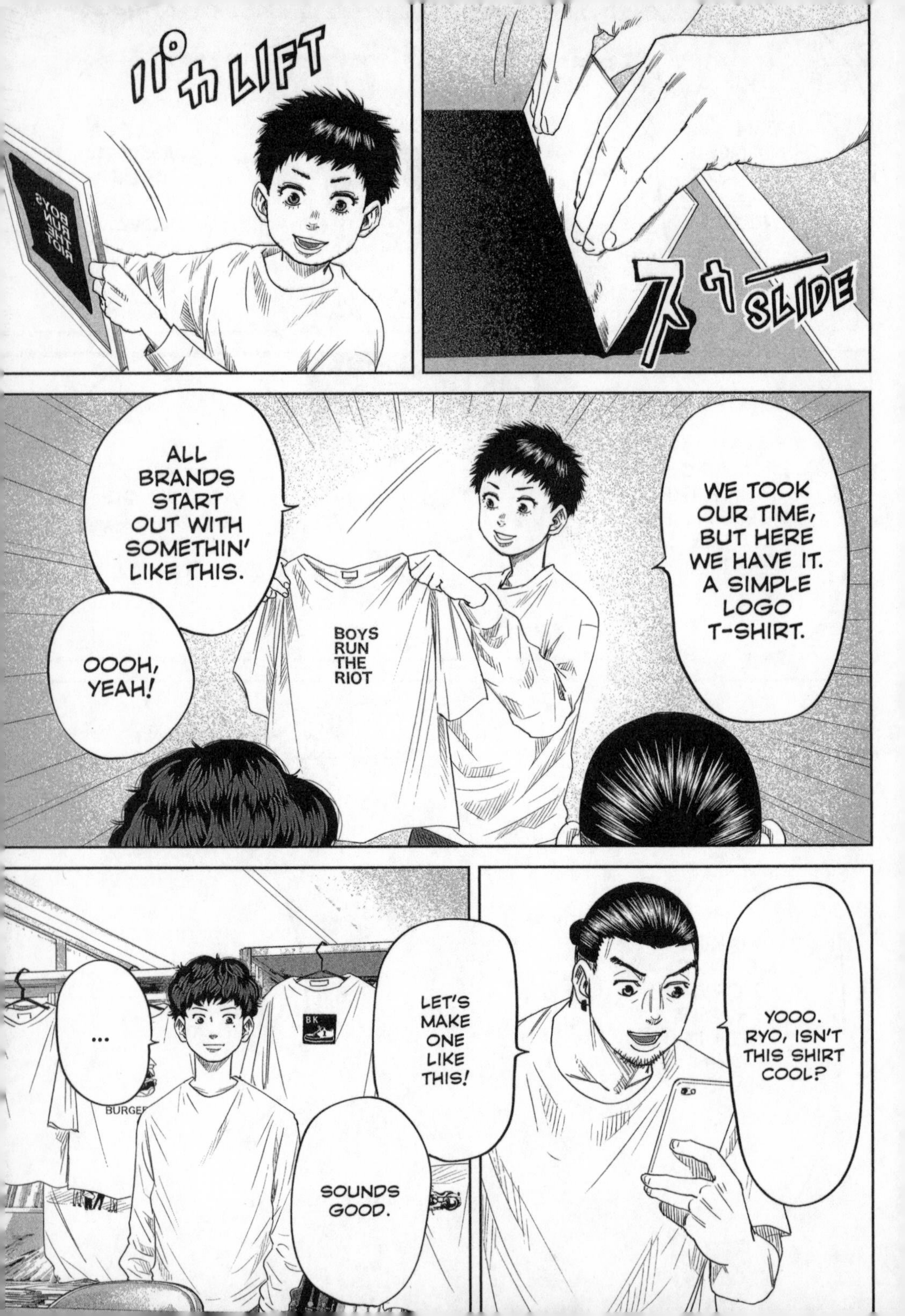
スゥ— SLIDE
パカ LIFT
WE TOOK OUR TIME, BUT HERE WE HAVE IT. A SIMPLE LOGO T-SHIRT.
ALL BRANDS START OUT WITH SOMETHIN' LIKE THIS.
BOYS RUN THE RIOT
OOOH, YEAH!
YOOO. RYO, ISN'T THIS SHIRT COOL?
LET'S MAKE ONE LIKE THIS!
...
SOUNDS GOOD.

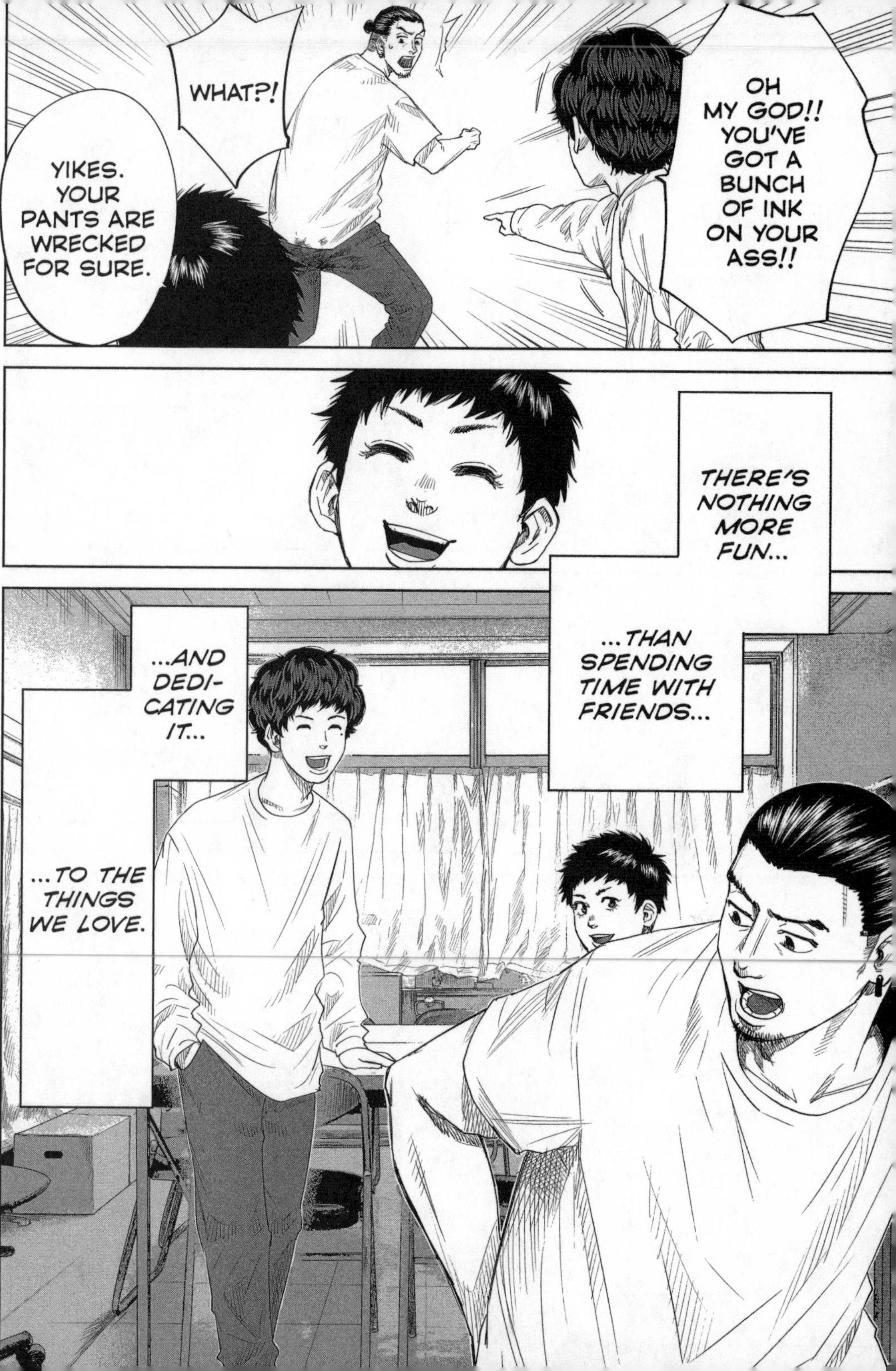
OH MY GOD!! YOU'VE GOT A BUNCH OF INK ON YOUR ASS!!
WHAT?!
YIKES. YOUR PANTS ARE WRECKED FOR SURE.
THERE'S NOTHING MORE FUN...
...THAN SPENDING TIME WITH FRIENDS...
...AND DEDI-CATING IT...
...TO THE THINGS WE LOVE.

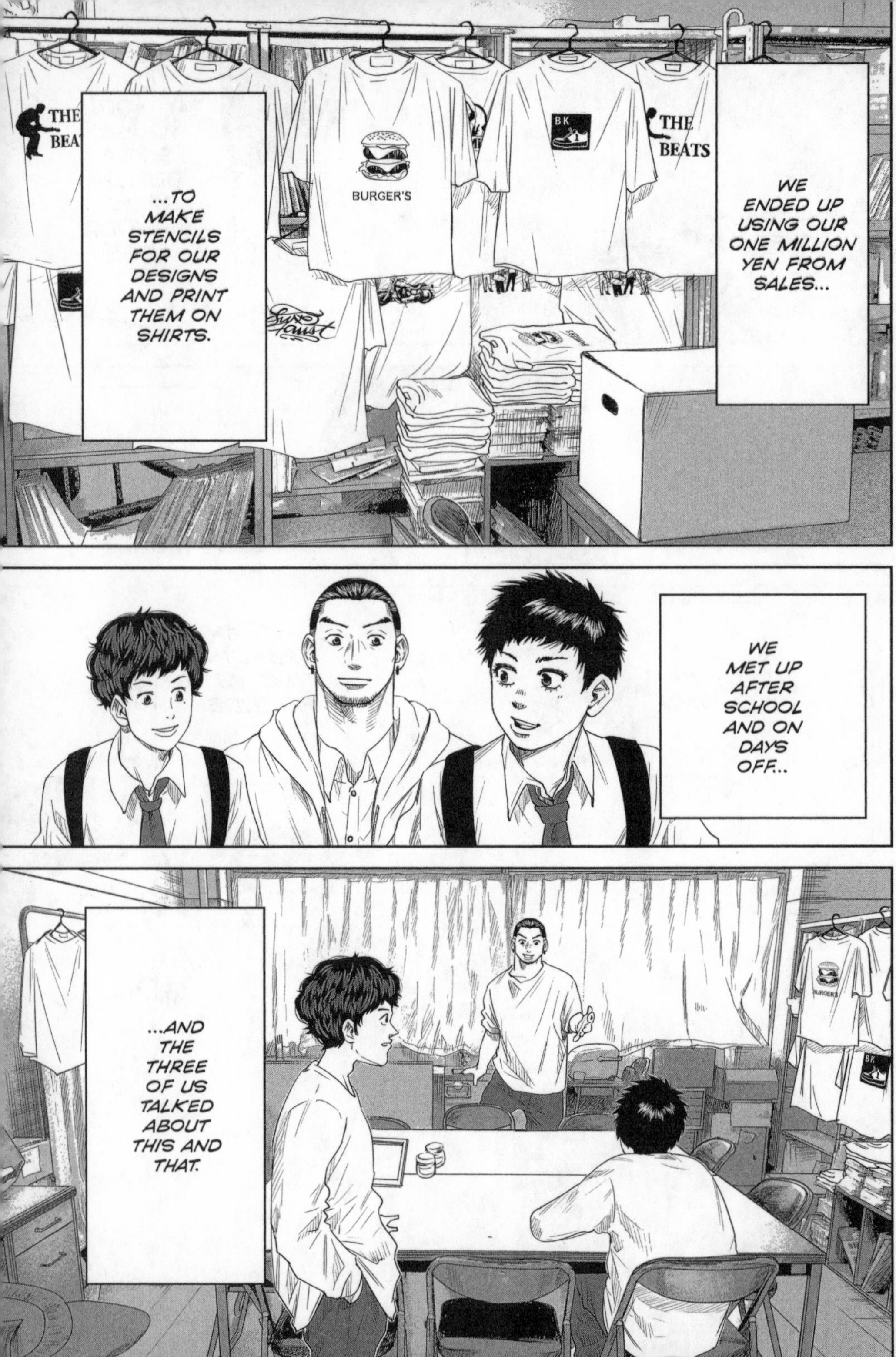
WE ENDED UP USING OUR ONE MILLION YEN FROM SALES...
THE BEATS
BK
BURGER'S
THE BEATS
...TO MAKE STENCILS FOR OUR DESIGNS AND PRINT THEM ON SHIRTS.
WE MET UP AFTER SCHOOL AND ON DAYS OFF...
BURGER'S
BK
...AND THE THREE OF US TALKED ABOUT THIS AND THAT.

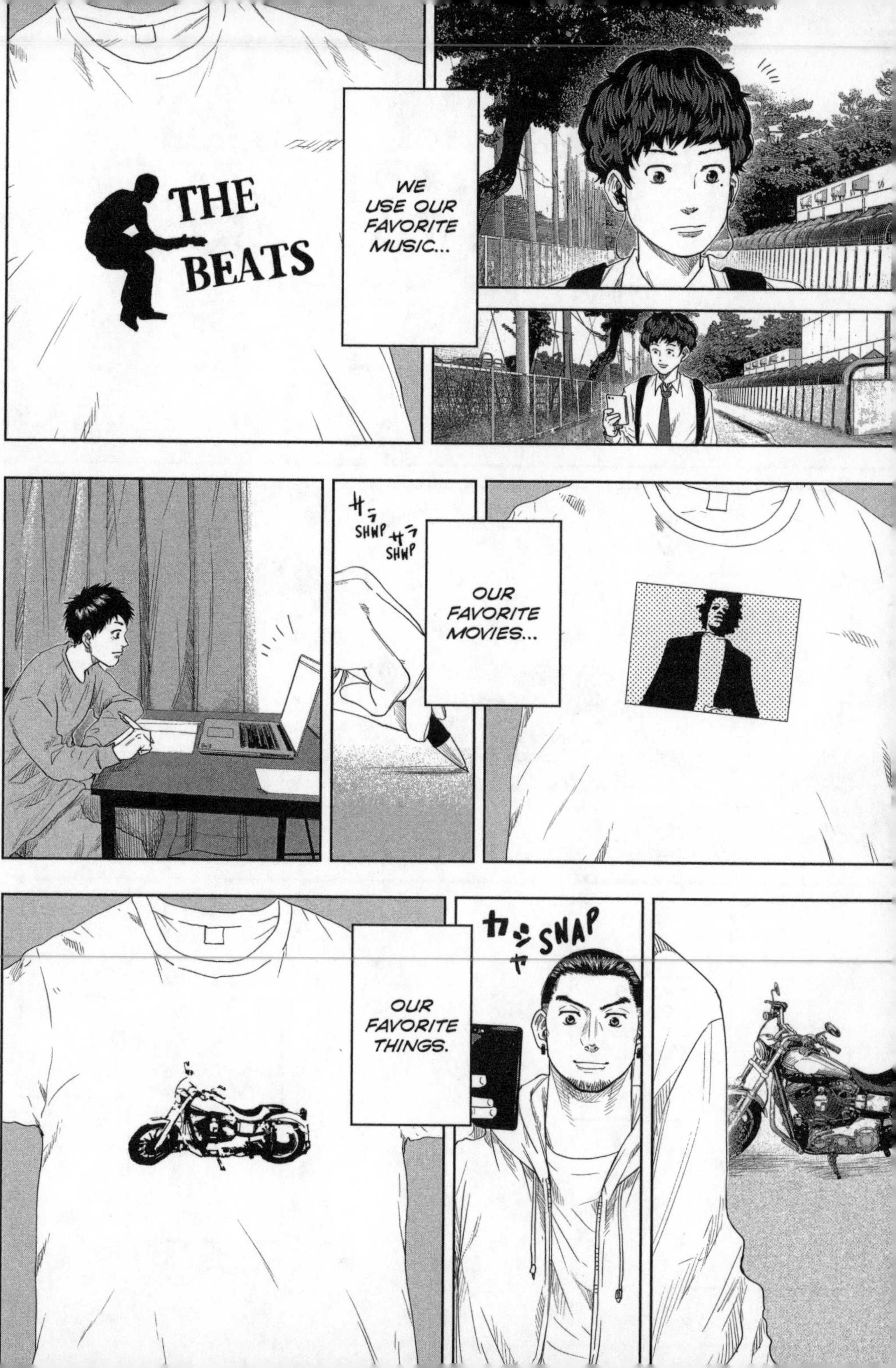
WE USE OUR FAVORITE MUSIC...
THE BEATS
OUR FAVORITE MOVIES...
SHWP
SHWP
SNAP
OUR FAVORITE THINGS.

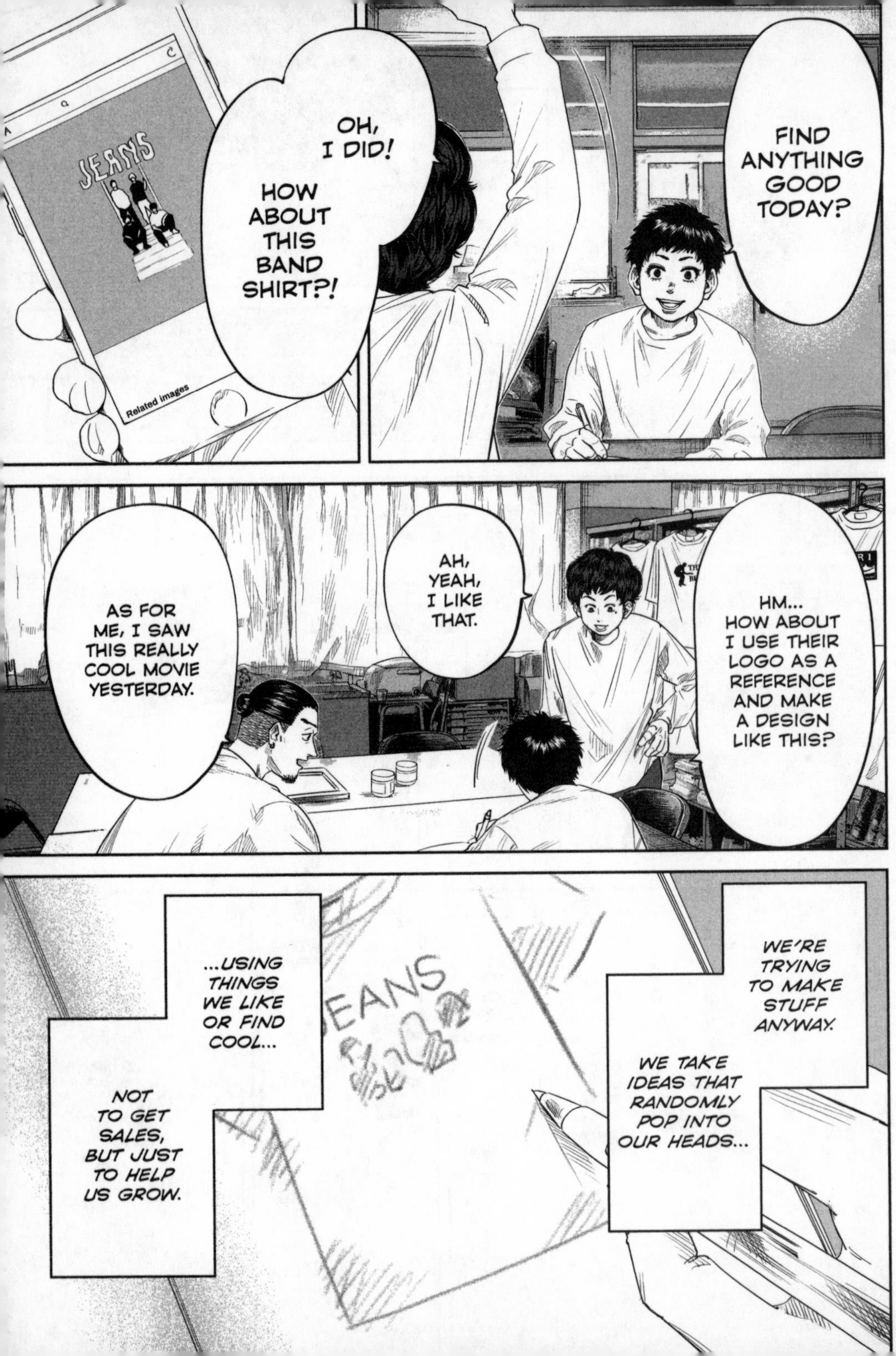
FIND ANYTHING GOOD TODAY?
OH, I DID!
HOW ABOUT THIS BAND SHIRT?!
JEANS
Related images
HM... HOW ABOUT I USE THEIR LOGO AS A REFERENCE AND MAKE A DESIGN LIKE THIS?
AH, YEAH, I LIKE THAT.
AS FOR ME, I SAW THIS REALLY COOL MOVIE YESTERDAY.
WE'RE TRYING TO MAKE STUFF ANYWAY.
WE TAKE IDEAS THAT RANDOMLY POP INTO OUR HEADS...
...USING THINGS WE LIKE OR FIND COOL...
NOT TO GET SALES, BUT JUST TO HELP US GROW.
JEANS

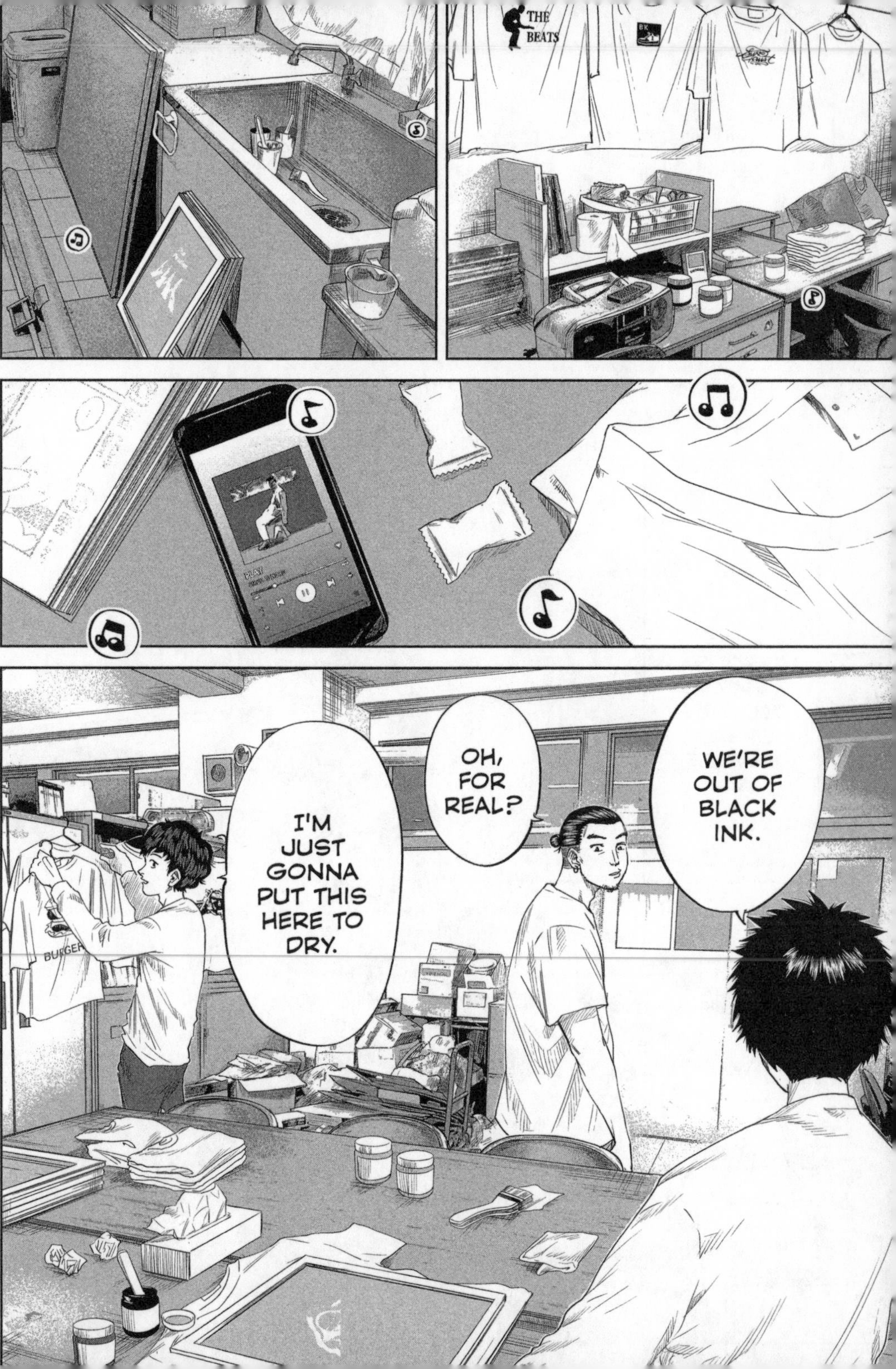
THE BEATS
WE'RE OUT OF BLACK INK.
OH, FOR REAL?
I'M JUST GONNA PUT THIS HERE TO DRY.
BURGER

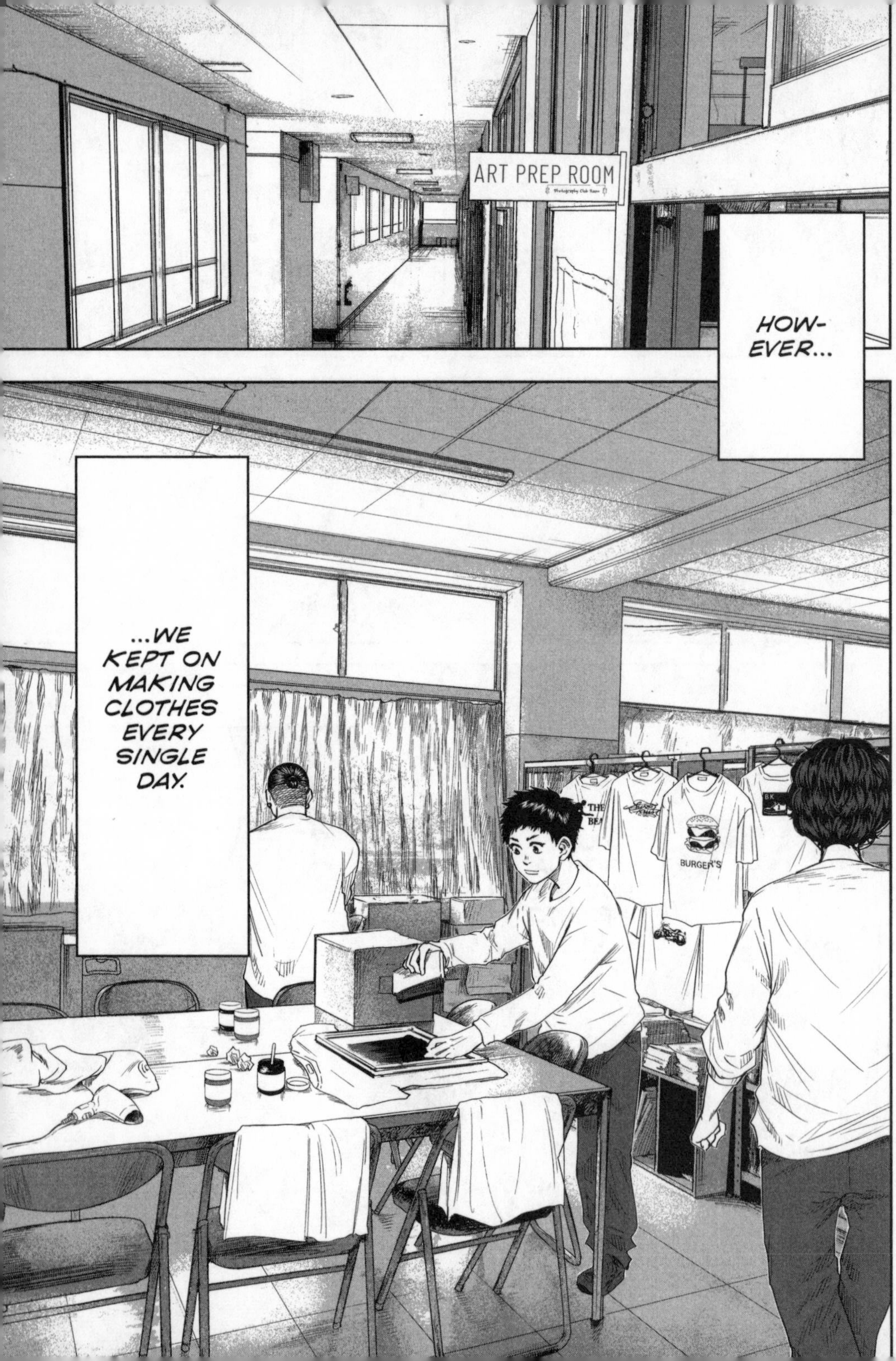
ART PREP ROOM
Photography Club Room
HOW-EVER...
...WE KEPT ON MAKING CLOTHES EVERY SINGLE DAY.
BURGER'S

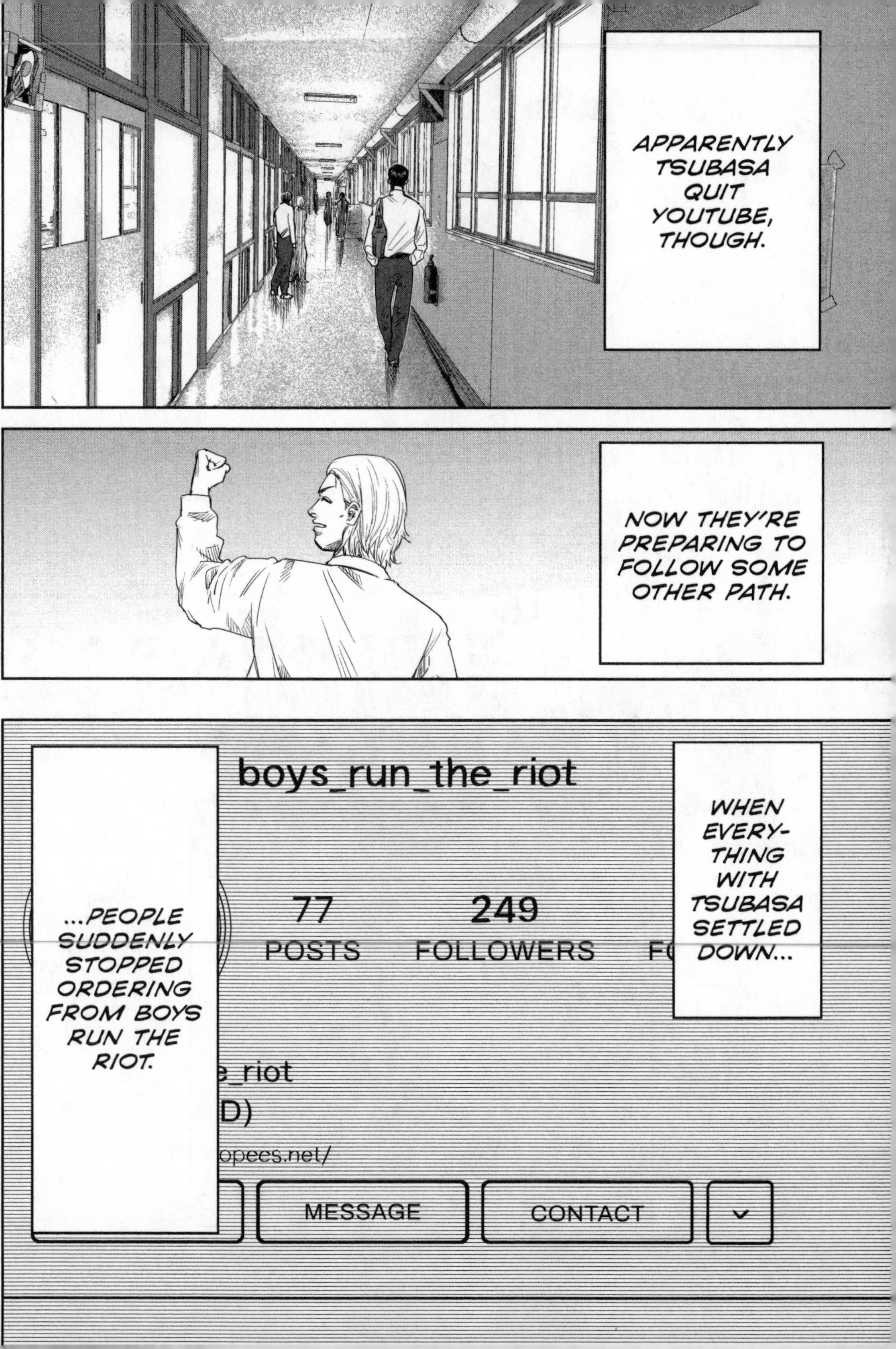
APPARENTLY TSUBASA QUIT YOUTUBE, THOUGH.
NOW THEY'RE PREPARING TO FOLLOW SOME OTHER PATH.
WHEN EVERY-THING WITH TSUBASA SETTLED DOWN...
boys_run_the_riot
...PEOPLE SUDDENLY STOPPED ORDERING FROM BOYS RUN THE RIOT.
77
POSTS
249
FOLLOWERS
MESSAGE
CONTACT

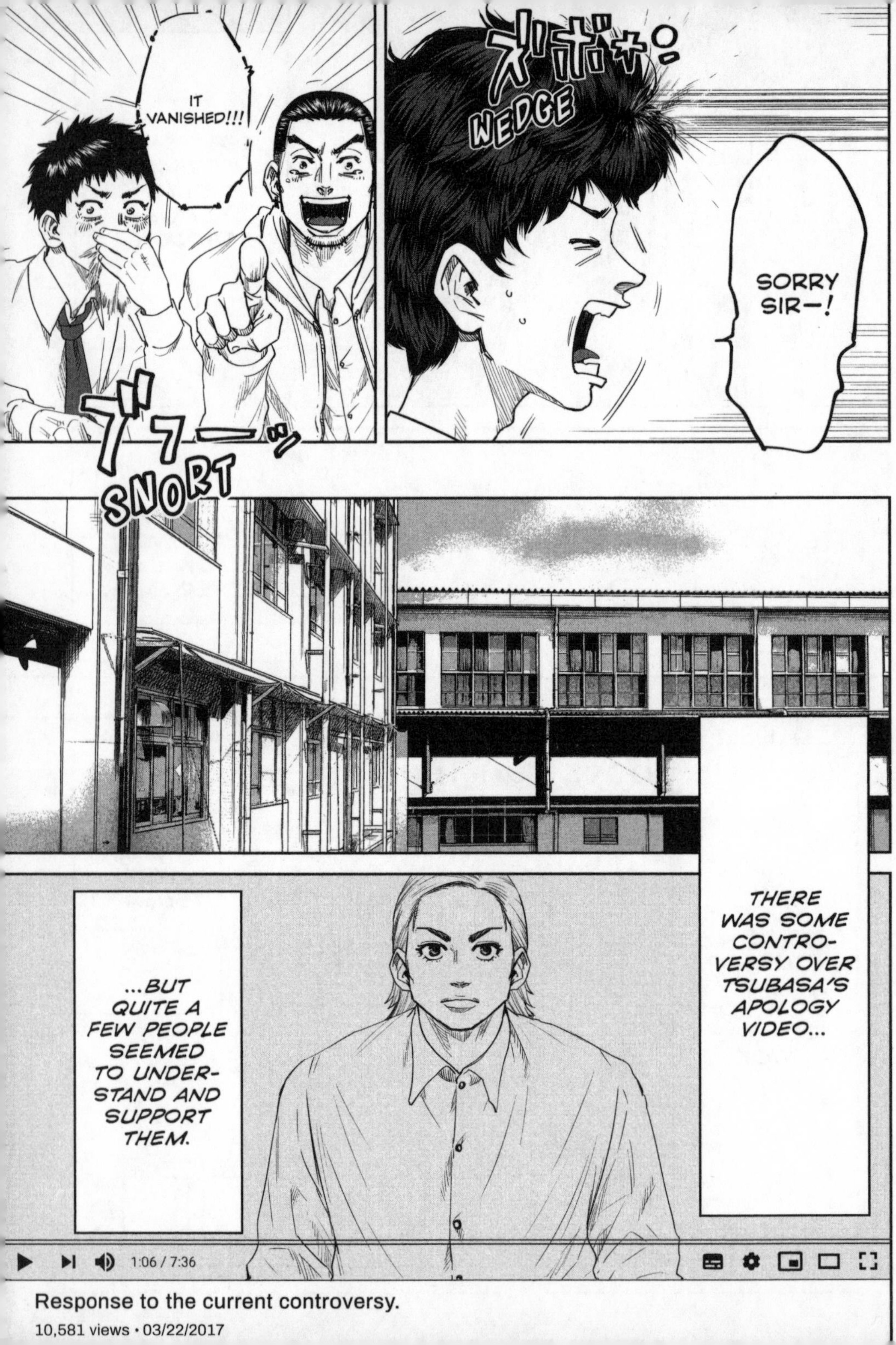
WEDGE
SORRY SIR—!
IT VANISHED!!!
SNORT
THERE WAS SOME CONTROVERSY OVER TSUBASA'S APOLOGY VIDEO...
...BUT QUITE A FEW PEOPLE SEEMED TO UNDERSTAND AND SUPPORT THEM.
1:06 / 7:36
Response to the current controversy.
10,581 views • 03/22/2017

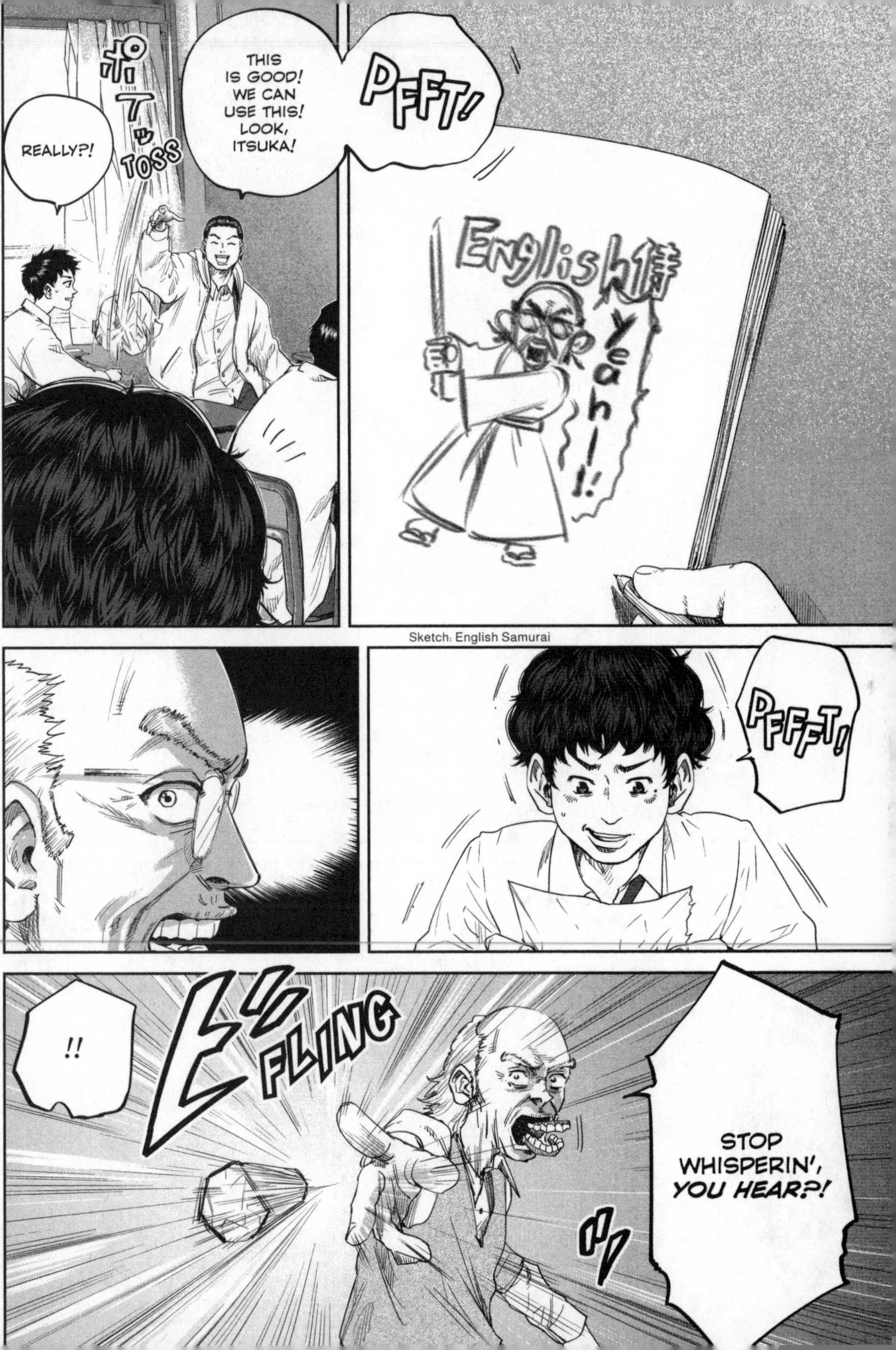
PFFT!
English侍
Yeah-!!
THIS IS GOOD! WE CAN USE THIS! LOOK, ITSUKA!
ポイッ TOSS
REALLY?!
Sketch: English Samurai
PFFFT!
STOP WHISPERIN', YOU HEAR?!
FLING
!!

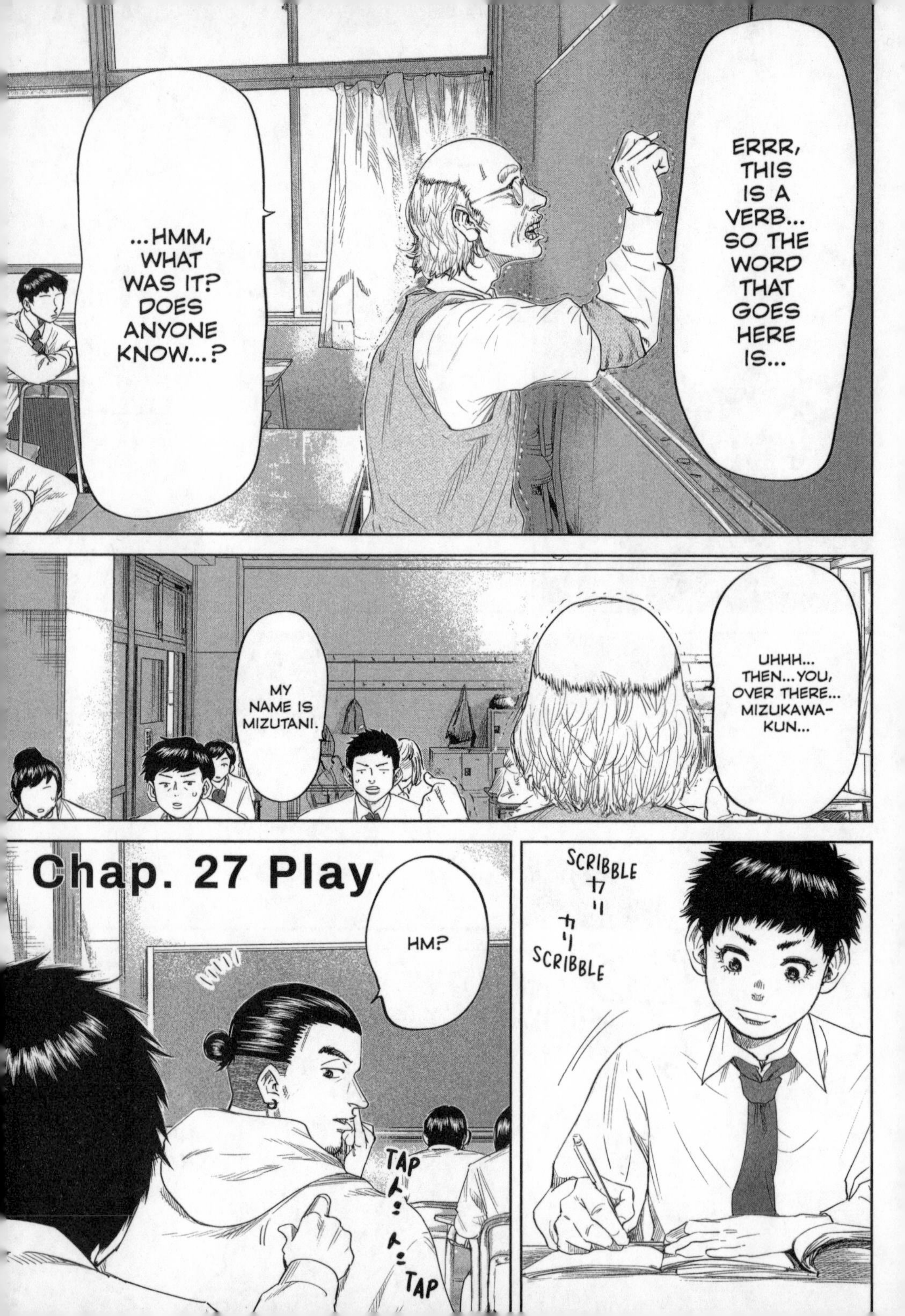
ERRR, THIS IS A VERB... SO THE WORD THAT GOES HERE IS...
...HMM, WHAT WAS IT? DOES ANYONE KNOW...?
UHHH... THEN...YOU, OVER THERE... MIZUKAWA-KUN...
MY NAME IS MIZUTANI.
SCRIBBLE
カリ
カリ
SCRIBBLE
Chap. 27 Play
HM?
TAP
トン
トン
TAP

The Undertaker's Widow

ALSO BY PHILLIP MARGOLIN

After Dark
Gone, But Not Forgotten
The Last Innocent Man
Heartstone
The Burning Man

Phillip Margolin

The Undertaker's Widow

LITTLE, BROWN AND COMPANY

A *Little, Brown* Book

First published in the United States in 1998 by Doubleday

First published in Great Britain in 1998
by Little, Brown and Company

Copyright © 1998 Phillip M. Margolin

The moral right of the author has been asserted.

A CIP catalogue record for this book is
available from the British Library.

ISBN 0 316 64648 2

Printed and bound in Great Britain by
Clays Ltd, St Ives plc

UK companies, institutions and other organisations wishing
to make bulk purchases of this or any other book
published by Little, Brown should contact their local
bookshop or the special sales department at the address below.
Tel 0171 911 8000. Fax 0171 911 8100.

Little, Brown and Company (UK)
Brettenham House
Lancaster Place
London WC2E 7EN

For Aunt Bea

Acknowledgments

Research is one aspect of novel writing that is always fun. I want to thank Bryan Ostrum, Dick Solomon, Mike Prahl, Joseph Ceniceros, Patricia Green, and Scott LaPine, who took the time to explain the technical information that I needed to write *The Undertaker's Widow*.

I also want to thank Vince Kohler, Steve Perry, Larry Matasar, Susan Svetkey, Norman Stamm, and Joseph, Eleonore, Jerry and Judy Margolin for reading early drafts and giving me the benefit of their wisdom.

Many thanks to Pat Mulcahy and Elisa Petrini for their unstinting editorial efforts, the crew at Jean V. Naggar's literary agency (the best agency in the known universe) for their terrific support and everyone at Doubleday and Bantam.

And, finally, just plain thanks to Daniel, Ami and Doreen.

Part One

The Undertaker's Widow

One

LEROY DENNIS began making dire predictions about the driving conditions as soon as the police dispatcher said that the scene of the shooting was a mansion on Crestview Drive. A week of torrential rains had devastated Oregon. Rivers were flooding, towns were being evacuated, power failures were the norm and mud slides were closing roads and highways around the state. The worst slides in Portland were in the hills that loomed above city center. Crestview Drive was at the top of Portland's highest hill.

Lou Anthony took the most direct route to the crime scene. A mountain of oozing earth almost stopped the homicide detectives halfway up Southwest Chandler Road. A series of flares had been spread along the pavement to warn off motorists. The unearthly rain, the devouring darkness on the edges of the headlights and the curling smoke from the flares made Anthony wonder if he had detoured into a corner of Hades.

"What have we got, Leroy?" Anthony asked as he maneuvered around the slide.

"A James Allen called in the 911," the slender black detective answered. "He works for the owner, Lamar Hoyt. Allen says that there are two dead. A man broke in and shot Hoyt. Then the wife shot the perp."

"Hoyt! That's Ellen Crease's husband."

"Isn't Crease the state senator who used to be a cop?"

Anthony nodded. "She was good, too, and a crack shot."

Dennis shook his head. "This guy sure picked the wrong house to burgle."

There were few streetlights on Crestview Drive and the road was pitch-black in spots, but Anthony and Dennis had no trouble finding the crime scene. This part of the West Hills had been carved into large estates and there were only a few homes on the narrow country lane. A high brick wall marked the boundary of the Hoyt estate. Just above the wall, the branches of a massive oak tree flailed helplessly against the elements like the tiring arms of a fading boxer. Anthony stopped in front of a wrought-iron gate. A yellow and black metal sign affixed to the seven-foot, spear-tipped bars warned that the estate was protected by an electronic security system. A black metal box with a slit for a plastic card stood even with the driver's window. Beside it was a speakerphone. Anthony was about to try it when Dennis noticed that the gate was slightly ajar. He dashed into the storm and pushed it open.

When Dennis was back in the car, Anthony drove slowly up a winding drive toward the three-story Tudor mansion that loomed over the landscape. Most of the house was dark, but there were lights on in a downstairs room. The driveway ended at a turnaround. As soon as Anthony brought the car to a stop the ornately carved front door swung open and a frightened man in a robe and pajamas dashed into the rain. He was just under six feet tall and slender. The rain matted his uncombed, graying hair and spotted the lenses of his wire-rimmed glasses.

"They're upstairs in the master bedroom," he said, pointing

toward the second floor. "She won't leave him. I've called for an ambulance."

The man led the detectives into a cavernous entry hall, where an immense Persian carpet covered a good portion of the hardwood floor. Before them was a wide staircase with a polished oak banister.

Anthony brushed the rain from his thinning red hair. He was a large man with a square jaw, a broken nose and pale blue eyes. The detective's shoulders were too wide and his clothes never fit properly. Under his raincoat he wore a brown tweed sports jacket that was frayed at the elbows and wrinkled tan slacks. Anthony had started buttoning the jacket to conceal an emerging beer gut. The blue knit tie his son had bought him for his fortieth birthday was at half-mast.

"Just who are you, sir?" Anthony asked.

"James Allen, Mr. Hoyt's houseman."

"Okay. What happened here, Mr. Allen?"

"I live over the garage. It's across from the master bedroom. There was a shot. At first, I thought it was thunder. Then there were more shots. I ran next door and saw a man on the floor near the bed. There was a lot of blood. And Ms. Crease . . . she was sitting on the bed holding Mr. Hoyt. I . . . I think he's dead, but I can't say for sure. She wouldn't let me near him. She's got a gun."

"Take us upstairs, will you, Mr. Allen?" Anthony said.

The detectives followed the houseman up the winding stairs with barely a glance at the oil paintings and tapestries that hung over the staircase. Dennis had his gun out but felt a little foolish. It sounded as if the danger was over. Allen led them to a room at the end of a dimly lit, carpeted hall. The door to the room was open.

"Please tell Senator Crease that we're with the police," Anthony instructed Allen. The detective knew Crease well enough to call her Ellen, but he had no idea what frame of mind she was in. He wasn't taking any chances if she had a gun.

"Ms. Crease, this is James. James Allen. I have two police officers with me. They want to come into the bedroom."

Allen started in, but Anthony put a restraining hand on his arm.

"I think it will be better if you wait downstairs for the ambulance and the other officers."

Allen hesitated, then said, "Very well," and backed down the corridor.

"I'm Lou Anthony, Senator. You know me. I'm a detective with the Portland Police. My partner and I are coming into the room."

Anthony took a deep breath and stepped through the doorway. The bedroom lights were off, but the light from the hall bathed the large room in a pale yellow glow. A man sprawled on the floor roughly halfway between the door and the west wall. The dead man's legs were bent at the knee as if he had crumpled to the floor. His feet were almost touching a French Provincial armoire that stood against the south wall across from a king-size bed. The doors of the armoire were partly open and Anthony could see a television. The man's head was near the foot of the bed, surrounded by a halo of blood. Near one of his hands lay a .45-caliber handgun.

Anthony pulled his attention away from the dead man and stared at the tableau directly in front of him. Seated on the side of the bed farthest from the door, as if posing for one of Caravaggio's dark oils, was Ellen Crease. She was facing away from Anthony and the back of her plain white nightgown was spattered with blood. Lamar Hoyt's naked body lay sideways across the bed. Crease's back shielded part of his upper body from Anthony, but he could make out two entry wounds and rivulets of blood running through the thick gray hair that covered Hoyt's bearlike torso. Hoyt's large head rested in his wife's lap and Crease was rocking slightly, making little mewing sounds. Anthony noticed that her right hand was resting on her husband's massive chest and that her left hand held a .38 Special.

"Senator," Anthony said gently, "I'm going to walk around the bed."

Crease continued to rock and sob. The detective edged past the armoire, then stepped over the dead man's faded jeans and took in his navy-blue windbreaker. The dead man's hair was wet from the rain and saturated with blood. His clothing was waterlogged.

Anthony looked away and focused on Crease. She was holding the gun, but lightly, and she was staring at her husband. What was left of Hoyt's face was covered with blood that was soaking through the white nightgown. As Anthony arrived at her side, Crease looked up. Her face was tearstained and torn by grief.

Forty-five minutes later, police cars, an ambulance and the van from the Medical Examiner's Office choked the driveway in front of the Hoyt mansion. While forensic experts worked the crime scene, Lou Anthony waited patiently for Ellen Crease in one of the deep, red leather armchairs in the library. The room was un-usually clean and he sensed that neither Hoyt nor Crease entered it much. Anthony had examined some of the hand-tooled, leather-bound volumes stacked tightly in the floor-to-ceiling, cherrywood bookshelves. His brief inspection had uncovered no book with a spine that had been cracked. The detective was holding a volume of Hemingway short stories when Ellen Crease entered the library wearing jeans, an Oxford-blue shirt, and a baggy, dark green, Irish wool sweater.

State Senator Ellen Crease was thirty-five, but she had the com-pact, athletic body of a woman ten years younger. Crease's per-sonality was as rugged as her physique. Her complexion was dark and her sleek black hair framed a face with features that were always on guard. There was nothing coy about Ellen Crease. She was an iron fist that never fit inside a velvet glove.

"Hello, Lou," Crease said, holding out her hand the way she might at a political rally. Anthony hastily replaced the book and shook it.

"I'm sorry about Lamar. How are you holding up?"

Crease shrugged. Anthony marveled at her composure. He had seen Crease's grief, but there was no trace of tears now. The detective assumed Crease was repressing any feelings she had about the death of her husband. She would also be repressing her feelings about killing the intruder, but Anthony knew the guilt would soon surface to haunt Crease as it had haunted him when he had killed a man in the line of duty. A board of inquiry had cleared Anthony. He had even been decorated. Still, it had taken several years before he could put the shooting behind him. For most people, taking a human life, even in self-defense, was very difficult to live with.

"Do you feel up to answering questions?" Anthony asked.

"I want to get this over, Lou, so let's do it."

Crease took a chair opposite Anthony and selected a slender Mouton Davidoff Cadet from a humidor on an oak end table. Anthony watched Crease light up the cigar. Her hand was remarkably steady.

"I have to give you your *Miranda* warnings, because there's been a shooting," Anthony said apologetically.

"Consider them given."

Anthony hesitated, uncertain whether to still read the rights. Then he thought better of it. He wanted to spare Crease as much discomfort as possible and speeding up his interview was one way to accomplish his purpose.

"Why don't you just tell me what happened?"

Crease drew in smoke from her cigar. It seemed to calm her. She closed her eyes for a moment. Anthony thought that she looked totally spent. When she spoke, Crease sounded listless.

"Lamar wanted to go to bed early, but I had to work. You know that I'm right in the middle of a primary campaign against Ben Gage for the Republican nomination to the U.S. Senate?"

Anthony nodded.

"There's a speech I'm supposed to give tomorrow night and a bill on the light rail I needed to study. Lamar wanted to make love before he went to sleep, so we did. Then I got up to change into a nightgown so I could go down to my study. I was going to go to the bathroom when there was a particularly bright flash of lightning. I walked over to the window. As I watched the storm there was another lightning flash. It illuminated the area around the pool. I thought I saw someone standing under one of the trees near the wall, but the light faded before I could focus on the spot. I wrote it off as a figment of my imagination."

"We found a set of footprints under one of the trees. The intruder must have been watching from there."

"Do you know who he is yet?"

"No. He wasn't carrying any ID, but it's only a matter of time before we identify him. Why don't you go on?"

For a second, Crease's self-control deserted her. She closed her eyes. Anthony waited patiently for the senator to continue.

"When I got out of the bathroom, Lamar wanted to cuddle, so I turned off the bathroom light, put on my nightgown and got in bed with him. We talked for a little while. Not long. Then I told Lamar I had to start working. I sat up on my side of the bed . . ."

"That's the side nearest the window and away from the bedroom door and the bathroom?" Anthony asked.

"Right."

"Okay, what happened?"

"The door crashed open and this man came in. I could see he had a gun, because there was a light on in the hall."

Crease's façade cracked again, but she caught herself and was back in control quickly.

"I keep a Smith & Wesson .38 snubnose under my side of the bed. It's always loaded with hollow points. I ducked over the side to get it. I heard three shots and I came up firing. I saw the man go down. When I was certain he was dead, I turned toward Lamar."

Crease's voice grew husky and her eyes grew moist. She shook her head and took an angry pull on her smoke.

"The bastard had killed Lamar, just like that. I didn't even get to say anything to him."

Crease stopped, unable to go on.

"Are you okay?"

"Shit, no, Lou."

Anthony felt awful. He gave her a moment to collect herself.

"Look, I'm gonna cut this short. If there's anything else I need to ask, I can get it later. Just two more things, okay?"

Crease nodded.

"When I got here I found the front gate open. With all the security your husband had, why wasn't it locked?"

"It was locked, earlier. There was a power outage. We never relocked it when the power came back."

"Is that why the house alarm was off?"

"No. I set the alarm when I'm ready for bed. I was going to work for an hour or so, like I said."

"This has been hard for me, Ellen. I want you to know that. You're a real star with everyone at the Police Bureau. No one blames you for this. You did the right thing."

"I know, Lou," Crease said, cold as ice now, "I'm just sorry I didn't kill the fucker sooner, so Lamar would be . . ."

A crash and shouts brought Anthony to his feet. When he opened the library door, he saw two men from the Medical Examiner's Office frozen in place halfway down the stairs to the second floor. Supported between them on a stretcher was a body bag containing the corpse of Lamar Hoyt, which they were maneuvering toward a gurney that sat at the foot of the stairs. Sprawled across the gurney was a tall, muscular man dressed in jeans, a plaid, flannel shirt and a raincoat. Three police officers were trying to pin him to the gurney, which slid back and forth across the hardwood floor during the struggle. One of the officers wrenched the man's arm behind him and a second tried to apply a chokehold. The man writhed and twisted until he was facing Anthony. There was no way of missing the resemblance to Lamar Hoyt.

The officer who had the chokehold applied pressure and the man stopped struggling. One of the officers cuffed his hands behind his back. Then the three officers dragged him off the gurney and wrenched him to his feet. Before Anthony could say anything,

Ellen Crease brushed past him and strode across the entryway. As soon as the intruder saw Crease his face contorted with rage and he lunged at her, screaming, "You did this, you bitch."

Crease paused in front of the man, stared at him with contempt, then slapped him across the face so hard that his head snapped sideways. Anthony grabbed Crease's arm before she could strike again.

"Who is this?" the detective asked Crease.

"This sniveling piece of shit is Lamar Hoyt, Jr."

Anthony stepped between Crease and her stepson, facing the furious man.

"Calm down," Anthony said firmly.

"That bitch killed him. She killed my father," Junior screamed.

The officers immobilized Junior, and Anthony grabbed the flannel shirt at the collar and jerked him upright. Anthony could smell liquor on his breath.

"Do you want to spend an evening in the drunk tank?"

"It wouldn't be the first time," Crease snapped. Junior lunged for her again but could not break Anthony's iron grip.

"Please wait for me in the library, Senator," Anthony commanded angrily. Crease hesitated, then strode away from the melee.

Anthony pointed toward the staircase. "That's your father's body, for Christ's sake. Let these men take care of him."

Junior stared at the body bag as if seeing it for the first time.

"Take him in there," Anthony told the officers, indicating a small sitting room just off the foyer. When the officers did as they were told, Anthony motioned them away. Junior dropped to a small sofa. Anthony sat beside him. Hoyt's son was a little over six feet tall and husky. His large head was topped by curly black hair, his eyes were brown and his nose was thick and stubby, like his father's.

"Do I have to keep these cuffs on?"

"I'm okay," Junior mumbled.

"I have these taken off and you act up, it's a night in jail."

Anthony motioned and the officer with the key unlocked the cuffs. Junior rubbed his wrists. He looked properly chagrined.

"What was that all about? That screaming?"

Junior's features hardened. "Why isn't she in custody?"

"Senator Crease?"

"I know she killed him."

"Mr. Hoyt, your father was murdered by a burglar. He broke into the bedroom and shot your father. Senator Crease shot him. Ellen Crease didn't kill your father, she tried to save him."

"I'll never believe that. I know that bitch is behind this. She wanted him dead and she got her wish."

Two

THE HONORABLE Richard Quinn, judge of the Multnomah County Circuit Court, was almost six foot
three, but he walked slightly stooped as if he were shy about his
height. Despite his size and position, the thirty-nine-year-old
judge was not intimidating. He smiled easily and seemed a bit
distracted at times. His blue eyes were friendly and his thick black
hair tended to fall across his forehead, giving him a boyish look.

Quinn's workday usually ended between five and six, but he
had stayed in his chambers until seven working on the *Gideon*
case. Then his normal twenty-minute commute stretched to fifty
minutes because of an accident on the Sunset Highway that had
been caused by the rain. When Quinn arrived at Hereford Farms,
he was famished and exhausted.

Homes in the Farms started at half a million. Quinn and Laura
could easily afford the place when they moved in five years ago.
Quinn was making a six-figure salary at Price, Winward, Lexington, Rice and Quinn, and Laura, an associate at the firm on the
fast track to a partnership, was pulling down high five figures

with the promise of more to come. Still, Quinn loved the old colonial in Portland Heights where he was living when he proposed to Laura, and he had fought the move to the suburbs.

Quinn could trace the strains in the marriage to the arguments over the house in Portland Heights. Laura felt it was too small for the parties she wanted to throw and too far from the country club she wanted to join. In the blush of new love it had been easy for Quinn to give in, but he had never felt comfortable in this house that seemed more like a display model than a real home. There was a vaulted ceiling in the dining room and living room and no walls to separate the areas. A chandelier hung high above the stone floor in the entryway. Walls of glass let light flood in everywhere during the day. A circular stairway led up to the second floor. Quinn had to admit the house was impressive, but Hereford Farms and all the houses inside its walled perimeter were sterile and Quinn doubted that he would ever feel at home in this suburban encampment.

Quinn opened his front door. He started to call out to Laura, then he remembered that she was competing in the club tennis tournament tonight. He hung up his saturated raincoat in the hall closet and fixed himself dinner in the kitchen. There were assorted salads from yesterday's meal and soup he could reheat. Meals for both of them were catch-as-catch-can and they usually ate out or grabbed prepared dinners from a local supermarket because of the hours Laura kept. None of the lawyers at Price, Winward worked a normal, eight-hour day. Many of them worked so hard that they developed health problems, burned out or drank excessively. Laura was one of the firm's hardest workers, but she was in excellent health and rarely touched liquor. The work exhilarated her.

Quinn was reading in bed when he heard the front door open. He checked the clock. It was a little before ten. Quinn listened to Laura as she rustled around in the kitchen. He heard the refrigerator door swing shut. There were small impacts as a glass or plate touched down on the counter where Laura liked to snack. Later, there were muffled footfalls as Quinn's wife climbed the spiral staircase to the second floor.

Laura entered the bedroom in her warm-ups. She was thirty-three, six years younger than the judge. Her skin was pale, her hair was caramel and her eyes deep blue. Even without makeup and with her hair in disarray, Laura was attractive. She was also one of the smartest women Quinn had ever met. Her rapid rise to partner was a testament to her intelligence and to the single-minded determination she brought to everything she did. But single-minded determination could also cause problems when there were conflicts in a marriage. Laura rarely gave in on something she wanted. She had prevailed on the house and she refused to consider children while her career was on the rise. The only issue of importance on which Quinn had not yielded to Laura's wishes was his judgeship.

"How did you do?" Quinn asked as Laura pulled off her sweats and unzipped her tennis whites.

"I beat Patsy Tang two sets to love," Laura answered matter-of-factly. "That puts me in the quarterfinals."

"Great. Did you have any problem driving?"

"No. They cleared that mud slide on Quail Terrace."

Laura stepped out of her clothes and took off her bra and panties. Quinn had seen his wife naked almost every day for seven years and she still aroused him.

"When did you get home?" Laura asked.

"About eight."

"What kept you so late?"

"Gideon. He had two supreme court justices, four circuit court judges, a mayor and several clergymen testifying on his behalf. We ran over."

Frederick Gideon was a Lane County Circuit Court judge who sat in Eugene, Oregon, a small city one hundred miles south of Portland that was best known for being the home of the University of Oregon. Gideon was a popular, conscientious jurist who had made several bad investments. The losses had left him unable to pay for his daughters' schooling. Gideon was severely depressed when the owner of a construction company, the defendant in a multimillion-dollar lawsuit, approached him with the offer of a bribe. In a moment of weakness, Gideon accepted the money and granted the defense a directed verdict in its favor.

The attorneys for the plaintiffs had been stunned by the ruling, which had no logical basis. A private investigator working for the plaintiffs unearthed evidence of the bribe. Judge Gideon, the owner of the construction firm and two other men were arrested. Gideon struck a bargain with the prosecution. He resigned from the bench, testified against the other defendants and was allowed to plead to a single felony that carried a maximum of five years in prison. Quinn was hearing the case because all of the Lane County judges had disqualified themselves. He had spent the day listening to witness after witness extol Gideon's virtues and plead for leniency. Tomorrow morning the attorneys would sum up and he would be expected to impose a sentence.

"What are you going to do?" Laura asked.

"I'm still undecided."

Laura bundled up her dirty clothes and sat beside Quinn on the bed.

"Did the D.A. bring up some new evidence against him?"

"No. Jane even let it drop that she wouldn't be upset if I gave him probation. Still . . ."

Quinn stopped, frustrated by the conflicting emotions that had been battling inside him ever since he had been assigned the *Gideon* case.

"I don't understand why this case is so hard for you," Laura said.

"He's a judge. Different rules apply when a judge breaks the law."

"A judge is also a human being."

"That's true, but he has to set his standards higher. When you put on the robe you separate yourself from the rest of humanity."

"Nonsense. You don't become some kind of god as soon as

you're sworn in. Gideon was under a lot of pressure. You might have done the same thing if you were in his place."

"No, never," Quinn answered firmly.

"How can you say that if you haven't been faced with Gideon's predicament?"

"Being a judge is more than just performing a job. Americans are brought up to respect the rule of law and they expect judges to administer the law fairly. When a judge takes a bribe, he undermines that faith."

"I think you're getting a little dramatic. We're talking about one judge in Lane County, Oregon. I don't think the country is going to self-destruct because Fred Gideon took some money so he could pay his kids' college tuition."

"So you'd go easy on Gideon?"

"I'd give him probation."

"Why?"

"For Christ's sake, Dick," Laura snapped, "he's a father. Send him to jail and you're destroying a family. And for what? Some theory you learned in high school civics?"

Quinn looked amazed. "How can you say that? You're a lawyer. Don't you respect the system you work in?"

"I work in the real world, not some ivory tower. Fred Gideon is a poor overworked and underpaid bastard who became desperate when he thought that his kids might have to drop out of college."

"Gideon's kids could have gone to the U. of O.," Quinn answered angrily. "They don't have to go to Ivy League schools. You worked your way through. Lots of kids do."

Laura's features tightened and Quinn was sorry the moment the words were out of his mouth. Until Laura was ten, she had lived in an upper-class suburb on the North Shore of Long Island, New York. Then her father had lost his job as an engineer. After a year of unemployment he became depressed. The family dropped the country club and beach club memberships, Laura's private tennis and piano lessons stopped and her mother started saving coupons and shopping for clothes at discount stores. Laura's father was forced to take a temporary job as a salesclerk, but he refused to let his wife work. His depression deepened and Laura's parents started fighting. By the time Laura was thirteen, her father had taken up with another woman, her parents were divorced and she was living with her mother in a tiny apartment in Queens.

Laura coped with her new situation by spending all of her time doing schoolwork and playing tennis. Although she had a partial athletic scholarship, she still had to work her way through college. She viewed her father's failure to contribute to her college education as more evidence of his betrayal.

"I'm sure you'll make the right decision," Laura told Quinn coldly. She went into the bathroom without another word. Quinn knew that he had hurt Laura and he felt bad, but his wife's lack of respect for his work depressed and upset him.

Quinn tried to read, but his book no longer held his interest. A little while later, the bathroom door opened. Laura walked over to her dresser and slipped into her nightgown. She still looked upset. Quinn did not want Laura to go to bed mad. When she was under the covers Quinn remembered that he had some good news.

"I'm going to be speaking at that judicial conference at the Bay Reef Resort on St. Jerome. The organizers confirmed late this afternoon."

Quinn's reading light was still on and he could see little interest on Laura's face.

"I thought maybe you'd come with me. We can go a few days early and make it a vacation. The only day I'm speaking is Thursday. We'd have the rest of the week free."

"I'm busy, Dick," she answered coldly. "There's the Media Corp. litigation and the Hunter Air contract."

"The conference is the last week in February. You have plenty of time to rearrange your work. Come on, Laura. It will be good for us. We haven't had a real vacation in two years."

Quinn waited.

"I'd really like you to come with me," Quinn said when he could stand the silence no more. "I can use the break, too. We'd have a great time on St. Jerome. I checked around and the island is supposed to be beautiful. Sand, sun. We'd lie out by the pool and sip banana daiquiris until we were blotto. What do you say?"

Laura began to thaw. "I can't promise right now," she told Quinn.

"It won't be anything but work if you're not with me."

"I'll talk to Mort Camden."

Quinn brightened and that made Laura smile. Quinn moved against her.

"I'll be miserable if you're not there."

Laura touched Quinn's cheek. "You're like such a little boy sometimes."

Quinn slid his hand under Laura's nightgown. She tensed for a moment, then relaxed and kissed him. Quinn made the kiss last. Laura stroked his neck. They had not made love for a week and a half. Her touch was like a live wire on his nerve endings and he was instantly erect. Quinn stroked down Laura's spine until he was cupping her backside. He enjoyed the tension in her muscles. Quinn felt Laura unsnapping his pajama bottoms. His mouth was dry with excitement. He longed to play with Laura so he could draw out their pleasure. His fingers found her nipples and he began stroking them to make them hard. Before he could finish, Laura was drawing him inside her and he was trapped in the rapid pull and push of her rhythm until, moments later, he exploded and collapsed, spent but not satisfied because of the rapidity of their intercourse.

Quinn felt the bed move as Laura left it for the bathroom. He replayed the quick sexual encounter in his mind and it occurred to him that sex with Laura had been less and less satisfying in the past year. Quinn stared at the ceiling and tried to remember when making love to Laura had stopped being fun. He knew he enjoyed sex with her tremendously before they were married and he was certain that the sex was still good when they lived in the old house in Portland Heights, but somewhere along the way he started suspecting that Laura was only going through the paces and he began to feel alone and lonely when they coupled.

Quinn was still excited by Laura and she never denied him sex. On the other hand, Laura rarely initiated the act the way she had when they were dating and she seemed to work hard at finishing quickly, as if sex was another chore, like dish washing, that she wanted to complete so she could move on to more important things.

Quinn wondered what would happen if he stopped having sex with Laura for a while, but he was afraid that her lack of interest was only in his imagination and that withdrawing from her would hurt her. Quinn could never do that to Laura. He was even more afraid that she would say nothing and that theirs would become a marriage of convenience.

The toilet flushed and Quinn heard the water running in the sink. He got out of bed and walked by Laura. It would have been so nice if she had touched him as they passed just to show that she was thinking of him. Quinn closed the bathroom door. All of a sudden he felt sad and defeated. He longed desperately to recapture the early days of their relationship when her passion matched his, sex left them both exhausted and fulfilled and he would drift off to sleep with a mind unclouded by doubt.

Three

LOU ANTHONY went straight from the Hoyt estate to the Justice Center to dictate his initial report. The last section recounted the incident with Lamar Hoyt, Jr., whose behavior was partially explained by the alcohol he had been drinking and partially by his intense hatred of Ellen Crease.

Lamar Hoyt, Sr., had been sixty-two when he was murdered. He was a hard-nosed businessman who had turned his father's funeral parlors into a business empire. Junior was the sole issue of Hoyt's first marriage. He had barely made it through college, where he had paid far more attention to football than academics, and had floundered around, failing at various jobs, until his father put him in charge of his mortuaries. Junior had not exactly thrived in the family business, but he had managed to keep it turning a profit. He had also earned himself a reputation as a drunk, a womanizer and a brawler, and he resented his father's refusal to let him play a bigger part in Hoyt Industries, his father's conglomerate. Anthony had learned all this from Ellen Crease, after Junior was escorted off the estate grounds and driven home by a Portland Police officer. Crease despised Junior for being a drunk and a weakling.

Anthony lived alone, so there was no one to disturb when he stumbled into the bedroom of his split-level at two-thirty in the morning. Lou's wife of twenty-two years had died of cancer three years before but he had kept the house for visits from their kids. The hostile invader had been discovered during a routine physical; the battle to save Susan's life had been furious but short. She was gone eight months later. Lou's son was a freshman in college at the time and their daughter had just been accepted at Oregon State. He was thankful that Susan had died knowing that they had turned out well. There wasn't much else that he was thankful for except the job, which kept him occupied and distracted him from his grief.

After a few hours of sleep, Anthony was back at his desk reviewing the draft of his report and waiting for the reports from the crime lab and the results of a house-to-house canvas for witnesses that he had instituted shortly after his arrival at the Hoyt estate. Anthony did not expect much from the canvas. A stolen car had been found near the wall that surrounded the estate. He assumed that it was the burglar's getaway car. The fact that it was still parked at the scene meant that the burglar had probably been working solo, but you never knew. There might have been an accomplice who left on foot, though he could not imagine that happening in the previous night's storm when a nice, dry car was available. The estates on Crestview Drive were all set so far back from the street that he doubted the neighbors would have seen an accomplice slogging from the scene, anyway. Still, stranger things had happened and some crazy neighbor might have been out jogging or walking a dog. Anthony was not holding his breath.

"Lou."

Anthony looked up and saw an excited Leroy Dennis bearing down on him with several sheets of paper in his hand.

"How do you feel about buying me lunch?" Dennis asked.

"Why would I buy you lunch, Leroy? The last time I sprung for you, you ate so much I almost had to file for bankruptcy."

One of life's great mysteries was how Dennis could eat and eat and still not put on a pound.

"I'm a growing boy, Lou. My body just needs more than the average man. It has something to do with my sexual prowess."

"Give me a break," snorted Anthony, "or give me a reason why I should assist you in committing suicide by cholesterol overdose."

Dennis not only ate like a machine, but he had an aversion to any kind of food that was even remotely healthy.

"This is the reason," Dennis said, shaking the documents he held at Anthony.

"What is that?"

"Uh-uh. No food, no facts. Hell, I'm so hungry I might just eat this exceptionally fine, and difficult-to-find, evidence."

Anthony laughed. "You have to be the biggest asshole in the bureau, Leroy, but I was going to eat soon, anyway."

Anthony stood up and walked over to the closet to get his raincoat. Dennis followed him.

"Now, what have you come up with?" he asked.

"The name of our perp," Dennis answered, his tone suddenly serious. "I ran the burglar's prints through AFIS," Dennis explained, mentioning the Automated Fingerprint Identification System that used computers to compare unknown prints to the prints stored in the computer's data banks. "We got a hit an hour ago."

"Who do we have?"

"Martin Jablonski. He's got the rap sheet for the job. Armed robbery, assault, burglary. He was paroled from OSP eight months ago where he was serving time for a pretty brutal home invasion that happened six years ago. Pistol-whipped an elderly couple. I talked to his parole officer. Jablonski's supposed to be living with his wife, Conchita Jablonski, and their two kids in an apartment off Martin Luther King near Burnside. He's been unemployed or working as temporary labor since he got out of prison."

"Let's get a D.A. to write up an application for a search warrant, then visit the little woman," Anthony said.

Dennis grinned. "Where do you think I've been this last hour? I'm two steps ahead of you. Sondra Barrett is working on the affidavit as we speak. She'll have it ready to take to a judge after lunch. Now, where shall we go?"

Anthony parked his car in front of an old brick apartment house a few blocks from the Burnside Bridge. The Jablonskis lived on the third floor. It was a walk-up. As they climbed the stairs, Dennis complained about the lack of an elevator and the god-awful smell in the stairwell.

The third floor was poorly lit. The outside light had to fight its way through a grime-covered window on one end of the corridor and was so weak from the effort that it ended up dull yellow. The lightbulbs that hung from the ceiling were either broken or of such low wattage that Anthony wondered why the super bothered to turn them on.

The Jablonskis' apartment did not have a bell, so Anthony bashed a meaty hand against the door and bellowed "Mrs. Jablonski" while he strained to hear if there was any movement inside. After his third try, Anthony heard a nervous "Who is it?" from the other side of the door.

"I'm Detective Anthony with the Portland Police, Mrs. Jablonski."

"I don't wanna talk with you," Conchita Jablonski answered. Her speech was thickened by a heavy Spanish accent. "Go away."

"What?"

"I said, I don't wanna talk to no cops. Leave me alone."

"I'm sorry, Mrs. Jablonski, but you have no choice. I have a search warrant. If you don't open the door, I'll have the super bring the key. It's about your husband."

There was no sound inside the apartment. When the silence stretched to thirty seconds, Anthony turned to Dennis.

"Wait here while I round up the key."

Dennis nodded. Anthony was about to walk to the stairs when he heard locks snap. The door opened a crack and Conchita Jablonski stared at Anthony through a gap in the door. The safety chain was still on. Anthony held up his badge so Mrs. Jablonski could see it through the narrow opening.

"This is Detective Dennis," Anthony told her as he pointed over his shoulder. Dennis flashed her a friendly smile, but Mrs. Jablonski continued to regard the men with suspicion. "We need to talk to you about Martin."

"For why?"

"Can we come in, please? I really don't want to discuss your business out here in the hall where all of your neighbors can hear."

Mrs. Jablonski hesitated. Then she closed the door for a moment and took off the safety chain. A second later, the door swung into the apartment and Dennis followed Anthony inside.

The apartment was small, with two narrow bedrooms, a small living room and a tiny kitchen area that was separated from the living room by a low counter. Both detectives were impressed by how clean Conchita Jablonski kept the apartment. Her two children huddled in the doorway of one of the bedrooms watching the detectives. They looked well cared for. A boy and a girl, both about six or seven, big-eyed and brown-skinned with soft black hair.

Conchita Jablonski was a heavyset, dark-complexioned woman with a pockmarked face. She led the detectives into the living room and seated herself in a frayed and shabby armchair. Dennis and Anthony sat across from her on a sagging couch.

"I have some bad news for you," Anthony said. Conchita Jablonski's facial features stayed frozen, but her shoulders hunched as if she were preparing for a blow. She clasped her hands in her lap. "Martin broke into a home last night." Conchita's features wavered. Her hands tightened on each other. "While he was in the house, he shot and killed someone."

Conchita began to shake. The children saw the change in their mother and they looked frightened.

"Martin was also shot. He's dead."

Conchita bent at the waist as if she had been punched in the stomach. She started to sob. Her shoulders shook. The children's eyes widened. They huddled together. Dennis stood up and walked over to the shaking woman. He knelt beside her chair.

"Mrs. Jablonski," he began in a soft and sympathetic voice. Before he could say another word, Conchita Jablonski spun in her chair and slapped him across the face. Dennis was off balance. He fell onto the floor awkwardly, almost in slow motion, into a sitting position, more stunned than hurt.

"You bastards!" Conchita shrieked. "You killed my Marty!"

Anthony raced to her chair and restrained Mrs. Jablonski.

"He was robbing a house, Mrs. Jablonski. He murdered a woman's husband. He would have killed her, too, if she hadn't shot him."

Conchita heard only parts of what Anthony said as she strained against him. Dennis struggled to his feet and helped subdue the distraught woman. She collapsed, sobbing, her head in her hands.

"Please, Mrs. Jablonski," Dennis implored. "Your kids are scared. They need you."

She fought for control, gulping air. The two children raced over to her and buried themselves in her skirt. She talked quietly to them, submerging her own grief. The detectives waited while she calmed them. Dennis brought her a glass of water, but she would not take it.

"Are you gonna be okay?" Dennis asked.

"What do you care?" the woman shot back angrily. "You cops never cared about me or Marty before. All you wanna do is lock him up."

Anthony saw no reason to argue with Mrs. Jablonski. He held out the search warrant. "This is a court order that gives us the right to search your apartment. Detective Dennis will sit with you while I conduct the search."

Mrs. Jablonski suddenly looked frightened. Anthony wondered why, but he did not ask. If there was something hidden in the tiny apartment, it would be easy to find. He decided to start in the bedroom that the adults used. He could hear Detective Dennis talking soothingly to Mrs. Jablonski as he tossed the covers off the small bed where the Jablonskis slept. He knelt down and looked under it but saw nothing.

There was men's and women's clothing in the cheap wooden chest of drawers but nothing else. When he was through with it, Anthony opened the door of the closet. Dirty men's clothes lay crumpled on the floor, but there was nothing under them. Anthony peered up at a shelf that was just above his head. He pulled over a wooden chair that swayed slightly when he climbed up on it. Toward the back of the shelf was a shoe box. Inside were stacks of currency bound by rubber bands. Many stacks. The top bills were hundreds, fifties and twenties. Anthony stepped down from the chair and carried the shoe box into the living room.

"I've read Marty's file," Anthony told her. "It says that you're on welfare and Marty was having trouble getting steady work. There's a lot of money in here. Where did it come from? Drugs? Was Marty selling drugs?"

"I ain't saying anything to you. You cops are all the same. I knew I shouldina let you in my house."

"Listen, Conchita, I'm not gonna mess around with you," Anthony said harshly. "Your husband killed a very important man. Now, all of a sudden, you're rolling in dough. You tell me where Marty got that money or I'll arrest you as an accessory to murder. What do you think happens to your kids if you're in jail?"

Conchita Jablonski wrapped her arms around her children and looked at Anthony with a combination of fear and loathing. He felt like a first-class heel, but Anthony did not let her know it.

"It's up to you, Conchita. You want your kids in foster care, keep playing games."

The fight went out of Mrs. Jablonski. "I don't know where Marty got the money," she answered in a small voice. "He just got it."

"He never said from who?"

"Just that it was from some guy."

"Did he tell you what this guy looked like?"

"No."

"Marty didn't say what this guy wanted him to do for this money?" Dennis asked.

"When he was doin' something bad he wouldn't tell me what it was because he didn't want me or the kids involved, but I knew it was no good." She shook her head and started to cry. "I tol' him to give back the money, but he said it was for me and the kids. He felt real bad how we lived and how he couldn't get no job because of his record. He wanted to do something for us. And now he's dead."

"I'm going to have to take this with me," Anthony said. "I'll give you a receipt."

"You can't take that money," she sobbed. "I got the kids. How I gonna feed them?"

"That's blood money, Mrs. Jablonski," Dennis told her. "Your husband may have been paid to kill someone for that money. You seem like a good woman. You take real good care of your kids and your home. You don't want that money. You know that money will only bring you grief."

Anthony and Dennis spent twenty more minutes with Conchita Jablonski, but it soon became clear that she did not know anything more about the money, the man who had given it to her dead husband or the reason he had been given it. While Dennis finished searching the apartment, Anthony counted the cash in the shoe box and gave Mrs. Jablonski a receipt for $9,800. The detective figured that the actual amount Jablonski had been given was $10,000. The bills were secured by rubber bands in five-hundred-dollar bundles. Anthony had discovered a solitary rubber band under three hundred dollars in loose bills.

"I don't like this," Dennis said when they were driving back to the Justice Center.

"I don't either. I didn't see anything in Jablonski's file about drugs. From what his wife says, he didn't score the money in a burglary. Some guy gave it to him because he wanted Jablonski to do something. Why would Jablonski run out in the middle of one of the worst storms in Oregon history to burglarize an estate with the security system Hoyt's had if that wasn't the job he was paid to do?"

"Yeah, Lou, that's what I was thinking. Only, robbery might not have been the motive. What if Jablonski was paid to hit Lamar Hoyt?"

"That's one possibility, but there's another."

Leroy Dennis carried the shoe box full of money to the evidence room while Anthony made the call. James Allen answered the phone and Anthony asked to speak to Senator Crease.

"I'm afraid she's resting, Detective. She does not wish to be disturbed."

"I can appreciate that, Mr. Allen, but this is an urgent police matter and I have to talk to her."

Two minutes later, Ellen Crease picked up the phone.

"I'm glad I got you," Anthony said. "I wasn't sure you'd be staying at your house."

"I'm using the guest room tonight," Crease said. She sounded exhausted. "Tomorrow is the funeral. Then I'm going out to eastern Oregon to campaign."

"Oh," Anthony said, surprised that she was going back on the campaign trail so soon after her husband's murder.

Crease could hear the note of censure in Anthony's tone.

"Look, Lou, everything I see in this house reminds me of Lamar. If I don't get out of here and keep busy, I'll go crazy."

"I understand."

"Did you call just to see how I'm doing?"

"That and one other thing. A few hours ago, we identified Martin Jablonski as the man who broke into your house. Does that name mean anything to you?"

"No. Should it?"

"Probably not. He was a real bad guy. Multiple arrests and convictions. Home burglaries accompanied by assaults. We thought we had ourselves a simple solution to what happened at your house. Then we discovered almost ten thousand dollars in cash in a shoe box in Jablonski's closet. His wife says someone gave it to him, but he wouldn't tell her why. We think Jablonski may have been paid to break into your estate."

"But why . . . ?" Crease started, stopping when the obvious answer occurred to her. "Lamar? You think this Jablonski was paid to kill Lamar?"

"We have no concrete evidence that is what happened. I just found the money an hour ago. It could be completely unconnected to the break-in."

"But you don't think so."

"The timing bothers me. The fact that he broke in when the weather was so bad."

"Thank you for letting me know about this, Lou. I appreciate it."

"This wasn't just a courtesy call. If Jablonski was paid to make a hit, Lamar may not have been the intended victim."

There was dead air for a moment. "You're suggesting that I might have . . . that Jablonski was sent to kill me?"

"I don't know. But I'm not taking chances. There's going to be a patrol car parked outside the estate while you're in Portland. You're going to have an around-the-clock guard until we sort this out. I suggest that you arrange your own security when you're out of the city."

"I don't believe this."

"I could be wrong. I just don't want to take any chances."

"Thanks, Lou. I'm not going to forget this."

"Yeah, well, let's hope I'm way off base. In the meantime, I'd appreciate it if you could work up a list of people who might want you or Lamar out of the way bad enough to pay someone to kill you. It could be a business thing, something personal. If there's even a possibility, write it down and let me look into it. I'll be discreet."

"I'll work on it right away." Crease sounded nervous, distant. "And thanks again."

Anthony hung up the phone and leaned back in his chair. He hoped he was wrong about the money. He hoped it was for drugs or a payoff for something Jablonski had already done, but he didn't think so.

Four

IT WAS STILL RAINING when Richard Quinn left for work on the morning after Lamar Hoyt's murder. Not the monster rain of the night before, but a steady, wearying drizzle that was profoundly depressing. The main roads had been opened during the night, but there were places where two lanes narrowed to one because of half-cleared mud slides or still active road crews. Quinn parked in the county garage shortly after seven-thirty and walked through the drizzle to the Multnomah County Courthouse, an eight-story, gray concrete building that takes up an entire block between Fourth and Fifth and Main and Salmon in the heart of downtown Portland. Quinn waved to the guard at the front desk and took the elevator to the fifth floor.

The door to Quinn's chambers was halfway down the marble corridor on the south side of the courthouse. Copies of the *Oregonian* and the *New York Times* were lying in front of it. The judge usually started his day by doing the crossword puzzle in both papers while drinking a cup of coffee, but he was too distracted by the *Gideon* case to try them this morning.

Quinn picked up the papers and opened the door to his chambers. After flipping on the lights in the reception area, Quinn started coffee in the pot that sat on the low, gray metal filing cabinet behind his secretary's desk. Then he switched on the lights in his chambers.

A large rain-streaked window looked out at the ornamental ribbons decorating the north side of Michael Graves's post-modern Portland Building. Behind Quinn's massive oak desk was a bookshelf filled with a complete set of the Oregon Supreme Court and Court of Appeals case reporters and the Oregon Revised Statutes. In front of the desk were two high-backed armchairs. A couch stood against the wall behind the chairs. Above it hung a modern oil painting that made no sense whatsoever. Given the choice, Quinn would have set the oil on fire, but Laura had bought it for him as a swearing-in present. Quinn was not about to destroy the only indication of support for his decision to ascend the bench that his wife had made since the governor's call, three years ago.

Quinn dropped the newspapers on the bookshelf and surveyed his desk. It was as he had left it the preceding evening. Every square inch was covered with paperwork pertaining to Gideon's sentencing. Quinn eyed the reports, letters and lawbooks as he hung up his jacket on the coatrack that held his judicial robes. He sat behind the desk and stared some more. He had read every piece of paper several times. He knew some of the documents by heart. What he did not know was the proper sentence to impose on Frederick Gideon.

On Quinn's wall was a framed quotation from Abraham Lincoln, which read: "I'll do the very best I know how—the very best I can; and I mean to keep doing so until the end. If the end brings me out all right, what is said against me won't amount to anything. If the end brings me out wrong, ten angels swearing I was right would make no difference."

The judge's father, Oregon Supreme Court Justice Patrick Quinn, had framed the quotation and it had hung in the elder

Quinn's chambers in the Supreme Court Building during his years on the bench. Justice Quinn had died when Richard was fifteen. If his father had faults, Richard never learned of them. His wife, who died in the same car accident that killed her husband, adored him. No one Richard had ever met had an unkind word for Patrick Quinn. Certainly not Frank Price, senior partner in Richard's old firm, former partner and best friend of Patrick, and the man who raised Quinn after his parents died. True or not, Patrick Quinn's perfection lived in his son's memory as a model and a challenge, and the framed quote that Quinn had inherited was the creed the judge tried to live by. But doing the right thing was not always easy.

Quinn reread the quotation. He thought about Lincoln's words. At this level, all decisions were hard and the certainty of mathematics was usually unattainable. He could only do his very best, then hope that, in the end, he had chosen correctly. That knowledge did not make the knot in his gut less painful, only a bit easier to bear.

"Your Honor," Stephen Browder said as he launched into the conclusion of his argument in favor of probation, "Frederick Gideon is a local boy who pulled himself out of poverty and worked his way through college and law school. Much of his early legal career was devoted to helping the poor. As his fortunes improved, he expanded his involvement in civic affairs. I am not going to repeat the testimony of the friends, business associates and community leaders who have testified in Judge Gideon's behalf at this sentencing hearing, but the gist of the testimony of these highly respected citizens is that Fred Gideon is a good man, a man worthy of your compassion. He is a man who made one tragic mistake in an otherwise blameless life."

Browder paused and Quinn studied the defendant. He knew that everything Browder said was true. Gideon was basically a good person and he was repentant. Quinn's mental image, formed during his brief contacts with Gideon at judicial conferences, was of a rotund and jovial man who was always quick with a smile and a joke. The months following his arrest had taken the heart out of the jurist. His skin was pasty and there were circles under his eyes. He had lost a lot of weight. He had also lost his pride. The eyes that Quinn remembered for their twinkle were lifeless and had not raised high enough to meet the eyes of Quinn or any witness during the sessions in court.

"No one, including Judge Gideon, is asking you to excuse what he did," Browder continued. "Frederick Gideon sold his judicial opinion for money and he will regret his decision to do so every day that remains to him in this life. But, Your Honor, Judge Gideon has been severely punished for his transgression in ways far more severe than any jail sentence this Court can impose on him. He is a judge no more, having voluntarily relinquished his position soon after his arrest in order to protect the bench from further controversy."

In the front row of the courtroom, Martha Gideon hid her face in her hands. Her shoulders shook with each sob. Gideon's daughters tried to comfort their mother while fighting back their own tears.

"In addition, my client will be disbarred and lose not only his means of earning a living but his right to practice a profession in which he has spent most of his adult life. A profession he loves.

"There is more, and it is the worst punishment. Before he brought this shame on himself, the name Frederick Gideon stood for integrity, honesty. My client was someone who was widely admired. Judge Gideon has disgraced his good name and he may never be able to reclaim his dignity."

Browder was an imposing attorney with wavy gray hair and a dignified bearing. He paused and placed his hand on his client's shoulder. Gideon flinched, as if the touch had burned him.

"The ability to show compassion is essential in a judge," Browder said. "I ask you to show compassion to this man. Please look beyond this single transgression to Fred Gideon's countless good deeds. He is a decent person who made one tragic mistake. Probation is the appropriate sentence for this man."

Browder sat down. Quinn could put off his decision no longer. He looked across his courtroom at the defendant.

"Mr. . . . ," Quinn began. Then he corrected himself. "Judge Gideon. Even though you are no longer on the bench, I will address you as a judge because you have served as a judge for a long time. By all accounts, with the exception of the incident that brings you to this sorry pass, you have been a good judge."

Quinn's voice caught in his throat and he was afraid that he might not be able to go on. There was a pitcher of water and an empty glass at his elbow. Quinn filled the glass slowly to give himself time to recover. He sipped the water until he felt his composure return.

"I'm relatively new to the bench. I suspect that's why I was assigned your case. You sat in another county, our contacts have been few. Most of what I know about you I have learned during this sentencing hearing. As I said, I'm new to the bench, but I suspect that I may never have to make a more difficult decision than the one I will make today."

In front of Quinn were notes he had made in his chambers the night before. He consulted them for a moment.

"Judge Gideon, some of the finest people in this state have spoken on your behalf and your lawyer has been eloquent in his plea for leniency, but there is a presence that speaks more eloquently than any of your lawyers or your witnesses. It is this courtroom with its high ceilings, marble floors and walls of dark wood. This courtroom reminds me of the dignity and majesty of the law and it speaks to the duties of a judge."

Gideon's head hung down and he stared at the top of the counsel table.

"We have a code of judicial conduct in Oregon. It forbids judges to commit criminal acts or engage in fraudulent conduct. You would expect that. But it also says that judges have to act honorably not just because fraudulent and criminal acts are forbidden by law but because acting at all times in an honorable way promotes public confidence in our judges and our courts."

Quinn paused. This was as hard as he thought it would be.

"Judge, I know how much you have suffered and will suffer every day of your life. You are a decent man who knows that you have committed a great wrong. When you sold your judicial decision for money, you did far more than simply rob a litigant of a fair hearing. You committed an act that called into question the integrity of the American system of justice. You committed an act that undermined the confidence of our citizens in the judiciary. In effect, you betrayed the people of this state. I know that you understand what you did and I can see how much you are suffering. I want to give you probation, but I would be committing a great wrong myself if I did not sentence you to prison."

Martha Gideon moaned. The defendant was sobbing quietly. His attorney looked as if it were he who would soon be behind bars.

"If you are the person I believe you are, you will know that I am doing the right thing today by sentencing you to the Oregon State Penitentiary for two years. If you are not able to appreciate your sentence, then I have probably been far too lenient."

[2]

Presiding Circuit Court Judge Stanley Sax found Quinn in his chambers shortly after noon. Quinn's secretary was at lunch and his clerk was also gone. An uneaten ham and cheese sandwich and a sealed bag of potato chips lay on Quinn's desk next to an unopened can of Coke in a small space that had been created by pushing aside some of the paperwork in Judge Gideon's case. Quinn was seated in shirtsleeves in front of his untasted food.

Sax sat in a chair across from Quinn without being asked. He was a small, solemn-looking man with a paunch. Except for a fringe of curly black hair that was going gray and a few odd strands on the top of his head, Sax was bald.

"You going to eat those?" Sax asked, pointing at the bag of potato chips. Quinn shook his head and Sax leaned across the desk and grabbed the bag.

"You look down in the dumps," Sax said as he wrestled the bag open.

"It wasn't easy sentencing a fellow judge to prison."

"That's why they pay us the big bucks."

Sax popped a few chips in his mouth. He chewed for a moment. Then he said, "There's something I want you to think about."

Quinn waited while Sax popped some more potato chips into his mouth.

"You gonna drink all of your Coke?" he asked.

Quinn opened the tab. As he handed the can to Sax, he asked, "Do you want my sandwich, too?"

"Thanks, but I ate already." Sax took a swig from the can. "Katherine Rowe is moving over to domestic relations from the homicide rotation. Craig Kittles was supposed to take her place, but it looks like he'll be getting the U.S. magistrate appointment. That leaves me a judge short."

It took Quinn a moment to catch on. In order to develop expertise, the judges in Multnomah County were assigned to rotations where they heard particular types of cases for set periods of time. Judge Rowe was transferring to the panel that dealt only with divorces, adoptions and other family matters. Some judges heard civil or criminal cases exclusively for a year or two. There were three judges who handled only homicide cases. The rotation was for one or two years, based on the judge's preference. Homicide was the most prestigious and demanding rotation and was usually reserved for judges with years of experience.

"You want me to go into the homicide rotation?" Quinn asked incredulously.

"You catch on fast. That's what I like about you. You're also not afraid to do what's right. You need brass balls to handle a death case. Not everyone can drop the hammer. You showed me a lot today."

"I'm flattered, but I've only been sitting as a judge for three years."

"Don't go modest on me, Dick. I've heard Frank Price say that you were giving out legal opinions on your daddy's lap when you were three, and you don't make partner at Price, Winward without getting a little bit of experience along the way. You're smarter than any other judge in this county with the exception of yours truly. Plus, and this is a big plus for someone who's going to deal in matters of life and death, you wanted to be a judge for all the right reasons. You didn't take this job because your practice wasn't going well or for the prestige or the power. I've been watching you. You're Pat Quinn's son, all right."

Sax paused. He ate another chip. While he chewed he looked Quinn in the eye.

"You want it, it's yours."

"How soon do you need to know?"

"Take a day or two to think about it." Sax stood up. "Don't let me down. And stop feeling guilty. If it's any comfort to you, I would have given Gideon the whole five years. So would your dad."

[3]

Francis Xavier Price, the Price in Price, Winward, Lexington, Rice and Quinn, had been a major force in Oregon legal and political circles for almost fifty years. He and Alan Winward had founded the firm in 1945, as soon as they were discharged from the army after serving with distinction in World War II. Both men jumped into the political arena at the same time they were forging their legal careers. Alan Winward became a state representative, a state senator and governor, while Frank Price maneuvered behind the scenes. By the mid-fifties, Roger Lexington, Bill Rice and Patrick Quinn were name partners. By the sixties, the firm had over one hundred attorneys and its political connections and its list of lucrative clients made Price, Winward the most powerful law firm in Oregon.

The relationship between Frank Price and Patrick Quinn had always been special. When politics began taking more and more of Alan Winward's time, the firm hired the slender, nervous young man as its first associate. Within three years, Price and Winward made Quinn a partner, partly to recognize his magnificent record of success and partly out of fear that he would leave and set up his own practice. Neither partner wanted to face his protégé in court.

When Quinn tired of the grind of a high-level law practice, Frank Price used his political connections to secure an appointment to the Oregon Supreme Court for the man who had become like a son to the Prices, who had no children of their own. When Richard's parents were killed three years into the justice's first term on the court, Frank and Anna Price had not hesitated to take in Richard and raise him.

Frank Price was a gaunt and wiry bantamweight who still went to work every day at the age of eighty. For most of his adult life, Price had lived in a large house in Dunthorpe, but he had moved to a condominium in downtown Portland soon after his wife died. Quinn visited his surrogate father after work whenever he could. He knew how much in love Frank had been with his wife and how lonely he was since Anna's death. Quinn hoped that his visits helped Frank get through his dark period.

By the time Quinn left the courthouse shortly after six, the rain had let up. When Price opened the door for Quinn, the judge could see the lights of cars streaming over the bridges that spanned the Willamette River through the wide and high windows that made up the outer wall of the apartment.

"Come on in," Price said with a smile. "Can I get you something to eat? Some coffee?"

"Just coffee. I'm meeting Laura for Thai food in half an hour."

Price walked into the kitchen. He was a little stiff. Arthritis. His complexion was pale, too, but he still swam fifteen hundred meters every weekday. Price had never surrendered in court and he was not giving in to old age.

"I heard about Gideon," Price called in from the kitchen.

"It was a tough call," Quinn said.

"A good result, though. I've never been able to stomach lawyers and judges who break the law. They always have an excuse."

Quinn shrugged. He still felt lousy about what he had done, even though he felt that his sentence could not be avoided.

Price returned to the living room, carrying two steaming mugs of coffee. Quinn was sitting on the couch in front of a low table. Price set one mug in front of him and took a seat in an antique wooden rocker.

"I bet you feel like shit."

Quinn smiled wearily. Frank had always been able to read his mind.

"It'll pass. Come this time next week, you'll be feeling a whole lot better. Know why? By next week, you'll have figured out that you did the right thing."

"I don't know—" Quinn started, but Price cut him off impatiently.

"Of course, you know. Gideon is a crook and a disgrace to the bench. He knew what he was doing when he took that money and he deserves every day of the sentence you imposed on him.

"Besides, if it's any comfort, you can count on the Parole Board cutting him loose inside of six months."

Quinn looked up.

"You don't think a man with that many friends is going to do hard time, do you?"

Quinn didn't answer.

"You're thinking of Gideon's wife and kids, right? Gideon didn't think about what would happen to them if he got caught. Why should you? He's an adult, Dick. He was a judge. The son of a bitch knew right from wrong and he chose to do wrong. Don't forget that. This was the sentence he knew he could get, but he probably convinced himself that he would skate if he was caught because he was a judge with friends in high places. Maybe the next judge who is tempted to cross the line will think twice because you hammered Gideon. Have you considered that?"

"No."

"Well, stop feeling sorry for yourself and think about it."

"I will."

Quinn took a sip of coffee. Then he said, "Stan Sax came to my chambers today. He wants me to go on the homicide rotation. What do you think?"

"It sounds interesting."

"I'm not that experienced in criminal law."

"You're a quick study, Dick. Stan wouldn't have asked if he didn't think you could handle the job."

"Yeah." Quinn smiled. "I've already made up my mind to do it."

"Good. Say hello to Stan for me, the next time you see him."

"I will. Say, did I tell you that I've been asked to speak at the National Association of Litigators' annual convention on St. Jerome next month?"

"No."

"Laura's coming with me. We'll go a few days early. It will be good for her to get away and just relax."

"St. Jerome should be beautiful this time of year. I'm jealous."

Quinn grinned. "I'll be thinking of you as I lie on the beach. The paper said it was eighty-four and sunny today."

Price laughed. "Go ahead, rub it in, you ingrate. I hope you get hit by a hurricane."

Five

SHORTLY AFTER NOON, one week after the Hoyt homicide, Lou Anthony returned to the Homicide Bureau and found two messages from Gary Yoshida, the lead forensic expert on the case. Anthony found the criminalist bent over a microscope in the crime lab.

"Lou," Yoshida said with a smile. He swiveled the stool on which he was perched. Anthony leaned against the counter. Around them, other forensic experts were testing drugs, examining objects under microscopes and recording observations on reports that were often the difference between a guilty and not guilty verdict.

"You called twice," Anthony said, and Yoshida's smile faded.

"Thanks for getting back to me so quickly."

Anthony shrugged. "What's up?"

"Has the Hoyt crime scene been turned back to Senator Crease?"

"Yeah. We released it two days ago."

"Damn."

"What's the matter?"

"I'd really like to look it over again."

"Why?"

Yoshida walked over to his desk and picked up a stack of photographs that had been taken in Lamar Hoyt's bedroom. When he found the two that he wanted, Yoshida brought them over to Anthony.

"I was going through the evidence again when I was writing my report and I spotted this," Yoshida said, pointing to a section of each photo that showed the armoire that held the television.

"Is that blood spatter?"

"Yeah. And it's got me concerned. I don't like to screw up, but I may have, big-time."

"I don't get it."

Yoshida explained the problem to Anthony. When he was finished, the detective looked upset.

"How certain about this are you?"

"I've got to see the scene in three dimensions to be sure. That's why I want to look at the bedroom again."

"Shit." Anthony took a deep breath. "Okay. Look, two days isn't that long, and I don't imagine Crease is staying in the bedroom. Maybe the scene hasn't been altered yet. We could take a drive out to the estate. Can you go now?"

"You bet."

"Then let's head out."

"Great."

"Not if you find what you're looking for," Anthony answered grimly.

Days of biting cold followed the heavy rains that had disrupted the commerce of the city. Low gray clouds drifted in an iron sky and threatened more rain. The winding country roads that led to the Hoyt estate were clear of debris, but the landscape looked bedraggled and grimy.

Anthony rolled down his window so he could use the

speakerphone at the front gate. A gust of cold wind rushed into the police car. After a brief wait, James Allen buzzed Anthony and Yoshida through the gate. The estate grounds had been hard hit by the weather. The colors had been leeched out of the hedges and the lawn by the pale light, and the foliage bowed down, cowed by the cold and the threat of rain. The house looked deserted and dispirited as if it were in mourning.

Anthony circled the turnaround and parked near the front door. The houseman was waiting for them. He had the door open as soon as Anthony and Yoshida were out of their car. The men hunched their shoulders and walked with speed into the entry hall.

"Good afternoon, Mr. Allen," Anthony said. "Is Senator Crease in?"

"No, sir. She's campaigning in eastern Oregon. I don't expect her back until Monday. Is there something I can do for you?"

"Yeah. It's actually better if we don't have to bother the senator. This is Gary Yoshida from our crime lab. We want to take another look at the bedroom."

"I'm not sure I can let you do that. Ms. Crease left me strict orders that no one but the cleaning people were to be allowed in the bedroom."

"Has the bedroom been cleaned up already?" Anthony asked, trying hard to hide his concern.

"No, sir. A crew is coming tomorrow morning."

"Senator Crease probably wanted to keep reporters out of the house. She wouldn't want to interfere with our investigation."

"I'm sure you're right, but I can't let you in the room without talking to her."

"Why don't you phone?"

"I can try. I have the number of her hotel in Pendleton. Do you want to wait in the living room?"

"Sure."

"Can I get you something to drink? Some coffee or tea?"

Anthony glanced at Yoshida. The forensic expert shook his head.

"No, thanks," Anthony told the houseman.

Anthony knew where the living room was from his official visit to the estate on the evening of the murder, but he let Allen direct him to it. The vast room was dominated by a massive stone fireplace. A Persian carpet, similar to the carpet in the entry hall, lay over the hardwood floor. Yoshida tried to be nonchalant, but as soon as Allen was gone, he said, "This room is almost as big as my house. We're in the wrong business, Lou."

"I don't know, Gary. The owner's dead and we're still ticking."

Anthony and Yoshida settled themselves on one of the large sofas that flanked the fireplace, and waited for the houseman to return. A fire had not been laid in the grate and the room was chilly. Anthony was beginning to regret turning down the offer of coffee when Allen reentered the room. The policemen stood up and met him halfway.

"I'm sorry. Ms. Crease has already left the hotel and I have no idea when I'll be able to talk to her."

"Thanks for trying, but we really do have to see the room."

"I thought the investigation was complete."

"For the most part, but we have a few loose ends to tie up."

"I don't want to impede your investigation, but without Ms. Crease's permission . . . ," Allen said hesitantly.

Anthony tired of diplomacy. He was all for civility, but he was used to getting his way, like most policemen.

"Look," Anthony said sharply, "this is an official police investigation into the death of your employer and Senator Crease's husband. You're telling me the bedroom is going to be cleaned tomorrow. By the time you talk to Senator Crease any evidence in that room will be destroyed. We need to get into the bedroom and we need to do it now."

"All right," Allen said reluctantly. "You can go up. The room is locked. I'll get the key for you."

"Thanks. We won't be long."

Anthony knew the way to the bedroom and he did not want the houseman tagging along, so Anthony told Allen that there was no need for him to accompany them. He sensed that Allen was relieved that he would not have to reenter the bedroom.

As soon as Yoshida opened the door, Anthony started to envy Allen. The room had been sealed and the windows were closed. The stench of death still hung in the stale air.

Anthony took a step into the bedroom, but Yoshida held out his arm to block him. Anthony stepped back into the corridor as Yoshida switched on the lights. The forensic expert stood in the doorway and slowly surveyed the room. He was carrying the Hoyt file in an attaché case. When he had seen what he wanted to see from the doorway, Yoshida walked over to the bed and set down the attaché on Lamar Hoyt's end table. Then he took out the crime scene photographs and the lab reports and shuffled through them. Every so often, he compared a photograph to the section of the room it portrayed. When he was through with the photographs, Yoshida began studying sections of the room. He stood at the door to the bathroom for a while, then inspected the armoire that stood opposite the foot of the bed against the south wall. After he was shot, Martin Jablonski had crumpled to the floor with his feet almost touching the side of the armoire that faced the west wall. A fine spray of blood that discolored the west-facing side of the armoire about six feet above the carpet attracted Yoshida's attention.

Occasionally, Yoshida made notes on a yellow pad. Other times he asked Anthony to hold one end of a roll of string over a particular patch of blood while he unrolled the string and straightened it at some point before squatting down and sighting back along it toward Anthony. Sometimes Yoshida employed a tape measure. Except to clarify Yoshida's instructions, Anthony kept quiet, even though he was anxious to learn Yoshida's conclusions.

Yoshida put everything back in the attaché and snapped the locks closed. Anthony looked at him expectantly. Yoshida looked very grim. He explained his conclusions to Anthony with scientific detachment while walking the detective through every step in his reasoning and showing him the physical evidence that supported his opinion. Anthony's mood grew more morose with each new detail.

When Yoshida was through, Anthony told him to wait in the living room while he went in search of James Allen. The detective found the houseman in the kitchen. A huge, tiled center island with several stove lights dominated the room. Anthony spotted two dishwashers and two ovens. Copperware hung from the ceiling. Allen was seated at a large wooden table polishing silverware. He stood up when Anthony entered.

"Are you through, sir?"

"Just about. I wanted to ask a few questions, though."

"Please."

"How long did you work for Mr. Hoyt?"

"A long time. Mr. Hoyt first employed me in the West Side Home of Heavenly Rest. When he purchased this estate, he asked me if I would work for him here."

"Was Mr. Hoyt a good employer?"

"He was the best, sir," Allen answered. He paused and it was clear to Anthony that the houseman was struggling.

"I want to be completely honest, Detective. I don't want you thinking that I have concealed information. When I was a young man . . . well, sir, I killed a man. There is no other way to put it."

Allen looked down, embarrassed by his confession.

"I was convicted of manslaughter and I served two years in prison. I was twenty when I was paroled. I was a high school dropout with no job skills who bore the stigma of a felony conviction. No one would hire me. I was sleeping in missions, barely able to keep myself together. I seriously considered suicide on more than one occasion. Then Mr. Hoyt hired me. He . . . well, sir, it would be quite accurate to say that he saved my life. Simply giving me a job would have been enough, but he did much more.

When my mother grew ill, Mr. Hoyt paid for her care and he financed my education."

Allen looked directly into Anthony's eyes. "Mr. Hoyt was not merely my employer. He was my savior. His death has been very hard on me."

"I appreciate your candor."

"Thank you, sir."

"If you worked for Mr. Hoyt since you were twenty, I guess you were with him through all three marriages."

"Yes, sir."

"I gather that the first two were pretty stormy toward the end."

"They were."

"How about his marriage to the senator? Did Mr. Hoyt and Senator Crease get along?"

Allen looked uncomfortable. "I shouldn't be discussing Mr. Hoyt's private life."

Anthony nodded. "I appreciate that, but this is a murder investigation and it's suddenly become important that I learn a little more than I already know about the personal life of Mr. Hoyt and Ellen Crease."

"Really, Detective Anthony, I don't feel it's proper for me to comment."

Anthony placed his slablike forearms on the kitchen table and leaned forward slightly.

"Mr. Allen, there is no place for delicacy here. Martin Jablonski splattered your boss's brains all over his expensive bed linens. Life doesn't get more indelicate than that. What I want to know is why he did that. If you respect Mr. Hoyt as much as you seem to, you'd want to help me out here."

Allen looked confused. "I thought Mr. Hoyt was killed during a burglary. What possible relevance could the state of his marriage have to your investigation?"

"Let's just say that we're looking into other possibilities."

"And you suspect Ms. Crease?"

"I'm afraid that I can't go into that."

Allen considered the implications of Anthony's answer. Then he said, "For most of their marriage, Mr. Hoyt and Ms. Crease got along quite well."

"Most?"

"Yes, sir."

"When did they stop getting along?"

"Recently."

"What made you think there were problems?"

"They quarreled. Not all of the time, you understand. But there were arguments."

"About what?"

"I really can't say."

"Do you think Senator Crease was in love with her husband?"

Allen thought about the question for a moment before answering.

"Yes. When he died she took it very badly. I know that she has not made a public display of her grief, but in the privacy of this house . . . in my opinion she is still grief-stricken."

"Was Mr. Hoyt in love with Senator Crease?"

"I believe so."

"Believe?"

"Well, there were the arguments."

"Was she cheating on him?"

"Not that I knew, but she wouldn't have brought men back here, would she?"

"What about Mr. Hoyt? Was he cheating on her?"

The houseman's eyes dropped briefly.

"Not that I knew," Allen replied.

"What does that mean?"

"If you're aware of Mr. Hoyt's marital history, you know that he has always had a problem with fidelity."

"Did you ever hear Senator Crease accuse her husband of cheating on her?"

"No."

"Did the senator ever threaten her husband?"

"I never heard any threats," Allen answered evasively.

"Let me put this another way. Did you ever get concerned for Mr. Hoyt because of anything Ellen Crease did?"

Allen considered the question.

"The arguments . . . some of them were very loud. I couldn't hear what was said, but the tone . . . I'm afraid that's all I can say."

Anthony stood up. "Thank you for talking to me. I know it wasn't easy."

"No, sir, it wasn't."

Anthony was grateful that Yoshida did not say much during the short ride back to the Justice Center. The detective liked Ellen Crease. He respected her. But there was no way of avoiding the implications of the blood spatter patterns in the master bedroom.

The discovery that Jablonski may have been paid to break into the Hoyt mansion had complicated the investigation by turning a simple burglary into a possible murder conspiracy. Now the discovery of the blood spatter evidence forced Anthony to add Crease to the list of people who might have paid Jablonski to murder Lamar Hoyt. If it turned out that Ellen Crease was behind her husband's murder, he would arrest her. He did not want to do that, either, but he would if his duty demanded it.

Six

CEDRIC RIKER looked around the interior of the Lumberjack Tavern with jerky head movements that betrayed his nervousness. The Multnomah County district attorney was not used to meeting people after midnight in workingmen's bars. He liked to conduct business over power breakfasts at upscale hotels or pricey dinners at trendy restaurants.

Riker was a slender man of medium height who wore wire-rimmed glasses and styled blond hair. He usually dressed elegantly, but he was wearing jeans, a flannel shirt and a navy-blue ski jacket for this clandestine meeting with Benjamin Gage's hatchet man, Ryan Clark. Riker's attempt to blend in with the customers in the Lumberjack was doomed to failure. None of the construction workers or bikers who drank there wore polished wing-tip shoes.

As soon as Riker's eyes adjusted to the dark interior, he spotted Clark waiting for him in a booth in the bar's darkest corner. Riker slid onto the bench across from Clark until he was pressed against the wall. There was an empty glass and a pitcher of beer between the two men, but Riker ignored them.

"Ben appreciates your meeting with me."

"He won't be so happy if some reporter sees us here," Riker snapped. "Let's get this over with."

Cedric Riker was an arrogant and insecure man who liked to throw his weight around. He could not afford to antagonize Benjamin Gage, a powerful political ally and a source of campaign funds, but Clark was only an employee. Riker detested Clark with his mysterious ways and intimidating scar, and he was never civil to him. Riker's bullying tactics had no effect on Clark. He despised Riker, but he kept his contempt well hidden because Riker was useful to his boss on occasion.

"We're very worried about the impact of Lamar Hoyt's murder on Ben's campaign," Clark said.

"You should be. Crease is playing this for all she can get. The press is making her sound like a cross between Joan of Arc and Annie Oakley."

"Ben understands that there are new developments in the case. He'd like to know what they are."

"What kind of developments?" Riker asked warily.

"Something to do with Jablonski and some money. Our source wasn't clear."

Riker was angry. Someone was leaking the details of the Hoyt investigation. Still, if Gage wanted to know, Riker was not going to keep the information from him.

"Jablonski's an ex-con with a history of violence. He just got out of the Oregon State Penitentiary eight months ago. He was serving time for a series of home burglaries in wealthy neighborhoods. In a few cases, he pistol-whipped the victims. He hurt one of them pretty badly. Killing Hoyt would be consistent with his modus operandi. But Lou Anthony's found a few things that don't look right."

"Such as?"

Riker took a quick and nervous look around the tavern. When

he was satisfied that no one was listening, he said, "The search of Jablonski's apartment turned up ten thousand dollars in cash in a shoe box. It was hidden in the bedroom closet. Jablonski may have been paid to make a hit."

"On Hoyt?"

"Or Crease. Then again, the money and the Hoyt break-in might be unconnected. Except . . ."

"Yes?" Clark prodded.

Riker leaned across the table and lowered his voice.

"Lou went back to the crime scene with a forensic expert. There's something wrong with the blood."

"The blood?"

Riker explained what Anthony had told him. When he finished, Clark looked thoughtful.

"What are you planning to do?" he asked.

"I know Ben's losing votes, but I've got to move very slowly. Ben should understand that. Everyone knows that he's one of my supporters. If I go after Crease without the goods, it will hurt both of us."

Clark nodded. Riker waited for him to say something else. Instead, Clark stood up.

"It would be better if we left separately. I'll let Ben know how helpful you've been."

Riker watched Clark walk out of the tavern. When the door closed, Riker shuddered involuntarily. He just did not feel right around Gage's A.A. The guy was spooky. A few minutes later, Riker left the Lumberjack. Outside, the rain had let up, but the wind was blowing. Riker hunched his shoulders and walked quickly to his car.

Seven

HOYT INDUSTRIES corporate headquarters was housed in a three-story, no-frills concrete box a few minutes from the Wilsonville exit on I-5. A parking lot surrounded the building and a field surrounded the parking lot. There were minimal attempts at landscaping. Anthony parked in a spot reserved for visitors. A receptionist sat behind a wide desk in the lobby. Anthony named the person whom he wanted to see. A few minutes later, he was sitting across the desk from Stephen Appling, Hoyt's senior vice-president.

Appling was dressed in a gray, pinstriped Armani suit and a silk Hermès tie. His curly salt-and-pepper hair had been styled and he had a tan in spite of the weather. He seemed the antithesis of someone who would work for a good old boy like Lamar Hoyt. Then, again, anyone as country smart as Hoyt would see the value in hiring a shrewd businessman who would feel at home with blue-blood bankers and wealthy investors.

Anthony noticed several golf trophies on a low credenza behind

Appling's desk and a framed Wharton M.B.A. next to several photographs of Appling playing golf with various celebrities.

"Is that Michael Jordan?" Anthony asked.

Appling smiled. "Hoyt Industries hosts a celebrity golf tournament every year to raise money for charity."

"Did you play with Jordan?"

"No. I played with Gerald Ford that time. I did get in a round with Michael at Pebble Beach, though. We were trying to recruit him for an endorsement contract. It didn't work out."

Anthony's brow furrowed. "What product was Jordan supposed to endorse? Not the mortuary business?"

Appling threw his head back and laughed.

"No, Detective, not the mortuaries. Actually, the funeral parlors were only a small part of Lamar's financial interests. Hoyt Industries owns a company that manufactures supplies for funeral homes nationally, a trucking company and Modern Screen Theaters."

"That's Hoyt Industries?"

Appling nodded. "We operate eighty percent of the movie theaters in Oregon, Washington and Idaho and we're expanding into northern California. We were talking to Michael about being a spokesman for the theaters."

"So this is a big operation."

Appling smiled sadly. "Lamar liked to come across as a hick, but he was anything but. His business expertise rivaled that of any of the M.B.A.'s he employed, yours truly included, even though he never graduated from high school. He is sorely missed around here."

"Who's running the company now that Mr. Hoyt is dead?"

"I'm the interim president, but the Board of Directors is going to have to select a permanent president."

"Is Senator Crease going to inherit her husband's stock?"

"You'll have to talk to Charles DePaul, Lamar's lawyer, about that."

"If she does inherit Mr. Hoyt's shares, will that give her a controlling interest in the company?"

"Yes," Appling responded. Anthony noticed that he was not smiling now.

"So she'll have a big say in how the company runs."

"If she wants to, no one can stop her."

"You don't seem happy about that."

"I'm sure that Senator Crease will do what is best for the company."

"But you're not certain?"

"Is this just between us, Detective?"

"Sure, if that's how you want it."

"Ellen Crease is a . . . how shall I say this? Headstrong is a good description. She has her own opinions about how to do things. Once those opinions are formed, it is difficult to change them. Unfortunately, the senator's views on how to run this company are not based on a background in business."

"You don't think she's competent to head up Hoyt Industries?"

"Don't get me wrong. I have the highest respect for the senator's intelligence, and I think she believes that she is capable of running Hoyt Industries. I'm not convinced, though."

"Who would profit if the senator had been murdered along with her husband?"

"You mean with regards to the company?"

Anthony nodded.

"I guess Junior, if he inherited."

"Could he run Hoyt Industries?"

"Off the record again?"

"Yes."

"Junior is a fool and a spendthrift. He would bankrupt this company."

"So you don't think Mr. Hoyt contemplated any part in running the company for his son?"

"I'm certain of it. They weren't even on good terms personally.

In fact, shortly before his death, Lamar and Junior had a yelling match right here."

"About what?"

"I don't know. Lamar wouldn't talk about it. I just caught the tail end. I was walking over to Lamar's office when his door burst open and Junior came storming out. He almost knocked me down. Junior looked furious. When I went into Lamar's office, he was just as angry."

"Mr. Appling, can you think of anyone who would want Mr. Hoyt dead?"

"No, and I have thought about it. We have union problems with the trucking concern, of course, and there are employees that we've had to let go, but that's just grasping at straws. If you're looking for serious suspects, I can't give you any."

"Thank you for your time, Mr. Appling," Anthony said as he stood up. He placed a card on the vice-president's desk. "If you think of anything else, please give me a call."

[2]

Charles DePaul's office was not as grandiose as Anthony had expected the office of a senior partner in a major law firm to be. It was sparsely furnished and functional. DePaul's desk was almost bare. There was an antique reading lamp, some correspondence neatly stacked under a glass paperweight, a picture of DePaul's wife and three daughters and a single file sitting squarely in the center of the desk. DePaul was as unimposing as his office, a short, balding, slightly overweight man who looked nothing like the image suggested by his reputation in the Oregon Bar.

"You said on the phone that you wanted to discuss the terms of Lamar's will. Can you tell me why?"

"This is confidential information, Mr. DePaul. So let me ask you first, who is your client?"

"Lamar Hoyt, Sr."

"Not Ellen Crease?"

"No, sir."

"Mr. DePaul, I need your promise that what is said here will not be repeated."

"You can trust my discretion."

"There is a possibility that the break-in at the Hoyt estate was more than a burglary. The man who broke in may have been paid to kill Mr. Hoyt, his wife or both of them. If Mr. Hoyt was the intended victim then I need to know who gains by his death . . ."

"And the beneficiary of the will is an obvious suspect," DePaul said, completing the detective's thought.

"Exactly."

"Aside from bequests to a few charities, Mr. Allen and some of the employees at Hoyt Industries, the major beneficiaries were Ellen Crease and Lamar's only child, Lamar, Jr. Senator Crease inherited the bulk of the estate. That would be the house, the controlling shares in Hoyt Industries and a number of other bequests."

"And his son?"

"Lamar left Junior the mortuary business, a quarter of a million dollars in cash and a home in the mountains. Junior is an avid skier."

Anthony remembered the incident with Lamar, Jr., at the mansion and asked, "How did Mr. Hoyt react when the will was read?"

DePaul shook his head with disapproval. "Junior caused quite a scene. He threatened to contest everything, then he stormed out after flinging a few choice words at Senator Crease."

"Inheriting a quarter million dollars and a going business would make my day. What was bothering Junior?"

"The amount that he left to his son was a very small bequest when you consider that Lamar's estate is worth twenty million dollars."

"Why didn't he leave Junior more?"

DePaul considered the question for a moment before answering. "Junior is not an idiot, but he's lazy and irresponsible. He's been able to run the mortuaries, but Lamar had to keep a close eye on the business. I believe that Lamar wanted to give Junior an incentive to work hard. He didn't want to leave him penniless, but he was afraid that Junior would not work at all if he had too much money."

"He obviously didn't feel that way about his wife."

DePaul hesitated. "Detective Anthony, I don't know if I should be telling you this, but Lamar and I go way back. If there is something amiss . . . well, I just want to make sure that you're fully informed. Shortly before his death, Lamar discussed the possibility of changing his will."

"In what way?"

"He didn't say specifically, but I had the impression that he was going to change his bequests to his wife and son dramatically."

"How?"

"He never came right out and said what he planned to do, but I believe that their stake in his estate would have been drastically diminished."

"So Senator Crease and Junior benefited when Mr. Hoyt was killed before the will was changed?"

"Yes. Senator Crease in particular."

DePaul paused. He looked troubled, as if a new thought had just occurred to him.

"Of course, if Ellen was involved in Lamar's murder, Junior would inherit her share."

"Why is that?"

"The law forbids a person to profit from a will if they cause the death of the person who made it."

Eight

KAREN FARGO heard the announcement of Lamar Hoyt's murder on the morning news while she was driving to work. She had pulled onto the shoulder of the highway because she could not see the traffic through her tears and she was shaking so badly that she was afraid she would lose control of her car. When she could drive, she took the first exit and returned home. She had called in sick that day and the next.

On her first day back to work, Mr. Wilhelm had called her into his office and fired her. Fargo was in a state of shock and her protests were feeble. Mr. Wilhelm had an explanation for his actions, but she barely heard them. She knew why she had been let go and who was behind the firing, though that person was so insulated by layers of middle management and executive power that she knew she would never be able to prove her suspicions.

After cleaning out her desk, Fargo drove straight home and called her parents in Michigan. She told them about being fired, though not about Lamar. Her parents were serious Baptists and would not have approved of her affair with a married man. They acted like cheerleaders, reminding her of how smart she was and what good work she did. Surely another company would hire her.

When Fargo ended her call to her parents, she was upbeat. She did not have very much money saved, but she had enough to get by until another job came along. There was always a market for a good secretary. Maybe, she thought, it was best that she not continue to work at Hoyt Industries, where every day would be a reminder of the life she had lost. Maybe being fired was a blessing in disguise.

The next day Fargo started her job search with high hopes. She had graduated at the top of her secretarial school class, she was attractive and friendly and she always received excellent efficiency ratings. Strangely, the jobs did not come. The interviewers were always enthusiastic and she left the interviews with high expectations, but her phone did not ring.

At first, she convinced herself that the companies had lost her number and she called them to see if a decision had been made. Most of the time, the person who had interviewed her would not take her call. A secretary would tell Fargo that the job had been given to someone else. On the few occasions that someone important did talk to her, they seemed embarrassed. It was only during the call that she had made two hours before to Durham Food Products that she found out why she was being turned down for job after job. Mr. Pebbles, the man with whom she'd had such a positive interview, sounded uncomfortable when they spoke. Toward the end of their short conversation, he told her sympathetically that he would have hired her if her reference from Hoyt Industries hadn't been so negative. When Fargo asked the man what he meant, Pebbles told her that he had said too much. He wished her luck and hung up.

Fargo was too numb to think straight. Then she remembered that all of the jobs for which she had applied required references. When she figured out that someone at Hoyt Industries was blackballing her, she became frightened, then she became angry. Fargo had driven to her old company to confront Mr. Wilhelm, but the security guard would not let her into the building. On the ride home, Fargo grew scared. What if she could not find a job? How would she live? She had broken down halfway home and she was still crying when she opened the front door of her small, rented Cape Cod.

Fargo had not bothered to raise her shades that morning and her front room was thick with shadows. She turned on a floor lamp. It took her a moment to realize that a man was sitting in the armchair near the window. Fargo took a step backward. The light from the lamp did not reach all the way to the armchair and she could just make out the man's profile.

"There's no need to be afraid, Miss Fargo," the man said quietly. "I'm a friend, and I think you need one."

Fargo reached behind her for the doorknob, but she made no move to open the front door.

"Who . . . who are you?" she asked anxiously.

"Someone who wants to help you. Are you upset because you've been turned down for another job?"

Fargo let go of the doorknob. "How did you know that?"

"That's not important. What is important is that you know the identity of the person who has been stopping you from getting a job. She's the same person who made certain that you were fired from Hoyt Industries.

"Miss Fargo, there are people who are concerned about you. People who don't think that it's fair that Ellen Crease used her power to have you fired and is using her power to keep you from finding work. These people want to secure a job for you. A good job that will pay you the salary you deserve."

"Why would these people do that for me?"

"They're the same people who believe that Ellen Crease is responsible for the murder of Lamar Hoyt. They want to see justice done."

The man stopped talking to let Fargo absorb what he had said.

"What . . . what do you want from me?" she asked.

"There is almost enough evidence for the district attorney to indict Ellen Crease. The one thing that is missing is a powerful motive. Crease was well taken care of by Lamar Hoyt, she had her own career and everyone says that she loved Hoyt and he loved her."

"That's not true," Fargo interjected.

"What isn't true?"

"Lamar didn't love her. He loved me."

"We know that, Miss Fargo, but the authorities don't. If you give that information to the police, they will know Ellen Crease's motive for murder."

"I couldn't go to the police," Fargo said.

"Of course you could. We would protect you and we would reward you. The day after you go to the police someone will call you with a job offer. A very good job offer. Someone else will deposit a substantial sum of money into your savings account. I believe it's down to three hundred and eighteen dollars, as of this morning."

"How . . . how did you know that?"

"We're concerned about you, Karen," the man said with compassion. "We were afraid that you were suffering financially, so we checked your account to see if you needed our help. It looks like we can help each other."

The man sounded so sure of himself, so comforting. Why, then, Fargo asked herself, did she feel so frightened?

"Why don't you tell me about your relationship with Lamar, so we can decide what you can say that will help the police?"

"I don't know if I should."

"Karen, Ellen Crease has already made Lamar Hoyt her victim. Do you want to be her victim, too? Crease did not give Lamar a chance to fight back. We are giving you that chance."

Fargo considered what the man said while he waited patiently. Then she started talking. When she was through, the man asked her questions and she answered them truthfully. When he was satisfied with what he heard, he told her what to do.

"How do I get in touch with you?" she asked as he crossed the room.

"Don't worry about that."

He stepped into the pool of light near the front door. Then he was gone and Fargo realized that the only thing she knew about her visitor was that once upon a time something had happened to him that was violent enough to leave a jagged scar on his right cheek.

Nine

HOYT & SON'S West Side Home of Heavenly Rest
was a white, three-story building that resembled a
plantation home in the antebellum South. Lou Anthony knew that
there were four other Homes of Heavenly Rest in Oregon, as well
as two Heavenly Rests in Seattle, Washington, one in Butte, Mon-
tana, and one in Boise, Idaho. Junior's office was here on the West
Side.

A crystal chandelier hung over the foyer, but the lighting was
subdued. As Anthony entered through the wide front doors, a tall,
solemn-looking man in a mourning coat approached him.

"Are you with the Webster party?"

"No, I'm not." Anthony flashed his badge. "I'm looking for
Mr. Hoyt."

The man examined the badge for a moment while Anthony
listened to the soft strains of organ music that floated toward him
from somewhere in the building.

"Take the hall on your right. There's a set of stairs at the end.
Mr. Hoyt's office is at the top of the stairs."

The interior of the funeral home was dark woods and dark red draperies, all under subdued lighting. There were two chapels on Anthony's left as he walked down the hall. One was empty, but a small group of mourners gathered in the other talked in hushed tones. A casket dominated the room. A heavyset woman wept in the front row. Two young men in ill-fitting black suits tried to comfort her.

Anthony found the office easily. An attractive blonde wearing too much makeup was talking on the phone when he entered. She glanced at Anthony, told the caller that she would get back to her and hung up.

"I'm here to see Mr. Hoyt," Anthony said when he had the woman's attention.

"What does this concern?"

Anthony showed the woman his shield. The secretary disappeared behind the only other door in the office. A moment later, she emerged and held it open.

The office had the same subdued decor as the rest of the funeral home. Junior was sitting behind his desk. He did not look pleased to see Anthony.

"What's this about?" Junior asked brusquely. "I'm pretty busy."

Anthony sat down across from the mortician without being asked.

"I have a few questions I want to ask you. I decided to wait until after the funeral. How did it go?"

Junior's aggression disappeared.

"We gave Dad the best we had. Our Royal Deluxe." Junior looked thoughtful. "It was so odd seeing him laid out. I see people every day like that, but when it's your own father . . ."

Junior caught himself, embarrassed by his show of emotion. "You said you had some questions?"

"Just a few. I'll try to make this quick. I understand that you and your father had an argument at Hoyt Industries headquarters a few days before he was killed. What was that about?"

Junior's face registered fear and surprise.

"Who told you that?"

"I'm afraid I can't reveal my sources."

"I bet it was that turd Appling. Well, the argument was a big nothing. Just a disagreement about some changes I made at Heavenly Rest."

"There wasn't any more to it?"

"No," Junior answered nervously. "Why are you interested in an argument I had with my father, anyway? I thought the police believed that this was just a burglary by that guy Jaworski."

"Jablonski," Anthony corrected Junior. "Martin Jablonski. You didn't happen to know him, did you?"

"Why would I know him?"

Suddenly, Anthony's reason for asking the question dawned on Junior.

"What the fuck is going on here? You're not suggesting . . ."

"I'm not suggesting anything."

"Well, I think you are. If you really want to find out who's behind my father's murder, investigate Ellen Crease."

"You made the same accusation against Senator Crease when you were at the mansion on the night your father was murdered. Why do you think your stepmother . . ."

"That cunt is not my mother . . ."

"Senator Crease, then. Why do you think that she had something to do with your father's murder?"

Junior snorted with derision. "You're some detective. Don't tell me you don't know yet."

"Know about what?"

"Dad was going to dump her. She was on the way out. Then good-bye, sugar daddy."

"Why do you think that your father was planning to leave Senator Crease?"

"You don't know much about my father, if you're asking that question. His wives all had a shelf life of about seven years and he began cheating on them way before he dumped them. Ask my mom."

"So you're going on your father's history with women? You don't have any concrete evidence that your father was going to divorce Senator Crease?"

"No. I just know my father," he answered bitterly. "He was a user."

"You don't seem to have liked him much."

Junior seemed suddenly subdued. "My father walked out on my mother and he never hid how he felt about me. No matter what I did, it was never good enough. He told me to my face what a disappointing incompetent I was, more than once."

"He let you run this business."

"I'll give him that. But he made it pretty clear to me that I could never expect anything more from him."

"Like letting you run Hoyt Industries. That was something you must have wanted."

"Are you kidding? That company is worth millions," Junior answered with a combination of anger and wistfulness. "The bitch will get those shares now. My only regret is that my father won't get a chance to see her run his life's work into the ground."

[2]

Lou Anthony reached two conclusions as soon as he saw the young woman who was waiting in the reception area of the Portland Police Bureau Detective Division. The first was a no-brainer. The woman was gorgeous, with smoky emerald eyes and hair the shade of auburn that takes your breath away when the leaves change color in the fall.

Anthony's second conclusion was that the woman would rather be someplace else. Her slender hands fidgeted in her lap and she sat too straight, as if preparing for flight. Anthony walked over to her and she stood up quickly. The detective figured her for five four, but she seemed taller because she was wearing heels.

"My name is Lou Anthony. I'm the detective in charge of the Lamar Hoyt case. I understand you have something you wanted to tell me."

The young woman looked lost. She glanced around the reception area. Anthony guessed that she had something to say but was not sure that this was the place she should be saying it.

"Why don't you come back with me?" Anthony said, holding open the door that led to the wide-open spaces where the detectives worked on the thirteenth floor of the Justice Center. The woman walked through the door and Anthony directed her to an empty interrogation room, where they would have some privacy.

"Can I get you something? Coffee?" Anthony asked. The room was small and barely held a gray metal table and four chairs.

"Coffee, please. Black," the woman answered.

"I'll be right back," the detective told her with a reassuring smile. When he returned with two steaming cups of coffee, she was still wearing her raincoat. Her hands were in her lap and she was twisting in her seat so she could look around the tan-painted, concrete-block room.

"Are you cold?" Anthony asked. The woman looked puzzled. "I noticed you're still wearing your raincoat."

Fargo looked down, as if she had not realized that she still had on the coat. She took it off and Anthony draped it over a chair. Drops fell from the coat onto the metal legs and ran down them toward the floor. When she sat, she picked up her coffee, wrapping both hands around the Styrofoam cup for warmth.

"I'm sorry," Anthony apologized, "but I didn't get your full name."

The woman nervously ran her tongue across her lips before answering.

"I'm Karen. Karen Fargo."

"Is that Miss or Mrs.?"

"I'm not married."

"The receptionist said you wanted to speak to someone about

Lamar Hoyt's murder. Like I said, it's my case, so you can tell me anything you have to say."

Fargo hesitated and Anthony waited. Then she said, "I read in the paper that a man broke in and shot Lamar. Is that what happened? I mean, are you certain that this man . . . that he killed Lamar?"

Anthony caught the use of Hoyt's first name but did not change his expression.

"We found the bullet that killed Mr. Hoyt and we gave it to the people at the police lab. They checked the gun we found next to the intruder. The bullet came from that gun, and the intruder's fingerprints were on the gun."

"Oh." Fargo looked down as if she were losing the courage that had brought her to police headquarters.

"Did you think that someone else may have shot Mr. Hoyt?" Anthony asked gently.

"I . . . Well, I thought . . ."

"Yes?"

When she answered, Anthony could see that Karen Fargo was very frightened. "It wasn't her? His wife? You're certain?"

"Why would you think that Ms. Crease shot her husband?"

Fargo looked down again. "I . . . I shouldn't have come here," she said, and started to stand.

"Miss Fargo, what was your relationship to Mr. Hoyt?"

Karen Fargo burst into tears and collapsed on her chair.

"I'm so sorry," she managed.

"Do you want some water?"

"No. I'll be okay."

Fargo took two deep breaths. "We loved each other. We . . ." Fargo looked down. "We were going to be married."

"Mr. Hoyt was already married," Anthony said carefully.

Fargo dabbed at her tears again. "He was going to divorce her. He told me so. Lamar was going to wait until after the campaign. Then he was going to divorce her and marry me."

"How long did you have this relationship with Mr. Hoyt?"

"About a year. A little less. It started six months after I went to work for his company. I'm . . . I was a secretary at Hoyt Industries."

"And you met Mr. Hoyt there?" Anthony prodded.

"At the company picnic. We just started talking. It didn't last for long. He asked me my name and how long I'd been there and if I was enjoying my job. I thought he was asking to be nice. I was sure he wouldn't even remember me. But he did. About a week later, he saw me in the cafeteria and he remembered my name. Then a week after that, he called me at my apartment and asked if he could come over. I didn't know what to say. I mean, he was the boss of the whole company. I couldn't very well say no, could I?"

She looked toward Anthony for approval and he gave it to her. She bit her lip and looked down at the tabletop.

"I was afraid. I . . . I thought . . . Well, I knew he was married and I'm not naive. But Lamar was a perfect gentleman. He was always a perfect gentleman.

"After that first time, he just started visiting. Sometimes he'd take me out to eat. Usually when his wife was busy in Salem at the legislature. He didn't come on to me. It was just to talk. He said he liked being with me and how he felt he could just be at ease when he was with me. There's so much pressure for a businessman like Lamar, you know, and he felt that his wife was so busy with her own work that she didn't have time for him."

"So you started sleeping with him?"

Fargo looked straight at Anthony.

"He was lonely. It was sad. He had all that money and his big house, but he was lonely."

"When did Mr. Hoyt start talking about marriage?"

"Right around when his wife said she was going to run for the U.S. Senate. That really upset Lamar, because it meant that she would be living in Washington, D.C., and he would never get to see her. He said that it would be like they weren't even married."

"Miss Fargo, Lamar Hoyt was murdered on January seventh. Why did you wait until now to come see me?"

Karen Fargo's eyes widened with fright. Then she looked away.

"I don't know," she answered. "It's just been eating at me. Lamar dying like that. It didn't seem right."

"Do you have anything concrete that would prove Ms. Crease was behind her husband's death?"

"No. Just that Lamar said he thought she might know about us."

"He did? When did he say that?"

"A few weeks before he was killed. He said she was acting funny around him and that we had to be careful. He wanted to know if anything unusual had happened. Strange phone calls or anyone watching or following me."

"And did any of that happen?"

"Not that I knew of."

Anthony tried to think of something else to ask Fargo, but he couldn't. He was not surprised to discover that Hoyt had a mistress. It fit his pattern. Ellen Crease was a little older than the first two wives when she'd become wife number three, but not much older. She was now around the age of the other exes when Hoyt cut his ties with them.

"Thank you for coming in to talk to me, Miss Fargo. I can see how hard it was for you."

Anthony thought Fargo looked relieved that he was not going to ask her any more questions. Anthony shook her hand and showed her out. Back at his desk, he swiveled his chair and looked out the wide windows. Rain again. Surprise, surprise. Some days he would give everything he owned for one sunny day.

Anthony felt sorry for Karen Fargo. He imagined that Hoyt's attentions must have seemed like something out of a fairy tale to a secretary who is suddenly transformed into the mistress of a millionaire. Was Hoyt really intending to dump Crease for Fargo or was he simply dangling the possibility of marriage in front of Fargo to keep her in his bed?

As Anthony went to get a fresh cup of coffee, he thought about a question Fargo had asked. Was he certain that Jablonski had killed Hoyt? Definitely, as far as the physical act went, but what about the blood spatter evidence and the money? And then there was the fact that all the security systems at the estate were off when Jablonski broke in. Crease had a reasonable explanation for that, but did he believe it? Crease had definitely benefited from Hoyt's death. She had skyrocketed in the polls, and there was the insurance and the will. These were all motives for murder. Now there was another motive for Crease to hire Jablonski.

Anthony let the thought hang in the air. He turned it around and examined it. He did not want to believe that Ellen Crease was a murderer. Anthony liked Crease. He had no doubt that Hoyt's death had really hurt her. She had shown little emotion other than anger in her press conferences, but he had seen her right after the murder and he would swear that her grief was real. That actually weighed against her. If Ellen really loved Lamar, the knowledge that he had a lover and was ready to leave her would be a powerful motive to kill. Anthony decided that it was time to have another meeting with the district attorney.

Ten

R YAN CLARK entered the pool house just as United States Senator Benjamin Gage began the final lap of his morning workout. Clark was six feet tall, darkly handsome and very fit. When he moved, he exuded a quiet confidence that warned off muggers and attracted the attention of beautiful women, who found the jagged scar on Clark's right cheek fascinating. They always asked about it and Clark had invented a story that seemed to satisfy their curiosity.

The only time Benjamin Gage had ever mentioned the scar was at the end of Clark's interview for a job at StarData, Gage's high-tech company. The conversation had taken place eight years earlier when Clark was twenty-nine and Gage was thirty-eight. Clark was wearing a beard at the time and the scar was barely visible. The formal part of the interview, which had been conducted in Gage's office at company headquarters, was over and the two men had adjourned to a smart restaurant in Northwest Portland for dinner. Their booth was in the back. Gage was a frequent customer. When he dined at the restaurant it was understood that the booth next to his would be kept vacant. Gage paid a premium for this that he could easily afford.

"Where did you get the scar?" Gage had asked. His own face was unmarked and ruggedly handsome.

Clark had hesitated before answering. That was when Gage knew that the scar had something to do with the five years on Clark's résumé that read "Naval Intelligence—Administrative Responsibilities." When Gage had asked Clark to describe his administrative duties during the interview at the office, Clark had been creatively evasive and Gage had let it pass. He knew he would pursue the question at dinner.

Gage had leaned back against the wine-red leather. There was no one else around. Their corner of the restaurant was suitably dark. When he spoke, Gage looked directly into Clark's eyes. A few years later, during Gage's first successful run for Congress, this ability to look people in the eye had convinced voters of Gage's sincerity. Clark was not affected at all and he was able to keep eye contact long enough to make Gage blink first, something few people could accomplish.

"Look, Ryan, you're not interviewing to be a security guard. If I wanted a rent-a-cop, I'd call Pinkerton. I wouldn't conduct my job search through the chairman of the Senate Committee on Covert Operations. I need a man who can be counted on to do odds and ends that other people can't, or won't, do," Gage had said, proving that he could be as creatively evasive as Clark. "You want me to pay you six figures to do these odd jobs. I'm not going to pay that kind of money or trust someone with this type of work without knowing everything there is to know about the man I'm hiring. So tell me about the scar."

There had been no more hesitation. Gage liked that. It meant Clark could make important decisions quickly. He also liked the fact that Clark did not touch the scar or do anything else to indicate that he even thought about it.

"This is a knife wound I received in a Mideast country. The man who stabbed me was lying next to two other bodies. I thought he was dead. When I leaned down to secure his weapon, he stabbed me."

"Who were these men?"

"It was two men and a woman," Clark had answered without emotion. "They were terrorists who directed the suicide bombing of the American Embassy in Paris."

"I remember the bombing, but I don't remember reading that the people behind it were caught."

"You wouldn't have."

"What happened to the man who stabbed you?"

"Another member of my team shot him."

"I see. Tell me, Ryan, did this incident occur when you were a navy SEAL?"

"No."

"Was this one of your 'administrative responsibilities' in Naval Intelligence?"

"I'm afraid I can't answer that question, Mr. Gage."

"Not even if refusing to answer costs you the job?"

Clark had smiled. He knew he had the job. He knew Gage was trying to play with him. Gage had held his ground for a moment. Then he had returned the smile. Clark had been doing this and that for Gage ever since.

Moments after Clark was admitted to Gage's house, a servant placed a pitcher of fresh-squeezed orange juice, a pot of steaming coffee and a plate with two croissants on a table that stood on the tiled deck of Gage's twenty-five-meter lap pool. The lap pool was four lanes wide and heated. Entering the humid air of the pool house caused beads of sweat to form on the brow and upper lip of Senator Gage's administrative assistant. Clark sat down at the table and watched Gage make his final turn. Then he lost interest and glanced out through the wall of glass on the east side of the pool house. On most days, Clark would have seen the apple orchards, lush farmlands and green foothills that stood between Gage's twelve-thousand-square-foot home of glass and cedar and the snow-covered slopes of Mount Hood. But today the landscape was gray with mist and there was little to see.

Gage boosted himself out of the pool. He was forty-six years old, but he was only slightly slower in the pool than he had been in his days as a competitive swimmer. Some of the hair that covered Gage's lanky body was starting to silver.

Gage toweled himself dry, then crossed the pool deck and sat opposite Clark.

"Have you seen the latest polls?" he asked Clark angrily.

"Crease has fifty-one percent, you've got forty-four and the rest are undecided," Clark answered calmly.

"That's right. Before the murder, we were dead even. Crease has gotten everyone's sympathy for losing a husband, and the press has made her out to be a female version of Rambo. I am sinking fast."

Gage took a bite of his croissant. Clark waited patiently.

"Did you listen to Crease's press conference in Bend?"

"I missed it."

"A reporter asked Crease how her husband's murder affected her. She stared him down for a second or so. Then she told him that she would be dead, too, if the gun control lobby had its way and that Hoyt would be alive if the tough crime measures she's advocating were law. After that, she looked into the camera for a few seconds more. Then she told all those voters that she couldn't bring her husband back, but she could dedicate the rest of her life to trying to prevent similar catastrophes from happening to them and to seeing that those who break the law regret it."

Gage smiled without humor and shook his head in wonder. "She is one heartless bitch and she has played Hoyt's murder like a violin virtuoso."

Clark allowed himself a rare smile.

"She may be playing a different tune by next week," he said.

"Oh?"

"Cedric Riker called me. He wanted to make certain that you

knew before the press. He's going to the grand jury this morning. It looks like Fargo tipped the scales."

Gage grinned broadly.

"That's that, then," the senator said with satisfaction. "Once the indictment comes down, she's dead."

"That's how I see it."

"Good work, Ryan. Very good work."

[2]

Henry Orchard knocked loudly on Ellen Crease's hotel room door because he knew she would be sound asleep after an exhausting day of campaigning. Crease's campaign manager was a slovenly, overweight dynamo who was uninterested in anything but politics. Until minutes ago, Orchard had been a happy man. His candidate had exploded in the polls, breaking away from a dead heat to take a substantial lead over Benjamin Gage.

"Who is it?" Crease snapped. She sounded wide-awake. Orchard was not surprised. Crease never seemed to tire and she needed little sleep. When she did sleep, she had a knack for waking up fully alert.

"It's Henry. Open up. Something's happened."

Orchard heard Crease cross the room. Her door opened and he walked in. Orchard was unshaven and there were dark shadows along his fleshy jowls. The shirt he had thrown on was dotted with stains and his socks did not match. Crease was wearing a quilted bathrobe over a floor-length flannel nightgown. Only the bedside light was on in the room, but Orchard did not turn on any other lights. He spotted an armchair near the window and dropped into it.

"I just talked to a source in the Multnomah County District Attorney's Office. Tomorrow Cedric Riker is going to ask a grand jury to indict you for murder."

"What?"

"He's looking for two counts. Lamar and the guy who shot him."

Crease looked stunned. "Is this the first you've heard about this?"

"Absolutely. I knew the investigation was still open, but I haven't heard a thing suggesting that you were under suspicion."

"What have they got? What's the evidence?"

"I don't know and neither does my informant. The first thing I asked him was what Riker's got, but only Riker and the investigating officer . . ."

"Lou Anthony?"

"Right, Anthony. They're the only ones who know for now. What do you think they have?"

"There's nothing out there, Henry," Crease answered bitterly. "And this really hurts. I loved that old bastard."

Crease found a cigar in her purse and lit it. Then she paced across the room until she arrived at a writing desk. She pulled out the desk chair and sat on it, facing Orchard.

"This is unbelievable. An indictment will kill us." Crease thought for a moment.

"It's Gage," she said angrily. "It has to be. He contributed heavily to Riker's campaign and they go way back. Gage and Riker cooked up this whole thing to help Gage climb back in the polls."

"I'd like to think that," Orchard replied cautiously, "but this isn't any old dirty trick. We're talking an indictment for murder. Riker would have to have some evidence to show the grand jury. And even if Riker's a prick, Lou Anthony isn't. He's an old friend of yours, isn't he?"

"I know Lou," Crease answered thoughtfully. She blew a plume of smoke toward Orchard. "You're right. Lou wouldn't phony up evidence."

Crease was quiet for a moment. Orchard watched her.

"What do you suggest I do, Henry?" she asked after a while.

"The same person who warned me about the grand jury is

going to call me the minute he hears that Riker has an indictment. Riker probably has your campaign schedule. I know the way he thinks. He's going to get the local sheriff to arrest you, preferably at some campaign function for maximum embarrassment. He'll work out the timing so you have to spend a night in the local jail, then he'll have you flown back to Portland in handcuffs and parade you through the airport the way the Romans used to display conquered enemy chieftains."

Crease shook her head in disgust. "Riker is such a creep."

Orchard smiled. "Of course, we won't let him do any of this. As soon as I hear that Riker's got his indictment, you'll disappear. When the sheriff arrives with his warrant, you won't be here. I've arranged for a private plane to fly us back to Portland. It's on standby. And I have Mary Garrett on retainer. She tells me that she'll set up a time to surrender you when it's convenient for us and she'll schedule an immediate bail hearing."

"Garrett, huh."

"We can't fuck around with this, Ellen. I've seen Garrett in court. She's a great white shark. More important, the press loves her and you need the press as much as you need a good lawyer."

Eleven

THE DECOR of Mary Garrett's office was ultramodern and disorienting, as if the decorator had artistic dyslexia. Ellen Crease could not find a straight line anywhere. She did see many gleaming aluminum tubes, myriad sheets of odd-shaped glass and numerous objects whose function was not easily identifiable. The lawyer Henry Orchard had chosen for her fit into this setting quite nicely. Her wardrobe and jewelry were expensive, but the clothes and accessories did not look quite right on the birdlike, five-foot woman. It was as if Garrett were under a court-ordered punishment to wear them as a means of emphasizing her dense glasses and overbite. Had this been true, the joke would have been on the court, because Garrett knew she wasn't a beauty queen and didn't care. What she did care about was winning and that was something she did very well.

As soon as the introductions were made, Garrett asked Henry Orchard to leave the room so she and Ellen Crease would have privacy. Crease sat in a director's chair. Its arms and legs were polished metal tubing and the back and seat were black leather that sagged a little, so that the height of the chair's occupant decreased. Garrett sat behind a wide glass desk on a high-backed chair of black leather. The chair could be elevated by pushing a button so that the diminutive attorney was always taller than her clients.

"I think your politics suck," was the first thing Garrett said to Ellen Crease when the door closed on Henry Orchard. "In fact, I can't think of a single thing you stand for that I agree with. I thought I should put that on the table right off."

Garrett had caught Crease completely off guard. There was a smirk on Garrett's lips and arrogance in the way she held her body. She was clearly communicating her opinion that she did not need Ellen Crease as a client but that Crease could not do without her as her attorney. If anyone else had treated her this way, Crease would have been out the door, but Garrett's combativeness endeared her to Crease. Perhaps it was the fact that her arrogance was wrapped in such a small and unattractive package. Instead of flushing with anger, Crease felt herself breaking into a wide grin.

"Then let's not talk politics," Crease said.

Garrett grinned back at her. "Good. I've been told that you have a thick skin. I wanted to see for myself. You're going to need it before this thing plays out."

"What exactly do you take 'this thing' to be?"

"The Prince of Darkness's dumber brother has an indictment charging you with two counts of aggravated murder. Aggravated murder, as you know from your days as a cop, carries a possible death sentence.

"Before I go any further, I'm going to explain the attorney-client relationship to you. And I want you to listen very closely to what I say, because this is not just a civics lecture.

"Anything you tell me is confidential. That means that, by law, I'm forbidden to tell anyone what you confide to me. It also gives you the freedom to tell me the most outrageous lies, but you may pay a price if you aren't completely honest. The best liar I ever represented is sitting in prison because I turned down a plea offer that would have kept him out of jail as a result of a fairy tale that he concocted. Do I make myself clear?"

"Perfectly. But I have no reason to lie to you."

"Then why did Riker go to the grand jury?"

"Isn't it obvious? Have you seen the latest polls? Cedric Riker is one of Ben Gage's tools. Gage was a major contributor to Riker's campaign and Riker owes him his job. Indicting me is a way of paying back Gage."

"I don't doubt that Riker is motivated by politics, but he can't go in front of a grand jury without evidence." Crease remembered that Orchard had said the same thing. "What does he have on you, Senator?"

"I don't know."

Garrett formed a steeple with her fingers and thought out loud.

"We know Jablonski fired the shot that killed your husband, so the only way you would be implicated in your husband's death would be if you hired him to do it."

"Ms. Garrett . . ."

"Call me Mary. We're going to be seeing a lot of each other."

"Mary, then. I didn't even know Martin Jablonski existed until my husband was murdered. Cedric Riker could not have any evidence implicating me in my husband's death, because I had nothing to do with it."

"Let's approach this problem from a different angle," Garrett said. "Was there something going on in your relationship with Lamar Hoyt that Riker could interpret as a motive for murder?"

Crease hesitated and Garrett concluded that her client was making a decision that would shape the direction of her representation. After a moment, Crease looked directly at her lawyer and said, "There's the money I'm going to inherit and the Hoyt Industries stock, which will make me the majority shareholder. But if I had hired Jablonski to kill Lamar, it would have been because Lamar was cheating on me with a woman named Karen Fargo."

"How long had you known?" Garrett asked softly.

"Since Lamar stopped having sex with me regularly."

"Did you confront your husband?"

"Yes. I wasn't surprised. In fact, I'd been expecting this for some time. I was Lamar's third wife and each marriage followed a pattern. Lamar would marry a woman in her twenties, then tire of her when she turned thirty or so. He began cheating on his first two wives when they were about my age and I expected him to cheat on me. The difference is that I'm not a docile airhead like the first two Mrs. Hoyts. I loved Lamar and I decided to break the cycle so I could keep our marriage intact."

"What did you do?"

"I made it crystal-clear to Lamar that I wasn't going to stand for his bullshit. He bought off his first two wives. I told Lamar that he'd be living on the street if he tried to pull this crap with me. Then I asked him point-blank if Miss Fargo could ring his bell the way I did. That got him thinking."

"And?"

"He stopped inventing excuses to avoid getting in the sack with me."

"So you think he broke it off with Fargo?"

"I'm not sure, but Lamar seemed like a loving husband again."

"Do you think Riker is aware of the affair?"

"I have no way of knowing."

Garrett made some notes on a pad. Crease waited patiently. When Garrett stopped writing, the lawyer said, "Why don't you tell me how you met Lamar?"

"I was a policewoman in Portland and there was a burglary at one of Lamar's mortuaries. I interviewed Lamar while I was conducting my investigation. He was charming in an old-boy sort of way. Very gallant. After the official part of the meeting, we drifted into small talk. Then I left.

"The next day, Lamar left me a message at work asking me to call him. I thought it had something to do with the case, but he wanted to take me out for dinner. I turned him down. I knew he was married. He was also a witness in a police investigation.

"About six months later, we arrested the perp who'd broken into the mortuary. He was an addict looking for something to sell for a rock of crack cocaine. I dropped by Lamar's office to let him know that the case was wrapped up and ended up at dinner with him."

Crease drifted off for a moment as if she were reliving the moment.

"Lamar was a charming bastard," Crease said with a small smile. "By the end of that dinner, I was hooked. See, I'd never had much. My father just took off about a year after I was born and my mom cleaned houses to put food on the table. I got through college on scholarships and waiting tables. The most money I'd ever seen was what I was pulling down as a cop. And here I was dining in elegance with a man whose pinky ring cost more than my mother made in a good year."

"Didn't the age difference bother you?"

"It's a funny thing. I never thought about the fact that he was almost thirty years older than me. He was a big bear, and so full of life. Lamar knew all the right things to say, too, and how to make you feel important. We spent most of that dinner talking about me. He had me believing that our backgrounds were pretty similar. You know, poor boy makes good, which was pretty much bullshit, since Lamar's daddy owned two funeral parlors when he died and Lamar's mother never worked a day in her life. Still, Lamar could make you think he was a sharecropper's son who rose from poverty.

"He also gave me a taste of how things could be for me if I continued to see him. There was the limousine, the waiters in tuxedos, his jewelry and the estate."

Crease spaced out again and Garrett could see her thinking about that good time with a man she loved and would never see again. It made Garrett feel sad. Then Crease laughed.

"What's so funny?" Garrett asked.

"I was just remembering Lamar. You know he looked like a

redneck hick with his cowboy boots and string ties, but he was smooth. When he asked to see me again, I didn't hesitate."

"Did the subject of his marriage ever come up?"

"He was the one who raised it. I don't remember how he did it, but I left that first dinner with the impression that Lamar thought that the second Mrs. H. was as dull as a dishrag, while finding me intellectually stimulating." Crease stared directly into Garrett's eyes. "That part was one hundred percent accurate. Mary Lou is a dim bulb. I know why Lamar was attracted to her. I've seen pictures of her during the Miss Oregon swimsuit competition. But I'll be damned if I know what they talked about outside of bed. Lamar was very smart. Country smart. I challenged him in a way no other woman ever did."

"What happened after the first dinner?"

"There were more dinners. They were wonderful. We talked and talked. Around the third time we met, Lamar took me back to his estate. Mary Lou was in New York on a buying spree. I suspect he sent her there to get rid of her for the weekend. I was bowled over. I'd never been inside a house like that before. That was the evening I made up my mind to marry Lamar. And it wasn't just the house or his money. I want you to understand that. I wanted those things, but I wanted Lamar more. I was fascinated by his intelligence, his energy . . ."

Crease trailed off, as if she had suddenly remembered that Lamar was dead and gone and all that energy and intelligence was now part of the void.

"Was that first evening at his estate the first time you slept together?"

"Yes."

"I get the impression that you two were good in bed."

"I thought so. That's why my antennae went up when Lamar started making excuses. At his age, he couldn't have sex as often as he used to, but he was pretty game whenever we made love."

"How did Lamar feel about your career?"

Crease's smile faded. "At first, my being a cop fascinated Lamar. I think it was a turn-on. But soon after we were married, he began complaining. Deep down, he wanted a traditional wife. Someone who looked good, had dinner waiting on the table when he got home and spread her legs whenever he was horny. He found out fast that I wasn't like that and never would be."

"What happened when he made this discovery?"

"There were a lot of hard words at first. Then I hit him straight on. I asked him if he wanted a partner or a doormat. I told him that we could be something together, but I made it clear that I wasn't going to lose my identity in order to make him happy. For a while, it was touch-and-go."

"But he came around?"

"He came around. And when I told him I wanted to quit the force to run for the legislature, he was my biggest supporter." A tear formed in Crease's eye and trailed down her cheek. Crease squared her shoulders. "He changed for me and he was always there for me. Damn, I miss him."

Garrett studied her new client. Crease's display of emotion seemed genuine. That did not mean that Crease was not a murderer, but it made Garrett, who was a cynic at heart, reserve judgment. She looked at her watch.

"We're due in court soon, so this is enough for now. Henry told you about my fee?"

Crease nodded. "I'll have it to you by tomorrow."

"Good. My secretary will give you my retainer agreement.

"Now, I know you've been a cop, so you have a good idea of what is going to happen as a result of these charges, but I want to spell it out for you. Your life is about to become a living hell. There's no other way to put it and I don't believe in sugarcoating the facts for my clients."

Garrett paused to judge how Crease was taking what she was dishing out. The senator was tense but alert.

"Bail will be the big problem. There is no mandatory bail in a murder case, but Riker is going to have to convince the judge that his case is very strong if he wants you held with no bail. If he succeeds, you'll be locked up with the type of people you used to arrest. I don't have to tell you what that will be like. The good news is that I think we've got a real shot at keeping you out of the pokey. And I mean completely out.

"That doesn't mean your life will be normal. The vultures of the press will be circling you twenty-four hours a day, and they won't have the slightest interest in your political views. You'll also find out who your real friends are."

Garrett leaned forward. She reminded Crease of the gargoyles she'd seen perched on the Notre Dame Cathedral the first time Lamar had flown her to Paris.

"I have some advice. Most clients aren't tough enough to follow it, but I think you are. Whatever has happened has happened. No matter how much you would like to you cannot change the past, so do not dwell on the murder of your husband. That's my job. That's why you hire an attorney. So you can go on with your life and let someone else do the worrying. I'll be doing enough for the two of us."

Garrett looked at her watch again and stood up.

"Stanley Sax, the presiding judge, is a friend of mine and he's got integrity. I talked to him this morning. He's set a special arraignment for ten-thirty. Your case will be the only one on the docket and we'll be taking up bail at the same time you're arraigned. That's unusual in a murder case, but this case is unusual because of the impact your incarceration would have on the primary. You'll plead not guilty. The press is going to be there in full force, so sing it out loud and clear. Then go back to campaigning and let me do my job."

[2]

Richard Quinn was studying a brochure from the Bay Reef Resort on St. Jerome when his secretary told him that Stanley Sax was on the way over from presiding court. The brochure showed a white sand beach, azure waters and clear blue skies. The hotel was new and he and Laura had a room with an ocean view. There was a casino, a huge pool, a four-star restaurant, water sports, tennis and more. Lately, Laura seemed excited about their week in paradise.

Quinn set down the brochure when Sax rapped his knuckles on the doorjamb.

"Come in, Stan," Quinn said cheerfully. "What's up?"

Sax did not return Quinn's smile. He dropped into a chair on the other side of Quinn's desk.

"I'm here to make your day."

"Oh?" Quinn answered cautiously.

"I know you're not scheduled to move into the homicide rotation until next month, but something has come up and I need you. Ced Riker has indicted Ellen Crease for the murder of her husband."

"What!"

"That was my reaction, too. He went to the grand jury yesterday. Crease is represented by Mary Garrett. Garrett called me to request an expedited bail hearing and I agreed because of the impact on the campaign if Crease has to sit in jail for a week while we schedule a hearing in the normal way. I'd like you to handle the case."

Quinn saw the brochure from St. Jerome in his peripheral vision. He owed Stanley Sax, but Quinn was counting on the week alone with Laura as his best chance to jump-start their ailing marriage.

"I can't do it, Stan. I've agreed to speak at a seminar in two weeks on St. Jerome. Remember? Laura's coming with me."

"That won't be a problem. I've scheduled the arraignment and the bail hearing for ten-thirty today. You take care of the hearing and I'll handle any emergencies while you're away."

"I don't know, Stan. This is a pretty big case for me to take on for my first homicide."

"Let me tell you something, Dick, every death penalty case is too big for any of us to handle. Only God should be deciding who should live and who should die, but we're stuck with the job.

"Now, it's true that you'll be under a spotlight in Crease's case that would not be shining on you if the defendant were some junkie lowlife. If you make a mistake, everyone in the country will know about it. But that won't make a difference to you. Want to know why?"

Quinn just stared at him.

"I know you, Dick. I know how conscientious you are and I know that you punish yourself for your mistakes much harder than anyone else can. That's why I want you on this one. You won't let yourself screw up. You'll make certain that both sides get a fair trial."

Quinn's bailiff pressed a button under his desk in the courtroom and a light on the desk in Quinn's chambers flashed bright red to let him know that both sides in *State v. Crease* were in the court-room. Quinn slipped into his judicial robes and opened the door that led directly to the bench. As he stepped through it, the bailiff rapped the gavel, commanded everyone in the packed courtroom to rise and announced that the Honorable Richard Quinn would be presiding over the docket. Quinn noticed several members of the press in attendance and saw the lights of the TV cameras that were shooting through the glass in the courtroom doors.

"You can be seated," Quinn said as soon as he had taken the bench. Cedric Riker remained standing, but the deputy district attorneys who accompanied him took seats on either side of the prosecutor. One deputy was a black woman and the other was an Asian male. They looked young and nervous.

Riker looked anything but nervous. He was dressed to kill and hungry for every second of publicity that this case would bring him. Quinn was willing to bet that Riker had held a news confer-ence in the corridor. Speaking with the marble and polished wood of the courtroom as a backdrop lent authority to Riker's words and made him look good to all the voters who listened to his sound bites on the eleven o'clock news.

Seated at the other counsel table were Mary Garrett and her client. Garrett was wearing black with a pearl necklace. None of Garrett's associates were at the counsel table, though Quinn suspected that there were one or two in the audience in case of an emergency. There were no lawbooks in front of Garrett, either. Quinn had heard that Garrett had an encyclopedic knowledge of the law and was known to give accurate volume and page cites to cases in the law reports from memory. She had already delivered a concise and expertly written brief on the bail issue to Quinn's chambers. Quinn was impressed by Garrett's ability to pump out a brief of such high quality on such short notice.

Ellen Crease sat quietly beside Garrett. She was dressed in a gray business suit and a cream-colored silk blouse. Aside from a pair of small diamond earrings, she wore no jewelry. Quinn's eyes rested on the defendant for a moment. It was hard to avoid looking at her. Crease was not classically beautiful, but even dressed in a conservative business suit, she exuded an animal sexuality that attracted and held a man's attention.

"Mr. Riker and Ms. Garrett, Judge Sax has assigned *State v. Crease* to me. However, I want to make counsel aware that I will be speaking at a legal seminar in St. Jerome in two weeks. That means that I will not be in Portland for approximately one week. During that time, if there are any emergencies, Judge Sax will take care of them. Is that a problem for counsel?"

Both lawyers answered in the negative.

"Good. Now, Mr. Riker, as I understand it, we're to hold an arraignment and bail hearing this morning."

"Well, Your Honor, we do intend to arraign the defendant on two charges of aggravated murder, but the People object to holding a bail hearing on such short notice in a case this serious."

Garrett was on her feet before Riker had finished his sentence.

"Your Honor, Senator Crease is in the middle of a hotly contested campaign for the Republican nomination for the United

States Senate. Her opponent is a political ally of Mr. Riker, who has done enough damage to her on behalf of his political cohort by bringing this spurious indictment during the campaign. Keeping the senator in jail for a week or more would cause her untold damage. She has had to cancel an entire day of campaigning already because of these absurd charges."

"I resent the implication that this indictment was politically motivated," Riker told Quinn self-righteously. "*I* did not charge the defendant with murder. This murder indictment was handed down by the people of this state through the agency of a duly impaneled grand jury."

"Nonsense, Judge," Garrett countered with a snort. "A grand jury is a tool of the prosecutor's office. Everyone knows that. Mr. Riker would fire any of his deputies who couldn't get an indictment charging the Pope with JFK's assassination."

The hearing was getting out of hand, so Quinn said sharply, "Ms. Garrett and Mr. Riker, I want this sniping to stop right now. This may be a long and contentious case, but it is going to be conducted with civility by all parties. Am I understood?"

"Of course, Your Honor," Riker assured the judge in a fawning manner intended to ingratiate him with Quinn. Garrett merely nodded.

"Good. Now, I assume you've been given a copy of Ms. Garrett's brief on the bail question, Mr. Riker."

"Well, I was, but so soon before court that I haven't had a chance to read it."

"Tell me why you believe holding Senator Crease in jail for a week or so during the height of this campaign would be in the interests of justice," Quinn commanded the prosecutor.

Garrett held back a smile. Having Quinn address her client as "Senator Crease" instead of "the defendant" was a small but important victory.

"The defendant is charged with two counts of aggravated murder," Riker blustered, and it was immediately obvious to Quinn that the prosecutor had not done any legal research on the issue of the proper timing for a bail hearing in a murder case. "These charges are serious. The defendant is a flight risk and a potential danger to others."

"The question of whether the senator is a flight risk or a danger to others is relevant to the amount of bail to be imposed, if I decide to grant bail. It is not relevant to the question of my authority to hold a bail hearing at the same time that I arraign Senator Crease. Do you have any other arguments you wish to make?"

"No, Your Honor."

"Then I must tell you that I find the arguments in Ms. Garrett's brief persuasive and I hold that the interests of justice require me to hold Senator Crease's bail hearing this morning.

"The question of whether bail will be granted is another matter. I have no opinion on it at this moment and I will hear counsel on the question as soon as Senator Crease is arraigned."

Quinn held the arraignment quickly. He read the charges to Crease and advised her of her rights. Then he asked her how she wanted to plead to the accusation that she had hired Martin Jablonski to murder her husband, then murdered Jablonski because he was a witness to her involvement.

Crease had been standing during the arraignment. When Quinn asked her how she wished to plead, she squared her shoulders and looked Quinn in the eye. Despite the tense atmosphere in the courtroom, Crease appeared to be confident and free of fear. When she spoke, her voice was firm and filled with resolve.

"I loved my husband very much, Your Honor. I would never hurt him. I don't know what is behind these allegations, but they are false and I am not guilty."

For a moment, the fire in Crease's eyes trapped Quinn. Then he pulled himself away and pretended to scan some papers that lay in front of him.

"Very well," Quinn said. "We'll record your plea of not guilty to both charges. Now to the issue of bail. Mr. Riker, I believe that you have the burden of convincing me that there is clear and convincing evidence of Senator Crease's guilt before I can hold her without any bail. How do you wish to do that?"

"This hearing has caught me by surprise, Your Honor. I'm not prepared to proceed with witnesses at this time."

"When could you have your witnesses here, Mr. Riker?"

Garrett was certain that Riker was not going to give her a chance to rip into his witnesses prior to trial, and she smiled when he said, "Well, I don't know. Perhaps I could give the Court the police reports in lieu of presenting live testimony?"

"That would deprive me of the opportunity to cross-examine, Your Honor," Garrett objected.

"I agree," Quinn said. "Mr. Riker, unless you want to call witnesses and subject them to examination by Ms. Garrett, I'm going to have to hold that bail is appropriate in this case and move on to the question of the proper amount of bail."

Riker looked very uncomfortable. He shifted from one foot to another. One of the deputies tried to whisper something to him, but Riker waved him off.

"You've put me in an impossible position, Your Honor," Riker complained.

"I'm sorry you feel that way, Mr. Riker, but you're going to have to tell me if you want to put on witnesses or argue the amount of bail."

"Let's proceed with arguments on the amount of bail," Riker said reluctantly. "The defendant is a wealthy woman who can fly to any country, including those without extradition treaties with the United States. She even owns her own airplane. This makes her a flight risk. Plus, she is a former policewoman. She knows how to use a weapon. She could be a danger to our witnesses."

Garrett stood up and addressed Quinn.

"Your Honor, until Mr. Hoyt's will is probated Ms. Crease has limited access to his wealth. She earns a salary as a state senator, but that hardly makes her rich. Furthermore, Senator Crease is in the middle of a political campaign. That, in addition to her complete innocence, is why we are fighting so hard for bail."

"Would the senator surrender her passport as a condition of my setting bail?"

"Of course."

Quinn reviewed the personal history that was part of Garrett's brief. He came to a decision.

"Instead of setting bail, I am going to release Senator Crease on her own recognizance . . ."

"But, Your Honor . . . ," Riker sputtered.

"Please do not interrupt me, Mr. Riker. I will give you an opportunity to make a record when I am finished."

Quinn dictated a series of conditions for Crease's release, then gave Riker an opportunity to vent his spleen. When the district attorney was finished ranting and raving, Quinn set a date for the state and defense to file motions and set a tentative date for hearing the pretrial motions and for the trial. When there was no further business to conduct, the bailiff rapped the gavel, everyone in the courtroom stood and Quinn returned to his chambers.

As soon as Quinn left the bench, Mary Garrett broke into a huge grin. "So far so good, Ellen."

"The judge seemed to be very fair."

"That he did."

"Will he be our trial judge?"

Garrett nodded. "This is my first time in front of Quinn. He's a surprise choice for the homicide rotation. Before he came on the bench he was a contract law specialist in the Price, Winward firm. But I like what I've seen so far. He seems bright and he's decisive."

"Do you think he'll work with us? He seemed to dislike Riker."

Garrett stopped smiling. "Don't get any ideas about Quinn being some sort of pro-defense, knee-jerk liberal because of what happened today. My book on him is that he is one hundred percent ethical and that he decides cases on the law. That means that he'll rule for Riker whether he likes him or not, if he thinks he is right. And he can be really tough. He just sent Judge Gideon to prison when everyone in the courthouse was putting money on probation.

"On the other hand, we won't have to worry about having a judge who is part of the prosecution. The bottom line is that we have the best kind of judge. He's smart, he's ethical and he'll give us a fair trial. Now it's up to me to make certain that the trial ends favorably for you."

[3]

Quinn found Laura hunched over the computer in their home office on the second floor. She was dressed in a flannel nightgown with the granny glasses she used for reading perched on her nose.

"Still working?" Quinn said.

"It's that condo deal in Maui," Laura answered without looking away from the monitor. "There are all sorts of problems and, of course, our client had to wait until the last possible minute to let us know."

"Ellen Crease was indicted for Lamar Hoyt's murder. Stan Sax assigned me the case."

Laura looked up and swiveled away from the screen.

"That'll keep you busy," Laura said.

"Didn't you handle some litigation involving Hoyt?"

"BestCo. We sued his ass. I deposed him."

"What was he like? I met him a few times but I never had a real conversation with him."

Laura thought about the question. She swiveled her chair and pushed her glasses back on her nose.

"Hoyt was a real cowboy. All ready to shoot it out at high noon with us, as if the lawsuit were some kind of nineteenth-century gunfight. He impressed me as the type of guy who thinks he can conquer every situation with the force of his personality." Laura thought for a moment, then added, "I guess he had a sort of primal charm, but he was also a real chauvinist. He couldn't keep his eyes off my breasts."

"Didn't he make his money in mortuaries?"

"Yeah, but that was only at the beginning. He diversified early on. Hoyt had his fingers in a lot of pies and," Laura added with a smirk, "up a few dresses."

"He was cheating on Senator Crease?"

"That's the rumor."

"I wonder if she knew."

"If *I* knew, she probably had a clue."

"I'm surprised she stood for it. From what I hear, that's not her style."

"Some women will put up with a lot for twenty million dollars. She was number three. Maybe she didn't want to become the ex–number three."

Laura paused. "Is this going to affect our trip to St. Jerome?"

"No way. Stan is going to cover for me when we're gone. I told him I wouldn't handle the case if I had to give up the trip. I'm really looking forward to spending some uninterrupted time with you."

"Me, too," Laura told Quinn. He bent down and kissed her and she returned the kiss.

"That's enough smooching," Laura said. "If I don't get back to work, I'll be up all night."

Quinn smiled and gave Laura a peck on the cheek. She seemed excited about the trip to St. Jerome. Maybe she realized how hard she had been working and how nice it would be to take some time off. Quinn hoped that spending time with him had something to do with Laura's good mood. When he walked downstairs to fix himself a snack, he was grinning.

Part Two

The Cove
of Lost Souls

Twelve

C"AN I GET you something to drink before we take off?" the flight attendant asked.

Quinn was lost in thought, oblivious to the attendant and the passengers who were filing past his aisle seat in first class while the flight crew prepared for the plane's departure from New York for St. Jerome. When he realized that the flight attendant was speaking to him, Quinn looked up at her with a blank expression and she repeated the question with a pleasant smile.

"Scotch on the rocks, please," Quinn answered without returning her smile. The attendant turned to the first-class passenger across the aisle and Quinn looked forlornly at the empty window seat beside him. Yesterday Laura had told him that she would not be able to go to St. Jerome.

"Honey, I have really bad news," she had said in a midday call from her office to his chambers. "A group of businessmen in Florida are putting together a condominium deal like the one in Maui. They heard about the job I did for Eddie Meyers. They have some of the same problems. The deal is going to be finalized this weekend and I have to fly to Miami tomorrow afternoon so we can meet on Wednesday. Then they want me with them during the negotiations through Saturday."

There had been stunned silence on Quinn's end. The conference on St. Jerome was from Thursday to Sunday. Quinn was speaking on Thursday morning. He had planned it so that he and Laura would leave on Tuesday and have every day but Thursday to themselves. If Laura had to be in Miami from Tuesday to Saturday, there was no way she could come with him.

"Can't someone else go in your place?" he had asked, but Laura had told him that the clients insisted on her handling the matter personally and were willing to pay a large retainer to secure her services.

"Turn them down," Quinn had snapped, unable to hide his anger and disappointment. "There must be hundreds of lawyers in Miami who can review their damn contract."

"I know you were looking forward to this vacation," Laura had answered calmly. "So was I. But this will give me a foothold in Florida. Do you know how many condo deals are made there?"

"I don't care, Laura. This vacation . . . I was hoping so much . . ."

Quinn could not finish the sentence.

"I'm sorry, Dick. I'm not in this just for myself. You were a partner at Price. How could I explain turning down a fee like this and losing the potential business?"

Quinn wanted to remind her that she was also a partner in their marriage. Instead, he hung up after assuring Laura that he understood in a tone that let her know that he did not.

The line of boarding passengers started to thin. To distract himself, Quinn took the airline magazine from the seat pocket in front of him and found the crossword. Completing the crossword before takeoff was a ritual that Quinn followed whenever he flew.

"Excuse me. I think the window seat is mine."

When Quinn looked up he saw a woman standing in the aisle. She was about five feet four and wore a white T-shirt under a red sports jacket. Her jeans were secured at the waist by a brightly colored red and yellow fabric belt with an unusual silver buckle that resembled a seashell.

"I have 2A," she explained, showing Quinn her ticket.

"Sorry," Quinn said as he stumbled awkwardly to his feet. As the woman edged by him, she smiled apologetically. Quinn guessed that she was in her mid-twenties. She was not wearing makeup and she looked tired. Her straight black hair was pulled back into a ponytail. Here and there, strands had escaped to add to the picture of an exhausted traveler. The woman had a small nose, full lips and almond-shaped brown eyes that were a little bloodshot. The overall effect was vaguely oriental. Just as the woman sat down, the flight attendant brought Quinn his drink.

"Can I get you anything?" the attendant asked the woman in the window seat. The woman looked at Quinn's drink.

"Is that a Scotch?" she asked him.

"Yes."

"Then make mine the same."

The attendant left to fill the order.

"I need a stiff drink," she told Quinn while flashing a tired smile. "I just got off a nonstop from Italy."

"Vacation?" he asked to be polite.

"I wish," she answered with a pleasant laugh. "I was in Bologna checking out leather suppliers for my business."

"What do you do?"

"I'm the president of Avalon Accessories, creators of the best custom-made belts in the known universe," the woman answered proudly. Then her shoulders sagged dramatically. "But sometimes I wish I had a partner. All the travel kills me. If I'm not in the shop, I'm on a plane."

"Do you sell your belts out of your shop?"

"I don't actually have a shop. That's just a figure of speech. I make the belts in a small factory. I sell through specialty shop customers and catalog sales. But I also work with a few fashion designers. They show me their designs for the season and I make belts that are appropriate for the collection." The woman pointed at her belt. "This is part of Gretchen Nye's spring collection. Do you like it?"

"I noticed it when you sat down. It's very nice."

"Nice?" the woman answered with mock indignation. "You're supposed to say that it's a startlingly innovative combination of style and color that knocked your socks off. Nice doesn't sell Gretchen Nye originals at two thousand a pop."

Quinn laughed. "I did mean to say that it was startlingly innovative. It came out wrong."

"You're forgiven."

The flight attendant brought the woman's drink just as the plane began taxiing toward the runway. She swallowed most of it, then sat silently during takeoff. Quinn could see that her knuckles were white from tension. As soon as they were airborne, she downed the rest of her Scotch.

"No matter how many times I go through that, I still get scared," she confided to Quinn. "A friend of mine was killed in an air crash."

"That's terrible."

"Yeah. It really shook me up. I'm a mess every time I fly."

The attendant passed by and the woman ordered a second drink. So did Quinn.

"Are you vacationing on St. Jerome?" the woman asked.

The question reminded Quinn that Laura was not with him and he lost the relaxed feeling he had been experiencing since his conversation with the woman began.

"Business, I'm afraid. Though I'm going to take advantage of the beach."

"What kind of work do you do?"

"I'm a judge."

The woman looked impressed. "I've never met a judge before."

Quinn smiled. "Well, this is what we look like."

She laughed. "Where are you a judge?"

"Portland, Oregon."

"I hear that Portland is a beautiful city. I'd like to visit someday."

"I like it."

Suddenly, the woman looked confused. "You can't be a judge on St. Jerome, can you?"

"No. I can only hear cases in Oregon."

"That's what I thought. So what kind of business do you have on the island?"

"I'm speaking at a legal seminar. I only hope I can keep my audience interested. My lecture is going to seem awfully dull compared to those white sand beaches outside the hotel."

"I'm certain you'll hold their interest, Judge . . . Say, I don't know your name. Mine is Andrea. Andrea Chapman."

"Richard Quinn," he said as they shook hands. "Dick, actually. And please don't call me Judge. That's for the courtroom."

"Okay, Dick. Are you staying at The Palms?"

"No. I'm at the Bay Reef Resort."

"Oh, the new one. They were just finishing it the last time I was on the island."

"It looks beautiful in the brochures. Are you going to St. Jerome on business?"

"God, no. This trip is strictly R and R. A friend of mine owns a villa on the island. He lets me use it when I need to get away."

"A boyfriend?"

Andrea giggled. "Freddy is gay. Flaming. But he's a great friend and one of my best customers. We met at a leather goods show in Milan about five years ago. He owns a catalog business and he really pushes my belts."

"Is the villa near my hotel?"

"No. It's on the other side of St. Jerome. You should see it. The place is unbelievable. The floors are these different-colored marbles, the walls are all glass, and the view is to die for. It's right on the ocean on this cliff. When I wake up and pull the drapes it's like I'm floating in space."

"It sounds fantastic."

"It is." Andrea leaned over toward Quinn and dropped her voice an octave. "There's a story behind the villa. The way Freddy got it. Some Guatemalan drug lord owned it, but he was busted in Rhode Island of all places. He gave it to this lawyer in Boston that Freddy knows as part of his fee and Freddy bought it from the lawyer for a song. I don't think the lawyer ever saw it. He just wanted cash."

Andrea lowered her voice even more.

"The last time I used the place, I found a stash of coke hidden behind a phony panel in the bathroom. It scared the hell out of me."

"I can imagine. Did you turn it over to the police?"

"On St. Jerome? You're kidding? I wouldn't go within a mile of an island cop if I was being murdered. St. Jerome is great, but everyone—and I mean everyone—in the government is on the take. If I told the police about the dope, I'd either be in jail or penniless now."

"So what did you do?"

"Flushed it as quickly as I could. Then I scrubbed down the toilet bowl to make sure there wasn't a trace of the stuff left. It was my last day on St. Jerome, thank God. If it had been my first, I would probably have been on the next flight out. As it was, I didn't sleep a wink. I kept expecting Governor Alvarez's Gestapo to kick in the door and throw me in prison."

Quinn laughed. "If you were so frightened, why did you come back?"

"You wouldn't ask that if you'd been on St. Jerome before. The place has got to be the most beautiful island in the world. Besides, Freddy swore to me that the place is clean now. He was just as scared as I was when I told him about the coke. Can you imagine what it would cost an American to buy his way out of a drug beef?"

Chapman paused. "Say, are you going to be working all the time?"

"Not the first two days."

Quinn realized where the conversation might be going and his wedding ring suddenly felt very heavy on his finger. He decided to make his marital status clear to Andrea.

"My wife was supposed to come with me, but something came up at the last minute. She's a lawyer, too, and there was a business emergency."

"That's too bad. I bet she would have loved St. Jerome. There's a lot to do if you know your way around."

"Such as?"

"Do you snorkel or scuba dive?"

"No. I'm a lousy swimmer."

"You don't have to swim great to snorkel. And there are these fabulous reefs where you can see all these tropical fish. You've never seen such bright colors," Andrea said excitedly. "Electric blues, iridescent greens. It's wilder than a Missoni fashion show."

"That sounds terrific. Are any of these reefs near my hotel?"

"Oh, sure. But the best one is on my side of the island, away from the hotels, where Freddy's villa is, off Cala de Almas Desoladas."

"What was that?" asked Quinn, who spoke no Spanish.

"The Cove of Lost Souls. Freddy said it's called that because of a ship that was wrecked on the reef in 1700 something. The captain was in love with a beautiful woman. They were going to be married. On their wedding day, the bride was kidnapped by pirates. The captain chased the pirates to St. Jerome just as a terrible storm struck the island and the captain's ship and the pirate ship were wrecked. Everyone died, including the captain and his bride.

"Freddy told me that if you go to the cove at night, sometimes you can hear the souls of the captain and his bride calling to each other across the water. Isn't that sad and romantic?"

"Yes, it is."

"There's more, though. Freddy says that there have been mysterious disappearances in the cove. Not often. Once or twice, every ten years or so. They occur when lovers come to the beach at night on the anniversary of the shipwreck. They swim out toward the reef. One minute they're there, the next they're gone. The locals think that the lost souls on the reef are harvesting other souls to keep them company."

"It's probably cramps," Quinn said with a smile.

"See, that's the lawyer in you talking," Andrea scolded Quinn. "Lawyers are so unromantic." She paused as if debating whether to say more. "Do you want to hear something spooky?"

"Sure."

"The last time I stayed on St. Jerome, a day before I found the coke, I went down to the cove at sunset and waited around to see if I would hear the lost souls calling. At first, I just heard what you usually hear on the beach at night, the surf and the wind. Soon after the sun went down, the temperature dropped and I got cold. I was just starting to leave when something very strange happened."

Andrea paused. She looked distant.

"What's the matter?" Quinn asked with concern.

"I was remembering the voices. Only they weren't really voices. It was more like a moaning sound and it was so sad."

Quinn was weaned on logic and had the overly rational mind of the contract lawyer, which has no cubbyhole where the supernatural can dwell comfortably.

"Do you think it might have been the wind?" he asked tolerantly.

"I knew you'd say that. Everyone I tell this story to says the same thing. If you'd been there, though, you'd know that it wasn't the wind. That sound . . ." Andrea shivered. "It was inside my bones." She shook her head. "I just don't know how else to describe it. And the way it made me feel. At first I was really scared, but suddenly I felt so lost and alone."

Andrea paused thoughtfully.

"What if it's true? It would be so tragic. The two lovers, so close to each other, but separated by the raging sea for eternity."

Quinn could not think of a thing to say that wouldn't sound

patronizing, so he was silent. He did not want to insult Andrea. He liked her. She was so different from Laura. Quinn thought of the way Laura would react to Andrea's ghost story and laughed.

"You don't believe me. I know. No one does."

"I'm sorry. I wasn't laughing at you."

"Oh, that's okay. No one takes my experience at the cove seriously. I'm used to it. Say, I just got an idea. You could hear the lost souls yourself. I could take you to the cove."

"I don't know."

It had been some time since he had spent a day alone with a woman other than Laura and the thought of it made him uncomfortable, especially with the way things were between them.

"Oh, come on. You'd love it. And it's not a place that the tourists get to see. They pretty much stay near the hotels. Freddy told me that the governor likes it that way. There's a lot of poverty away from The Palms and Bay Reef. Freddy said that poor people are bad for tourism, so Governor Alvarez only paved the road on one section of the island. You have to drive on a dirt road to get to the villa and the cove. It goes through these shantytowns."

Quinn knew he was being foolish. He didn't believe for a moment in the lost lovers, but the cove and the reef with the tropical fish sounded fascinating, and he did have two days with no plans. Spending one of them in the company of an attractive woman suddenly sounded like a good idea.

"The invitation sounds tempting," Quinn hedged.

Andrea turned slightly and put her hand on his arm.

"I insist. I'll even teach you how to snorkel. You'll love it. What do you say?"

"I . . ."

"I'm not taking no for an answer. There's no way I'm going to let you leave St. Jerome without learning how to snorkel. I can pick you up at the hotel around four, tomorrow afternoon. That will give us both time to get over our jet lag and catch up on sleep. It takes about three-quarters of an hour to get to the cove from the hotel. I'll bring a picnic basket. We can swim for a while. I have snorkeling equipment and I'll give you a lesson. Then we'll eat and wait for the sun to go down."

Andrea grinned mischievously. "I just got a great idea. If we hear the sound of the lost souls and you can't explain it, you have to treat me to dinner. But it's my treat if you can come up with a rational explanation. What do you say?"

Quinn made a decision. He would go and have a good time. Maybe an evening with Andrea would help him get rid of his melancholy mood. But Quinn did not want anyone connected to the conference seeing him drive off with Andrea: judges had to avoid even the appearance of impropriety.

"Why don't you give me directions to the cove and I'll meet you there? I'll rent a car."

Andrea's smile widened. "So, you'll come?"

"I'll come. And, if you win, we can invite the ghosts along. I'll even spring for their dinners."

Quinn's first glimpse of St. Jerome was filtered through gauzy white clouds. A patch of sugar-white sand, a strip of crystal-clear blue water, groves of swaying emerald-leafed palms. When the plane dropped beneath the clouds and Quinn had an unobstructed view of the island, he was certain he had found paradise. After the steady diet of gray and rain he had dined on in Portland, the sight of the sun, the palm trees and the clear blue water was exhilarating.

The exhilaration ended when the hatch of the airplane opened and Quinn was engulfed by a thick soup of hot, sticky air. He had rarely experienced such all-consuming heat. It bounced off the railings of the portable, metal steps that descended to the tarmac, melted the black asphalt and stirred the tar into a sucking mixture that threatened to wrench his shoes from his feet during the walk from the plane to the one-story terminal building that shimmered before him in the undulating waves of heat. Only the breeze from the sea made the heat bearable.

The lime-green paint on the exterior walls of the terminal had been savaged by the salt-heavy sea air. On one wall hung a huge poster of a smiling, mustachioed man in a military uniform. Quinn could not read the Spanish words on the poster. A large tear almost disconnected the top of the poster from the bottom. It looked to Quinn as if the damage had been done with a knife. Lounging against the wall next to the poster were two soldiers carrying automatic weapons. Quinn could not help noticing several other soldiers who were similarly armed.

"Why all the heavy artillery?" Quinn asked.

Andrea lowered her voice.

"The soldiers are here to protect the tourists. Governor Alvarez lets drug smugglers use the island for a fee. About five years ago, he executed six dealers who tried to cheat him. They were members of a South American cartel. A few weeks later, six tourists were gunned down in an ambush in retaliation. The island's economy is dependent on tourism. The massacre had a disastrous impact."

"You're making St. Jerome sound pretty dangerous."

"Oh, you don't have to worry. There hasn't been any trouble since. Freddy told me that a lot of money changed hands and Alvarez worked out the problem."

"This Alvarez sounds like a petty criminal."

Andrea looked alarmed. She cast a quick look around to see if anyone had heard the judge's comment.

"You don't criticize Governor Alvarez here," Andrea warned. "Enjoy the beaches and forget politics. It's not a healthy subject for discussion on St. Jerome."

Louvered windows let air into the terminal, but it was still hot. Quinn looked for the baggage carousel before noticing two black men in shorts and sweat-stained shirts taking luggage off a cart and stacking it near one of the interior walls. He found his bags and looked around for customs.

The dominant language on the signs inside the terminal was Spanish, the official language of the island, but there were translations in English, French, German and Japanese. Quinn heard most of these languages being spoken by the tourists who queued up in front of the customs officials. The heavyset, sleepy-eyed man who checked Quinn's passport spoke broken English. After a few perfunctory questions, he smiled at Quinn and welcomed him to St. Jerome.

"The Bay Reef Resort is supposed to provide a shuttle service between the airport and the hotel," Quinn told Andrea.

"Don't worry about me. Freddy's driver will pick me up."

A brand-new air-conditioned van with the Bay Reef logo was waiting at curbside.

"I'll see you at the cove at four tomorrow," Quinn said before boarding it.

"At four."

The air-conditioning in the van made Quinn forget about the debilitating heat. Two middle-aged couples were the only other passengers on the shuttle. From what Quinn could hear, they were Australian and they were on holiday together. Quinn turned his attention to the royal palms with their thick tan trunks and broad green leaves that shaded the highway. Beyond the palm trees, waves rushed across a white sand beach. Everywhere Quinn looked he saw the sea or lush tropical vegetation. St. Jerome was every bit as beautiful as the brochure from the Bay Reef Resort had promised.

After a fifteen-minute ride, a high white stucco wall appeared on the ocean side of the highway. They drove alongside the wall for a mile. Then the van pulled up in front of a guardhouse and waited while a black man in a clean, white short-sleeved shirt and tan slacks opened a gate topped by black spikes. The bold black letters on a copper sign affixed to a column next to the gate identified the enclave as the Bay Reef Resort.

The van drove for a short distance down a wide road lined with pink bougainvillea and more palms, then stopped in front of a one-story white stucco building. To the left, Quinn could see the beginning of a line of elegant shops. To the right was a row of two-story suites. High hedges blocked Quinn's view in both directions.

Quinn got out of the van and identified his bags for a porter, who directed him through an arched portal toward the reception area. Quinn noticed that there were almost no doors in sight. The reason was soon obvious. As he stepped through the archway, the breeze that blew in from the ocean cooled him.

There was a red and yellow terrazzo floor and a dozen varieties of flowering plants in the lobby of the Bay Reef. Beyond the reception area was a wide flagstone terrace. Guests in shorts and bathing suits were eating lunch at tables covered with white cloth under the shade of sea-grape trees. The trees were strung with lights that illuminated the open-air restaurant after the sun set.

After he checked in, a porter showed Quinn to his suite. A king-size, four-poster bed dominated the bedroom. The sight of it made Quinn sad. He had requested it after seeing pictures of the suite in the brochure for the resort. Before Laura's abrupt withdrawal from their trip, he had imagined the pleasure they would both take in making love in that bed.

Quinn tipped the bellman, put away his clothes, and switched on the air conditioner and the overhead fan. The judge was tired from his nine-hour flight, but he did not want to nap. As soon as he showered and changed into shorts and a T-shirt, Quinn wandered onto the balcony. Oleander, coconut palms and more sea grape were planted liberally along the edge of the beach, providing some shade for the bathers who lounged around, soaking up the sun. To the left, Quinn could see the thatch-roofed bar at the end of the flagstone terrace. Brown-skinned waiters and waitresses cruised back and forth between the bar and the guests with drink-laden trays. The ocean near the resort was dotted with sailboats, catamarans and splashing, laughing vacationers. Quinn checked his watch. Laura's plane would be in by now. He walked inside, lay down on the bed and called Laura at her hotel.

"Hi," Quinn said as soon as they were connected. "I just wanted to make sure you got in okay."

"No problems here. How was your flight?" Laura asked.

"The flight was fine."

"Does St. Jerome live up to your expectations?"

"Yeah, it does. It's even more beautiful than I thought it would be. The resort is unbelievable."

"You know I want to be with you, don't you, Dick?"

Quinn wanted to tell Laura that she would have turned down her new clients or had someone else from the firm handle the business if she really wanted to be with him, but he did not want to start a fight. So he said, "I know, honey." Then he added, "I really miss you," which was true.

"I miss you, too. Maybe we can get away together soon. Just the two of us."

Quinn wanted to remind her about the Crease trial and his other cases, which would eat up most of the year, but he didn't.

"That would be great," he answered with as much enthusiasm as he could muster. "I love you."

"Love you, too," Laura answered before she hung up.

Quinn replaced the receiver and lay back, staring at the long-bladed ceiling fan that spun slowly overhead. It dawned on him that he had not mentioned Andrea Chapman or their plans for the next day. Quinn wondered why it had slipped his mind. He felt vaguely guilty about not mentioning Andrea, but there was nothing he could do about it now.

Quinn walked onto the balcony again. He missed Laura terribly. There were so many happy couples frolicking on the beach. The sight of them made Quinn feel worse. He wished he were with Laura lying in the sun, reading a trashy novel and getting smashed on banana daiquiris. But Laura was working and he was alone.

Thirteen

THE HEAT AND LIGHT of the sun woke Laura Quinn. It was a pleasant change from the alarm clock that usually shocked her out of bed in Portland. She stretched and turned so she could see the clock on the hotel nightstand. It was eight-thirty. Laura could not remember the last weekday when she had been in bed at this hour.

Laura rolled onto her back and contemplated a lazy morning. Her client had left a message saying that she would be contacted at ten. That left her time to shower and have a leisurely breakfast. She got out of bed wearing the T-shirt and panties she'd slept in. It was hot in Miami, but Laura had switched off the air conditioner so she could enjoy the warmth after the cold and gray of the Oregon winter.

Laura found a space on the hotel carpet that was wide enough for her to do some stretching and proceeded to go through the routine she followed every morning at home. Repeating the familiar exercises made her think of Quinn, who was usually shaving and showering while she worked out. She missed her husband, and her good feelings were replaced by pangs of guilt.

Laura completed fifty crunches and twenty push-ups. The Florida heat and the exercise had covered her in a thin sheen of sweat. She stripped and went into the bathroom. Quinn had sounded so lonely during the call from St. Jerome, but it was his reaction when she told him that she could not make the trip to the island that haunted her. He had sounded betrayed and abandoned and, she admitted to herself, he had every right to feel that way.

Affection for Quinn had crept up on Laura. Bushwhacked and ambushed her. It was something she never anticipated when the two of them were teamed to work on the Remington litigation. Quinn was someone who rarely entered Laura's thoughts before the *Remington* case. He was nice-looking, but not handsome enough to moon about. He was also shy and clumsy. Laura knew that Quinn had been a varsity basketball player in college, but she still had trouble imagining him playing with grace. Of course, Quinn was very smart, even brilliant at times, but so were most of the lawyers at Price, Winward. You didn't get invited to join the firm unless you were a superstar in law school and you didn't make partner unless your talent sparkled in the real world.

Laura turned off the shower. While she toweled off, she thought about the first time she and Quinn had made love. It had been in a hotel room. They were staying at the Adolphus in Dallas while they took depositions in *Remington*. She had a small room, but Quinn was a partner, so he was staying in a suite. It was the end of a grueling fifteen-hour workday. They were in the living room of the suite under a wide skylight going over their notes of the depositions they had conducted from nine to five at the offices of Remington's attorneys. The night had been clear and Laura remembered a moment when she had leaned her head back against the couch and stared up through the skylight at a swirl of stars and a bright, white quarter moon.

Quinn had been brilliant that day. He had broken Remington's CEO and they were both excited. Laura remembered feeling like a timber wolf circling a terrified calf as she watched the CEO's expression change slowly from disdain to despair. They could both taste blood when they packed their attaché cases and left the offices of Remington's attorneys. Hours later, Quinn and Laura, exhausted by the long day and tipsy from the wine they'd drunk at dinner, were sitting next to each other on the couch when Laura said something that had struck them both as funny. What normally would have merited a good chuckle made them giddy in their weakened state. When their laughter was spent they found themselves pressed together. Laura remembered Quinn looking at her with such longing the moment before their lips touched.

The morning after their first sex, Laura had been in torment. Quinn was not a particularly good lover, but he did love her. That much Laura knew. As they lay together in the dark, Quinn had confessed the feelings that had exploded in him during the past year. He told her how he had come to care for her but had been afraid to tell her. He was a partner and she was an associate. He was concerned with appearances, worried about the difference in their ages. But he was also helplessly in love with her, he admitted, laying himself open for rejection.

Quinn's honesty impressed Laura, but intimacy terrified her. Laura's father had adored her and her mother, or so Laura had believed. Then he had left them. How could Laura trust Quinn's feelings? How could she trust her own? Laura had slept with men, but she had never let herself expose her emotions to a man. Quinn wanted that. He needed it.

Laura had told Quinn that she did not want to rush into a serious relationship. Quinn backed off. She could read the pain in his eyes. The sag in his shoulders reminded her of the defeated CEO. It upset her to think that she had hurt him.

In the week after their return from Texas, Laura thought long and hard about her feelings for Quinn. She had learned to admire and respect Quinn during the time they'd worked together, but did she love him? What was love, anyway? Her emotions were so jumbled by the life she had led that she wasn't certain that she would ever be able to answer that question. If love existed, she knew that it did not last forever. Her mother had loved her father, and her father said he loved her mother, but neither loved the other now. Laura was convinced that love could be a lie. Still, she did feel something for Quinn that she had never felt for another man. He was gentle and considerate and he respected her legal abilities. She felt safe and comfortable when she was with him. Was that the way someone in love was supposed to feel?

Laura suggested that they spend time together. Quinn agreed eagerly. He did not pressure her and he seemed to understand the difficulty she had committing herself emotionally. When Laura thought about their future, she imagined herself and Quinn working together with the same verve and success they'd had in the Remington case. Only, in her thoughts, she, too, was a partner at Price, Winward. When she agreed to marry Quinn she was still not certain that her feelings for him were love, but they were what she thought love was supposed to feel like.

Laura took the elevator to the lobby and treated herself to fresh-squeezed orange juice, cold cereal and coffee in the hotel restaurant. As she ate, she wondered what had happened between her and her husband. There had not been anything dramatic. No affair, Quinn did not drink like her father or suffer from depression. He was the same man she had married, but somewhere during the past seven years, the marriage had started to die.

Who was to blame? Laura thought that their problems started with Quinn's ascension to the bench. When Quinn told her that the governor had approached him about the appointment she had been stunned. Laura knew that Dick was Patrick Quinn's son. Everyone knew that. She knew that he was basically an intellectual who enjoyed the law because of its mental rigor and not because of the money and thrill of combat that drew her to its practice. What she could not understand was how anyone could achieve her dream of making partner at Price, Winward and abandon it for the bench. As an associate, she was making almost as much as an Oregon Supreme Court justice. When she made partner, their combined salaries would be more than $300,000 a year. How could Quinn throw away the prestige and financial security of his present position? Laura tried to understand her husband's motivation, but she could not accept what he wanted to do. Should she have tried harder to understand Quinn's feelings? The thought nagged at her. Had she lost respect for Quinn simply because his job paid less than hers? Was that fair?

Laura returned to her room. Her client had not called by ten-fifteen. She took out the letter in which the retainer check and first-class plane ticket had been enclosed. The letter had been FedExed to the firm and there was a phone number on the letterhead. Jerome Ross, the man she had spoken to on the phone, had also signed the letter. She reached for the phone, then stopped herself. Ross would call when he was ready.

Laura walked to the window and stared out at the ocean. Since Quinn's ascension to the bench, and her promotion to partner, Laura had increased her workload. Was she working hard to establish a reputation and to prove her worth to the firm, or was she hiding in her work? One thing was certain, she and Quinn were growing apart and she had to decide what she wanted to do about it. There were two choices: seal the rift or separate.

At ten-thirty, Laura dialed the number for SeaCliff Estates. The phone rang twice. Then a recording told her that the number she had dialed was not in service. Laura redialed, assuming that she had misdialed the first time. She heard the same message again. There was a phone book in her end table. Laura could not find a listing for SeaCliff Estates or Jerome Ross, so she rang the front desk.

"This is Laura Quinn in room 517. I have a reservation for five nights. I need to call the company that made it for me and I've misplaced the phone number. Did they give it to you when the reservation was made?"

"Let me check, Mrs. Quinn."

A moment later, the desk clerk read her the same number that was on the letterhead.

"You're certain that there aren't any other phone numbers for the company?" Laura asked.

"That's the only one."

"Thanks."

"Uh, Mrs. Quinn. Did you say that the reservation was for five nights?"

"Yes. I'm supposed to fly out Sunday."

"We only have you down for two nights. Yesterday and today."

"There must be some mistake."

"That's what I have here."

Laura thought for a moment. Then she asked, "Have I received any messages?"

"Your box is clear."

Laura hung up. She called Portland and asked for Mort Camden, another partner at Price, Winward. They talked for a few minutes, then Camden told her he would get back to her. Jerome Ross had still not contacted her when Camden called twenty minutes later.

"This is fucked, Laura. The retainer check is drawn on an account in a Miami bank that was opened a week ago, but there's only one hundred dollars in it."

"One hundred! The damn retainer is twenty thousand."

"I don't know what to say, but something stinks. I think you should hop on the first plane back to Portland."

"What do you think is going on, Mort?"

"Beats me. Maybe someone is playing a joke on you."

"It's one expensive joke. The first-class round-trip ticket and the hotel reservations cost several thousand dollars."

"I don't know what to say."

Laura threw her file on the floor. She was livid.

"I'm checking out. I'll see you tomorrow."

As soon as Camden hung up, Laura angrily jabbed out the number of the airline. The phone rang. She planned to ask for a seat on the next flight from Miami to Portland, but a thought occurred to her and she hung up the phone. She had hurt Quinn when she chose a business deal over a vacation with him. It was only Wednesday morning and St. Jerome was not far from Miami.

Laura's arm dropped to her side. Quinn had given her seven good years. The hurt in his voice when she told him that she could not go to St. Jerome was proof that he still cared for her very much. If she wanted her marriage to survive, she had to act. Laura dialed the airline and asked for a seat on the next flight to St. Jerome.

Fourteen

ANDREA WAS RIGHT about the difference between the resort side of St. Jerome and the other side of the island. The Bay Reef and The Palms were palaces where the wealthy, dressed in the latest fashions, dined on lobster and caviar, played golf and sunned themselves while sipping cool drinks by the pool. Puerta del Sol, the brightly colored capital city, was filled with fashionable shops and upscale restaurants. The buildings were freshly painted sunny yellow, happy blue and festive red, and the shop owners greeted everyone with a laugh and a smile. Poverty had been banished from the immaculate streets of the capital by order of Governor Alvarez. True, the taxis were dilapidated and there were some beggars who managed to evade the ever-present police patrols, but this was local color, the source of quaint Third World stories that could be told back home for the amusement of neighbors and friends.

The far side of St. Jerome was another story. The island's only paved highway was an oval that passed through Puerta del Sol, then swung around behind the hotels on the way to the airport before curving back to the resorts. Seven miles past the capital, a dirt track branched off toward the far side of the island. This road was the only open space in a jungle of towering trees whose branches interlocked to form a dense, dark green canopy that blocked out the sun and cast thick shadows over the narrow highway. The air was filled with the sweet smell of flowering plants and the wet, fetid smell of rotting vegetation. Quinn passed only a few people during the forty-minute, cross-island trip. More than once, he nervously checked his fuel gauge, having no desire to be stranded in the dense jungle.

At the suggestion of the concierge, Quinn rented a Land-Rover and soon discovered why the recommendation had been made. The road was not well maintained. Quinn felt his kidneys suffer each time the Rover hit a pothole, and the billowing dust clouds kicked up by the thick tires completely obscured the scene in the rearview mirror.

The jungle thinned, then disappeared when the road descended toward the ocean and into a civilization quite different from the one most St. Jerome tourists saw. Scattered along both sides of the road for half a mile were rusting shacks constructed from corrugated tin and a few more-substantial buildings made of concrete blocks. Some of the structures had colorful curtains strung across the doorway. None had glass windows, but some of the more solidly constructed buildings had louvered shutters. An emaciated goat was tethered to one shack and scrawny chickens wandered among many of the buildings pecking at the dusty ground.

A group of children was playing soccer with a tin can in a dirt field. They stopped when they heard the Rover and watched it drive by. An old man with nappy gray hair smiled and waved at Quinn and Quinn waved back. The old man's teeth were yellowed and decaying and there were gaping holes in his mouth where some teeth had rotted out. His T-shirt and shorts were in the same state of decay as his teeth. The clothing worn by the children who were playing soccer was also torn and tattered. All of the people he saw as he passed by the shacks were barefoot. A group of women in colorful skirts and blouses, their hair covered by multicolored scarves, walked along the road balancing tin basins filled with fruit on their heads. They also stopped to watch the Rover pass. Except for the old man with the rotting teeth, no one smiled.

Quinn drove through the village and around a curve that put it out of sight. The road straightened out. Quinn noted the location of the village on the map Andrea had drawn for him. According to her notes, four miles after the village a narrow dirt trail branched off toward the sea. Quinn looked up from the map and saw a jeep with two soldiers closing fast in his rearview mirror. The jeep pulled around Quinn to pass, then slowed when it was next to the Rover. The soldier in the passenger seat studied Quinn. His expression was hard and he cradled an automatic rifle. Quinn flashed a nervous smile at the soldier, but the soldier did not smile back. His cold appraisal was intimidating and Quinn looked away. After what Andrea had told him, Quinn was not certain that tourists were safe on St. Jerome. The land on either side of the road was flat and sandy and totally deserted. If something happened to him here, there would be no witnesses.

The jeep drove parallel to the Rover for a few seconds more, then cut in front of it and sped up. Quinn did not relax completely until the jeep was out of sight.

The dirt trail to the cove was right where Andrea's map said it would be. The sandy track was flat for a short distance. Then the Rover climbed upward to the crest of a hill and the road ended. Quinn stopped the car and got out. He was on the edge of a high cliff. Below him was the sea, which the cliff surrounded on three sides. An overhang blocked Quinn's view of the beach except for a strip that was adjacent to the ocean. Quinn looked for Andrea's car but did not see any other vehicles. He checked his watch. It was only a few minutes after four.

Quinn grabbed a towel and locked the Rover. A moment later, he found a narrow pebble-strewn path that wound downward along the cliff side. A stiff breeze messed with his hair. He was wearing a pair of baggy, khaki Bermuda shorts over a blue boxer swimsuit and a T-shirt with a colorful map of the world on the back. His sandals had smooth soles and twice he slipped sideways on small rocks.

When he was halfway down the trail, Quinn spotted Andrea lying on a large blanket. Beside her was a towel, some clothes, a large wicker picnic basket and snorkeling equipment. During the plane trip, Andrea had looked tired and bedraggled and her clothes had concealed her figure. Today she was wearing dark glasses and a bikini that was no more than three minute patches of yellow fabric. Her trim figure impressed Quinn. Andrea's legs were smooth and faintly muscled and her waist was narrow. He could see her ribs just below the bra of the bikini, then a flat stomach. Andrea's only imperfection was a pale, half-moon-shaped scar that stood out on her hip just below the string that secured the right side of her bikini bottom. The sight of Andrea's near-naked body aroused Quinn. Before he had time to think about his feelings, Andrea sat up and waved. Quinn waved back, then walked down the trail slowly to give his erection time to subside.

"You found me," Andrea said with a smile.

"Your directions were excellent and you're right about this place. It's beautiful."

"Wait until you see the reef."

Quinn lowered himself onto the blanket and eyed the snorkeling equipment nervously.

"I'm not a very good swimmer. Are you certain I can do this?"

"If you can swim at all, you can snorkel. All you really do is paddle around with your face in the water. It's a piece of cake. You'll see. I won't let you drown."

Andrea stood up. Quinn could not help noticing the way her breasts moved under the thin fabric of her bikini top. For a second, he fantasized Andrea naked, lying next to him on the blanket in the hot sun.

"I'm going to cool off. Come on."

Andrea reached out for Quinn and he took her hand. Her palm felt warm and smooth and she held on for a second before pulling him toward her. Quinn lurched to his feet and stumbled forward. Their bodies touched. Andrea laughed. Quinn was aroused again. The sensation was exciting but disturbing. He was certain that nothing would happen between them, but a part of him wished it would.

Quinn tossed his T-shirt and shorts on the blanket. Andrea jogged toward the water. Quinn followed, entranced by Andrea's muscular thighs and the way the movement of her buttocks made the fabric of her bikini bottom undulate. Quinn wondered what Andrea would be like in bed. She seemed so carefree and he imagined that her lovemaking would be loose and spontaneous. He remembered how quick and unsatisfying sex with Laura had become. Instantly, a wave of guilt washed over him.

Andrea ran into the surf, slowing as the water got higher and diving in when the ocean was at her waist. When she surfaced, her long black hair was wet and it gleamed in the strong sunlight.

"Come on in."

Quinn walked into the water. From his experiences in Oregon, he expected the ocean to be freezing, but when the water touched his skin, it felt like a cool shower on a warm summer day. At first, the water was shallow and the sand was smooth. Then fields of dark green seaweed grabbed at his ankles, snarled between his toes and obscured the bottom. Without warning, the seafloor dropped abruptly and Quinn stumbled into water that reached his waist. He bucked a small wave and nearly lost his balance. When he recovered his footing, he squatted and let the waves wash over him. Quinn was still not used to the torrid heat, and the cool water felt great. He closed his eyes, stretched out flat in the water and windmilled his arms, swimming gracelessly for a short distance. When he was winded, Quinn rolled onto his back. Unlike pool water, the salt water supported Quinn and he relaxed a little.

Andrea was a polished swimmer and she swam over to him with a natural stroke.

"Feels good, doesn't it?"

"It feels great. The sun is really hot."

Andrea rolled onto her back and closed her eyes.

"This is the most wonderful place in the world, don't you think?"

The water slipped under Andrea's bikini top and the fabric rose and fell with the motion of the sea. Andrea drifted next to Quinn and he watched as the water washed across her breasts when the fabric shifted. Andrea opened her eyes and caught Quinn staring. He blushed and she smiled. Their eyes met and Andrea rolled against Quinn. Her arms snaked around his neck. Quinn froze. He knew what was happening and he knew he should stop it, but he couldn't. He did not want to.

Andrea's lips were cold and tasted salty. Her kiss was gentle. She teased him with her lips and he responded. The kiss was long and deep. Quinn closed his eyes and savored it. When her breast brushed his chest, Quinn cupped it. Andrea let Quinn caress her breast for a moment, then broke away, laughing. Quinn was confused. Andrea's fingers brushed his cheek, a feather touch. Quinn felt desire and guilt simultaneously.

"The sun will start to go down soon," Andrea said. "If you want to snorkel, we better do it now."

Quinn's mouth was dry from sexual excitement. He nodded instead of speaking, grateful for the chance to sort out what had just happened and to think about what he wanted to happen later when the sun was down and they left the water for the blanket Andrea had so carefully spread out on the sand.

Andrea swam in easily. Quinn followed her using an ungainly crawl. He was a slow swimmer and he used his time in the water to calm himself. Andrea's kiss had shaken Quinn and made him want more. He and Andrea lived on opposite coasts. They would probably never see each other again after St. Jerome. If he slept with Andrea, Laura might never know. But Quinn would know and he had no idea how that would affect his marriage.

Andrea was gathering up a set of fins, a mask and a snorkel when Quinn swam ashore. She held up the mask. "This is the key to snorkeling," she instructed. Quinn was still in a state of sexual confusion, but Andrea's tone gave no hint that anything had happened between them. "Without this, you'd be blind underwater. With it, you can see clearly."

Quinn concentrated on what Andrea was saying to distract himself.

She held up the snorkel. "This is basically a tube with a U-bend at one end that's fitted with a mouthpiece. With the snorkel, you can breathe while you're swimming facedown on the surface of the water without raising your head."

Andrea sat on the sand and slipped on her fins. Quinn copied her. He tried to stand up but he had trouble. When he was on his feet he took a few tentative steps and almost fell.

"God," he laughed self-consciously, "I feel like I'm a clown in the circus."

"You're doing fine." Andrea handed Quinn his mask and snorkel. "Let's wade out a ways."

Quinn struggled through the surf. He noticed that Andrea was holding her mask and snorkel out of the water and he did the same. When they were in waist-deep, Andrea said, "Spit on the glass on the inside of your mask like this and rub the spittle all over it, then rinse it off. This will stop the glass from misting when you're underwater."

Quinn did as he was told. Andrea put on the mask and slid the snorkel under the thick black rubber strap that secured the mask to her head.

"Breathe through the mouthpiece," Andrea said, "then bend forward and stick your face in the water. Just stand there. I want you to get used to breathing through the snorkel. I'll hold onto you so you can concentrate on what you're doing."

Quinn bent forward hesitantly until the mask was submerged.

Andrea's hands were firm and her touch aroused him again, so he tried to concentrate on her instructions. He put his face in the water and tried to breathe through the mouthpiece, immediately sucking in a mouth full of seawater. The salty taste panicked him and he stood up, spitting. Andrea showed him the correct way to breathe so he would not get water in his mouth. Quinn got it right after a few tries.

The first thing that amazed Quinn was the clarity with which he could see the underwater world beneath him. A small crab scuttled across a rock on the sandy sea bottom. Then a bright blue and indigo fish that shot into and out of his vision startled Quinn. He jerked up and spit out his mouthpiece.

"Did you see that?" he asked excitedly. "This fish . . . it was incredible . . ."

Andrea laughed. "You ain't seen nothing yet. Wait till we get to the reef."

Andrea spent a little longer in the shallow area close to the beach getting Quinn used to swimming with the snorkel. The memory of the solitary blue and indigo fish spurred Quinn to learn quickly. Finally, Andrea motioned Quinn to head for the reef.

"You think I'm ready?" he asked anxiously.

"No question. Let's do it."

Quinn was nervous about leaving the area near the beach, but he was soon swimming slowly but steadily into deep water. The most frightening thing was how far away the bottom seemed and the fact that it kept receding, but the sheer beauty of the world below kept him from turning back. He was soon looking down on chasms of coral divided by rivers of white sand on which the wave action had inscribed ripple patterns. The coral was shaped like knobs, spines, fingers and fans. Andrea pointed out several round gray boulders covered by a maze of ridges and grooves that looked remarkably like a human brain. Quinn crossed over a coral cliff from which strands of seaweed waved. Attached to the cliff were clusters of brown coral shaped like the antlers of a great stag and reddish brown spines that jutted high up in the water like the fingers of a drowning man.

Quinn noticed two small plastic bags filled with bread crumbs tied to Andrea's bikini bottom. He watched as she opened the tie that secured one of the bags and took out some bread. Andrea motioned to Quinn to look down. He could see a large section of whitish brown coral directly below him, but no sign of life. Andrea let the bread fall. The crumbs floated downward undisturbed until they were almost touching the coral. Suddenly, the sea was filled with multicolored fish. Flashes of bright yellow, garish red, electric blue and neon green swooped below him. Andrea handed Quinn the other bag. He opened it quickly, anxious to keep the sea filled with tropical fish.

Quinn shredded a piece of bread and dropped some of it into the water. A bright yellow goatfish darted out of a hole in the coral and nipped at a bread crumb, while a butterfly fish with a fat white body and broad black stripes attacked another piece.

Quinn was so absorbed by the swirl of colors that he forgot about Andrea. When he remembered, he looked along the surface for her. She wasn't there. Quinn treaded water to keep himself upright and spun in a circle. The endless ocean and limitless sky gave way to the shoreline, the beach and the high cliff walls, then the ocean and sky returned. Quinn grew anxious. Andrea had been beside him a moment ago. He started to spin again when Andrea erupted from the ocean a few feet from his face. Quinn started to laugh, then Andrea screamed. Quinn froze. Something jerked Andrea underwater and Quinn dove after her without thinking. Through the glass plate in his facemask he saw Andrea clawing at the arms of a diver in scuba gear, her legs and arms flailing helplessly.

Quinn grabbed the arm that was wrapped around Andrea's throat and tried to pry it from her neck. Andrea's eyes were wide with fear behind her mask. Quinn used all his strength and the diver's arm loosened. Then Quinn's snorkel filled with salt water. Quinn gagged, panicked and bolted straight up. When he cleared the surface, Quinn spit out his mouthpiece, gulped in air and dove again. Andrea and the diver were fading away. She was no longer struggling and she looked like a rag doll in the diver's grip. Quinn took a few desperate strokes in Andrea's direction even though he knew that he could not save her. He came up for air and dropped under the water once more, but Andrea and the diver had disappeared.

Quinn surfaced and scanned the horizon. The sun was setting, the air was suddenly cold and uninviting and the stunningly beautiful ocean floor had been transformed into a frightening abyss. Andrea had been snatched away and he could be next. Terror propelled Quinn toward the beach. Each time he kicked, he expected to feel a hand clamp onto his ankle. He wanted to look down so he could see if he was in danger, but he was afraid to stop.

The shore seemed miles away and Quinn's lungs burned. Though he swam with all his might, the beach never seemed closer. He struggled forward, but his arms felt heavy and he could barely kick his legs. He wanted to rest, but terror drove him on. Just when he thought his arms and lungs would give out, a wave carried him into shallow water and he waded ashore.

The panic-driven swim had exhausted Quinn. He threw himself onto the beach and gasped for air. When he had recovered a little of his strength, Quinn struggled to his knees and threw up. Then he collapsed on the sand and experienced a momentary rush of joy because he was alive. That feeling was rapidly replaced by fear for his own safety and guilt over his failure to save Andrea.

Quinn scanned the beach and the ocean for any sign of Andrea or the diver, but he was completely alone. He threw on his clothes and collected everything else that he had brought to the cove. The sun was starting to set. Quinn hurried up the trail. The Land-Rover was the only vehicle in sight. If Andrea had not driven to the cove, Freddy's villa had to be nearby. There would be a phone he could use to call the police.

Andrea had told Quinn that the villa overlooked the ocean. He had not noticed any turnoffs between the village and the cove, so he headed away from the village. He assumed that Andrea had not walked far in the heat. After driving two miles without spotting a side road, Quinn began to wonder if Andrea had been dropped off at the cove and was counting on him to drive her back to the villa.

Another roadside collection of shacks appeared a short distance ahead. Quinn slowed, looking for someone he could ask for directions to the villa. Halfway through the makeshift town, Quinn saw a concrete-block building slightly larger than the rest. A sign dangled from a roof that overhung a small porch. Quinn guessed that the building housed a shop. He started to slow down when he spotted a metal cooler advertising Coca-Cola at the far end of the porch. The soldiers in the jeep were sitting next to it, drinking sodas. As the Rover neared the shop, they stopped sipping their drinks and watched it.

It occurred to Quinn that he knew very little about Andrea and that the subject of drugs had come up several times since they had met. There was the drug dealer who owned the villa where she was staying and the cocaine she had found there. Andrea was also knowledgeable about Governor Alvarez's drug connections. If Andrea's murder was drug related, the authorities could be involved.

Even if Andrea's death had no connection to drugs, it might not be smart to tell the soldiers about the murder. Would they believe Quinn if he said that a diver appeared out of nowhere and spirited Andrea away? The story sounded fantastic even to Quinn, and he had witnessed the murder. It was possible that the soldiers would conclude that Quinn and Andrea were lovers who fought and that Quinn, afraid that Andrea would ruin his marriage and career, had drowned her.

Quinn made a quick decision. He would drive back to the Bay Reef Resort and explain what happened to the manager or one of the organizers of the convention. There might even be an attorney from St. Jerome at the conference with whom he could consult.

Quinn made a U-turn and hoped that the soldiers did not follow him.

When Quinn arrived at the Bay Reef the sun had almost set and he was in the grip of a mind-numbing depression. Quinn dropped off the rental car with the valet and entered the lobby. Heat and fear had caused him to sweat through his T-shirt. As he walked across the terrazzo floor, he imagined that everyone was staring at him. Quinn jumped when someone touched his elbow.

"Judge Quinn?" asked a heavyset man wearing wire-rimmed glasses and a Hawaiian shirt. Quinn's vision blurred from fatigue. He could not place the man, but he faked a smile.

"Cliff Engel. We met at the ABA convention in Chicago."

"Oh, right," Quinn answered, vaguely remembering Engel as someone he'd had lunch with after a committee meeting.

"Been down by the beach?" Engel asked after spotting the top of Quinn's swimming trunks poking out above the waist of his shorts.

"Yes. I'm pretty wiped out," Quinn added hastily. "This sun takes it out of you. I thought I'd take a nap."

"Oh, too bad. I was hoping you'd join Nancy and me for a drink and dinner. We're with the Lyles. You met Gary at the ABA. He's one of my partners."

"Sorry," Quinn said, forcing his smile to widen, "but I'm all in. I'll see you tomorrow, though."

"Sure thing. I can't wait to hear your talk. Maybe we can have that drink after you speak."

"Sounds good."

Engel pumped Quinn's hand and strode off toward the bar. Quinn sagged. When Engel had touched him, Quinn was certain it was a policeman making an arrest. His heart was still beating hard.

Quinn crowded into an elevator with two couples who were speaking French, and stood at the back of the car. He could not wait to get to his room. He planned to take a cold shower and clear his head, then figure out his next step.

Quinn opened the door to his room and froze. Laura was sitting in a chair, looking cool and beautiful in a T-shirt and shorts.

"What . . . what are you doing here?"

Laura laughed. "You should see your face."

"I . . . I thought you were in Miami all week."

"Aren't you glad to see me?" she asked with a grin.

"Of course," Quinn lied.

Laura stood up and started across the room toward him. Under any other circumstances, Quinn would have been overjoyed to see Laura. Two days ago he had been crushed when she refused to fly with him to this island paradise. Now, the last thing he wanted was to find Laura in his hotel room, and the thought that she might want to make love terrified him.

Laura started to put her arms around Quinn, but he stopped her.

"You're all clean and I'm sweating like a pig," he said. "Give me a rain check on that kiss until I've showered."

Laura sniffed. "You are a little ripe."

Quinn faked a laugh and forced a smile. "So what happened in Miami?"

Laura followed Quinn into the bathroom and told him about her experience while he got ready to shower. He only half listened as Laura told him about Miami. What, he wondered, was he going to tell his wife about his day at the beach, if she asked?

"I was pissed, as you can imagine," Laura concluded. "Mort told me to fly home. I was going to, but I thought about you being alone on St. Jerome. I really did feel lousy about ruining your vacation. Fortunately, there was a seat on the early morning flight."

"Well, that's . . . that's great."

"What have you been doing all day?"

"I, uh, I rented a car and drove around the island."

"See anything interesting?"

"Not really. Everyone is pretty poor. Except for the capital, there's not much here. But the resort is great."

"How's the food, because I'm starved?"

"Good. Why don't you make a reservation for us at the Plantation Room while I shower? It's a four-star restaurant."

It was seven-thirty. Laura was able to get a reservation at eight. Quinn drew out his shower for as long as possible, using the time to decide how much he could tell Laura about the murder and Andrea. Quinn wanted to confess his infidelity and seek her counsel, but he also wanted to protect her from involvement in his nightmare, and he was terrified of her reaction to what had happened between him and Andrea.

By the time Quinn finished shaving, it was time to eat. Many of the attorneys who were enrolled in the seminar were eating in the Plantation Room and several of them recognized Quinn from American Bar Association functions. After dinner, Quinn and Laura found themselves barhopping in Puerta del Sol with Cliff Engel, Gary Lyle, their wives and two other couples. Quinn was glad to be hijacked. Laura and Cliff Engel got into a discussion about real estate transactions and Quinn was able to use the time to think about what he should do while the others became more rowdy from drink.

It was two in the morning when Quinn and Laura stumbled into their hotel room. Laura was mildly intoxicated. Quinn had hardly touched any of the drinks that had been thrust upon him. He was afraid of what he might say or do if he got drunk.

"Gary Lyle is a horse's ass," Laura said as she collapsed on the bed fully clothed, "but I like his friend Cliff."

"He seemed okay," Quinn answered as he shucked his jacket and sat down on the edge of the bed to take off his shoes.

Laura sat up and draped an arm across her husband's shoulders.

"You were quiet tonight."

"Was I? I'm just tired, I guess."

Laura leaned into Quinn. She slipped her hand inside his shirt and ran it slowly back and forth across his chest.

"Not too tired, I hope."

Before Quinn could answer, Laura's lips were melting onto his. Laura pressed Quinn onto his back and finished unbuttoning his shirt. Then she slid down the straps of her dress and shrugged it off. Quinn's throat was dry. It had been so long since Laura had initiated sex.

Laura slid out of her bra and panties. Her breasts were high and firm and her skin was the color of cream. She sank to her knees between Quinn's legs and unzipped his pants. He did not move as she slid them down his legs, then did the same with his underpants. He closed his eyes and began to swim in sensation. There was a feeling of silk on skin as Laura slid against him and up the length of his body. He could smell her hair. He could taste her lips and her tongue. Then he saw Andrea's face frozen in terror as she burst from the sea.

Quinn's eyes opened. He was sweating. He held Laura tightly. Laura could not hear Andrea's scream, but she must have heard the rapid beat of his heart, because she pulled back and looked at Quinn.

"What's wrong?"

Quinn did not answer. He sat up and put his feet on the floor. His breathing was ragged. Laura's eyes widened. She was afraid that Quinn was having a heart attack.

"Are you all right?"

Quinn needed to confess, to unburden himself. But how could he talk to Laura about the things that had happened in the cove? The bed moved as she slipped to the floor in front of Quinn and took his hands in hers. She looked so concerned. Quinn saw with crystal clarity that this was the pivotal moment in their marriage. Laura was his wife, but for months he had not been certain that she loved him. If she did, they would ride out this tragedy together. If she did not, his confession could sever the slender thread that bound them together.

Laura squeezed his hand. "Dick?"

Quinn could not keep his terror and despair inside any longer. He needed help and he prayed that Laura was the person to turn to for it.

"Something happened today," Quinn managed. "Something very bad. I . . . I was with a woman."

"What?"

"She was someone I met on the plane. She sat next to me on the flight from New York. Her name was Andrea Chapman. She's dead. She was murdered."

Laura stared at Quinn, too stunned to speak. Quinn focused on the floor as he told Laura about Andrea's invitation to spend the day at the Cove of Lost Souls. Then Quinn told Laura how Andrea died.

"One minute she was there, then she was gone. I thought she was playing a game until she screamed." Quinn shook his head to rid himself of the image. "I tried to save her. I dove down and grabbed the diver's arm, but I swallowed water and I had to come up for air. I was choking." Quinn paused. He was having trouble breathing, as if he were underwater again. "When I dove the second time, Andrea and the diver were almost out of sight. When I went under the third time, they were gone."

"Have you told the police?"

"No. I was afraid."

"Of what?"

"Andrea talked about drugs. She said the police are corrupt. That they work with drug dealers. The killing could be drug related. And . . ."

Quinn's voice trailed off. Laura studied him.

"Did anything happen between the two of you, Dick?"

Quinn did not answer. His head hung lower.

"Did you . . . were you . . . intimate?" Laura asked, using this bland term because it provided a barrier between her feelings and her fear.

"We didn't . . . It never got that far," Quinn answered, his voice barely above a whisper.

"How far did it get?"

Quinn tried to answer the question, but he could not. Laura stood up and walked away from the bed.

"I don't know what happened," Quinn told her without conviction. His eyes begged for forgiveness, but he did not see any give in Laura's rigid features.

"It was just a kiss. We . . . we only touched one time."

Quinn wanted to tell her that nothing would have happened, that he would have remained faithful, but the lie died unspoken.

Laura paced back and forth. Quinn felt smaller and smaller as each moment passed in silence. Laura sat in a chair near the window. She was thinking like an attorney so she would not have to think like a woman.

"How certain are you that you can't be connected to the murder?" Laura asked.

"I don't know. I don't think my fingerprints are on anything, but I can't be certain. Even if they are, the St. Jerome Police won't have the technology to match them unless I become a suspect."

"Were there any witnesses? Anyone who knows that you were with this woman?"

"I don't think so."

Quinn told Laura about the soldiers in the jeep and the people in the village.

"But they didn't see me with Andrea. I did sit next to her on the plane. Another passenger may have heard us make plans to meet, but I doubt it."

"How certain are you about the corruption on St. Jerome?"

"Andrea was pretty emphatic about it. I have heard other things. One of the organizers of the conference made some remarks while we were talking."

"Given what you know about the government of St. Jerome, I think going to the authorities would be a mistake, especially now that you've waited to come forward. That looks very suspicious.

If you went to the police, you wouldn't be able to tell them anything, anyway."

"You're right. I'm not even sure of the sex of the diver."

"If this came out, you being with this . . . this woman in the cove, the murder. If you became a suspect . . . The effect on your career would be devastating."

"Then, you think I should say nothing?"

"It's a gamble. There's no telling when the body will be discovered. With luck, you'll be back home and no one will connect you to the crime."

"Thank you, Laura."

"Don't thank me," Laura answered harshly. "I'm doing this for me as much as for you. Do you think I want to be involved in your sordid affair or with the police?"

Laura walked over to the desk and picked up the phone.

"What are you doing?"

"I'm going to get a seat on the next flight back to Portland."

"Don't leave me. Please. I need you."

"You should have thought about that when you cheated on me."

"Don't do this, Laura. I love you. We need to discuss this calmly."

"We do, but I am not calm now. I am very, very angry, and I need some time away from you to think about what I want to do. We can talk when you get back. Right now, I can't stand the sight of you."

Fifteen

QUINN'S PLANE landed in Portland at eight-thirty Friday evening. Laura knew his flight number and the time of arrival, but she was not waiting for him. Quinn found a taxi.

There were lights on in the house when the cab arrived at Hereford Farms. Quinn paid the driver and carried his suitcases to the front door. Laura opened it before he could ring the bell. She was wearing dark jeans and a black turtleneck. Her hair was combed, but she wore no makeup. There were circles under Laura's eyes and her complexion was paler than usual. He forced a smile, but Laura did not return it.

"We have to talk," Laura said without any preliminaries.

Quinn left his bags in the hall and followed Laura into the living room. She sat in an armchair and Quinn took the couch.

"You don't know what you've done to me," she said.

"Laura, I . . ."

"No. Let me say this." She looked down. Her hands were clasped so tightly in her lap that her knuckles were white where the blood was cut off. "I trusted you completely. You have no idea how hard that is for me. I know we've had trouble. I know I'm not the easiest person to live with. But I was certain that I could trust you."

Laura's eyes began to tear and she swiped at the drops angrily. Quinn was shocked. Laura never cried. The sight of his wife in tears made Quinn sick. "You don't know how difficult it was for me to fall in love with you. I swore that I would never give myself to a man the way my mother did."

Laura shook her head, too choked with anger to go on. Quinn watched helplessly, knowing that there was nothing he could say.

"I don't want to live with you."

"You want a divorce?" Quinn asked incredulously.

"I haven't thought that far. What I do want is to be alone for a while."

"Can't you forgive me? Don't you see how sorry I am? I love you, Laura."

"I don't know that. Right now, I don't want to be around you. I've made up the bed in the guest room. You can stay here until you've found somewhere else to live."

Quinn was desperate.

"Don't do this. Don't destroy our marriage."

Laura's head snapped up.

"Don't you dare put this off on me. No one made you go with that woman."

Quinn could see that Laura was so angry that nothing he said would change her mind.

"I'll get an apartment for a while," he said softly. "Whatever you want, as long as you promise me you'll think about what we have. No matter what I've done, I still love you and I don't want our marriage to end."

Part Three

Hell Week

Sixteen

I T WAS ALMOST THREE when Quinn signed in with the guard at the front desk of the Multnomah County Courthouse on the Sunday afternoon following his return from St. Jerome, then took the elevator to his chambers on the fifth floor. He was depressed and a little hung over, having had way too much to drink the night before. Quinn rarely drank excessively, but Laura would not take his calls and his small apartment with its ugly rented furniture had gotten him down.

Quinn hung up his raincoat and put on a pot of coffee. He was in for a solid afternoon of legal research and he hoped the caffeine would clear the cobwebs from his brain. The pretrial hearing in *State v. Crease* was set to start Monday afternoon. The defense had filed several motions. Quinn's ruling on three of them would have a significant impact on the trial. Mary Garrett was asking Quinn to suppress all of the evidence found during the search of the crime scene that had been made a week after the shootings. Ellen Crease's defense attorney was also asking Quinn to suppress certain statements as hearsay.

The State had filed only one motion of importance. Mary Garrett wanted to introduce evidence concerning Martin Jablonski's prior crimes. Cedric Riker opposed the introduction of this evidence.

Quinn organized the materials relating to each motion into a separate pile while he waited for the coffee to perk. When the coffee was ready, Quinn filled a mug and started reading the memos relating to the motion to suppress the evidence found at the crime scene. Three hours later, he was slogging through the police reports detailing Martin Jablonski's criminal history so he would have a better idea of how to handle the district attorney's motion. He finished deciphering Portland Police Officer J. Brademas's handwritten account of a six-year-old, extremely violent, home burglary and was about to start Officer K. Raptis's report of an older liquor store holdup when he heard the phone ringing in the outer office and saw one of his lines flashing.

"Hello."

"Is this Richard Quinn?"

"Yes."

"My name is Kyle Fletcher. I'm a detective in Missing Persons." Quinn straightened up, suddenly alert. "I'm looking into the disappearance of a woman named Andrea Chapman. Does that name ring a bell?"

Quinn's heart rate accelerated.

"Judge Quinn, you there?"

"Uh, yes. I was just thinking," Quinn said to stall for time while he tried to figure out why a policeman was calling him about Andrea.

"This woman disappeared last week while she was vacationing on the Caribbean island of St. Jerome. You were there the same time she was."

"That's right. I was speaking at a legal seminar."

Quinn wanted to forget about St. Jerome. His failure to tell the police about Andrea's murder haunted him. Detective Fletcher's call gave Quinn a chance to tell someone about the terrible thing that had happened in the cove.

"I believe Miss Chapman sat next to you on the flight from New York to the island. I got your name from the manifest." Quinn heard a deep sigh. "I'm stuck here calling everyone in first class. Then it's on to economy. If you could tell me what you remember about her, it would be a help."

Quinn wanted to tell the truth, but he was afraid. So much time had passed. If he confessed to witnessing the murder now, he had no idea of the consequences.

"Okay. Now I know whom you're talking about. I didn't remember her name. The woman who sat next to me on the flight from New York to St. Jerome designed belts. She was wearing a very attractive belt that she'd designed for some collection."

"That's her. What did you two talk about?"

"Not a lot. The type of things you discuss with a seat companion on a flight. I was reading a book for part of the time."

"Just what you remember."

"I believe she mentioned that she was flying back from a show for leather suppliers in Bologna, Italy. We talked about her job. That's about all I remember, except that she didn't like flying, but she had to because of her work."

"Did she tell you her plans on St. Jerome?"

Quinn was sweating. This was his last chance to tell Fletcher what had happened, but he could not do it.

"She was going to stay at a friend's villa," Quinn said. "I don't remember his name."

"That fits in with what I have so far. Did she mention someone she was going to meet or someone she knew on the island?"

Quinn felt sick and he hoped that his voice did not betray him.

"I don't remember her saying she was going to meet anyone. I got the impression that she just wanted to relax."

"Is there anything else you can recall?"

"No. I think that's it."

"Say, did you see her after the flight? On the island?"

Quinn froze. "What was that?" he asked to cover his hesitation. "You faded out there for a moment."

"Sorry. Must be my line here. I asked if you saw Miss Chapman after you landed. Maybe at your hotel?"

"No. Not after the airport."

"Okay. Well, thanks."

Quinn knew that he should hang up, but he could not help asking, "Uh, what happened? I mean, what do you think happened? She seemed like a nice person."

"What we know for sure is that the day after she landed she went to the beach late in the afternoon. We think she might have planned to meet someone, because she took two sets of snorkeling gear. However, the local police questioned the servants and she never said anything to them about meeting anyone.

"The St. Jerome Police tell me that there are lots of safe beaches on the island. Then you get some with real strong currents. A person could be swept out to sea. They get a tourist drowning every couple of years. There's warnings posted, but people don't listen. The locals think that's what happened."

"And you? Is that what you think?"

"No reason to think otherwise. Except, of course, there's the extra snorkeling gear. The cops did find her blanket and stuff along with one set of equipment, not two. And the cove where they found this stuff, it's supposed to be safe. Then, again, there have been several reported disappearances in it over the years. So who knows? Anyway, thanks for your time, Judge. I'll let you get back to your work."

Quinn hung up. His hands were sweaty and he was breathing hard. He had just lied to a police detective. If he was ever linked to Andrea . . . But he wouldn't be. If they knew that he was the person that Andrea was meeting, the detective would have questioned him further. Or would he? What if they did know and the conversation was a trap? The conversation could have been taped. He was getting a headache. Quinn stroked his temples. He should have told the detective what he knew, but anything he said would incriminate him. He could not call back, anyway, he suddenly realized. The detective had not left his phone number or the city he was calling from.

The call from the detective had drained Quinn of energy. He went into the bathroom in his chambers and took two aspirin. While he was washing them down, he saw his reflection in the mirror. He looked pale and shaken. Since his return from the island, the murder had taken on a dreamlike quality. Andrea still haunted his dreams, but her features were blurring and there were times when Quinn did not think about St. Jerome at all. The detective's call had made Quinn relive the horror in the cove and the cowardly way that he had dealt with it.

Seventeen

THE ATTORNEYS were raring to go when Quinn took the bench Monday afternoon to hear the motions in *State v. Crease*. Cedric Riker looked bright-eyed and dressed for success. He was always most excited when the gallery was full and the press was in attendance. Mary Garrett looked intense. She was wearing a gray pinstriped suit that was all business.

It was Ellen Crease that Quinn studied most intently. Her black dress reflected a somber mood, but she seemed unafraid. Crease did not slump in her seat or look down as Frederick Gideon had. From the moment Quinn took the bench she sat square-shouldered and straight-backed, coolly confident and self-assured.

Quinn let his eyes rest on Crease for a moment too long. She sensed the judge's interest and turned her head toward him. Quinn colored and looked down at a pleading on the dais. He recovered his composure just as Lamar Hoyt, Jr., entered the courtroom. Quinn saw Junior smirk at Crease, who flushed with anger, held his stare long enough to let him know that she was not intimidated, then turned her attention to the proceedings. Just before she did, Quinn noticed Ryan Clark sitting in the back of the courtroom. Quinn had met Benjamin Gage's administrative assistant at a Republican fund-raiser. Quinn was not surprised to see Clark, given Gage's interest in the outcome of Crease's case.

"Good morning, Counsel, Senator," Quinn said. "For the record, this is the time set to discuss the motions filed by the parties in this case. Am I correct that only the motion to suppress the evidence found in Senator Crease's bedroom will require me to hear witnesses and that I'll be deciding Ms. Garrett's hearsay objections to the testimony of Karen Fargo and Conchita Jablonski after reading the briefs and affidavits you have submitted?"

"That's correct, Your Honor," Mary Garrett said. Riker nodded his agreement.

"Why don't you state your positions? Then we'll hear the witnesses in the motion to suppress."

Riker sat down and pulled a legal pad in front of him.

"We are asking the Court to suppress all of the evidence obtained as a result of the warrantless search of my client's bedroom by Detective Anthony and Gary Yoshida of the crime lab after the crime scene was released back to my client," Garrett told Quinn.

"I want to be clear on this," Quinn interrupted. "As I understand it, you have no objection to the introduction of any evidence found in the bedroom on the evening of the murder?"

"That's correct," Garrett responded. "The police were legally on the premises at that time. The bedroom was a crime scene, there were two dead bodies present. The situation changed when the bedroom was released back to Senator Crease. After that point, it became incumbent on the authorities to obtain a warrant to search the bedroom."

"I'm with you. Now, why don't you think the search was legal?"

"The obvious reason is that the search was conducted without a warrant when the police had adequate time to obtain one. Our second point is that James Allen, the houseman, was coerced into opening the locked bedroom for the police. Finally, even if he was not coerced, Mr. Allen had no authority to let the police into his employer's locked bedroom."

"Thank you, Ms. Garrett," Quinn said as he made some notes. "Mr. Riker?"

Riker stood slowly, then paused for effect before shaking his head.

"Your Honor, this whole motion is a ridiculous waste of time. There is a well-recognized exception to the warrant requirement that permits the police to search without a warrant if emergency conditions make an immediate warrantless search necessary to prevent the destruction of evidence. If Detective Anthony and Officer Yoshida had waited to search the bedroom, the most important evidence in this case would have been destroyed.

"Even if exigent circumstances did not exist, the entry into the bedroom was perfectly legal. The defendant was in eastern Oregon campaigning. In her absence, Mr. Allen was in charge of the house. He had authority to let people into the bedroom and he let Detective Anthony and Officer Yoshida into the bedroom willingly. The courts have long recognized that third parties may give binding consent to officials to search the premises of a defendant and seize evidence found inside the premises. This is an exception to the requirement that the police obtain a warrant before searching and to the requirement that the person searching have probable cause to believe there is evidence of a crime in the place searched."

"As I understand it," Quinn said, "it's the position of the defense that the person who gave consent did not have the actual authority to give it."

"We disagree with that assertion, but it would make no difference if the defense was correct, Your Honor. Even if Mr. Allen did not have actual authority to let the officers into the bedroom, he appeared to have that authority. As the Court knows, if a police officer has a reasonable belief that a person has authority to consent to a search, a warrantless search will be legal, even if it turns out that the officer was mistaken."

"Okay. Why don't you call your first witness, Ms. Garrett?"

"Senator Crease calls James Allen, Your Honor."

James Allen took the oath and sat in the witness box. He looked uneasy.

"Mr. Allen, how are you employed?"

"I work . . . worked for Mr. Lamar Hoyt as his houseman until his death. I am now employed in that same capacity for your client, Ms. Crease."

"Do you remember the time, several days after Mr. Hoyt was murdered, when Detective Anthony and an Officer Yoshida came to the estate and told you that they wanted to reenter the master bedroom?"

"Yes, ma'am."

"Did either gentleman show you a search warrant?"

"No."

"What reason did they give you for wishing to look at the room?"

"Detective Anthony told me that there were loose ends in the investigation that needed to be tied up and that they had to look at the bedroom again to do that. He was never very specific."

"Where was Senator Crease on that day?"

"She was campaigning in eastern Oregon."

"What did you tell Detective Anthony when he asked to look in the bedroom?"

"I told him that Ms. Crease had given me strict orders to let no one into the bedroom except the cleaning people, who were coming the next day."

"What happened when you told Detective Anthony that you had strict orders not to let anyone but the cleaners into the bedroom?"

"He said that Ms. Crease couldn't have meant to keep out the police. He said she probably just wanted to keep reporters out."

"What happened next?"

"I told the detective that he was probably right, but I didn't feel that I could let him in without speaking to Ms. Crease, so I tried to get in touch with her at her hotel in Pendleton. Unfortunately, she was not in."

"What happened after you told the detective that you couldn't reach Senator Crease?"

Allen looked nervous. He licked his lips. "Uh, well, at that point, Detective Anthony became quite agitated. He reminded me that he was investigating Mr. Hoyt's murder and said that any evidence in the room would be destroyed by the cleaners if I waited to talk to Ms. Crease before letting them into the room."

"You said that Detective Anthony grew agitated when you refused to let him into the bedroom. Please describe his demeanor."

"His tone grew sharp and he leaned very close to me. He was quite insistent."

"What did you do after his demeanor changed?"

"I . . . I didn't want to impede the investigation, so I gave Detective Anthony the key to the bedroom."

"Thank you, Mr. Allen. Your witness, Counselor."

Riker stood up and walked over to James Allen.

"Good morning, Mr. Allen," he said in a tone that lacked sincerity. Allen nodded.

"It's in your best interest to say things that help the defendant, isn't it?"

"Pardon me, sir?" Allen asked, clearly offended by the question.

"The defendant pays your salary. You're dependent on her for your living, for the roof over your head?"

"I have testified to the truth, Mr. Riker," Allen answered with great dignity.

"Certainly. But what I've said is true, is it not?"

Allen started to say something, then thought better of it and ended by answering, "Yes," tersely.

Riker opened a thick folder and reviewed some papers. He selected one of them and looked up at the witness.

"Mr. Allen, have you ever been convicted of a crime?"

Allen paled and answered, "Yes," in a shaky voice.

"What crime was that?"

"Man . . . manslaughter."

"You stabbed a man to death in a bar fight, did you not?"

Allen looked like he was going to be sick.

"Please instruct Mr. Allen to answer, Your Honor," Riker asked the Court.

"Please answer the question," Quinn instructed the witness.

"That is true," Allen answered.

"Did you know about this?" Garrett whispered to Crease.

"Yes, but I forgot. It's ancient history. James is gay. When he was eighteen, two men attacked him. They were gay bashing. James had a knife and he fought them off. Lamar said that it would have been self-defense, but James ran the men down after they quit the fight and killed one of them. He gave James a break when he got out of prison and hired him. He hasn't been in trouble since."

"You're the housekeeper at the Hoyt estate, right?" Riker asked Allen.

"Yes."

"When Mr. Hoyt and the defendant were away, you were in charge of the house, weren't you?"

"Yes."

"That's why you had the keys to all the rooms, including the bedroom?"

"Yes."

"And you could go into any room in the house to clean or to get something, right?"

"Yes."

"In fact, it was part of your duties to let people, like the cleaners, into various rooms in the house, including the bedroom, when Mr. Hoyt and the defendant were away?"

"Yes."

"Mr. Allen, did you like Mr. Hoyt?"

"Yes, sir."

"You'd worked for him for more than twenty years?"

"Yes."

"And you wanted his killer brought to justice?"

"Yes."

"How did you feel when Detective Anthony told you that keeping him and Officer Yoshida out of the bedroom might lead to the destruction of evidence that could prove who killed Mr. Hoyt?"

"I . . . Well, I didn't want to be responsible for something like that."

"So you wanted the officers to enter that bedroom, didn't you?"

"I . . . I guess . . . Yes. I wanted to help."

"Thank you, Mr. Allen," Riker said before turning away from the witness and returning to his seat. Quinn noted Riker's satisfied smile and the brief look of concern on Garrett's face.

"If I might, Your Honor," Garrett said.

"Certainly."

"Mr. Allen, your instructions from Senator Crease were quite explicit, were they not? Didn't she tell you to keep the bedroom locked and let no one but the cleaners into it?"

"Those were my instructions."

"She did not tell you to make an exception for the police, did she?"

"No."

"You made it clear to the officers what your instructions were?"

"Yes."

"And when you refused Detective Anthony admission, that is when he became agitated, sharp with you and demanding?"

"Yes."

"Did his tone have anything to do with your decision to give him the bedroom key?"

"Well, he was a policeman and he seemed very upset with me. I didn't feel that I could refuse him."

"Nothing further."

Riker was already on his feet. "Mr. Allen, did the defendant give you specific instructions to keep the police out of the bed-room."

"No."

"So you never discussed with the defendant what you should do if a policeman came to the house and needed access to the bedroom so he could try to secure evidence that would help find Lamar Hoyt's murderer?"

"No."

"Before you gave Detective Anthony the key, did you try to figure out what the defendant would have told you if you had been successful in talking to her in Pendleton?"

"I . . . Yes, I did."

"Was it your impression that the defendant wanted her hus-band's killer found?"

"Most assuredly."

"So you concluded that she would never want to impede the investigation, didn't you? That she would have gladly allowed the police access to that bedroom if it would help find her husband's killer?"

Allen looked down and answered, "Yes," in a tone so low that Quinn had trouble hearing him.

"And that was why you gave Detective Anthony the key, wasn't it? Not because he grew sharp with you, but because you realized that his agitation stemmed from his desire to solve the murder of your employer of twenty years? Isn't that so?"

"I . . . I guess . . . Yes, that had a lot to do with it."

"Thank you, Mr. Allen," Riker said with a self-satisfied smile.

Quinn asked Mary Garrett if she had any other questions for the witness. Garrett thought about trying to rehabilitate Allen, but she realized that the damage had already been done. She dis-missed the witness. Allen took a seat in the back of the court-room. He looked very upset.

"How bad were we hurt?" Crease asked in a whisper.

"Riker did a good job. We can argue that Allen was bullied into consenting to the search, but Riker can argue that he was only doing what he thought was best and that he had concluded that you would have consented, too."

"Would it do any good to call me as a witness?" Crease asked. "I definitely told Jim to keep the bedroom locked, except to let in the cleaners."

"Riker would ask you if you intended to keep out police officials who were trying to solve the murder of your husband," Garrett answered. "We both know how you would answer that question."

"Any more witnesses, Ms. Garrett?" Quinn asked.

"No, Your Honor."

"Then let's hear from your people, Mr. Riker."

"The State calls Lou Anthony, Your Honor."

The bailiff went into the hall and returned with the detective. The bailiff gave Anthony the oath, then motioned him toward the witness box. Quinn thought that the detective seemed very uncomfortable and the judge noticed that the witness avoided looking at Ellen Crease.

"Detective Anthony, are you the detective in charge of the investigation into the death of Lamar Hoyt?" Riker asked after establishing Anthony's background in police work.

"Yes, sir."

"Were you at the crime scene on the evening of January seventh?"

"Yes, sir."

"Did you interview the defendant and speak to the medical examiner, forensic experts and other investigators?"

"Yes, sir."

"What conclusion did you come to about the defendant's responsibility for the death of her husband and Martin Jablonski on the evening of the shooting?"

"On the evening of January seventh, I concluded that a burglar, who we later learned was an ex-convict named Martin Jablonski, had broken into the home of Mr. Hoyt and the defendant to commit a burglary and had shot Mr. Hoyt during its commission.

I also concluded that the defendant shot and killed Mr. Jablonski to protect herself."

"Did you believe that Mr. Jablonski was working alone?"

"At that time, yes."

"Did you later suspect that Mr. Jablonski had been hired to break into the Hoyt estate and shoot Mr. Hoyt?"

"Yes."

"What caused you to form that opinion?"

"During a search of Mr. Jablonski's apartment, I found ten thousand dollars that his wife said Jablonski received shortly before the break-in."

"Subsequent to learning about the ten thousand dollars, did you become aware of evidence that called into question the defendant's version of the shooting?"

"Yes, sir. Gary Yoshida, a forensic expert in our crime lab, told me that blood spatter evidence at the crime scene contradicted the defendant's version of the way the shooting occurred."

"When did Officer Yoshida tell you about the blood spatter evidence?"

"On January 14, a week after the shooting."

"Did Officer Yoshida tell you he needed to visit the crime scene to confirm his suspicions about the blood spatter evidence?"

"Yes. He said that he had to see the scene in three dimensions. His initial conclusions were drawn from examinations of photographs and he felt that wasn't good enough."

"When Officer Yoshida informed you that he needed to see the bedroom again to confirm his suspicions about the blood spatter, did you drive to the estate immediately?"

"Yes."

"Why did you go so quickly?"

"It had been a while since the murder and we had just turned the scene back to the defendant. We were both worried that the scene had been altered. I felt time was of the essence."

"What happened at the estate?"

"Mr. Allen, the housekeeper, let us in. He told us that the bedroom was going to be cleaned the next day. I asked for his consent to enter the bedroom with Officer Yoshida so we could find any evidence that might exist before the cleaners destroyed it. He gave his consent and we conducted our investigation."

"Why didn't you get a search warrant for the bedroom?"

"There wasn't any reason to do that. We are taught about the law of search and seizure at the Police Academy and we get updates from time to time. It has always been my understanding that a warrant was not necessary if someone with the authority to give it consents to a search of the premises."

"Did you believe that Mr. Allen had the authority to consent to your entry into the bedroom?"

"Yes, sir. He was the housekeeper. He had the key. The defendant was away campaigning. He was the only one home."

"No further questions. Thank you, Detective."

"What's your take on Anthony? Is he an honest cop?" Garrett asked Crease in a whisper.

Crease thought about the question before answering. Then she leaned close to her attorney.

"Lou's a straight arrow. He won't lie."

Garrett looked at the witness.

"As I understand your testimony, Detective, you and Officer Yoshida went to the Hoyt estate, James Allen met you, you told him you wanted to enter the bedroom, he said that was great and he took you upstairs and let you in. Do I have that right?"

"No, ma'am. That is not what happened."

Garrett looked astonished. "Oh! What part do I have wrong?"

"When I first asked Mr. Allen if Officer Yoshida and I could go into the bedroom, he wasn't sure that he could let us in."

"In fact, he specifically told you, did he not, that the room was locked and that Senator Crease had instructed him to unlock the room only for the cleaners?"

"Yes, ma'am."

"Did you take 'no' for an answer?"

"No, because the defendant had no reason to believe we would need to take a second look at the room when she left for eastern Oregon. I assumed that she wouldn't want to block a police investigation."

"Well, Detective, weren't you also assuming at this time that Senator Crease may have hired Martin Jablonski to kill her husband?"

"That was a theory."

"If that was true, she would have every reason to impede a police investigation, wouldn't she?"

Anthony hesitated before answering, "I guess so."

"And every reason to want to forbid you access to the crime scene."

Anthony did not know what to say.

"I'll assume your lack of response constitutes agreement, Detective," Garrett said.

"Objection," said Riker, who was obviously upset by the course of Garrett's examination. "Detective Anthony did not just agree. Ms. Garrett is putting words in his mouth."

"Sustained," Quinn said. "Detective, we need a yes or no for the record."

Anthony looked helpless. Finally, he answered, "I guess she would have a reason to deny us access to the room if she was the killer."

Garrett's lips twitched. It was bad form to grin in court when you scored points, so she had to suppress a big smile.

"It is true, is it not, that Mr. Allen tried to reach Senator Crease by phone to see if she would agree to let you in the room, but he was unable to talk to her?"

"Yes."

"He then reiterated to you that his instructions were to keep everyone but the cleaners out of the room?"

"Yes."

"That upset you, didn't it?"

"I wasn't upset."

"You didn't become agitated and raise your voice?"

"I . . . I was concerned about the cleaners and I was certain that . . . I mean, well, it seemed to me that Senator Crease would have let us in if she was asked. That she wouldn't have objected to the police going in."

"Even though you just said that she had every reason to keep out the police if she was a murderer?"

"I . . . Honestly, that didn't go through my mind, about her refusing."

"You just wanted to get into the room?"

"Yes."

"So you applied pressure to Mr. Allen."

"No."

"You didn't lean into him?"

"I may have."

"You didn't sound annoyed?"

"I . . . That may be so. I was concerned."

"You made Mr. Allen change his mind, did you not?"

"He changed his mind. I couldn't force him. I didn't. It was his decision."

"You're telling Judge Quinn that you didn't use your authority as a policeman and your size to intimidate Mr. Allen?"

"No. It wasn't that way."

Garrett hesitated for a moment. Then she said, "No further questions, Your Honor."

Quinn studied the detective. He sounded a little desperate, but he also sounded like an honest cop. The judge did not doubt that Anthony had applied some pressure to Allen to convince him to change his mind, but it made a difference if the detective simply used his powers of persuasion as opposed to coercing the housekeeper to open the bedroom door. However, the line between persuasion and coercion could be very thin when the person who wants a result is a police officer.

"Our next witness will take a while, Your Honor," Cedric Riker said. "This might be a good time to break."

"Who is the witness?"

"Officer Yoshida. He'll be explaining the basis for probable cause and talking about the exigent circumstances."

"All right. Let's break for the day. I'll see everyone at nine in the morning."

[2]

Quinn did not want to go back to his barren apartment, so he stayed in his chambers to work on cases that he had not been able to get to because of *State v. Crease*. The corridors of the courthouse were deserted when Quinn turned out the lights in his chambers and locked the door shortly before seven. The courthouse floors were marble and the ceilings were high. The slightest noise was magnified. At night, the silence in the darkened halls was eerie. Quinn walked down the corridor. The elevators were around the corner. When he was almost at the end of the hall, Quinn paused. He thought he heard a footfall. He stopped to listen, but the hall was silent. Maybe a security guard was walking rounds on the floor below. Sound carried in odd ways in an empty building at night.

Quinn turned the corner. There was a bank of two elevators on either side of the wide marble stairs. Just as the judge pressed the Down button to summon one a scraping sound made Quinn's breath catch in his chest. He stepped away from the elevators and peered down the deserted hallway in both directions. Quinn jumped, then sagged, startled by the bell that signaled the arrival of the elevator.

Quinn took the car to the lobby. The empty courthouse had spooked him and the dark, deserted streets looked threatening. The rain had stopped, but a stiff wind forced Quinn to turn up the collar of his raincoat. He hurried along the three blocks between the courthouse and the garage where the county rented parking spaces for the judges.

During the ride home, Quinn tried to think about the evidence he had heard, but he found himself thinking about Laura and how lonely he would be all evening. Quinn decided to call Laura as soon as he got home. Maybe she was ready to talk about their future.

Quinn opened his door and turned on the light. He shut and locked the door. A man in a black ski mask, turtleneck and jeans stepped out of the judge's bedroom and pointed a gun at Quinn.

"Stay calm," the man said. "I'm not here to hurt you or rob you, but I will hurt you if you don't do as you're told. If you're smart, I'll be gone in a few minutes and you'll be just fine. Do you understand me?"

"Yes," Quinn answered, trying to keep his tone neutral so the gunman would not hear how frightened he was.

The intruder gestured toward a chair that stood in front of a low coffee table.

"Sit down."

Quinn did as he was told.

"How did Andrea Chapman die?" the man asked.

"I told the police that I don't know anything about that."

The man reached behind his back and pulled a manila envelope out of his waistband. He tossed it onto the coffee table.

"Open it," he commanded.

Quinn raised the flap.

"Now, take out the photographs."

Quinn removed three 8 ½ by 11 black-and-white photographs. All three shots showed Quinn and Andrea Chapman in the Cove of Lost Souls. Quinn's stomach rolled. The man pulled back the hammer of the gun and pointed the barrel at Quinn's head. Quinn blanched.

"I repeat, how did Andrea Chapman die?"

"She was murdered," Quinn stammered.

"Yes, but how was she murdered?"

"Drowning. She was drowned."

There was a slit for the mouth in the ski mask and Quinn saw the man's lips curl into a cruel grin.

"I hear that drowning is a peaceful way to die once you give in to it. Andrea didn't have it that easy."

The man paused as if recalling a fond memory. When he spoke again, it was in the tone that confidants use with one another.

"Andrea's skin was smooth and her body was very firm. You would have enjoyed playing with her. I did. Oh, she cried and begged at first, but I soon put an end to that. Do you want to know how?"

This time the man's smile was wide and self-satisfied. Quinn's stomach clenched and bile rose in his throat. The man chuckled.

"Don't go in much for rough foreplay, do you? It's one of my favorite things. After a while Andrea was willing to do anything I asked, even to the point of inventing her own little sex games, to avoid the pain."

The man paused. He eyed Quinn curiously, holding the judge's gaze the way a hypnotist traps his subject. The smile faded suddenly.

"Unfortunately, I had business to attend to, so I was forced to rape Andrea brutally, several times. Then I selected a very sharp hunting knife and engaged in some creative dismemberment."

Quinn gagged and fought with all his might to keep from throwing up.

"Don't worry, Judge. You won't have to see any pictures. In fact, if you do as you're told, neither you nor anyone else will ever view my handiwork. But if you disobey me there will be terrible consequences for you.

"Tell me, Judge, what do you think would happen if the St. Jerome Police received an anonymous call telling them where to find the body of Andrea Chapman? What do you think would happen if the St. Jerome Police received copies of these photographs? Did you know that there is an extradition treaty between the United States and St. Jerome? Did you know that hanging is the punishment for murder on St. Jerome?"

Quinn had trouble breathing. He felt as if his body had turned to water.

"What do you want from me?" Quinn managed.

"One thing. If you do that one thing, you'll be safe. If you don't, Andrea Chapman's body will be found, the police will get these pictures and you will rot in a rat-infested prison on St. Jerome until the day you are hanged by the neck in the prison courtyard. Now, ask me what the one thing is."

Quinn hesitated.

"Come on. You can do it. Ask me how you can save your life."

"What do you want me to do?"

"Everything in your power to see that Ellen Crease is convicted of the murder of her husband. Once the jury returns a verdict of guilty, Andrea Chapman's body will disappear forever and all copies of the photographs you are holding will be destroyed."

"I . . . I can't rig the trial. She could be sentenced to death."

"So could you. Do you have an alibi for the day Andrea died? Can you explain where you went in your rented car?" The man walked over to Quinn and held out his hand. "Please hand me the photographs, Judge."

Quinn's hand shook as he picked up the pictures. The man took them and walked to the front door.

"You know what you have to do to save your life. Keep your mouth shut, do it, and you'll survive."

The door closed and the man was gone. Quinn concentrated on fighting the nausea, but it was no good. He raced into the bathroom and threw up several times. Then he collapsed on the bathroom floor. Quinn remembered Andrea's smile, her laugh. An image of her running toward the sea came to him unbidden. Then, superimposed on that vision was an image of her body beaten and mutilated. Quinn squeezed his eyes shut and willed the vision away. He leaned against the bathroom wall and breathed deeply.

After a while Quinn struggled to his feet, cupped his hands and gulped cold water from the tap, then splashed it on his face. He had almost regained his composure when he remembered the call from the detective. Quinn had told him that he had not seen

Andrea after he left the airport. The photographs would destroy him.

Quinn went into his kitchen and poured a glass of Scotch, which he drank quickly. The Scotch burned away some of his fear. Quinn took the liquor bottle into the living room, refilled his glass and collapsed on the couch. He reviewed everything that had happened to him since Andrea sat next to him on the plane trip to St. Jerome.

The first thought that occurred to Quinn was chilling. Until this evening, Quinn believed that Andrea Chapman's murder was not connected to him in any way. Now Quinn knew that Andrea Chapman had been killed to set him up. It was the only way to explain what happened to Laura in Miami. The people who wanted Crease convicted had learned about Quinn's trip to St. Jerome. They had lured Laura to Miami with a fat retainer check so they could make certain that the first-class seat next to Quinn would be vacant. He had been played for a fool from the beginning.

[3]

Frank Price eyed Quinn as he let him into the apartment. The judge's tie was loose, his suit coat was rumpled and there were stains on his wrinkled white shirt. His complexion was pasty and there were dark shadows under his eyes.

"For someone who's just been on vacation in a tropical paradise, you don't look so hot."

"Too much work," Quinn mumbled without conviction. Price gave him a harder look.

"How are things with you and Laura?" Price asked as he led Quinn into the living room.

"Fine. Everything is fine," Quinn said.

Only after he answered did it occur to Quinn that Price had asked about the health of his relationship with Laura and not the usual small-talk question about the state of his wife's health.

Quinn wondered if Laura had talked to Frank at work. Price was watching him closely.

"We're separated," Quinn confessed.

Suddenly, Price looked every bit of his eighty years.

"I'm sorry to hear that," he said.

Quinn heard a slight tremor in Price's voice. Quinn knew that the old man loved him and hoped he would have a good marriage. He could see how much his separation from Laura hurt Frank.

"I'm living in an apartment. It's just temporary."

"Do you want to talk about it?"

Quinn shook his head. "We'll work it out. I still love her. I think she loves me."

"If you need my help I'm always here for you."

"I know that."

"I put up some coffee, but you look like you can use something stronger."

Quinn wanted a glass of Scotch, then thought better of it.

"Coffee will be fine."

Price carried two mugs of steaming coffee into the living room.

"I came for some information and I need it in confidence," he told Price.

"Oh?"

Quinn wrapped his large hands around the mug for warmth.

"I'm hearing the pretrial motions in Ellen Crease's case. Do you know her?"

"We've met at political functions and I know people who know her. We're not friends."

"What about her husband, Lamar Hoyt?"

"He was a major contributor to the Republican Party. I've had dinner with him."

"Frank, can you think of anyone with a grudge against Ellen Crease? I'm talking about something very serious. Something that would motivate a person to want to hurt Crease very badly."

Price was clearly uncomfortable.

"This is highly irregular, Dick. This extra-judicial inquiry into the background of a defendant whose case you're hearing. Do you mind telling me what prompted this visit?"

"I . . . I can't explain why I'm here. You're going to have to take it on faith that the information I'm asking for is crucial to a decision I have to make."

"If you're in some kind of trouble . . . ," Price started.

"Frank, I know I can trust you. I just can't confide in you."

"Does this have anything to do with Laura?"

"No," Quinn lied.

Price hesitated for a moment, but he could see how desperate Quinn looked.

"Ellen Crease has always been confrontational and she's made several political enemies, even in her own party. We never minded her ambition when she was running aggressive campaigns against Democratic opponents, though I, and others, did find her methods objectionable on occasion, but I can tell you that she has not endeared herself to the party by challenging an incumbent Republican senator."

"How did she get away with going after Gage?"

"Crease doesn't feel that she's accountable to anyone. She has a very committed following on the far right and her husband's money."

"Is there anyone you can think of who would be so upset with Crease that he would try to have her killed?"

"Why do you need to know that?"

"What if the man who broke into the Hoyt mansion came to kill Ellen Crease and not Lamar Hoyt? Crease would be innocent."

"Dick, do you realize what you're doing? You're a judge, for Christ's sake. You have to remain impartial. You have no business playing detective like this. In fact, you're violating your oath by taking sides in this case."

"I know that, and I can't explain why I'm asking you these questions. Please, Frank, I need your help."

"What have you gotten yourself into?"

Quinn looked away. Price was very troubled. For a moment, Quinn worried that he was going to end the meeting. Then Price said, "There are two people I can think of who would have the motive and personality to do what you're suggesting. Lamar Hoyt, Jr., was a constant source of concern to Lamar since he was a child. He is irresponsible and he has a history of violence. I know of two assault charges that Lamar was able to settle out of court by paying off the complaining witnesses. Junior has been quite vocal about his hatred of his stepmother. I assume you've heard about the will contest?"

Quinn nodded.

"Then, there's Benjamin Gage. Have you heard the rumors about his connection to Otto Keeler's death?"

"I never paid that much attention to them."

"I have no idea if there's any truth to them, but they won't go away. Gage made his fortune in the computer industry with a company called StarData. Otto Keeler and Gage started the company. For a while, StarData looked like it might take off, but it experienced a serious funding problem. Just when things looked darkest, the StarData building burned down. Otto Keeler was killed in the blaze. Gage assumed total control over the company and he used the millions the company received from Keeler's key man insurance and the fire insurance to help StarData turn the corner financially. The origin of the fire was unquestionably arson and there was no reason anyone uncovered for Keeler sleeping in the building on the evening of the blaze. There was never any evidence connecting Gage to the fire, but the police took a very hard look at him for a long time.

"Other than Gage and Lamar, Jr., I can't think of anyone else who would have a reason to try to do what you're suggesting."

Quinn stood. He looked drained and distant. Price gripped Quinn's shoulders.

"Let me help you, Dick."

Quinn smiled sadly. Then he embraced Price.

"I love you, Frank. But I've got to do this on my own."

Quinn let Price go and headed for the door.

"If you change your mind . . . ," Price said.

"I know," Quinn answered.

Eighteen

"OFFICER YOSHIDA, how are you employed?" Cedric Riker asked.

"I'm a criminalist with the Oregon State Police Forensic Laboratory in Portland."

"Please give Judge Quinn your academic background."

Yoshida turned toward Quinn. He had testified in his court on a few occasions and was perfectly relaxed on the witness stand.

"I graduated from Portland State University with a B.S. in chemistry in 1989 and returned to PSU for courses in genetic biology and forensic DNA analysis. From 1989 to 1990, I worked as an analytical chemist. Then, in 1990, I became an Oregon State Police officer assigned to the crime lab."

"Over the years, have you had training in crime scene investigation and, more specifically, in the analysis of bloodstain patterns?"

"Yes, sir. I attended the Oregon State Medical Examiners' death investigation class in 1990, a blood pattern analysis training program at the Police Academy in 1991, an advanced crime

scene training program in 1992, and I completed a basic, interme-
diate and advanced serology training program in 1992. Over the
years, I have read numerous articles in the area and attended
many seminars where these subjects were discussed."

"As part of your duties, do you go to crime scenes and collect
evidence?"

"Yes."

"How many crime scenes have you investigated?"

Yoshida laughed. "Gosh, I don't know. I never kept a count.
It's a lot, though. I investigate several homicides each year. Then,
there are other scenes."

"Okay. Now, were you one of the criminalists who went to the
Hoyt estate on the evening that Lamar Hoyt and Martin Jablonski were shot to death?"

"I was."

"Please describe the scene for Judge Quinn."

Yoshida left the witness box and walked over to a large diagram of the murder scene that he had prepared. The diagram was
resting on an easel.

"The crime scene we are interested in is the master bedroom on
the second floor of Mr. Hoyt's mansion. To get to that room, you
climb a set of stairs to the second floor, then go down a long
corridor in a westerly direction."

Yoshida picked up a wooden pointer and placed its tip on a
section of the drawing that represented the door to the hall.

"The master bedroom itself is a rectangle. The door between
the bedroom and the hall is in the east wall at the southeast corner
of the bedroom."

Yoshida moved his pointer to the bathroom doorway.

"The northern wall in the hall is also the south wall of the
bathroom. When you enter the bedroom, you can see the bathroom door if you look to your right."

Yoshida moved the pointer again.

"If you are standing in the doorway and you look directly
across the room, you'll see the west wall. A good portion of that

wall is a large window with a view of the pool and part of the yard. Halfway between the west and east walls is a king-size bed. The headboard touches the north wall. Directly across from the foot of the bed is an armoire approximately seven feet high. It contains a television and its back touches the south wall. My information from the first officers on the scene and an interview with the houseman, James Allen, is that the lights in the room were off when the crime occurred and that the television was also off."

"When you entered the crime scene, what did you see?"

Yoshida pointed to a stick figure that had been positioned between the small box that represented the armoire and the slightly larger box that represented the king-size bed.

"The first thing I saw was the body of Martin Jablonski. He was facedown with his feet almost touching the armoire and his head facing the bed. There was a pool of blood under his body approximately ten feet from the foot of the bed and one foot from the west-facing side of the armoire. There was also a .45-caliber handgun lying on the floor near Mr. Jablonski's right hand."

"Did you determine how Mr. Jablonski was killed?"

"Yes, sir. The defendant told the investigating officers that she shot Mr. Jablonski twice with a Smith & Wesson .38 snubnose loaded with hollow point bullets. When Mr. Jablonski was autopsied, the medical examiner recovered two bullets that had lodged in the body. One was recovered from Mr. Jablonski's head and the other from his torso. They were the type of bullet that the defendant described. Ballistics tests confirmed that the defendant's gun, which was recovered at the scene, fired the two shots."

"Why didn't the bullets exit the body?" Riker asked.

"Hollow point bullets are designed to stay inside the body so they can bounce around and cause more damage."

"Did you see another body in the room?"

"Yes, sir. The body of Lamar Hoyt was sprawled on his back on the bed. I was told that he had been shot while in the bed, but that the defendant had been found holding him with his head in her lap. From blood spatter patterns on the headboard and bed, I concluded that Mr. Hoyt was probably sitting up on the east side of the bed when he was shot. Then he fell sideways onto the west side of the bed. The defendant pulled him even further sideways when she sat down and cradled his head."

"Did ballistics tests identify the .45-caliber handgun found next to Mr. Jablonski as the weapon that was used to kill Lamar Hoyt?"

"Yes."

"Now, Officer Yoshida, did the defendant explain what happened on the evening of the shooting?"

"Yes, sir. To Detective Anthony."

"Please tell the Court how the shooting scenario was explained to you."

"As I understood the defendant's version, she and Mr. Hoyt had engaged in sexual intercourse. The defendant has the side of the bed closest to the window. She stated that after they finished, she got up from the bed, went to the window in the west wall, then crossed in front of the bed and entered the bathroom, turned on the bathroom light and washed up.

"After finishing in the bathroom, she put on her nightgown, turned off the bathroom light and crossed back in front of the bed. She got back in the bed on her side and talked with Mr. Hoyt for a while. As they were talking, the door opened and Mr. Jablonski entered the room. The defendant said she saw that Mr. Jablonski was armed, so she ducked over her side of the bed and secured the .38 that she keeps under it. She heard three shots and came up firing. Mr. Jablonski fell and she turned her attention to her husband, whom she determined to be dead."

"Officer Yoshida, when you looked at the crime scene on the evening of the shootings, did you see anything that called the defendant's version of the shootings into question?"

Yoshida looked embarrassed.

"The evidence was there. I just didn't pick up on it."

"What did you conclude on the evening of the crime?"

"That the defendant was telling the truth."

Yoshida's embarrassment deepened. He looked up at Quinn and tried to explain his failure to correctly interpret the crime scene's story.

"Everyone thought we were dealing with a burglary that went wrong. I mean, Jablonski was dead, there was no question his gun fired the shots that killed Mr. Hoyt. I guess I just assumed there was nothing to look for."

"Did something happen after the first crime scene investigation that caused you to question your first impression?" Riker asked.

"Yes, sir. I took a second look at the evidence while I was writing my report."

"When you reexamined the evidence, did you discover something you'd missed the first time around?"

"I did."

"What was that, Officer Yoshida?"

"I spotted a blood spatter pattern in two of the crime scene photographs that had not made an impression on me when I was at the scene. It made me question the defendant's story of how the shooting of Martin Jablonski occurred."

"Did you tell Detective Anthony that you had to visit the scene again?"

"Yes. I needed to see everything again in three dimensions to confirm my suspicions."

"Did you feel time was of the essence?"

"I did. It was already a week since the shooting and I was afraid that the blood pattern would be destroyed or contaminated."

"Can you explain to the judge what you can tell from blood spatter analysis that is relevant to this case?"

"Certainly," Yoshida told Riker before addressing the judge. "If I asked you to tell me what shape a drop of blood takes when it falls straight down, you would probably tell me that it would look like a teardrop, but that is a popular misconception. Actually, falling drops of blood are shaped like a sphere. The type of surface the drop strikes and the angle at which it hits affect the pattern the drop makes when it strikes a surface.

"If a drop of blood falls straight down at a ninety-degree angle it should leave a pattern that looks like a circle. As the degree of the angle changes so that the drop is hitting the surface at an angle that is moving from the vertical to the horizontal, the pattern will become more and more elongated. There is an equation that will give you the angle of impact using measurements of the length and width of the bloodstain. This helps a forensic scientist determine if the victim was standing or sitting when his blood was spattered onto a surface. You can also tell the direction in which the blood was cast by examining the shape of the blood drop after it strikes a surface."

Yoshida placed blowups of two crime scene photographs on the easel. The first had been taken from the west side of the room shooting back toward the hall. It showed Martin Jablonski's body in front of the armoire. The second photograph was a close-up of the west-facing side of the armoire. Quinn could see a discoloration on the side of the armoire approximately six feet from the floor in the first photograph. In the close-up, the discoloration could clearly be seen as a fine spray of blood.

"When a person is struck with sufficient force to cause blood to spatter, the blood may spatter at low, medium or high velocity," Yoshida instructed Quinn. "If I punched you in the nose, the spatter would likely be low-velocity and would not carry very far. If the force is stronger, say because I use an object like a club or a brick, the blow may result in a medium-velocity pattern. Gunshots create high-velocity spatter patterns with an extremely high percentage of very fine blood specks. The result is a mistlike dispersion similar to an aerosol spray. Because of their low mass, these particles seldom travel a horizontal distance of over three or four feet."

Yoshida put the tip of the pointer on the spatter pattern in the first blowup.

"The first bullet that hit Mr. Jablonski struck him in the right temple. From the high-velocity spatter pattern on the side of the armoire, I conclude that Jablonski was struck by that bullet when he was standing with the right side of his head approximately one foot from the side of the armoire facing directly forward toward the bed. When the bullet struck Mr. Jablonski in the temple area on the right side of his head, his blood sprayed onto the west-facing side of the armoire. He had to be close to the armoire for the blood to spray onto it.

"Now, here is the problem," Yoshida continued. "I've lined up the angles. For the bullet to enter Mr. Jablonski's right temple at an angle that would leave the spray pattern on the west-facing side of the armoire, the shot had to come from the bathroom, not the west side of the bed."

Movement in the corridor outside the courtroom caught Quinn's eye. He turned pale and his breath caught in his chest. The woman who had passed by the door reminded him of Andrea Chapman.

Cedric Riker picked up a brown paper bag and turned to Yoshida. Quinn tried to calm down so he could pay attention to the testimony. The woman could not have been Andrea, Quinn told himself. Andrea Chapman was dead. The woman he saw simply resembled Andrea. She had passed by quickly, the distance between the bench and the corridor was considerable. The glass in the door must have distorted the woman's image. Quinn wrenched his attention back to the testimony.

"Officer Yoshida, I am handing you State's exhibit 113. What is that?"

Yoshida pulled a white nightgown out of the bag. The front was saturated with dried blood, but the back was only covered with a fine spray.

"This is the defendant's nightgown. Lab tests have determined that the blood on the front and back is her husband's."

"According to the defendant, where was the nightgown when Lamar Hoyt was shot by Mr. Jablonski?"

"She said that she was wearing it."

"Is the physical evidence consistent with the defendant's claim that she was wearing the nightgown when her husband was shot?"

"No." Yoshida held up the nightgown and displayed the backside to Quinn. "This is also high-velocity spatter. If the defendant was wearing the nightgown when Mr. Hoyt was shot, the spray would have covered the front of the nightgown. It is my conclusion that this nightgown was not on the defendant when Mr. Hoyt was shot. I believe it was lying on the bed with the backside up."

"What conclusions did you draw concerning the way in which the shooting occurred from your analysis of the blood spatter evidence?"

"It is my conclusion that the defendant was not wearing the nightgown when the shooting occurred. I believe that she left the nightgown front-down on the bed after having intercourse. Then she went to the bathroom. She was in the bathroom when Mr. Jablonski was in front of the bed and to the left of the armoire. Mr. Jablonski fired the three shots that struck and killed Mr. Hoyt. Then the defendant fired her first shot into Mr. Jablonski's temple from the area near the bathroom door. This shot caused high-velocity blood spatter to spray onto the side of the armoire. As soon as he was shot, Mr. Jablonski turned toward the bathroom and was shot front to back. The second bullet left no blood spatter because Mr. Jablonski was wearing heavy clothing and the bullet stayed in the body. Mr. Jablonski then crumpled to the floor with his head toward the bed and his feet almost touching the armoire."

"I have no further questions of Officer Yoshida," Riker said.

Mary Garrett began her cross-examination, but Quinn had trouble paying attention to it. Yoshida's testimony stunned him. Quinn had reached a tentative conclusion about how he would deal with the blackmailer's demand that he assure the conviction of Ellen Crease, but that decision had been based in part on a belief that Ellen Crease was an innocent person who was being framed by her enemies. Yoshida's testimony changed everything. He had to know if there was a flaw in Yoshida's interpretation of the blood spatter evidence.

"We have no further witnesses," Riker said when the examination of Yoshida was concluded. Quinn glanced at the clock. It was almost noon.

"Let's break for the day and I'll hear the legal arguments tomorrow. We'll reconvene at two. I have some matters I need to attend to in the morning."

Quinn turned to his court reporter.

"Miss Chan, please see me in chambers."

Quinn left the bench. He took off his robes as soon as he was through the door to his chambers. An idea had occurred to him as Garrett was questioning Yoshida. He buzzed Fran Stuart just as Margaret Chan walked in.

"Fran," Quinn said over the intercom as he motioned for Chan to sit down, "get me the file in *State v. Schwartz,* please."

Quinn released the intercom button and addressed the court reporter.

"Can you get me a transcript of Gary Yoshida's testimony today?"

"Sure. I should be able to finish it before five."

"Please drop it by when you're done."

Chan left just as Fran Stuart put the *Schwartz* file on his desk. Quinn thanked her and she returned to the outer office. Court-appointed counsel had represented the defendant in *Schwartz.* Quinn remembered signing an order authorizing payment of indigent defense funds for a court-appointed defense witness who was an expert in blood spatter. Quinn had been impressed by the testimony. The man's name, address and phone number were on the form on which the request for payment was made. Quinn jotted down the information and picked up the phone.

"Paul Baylor?" Quinn asked when the phone was answered.

"Yes."

"This is Judge Richard Quinn of the Multnomah County Circuit Court. You testified before me in *State v. Schwartz.*"

"Oh, yes, Your Honor. What can I do for you?"

"I'd like to consult with you privately. The matter is confidential. Would you have time to meet with me tomorrow morning?"

"Do you want me to come to the courthouse?"

"No. I thought I could come to your office."

"Sure."

"Is eight A.M. too early?"

"No, that's fine. Uh, what is this about?"

"I'm looking for an opinion on an issue involving blood spatter evidence. I'll be bringing some pictures and a transcript."

"Fine. See you tomorrow."

"One more thing. Please don't mention this conversation or our meeting to anyone."

Quinn hung up and buzzed his secretary.

"Fran, please bring all of the evidence in the *Crease* hearing into my chambers. I want to study it."

A few minutes later, Fran Stuart placed a large cardboard box on the floor next to Quinn's desk.

"I'm going to get my lunch, Judge. Can I get you anything?"

"I brought my lunch. Thanks, Fran."

"I'll lock the front door to give you some privacy. I won't be long."

Fran Stuart closed the door to Quinn's chambers. A moment later, Quinn heard the door between the corridor and the reception area close. There was a small refrigerator in Quinn's private bathroom. Quinn took out a can of Coke and a brown bag with a ham and cheese sandwich and a bag of potato chips. He had made the sandwich that morning, but he had no appetite now. Still, he forced himself to take a bite. He knew it would be a mistake to skip lunch. He needed all his energy to cope with the crisis he was facing.

While Quinn ate he mulled over Yoshida's testimony. Loud and repeated knocking on the outer door interrupted Quinn's chain of thought. He did not want company, but the knocking was insistent. Quinn went into the reception room. There was a peephole in the door to the hall. Quinn looked through it. The blood drained from his face and he felt dizzy. The woman in the corridor was the woman who had passed by the courtroom door. Quinn stared harder through the peephole. The glass distorted the woman's image but there was no getting around her resemblance to Andrea Chapman. Quinn opened the door.

The woman was Andrea and she was not. Andrea had long black hair. The woman in the hall was blonde and her hair was cut short to frame her face. She also wore glasses. Beneath her raincoat, her clothing was conservative and cheap: a drab, colorless dress, no jewelry and very little makeup.

"Are you Judge Quinn? Richard Quinn?"

"Yes. Can I help you?"

"My . . . my name is Claire Reston. I need to talk to you. It's very important."

Quinn saw none of Andrea's breezy self-confidence in the woman. They were almost the same height, but Claire Reston slouched and her shoulders were hunched and folded in as if she were trying to hide behind them. She also had trouble looking Quinn in the eye.

"Why don't you come into my chambers?" suggested Quinn, who was anxious that no one see him with the woman.

Reston took one of the chairs across the desk from Quinn. She folded her hands in her lap.

"I . . . I know about you and Andrea," Reston said without conviction.

"Who?"

Reston looked up. The lenses in her glasses were thick and made her eyes look large. Quinn felt terrible about lying to the woman, but he had no choice.

"Andrea Chapman is my sister. The . . . the day before she disappeared, she told me about you."

"Okay. Now I understand. Look, Miss Reston, a police detective called me about your sister's disappearance. I'll tell you what I told him. I sat next to her on the flight to St. Jerome, but I didn't see her after we landed."

Reston looked down. She seemed on the verge of tears.

"That's not true." Reston's voice quivered as if the effort to disagree with Quinn was monumental. "She told me your name. She was upset. She didn't want to do it. I want you to know that."

"Do what, Miss Reston? I don't understand."

"They wanted her to seduce you. They were going to blackmail you."

"Who was going to blackmail me? What are you talking about?"

"She didn't tell me anything else. Just that she had been hired to seduce a judge. She told me your name. She was very nervous, very tense."

"Miss Reston, I assure you that I did not see your sister after we left the plane. If she was hired to do something to me, maybe she changed her mind. I only talked to her during the flight. She was friendly, but she made no attempt to seduce me. I'm married."

Reston looked confused.

"Have you told the police that I had something to do with your sister's disappearance?"

"No. I . . . Andrea and I . . . we're not close. I don't even see her that much. In fact, the call from St. Jerome surprised me. I didn't even know that she had disappeared until the detective called to ask about her. I . . . Well, I didn't know anything but your name and that you were a judge, so I didn't tell the detective what Andrea said." Reston looked down at her lap. She seemed embarrassed by her lack of courage. "Then I read about Senator Crease's trial and the story gave the name of the judge . . ."

Reston trailed off. She looked very unsure of herself and Quinn believed his bluff would work.

"Miss Reston, I am sorry that your sister has disappeared. She seemed very nice. But I really can't help you. I talked to her a little on the plane. That's all. I probably mentioned where I was staying, but she never called my hotel. If she did, she didn't leave a message."

Reston sat up a little straighter. She studied Quinn.

"I . . . I don't believe you. I think you do know something about Andrea's disappearance."

Quinn heard the hall door open and close. Reston looked over her shoulder toward the sound. She stood up quickly and opened the door between Quinn's chambers and the reception area. Quinn saw Fran Stuart over Reston's shoulder.

"I'm staying at the Heathman Hotel in room 325. You . . . you have to be honest with me. If you know something . . ." Reston was on the verge of tears. "I'll give you until tomorrow."

Reston saw Stuart. She ran out of courage and bolted past the secretary.

"Who was that?" Stuart asked.

Quinn shook his head. "Forget about her. She's confused. It wasn't anything important."

Stuart started to say something, then thought better of it. Quinn closed the door to his chambers.

Nineteen

THE OFFICES of Oregon Forensic Investigations were located in an industrial park a few blocks from the Columbia River. Quinn had to wind through narrow streets flanked by warehouses to find the entrance to the parking lot. After parking in a space reserved for visitors, Quinn walked up a concrete ramp, then followed a walkway that led past several businesses. A door with the company name opened into a small anteroom. There were two chairs on either side of an end table that held a lamp and several copies of *Scientific American* and *Time*. In one wall of the reception area was a door and a sliding glass window. Quinn looked through the window and saw a receptionist's desk with a telephone and a second door in the back wall. The door to the receptionist's area was locked. A sign above a button on the wall instructed Quinn to ring for assistance. He pressed the button and heard a muted buzzing somewhere in the building. Moments later, the doors opened and Paul Baylor greeted Quinn.

Baylor was a slender, bookish African American with a B.S. in forensic science and criminal justice from Michigan State who had worked in the Oregon State Crime Lab for ten years before opening his own forensic consulting firm with another OSP forensic expert. Quinn had been impressed by the slow, thoughtful manner with which Baylor handled the prosecutor's questions when he testified in his courtroom. He did not appear to be taking sides and had answered truthfully, even when the answers were not favorable to the defense. Baylor was wearing a brown tweed sports jacket, a white shirt, a forest-green tie and tan slacks. After shaking hands with Quinn, Baylor brought him into a cramped office outfitted with inexpensive furniture.

"How can I help you, Judge?" Baylor asked when they were seated. Quinn was carrying a box containing the transcript of Gary Yoshida's testimony, several police reports, a sketch of Yoshida's diagram of the crime scene, a complete set of the crime scene photographs, including the two that showed the blood spatter pattern on the side of the armoire, and a brown paper bag with Ellen Crease's nightgown inside. He set the box on top of Baylor's desk.

"You may have read that I'm hearing motions in *State v. Crease.*"

Baylor nodded.

"Do you know Gary Yoshida?"

"Sure. We worked together for several years when I was with OSP."

"What's your impression of him?"

Baylor looked uncomfortable about being asked to comment on another professional, but he answered the question.

"Gary does good work and he's very honest."

"Is he an expert on blood spatter?"

"He's knowledgeable about it."

"How exact a science is blood spatter analysis?"

Baylor thought about the question before answering.

"Blood spatter analysis is very helpful in determining what happened at a crime scene, but it's not like fingerprint examination.

There is a certain amount of subjectivity involved. A fingerprint is not open to interpretation, if you have enough points of comparison. That's not true with blood spatter. You can't just look at an individual blood spot and draw indisputable conclusions. You have to look at the spot in the context of the whole scene. Bloodstains just tell you in general what happened."

"So two honest experts can look at the same scene and draw different conclusions as to what happened?"

"Sure, in certain instances."

"I would like you to look at the evidence I've brought and read Officer Yoshida's testimony. Then I would like you to tell me if there is any analysis of the evidence that would support Ellen Crease's version of how the shoot-out in her bedroom occurred."

Baylor's brow furrowed. He looked concerned.

"Are you questioning Gary's honesty?" he asked.

"No, no. I just want to know if there is a reasonable explanation of the evidence that is different from his conclusions. There isn't any question in my mind that Officer Yoshida gave an honest opinion in court. I want to know if he could be wrong."

"I assume Gary had the advantage of visiting the crime scene?"

Quinn nodded. "He was out there twice."

"Can I visit it?"

"No. Besides, my information is that it has been cleaned."

"That's going to put me at a disadvantage."

"I realize that. Just do your best. And let me know if working on the problem without visiting the scene has a critical impact on your conclusions."

"Okay. When do you want me to get back to you?"

"Actually, I thought I'd wait. Is this something you can do right away?"

Baylor looked surprised. "I can get to it now. It might take a while."

"Is there someplace nearby I can eat breakfast?" Quinn asked. He did not have much of an appetite, but a restaurant would give him a place to pass the time while Baylor worked.

"Yeah. Sue's Cafe is pretty good. It's two blocks down just when you turn out of the lot on the right."

"Okay. I'll be back in an hour."

"I'll see what I can do by then. Uh, one other thing. Should I submit a court-appointed witness voucher for my work?"

"No. I'll be paying for this personally."

When Quinn returned to Oregon Forensic Investigations, he found Paul Baylor in shirtsleeves with his collar open and his tie at half-mast.

"You find Sue's okay?" Baylor asked as he led Quinn through a door into a large work area. The walls were unpainted concrete blocks and there was fluorescent lighting hanging from the ceiling. The laboratory equipment that sat on several wooden tables looked new and Quinn figured that this was where Baylor and his partner had sunk their capital.

"It was a good suggestion." Quinn noticed the papers and photographs that covered one of the worktables. "Are you through?"

"Yeah. It didn't take as long as I thought it might."

"Were you able to draw any conclusions?" Quinn asked anxiously.

"Yes."

"And?"

"Okay. First thing, I can't disagree with Gary's findings."

"You mean the evidence contradicts Ellen Crease's version of the shootings?"

"I didn't say that. Look, as I said before, blood spatter analysis is not an exact science. People can draw different conclusions from the same evidence in some situations. Gary's conclusions are valid. However, Gary's analysis of the significance of the blood spatter patterns on the nightgown and the side of the armoire is not the only analysis one can make."

Crease's nightgown was lying facedown on top of butcher paper on a long table. Baylor led the judge over to it.

"The spatter pattern on the back of the nightgown was the

easiest to deal with." Baylor pointed at the dried blood that had sprayed over the back of the white fabric. "In the transcript, it says that the lab concluded that the blood on the front of the nightgown and the spray on the back are Lamar Hoyt's blood, so I'm accepting that as a fact. No question that's high-velocity spatter. So far so good.

"Now, as I understand it, Crease said that she was in bed with the nightgown on, talking to her husband, when Jablonski entered the bedroom and shot him."

"That's how I heard it."

"Okay. Now, Gary concludes that she was lying about wearing the nightgown because the spray pattern from the high-velocity spatter is across the back of the nightgown. His conclusion is that she's in the bathroom lying in wait for Jablonski and the nightgown is flat on the bed, front side down. That's one explanation for the pattern being on the back, but there is another that's consistent with Crease's story."

Baylor grabbed two wooden chairs and set them side by side. Then he motioned to Quinn.

"Stand over by that filing cabinet and face me." Baylor sat in the chair that faced Quinn's left side. "You're Jablonski and I'm Crease. The filing cabinet is the armoire. I'm sitting on my side of the bed. I've got my nightgown on. The other chair is the side of the bed closest to the bathroom. That's Lamar Hoyt's side.

"Jablonski comes into the bedroom. He moves to the middle of the bed and to the left of the armoire and raises the gun to shoot Hoyt."

Baylor bent over the side of the chair to his right.

"I'm going for the gun that is under the bed. See how my back is suddenly facing my husband? The fabric is stretched out. If you shoot while I'm bent like this and Hoyt is hit at a certain angle, the spray will cover my back, not my front. Then, when I straighten up, the fabric will rumple a little, making it look like the nightgown was tossed on its front on the bed."

Baylor straightened up.

"So Crease could have been telling the truth about wearing the nightgown," Quinn said slowly, more to himself than to Baylor. "If she was, she would have had to bend over the west-facing side of the bed for the spatter pattern on the nightgown to look like that? She couldn't have been in the bathroom."

"Yes. But Gary's explanation could also be correct."

"What about the blood on the armoire?"

"That gets trickier, but there is a way that the spray could have gotten on the armoire with Crease shooting from her side of the bed.

"Let's keep Jablonski on his feet on the west side of the armoire, exactly where Gary placed him. He shoots Hoyt as Crease goes for her gun. Crease's movements distract Jablonski. He turns his head toward the window but does not turn his body. Now Jablonski's right temple is facing Crease's side of the bed. Go on, turn your head."

Quinn did as he was told.

"Now, the next part gets tricky." Baylor raised his hand and pretended to fire a gun. "Bam. Crease's first shot enters the right temple, high-velocity spatter sprays from the wound, but the spray would go forward, in front of Jablonski's body and onto the floor, and it would not travel far, since the amount of spray is small and high-velocity spray is atomized. When Jablonski collapses after the body shot, he would fall on top of the high-velocity spray and obliterate it."

"If the high-velocity spray from the head shot landed on the floor, what caused the blood spatter pattern on the side of the armoire?"

"Aspirated blood from Jablonski's lungs. A shot to the body frequently causes people to cough up blood. If Jablonski turned his head toward the armoire after he was shot in the body, he could have coughed blood on the armoire before collapsing onto the high-velocity spatter from the head wound. Aspirated blood can resemble high-velocity spray."

A thought occurred to Quinn. "Is there a difference between

blood that is sprayed from a head wound and aspirated blood from the lungs?"

"You mean, could we test the blood on the armoire to see if it is aspirated blood?"

"Exactly."

"Not anymore. If the blood on the armoire was tested shortly after the crime, it's possible that amylase, an enzyme from saliva, could have been detected. Amalyse could have been caught up in the blood when Jablonski coughed. But amalyse breaks down and becomes undetectable in a week or two, depending on the temperature and humidity in a room. Additionally, amalyse is not always found in aspirated blood, or it may go undetected because it's below the detection limit of the test that's used. Even if Gary had tested the blood on the armoire as soon as he caught on to its possible significance, I doubt that it would have told him anything."

"So there's no way to tell if the blood on the side of the armoire is aspirated blood or high-velocity spatter."

"Correct."

"And there's no way to say for certain where Ellen Crease was when she shot Martin Jablonski."

"Also correct."

Quinn's shoulders sagged. He was hoping that Baylor would debunk Yoshida's analysis. All he had done was confuse the situation.

[2]

Quinn's head was pounding by the time he arrived at his chambers. If Baylor had told him that the blood spatter evidence proved that Ellen Crease was a liar, Quinn would have let the trial run its course. But Baylor could not say that the shooting of Martin Jablonski had not occurred exactly as Crease described it.

Quinn gave the exhibits to Fran Stuart and instructed her to hold all of his calls. He reviewed the memos on the law of search and seizure and the rules of evidence filed by the parties. From what he could determine, the blood spatter evidence was the key to the State's case. If Quinn granted all of Garrett's motions, the only evidence left in the case would be Jablonski's history as a burglar who resorted to violence and the indisputable fact that Jablonski had broken into the Hoyt mansion and shot Lamar Hoyt. If this was the way that the evidence stood when the State rested, any judge would have to grant a motion for judgment of acquittal to the defense.

Quinn rested his head in his hands. He had slept little the night before and he was exhausted and not thinking clearly. He needed to rest, he wanted time to think out his course of action, but court was scheduled to convene in five minutes.

When Quinn looked up, he saw Lincoln's framed quote on his wall. Lincoln's counsel to do one's best while trying to do what was right had helped him reach his decision to impose a prison sentence on Frederick Gideon when everyone expected him to grant the judge probation. Doing the right thing was the center-piece of Quinn's personal philosophy. It was something you did regardless of the consequences. Sometimes doing the right thing required courage. Quinn had not been courageous on St. Jerome. He did not report Andrea's murder to the authorities for selfish reasons. While his cowardice protected him, it helped Andrea's killer get away with murder. Now he wanted Quinn to help him destroy another life. Quinn decided that he was not going to do that. This afternoon he would act with the courage he had not shown on St. Jerome.

"Before I rule on these motions, I want to thank counsel on both sides for their excellent briefs and oral argument. They have been of great assistance to me in framing and resolving some difficult issues."

Quinn paused. Cedric Riker leaned back, looking as if he did not have a care in the world. He was so self-centered that he could not conceive of losing a motion. When he did lose, he always found someone else to blame. Mary Garrett shifted nervously on her chair. She was self-confident, but she had none of Riker's egomania to blind her to the fact that the questions were close. Ellen Crease watched Quinn with cool detachment.

"I'll start with the most complex question. Did the search of the defendant's bedroom violate the Oregon and United States Constitutions? The burden is on the State to prove that the search was legal because the search was conducted without a warrant. Warrantless searches are presumed to be illegal, unless the State can show the existence of an exception to the warrant requirements of the Oregon and United States Constitutions.

"Mr. Riker has argued that exigent circumstances excused Detective Anthony and Officer Yoshida from obtaining a warrant. I do not find this argument convincing. Officer Yoshida gave no scientific opinion as to why waiting a few hours while a warrant was obtained would make it any more likely that the blood spatter would be degraded or destroyed. After all, it had been over a week since the crime scene was created. True, the cleaners would have destroyed the evidence, but they were not scheduled to appear until the next day. Additionally, Detective Anthony and Officer Yoshida did not know that the cleaners were coming until after the decision was made to go to the estate without a warrant."

Garrett leaned forward, hanging on Quinn's every word.

"The State argues that James Allen gave a valid consent to the police to enter the bedroom. I find that Mr. Allen did not have real authority to do that. He and the police were both aware that Senator Crease had specifically instructed Allen to keep everyone except the cleaning crew out of the bedroom.

"However, I do find that James Allen did have apparent authority to open the locked bedroom for the police. He was the housekeeper. He had the keys to the room. Detective Anthony could reasonably assume that the person left in charge of the house by Senator Crease could let him and Officer Yoshida into the bedroom if he wished to let them in and there was a valid reason to do so."

Garrett's shoulders sagged and Riker smiled.

"Despite my finding that James Allen had the apparent authority to consent to a search of Senator Crease's bedroom, I must still suppress the evidence obtained during the search."

Riker shot up in his chair. He looked stunned. Garrett looked like she could not believe what she was hearing.

"I find that Detective Anthony intentionally coerced Mr. Allen into opening the bedroom after he had been told unequivocally by Mr. Allen that he was under instructions from his employer to keep everyone but the cleaning crew out of the bedroom. I hold that Detective Anthony was not credible when he testified that he did not intentionally coerce Mr. Allen into giving consent."

Riker was on his feet. "Your Honor," he started, but Quinn cut him off.

"The time for argument is over, Mr. Riker. Please sit down."

Riker collapsed onto his chair.

"As to the other motions, I have read the briefs submitted by the parties and I have examined the affidavits submitted by the State detailing what Conchita Jablonski and Karen Fargo would testify to if called as witnesses. I will not allow Conchita Jablonski to testify to anything her husband told her concerning how he came by the money that was found in the Jablonski apartment. That is pure hearsay.

"Similarly, I am excluding any statements that Lamar Hoyt may have made to Karen Fargo about the state of his marriage and his desire to leave his wife for her on the grounds that they, too, are hearsay."

Riker could only gape at the judge. His case against Ellen Crease was being destroyed beyond repair.

"Finally, I will allow the defense to introduce evidence concerning Mr. Jablonski's criminal background to support its position that he was acting as a burglar on the evening of the shooting.

"I'll prepare the order," Quinn said as he stood. "Mr. Riker, you have thirty days to decide if you want to appeal my order to the court of appeals. Court is adjourned."

As soon as Quinn left the bench, Cedric Riker streaked out of the courtroom with his assistants in tow and Ryan Clark headed down the hall to the pay phones to let Benjamin Gage in on the bad news. James Allen stayed seated. He watched Mary Garrett and Ellen Crease discuss the outcome of the case at their table. Allen looked grim and undecided. After a moment's more thought he mixed with the spectators and left the room.

"What does this mean?" Ellen Crease asked her lawyer.

"It means we won everything," Garrett told her as the enormity of Quinn's ruling dawned on her. "He suppressed everything Riker can use to convict you. He left him with nothing."

Garrett hoisted her attaché case and they headed out of the courtroom.

"You sound surprised."

"To tell the truth, I am. I had some hope of winning the motion to keep out the hearsay, but the blood spatter motion was a real long shot."

"Does this mean that the case is over? That I'm free?"

"Technically, the charges still exist. But Riker's choice is to appeal or dismiss and . . ."

Garrett stopped. Bearing down on them was Lamar Hoyt, Jr.

"This isn't over, bitch!" he screamed in Crease's face. "I'm contesting the will and I'm gonna sue you civilly for wrongful death."

"Get away from my client," Garrett commanded.

"Shut up, you . . ."

Suddenly, Junior was up on his toes with his left arm cranked behind his back in a hammerlock. Applying the pressure was a tall man with a swimmer's wide shoulders and narrow waist. Long black hair swept across his forehead. His blue eyes looked sleepy and his thick black mustache was shaggy. The man did not look angry and he sounded unexcited when he said, "Come on, Junior. Let's calm down here."

"Ah, ah," Junior managed as the man pressed his arm toward his shoulder blade and beyond.

"I don't want to hurt you," the man said, "but I can't have you threatening the senator and Ms. Garrett."

"Let go! Ah!" Junior gasped. His face was cramped with pain and Garrett thought he was going to cry.

"If I let go, will you behave?"

"Yes!"

"Okay," the man said as he released some of the pressure on Junior's arm. "Now, I'm taking you at your word and I'm going to let you go. When I do, I want you to head out of here as fast as your fat legs will carry you. If you're lying to me, I'll break both your arms. We on the same wavelength?"

"Yeah! Yeah! Let me go."

The man released Junior and took a step back. Junior grabbed his shoulder and bent forward.

"On your way. Let's not dawdle," the man said.

Junior glared, but kept his mouth shut and headed for the elevators.

"Thank you, Jack," Ellen Crease said calmly. She had not blinked during the encounter with Junior.

"My pleasure," the man said, flashing her a boyish smile.

Mary Garrett had noticed the man sitting in the back of the courtroom throughout the hearing. She had assumed that he was a policeman.

"Mary, this is Jack Brademas," Crease said. "He's the head of security at Hoyt Industries. Jack's been protecting me since I learned about the money that was paid to Martin Jablonski."

"Pleased to meet you, Mr. Brademas."

"Jack, please. Especially after that coup you just pulled off in court. Was Judge Quinn's ruling as good for the senator as it seemed?"

"Better," Garrett answered. "For all intents and purposes, this case is over."

[3]

"Ced, this is Lou Anthony. I just got back to my desk and there was a note to call you. What happened at the hearing?"

"Quinn fucked us, Lou."

"How?"

"He suppressed everything. The blood spatter evidence, Fargo's statements about what Hoyt told her. Everything."

"All the evidence?" Anthony repeated as if he could not believe his ears.

"Everything he could suppress, he threw out."

"Jesus. Where does that leave us?"

"In outer fucking space without a ship. Quinn gutted our case."

"Can't you appeal?"

"Sure, but it would be useless. The court of appeals can reverse a judge who misinterprets the law, but Quinn based his decision to suppress the blood spatter evidence on his personal evaluation of your credibility. The court can't review that."

"What do you mean, my credibility?"

"He said you were a liar, Lou. That's as plain as I can say it."

"He what?"

"He said you lied under oath when you testified that you did not intentionally pressure James Allen to let you into the bedroom."

"But I didn't. I mean, I persuaded the guy, but I never leaned on him. We just talked."

"That may be what really happened, but Quinn put it on the record that you are a liar. The court of appeals cannot reverse a decision that rests on a judge's evaluation of the credibility of a witness, unless there is no evidence in the record to support the finding."

"I wouldn't lie under oath. You know that."

"I know it, Lou, but everyone who reads Quinn's opinion is going to think otherwise."

[4]

While she was driving home, Karen Fargo caught the end of a news story about Ellen Crease's case, but she did not hear enough to let her figure out what had happened. Fargo turned on the television as soon as she walked into her house. The case was the lead story. A reporter was talking about Richard Quinn's dramatic decision while the screen showed a triumphant Ellen Crease waving to supporters from the courthouse steps.

"I want to thank all of the people who had faith in me during these dark days," Crease told the reporters who were massed around her. "I loved my husband. Losing him to senseless violence was a great blow, but being accused unjustly of murdering someone you love is the cruelest blow. I thank God for Judge Richard Quinn's courage."

"Will you continue to campaign, Senator?" a reporter shouted.

Crease stared directly into the camera. Her mouth was set in a grim line. When she spoke, there was no doubting her determination.

"I have never stopped campaigning. The Republican Party should not be represented by a man who is soft on crime, for gun control and sympathetic to the liberal forces in our society that would pervert the values that have made America the greatest country on earth. I represent the true values of our party, and the voters will validate that statement in the May primary."

The screen was suddenly filled with a picture of Benjamin Gage dressed in a tuxedo with his beautiful wife on his arm entering the Benson Hotel to attend a fund-raiser.

"Senator," asked a reporter from Channel 6, "what is your reaction to Judge Quinn's ruling in Ellen Crease's case?"

Gage halted. He looked serious and thoughtful.

"Ken, it would be inappropriate for me to comment on Ellen Crease's criminal case. However, I do feel that it would be ironic if Ms. Crease was to have her case dismissed on one of the technicalities that she so frequently derides in her speeches. It would also be unfortunate for the voters if the public was deprived of a clear resolution of the murder charges against Ms. Crease because of the suppression of the evidence that the State believes will prove its allegations."

"So you do not feel that justice is being done in Senator Crease's case?"

"Now, Ken," Gage answered with a patient smile, "you know better than to put words in my mouth. I will leave the business of solving Lamar Hoyt's murder to the police. My job is to represent the people of Oregon in the United States Senate."

Gage turned from the reporter and entered the hotel. The reporter made a closing comment, but Karen Fargo did not hear him. She was concentrating on the man who followed Senator Gage into the Benson. He was tall, good-looking, dressed in a tuxedo, and he had a jagged scar on his right cheek. Fargo only had a moment to study him, but he definitely looked like the man who had offered her money and a job if she would tell the police about her involvement with Lamar Hoyt. Did the man work for Senator Gage? She wondered if the film footage showing the man with the scar would be aired again at eleven. She decided to watch the late news so she could be certain about what she had seen.

The phone rang. Fargo switched off the set and picked up the receiver.

"Ms. Fargo?"

"Yes?"

"This is Detective Anthony."

"Yes?" Fargo answered tentatively.

"I wanted to tell you what happened in court."

"I . . . It was on the news. That the judge suppressed the evidence. What does that mean?"

"It means that Mr. Riker cannot use the evidence we found in the second search of the crime scene to convict Ellen Crease. Mr. Riker will appeal the judge's ruling, but that could take a while. Maybe years."

"So I won't have to go to court?"

"It's possible you might, but not in the near future."

Fargo sagged with relief. She would never forget Lamar, but she was terrified of having to appear in court.

"Thank you for calling," Fargo said.

"I wanted to be certain that you understood what happened," Anthony answered kindly. "Feel free to call me anytime if you have questions."

Fargo thought about the man with the scar. Should she tell Detective Anthony about him?

"Detective," she started. Then it occurred to her that she might lose her job and the money if she said anything. And it might involve her further in a matter that she wanted to put behind her.

"Yes?"

"Nothing. Just thank you."

[5]

Quinn told Fran Stuart to hold all of his calls. Then he asked her to stay late so that she could type up the drafts and final version of the Findings of Fact, Conclusions of Law and Order in the *Crease* case. Quinn shut his door and collapsed in the chair behind his desk. He felt sick to his stomach from what he had done and sick with fear of the consequences.

Quinn gathered the materials that he would need to write the order. It took him an hour to write and polish a draft. Quinn gave it to his secretary. Fran typed it quickly and Quinn sent her to dinner while he worked on the final draft. It was already after six and night had fallen.

Fran returned around seven and typed the final draft. Quinn read it through.

"This is fine, Fran. You can go home now. I'll sign it and leave it on your desk. File the original with the clerk's office and send a copy to Cedric Riker and Mary Garrett. And thanks for staying late."

Fran closed the door. Quinn rubbed his eyes. Then he read through his order a final time, checking the facts, rereading sections of cases he had cited and statutes he had quoted. When Quinn was convinced that he had constructed the document in a way that would make reversal in an appellate court impossible, he signed the order.

Quinn closed his eyes and rested his head against the back of his chair. He had put off thinking about the future until he had made his ruling out of fear that he would be too afraid to act. He could put off thinking about his career no longer. Quinn's life was the law, but he had violated his oath by ruling for Crease. If he had ruled honestly, he would have held that Allen's consent was not coerced. By ruling as he had, he had betrayed the trust that had been put in him by the people of his state.

Quinn looked around his chambers at the bound volumes that contained the Law. His father had written some of the opinions in those books. As a boy, he revered them and dreamed of following his father's example and career. Now Quinn saw that the cases in the reporters were nothing. You could write the most beautiful words, but they were meaningless without the will and the desire to follow them. Quinn had betrayed his trust. He had turned the words to dust.

Twenty

THE NEXT MORNING Quinn overslept. By the time he arrived at the courthouse Fran Stuart had filed the order in *Crease* and sent copies to the parties. Quinn told Stuart that he did not want to be disturbed. He shut the door to his chambers and began work on a draft of the letter of resignation that he planned to submit to Stanley Sax. Writing the letter was more difficult than he imagined. It was almost like writing a suicide note. There were many false starts and a lot of time spent staring into space. When Fran buzzed him at eleven forty-five, she startled Quinn out of one of his reveries.

"What is it, Fran?"

"There are two Portland Police detectives to see you. I told them that you didn't want to be disturbed, but they insist on speaking to you."

"What do they want?"

"They wouldn't say."

"Okay. Send them in. I'll talk to them."

The door to Quinn's chambers opened and a slender black man

Quinn did not recognize followed Lou Anthony into the room. Anthony looked like a man who was controlling his anger. Quinn colored as it dawned on him how much the detective must dislike him.

"Good morning, Judge," Anthony said with strained civility. "This is my partner, Leroy Dennis."

Quinn nodded at Dennis and asked, "What brings you here?"

"Police business. I'd like you to come with us."

"Come where?"

"There's been a murder and I want you to accompany Detective Dennis and me to the crime scene."

"If you need to have a search warrant authorized, I can do the work here."

"If I needed a search warrant, you'd be the last judge I'd contact," Anthony snapped. Dennis put his hand on his partner's arm and Anthony looked down, embarrassed by his outburst.

"There are some things that we need to talk over with you and we can't do it here," Dennis said.

"This is getting a little too mysterious, Detectives."

"Sorry, but this is all we can tell you before we get to the scene," Dennis said. "Everything will become clear to you there."

The Heathman Hotel was only a few blocks from the courthouse. The detectives were silent during the short walk and Quinn's imagination ran wild. When they arrived at the hotel the judge noticed several police cars parked near the entrance. Dennis and Anthony led Quinn through the lobby to the reception desk, where an officer and a harried-looking man in his forties were examining hotel records.

"Mr. Abrams," Anthony interrupted. The man who was talking to the officer looked up. "Did you see this man in here yesterday evening?"

Abrams studied Quinn for a few moments, then shook his head.

"It's impossible to say. We were extremely busy. The lobby was very crowded."

Suddenly, Quinn guessed why the detectives had brought him to the hotel. Claire Reston, Andrea Chapman's sister, was staying at the Heathman. Anthony had said that there had been a murder. Was Reston the victim? If she was, why did the police think that Quinn would know anything about her death?

"What's going on here?" Quinn demanded.

"You'll see in a moment," Dennis answered as the detectives led Quinn to the elevators. Once inside the car, Anthony pressed the button for the third floor. Reston had told Quinn that she was staying in room 325. Now Quinn was certain that he was being taken to view Reston's dead body. He remembered that Fran Stuart was standing inches away when Reston had told him her hotel and room number.

The door to 325 was open. A large Portland Police officer was guarding the entrance. The room was a corner suite. Criminalists from the Oregon State Crime Lab were moving around inside the sitting room, photographing, dusting and measuring. Everything in the room looked orderly, except for a room service tray with a half-eaten dinner on it that sat on a coffee table across from the television.

Anthony led Quinn through the crowd to the door to the bedroom. The door was partially closed, but Quinn could see the edge of the bed and a bare foot. He knew he did not want to go into the room, but he had no choice.

"Do you recognize this woman, Judge?" Anthony asked as he thrust the door open. The bedroom looked and smelled like a slaughterhouse. Objects had been knocked onto the floor from a dresser, a chair had been overturned and the bed had been stripped of its blankets, which lay in a bundle on the bloodstained carpet. The blood on the carpet was nothing compared to the quantity of blood that saturated the bare undersheet upon which Claire Reston lay spread-eagled. Her hands had been bound to the headboard and her feet were secured to the foot of the bed.

Blood had spattered on the wall behind her. She was naked. A crude gag had been stuffed inside her mouth.

Quinn's knees buckled and he leaned against the wall.

"Are you okay, Judge?" Dennis asked when he noticed Quinn's ashen pallor.

Quinn wanted to turn away from the bed, but he was mesmerized by the tableau of wanton violence.

"This is the first time . . . I've seen pictures, but . . ."

"Maybe we better go next door," Dennis said. "Get you outta here. You want some water?"

"Please."

Quinn began to turn from the bed. Then he froze. The hair on Reston's head was blond, but her pubic hair was black like Andrea Chapman's. Quinn moved slightly so he could see Reston's right hip. What he saw caused his stomach to roll.

"Hey," Dennis said, gripping Quinn's elbow. "Come on, now. Take some breaths."

Quinn turned from the bed. He gulped in air. Dennis led him from the room, but Quinn did not even notice that he was moving. He was trying to absorb what he had just seen. Not the corpse or the gaping wounds that covered it or the blood or the stench, but the pale, half-moon-shaped scar that Quinn had seen on the dead woman's hip: a scar identical to that which he had seen on Andrea Chapman's hip on the beach in the Cove of Lost Souls. Claire Reston did not just look like Andrea Chapman. She was Andrea Chapman. Chapman had not been murdered on St. Jerome.

Dennis led Quinn out of 325 and into the suite next door. The police had commandeered it as a temporary headquarters. Anthony followed them. A detective was on the phone in the sitting room and two police officers were drinking coffee on the couch. Dennis brought Quinn into the bedroom and Anthony shut the door. The judge sank onto the bed and held his head in his hands.

"Must be quite a shock," Dennis said sympathetically as he walked into the bathroom to get Quinn a glass of water. "Seeing that poor young woman like that. 'Specially if it's your first time. I got light-headed my first time, too. Couldn't eat all day."

Quinn's senses were overloaded by the horror he had witnessed in the bedroom next door and by the discovery that no one had been murdered on St. Jerome.

"Here," Dennis said, handing the glass to Quinn. Quinn took it gratefully and sipped a little. Dennis pulled up a chair next to the bed. "How long you known her, Judge?"

Dennis had slipped the question in so smoothly that Quinn almost answered it. Should he admit he knew the dead woman? Should he admit to knowing her as Claire Reston or Andrea Chapman? If he admitted to knowing that the dead woman was Andrea, how could he explain that the scar was the tip-off without revealing that he had seen Andrea in a bikini? Once he admitted that, he would have to confess to seeing her after the flight to St. Jerome. Quinn made a decision.

"I . . . I just met her. I was asked to speak at a legal seminar on St. Jerome in the Caribbean in late February. My wife was supposed to accompany me, but she had to cancel at the last minute because of a business emergency. My wife's seat on the plane was taken by a woman named Andrea Chapman."

Quinn paused and drank some more water.

"A few days ago, I received a call from a police detective who was looking into Ms. Chapman's disappearance . . ."

"Where did he call from and what was his name?" Anthony interrupted.

"I think his last name was Fletcher. He mentioned his first name, but I can't remember it. If he told me where he was calling from, I forgot. I don't think he did, though."

"So this Chapman woman disappeared?" Dennis said.

"From St. Jerome. I didn't know anything about that."

"You didn't see Chapman after the flight?" Anthony asked.

"Well, in the airport, but not after that."

"You were saying that you just met the deceased?" Dennis prodded.

"Yes. She came to my chambers during the lunch break in the hearing on the pretrial motions in Ellen Crease's case. She said her name was Claire Reston and that Andrea Chapman was her sister. She wanted to know if I had any information about her sister's disappearance."

"Why would she think you knew anything about that?" Anthony asked.

Quinn froze. He had not thought about that.

"I, uh, I assumed that she'd gotten my name from the detective who called me. He got my name from the airline manifest. She never told me how she got my name, but the detective must have told her that I sat next to her sister."

"So that's when you talked to the sister? On the plane and in the airport?" Anthony asked.

Quinn felt panicky. Why did Anthony repeat his question? Could he prove that Quinn had seen Andrea the next day?

"Yes."

"Not after the flight?"

"No. Not after."

"Judge Quinn, I am going to give you the *Miranda* rights now," Anthony said. Quinn's pulse rate jumped. Anthony would only do that if Quinn was a suspect in Claire Reston's murder.

"You have the right to remain silent . . ."

"Why is this necessary?" Quinn asked.

"I'll answer that when I'm done," Anthony answered curtly. Quinn sat silently while Anthony finished reading him his rights, trying to guess what the police knew.

"Judge, I'm going to ask you again. Did you see Andrea Chapman after the flight to St. Jerome?"

Quinn suddenly noticed the manila envelope that Anthony was holding. The detective had shielded it from Quinn's view while Dennis was talking to him. Anthony withdrew from the envelope a photograph of Quinn and Andrea talking on the blanket in the cove. The photograph had been taken with a telephoto lens. If they blew it up further, Quinn was certain that the scar on Chapman's hip would become visible and the police would figure out that Reston and Chapman were the same person, if they did not know that already.

"We found these photographs in the dead woman's suitcase, Judge Quinn. Would you care to explain them?"

Quinn was having trouble breathing.

"Can I get you some more water, Judge?" Dennis asked solicitously. "You okay?"

Quinn sucked in air. He was on the verge of breaking down.

"Did you fuck Chapman on St. Jerome?" Anthony asked angrily. "Did her sister trail you to Portland and threaten to tell your wife?" They didn't know that Reston and Chapman were the same person, Quinn realized. "Did you slash her to ribbons to shut her up?"

"No. It wasn't like that. I didn't have sex with Andrea."

"You want us to believe that you were all alone with this woman and you didn't try to fuck her?"

Quinn did not know what to say.

"It is a strange coincidence that this Chapman woman disappears right after you meet her, then her sister talks with you and she's dead the next day," Dennis said.

"You have to believe me," Quinn pleaded. "I met Andrea on the plane. She was very nice. We talked during the flight. She told me that there was a cove on the far side of the island with a beautiful reef. It's the cove in the picture. We spent the afternoon there. That's all."

"Why didn't you tell us that before?" Dennis asked.

"I was afraid that someone would think I was involved in her disappearance," Quinn answered lamely.

"Did you ever see these pictures before?" Dennis asked.

"No."

"That's funny, because you haven't asked us where we got them or who took them. You didn't even seem surprised to see them."

When Quinn did not respond, Dennis asked, "Judge, can you tell us where you were last night between six and eight?"

"Six and eight?" Quinn repeated inanely.

"Yes, sir."

"I was at the courthouse, in my chambers. I . . . I was working on the order in the *Crease* case."

"Can anyone vouch for you?"

"My secretary, Fran Stuart. She was there."

"The whole time?"

"No. She typed up a first draft for me, then went to dinner sometime between six and seven. Then she came back and typed the final. I think she left around seven-thirty."

"So there was an hour and a half between six and eight when you were alone?"

Quinn nodded.

"No cleaning people came in, no one called?"

Quinn shook his head. He felt completely helpless.

"You see our problem here, Judge?" Dennis asked. "The Heathman is only a short walk from the courthouse. I'd bet five minutes max. And there was a lot going on in the hotel between six and eight, which is the time when the medical examiner estimates that Claire Reston was murdered. It would have been easy for you to walk from the courthouse to the hotel, slip up to the third floor unnoticed and . . ." Dennis shrugged. "Can you help us out here?"

Quinn looked back and forth between the two policemen. Both men watched him with blank expressions.

"You can't think . . . My, God, I could never do something like . . . like what was done to that poor woman."

"Nice people sometimes do terrible things under stress, Judge," Dennis said sympathetically. "She showed you the photos, you see your marriage and career going down the toilet. We see a lot of this kind of thing. If you did it, let us know so we can help you."

"That . . . that woman wasn't just killed. That was methodical. That was torture."

"Maybe you got a taste on St. Jerome," Anthony said harshly. "The thrill of having Chapman helpless, begging. It can be a turn-on for some people. Was it a turn-on for you?"

Quinn stared at Anthony in disbelief. Then he looked at Dennis. They had been playing with him and he was too distracted to see it. They really believed that he could tie up and torture a defenseless woman.

"Gentlemen, I've tried to be cooperative, but it is now clear to me . . . I don't want to continue this conversation, except to say that I did not hurt Claire Reston. I want to go now. I won't talk to you anymore without a lawyer."

"Why don't you sit and think a minute while I discuss this with Detective Anthony?" Dennis said as he motioned Anthony into the outer room.

Quinn let his head fall into his hands. He wanted to tell the detectives the truth, but he would be providing them with a massive motive for murder if he revealed that the dead woman had been used to blackmail him. Dennis and Anthony would believe that Quinn, enraged by her betrayal, had murdered Reston. The conclusion was logical, even if it was false.

The door opened and Dennis and Anthony reentered the bedroom.

"We're going to let you go, Judge," Dennis told Quinn. "Neither one of us thinks you've told the truth, but we don't want to rush this investigation. I advise you to think very seriously about your duties as a citizen. If you have information that would help us solve the death of the poor girl in the other room, you have to tell us. You're not just some nobody on the street. You're a judge. From what they say, that means something to you. Think about how you should be acting here."

[2]

Fran Stuart stood up as soon as Quinn walked into the reception area. She looked very upset.

"I waited for you to come back. I didn't know where to reach you."

"Calm down, Fran. What's wrong?"

"It's Mr. Price. He's had a heart attack. Richard Kahn called you ten minutes after you left with the detectives."

"Is he . . . ?"

"No. Mr. Kahn said they were talking about a case in Mr. Price's office when he complained about chest pains. He's at St. Vincent's Hospital. They're in surgery right now."

Quinn was nursing a cup of coffee in the hospital cafeteria when a tall, middle-aged woman wearing a black skirt and a gray sweater approached his table.

"Judge Quinn?"

"Yes."

"I'm Dr. Loerts. I operated on Mr. Price."

"Sit down, please. Can I get you some coffee?"

"No, thanks," the surgeon answered with a weary smile. She looked tired. Her red hair was pulled back in a ponytail and she rubbed her eyelids as soon as she slid onto the chair across from the judge.

"Mr. Price is going to be fine. We performed a triple bypass. That sounds scary, but we do a ton of them and it's routine for my team."

"What happened?"

"Three of Mr. Price's arteries were clogged and that was keeping an adequate supply of blood from reaching his heart. We took one vein from his leg and another from his chest and attached them to the arteries at a spot in front of and behind the area that was blocked. In other words, we literally bypassed the area. Everything is working just fine now. In fact, he's probably in better shape because there isn't anything blocking the flow of blood to his heart."

"Can I see him?"

"Not right now. He's in the recovery room and he'll probably be there for another hour or two. He'll go to the coronary care unit when he's ready. You can see him there but he's going to be heavily medicated. He probably won't even remember your visit. When he's well enough, he'll go up to the sixth floor for the rest of his stay. That floor is reserved for people with heart problems. I expect him to be out of the hospital by next week."

"I'd still like to see him today, even if he doesn't know. When can I do that?"

The doctor looked at her watch. "We'll transfer him to coronary care in an hour or so. You can only stay for a short time, but I'd guess that you'll be able to see him around six."

"You're certain my . . . my father is okay?"

Dr. Loerts pushed herself to her feet. "Your dad is going to be fine, so don't worry."

[3]

Quinn could not return to the gloomy solitude of his rented apartment. The only other place he could think to go was his chambers, where he planned to finish writing his letter of resignation and put his cases in order for the judges who would inherit them. Quinn drove the route to the courthouse in a mental fog. Dr. Loerts had assured Quinn that Frank would be okay, but Frank was eighty years old and Quinn knew that the years they had together were growing short.

Quinn's eyes watered and he felt a painful lump in his throat as he recalled asking Dr. Loerts if his "father" was okay. It was the first time that he had ever referred to Frank Price as his father, even though the quiet, taciturn man had slowly insinuated himself into Quinn's consciousness in that way.

Quinn remembered the day that he moved into the Price home. It had been the day of his parents' funeral. He'd been putting his clothes away, still dressed in his black suit and too stunned to change, when Price came into his new bedroom. Quinn could picture him standing in the middle of the room, his arms dangling at his side, looking ill at ease. Quinn had been holding a stack of white crew-neck undershirts in his hand.

"I know you're about all in, so I'll make this short," Frank had said. "Anna and I don't have children. We didn't plan it that way. It's just the way it worked out. Your father is as close as we came. He was a great lawyer and one of the best men I ever met. When he married your mother, we were overjoyed and we came to love her as much as we loved Pat. Anna and I can't take the place of your parents. We'd never try. But we're here for you whenever you need us."

Quinn warmed quickly to Anna, but it took him years to feel comfortable with Frank Price. Now, when he was close to losing him, the full import of what the feisty old man had done for him flooded in and it made him realize what it would mean to lose Laura, too. Love was a precious commodity, which people possessed rarely in this life. When you found it, you could not let it slip away. Quinn loved Laura and he was going to fight for her. He vowed to call her as soon as he arrived at the courthouse. He would tell her how much he loved her and he would beg her to take him back.

The Multnomah County Courthouse had been constructed in 1914 when there were few cars and parking was easy, so it did not have a garage. Judges with seniority were assigned spaces across the park across from the courthouse in the basement of the Justice Center, but Quinn's parking space was in a garage three blocks away where the county rented space. Quinn stopped at the entrance and put a plastic card in a slot. A metal bar rose and Quinn drove in. His space was in a corner far from the entrance on the lowest floor. The ceiling above the space was low where the ramp from the floor above sloped down and the corner was always in shadow.

There were no other cars around when Quinn parked his Volvo, which was not surprising since it was after nine at night.

He knew a security guard patrolled the garage but he did not see him and assumed that he was making his rounds on another level.

Quinn's attaché case was in the backseat of the car. He opened the front door and stepped out, closing it behind him. He opened the back door on the driver's side and bent down to retrieve the attaché. When he straightened up, he saw movement in the side view mirror. Quinn turned and raised the case reflexively. Whatever the attacker had in his hand bounced off its side, but the blow was hard enough to drive Quinn backward into the side of the car.

Quinn lowered the attaché enough to see a tall man wearing jeans, gloves, a dark blue windbreaker and a ski mask. There was a sap in his right hand. Quinn was certain that he was the same man who had broken into his apartment. Quinn was taller and heavier than his assailant but he had never been good with his fists. He had won his only fight in high school because of his size, not his skill. Quinn circled warily, holding the attaché in front of him like a shield. The attacker edged closer. Quinn yelled for help. As the scream echoed off the concrete, the attacker feinted with the hand that held the sap. Quinn raised the attaché and the man kicked him in his shin. Quinn gasped. His right leg gave way and Quinn dropped his arms while still holding onto the attaché. The attacker smashed the sap into the left side of Quinn's head. Quinn's hands flew to his face and he dropped the case. The man hit Quinn in the solar plexus to silence him. Quinn fell against the car, hitting his head hard on the edge of the roof. He started to slump to the floor, but his attacker propped him up.

Quinn was almost unconscious. He heard the driver's door open and felt his attacker push him into the front seat. He wanted to sit up, but his body would not obey him. His vision blurred. Quinn thought he saw his attacker take a handgun out of the windbreaker and place it on the hood of the car. Quinn tried to struggle up, but rough hands grabbed both of his legs. He heard his assailant swear. The man was trying to stuff Quinn's legs into the car.

Quinn suddenly remembered his car keys. The Volvo could be opened or locked from a distance using a small keypad that was attached to the key. The lock button on the automatic door opener doubled as a panic alarm. Quinn groped in his pants pocket until he felt the plastic keypad. Just as his assailant finished pushing one of his legs into the car, Quinn held the lock button down for a count of three. The locks on all four doors clicked down. The attacker stopped, surprised by the sharp sound. The car alarm blared. Adrenaline coursed through Quinn. He kicked out with both feet. They struck solidly and drove the man back. Quinn launched himself out of the car and landed a wild right to the side of his attacker's head. The punch had no force and the man rolled with it, then connected solidly with Quinn's ribs. Quinn grunted and the man struck him in the throat.

"Hey! What's going on here?" a security guard yelled from the far end of the garage. Quinn's attacker glanced toward the guard, doubled up Quinn with a front kick and ran toward the exit. Quinn slumped over the hood of the Volvo just as the guard ran past him. The guard was overweight and out of shape. He chased the attacker for a short distance, then turned back to Quinn. The judge looked down and saw the handgun. He pocketed it just as the guard asked, "Are you okay?"

Quinn slumped against the car. His throat hurt and he had trouble talking for a moment, so he just nodded.

"You're lucky I came down here on my rounds."

The guard took Quinn's elbow and helped him to straighten up. He picked up Quinn's attaché.

"Is this what he was after?" the guard asked.

"That's just a file in one of my cases," Quinn croaked.

The guard realized the area of the garage he was in.

"Are you a judge?"

Quinn nodded.

"You don't think this was some guy you sentenced?"

"No. He was probably after my wallet."

Quinn sat in the car until he caught his breath. He touched the side of his head where he had been sapped, and winced. The back of his head also hurt where it had smacked against the roof of the car, but the skin was not broken. His ribs, shin and head hurt and felt a little sick from being kicked and punched in the body.

"Do you want to go to the hospital?" the guard asked.

"No."

Adrenaline had made the attack seem surreal. Now it was wearing off and Quinn began to shake, as it dawned on him that he could have been killed.

"I'd really like to go to my chambers in the courthouse."

"You're certain?"

"Positive."

He was afraid to return to his apartment, which his assailant had penetrated with ease.

"I'll walk you over to make sure nothing else happens."

"Thanks. And thank you for saving me."

As the guard and Quinn walked to the courthouse, Quinn asked, "Do you have to report this?"

"Definitely."

"It's just that I can't identify the man who attacked me. He was wearing a mask. And he didn't get anything. I don't want to waste police time when there's nothing I can say that will help them."

"This is pretty serious. This guy may have attacked someone else. Besides, it's the rules."

"Will the police have to talk to me right away? I'm pretty tired. I'd rather give my statement tomorrow."

"I'll see what I can do."

The security guard rode up with Quinn to his floor. Quinn unlocked the door to his office. He heard the guard report the attack on Fran's phone while he washed his face in the bathroom.

The guard rapped on the doorjamb and Quinn stepped out of the bathroom.

"You're okay for tonight. They're gonna send over a patrolman in the afternoon."

The guard left. As soon as the door closed, Quinn took a step forward and the gun slapped against his side. Quinn took it out. When the policeman interviewed him about the attack tomorrow, he would give it to him. As he looked at the weapon a thought occurred to Quinn. He went through the sequence of the attack. The man had used a sap, so he wanted Quinn unconscious. When the assailant believed that Quinn was unconscious, he put the gun on the hood of the car and tried to stuff Quinn's legs into the car. Why do that? Why not just use the gun?

An answer occurred to Quinn. He felt ill. The police had the photographs of Quinn and Andrea in the Cove of Lost Souls. They suspected him of killing the woman at the Heathman. His assailant was planning on making it look like Quinn had committed suicide in his car. The gun would be placed in Quinn's hand. When the body was discovered it would look like Quinn had killed himself rather than face disgrace. An investigation might have cleared Quinn. Suicide would end the case.

Quinn let the gun rest in his hand and he flashed back to the fight in the garage. He'd been beaten, but he had fought back and it had felt good. For the first time since this insanity had started, he had not been a punching bag. He wondered what he would have done if he'd had the gun when he was attacked. He knew nothing about guns, but he believed that he would have fired it. The thought unsettled Quinn. He had experienced many emotions since Andrea Chapman was murdered, but anger was not one of them. Anger was not an emotion that Quinn felt often. He rarely had a reason to be angry, but he was angry now. Someone was playing with his life and he was going to find out who it was.

Quinn suddenly realized that there was someone else who was in danger, someone who had a motive as strong as Quinn's to discover the people behind the plot to fix the *Crease* case and the resources to fight back. Quinn went to his desk. He opened Ellen Crease's file and found the form that she had filled out so that she could be released on her own recognizance. Then he dialed her unlisted phone number.

[4]

Two armed and uniformed guards were waiting for Quinn just inside the front gate of the Hoyt estate in a patrol vehicle with the markings of a private security company. As soon as Quinn stopped his car, the passenger door of the patrol car opened and a man with the build of an offensive lineman walked to the gate.

"Please step out of the car, sir, and show me some identification," he commanded. Quinn noticed that he kept one hand on the butt of a holstered revolver. The guard in the car also watched Quinn's every move.

A gray mist covered Portland and the air was cold and clammy. Quinn shivered and hunched his shoulders. He slid his driver's license through the bars of the front gate. As soon as the guard was satisfied that the judge was the person he claimed to be, he told Quinn to return to his car. Quinn waited while the guard radioed the house, glad to be in a warm place again. Moments later, Quinn heard a low hum. The gate opened wide and the guard told him how to reach the house. Quinn drove through the gate. In the night sky was a dim quarter-moon. Quinn's headlights only made the barest incursion into the thick fog that obscured most of the grounds. Twice he saw an armed guard on patrol.

A handsome man in a gray business suit was waiting for Quinn when he parked in front of the mansion.

"Come in, Judge," the man said, extending a hand. "I'm Jack Brademas, head of security at Hoyt Industries. The senator wanted me to sit in on this meeting."

Quinn shook hands and Brademas led him into the library, where Lou Anthony had talked to Ellen Crease on the evening of the murder. Crease stood up when the men entered. She was wearing jeans and a white shirt under a baggy sweater. A cigar smoldered in an ashtray at her elbow.

"You look cold, Judge," Crease said. "Would you like tea, coffee, or something stronger?"

Quinn noticed a coffee urn and a teapot sitting on a cherrywood sideboard next to several fine-china cups and saucers.

"Coffee, please."

"Would you, Jack?"

Quinn sat down across from Crease in a high-backed chair and Brademas handed him a cup. The senator waited patiently while Quinn took a sip. Quinn's exhaustion was apparent, as was the discolored swelling on the side of the judge's face.

"When you called me, you sounded so upset that I agreed to meet with you," Crease said. "Now that I've had some time to think, I'm wondering if this meeting doesn't violate some code of ethics. I am the defendant in a case you're hearing."

"Matters have gone way beyond that, Senator. There are events happening on the periphery of your criminal case of which you have been completely unaware. Both our lives are in danger."

"Please explain that."

"Senator, you have some very powerful enemies. People who will stop at nothing, including murder, to harm you. They have already effectively destroyed my career as a judge. Tonight they tried to kill me."

"What?"

"Monday evening, a man in a ski mask broke into my apartment. He had photographs of a young woman and me that have the potential of destroying my career and my marriage. The man threatened to make the pictures public if I didn't fix your case so that you would be convicted of murdering your husband and Martin Jablonski."

"But you ruled for me. You destroyed the State's case."

"Yes. I did the only thing I could think of to protect you," Quinn said softly. "Because of what I did, a woman was murdered and an attempt was made on my life."

"Judge, this is getting a bit confusing," Jack Brademas interrupted sympathetically. "If we're going to help, we have to know everything that's happened to you. Why don't you start at the beginning?"

Quinn recounted the trip to St. Jerome, the ruse that was used to trick Laura into flying to Miami, the visit from Claire Reston, his discovery of the second explanation for the blood spatter evidence found on the armoire, Reston's murder, and the recent attempt on his life.

"I think that Martin Jablonski was paid to murder you, Senator," Quinn concluded. "When he failed and you were arrested for your husband's murder, I was set up. Now that I've double-crossed the blackmailers, they're trying to frame me for Reston's murder and kill me. But I'm not the main focus of these people. You are. And that means that you're also in danger."

"Judge, I can't begin to thank you for the sacrifices you've made for me. I owe you everything. Quite possibly my life."

Quinn looked down, embarrassed. Crease thought silently for a moment. Then she blew an angry plume of smoke into the air and said, "Benjamin Gage has to behind this. He and Junior are the only people I can think of who hate me enough to want me dead, and Junior is too stupid to dream up a scheme this complex."

Brademas nodded. "I drew the same conclusion."

He turned to Quinn.

"Benjamin Gage's administrative assistant is a man named Ryan Clark. He's an ex–navy SEAL. As soon as you told us that a man in scuba gear snatched the Chapman woman I thought of Clark. Pulling off a fake abduction underwater would be a piece of cake for someone with Clark's skills."

"How did he do it?" Quinn asked. "I never saw Andrea surface for air."

"She wouldn't have to. There's an emergency breathing apparatus attached to all air tanks. She could have used the one on Clark's tank while they were underwater."

"What do you think we should do next, Judge?" Crease asked.

"I think that the key to discovering the person behind this plot is learning the true identity of Andrea Chapman or Claire Reston or whatever her real name is. If we find out who she is, we might be able to find a link between her and the people who are after us."

"Jack can trace her, Judge," Crease said. "He was a Portland Police officer before he came to work for my husband's company. We knew each other on the force. He still has contacts in the bureau.

"Jack, can you get copies of the investigative reports of the murder at the Heathman? We need to know the identity of the murdered woman and where she lived. Then we can try to find out how she got mixed up in this."

"I'll have the information by tomorrow afternoon," Brademas assured his boss.

"Good. Why don't you also think about the information that Judge Quinn has given us and see if you can come up with any other avenues of investigation?"

Brademas left and Crease turned to Quinn. "It looks like we're both in more trouble than we ever wanted to be." Crease sighed heavily. "If the latest polls hold, my political career will be over. The only way I can save it is by proving that I was framed. Otherwise, people will always believe that I hired Jablonski and beat the rap on a technicality."

"It might help if I went public and told everyone about the blackmail attempt."

"It would only help if we can prove that we were both set up and who is behind this conspiracy. Otherwise, anything you say will sound like an attempt to exonerate yourself in the Reston murder. Besides, going public would destroy your career and I couldn't let you do that for me."

"My career is over, anyway. I'm stepping down from the bench tomorrow. When I was attacked, I was going back to the courthouse to write my letter of resignation."

"Don't do that. You're a good judge. If you resign from the bench, you're letting the bastards who set us up win. It took guts to rule for me. It was the right thing to do. Let Jack and me work on this. And don't give up hope. That's what you'd be doing if you resign."

Twenty-one

W HEN QUINN walked into Stanley Sax's chambers, the presiding judge took a hard look at the yellowish purple bruise that spread across the left side of Quinn's face.

"Are you okay?"

"Physically, I'm fine. Emotionally . . . that's something else."

"I can imagine. You're the talk of the courthouse. First that ruling in *Crease*, then this attack in the garage."

"I want to take some time off, Stan."

"That makes sense. How long do you want?"

"I cleared my desk when I thought that the *Crease* trial would take most of the month. I can take a few days off without disrupting the work of the court. I'll write memos in all of my cases so that any judge you assign will be able to get up to speed easily."

"All right. Being attacked like that has to be frightening. Go home and rest. Call me next week and let me know how you feel. Maybe you and Laura should head for the coast. Lily and I used to rent a little bungalow in Cannon Beach and watch the storms with hot buttered rums and a good fire." Sax smiled. "A little romance is a great remedy for the blues."

Sax's reminder of his empty marriage hurt, but Quinn faked a smile and said, "Thanks for the advice and for being so understanding."

Sax waved off Quinn. The judge left Sax's chambers and headed for his own. Fran Stuart examined Quinn's face. Before she could ask, Quinn said, "This looks pretty bad, but I'm fine."

Fran handed Quinn a stack of messages. As Quinn thumbed quickly through the stack to see if there was one from Crease or Brademas, his secretary said, "Most of these are from friends asking if you're okay or from reporters who want to interview you. There was also a call from an Officer Ramirez. He wanted to set up an appointment for this afternoon so he can get a statement about the attack."

Quinn looked at his watch. It was a little after three. He could probably fit in Ramirez around four-thirty. Quinn started toward his office.

"And your wife called several times." Quinn's heart jumped. "She wanted you to call her as soon as you got in."

Quinn had been too exhausted physically and emotionally to call Laura after his visit to Ellen Crease. Her calls made Quinn anxious. Was she calling to reconcile or to ask for a divorce?

"Oh," Fran said, "there was one unusual call. It came in ten minutes ago. A woman named Denise Ritter. She said it was urgent. She wanted to talk to you about that woman who was murdered at the Heathman Hotel. She said that she's the woman's sister."

"Her sister?"

"Yes. She sounded very upset."

"Thank you, Fran."

Quinn thumbed through his messages until he found the slip with Ritter's phone number. It had a Seattle area code. The phone rang twice, then a woman answered.

"Is this Denise Ritter?" Quinn asked.

"Yes?"

"This is Judge Richard Quinn."

Quinn could hear breathing on the other end of the phone.

"Ms. Ritter?"

"I'm sorry. Maybe I shouldn't have called."

"Is this about the woman who was murdered?"

"Yes. Marie is . . . was my sister."

Quinn heard the woman's breath catch. Then he heard a sob.

"Are you all right?"

"I'm sorry. I . . . I flew down this morning on the shuttle to identify Marie's body."

"That must have been awful."

"The detectives were very kind, but . . ."

Ritter's voice trailed off and Quinn heard her blowing her nose. She apologized again.

"Ms. Ritter, why did you call me?"

"The detectives showed me a picture of you and Marie on a beach."

"You told them that the woman in the pictures was Marie?"

"Yes."

"Did they seemed surprised?"

"Now that you mention it, they did."

"What did they ask you when you said that?"

"They wanted to know if Marie had ever mentioned you, but they wouldn't tell me why they were asking."

Ritter hesitated. Then she said, "Judge, Marie and I weren't close. Especially these past few years. I was hoping you could tell me what went wrong. How this happened."

"Ms. Ritter, I would like to talk with you about Marie, too. If I took the shuttle to Seattle, would you meet with me tonight?"

[2]

The shuttle touched down a little after six P.M. Twenty minutes later, the cab Quinn hired at Sea-Tac Airport rounded a curve on the freeway and the judge saw the massive, glass and concrete structures that dominated Seattle's city center. Seattle had its share of interesting architecture: the Space Needle towered over everything, and the Pike Place Market, a collection of ramshackle stalls, shops and restaurants seemingly held together by glue, tottered on a hillside overlooking Elliott Bay. However, Seattle's buildings were nowhere near as spectacular as its geography. The "Emerald City" sat on a narrow strip of land between Puget Sound and eighteen-mile-long Lake Washington. Massive Mount Rainier dominated the landscape east of the city, and to the west were the jagged peaks of the Olympic Mountains.

Shortly after reaching the city, the cab turned off the interstate and traveled downhill toward the Pioneer Square Historic District, an area of late-Victorian and early-twentieth-century buildings that had been built up after the Great Fire of 1889. Day and night, the district swarmed with crowds attracted to its galleries, restaurants, antique shops and theaters. Denise Ritter had agreed to meet Quinn in an espresso bar at First and James near the original Pioneer Square. Quinn spotted the totem pole in the square before he located the café, a dark and narrow space squeezed between a gallery featuring Native American art and an occult bookstore. Toward the back of the espresso bar, a woman wearing a peasant dress nervously scanned the door.

Denise Ritter bore little resemblance to her sister. She was five nine and stoop-shouldered. Her hair was black like Marie's, but it was frizzy and collected behind her in a barrette, and her blue eyes hid behind thick, tortoiseshell glasses. Behind the thick lenses, Ritter's eyes were red from crying. When she noticed Quinn walking toward her, Ritter seemed to pull into herself. It took Quinn a moment to realize that Marie had modeled her Claire Reston persona on her real sister.

"I'm Richard Quinn," the judge said when he reached Ritter's table. Ritter held out her hand self-consciously and Quinn took it. The skin felt cold and she looked exhausted.

"Are you all right?" Quinn asked as he sat down.

"No," Ritter answered frankly. "Seeing Marie like that was really hard for me."

She could not go on and Quinn was relieved when a skinny waiter in jeans and a T-shirt walked up to the table. Quinn asked for coffee. Ritter was nursing a latte.

"I appreciate your willingness to meet with me, under the circumstances," Quinn told Ritter.

"I'm doing this as much for me as for you. Marie was my sister. What I don't understand is your interest."

"What did the police tell you about me?"

"That you knew Marie."

"Did they say that I was a suspect in Marie's death?"

The question startled Ritter. She shook her head while examining Quinn more closely.

"And Marie never mentioned me to you, or talked about a judge that she knew?"

Ritter looked down at the tabletop. "I rarely talked to Marie about her business."

"What exactly did you understand Marie's business to be?"

Ritter sighed sadly. "Marie was a call girl, Judge. A prostitute."

Quinn should have been shocked, but he wasn't. If you wanted to hire a woman to seduce a man, seeking the services of a professional made sense.

"Did Marie work in Seattle?"

"Yes."

"Did she ever work in Portland?"

"I don't know. She never told me she did, but I disapproved of Marie's . . . lifestyle and she knew it, so it was rare for her to discuss her profession with me."

"I want you to know that before today I did not know that Marie was a prostitute," Quinn said firmly. "She told me that she designed belts. I thought she worked in the fashion industry. Did she ever do anything like that?"

"Marie! Not that I knew of."

"Would you mind talking about your sister?"

Ritter brushed at her eyes. Her lower lip trembled.

"Marie was two years younger than me. She was always rebellious. I was a good student. Marie was at least as intelligent as I am, but she barely passed. She was into drugs, boys. My parents tried everything. Eventually, they gave up. When she was eighteen, Marie was arrested for prostitution and my parents kicked her out of the house. She wasn't really living at home then, anyway. After that, they wouldn't have anything to do with her."

"Do your parents know that Marie is dead?"

"No. I haven't told them. I don't know what to say. They wrote Marie off years ago."

"How close were you to your sister?"

"That's hard to answer. We saw very little of each other when I was at college and graduate school. After I moved back to Seattle to take a teaching job we started meeting a little more, but there wasn't any plan to it. Sometimes she would just drop by or she'd call on the spur of the moment and we'd go out for dinner. A lot of the times when she called I thought it was because she was lonely, but, if I asked her, she would always pretend to be upbeat and tell me how great her life was."

Ritter paused and took a sip of her latte. When she looked up, there were tears in her eyes.

"There were other times when she would show up out of the blue, strung out or just needing a place to stay. I knew she wanted help when she came to me like that. I even got her to go into a rehab program once. The last few times I saw her I think she was clean, but I'm so naive I don't think I could really tell if she was using."

Quinn handed Ritter his handkerchief.

"I'm sorry," she apologized. "I guess we really weren't that close. We were so different. But she was my sister and she was so lost. The last time we were together I tried to talk her into getting a straight job. She just laughed. She said she was doing great and was going to do better. She looked like she was, too. She was wearing expensive clothes and jewelry I hadn't seen before."

"Where was she getting her money? I know you said that she was a call girl. Was that her only job? Did she have a pimp?"

"No, not a pimp. From what I could figure out, she worked for an escort service. But it was a front for a call girl operation."

Denise paused. She suddenly looked very thoughtful.

"That last time I saw Marie, the time I told you about, when she was dressed in the expensive clothes, that was in mid-February. She was very up, very excited, and that was strange, because I knew she didn't enjoy earning her money the way she did. She'd told me that much."

Quinn had been in St. Jerome in late February. He was sure that Marie Ritter's sudden, mid-February good fortune was connected to the blackmail plot.

"Did Marie tell you why she was excited or how she got the money for the clothes?"

"Not specifically. She did talk about making a lot of money and I had the impression that the money she was going to make wasn't connected to the escort service. That it was something that she had going on the side. But I can't be certain of that."

"Did your sister have any friends I might talk to?"

"Marie mentioned someone named Christy a few times and another woman named Robin, but all I know about them is their first names."

"Did your sister ever talk about her customers?"

"I didn't encourage Marie to talk about what she did. It was very distasteful to me, that kind of life." Ritter shuddered. "I can't even imagine it.

"When she did speak about the men she'd been with, it was usually with contempt, but she never mentioned their names and I didn't ask. She thought most of them were pathetic. There were a few she said were okay, but generally she would laugh about them. As I said, I didn't enjoy discussing what she did, except to try to get her to stop."

"Denise, did your sister ever mention any customers from Portland?"

"Not that I can recall." Ritter paused. "She did tell me that there was a man she had seen more than once who lived in Oregon. He had some kind of business in Seattle. It was something odd."

"Can you remember what it was?"

Ritter brightened. "She said he was an undertaker. Marie thought that was funny."

Quinn felt a surge of excitement. "Denise, this is important. Did she describe this man? Can you remember anything she said about him?"

Ritter frowned, then shook her head.

"All I remember was his business."

"She never said how old he was?"

"She said he didn't dress or act like she thought an undertaker would. I think he was a flashy dresser and he liked to dance all night, so I assumed that he was young, but she never told me his age."

"Do you have any idea how I can get in touch with Marie's escort service?"

"No. I don't even know where Marie was living these past few months."

Ritter paused. Then she looked directly at Quinn.

"I've been trying to build up the courage to ask you something since you walked in, Judge."

"Go ahead and ask your question."

"What was your connection with my sister?"

"I met her on a plane when I flew to the Caribbean to speak at a legal conference. We spent the next day on the beach you saw in the picture. I think Marie was hired to make friends with me, then seduce me. When the police searched the hotel room where Marie was murdered, they found those pictures in her suitcase and they brought me to the hotel room. They thought that I might have killed her, but I didn't. I could never hurt someone the way your sister was hurt."

Ritter digested this information. Then she took a deep breath and looked directly at Quinn.

"The detectives . . . They only pulled back the sheet enough to show me Marie's face and I was too upset to ask. Was she . . . ? Did she feel much pain?"

Quinn flashed back to the room. For a brief moment, he saw Marie Ritter's savaged body.

"I'm afraid she did," the judge answered gently.

Ritter's eyes watered. She bit her lip.

"Please tell me what happened."

"Marie, you don't want to know that. That isn't going to do you any good."

"Please," Ritter pleaded.

Quinn sighed and described what he had seen in the hotel room as delicately as was possible. When he was through, Ritter spaced out for a moment.

"I knew this would happen if she stayed in that life. I tried to talk to her, but she wouldn't listen to me."

"You can only do so much. Don't make the mistake of thinking that this was your fault or that there was some way that you could have saved her. Some people don't want to be saved. Promise me that you're not going to take this burden on your shoulders."

Ritter sighed. "No, I won't make that mistake."

"Good. That's good. The killer took your sister. Don't you let him take you, too."

[3]

Quinn was barely conscious of the fifty-minute flight back to Portland. All he could think about was the information that Denise Ritter had given to him. Mary Garrett had filed a pretrial discovery motion claiming that she had not received all of the police reports in the possession of the prosecution. To resolve the issue, Quinn had been forced to review the reports. He had read

Detective Anthony's interview with Charles DePaul. If Junior knew that his father was going to change his will, he would have a clear motive for hiring Jablonski to kill his father and Ellen Crease. If Junior knew that Crease could not benefit from the will if she was convicted of her husband's murder, Junior would have a motive to blackmail Quinn. Quinn suddenly remembered the argument between Junior and his father at Hoyt Industries that Anthony had learned about during his interview with Stephen Appling. Were they arguing about the will?

How could he find out the cause of the argument? Only Junior and his father were present. An idea occurred to Quinn. Karen Fargo had to be the woman who was going to be the new beneficiary of Hoyt's will. She was his mistress when the argument occurred. Men talked to their mistresses about the things that bothered them.

Quinn's first impulse was to tell Ellen Crease about his discovery in Seattle. Jack Brademas could talk to Fargo. He was a professional investigator, a former policeman. But that wouldn't work. Fargo would never talk to anyone connected to Ellen Crease. He would have to do it.

A light rain was falling when Quinn's flight landed at nine-thirty. He found Fargo's address in the phone book and drove straight from the Portland Airport to her yellow and white Cape Cod. The judge parked out front shortly after ten o'clock. There were lights on in the front room. Quinn dashed across the street and huddled under the overhang that shaded the front door. He rang the bell. The sound from a television show stopped and a curtain moved. Moments later, the front door opened as wide as the safety chain would permit.

"Ms. Fargo?"

"Yes?" she responded warily.

"I'm Richard Quinn. I'm a judge. I heard the case against Ellen Crease."

Fargo recognized Quinn from the television broadcasts about the case.

"What do you want from me?"

Quinn smiled to put Fargo at ease. "It would be great if I could get inside. I forgot my umbrella."

Water was running down Quinn's face and beading on his raincoat. Fargo opened the door and let Quinn inside. He ran a hand through his hair to rid it of some of the rain.

"I apologize for coming so late and not calling first. I wouldn't disturb you if this wasn't important."

Fargo walked into the living room and gestured toward the couch. Quinn took off his coat so he would not dampen her furniture. Fargo sat forward on her chair watching Quinn.

"You know that I ruled against the State in the pretrial hearings?"

Fargo nodded.

"Some new information has come to me that I didn't have when I made the ruling. I'm afraid I can't tell you what it is. I hope you understand."

"Certainly."

"I've learned that Lamar Hoyt and his son had an argument shortly before Mr. Hoyt was murdered. It's suddenly become important to find out the substance of the argument, but no one knows what they talked about. I was wondering if Mr. Hoyt mentioned it to you."

"Yes. He did. I . . . I never told anyone about it because I didn't think that it was important."

"That's okay, Ms. Fargo. You wouldn't have understood why I need to know about the argument. Can you tell me what Mr. Hoyt said?"

"I don't remember the date."

"That's okay."

"I do remember Lamar visiting in the early evening. He was very angry about Junior."

"Why?"

"He thought he was skimming money from the mortuary business. Profits were down and he was furious. He was having Junior investigated and the investigator had found out that Junior was living way beyond his means. The argument occurred when Lamar confronted Junior with the things that the investigator found."

"Did Mr. Hoyt mention anything specific that the investigator had found?"

Fargo colored. "Most of it had to do with women."

"Dates?"

Fargo shook her head. "There was some of that, but Lamar said that Junior was also paying expensive prostitutes. Lamar also thought that Junior was using cocaine. It was very sordid and Lamar was furious."

[4]

Laura's calls had been on Quinn's mind all day, but he had been either too busy to call her or too afraid. If she wanted a divorce, he did not want to learn about it when he was tired and rundown. But what if she wanted him back? As soon as he returned to his apartment, Quinn poured himself a stiff drink and phoned Laura.

"Dick!" Laura responded with obvious relief when she heard his voice. "Where are you? I've been trying to reach you all day."

"I'm at my apartment, but I was in Seattle earlier today."

"What were you doing there?"

"It would take too long to explain. Fran told me that you called several times. What did you want to talk to me about?"

"I need to see you." Laura's voice wavered. "Can you come home?"

"Now?"

"Yes. Please."

Quinn had rarely heard uncertainty in Laura's voice and this was the first time he had ever heard her plead. If she was anything, Laura was a model of self-confidence, always certain that she was right, always the one who made the demands, never the supplicant.

"I'll come over right away."

"Thank you, Dick."

Quinn hung up the phone and stood quietly for a moment. He had wanted to say something more, to tell Laura that he still loved her, but he couldn't, because he was afraid of what she would say.

Laura looked tense when she opened the front door for Quinn. She was dressed casually in a blue warm-up suit, but she had put on makeup and her hair was combed carefully. He hoped that was a good sign.

"Take off your coat. Let's sit down." Laura pointed toward the living room. "I even made you a drink."

Quinn saw a glass of Scotch resting on an end table next to the couch. He shucked his coat and followed Laura. She sat opposite him with a coffee table between them.

"I've been rehearsing this, so let me just talk, okay? When I married you we seemed to have the same goals. Then you left the firm to become a judge. It was hard for me to accept that. I felt betrayed. It wasn't just the money. It was the life I'd planned for the two of us. I couldn't understand how you could walk away from your partnership, something that I coveted so much. I think we started drifting apart after you made that choice. I'm not saying it was your fault. But it's true. Something changed in the marriage. Or maybe I changed. It doesn't matter.

"I really was sorry when the Miami client hired me, but I honestly believed that I owed it to the firm to take him on. Then the job turned out to be a hoax. I was furious. All I wanted to do was to fly back to Portland. I started to phone the airline when I remembered how sad you had been when I told you I couldn't go with you to St. Jerome. I remembered your voice on the phone. You sounded so . . ."

Laura shook her head. "I stopped with my hand in the air. It was . . . I don't know . . . like a light going on, like I was suddenly hearing something clearly that had only been a murmur. I realized how much pain you were in and that I was the cause of that pain. I asked myself what I wanted to happen to our marriage and I didn't know the answer to that question. That's why I flew to St. Jerome. I hoped that I could figure out how I really felt about us by being there with you, away from Portland and the law office and my work. I knew that there was something terribly wrong with our marriage and I wanted to try and cure it. But everything fell apart after I arrived."

Laura stopped to collect herself. She was a person who kept her feelings to herself and Quinn could see how painful it was for her to reveal her emotions.

"I was in Los Angeles on business on Wednesday and Thursday. Today, two detectives visited me at the office. They told me about the woman who was murdered at the Heathman. They wanted to know about the woman who disappeared on St. Jerome. They showed me pictures of the two of you on the beach.

"I didn't understand where they were going, at first. The black detective, Dennis, is very smooth. When it became clear that they thought you might have killed the woman at the hotel, I had to make a decision. I asked myself if I truly believed that you could murder someone the way they said that poor woman was killed. I had to decide what type of person I married and I decided that you could never do that."

"Laura, some other things have happened to me this past week that you don't know about. They explain why the woman at the hotel was murdered. I love you very much. The one thing I want more than anything in the world is for us to be together again. But I don't want to hide anything from you."

Laura waited for Quinn to continue. The look of wariness on her face frightened Quinn. By the time he finished explaining about the blackmail attempt by the man in the ski mask, Claire

Reston's visit to his chambers and the way he had decided the *Crease* case, her expression was unreadable.

"After I suppressed the evidence, I prepared for the worst, but I never dreamed that the blackmailers would murder someone to frame me. I've been sick about it. The way that woman died . . ."

"Why didn't the blackmailers just carry out their threat and send the photographs to the authorities on St. Jerome?"

"They couldn't, Laura. Andrea Chapman did not die on St. Jerome."

"What?"

"It was a hoax. The woman who posed as Andrea Chapman on St. Jerome and the woman who pretended to be Claire Reston were the same person, Marie Ritter, a Seattle call girl. Ritter has a distinctive scar on her hip. I saw it in the cove and I saw it on Reston's body in the hotel room. By killing Ritter, the blackmailer got rid of a witness at the same time that he set me up for her murder. Last night he tried to wrap everything up by killing me."

Laura's eyes widened. "Fran told me that someone attacked you in the parking garage. I thought that was a robbery attempt."

"The man who attacked me is the same man who broke into my apartment."

"God, Dick. Do you have any idea who's behind this plot?"

"Benjamin Gage has an aide who is an ex-SEAL. He'd have had no trouble faking the underwater murder on St. Jerome. But I talked to Marie Ritter's sister in Seattle. She told me that Marie had a customer who lives in Oregon. Denise didn't know his name, but she had the impression that he's young and he's an undertaker."

"Lamar Hoyt's son."

"Yes. And I've also learned that Junior and his father quarreled shortly before Hoyt's death because Senior believed that his son was skimming money from the mortuary business."

"Then you think Junior is behind everything?"

"That's where the evidence seems to be pointing, but Lamar,

Jr., and Ryan Clark are both the same size as the blackmailer and the man who attacked me in the garage."

"Have you given this information to the police?"

"No. I just learned the information about Lamar, Jr., tonight and I really can't prove that Junior knew Ritter. Marie never told Denise the name of her client. If Junior denies knowing Ritter, we can't prove he's lying."

"And Hoyt's statements to Fargo are hearsay."

Quinn closed his eyes and let his head fall back.

"I don't know what I'm going to do, Laura."

"One thing you are not going to do is give up," Laura said forcefully. "We are going to get through this."

Quinn opened his eyes and he looked at his wife hopefully.

"Does that mean that you want me back?"

Laura reached out and took Quinn's hand.

"I put up a good front, Dick, but I'm always scared. I've been scared since my parents divorced. Scared for years and years. Scared that I'll lose everything if I don't work harder than everybody. That I'll end up like my father."

"I have a hard time picturing you failing at anything, Laura."

"Our marriage almost failed, but I'm not going to let it. I do want you back. I want us to try to . . . to be together like we were when . . . when we first . . ."

Quinn took Laura in his arms before she could finish. Her body shuddered and so did his. Quinn stroked Laura's hair and kissed the top of her head. She raised her face and Quinn kissed her lips. The kiss was tentative at first, then they were sprawled on the carpet and Laura was opening Quinn's belt. Quinn broke away only for the brief time that it took them to struggle out of their clothes. Then they became a tangle of bodies, soft and hard, the kisses so eager that they both wondered if there would be anything left of them when they were through.

After their first frenzied bout of lovemaking, Quinn and Laura gathered their clothes and went upstairs to the bedroom. The second time they made love it was less frantic and Quinn took his time renewing his acquaintance with a body that had become foreign to him. When they were sated, Quinn collapsed beside Laura. Her hand found his and she said, "I love you."

"I never thought I'd hear you say that again."

"Well, I have. I want our marriage to work, Dick. I want it more than I want anything else. No matter what happens from now on, I'm standing with you."

[5]

Benjamin Gage listened to the recording of Richard Quinn's meeting with Ellen Crease and Jack Brademas for a second time. When the minicassette stopped spinning, Ryan Clark turned off the tape recorder. Gage looked grim.

"Can we use this?" Gage asked.

"No. The recording was obtained illegally. We'd also be forcing Quinn to go public."

"And he'd have to admit that he fixed Crease's case. She'd be discredited."

"Maybe not. Quinn would say that the blackmailer wanted him to make sure that Crease was found guilty. Now that there is an alternative explanation for the blood spatter evidence, a lot of voters will conclude that she's been framed. I don't think we can afford to gamble. Not with you leading in all of the polls."

"You're right." Gage picked up the minicassette. "Have there been more of these?"

"One other. The information wasn't useful, but the intelligence on this cassette is certainly interesting."

"Our man seems to be on top of things. Make sure he's taken care of. I want him working hard for us."

Twenty-two

WHEN LOU ANTHONY arrived at work Saturday morning there was a message from Denise Ritter asking him to call. Ritter sounded nervous when the detective identified himself.

"Something happened yesterday. I wasn't going to call, at first. I . . . I don't want to get anyone in trouble. But I thought about Marie. That this might help find the person who killed her."

"Finding your sister's killer is very important to me, Ms. Ritter. If you have information that might help, please tell me."

"When you and Detective Dennis interviewed me you asked if Marie ever mentioned Richard Quinn. She didn't. She never said that she knew any judge."

Denise Ritter hesitated. Anthony waited patiently for her to continue.

"I hope I didn't do anything wrong, but I couldn't stop thinking about that question, so I called Judge Quinn. He flew to Seattle yesterday evening."

"Quinn flew up to see you?"

"Yes."

"What did you two talk about?"

"Marie mostly. He told me how they met on St. Jerome . . ."

"He knew that the woman in the photograph I showed you was your sister? The woman who was murdered at the Heathman?"

"He seemed to know. Why?"

"Nothing. It's not that important. Go on."

"I did tell Judge Quinn one thing that I didn't tell you. That's why I'm calling. I thought about it all night. Judge Quinn seemed to think it was important, so I decided that you should know, too."

"What is it that you think I should know?"

"The judge asked me if Marie had any clients from Portland. I told him that Marie didn't tell me the name of any of the men she had been with, but she did tell me that one of them lived in Oregon. The only reason I remembered what Marie said was because he had an odd job. She said he was an undertaker."

Anthony and Ritter talked for a few more moments. The detective was thanking her when Leroy Dennis strolled over to Anthony's desk. Anthony waved him into a seat, finished with Ritter and hung up.

"The person on the phone was Denise Ritter. She called to tell me that Judge Quinn flew up to Seattle yesterday and pumped her about her sister's background."

"No kidding?"

"No kidding. She also told me that Quinn knew that Andrea Chapman and Claire Reston were the same person. But that's not the most important thing Denise told me. It seems that one of her sister's customers was an undertaker from Oregon."

"Whoa."

"Yeah, whoa."

"What are you thinking, Lou?"

"What if Junior learned that his father was going to marry Karen Fargo and alter his will in her favor? Steve Appling said that the two Lamars had a pretty bad argument shortly before the murder. Maybe that's when Junior discovered Senior's plan."

"So you think Junior may have hired Jablonski to kill his father?"

"And Crease. With both of them dead, he would inherit everything. But Jablonski screwed up and got himself killed, so Junior's plan failed. Then Crease was arrested and Junior had a second chance. If Crease was convicted of hiring Jablonski to kill her husband she couldn't benefit from the will. I think Junior used Ritter to blackmail Judge Quinn."

"Damn, you may be right."

"It would certainly explain the way Quinn is acting. Those photographs scream blackmail, Leroy."

"And Denise Ritter has just supplied the link between Junior and her sister," Dennis answered thoughtfully. Then he frowned. "But there are problems with your scenario, Lou."

"Such as?"

"Jablonski for one. He was in prison for a long time. When he was out, he wasn't running in Junior's circle. How did they meet?"

"I don't know, but I'm gonna nail Junior's ass as soon as I find out."

"And another thing," Dennis continued. "Until you learned about this possible connection between Marie Ritter and Hoyt, you thought Crease killed her husband."

"She still could be good for it," Anthony answered grudgingly. "That blood spatter evidence bothers the hell out of me."

"Exactly. And don't forget Judge Quinn. If Ritter was blackmailing him, he'd have a powerful motive to kill her."

Anthony sighed. "I have to admit that I've been really pissed at Quinn since he accused me of lying, but I have a hard time seeing him as Ritter's killer."

"Quinn has been acting like a man with something to hide."

"No doubt about that. The judge flat out lied about knowing Ritter and he continued to lie after being confronted with the pictures, but I still don't make Quinn for the Ritter killing. Any man can commit murder under the right circumstances. Ritter threatens to ruin Quinn, go to his wife, go to the press. Quinn hits her in a rage. One moment of passion, one dead woman. But that isn't what we have here. Marie Ritter was raped and systematically tortured. My gut tells me that Quinn couldn't kill her like that."

"So you think that the judge is concealing information about the murder because he's being blackmailed?"

"That's the only way I can explain the way the judge has been acting. Quinn definitely saw those pictures before we showed them to him at the Heathman. He almost peed his pants when he saw them, but he didn't ask a single question about where they came from or how we got them. And why else would he be playing detective in Seattle? I think he's trying to figure out who killed Ritter himself."

Dennis thought about what Anthony had just said. His brow furrowed. Then Dennis shot up in his seat.

"Hot damn. If someone did use those pictures to blackmail Quinn it might be our lucky break."

"I don't follow you."

"If Junior was the blackmailer he would have ordered Quinn to fix the case so that Crease would be convicted."

Anthony frowned. "Quinn rigged the case *for* Crease."

"Right."

"That puts us back to square one again with Crease as the main suspect."

"Not necessarily. I've been checking on Quinn. Everybody says that the man's a saint, and I mean everybody. Real high principles. Look at the way he sent that Eugene judge to jail. Everyone was betting that he'd give him probation. It's possible that the blackmailer ordered Quinn to make certain that Crease was convicted and Quinn just couldn't do it."

"So where does that leave us?"

"I think the key to identifying the blackmailer is finding out what Quinn was told to do, not what he really did. And to do that, we've got to ask the judge."

[2]

On Saturday morning, Quinn and Laura slept until nine-thirty. They decided to visit Frank Price at the hospital. After that Quinn would go to the courthouse. He had put his decision to resign on hold, but he still had to prepare the memos on his cases so he could take time off.

Quinn was washing the breakfast dishes when the doorbell rang. Laura looked up from the paper when her husband walked to the door. Quinn peered through the peephole. Lou Anthony and Leroy Dennis were standing on the welcome mat.

"Good morning, Judge," Dennis said. "May we come in?"

"What's this about?" Quinn asked warily.

Dennis glanced at Laura. He looked uncomfortable.

"Maybe we should talk in private, Judge."

"I have nothing to hide from my wife."

Dennis hesitated. "Some of the questions we're going to ask . . . The subjects are delicate."

"I repeat. I have nothing to hide from my wife."

Quinn led the detectives into the living room.

"What do you want to know?" he asked when they were all seated.

"Denise Ritter called me this morning and told me about your trip to Seattle," Anthony said. "What were you doing up there?"

"She called me. She said that she wanted to talk to me about her sister."

"So you hop a jet and fly to Seattle?"

Quinn did not respond.

"Why didn't you tell me that Andrea Chapman and Claire Reston were the same person when we were at the crime scene?"

"I only suspected that the two women were the same when I

saw the dead woman at the hotel. I wasn't certain. I was pretty upset."

"I remember," Dennis said, "and I can't believe that you want the person who tortured Marie Ritter to death to get away with it."

"I don't."

"That's not the way you're acting," Dennis said.

"We think that you have information that will help us identify Marie Ritter's killer," Anthony told Quinn.

"We're counting on your decency, Judge," Dennis said. "We're counting on you coming through for us."

"What is this information that you believe I have?"

"I'm gonna put my cards on the table," Anthony told Quinn. "We have evidence that points to a suspect other than Senator Crease. You know who I'm talking about. Denise Ritter told you that her sister had a customer from Oregon who was an undertaker. If Lamar Hoyt, Jr., is the customer, he becomes suspect number one.

"Now we come to you, Judge. I've been on the losing side of motions before. Hell, everyone screws up. But no judge has ever accused me of intentionally lying under oath. When I calmed down I asked myself why you did what you did. It was a mystery, until we found those pictures of you and Ritter. Then everything fell into place."

"Lou and I are certain that you were blackmailed to fix Ellen Crease's case," Dennis said, feeling vindicated by the swift shift of emotions on Quinn's face. "What we need to know is whether the blackmailer wanted you to acquit Crease or convict her. We figure that Junior would have asked you to make certain that Crease was convicted. If Senator Crease was blackmailing you, she would want you to fix the case so that she couldn't be convicted."

"So there it is, Judge," Anthony told Quinn. "If you tell us that the blackmailer wanted you to convict Ellen Crease, we'll concentrate on Lamar Hoyt, Jr. If you tell us that you were ordered to acquit Crease, we'll go to the D.A. with that."

"And you'll ask Cedric Riker to move to set aside Dick's order on the grounds that it was obtained by fraud," Laura told Anthony.

"Yes, ma'am," he answered without hesitation. "We'd have to."

"That would expose my husband to disbarment, criminal charges and disgrace."

"There is no way around that."

"Of course," Dennis said quickly, "we could work out something with the criminal charges."

"Like the Eugene Police did with Frederick Gideon?" Laura said.

Dennis blinked.

"Detectives," Laura said, "my husband won't answer any more of your questions without consulting an attorney."

Dennis and Anthony sagged.

"Laura," Quinn started.

"Listen to me on this, Dick."

Quinn wanted to talk to the detectives, but he realized that Laura was right.

"I appreciate the way you've handled this case and the consideration you've shown me," Quinn told the detectives. "I'm not ruling out our talking further. But you know how serious a decision this is for me."

"I know that, Judge," Dennis agreed.

"Just give me some time to think."

"Cedric Riker also suspects that you fixed Crease's hearing and he wants your blood. If Riker had his way, we'd be questioning you at the station with a rubber hose and klieg lights shining in your eyes. I'd rather trust your good instincts and have you cooperate because you know it's the right thing to do, but we can't wait very long for you to decide."

"You see our position?" Dennis asked. "We have a very dangerous person running free. That person has murdered Marie Ritter and was responsible for the death of Lamar Hoyt. He also attacked you. Remember, Judge, you're the key witness here and the killer knows that. He tried to kill you once. You can bet he'll try again."

Quinn thought about that. If he were attacked at home, Laura would be in danger.

"Before you go," Quinn said, "there is something else I learned that might help you. Lamar Hoyt suspected that Junior was skimming from the mortuary business. That's why they argued at Hoyt Industries headquarters."

"How do you know that?"

"Karen Fargo told me last night."

Anthony colored. "Damn it, Judge, you are not one of the Hardy Boys. Stay the hell out of this investigation. You hear me?"

Laura showed the detectives to the door. Then she returned to the living room, where she found Quinn looking totally lost.

"What should I do?" he asked as soon as Laura sat beside him.

"If you admit to the police that you fixed Ellen Crease's case you can bank on being forced to resign from the bench and you face the additional threats of being disbarred and prosecuted criminally."

"Maybe I don't deserve to stay on the bench. I covered up what I thought was a murder. I fixed a case."

"You had good reasons for not going to the authorities on St. Jerome and you decided the motion to suppress the way you did to protect Ellen Crease."

"I could have told the police about the blackmail threat, withdrawn from the case and let another judge take over."

"Yes. You probably should have, but you didn't. We have to deal with what really happened. I guess the problem is that anything you do puts you in jeopardy. The ideal solution would be for the police to arrest the killer without your assistance."

"Without my help they might never be able to do that."

[3]

Anthony dropped off Leroy Dennis at the police station, then drove to Karen Fargo's house. He got along well with the witness and he had explained to Dennis that Fargo might be more comfortable speaking to him alone.

"I just came from talking to Judge Quinn," Anthony said when they were seated at a table in Fargo's tiny kitchen. "He said he talked to you last night, and you told him why Lamar and his son quarreled."

"It was okay to talk to him, wasn't it?" Fargo asked anxiously. "He's a judge."

"Oh, sure. No, you did the right thing. I just wanted to find out if there's anything else you remembered that you think is important."

Fargo hesitated. Anthony thought that she seemed agitated.

"Is something wrong?" he asked.

"No, I . . ." Fargo could not meet Anthony's eye.

"Karen, if you know something that will help in this investigation, you've got to tell me. There have been three deaths already."

"I never lied. Everything I said to you and the grand jury was true, but . . ."

"Yes?"

Fargo looked desperate.

"Is it illegal if I was paid to come to see you? Would I be breaking the law?"

"Someone paid you to come forward?"

Fargo told Anthony about the visit from the man with the scar.

"How much were you paid?" Anthony asked when Fargo was through.

"Five thousand dollars."

"Did this man who visited you say who he was or who he was working for?"

"No, but I saw him again."

"Where?"

"On the evening news."

"Did the newscaster say his name?" Anthony asked excitedly.

"No. He was just someone in a news story, but . . ."

"Yes?"

"It was right after Judge Quinn suppressed the evidence. That's what the story was about. And this man, the one who came here, he looked like he was with Senator Gage."

[4]

The courthouse was deserted when Quinn arrived. He went directly to his chambers and put up a pot of coffee. While the coffee perked, Quinn went into his office and surveyed the paperwork that was strewn across the top of his desk. Most of it was from the motions in the *Crease* case. Quinn went back into the anteroom and looked through the filing cabinet behind Fran Stuart's desk. By the time he had pulled the files in the other cases that had to be dealt with, the coffee was ready.

Quinn poured himself a mug and shut the door to his office. After tuning his radio to a classical music station, the judge began organizing the documents on his desk into piles so he could return them to the file in *State v. Crease* with some sense of order. Quinn put a rubber band around the police reports that he had examined when he was deciding Cedric Riker's motion to exclude evidence of Martin Jablonski's criminal record. He was about to put them in the accordion file where he kept all of the documents pertaining to the motion when he noticed something that was written on the top report. Quinn slipped the report out from under the rubber band and examined it. It was the arresting officer's account of a six-year-old home burglary committed by Jablonski. His conviction for this crime had sent him to the penitentiary until his release last year. As Quinn reread the report his heartbeat accelerated. He tried to calm down so he could figure out what his discovery meant. When he was certain of his reasoning, Quinn phoned Ellen Crease.

"Crease residence," James Allen said.

"Mr. Allen, this is Judge Quinn. Is Senator Crease in?"

"Yes, sir."

Allen put Quinn on hold. When the phone came back to life, Ellen Crease was on the other end. Quinn told her about Junior's connection to Marie Ritter and what he had learned from Karen Fargo. Then Quinn explained his discovery of the police report and the conclusions he had drawn from it.

"My God," Crease said when Quinn was finished. "This is so hard to believe."

"But it makes sense."

"Yes, it does."

Crease sounded like she was in shock.

"What do you think we should do?" Quinn asked.

Crease thought for a moment.

"The courthouse is only a block from the Justice Center. Wait for me in your chambers. I'm coming down. We'll go to the police together."

While Quinn waited for Crease, he organized his files. The busywork helped him take his mind off the terrible events of the past few days. Periodically, Quinn checked the time. He thought it would take Crease about half an hour to drive downtown. Quinn had placed the call to Crease a little after three and it was already three-thirty. Quinn expected the phone to ring at any moment.

At three-fifty, Quinn heard the door between the anteroom and the corridor open. Quinn walked to the door to his chambers. He reached for the doorknob, then stopped himself. A peephole had been installed for security purposes. Through it, Quinn saw the man who had attacked him in the garage quietly closing the door to the corridor. His face was still concealed behind a ski mask and he was carrying a large hunting knife.

Quinn locked his door just as the man reached for the knob. Quinn saw the knob turn slowly. He backed against the desk. There was a second door in his chambers that opened onto the bench. Quinn realized that he could escape through it into the courtroom, then he could get out through the courtroom door.

Quinn started to leave when he remembered the gun that had been left on the hood of his car. It was in his desk drawer. He had meant to turn it over to the police, but he never had the chance. Quinn raced around the desk and got the gun. He had never fired one and had only a vague idea, picked up from television and the movies, of how to shoot it, but he felt better holding the weapon.

Quinn opened the door behind the bench as quietly as possible and slipped into the courtroom. He closed the door silently and crept down the stairs from the bench to the bar of the court, praying that the person in his anteroom would not think of his escape route.

Rain clouds had darkened the sky and very little light came through the courtroom windows. The weak light that illuminated the courthouse corridor seeped into the courtroom. The empty benches were cloaked in shadow. Quinn hurried to the door. It was locked, but he had the key. As he stepped into the corridor, the door to his chambers opened and he and his attacker were suddenly face-to-face.

Both men paused for a second. Then the man in the mask took a step toward Quinn. Quinn pointed his weapon down the corridor and fired. In the narrow confines of the marble hallway the gunshot roared like a cannon. Quinn's aim was terrible. The bullet ricocheted crazily as it bounced off the walls. The man ducked back into Quinn's chambers.

The courthouse was a square. The fifth floor consisted of four corridors built around an open center. At the front of the courthouse were the elevators and broad steps that led down to the front door. Quinn wanted to run down those stairs, but that would mean passing the door to his chambers, so he headed to the hall in the rear of the courthouse. There, two enclosed staircases at either end of the hall went down to the back corridor on the first floor. If he could make it to the first floor, Quinn could run into a tiny alcove where he would find the elevator that went up to the courthouse jail. If he got that far, he could call for help through an intercom on the wall of the alcove. Armed corrections deputies would be moments away.

Quinn took off. As he rounded the corner, he heard pounding footsteps racing after him. Quinn flung open the door to the near stairwell and leaped down the steps. He slipped on the third-floor landing and slid down half a flight before checking himself. In the second it took Quinn to regain his feet, he strained to hear his pursuer and thought he heard the sound of feet descending.

Quinn hit the bottom stair. The corridor in the back of the courthouse was dimly lit. He held his gun in front of him. His stomach was cramped and his breathing grew ragged. His senses were intensified. All he had to do was make it to the end of the hall.

Quinn sprinted for the alcove. The moment he reached it the door to the other stairwell flew open and the man in the ski mask ran into the hall. Quinn had been certain that he had heard footsteps in the stairwell he had just descended. Could there be two people hunting him? Before he could consider the question, the masked man sprang. Quinn backpedaled into the alcove and raised his gun, which was halfway up when the knife struck it. The impact jarred the gun and the knife loose and sent Quinn stumbling backward. He tripped on his own feet and fell heavily to the floor. His head smacked against the wall. Quinn's eyes wouldn't focus. He shook his head. When his vision returned, Quinn saw that the masked man was holding the gun.

Time slowed to a crawl and a feeling of overwhelming calm flooded through Quinn as he accepted his death. He saw the attacker sight down the barrel of the gun. His eyes locked on Quinn's. Then there was an explosion. The assailant's knees buckled, the gun fell and the front of the ski mask dampened with blood. There was a second shot. Quinn tried to push his way through the wall. The attacker collapsed at Quinn's feet and Ellen Crease stepped into the alcove holding a smoking .38-caliber revolver.

The jail elevator opened and two men stepped into the alcove. They were dressed in the light green shirt and dark green pants worn by the Multnomah County Corrections deputies. The first person out was Sergeant Art Bradford, a huge man with a marine crew cut who had been in Quinn's court guarding prisoners on many occasions. Clyde Fellers, the second deputy, was a black man with massive arms, a thick neck and a gut who had played football for Portland State. Bradford and Fellers stared at the dead man. Then they stared at Quinn, who was slumped on a bench outside the alcove.

"The judge is okay. He's just shaken up," Ellen Crease said.

Quinn looked up. He was pale and spoke softly.

"The dead man attacked me in the parking garage two days ago. He just broke into my chambers and chased me downstairs. Senator Crease shot him."

"I was supposed to meet Judge Quinn in his chambers," Crease explained. "I took the elevator up to the fifth floor. Someone raced around the far corner of the hall just as I came into the corridor where the judge's courtroom is located. No one was in the judge's chambers, so I ran down the back stairs looking for him."

Crease stopped her narrative. She looked as bad as Quinn.

"I had to shoot. He was aiming at the judge."

"Someone should call Portland Homicide," Quinn said. "Ask them to send Detectives Lou Anthony and Leroy Dennis over here. This is connected to one of their cases. And make sure that Anthony and Dennis are told that I know who murdered Lamar Hoyt."

"You can turn him over now," Dr. Marilyn Kinsey, the assistant medical examiner, said to Sergeant Bradford. Quinn, Detectives

Anthony and Dennis, Ellen Crease and the other people in the group surrounding the dead man waited expectantly as Bradford rolled the corpse onto its back. Kinsey knelt down and slowly peeled back the ski mask.

"Looks like you were right," Anthony told Quinn.

The judge looked down on the lifeless face of Jack Brademas.

"Let's go up to your courtroom so you can show us that report," Dennis suggested.

Anthony, Dennis, Crease and Quinn went up to the fifth floor. Quinn preceded everyone into his courtroom and switched on the lights. While the others sat at the counsel table that Garrett and Crease had used during the hearing, Quinn went into his chambers through the door behind the bench and retrieved the document that had cleared up the case for him.

"Why don't you tell us how you figured out that Jack Brademas was involved, Judge?" Dennis said as soon as Quinn laid the police report of Martin Jablonski's home burglary on the table. The report was the one he had just finished reading last Sunday when the police detective called to see if Quinn could provide information about the disappearance of Andrea Chapman. It was only while Quinn waited for the police to arrive at the courthouse that the judge realized that the man on the line could not have been a police detective. The incident on St. Jerome had been staged. Andrea Chapman never existed and Marie Ritter did not disappear on St. Jerome. The call from the phony detective was part of the plan to unnerve him so that he would be easy prey for the blackmailer. The caller had probably been Jack Brademas.

"This is the police report of the arrest that sent Martin Jablonski to prison this last time," Quinn said. "This was the crime for which he was serving time until he was paroled last year. It was a brutal home invasion. A nighttime burglary accompanied by a violent assault on the homeowners. Take a look at the report."

Anthony and Dennis studied the handwritten report. They looked confused.

"I don't see . . . ," Anthony started. Then he looked as if he had been shot. He pointed at the bottom of the report where the arresting officer had signed his name.

"J. Brademas," Dennis said out loud.

"Exactly," Quinn said. "Brademas knew Jablonski. He arrested him. I think he hired Jablonski to break into the Hoyt mansion and kill Lamar Hoyt and Senator Crease. If Jablonski was caught later, the crime would fit his M.O., but Brademas was probably going to murder Jablonski after Jablonski committed the double murder at the estate."

"I've been sick ever since Judge Quinn told me about the report," Crease said. "Jack was my friend. I helped him get his job and Lamar treated him very well. Why did he do it?"

"I think I can answer that, Senator," Lou Anthony said. "Your husband suspected Junior of embezzling from the mortuary business. He had Jack Brademas investigate. My guess is that Brademas went to Junior and made a proposal. He would arrange to have you and your husband murdered for a cut of the estate. The plan must have looked great on paper. Junior had no ties to Jablonski and Jablonski was known for this type of violent crime. But neither Brademas nor Junior counted on you killing Jablonski."

"Our problem now will be proving that Junior was Brademas's partner."

Dennis stood up. "You people have been through enough for one night. Wait here and I'll see if there's any reason to keep you further."

Dennis left and Crease slumped in her seat. She looked exhausted.

"I still can't believe that Jack was behind all this. I've known him for years."

"If Junior confesses, maybe you can salvage your election campaign," Quinn said in an attempt to cheer up Crease.

"Winning the primary seems less and less important to me, Dick. I've lost Lamar. Now I find out I've been betrayed by someone I really trusted. Besides, I'm so far down in the polls . . ."

Crease smiled sadly and shook her head. The courtroom door opened and Dennis returned.

"You can go," the detective said, "but you'll have to run the gauntlet. Someone notified the press."

Quinn walked toward the courtroom door. Crease started to follow him, but Anthony stopped her and said, "Wait a minute, Ellen. I know I put you through hell by arresting you."

"I don't hold it against you. You thought you were doing the right thing."

"I did, but I might have cost you the campaign, so I figure I owe you one. I need your promise that you won't reveal where you got this information."

Crease gave it.

"Karen Fargo was paid five thousand dollars to tell her story to me."

"Who did it?"

Anthony repeated Fargo's description. As soon as he mentioned the scar, Crease said, "That's Ryan Clark, Benjamin Gage's A.A., and he doesn't spit without Gage's say-so. If he bribed Fargo, Gage is behind it."

Part Four

Political Necessity

Twenty-three

[1]

HENRY ORCHARD popped the videotape into the VCR and pressed the Play button on the remote. Ellen Crease drew in smoke from her Cuban Cohiba Panatela. The anchor on the evening news suddenly appeared on the forty-eight-inch television screen in her home entertainment center.

"This is the Saturday night news report on Channel 6, but it's representative of the stories that the other local channels carried as the lead story last night," Crease's campaign manager told the senator. "The networks used local feeds."

Crease watched herself leave the courthouse protected by a phalanx of policemen. She saw herself ignore the outstretched microphones and the reporters' entreaties. Then Judge Quinn came down the courthouse steps. He stopped at the bottom and turned to the reporters.

"This is good," Orchard said as he turned up the volume.

"The police have asked me to refrain from making a statement or answering questions, and I am going to follow their instructions with one exception. Senator Ellen Crease saved my life tonight and I want to acknowledge her heroism and my debt to her."

"How did she save your life?" several reporters asked simultaneously, as others asked what had happened in the courthouse, but Quinn refused to say anything more. The next shots were of Quinn's and Crease's cars driving from the scene while a voice-over informed the viewers that Senator Benjamin Gage had refused to comment on the incident at the courthouse.

"Now, here's where they hurt us," Orchard said.

"Although Senator Gage refused to comment on the shooting, United States Congresswoman Renata Camp, a strong supporter of Senator Gage, did have this to say."

The screen showed a stern-looking woman of fifty with short gray hair. When she spoke into the camera, she looked very concerned.

"I want to preface this statement by saying that I know very little of the facts surrounding tonight's shooting incident. I do know that the man who attempted to murder Circuit Court Judge Richard Quinn at the Multnomah County Courthouse was a longtime friend and associate of Senator Ellen Crease and the current head of security at her husband's company. I hope that the authorities will look more deeply into the facts surrounding the murder of Lamar Hoyt."

"The information we have," a reporter told Congresswoman Camp, "is that Senator Crease saved Judge Quinn's life by shooting Jack Brademas. You seem to be suggesting that there was something more sinister going on here."

"I'm not saying that at all. I do find it interesting that the senator hid behind a legal technicality in order to escape a trial of the facts of her murder charge, after spending her political career decrying the so-called legal loopholes that murderers, rapists and child molesters use to escape punishment. Then we have her good friend and associate trying to murder the judge in her case. I think these kinds of facts deserve investigation."

Orchard stopped the tape and switched off the set.

"You don't need to see the rest, unless you want to."

Crease waved her cigar at her political adviser.

"It's more of the same," Orchard continued. "What hurts is the innuendo and the accusation that you're hiding behind legal technicalities to keep the voters from learning the truth about Lamar's murder."

Orchard leaned toward Crease. "There's just over a month to the primary and you are way back in the polls. You've got three choices. You quit, you sit and take it or you fight back. If you choose column A or column B, you might as well concede the election and go on vacation."

Crease blew a stream of smoke toward the ceiling. Then she looked at Orchard.

"You know the first thing I'm gonna do when I'm elected to the United States Senate, Henry? I'm going to get the embargo of Cuba lifted so I can smoke these cigars in public."

Orchard grinned broadly. "That's my girl! Now, I've got some ideas about how we can use Judge Quinn's statement."

"Hold on to them until tomorrow, Henry. I'm meeting with Mary Garrett tonight. I might have something that will bring us back, but I've got to talk to her before I tell you about it."

"What's Garrett have to do with your campaign?"

"I can't tell you. But it will be worth the wait. If I decide to go public with what I know, I've got to make sure that I don't burn myself. So hold on until tomorrow. Then we'll see."

[2]

The Multnomah County District Attorney's Office was deserted on Sunday afternoon, so Leroy Dennis and Lou Anthony were the only people who witnessed Cedric Riker's tirade.

"Can you tell me what the fuck is going on here?" Riker swore when the detectives finished their account of the Saturday shootout at the courthouse.

"It's confusing, Ced," Leroy Dennis told the D.A.

"Confusing?" Riker raged. "What do you find confusing? It looks like simple math to me. By my count that bitch has now killed two people. We usually send serial killers to death row. What are you two geniuses proposing? That I give her a marksmanship medal?"

"Just listen to Leroy, Ced," Anthony told the D.A. in his most conciliatory tone.

"I'm all ears."

"Before Saturday, it looked like Senator Crease paid Jablonski to kill her husband. Then the evidence started pointing to Lamar, Jr. Now there's a possibility that Senator Gage is involved."

"Gage! What are you talking about? Are you accusing Benjamin Gage of murder?"

"We're not accusing anyone right now."

"Well, that's a relief. Ben happens to be a close personal friend of mine and one of my staunchest supporters. Not to mention the fact that he is a United States senator."

"I'm just saying that there is a lot of circumstantial evidence pointing at people other than Ellen Crease. We may have acted too hastily when we arrested her."

"Lou, I went to the grand jury on Crease on your say-so. Are you telling me that we indicted an innocent woman?"

Anthony flushed. "We might have."

"Where does Senator Gage come in?" Riker asked.

"Karen Fargo was paid to come forward. The day after she came in to see me five thousand dollars was deposited in her bank account and she was offered a job at a business owned by one of Gage's supporters. This morning I took Fargo to a TV studio to view a videotape that showed Ryan Clark, Gage's administrative assistant. She identified him as the person who bribed her."

"Shit!" Riker swore as he paced back and forth in front of the detectives.

"There's a lot of circumstantial evidence linking Brademas to Junior," Leroy Dennis said, "but Brademas could have sold out

Crease to Gage. We think we have enough to bring in Gage for questioning."

Riker spun around and glared at Dennis.

"You are not going to drag a United States senator down to the station house."

"Where do you suggest that we question him?" Anthony asked calmly.

"Damn," Riker muttered. He paced to the window and back. "I'll call Gage. We'll talk to him someplace where the press won't see us." Riker pointed a finger at Anthony. "I don't want one word of this getting out. Meanwhile, you concentrate on Lamar Hoyt."

Anthony did not say anything. He knew Riker owed Gage. Everyone knew that. But he didn't owe Gage a thing and he would follow the investigation where it led him.

[3]

Mary Garrett closed her office door behind Ellen Crease and studied the senator as she crossed the room. After what her client had been through, she expected some sign of wear, but Crease looked confident, poised and full of fight. Crease had asked for this emergency meeting, so Garrett waited for her client to explain what she wanted.

"Mary, I need your advice," Crease said without preliminaries.

"That's what you pay me for."

Crease told her lawyer what had happened at the courthouse. When she finished, she hesitated and suddenly looked troubled.

"This is the difficult part, Mary, because it may mean betraying the trust of someone who came to me for help. But we're also dealing with political realities here and the current reality is that I don't stand a chance in hell of winning the primary if something dramatic doesn't happen quickly."

"If the police pin your husband's murder on Jack Brademas and Junior, that will be pretty dramatic."

"We don't know if that will happen. Gage is already using his stalking horses to suggest that I may still be guilty and that Brademas could have been my accomplice. If Junior doesn't confess, the killing will remain officially unsolved."

"What about going public with the fact that Gage bribed Fargo to come forward?"

"I've thought about that. Gage can admit he paid Fargo, then claim credit for bringing a witness forward. Some people will think what he did was sleazy, but they're not going to vote for me if my name hasn't been cleared."

Crease looked very uncomfortable. "Before I tell you anything more, I need your promise that nothing I say will leave this room unless I consent to it."

"Of course. That's all covered by attorney-client confidentiality."

"Would attorney-client confidentiality cover information I gave you about the criminal actions of another person?"

"Yes. It covers anything you tell me with a few exceptions that don't apply here."

"Would the privilege apply even if the person who committed the criminal acts was a judge and he committed them while acting in his capacity as a judge?"

Garrett frowned.

"What's this all about, Ellen?"

Garrett had never seen her client look so uncertain.

"I feel awful about this, but my political future and my reputation are at stake."

Crease told Garrett what Richard Quinn had confided to her on the night that he was attacked in the garage. As Crease related the details of the blackmail plot, Garrett looked incredulous. When she explained Paul Baylor's alternative explanation of the blood spatter evidence, Garrett took careful notes. When Crease told Garrett that Quinn had confessed that he fixed the motion to suppress, the lawyer looked stunned.

"This is very bad. I've never heard of anything like it."

"It happened. Brademas hired Jablonski to kill me and Lamar, then he used this call girl that Junior knew to coerce the judge into assuring my conviction."

"And you think that Junior was Brademas's partner?"

"Junior is the most likely person to have been in this with Jack, but there is another possibility. Benjamin Gage could have learned about the Ritter woman while trying to find dirt to use against me in the campaign. That must be the way he found out about Fargo."

"Do you have any proof of that?"

"No, but the blackmail plot required money and a high level of planning. Jack could have worked it out, but Junior never could have. Whatever else I think about Gage and Clark, there is no denying that they are extremely intelligent."

"You still haven't told me what you want from me, Ellen?"

"Advice. If I hold a press conference and go public with the fact that I was the victim of a conspiracy, I might turn the voters around. But Judge Quinn trusted me. He saved my life by ruling as he did. I don't want to hurt him. And there's the legal problem. I need to know what would happen to Quinn's order if Riker learns that the judge fixed my case. Would I be back facing a murder charge?"

"I'm pretty certain that the order would be null and void if Quinn admits he lied about his legal conclusions, but Riker would have real problems continuing his prosecution. Even if the blood spatter evidence was ruled admissible by a new judge, we now have a reasonable explanation for it, and that's the only concrete evidence the State has to contradict your version of what happened on the night of your husband's murder.

"Then, there's all this new evidence about Jack Brademas and Junior, and Gage bribing Fargo to come forward. The fact that someone tried to blackmail Quinn into assuring your conviction also makes it look like someone else was behind your husband's murder."

"What will happen to Judge Quinn if I go public with the information that he fixed my case?"

Garrett sighed. "He'll be ruined. Even if he fixed the case with the best of intentions he'll be removed from the bench. He could be disbarred. He could even face criminal charges."

"So Judge Quinn will be destroyed if I go public."

"I'm afraid that's what it comes down to."

"And if I don't go public, my reputation and my political career are over."

Twenty-four

HENRY ORCHARD and Ellen Crease sat in the back booth of a dimly lit downtown restaurant and discussed the campaign.

"I don't know what to do, Henry."

"It's a no-brainer, Ellen. You've got to hold the press conference and blow this blackmail scheme wide open. It's the only way you can give yourself a real chance to become a United States senator."

"I'd be climbing into national politics over the judge's body. It'd kill him, bury him so deep he might never crawl out."

"What if Gage is behind Lamar's murder? If you do nothing, Gage will win. You could be sending a murderer to the United States Senate. There's more at stake here than the career of one person. Quinn will still be alive. You've got money and influence. You can help him after you're elected."

Crease leaned her head against the back of the booth and shut her eyes.

"I wish this would all go away, Henry. I wish Lamar was still alive and I never decided to challenge that son of a bitch Gage."

"Yeah, well, those are wishes that won't come true, Ellen. And you're going to have to decide what you're going to do now. The days are slipping away. The primary is in May. If we're going to repair the damage caused by your murder indictment, we have to act. I agree with Garrett. Riker would be a fool to pursue his case once you reveal what you know. It's true that there are going to be casualties and Quinn will be one of them, but we're talking about your life here and about bringing your husband's murderer to justice.

"Look, why don't you talk this over with Quinn? Maybe he'll join you at the press conference and tell everyone how you saved his life and how this masked guy tried to force him into convicting you. If Quinn will help, it could be the break we need."

Crease sighed. "How soon can you set up the press conference?"

"I'll have you on the air Thursday night, prime time. We might even get national coverage."

"Then, God help me, let's do it. And God help Richard Quinn."

[2]

Quinn threw two more logs into the stone fireplace in the living room of Frank Price's beach house.

"You warm enough?" Quinn asked Laura.

"Uhm."

Laura was bundled up in a wool sweater and jeans. A glass of wine sat on a low table at her elbow. Quinn settled on the floor beside Laura and they both stared through the huge picture window at the rain that pounded the beach and the boiling whitecaps that rolled over the beleaguered sand. The fire crackled and Quinn felt the heat on his face. He had good memories of this rustic cabin where he had spent many of his summers growing up.

He was sorry that he would have to drive back to Portland tomorrow.

"What are you thinking about?" Quinn asked. "If it's business, you're in big trouble."

Laura laughed. "Believe it or not, I haven't thought about my practice since we crossed the coast range. The mountains must block the brain waves from Price, Winward."

Quinn put his arm around Laura's shoulder. He, too, had felt a lessening of tension as the landscape changed from urban sprawl to farmland and forest during their Sunday morning drive to the coast. By the time he and Laura were finishing bowls of thick, steaming clam chowder at a ramshackle restaurant of weathered wood on the Newport waterfront, he was a different person. An hour after lunch, Quinn and Laura were making love to the sound of rain pattering on the shake roof of the beach house and the murders were a universe away.

When they awoke Monday morning, a storm was brewing in the Pacific, but the rain held off until three. Quinn and Laura had walked the beach, driven into town for lunch, then spent the afternoon reading in front of the fire.

"If it's not business, then what caused that glazed look in your eyes?"

Laura looked a little guilty.

"You won't be mad at me?" she asked sheepishly.

Quinn squeezed her shoulder and kissed the top of her head.

"Speak. I know you. You'll brood all night if you don't get whatever is bothering you off your chest."

"Why do you think Brademas told Lamar, Sr., that Junior was embezzling the money?"

Quinn groaned.

"You said you wouldn't be mad."

Quinn sighed. "Brademas was Hoyt's head of security. He was supposed to tell him."

"I know, but wouldn't it have made more sense for Brademas to keep Hoyt in the dark? If Brademas hired Jablonski to kill

Hoyt and Senator Crease so he would get a share of the estate when Junior inherited, wasn't Brademas risking a lot by going to Senior? What if Hoyt called in the police immediately after finding out about Junior? What if he changed his will the same day?"

"I see what you mean. Maybe Brademas didn't think of the plan until after he spoke to Hoyt."

"That would explain it," Laura said in a tone that let Quinn know she was not really convinced. "And there's something else. That visit from Marie Ritter when she was pretending to be Claire Reston."

"What about it?"

"What was the point? What possible purpose was served by having Ritter pretend to be her sister?"

Quinn shrugged. "I guess Brademas and Junior wanted to shake me up so I'd go along with their blackmail scheme."

"But you were already a mess. They'd threatened to frame you for murder. You thought you'd be disbarred, disgraced and incarcerated in a rat-infested prison on St. Jerome. Ritter's visit was really overkill."

"Wait a minute. Ritter told me where she was staying just when Fran Stuart walked in. Brademas and Junior were creating a witness. After Ritter was murdered, Fran could testify that Ritter was upset when she left my chambers and that I knew her hotel room number."

"That makes sense, but what if you saw through Ritter's makeup and figured out that Claire Reston and Andrea Chapman were the same person? You'd know Ritter wasn't murdered on St. Jerome. Brademas and Junior would have lost their leverage. Why put Marie Ritter in the same room with you when everything was going so well? Why take the risk?"

"They probably figured that I'd be so shaken up that I wouldn't be able to figure out that Reston and Chapman were the same person. And they were right. If I hadn't seen the scar on Ritter's hip I would still believe that Claire and Andrea were different women. They took a risk, but given my state, it wasn't all that big a risk."

Laura snuggled close to Quinn. "You're probably right."

Quinn kissed Laura. "Even if I'm not right, I don't care. I want to forget about Ellen Crease, Lamar Hoyt, *fils* and *père,* and Jack Brademas."

Laura kissed Quinn. "I've been a bad wife. I promise not to mention the case or anything even remotely connected to law for the rest of our stay."

"Good. Because even a single slip of the tongue will be severely punished."

"Oh? What might you do?"

"Hmm. Ravishing comes to mind."

Laura fluttered her eyelids. "You mean that I'll be ravished if I say anything connected with law?"

"You betcha."

Laura smiled seductively and whispered, "Habeas corpus."

[3]

Lamar Hoyt, Jr., lived on the eighth floor of a brick and glass condominium near the Vista Bridge. Anthony flashed his badge at the security guard and told him not to announce the arrival of the detectives and the four uniformed officers who accompanied them. When they arrived at Junior's apartment, the officers stationed themselves on either side of the door and Dennis rang the bell. He had to press the button five times before an angry voice, thick with sleep, asked, "Who is it?"

Anthony held his badge in front of the peephole and said, "Open up, police."

The door swung open, revealing a huge living room decorated with low-slung, modern furniture of polished metal, glass and smooth woods. Anthony saw the lights of Portland through a floor-to-ceiling window that stretched across the outer wall of the apartment. The other walls were decorated with framed posters or paintings with a skiing theme. The top of a glass coffee table was covered with empty beer bottles, a half-filled bottle of red wine and an open pizza delivery box containing only the half-eaten remains of a slice of pepperoni and cheese.

"Real class, Junior," Anthony said.

"Ah, shit," Junior replied when he recognized the detective.

Junior was wearing a dark blue silk bathrobe belted loosely at the waist. The robe hung open a little, exposing Junior's hairy legs and torso and a pair of bright red bikini underpants.

"May we step inside, Mr. Hoyt?" Dennis asked.

"No, you may not."

"I'm afraid we have to insist," Dennis responded patiently.

"I'm calling my lawyer."

"Maybe you'd better do that," Anthony said. "Tell him to meet you downtown."

"Down . . . It's the middle of the night. I'm not going anywhere unless you've got a warrant."

Dennis smiled and handed Hoyt his copy of a search warrant.

"What's this about?" Junior asked nervously.

"Why don't we talk inside?"

Junior backed away from the door. Dennis noticed a dining area in front of the picture window that was relatively clean. He motioned Junior toward it. Anthony took a seat at the head of a large dining table and Dennis sat beside him. Two policemen stationed themselves near Junior and he eyed them anxiously.

"We have a new lead in your father's death and we need your help, Mr. Hoyt," Dennis said.

"What kind of new lead?"

Anthony took an autopsy photograph of Marie Ritter out of a manila envelope and handed it to Junior.

"Jesus!" Junior said, dropping the picture the moment he saw what it was.

"That's a curious reaction for someone who works in a funeral parlor," Dennis told Junior.

"You didn't happen to know this woman, did you?" Anthony asked.

Junior forced himself to look at the picture. He looked confused at first, then his expression changed. When he looked up, Junior's eyes shifted nervously between the detectives.

"You are two sick fucks, you know that?"

"Not as sick as the person who did this," Anthony answered, pointing at Marie Ritter's mutilated body. "This is a call girl named Marie Ritter. She was murdered a few nights ago at the Heathman. I understand that you were one of her customers."

Junior twitched. He cast another anxious glance at the autopsy photo.

"Look, I'll be honest with you. I, uh, I knew this woman, but not down here. I knew her in Seattle. And not as Marie Ritter. She called herself Crystal. All these whores have whore names." Junior forced a smile, but Anthony and Dennis did not respond. "But I didn't know that she was dead." Junior fidgeted nervously. "This isn't my normal thing, you understand. A friend of mine turned me on to her. Said she was, uh, exotic. I usually don't pay for sex, if you know what I mean."

"I'm sure you get lots of pussy, Junior," Anthony said. "But we're more interested in the last time you saw Marie Ritter than we are in your love life. When was that?"

"Uh. Let's see. It would be sometime in January. Late January."

"So soon after your father's death?" Dennis asked.

"So much for a period of mourning," Anthony added.

"Hey, I don't have to take this shit," Junior said, half standing and glaring at Anthony. "Especially from the person who blew the investigation of my father's killer."

Anthony paled and he started to stand, but Dennis put a restraining hand on his partner's arm.

"Why don't you relax, Mr. Hoyt?" Dennis said. "I'm sure it just seemed odd to my partner that you would be cavorting with a high-priced call girl so soon after your father passed away."

"Yeah, well, it happened," Junior answered sullenly. He settled back onto his chair. "I was in Seattle on business and I called her."

"Directly?"

"No. She works for an escort service. I arranged it through them."

"I bet Crystal didn't come cheap, Junior. No pun intended," Anthony said.

"You think you're funny?"

"Where do you get all the money for these expensive toys, Mr. Hoyt?" Dennis asked.

Junior barked out a harsh laugh. "You are two pathetic civil servants. For a guy like me, a couple of hundred a night is nothing. I'm making a bundle from the mortuaries."

"You must be spending a bundle, too," Dennis said casually. He didn't sound the least offended by Junior's outburst. "Wine, women and song, heh, heh. You know, the credit check I ran on you has you maxed out on just about every credit card there is and your bank balance . . ." Dennis shook his head sadly and Junior turned pale.

"Do you remember where you were on Wednesday evening?"

"Wednesday?" Junior asked nervously. "Why do you need to know that?"

"That's when Ms. Ritter—Crystal—was killed."

"Hey, I didn't have anything to do with that."

"Of course," Dennis said soothingly, "but it would help if we could eliminate you as a suspect. See, so far, you're the only person connected with this case who knew Ms. Ritter."

"I . . . I'm pretty sure . . . Yeah, Wednesday, I was by myself. I stayed home alone."

"No one called you or dropped in to visit?" Dennis asked.

"No."

"That's too bad. You're certain you were home and not at the Heathman with Miss Ritter?"

"Absolutely."

Dennis smiled. "Well, we'll know soon enough. The lab reports are expected back soon." Dennis shook his head sadly. "You know, it just isn't fair anymore. A good crook used to be able to beat the rap by just wearing gloves so he didn't leave fingerprints. But now with this DNA if you spit or leave a teensy-weensy head hair or an itsy-bitsy drop of semen, you're doomed."

"You won't find any of my prints or DNA on that woman."

"Mr. Hoyt," Anthony asked, "do you think you can remember a little more about that argument you had with your father? The one at Hoyt Industries headquarters. You were pretty vague about what made you and your father so upset."

"I've had enough of this. First, you drop a picture of a dead woman on my table, then you suggest I killed her, now you're asking about some argument I already told you about . . ."

"Let me help you out here. You know Jack Brademas, the head of security for Hoyt Industries, don't you? Probably heard all about his getting killed on the TV."

Junior did not answer. He looked desperate.

"We know that Brademas told your father that you were skimming money from the mortuaries. That's what you and your father argued about."

"That's bullshit, pure bullshit, and I'm not talking to you two anymore without a lawyer."

"That's your choice," Dennis said, "but it might be smart to cooperate with us now. That way we can tell the D.A. to give you a break."

"What D.A.? Are you gonna charge me with some crime?"

"Why, have you done something you're worried about?"

"No, I haven't," Junior said, but he looked confused and scared. "Now, why don't you two get out of here?"

"We're going to leave, but you'll be coming with us while these officers search your apartment.

"Take him into the bedroom and let him dress," Anthony told

two of the officers. Two men surrounded Junior. He hesitated and Anthony said, "We can take you downtown dressed in those skivvies and put you in the drunk tank, if you'd like."

Junior wrenched his elbow free and strode angrily out of the room.

Twenty-five

LOU ANTHONY and Leroy Dennis met Cedric Riker at Benjamin Gage's house at three o'clock, Tuesday afternoon. Benjamin Gage ushered Anthony and Dennis into his den, where Riker was waiting drink in hand. It looked like their arrival had interrupted a chat between old friends.

"I know that you gentlemen are busy, so why don't you tell me how I can help you?"

"Do you know a woman named Karen Fargo, Senator?" Anthony asked quickly to keep Riker from conducting the questioning.

"No. I don't believe I've ever met her."

"But you know who she is," Dennis said.

Dennis smiled disarmingly, but Ryan Clark had briefed his boss on both detectives and he knew that he was not dealing with fools.

"Of course. I've followed Senator Crease's case very closely."

"Have you ever paid her any money, Senator?" Dennis asked.

"Now, wait a minute," Riker interjected, "we're not here to . . ."

Gage held up his hand and Riker's sentence squealed to a halt.

"I have great respect for the law, Ced. I want to be completely candid with these men."

Gage turned to Dennis. "I hope I didn't do anything wrong in urging Miss Fargo to go to the police with what she knew, but I felt that her evidence would be of use in finding Lamar Hoyt's killer. Was it illegal to find Miss Fargo a job after Ellen Crease had her fired? Was I wrong to help her with her rent and food until she could get back on her feet?"

"No one is accusing you of doing anything illegal, Senator," Riker assured Gage.

"I appreciate that, because, after the fact, I wondered if I'd been out of bounds."

"Mr. Clark, he's your assistant?" Anthony asked.

"Administrative assistant. A true patriot. He was a navy SEAL. Decorated extensively."

"Do you happen to know his whereabouts on last Wednesday?"

"I'm afraid you'll have to ask him about that. I'm sure he'll answer all your questions."

"Do you know where we can reach him?"

"Certainly."

Gage told them a phone number.

"Senator, did you or Mr. Clark know Marie Ritter or Martin Jablonski?"

Gage smiled patiently. "I can only speak for myself. I recognize Mr. Jablonski's name, of course, and I can assure you that we never met. I'm unfamiliar with the other person you mentioned. I can't speak for Mr. Clark. You'll have to ask him."

Riker stood up. "Thank you for taking the time to talk to us."

"Anytime, Ced. I'm a strong supporter of the police."

Gage walked the detectives and the district attorney to the front door. When they were on their way, the senator returned to his study and phoned Ryan Clark.

"How did it go?" Clark asked.

"Piece of cake."

[2]

The message light on the answering machine was blinking furiously when Quinn and Laura returned home from the beach late Tuesday afternoon.

"Probably reporters," Quinn said as he carried the last of the bags in from the car.

"Or my office," Laura answered as she hit the Play button.

They were right about the first four messages, but the fifth was from Ellen Crease.

"Judge, I've tried calling you every place I could think of, but no one knows where you are. It's urgent that we speak as soon as possible. Please call me immediately."

"I wonder what that's about," Laura said.

"I'd better call. She sounded upset."

Quinn dialed the number Crease had left. James Allen answered the phone. Quinn gave his name and Ellen Crease picked up a moment later.

"I just got your message. Laura and I have been hiding out at the coast since early Sunday. What's up?"

"We need to talk."

Crease sounded very tense.

"About what?"

"It's not something that we should discuss over the phone. Can you come to my house?"

"Now?"

"Right away."

"Can't this wait until tomorrow? We just walked in the door and I'm bushed."

"It has to be now. Please. This concerns both of our futures. I wouldn't ask if it wasn't important."

Quinn hesitated. Then he gave in.

"Use the back entrance to the estate. That way, no one will see you. I'll leave the gate open. It's a little tricky to get to. You have to take some back roads."

"Give me the directions."

Quinn grabbed a pencil and wrote down Crease's instructions on a pad, then read them back.

"What was that about?" Laura asked when Quinn hung up.

"I have no idea."

"Can't it wait until tomorrow?"

"She sounded very uptight, so she must think that it's important we meet. She even wants me to come by a back way so I won't be seen."

"Call her back and tell her you'll talk to her tomorrow."

"She saved my life, Laura."

Laura sighed. "You're right. Do you want me to come with you?"

Quinn squeezed Laura's hand. "There's no reason why both of us should run out. I won't be gone long."

Quinn left and Laura carried their bags upstairs to the bedroom. She was unpacking them when something Crease had said on the answering machine flitted in and out of her consciousness. Laura paused and tried to recapture the thought. She frowned, then shook her head. It was gone. She was tempted to replay Crease's message but that would mean going downstairs. She felt sticky from the ride. She decided to shower first. It was probably nothing, anyway.

Quinn took the back roads to the Hoyt estate and ended at a small gated entrance surrounded by woods. The gate was open, just as Crease said it would be. It was almost a mile to the house on a narrow unpaved road.

Ellen Crease was waiting for Quinn at the rear door.

"I've given James Allen the night off and I've dismissed the security guards so we can have privacy," Crease said as she led Quinn into a sunroom in the rear of the mansion. The room was painted white and floored with terra-cotta tiles. Wide-leaf plants filled the corners of the room. Three of the walls were floor-to-ceiling windows divided into small panes through which the pale evening light entered.

Crease gestured Quinn onto one of four wicker chairs that surrounded a glass-top table. Outside the room was a garden. None of the flowers were in bloom and there were no buds on the limbs of the trees. The foliage looked cold and exposed. Just beyond the garden were heavy woods that stretched to the boundary of the estate. Crease got to the point immediately.

"I need your help, Dick. Believe me, I've thought long and hard before asking you for it, but I have no choice."

"I'll help any way I can," Quinn assured her.

"Don't say that so quickly. Wait until you hear what I want from you."

Crease sighed. She seemed sad.

"I've only known you for a short time, but you've impressed me with your integrity and character. That's what makes my request so difficult. I am going to lose my bid to win the primary unless I go public about the conspiracy against me. I trust the voters. If they know that I was framed for Lamar's murder, I believe they will swing over to me."

Crease's features hardened. She captured Quinn with her eyes. He could feel her power.

"Dick, the voters have to be told that you were threatened with blackmail if you did not fix my case. Benjamin Gage is taking the position that I've been hiding behind a legal technicality to keep the public from finding out the truth about Lamar's murder. You can tell everyone that you ruled as you did to protect me from a plan to frame me. I know it's a lot to ask. I tried to reach you yesterday, so you would have time to think about what I'm asking you to do. When I couldn't find you I had to go forward. I've planned a news conference for Thursday night. I'm going public with everything."

"You can't do that."

Crease looked sad. She shook her head wearily. "You have no idea how difficult this decision was for me, Dick, but I'm convinced that I must go ahead with the news conference."

"Do you appreciate what could happen to me if it gets out that I fixed your case?"

"Yes. I consulted Mary Garrett before I made this decision. She told me that you will probably have to resign from the bench and that you might face criminal charges."

"There is no 'might.' Cedric Riker is a political crony of Benjamin Gage. If my confession costs Gage the election he'll definitely come after me."

"I've got money and influence, Dick. I won't desert you if things start to go bad."

Quinn shook his head as if he could not believe what he was hearing.

"I know I'm asking a lot. If you go public at my press conference, I am prepared to back you with every penny I've got. You'll have the best lawyers, and I'll work behind the scenes for you. Gage isn't the only person with political influence."

Quinn leaned back and closed his eyes. He had been prepared to resign from the bench on the evening that Brademas attacked him in the garage. Crease had convinced him to reconsider that decision. Now she wanted him to make a public confession.

"I have to talk this over with Laura. If I'm disbarred or go to prison, it will affect her, too."

"Of course. But I'm going to go ahead with the news conference whether you help me or not. If you confess publicly, it may help you later."

Quinn was about to respond when the rear doorbell rang.

"Stay here," Crease said. "I'll see who that is."

A moment later, Quinn heard raised voices in the hall. One of them was Laura's. Quinn walked into the hall. Laura saw him and walked down the hall with Crease close behind her.

"What does she want from you?" Laura demanded.

"Your husband was just about to drive home and tell you," Crease answered calmly. "Why don't we discuss this in the sunroom, instead of standing in the hall?"

Quinn and Laura followed the senator into the sunroom. When they were seated, Quinn said, "Ellen wants me to go public about the blackmail plot. She thinks it will help her win the election if the voters learn that someone tried to coerce me into fixing her case so that she would be convicted."

Laura turned on Crease. "You want my husband to risk prison so you can win an election?"

"The decision to go public has already been made. The only question is whether Dick helps me. I'm sorry, Laura."

"I don't think you are. There's something very wrong here, something that I don't understand. I listened to the message that you left on our answering machine. You said that you tried to find Dick, but no one knew where he was."

"Yes?" Crease answered with obvious confusion.

"You couldn't find us because Dick and I didn't tell anyone that we were going to the coast."

Now Quinn looked confused, too.

"What are you getting at?" Quinn asked.

"How did Jack Brademas know that my husband was working at the courthouse on Saturday?" Laura asked Crease. "It was a weekend afternoon. No one would expect him to be there. The only person besides me that he told was you, Senator, when he phoned to tell you about the police report."

"Jack must have followed your husband," Crease said.

"That's possible, but it wouldn't explain why he was so desperate to kill Dick. Only one thing could have caused that urgency. Knowing that Dick had discovered his link to Jablonski and was going to tell the police. And you are the only person who knew about Dick's discovery."

"You think I sent Jack to kill your husband?" Crease asked incredulously.

"There were a few things that never added up. If Brademas was working with Junior so he could get a cut of the estate, it made no sense for him to tell your husband about the embezzlement scheme and run the risk that Lamar would go to the police or disinherit Junior. I think Jack Brademas was your accomplice all along, Senator."

"You've got it all wrong, Laura," Crease said without rancor.

"I don't think so. Jablonski was your sacrificial lamb. You hid in the bathroom while he murdered your husband. Then you ambushed him and became a grieving widow and a law-and-order avenger overnight. It was a terrific little coup that helped you to skyrocket in the polls and become a multimillionaire. Everything was going great until Gary Yoshida stumbled across the blood spatter pattern on the armoire and Gage bribed Fargo to go to the police. When you were indicted for Lamar Hoyt's murder, you lost everything you had gained. Now your priority was to escape death row. That's when you dreamed up your blackmail scheme. You knew that Dick was going to St. Jerome because he announced it at your bail hearing. I bet Brademas found out about Marie Ritter while he was investigating Junior. You used her to ensnare Dick, then you killed her when she had served her purpose."

"There's a problem with your theory, Laura," Crease said calmly. "If Jack and I were working together, why would we tell your husband that he would be ruined unless he did everything he could to see that I was sent to prison?" Crease flashed Laura a condescending smile. "That doesn't sound like a very good plan to me."

"That was the cleverest part of the plan, Senator, and it hinged on an excellent reading of the character of my husband. I could never understand why the blackmailers sent Marie Ritter to see Dick during the hearing. They were running an incredible risk that he would figure out that Claire Reston and Andrea Chapman were the same person. If that happened, the blackmail plan would be useless because Dick would know that Andrea Chapman was not murdered on St. Jerome. The blackmailers' leverage would be lost.

"On top of that, Reston let Dick know that she could go public with the fact that he was with Chapman in the cove. It was a ridiculous thing to do if the blackmailers wanted their plot to succeed, but it was a very clever thing to do if the blackmailers wanted their plan to fail."

For the first time since Laura arrived, Crease looked uncertain.

"You sent Reston to see Dick because you wanted him to do exactly the opposite of what Brademas ordered. You knew that my husband would never give in to blackmail if you told him to fix the case so that you would be acquitted. He would have gone to the police even if it meant his career. You used reverse psychology to get Dick to do what you wanted. You knew how decent Dick is. You gambled that he would sacrifice his career to save you."

"This is absolute nonsense," Crease said.

"Look at the evidence. Paul Baylor didn't say that Gary Yoshida's interpretation of the blood spatter evidence was wrong, he only gave a theoretical alternative to Yoshida's explanation. If Yoshida was right, you lied all along. You also profited the most when your husband died. You and Brademas go way back. Who does it make more sense for him to work with? And you were the only one who knew about the report that implicated Brademas, the only one who could tell him where to find Dick."

"She saved my life, Laura," Quinn said.

"No, Dick, she didn't save your life when she killed Brademas. She took care of a witness who could hang her. Brademas became a liability as soon as you found his name on that report."

"But why didn't she wait until Brademas killed me? With both of us dead there would be no way to prove that her case was rigged and she would be free of the murder charges."

"With you dead, there would be no one who could tell the

voters about the conspiracy to frame her. She needed you alive to save her campaign. It all fits, Dick. She's been playing you since you were assigned to her case."

Quinn stood up. He should have been furious, but he was too stunned to be angry.

"Where are you going?"

"To the police."

"Don't do that, Dick," Crease implored desperately.

"Don't be ridiculous."

"I'll make you a deal."

"There's nothing you can offer me."

"But there is. I can offer you your career. In order to implicate me, you'll have to confess to fixing my case. No one can prove what you did if you don't go to the police. Keep quiet and you'll stay on the bench, you won't be disbarred, you won't have to worry about criminal charges and the disgrace."

Quinn suddenly saw Crease's real face. An image of Marie Ritter spread-eagled on the hotel bed flashed in his mind and he remembered the terror he felt in the garage and as he lay waiting for death on the cold marble floor of the courthouse.

"Not a chance. If I have to go to jail, I will, but you're not walking away from this."

Quinn turned his back to the senator.

"God damn it, Quinn, you'll ruin us both," Crease shouted.

Quinn and Laura kept walking. There was an end table at Crease's elbow. She opened a drawer and pulled out a gun.

"Stop," she yelled. When Quinn did not look back, Crease squeezed the trigger. Quinn's right leg flew out from under him and he fell to the floor. Laura screamed. Quinn stared at Crease, dazed. Blood was spreading along his pants leg near his knee. Crease took a pair of handcuffs from the drawer and tossed them to Laura. She made no move to catch them and they fell at her feet. Crease cocked the gun and pointed it at Laura.

"Pick them up and cuff him," she ordered.

"I'm not . . . ," Laura started, but Crease smashed her across the cheek with the revolver, driving her to her knees. Quinn threw himself at Crease, but she stepped out of reach and he collapsed sideways, grimacing with pain. Crease pointed the gun at Quinn's head and spoke to Laura.

"Do as you're told or I'll kill him."

Laura looked at Crease wide-eyed. Crease cocked the revolver and Laura retrieved the cuffs.

"Get your hands behind you," Crease told Quinn. Laura snapped on the cuffs.

"Was it the money? Did you kill your husband for his money?" Quinn asked to stall for time.

Crease shook her head wearily.

"I didn't care about Lamar's money. I cared about Lamar and I killed the bastard because he was going to leave me."

Crease's voice caught and her eyes watered.

"I loved him. He's the only man I ever loved. I gave Lamar everything and he threw my love in my face." A tear ran down Crease's cheek. "Fargo wasn't the first tramp he'd played around with, but she was the one he was going to substitute for me. It was history repeating itself. As soon as one of his wives started to age, Lamar would trade her in. I tried to talk him out of it. I did everything I could. I really loved that son of a bitch, but I told him I'd see him dead before I'd let him make me into one of his discards. He didn't believe me."

"What if you were wrong about me? What if I did fix the case so that you were convicted?"

"I thought of that possibility. If I saw that you were trying to help the prosecutor convict me I would have released the photographs to the media and moved for a mistrial claiming that you had been blackmailed into fixing the case. But I never had to do that, because I had you doped out one hundred percent."

Quinn felt like a complete fool.

"What we didn't count on was that police report with Jack's name on it," Crease said. "If it weren't for that . . ." She shook her head.

"Did Brademas help you for the money?"

"Of course. And he was in love with me. He had been since we were on the force together. We were even lovers before I married Lamar. Jack had been shaking down drug dealers. Internal Affairs was after him, but they didn't have the evidence to make a case stick. He resigned to avoid a further inquiry. I got him his job in security at Hoyt Industries for old time's sake.

"When Lamar started cheating on me I became Jack's lover again, out of spite. But he never meant anything to me. When I decided to kill Lamar, persuading Jack to help me was easy. Then he started to get out of control. He was just supposed to kill Ritter, not torture her. I was furious when I heard what he'd done. I wanted to frame you for Ritter's murder, but you would never have killed her like that. Then you told me about the police report and I knew Jack was a liability I could not afford.

"When we got to the courthouse, I told Jack that I would follow him as backup. He thought that he was supposed to kill you and take the report. But I would never have let him kill you. Laura is right. You were worth more to me alive so you could tell everyone how I saved your life."

"Why did Brademas go after me in the parking garage?"

"We wanted to make sure that the order suppressing evidence would stand. I couldn't risk having it set aside if you told someone that you had fixed my case. Then you came to me for help. I decided that you would be of more use to me alive, because you would be my proof of the plot to frame me for Lamar's murder."

Crease suddenly looked very tired.

"We've talked long enough," she said. "Are both of your cars in back of the house?"

Quinn and Laura nodded.

"Get him up and help him outside," Crease told Laura.

"Don't do this," Quinn begged. "I'll make the broadcast."

Crease shook her head. "It's too late for that. I'd never be able to trust you."

"For God's sake," Quinn started.

"Move," Crease ordered, "and no more talking."

Quinn hobbled forward into the hallway. Crease followed at a safe distance.

"I love you," Quinn whispered to Laura.

"What did I say about talking?" Crease asked angrily.

A second later, a gunshot exploded in the hall.

Twenty-six

A YOUNG COP was waiting at the front door of the Hoyt mansion when Anthony and Dennis drove up. Two marked cars were parked along the other side of the turn-around. The officer told them where everyone was and Anthony and Dennis walked along the front of the mansion until they found a slate path that led toward the pool. The path continued along the side of the house. Eventually, they rounded a corner and saw an ambulance and two parked cars. Richard Quinn was lying on a stretcher. A medic was working on his leg. A second medic was working on a nasty gash on Laura Quinn's cheek. Through the open back door, Anthony saw a forensic expert circling a third person who was lying facedown in the hall. He was carrying a camera. Every so often he would stop and take a photograph. Another cop was videotaping the scene.

Anthony walked inside and knelt next to the body of Ellen Crease. He spotted the entry wound in the back of her head. He had no desire to see the mess the bullet had made when it exited. It was enough to know that Crease was dead.

Anthony walked outside just as Quinn gasped in pain. The medic apologized and Quinn gritted his teeth. He looked spent, but Anthony needed to find out what had happened. He squatted down beside the judge.

"Feel up to talking?"

"I can manage a little."

"We're gonna have to take him to the hospital," the medic said. "Make it quick."

"She was in it with Brademas," Quinn said. "She hired Jablonski to make the hit on Lamar because he was going to leave her for Karen Fargo."

Anthony remembered his interview with Crease in the library on the evening of her husband's murder. He had been impressed by the dignity with which she had conducted herself despite her grief. Maybe the grief had not been an act.

"Crease was going to go on television Thursday night and tell everyone that I had been blackmailed to fix her case. She wanted me to speak at her press conference. Laura figured out what happened. She came here and confronted Crease. We were going to the police. Crease shot me and hit Laura. She was going to kill us."

"Gotta go," the medic said as he signaled his partner.

"You take care," the detective said as the medics started maneuvering the stretcher toward the ambulance. "I'll talk to you at the hospital."

Anthony walked over to Leroy Dennis, who was finishing up with Laura. She joined Quinn in the back of the ambulance. When the ambulance drove away, Anthony said, "Let's talk to the man of the hour."

The detectives found James Allen in the sunroom.

"Mr. Allen?" Anthony said.

Allen looked up, but he seemed to have trouble focusing and he looked unstable.

"Do you remember me, sir?"

Allen made an almost imperceptible nod. Anthony sat across from him.

"I had to do it," he said, his voice slightly louder than a whisper.

"I know, Mr. Allen," Dennis said. "She was going to kill them."

"How did you happen to come back to the house? I understand from the officer who talked to you that this was your night off."

"I didn't feel well, so I came home. I wanted to make myself some tea to calm my stomach before going to my quarters. I was going toward the kitchen when I heard them. Judge Quinn said he was going to the police. Then there was a gunshot."

Allen paused and shook his head in disbelief.

"I froze for a moment. Then I went into the den where the gun collection is kept. She was raising the gun to fire again when I reentered the hall. I . . . I didn't feel that I had a choice."

Allen began to sob. Anthony watched helplessly. Dennis went into the hall and returned with a doctor. Then the detectives left.

"Let's take a walk," Anthony said. "I want to talk to you about something."

"Such as?"

"This blackmail business," Anthony told Dennis as they headed back toward the pool where the other policemen would not overhear them.

"We don't have any proof that Quinn fixed Crease's case. With Crease and Brademas dead, it doesn't look like we'll get any unless the judge confesses."

Anthony stood on the edge of the empty pool. Debris had settled on the bottom. Leaves mostly. Anthony figured the pool man would have cleaned it eventually, but he wondered what would happen now with everybody dead.

"Quinn's a good judge," Anthony said.

"If he fixed a case, he violated the law."

"I know that, but I'm wondering about the value of pursuing our investigation now that Crease is dead."

"Value? That's a funny word to use, Lou. We don't get paid to deal in values. That's for philosophers. We're lawmen. The senators and representatives write the laws, the governors sign them, we enforce them. Cops aren't supposed to think about whether the laws are good or bad."

Anthony walked away from the pool and into the garden. He could see the setting sun through the denuded tree limbs.

"Do you believe in second chances, Leroy?"

"That's what bleeding-heart defense lawyers are always whining for. Isn't that what you've told me?"

Anthony smiled. "You got me there. Well, I'm just one part of this team. You've got a vote, too, but I think that we should put this case to rest and leave Richard Quinn alone."

Dennis thought about Anthony's proposal for a moment. Then he shrugged.

"I'll go along with you for now. But I won't do it for nothing."

"What do you want, Leroy?"

"A Captain Neon burger and a pint of Terminator stout."

Epilogue

A RE YOU all right?" Laura asked when Quinn stopped. "I'm a little winded. Just let me rest for a moment." Quinn was home from the hospital and trying to get some exercise by walking along the streets in Hereford Farms, but he did not have much stamina. Quinn leaned on his cane for a moment while Laura waited patiently. It was not hard to do. Balmy spring weather had suddenly appeared. Flowers were starting to show up, the temperature was perfect and the sky was children's-book blue.

"Okay," Quinn said. Laura took his arm and they started down Peacock Road toward the swimming pool and the tennis courts.

"Stanley Sax stopped me in the courthouse hallway," Laura told Quinn, introducing a subject they had avoided. "He wants to know when you'll be ready to go back to work."

Quinn looked straight ahead.

"What did you say?" he asked.

"I said it's up to your doctors. Is that what I should have said?"

"Be honest with me, Laura. Do you think I deserve to be sitting as a judge?"

Laura stopped walking. She faced Quinn.

"I love the fact that you're so principled, Dick, but I wish you would recognize your humanity a little more often. You're going to make wrong choices. Don't punish yourself when you do because that's ego; that's crediting yourself with infallibility.

"You asked me if I think you should go back to the bench. I think you should do what makes you happy, and that's being a judge. I wouldn't tell you to go back if I didn't think it was right. The people of this state need good judges. If you leave the bench, you'll be letting them down so you can punish yourself."

Quinn and Laura walked in silence for a while. Finally, Quinn said, "I want to go back, I just . . ."

"You just acted like a human being."

Quinn looked anguished. "You really think it's the right thing to do?"

"Yes, Dick."

"Then the next time you see Stan tell him I'm anxious to get back to work."

[2]

"Un autre, s'il vous plaît," James Allen said.

"Immédiatement, monsieur."

The waiter took Allen's empty cup and saucer and carried it inside the café. Allen smiled. He was especially pleased because the waiter was conversing in French. Allen had noticed that many of the waiters switched to English the moment an American tried to converse in French if the American's accent or grammar was not perfect.

While Allen waited for the waiter to return with his cappuccino, he looked across the waters of Lake Geneva to the French Alps. The mountaintops were dusted with snow even though the weather in Lausanne was balmy. Every year, James Allen took his

vacation on the Continent. This was his second time in Switzerland and he was enjoying it very much. It was especially nice
because the $50,000 he had received from Benjamin Gage and the
money in Lamar Hoyt's bequest permitted him to travel in luxury
for the first time.

As per his agreement with Ryan Clark, Allen had told the police
nothing about the arrangement with Senator Gage that Allen had
initiated soon after the hearing on the motion to suppress. It was
the blood spatter evidence that had convinced Allen that Ellen
Crease had been behind the murder of his employer. Allen had
never liked the woman. She was too insensitive to Mr. Hoyt's
needs, too domineering. If she had won election to the United
States Senate, Mr. Hoyt would have been left alone for most of
the year. He knew how much that would have upset Mr. Hoyt
because he had overheard several arguments in which this matter
was the main subject.

Just when Allen decided that Crease was guilty, Judge Quinn
had destroyed the case against her. It was then that Allen decided
to give campaign intelligence to Benjamin Gage in the hopes that
his information would lead to Crease's defeat. When Ryan Clark
supplied him with the bugging equipment, Allen secretly hoped
that Crease would confess the murder on tape, but that had never
happened. Still, it was the phone conversation between Crease
and Judge Quinn that Allen had overheard that eventually put the
houseman in a position to avenge his employer's murder. Allen
had rigged the sunroom with a listening device and had acted as
soon as Crease threatened to kill Laura and the judge.

Life had been hectic following the shooting. There were the
police interrogations and the interviews with the press. Appearing
distraught through it all drained him, but Allen knew enough
about the authorities to understand that they would not have
reacted favorably if he expressed the joy he felt when he ended the
life of the woman who had taken Lamar Hoyt from him.

A ferry cruised by on the lake heading toward Montreaux. Tomorrow Allen was planning to travel by ferry a little farther to

Château Chillon, the fortress where Lord Byron had set his famous poem. He was looking forward to the slow ride during which he planned to reread "The Prisoner of Chillon."

"Monsieur," the waiter said with a warm smile as he placed the cappuccino in front of Allen. Allen thanked him in fluent French perfected during years of night school study and trips to France and Switzerland.

A cloud slipped in front of the sun. For a moment, the air cooled. Allen sipped his drink. The hot liquid cut the chill. He checked the time. In four hours he would be dining in one of Europe's finest restaurants. He picked up the book he was reading and took another sip of his cappuccino.